MORE
DYNAMITE

MORE DYNAMITE

CRAIG RAINE

Essays 1990–2012

Atlantic Books
London

First published in Great Britain in 2013 by Atlantic Books,
an imprint of Atlantic Books Ltd.

The author is grateful to the following publications in which the essays of this book
originally appeared, sometimes in slightly different form:
Areté, the *Times Literary Supplement*, the *Kipling Journal*, the *Financial Times*, Peter Lang,
Penguin Books, the *New Statesman*, the *Daily Telegraph*, the *Guardian*, *Another Magazine*,
the *London Review of Books*, *Modern Painters* and *Memory: An Anthology*.

1 3 5 7 9 10 8 6 4 2

A CIP catalogue record for this book is available from the British Library.

Hardback ISBN: 9781848872875
E-book ISBN: 9781782392057

Printed and bound by CPI Group (UK) Ltd, Croydon, CR0 4YY

Atlantic Books
An Imprint of Atlantic Books Ltd
Ormond House
26–27 Boswell Street
London
WC1N 3JZ

www.atlantic-books.co.uk

For Patrick Marber and Debra Gillett

Contents

Part Two: Art – Reading the Detail

PART ONE

Books – Reading the Fine Print

Isaac Babel

(2002)

My wife, Ann Pasternak Slater, met Nadezhda Mandelstam in Moscow in 1971, shortly after the publication of *Hope Against Hope*. The sequel, *Hope Abandoned*, was finished and waiting in another room. The poet's chain-smoking widow jerked her thumb over her shoulder: 'More dynamite in there.'

Isaac Babel was another dynamitist – a writer whose explosive force derives from his terse transcriptions of first-hand experience. He wrote to his friend Paustovsky: 'on my shield is inscribed the device "authenticity".' Some paragraphs of his prose are acts of deliberate terror. The simple shock-waves of the actual, the cruel, the irrefutable, are his speciality. His sudden, ruthless, marvellous gift leaves the reader trying – too late – to look away from what Babel is compelled to show us. There is no escape. The violence is calculated to injure the reader's bourgeois sensibility, to destroy his good taste, to trap him in the epicentre of the blast – to terrorise him.

Dulgushov is fatally wounded: 'He was sitting propped up against a tree. He lay with his legs splayed far apart, his boots pointing in opposite directions. *Without lowering his eyes from me*, he carefully lifted his shirt. His stomach was torn open, his intestines spilling to his knees, *and we could see his heart beating*' (my italics). The narrator lacks the 'courage' to finish him off, as the wounded man asks.

'Afonka Bida' tells the story of a Cossack whose wounded horse has to be shot. First, he feels in the wound with his copper-coloured fingers, then a comrade shoots the horse: 'Maslak walked over to the horse, treading daintily on his fat legs, *slid* his revolver into its ear, and fired' (my italics). Deranged with grief, Afonka Bida goes on the rampage and returns with a replacement mount. It has cost him an eye: 'he had combed his sweat-drenched forelock over his gouged-out eye.'

Afonka expresses his sorrow in a phrase – 'Where's one to find another horse like that?' – which recalls another story in the collection, 'Crossing the River Zbrucz'. The narrator is billeted on a family of Volhynian Jews in Novograd. He lies back on 'the ripped eiderdown' and dreams restlessly about battle.

The Complete Works of Isaac Babel, edited by Nathalie Babel and translated by Peter Constantine (W. W. Norton & Co., 2002).

He is woken by a pregnant Jewish woman tapping him on his face. I quote the rest of the two-page story, about one quarter of the total:

> 'Pan,' she says to me, 'you are shouting in your sleep, and tossing and turning. I'll put your bed in another corner, because you are kicking my papa.'
>
> She raises her thin legs and round belly from the floor and pulls the blanket off the sleeping man. An old man is lying there on his back, dead. His gullet has been ripped out, his face hacked in two, and dark blood is clinging to his beard like a lump of lead.
>
> 'Pan,' the Jewess says, shaking out the eiderdown, 'the Poles were hacking him to death and he kept begging them, "Kill me in the backyard so my daughter won't see me die!" But they wouldn't inconvenience themselves. He died in this room, thinking of me ... And now I want you to tell me,' the woman suddenly said with terrible force, 'I want you to tell me where one could find another father like my father in all the world!'

That sudden 'terrible force' is Babel's speciality, too. But it depends not just on the way the mundane nightmare is succeeded by the infinitely worse waking nightmare. It depends also on what follows the dark blood in the beard – *shaking out the eiderdown*. In those four alert words is all the shock, all the tragic incongruity, of ordinary life's unbearable, bearable continuities.

This is 'Berestechko' and more Jews:

> The old man was screeching, and tried to break free. Kudrya from the machine gun detachment grabbed his head and held it wedged under his arm. The Jew fell silent and spread his legs. Kudrya pulled out his dagger with his right hand and carefully slit the old man's throat *without spattering himself.* He knocked on one of the closed windows.
>
> 'If anyone's interested,' he said, 'they can come get him. It's no problem.' (my italics)

You know it is true. No fiction writer would dare this black farce – the fastidiousness of the barbarian's meticulous barbarity, the etiquette observed by the executioner knocking on the closed window. It is writing with the greatest possible specific gravity. It exerts an awful, irresistible pull on the reader. There are the ingredients for a sick joke here, the shape of perverse laughter – but Babel skirts the absurd and renders it as sober, almost off-hand, factual, unquestionable.

The casual cruelty and the laconic prose recall the italicised prefatory micro-bulletins above the stories in Hemingway's *In Our Time*. Quoted like this, the

Babel stories satisfy the imperatives set down in his diary: 'short chapters saturated with content'; 'very simple, *a factual account*, no superfluous description'; 'rest. New men. Night in the field. The horses, I tie myself to the stirrup. – Night, corn on the cob, nurse. Dawn. Without a plot.'

Of course, there are moments of more insidious vividness – a prostitute *squinting* to squeeze a pimple on her shoulder, a Jew on his way to synagogue ('he fastened the three bone buttons of his green coat. He dusted himself with the cockerel feathers'), 'a moaning hurrah, shredded by the wind'. Babel knows the 'round shoulders' of plump women. He is as expert on backs as a chiropractor: 'scars shimmered on her powdered back'; passion means that 'blotches flared up on her arms and shoulders'; 'her back, dazzling and sad, moved in front of me.' Or there is the mistress of Division Commander Savitsky, 'combing her hair in the coolness under the awning', smilingly chiding her lover as she buttons up his shirt for him. Not unbuttoning, but the far greater intimacy of buttoning up.

This is an utterly authentic vignette of a landscape transformed by battle:

> Cossacks went from yard to yard collecting rags and eating unripe plums. The moment we arrived, Akinfiev curled up on the hay and fell asleep, and I took a blanket from his cart and went to look for some shade to lie down in. But the fields on both sides of the road were covered with excrement. A bearded muzhik in copper-rimmed spectacles and a Tyrolean hat was sitting by the wayside reading a newspaper.

The fatigue we might have guessed – and even the excrement – but it took Babel's being there to assure us so confidently of those *unripe* plums and that implausible yet irrefutable Tyrolean hat. Equally, Babel's first-hand knowledge can assure us that cooking pots are stirred with a twig, or that sleeping cavalry tie their horses to their legs. Or consider the narrative hypnosis that holds us while a Cossack, Prishchepa, executes a bloody revenge to restore the looted furniture to his family hut. He arranges it as he remembers from childhood, drinks vodka for two days, sings, cries – and finally sets fire to the hut. Before he vanishes, he throws 'a lock of his hair into the flames'. A remarkable, inexplicable, unforgettable final touch.

Elsewhere, Vytagaichenko, the regiment commander, is woken by a Polish attack. 'He mounted his horse and rode over to the lead squadron. His face was creased with red stripes from his uncomfortable sleep, and his pockets were filled with plums.' The creases are good, but they are to be expected. The plums are the surprise – the authenticating detail, the guarantee of genuineness, by this alert connoisseur, this calm Berenson of the battlefield. Both Lionel Trilling and Henry Gifford are exercised by the perceived conflict between the timorous intellectual and the warriors he fought alongside. (See Trilling's introduction to *Collected Stories* (Methuen, 1957) and Gifford's shrewd and learned essay in *Grand Street* (Autumn, 1989).) In a revisionist spirit, Gifford offers the testimony of Viktor Shklovsky, the Russian formalist, who knew one of Babel's comrades-in-arms: 'They liked Babel very much in the army. He had a calm fearlessness of which he was quite unconscious.' The internal evidence of the stories suggests how closely this was related to an almost scholarly impulse. Those plums are recorded twice in the unflinching spirit of thoroughness – the pedantry of genius.

But selective quotation is distorting. It ignores the aesthetic pleasure of form and shapeliness. The stories are wholes. Who can tell from fragmentary quotation whether that verbal parallel lamenting the loss of a father and the loss of a horse is intentional and ironic, or inadvertent repetition? (There are unintentional repetitions in Babel, but here I think he is covertly ironising horse-centred Cossack morality.) A weak, early, overwritten, knowingly improbable story like 'Shabos-Nakhamu' can look intriguing if you quote only the last paragraph: 'The innkeeper, naked beneath the rays of the rising sun, stood waiting for her huddled against the tree. He felt cold. He was shifting from one foot to another.' And, up to now, most of my quotation has been sensationalist and Babel's subtler registers under-represented. For example, 'Dolgushov's Death' is more than its core – the slow cascade of intestines and flexing heart of Dolgushov, who is eventually put out of his misery by Afonka Bida. He shoots the dying man in the mouth. Bida despises the bespectacled, ineffectual narrator, whose fastidious tenderness is actually a form of cruelty – and he threatens to shoot him, too. The story ends like this: '"Well, there you have it, Grishchuk," I said to him. "Today I lost Afonka, my first real friend." Grishchuk took out a wrinkled apple from under the cart seat. "Eat it," he told me, "please, eat it."' A quiet, indirect, apparently inconsequential, Chekhovian close. But the soothing gesture is germane. Grishchuk, the subordinate, is consoling his friend and superior, whose feelings have been wounded in parallel to Dolgushov's physical wounding. The wrinkled apple is a token of friendship. It also carries an edge of impatience, a hint of rebuke, as the lowly driver confronts the narrator's self-indulgent egotism with an act of self-sacrifice, the giving up of the precious apple.

Consider 'A Letter', a four-page masterpiece about the civil war. In it, a father butchers his son Fyodor and is in turn butchered by another son, Semyon. The narrative is contained in a letter dictated to Babel by yet a third son, Vasily. The appalling cruelties are matched by the calculated subtlety of the narrative's ironies. The main thrust of the letter is prefaced by the tenderest of digressions – tenderness which, as it turns out, indicates a lack of affect. It concerns Stepan.

It is several unpunctuated sentences before we realise that Stepan is not a child but a horse. 'Write to me a letter about my Stepan – is he alive or not, I beg you to look after him and to write to me about him, is he still scratching himself or has he stopped, but also about the scabs on his forelegs, have you had him shod, or not?' The father makes his first, unfavourable appearance in the context of the horse: 'I beg you, dearest Mama, Evdokiya Fyodorovna, to wash without fail his forelegs *with the soap I hid behind the icons*, and if Papa has swiped it all then buy some in Krasnodar, and the Lord will smile upon you' (my italics). The tenderness privileges the horse over the human being.

Like the peasant boy this soldier is, he then describes the local inhabitants, the crops, the poor soil, *before* broaching the story of his father's brutality: 'In these second lines of this letter I hasten to write you about Papa, that he hacked my brother Fyodor Timofeyich Kurdyukov to pieces a year ago now.' When the revenge is achieved, it is Greek in its restraint: 'Semyon sent me out of the yard, so that I cannot, dearest Mama, Evdokiya Fyodorovna, describe to you how they finished off Papa, because I had been sent out of the yard.' Who could have guessed that a null tautology – 'because I had been sent out of the yard' – in conjunction with the formulaic endearment and patronymic would manage to convey so vividly the hideously inept offstage murder? In the hobbled clumsiness of the prose, in the awkward, inappropriate expression of affection, Babel's oblique mimesis is horrifyingly exact. The letter concludes with other 'news' about the wet town of Novorossisk – which situates the letter's moral tone somewhere between the affectless and a misplaced sense of naive politesse.

(Babel is uniformly good on letters: 'Trunov scrawled gigantic peasant letters on a *crookedly torn* piece of paper' (my italics); Khlebnikov 'asked me for some paper, a good thirty sheets, and for some ink. The Cossacks planed a tree stump smooth for him, he placed his revolver and paper on it, and wrote till sundown, filling many sheets with his smudgy scrawl.' His comrades tease him as 'a regular Karl Marx'.)

The story of Vasily's letter concludes with a family photograph, showing his father and 'next to him, [his mother] in a bamboo chair, a tiny peasant woman in a loose blouse, with small, bright, timid features. And against this provincial photographer's pitiful backdrop, with its flowers and doves, towered two boys, amazingly big, blunt, broad-faced, goggle-eyed, and frozen as if standing at attention: the Kurdyukov brothers, Fyodor and Semyon.' What is the photograph telling us? Beyond, that is, the blunt irony of the photographer's 'flowers and doves' and the record of family togetherness? The photograph is eloquent about how little it is telling us. It confesses its fraud, its nugatory pretence. It keeps us out like that earlier repetition: 'because I had been sent out of the yard.'

'A Letter' is a story perfect in every particular – and therefore rare in Babel's consistently imperfect œuvre. And the cause of the imperfections? So far selective quotation of the high points might imply that Babel is a realist – 'sisters with their little moustaches' – whereas he is only partly a realist. He has a fatal hankering for poetry, too. By which he understands something essentially anti-realist. Babel was a *writer*, uneasy with the idea of documentary. The editor of this sumptuous and thorough *Complete Works*, the writer's daughter, Nathalie Babel, emphasises in her headnote to the Red Cavalry stories that they were, 'as Babel himself repeatedly stressed, fiction set against a real backdrop'. Art, then, not reportage. According to Henry Gifford, Babel was a great reviser, taking twenty-two drafts to finish 'Lyubka the Cossack': he didn't want posterity to think him a passive onlooker and recording stenographer-angel merely taking down dictation. Lest we should undervalue the writing itself, Babel's opus includes a number of characteristically Russian over-statements about the writing process. They are fondly quoted by credulous admirers like Cynthia Ozick, who here contributes a breathless, brainless introduction. 'I spoke to her of style,' he writes in 'Guy de Maupassant', 'of an army of words, an army in which every weapon is deployed. No iron spike can pierce a human heart as icily as a period in the right place.' This self-vaunting credo might carry more weight were it not for another *obiter dictum* about repetition on the same page: 'When a phrase is born, it is both good and bad at the same time. The secret of its success rests in a crux that is barely discernible. One's fingertips must grasp the key, gently warming it. And the key must be turned once, not twice.' This is sound, subtle, tactful – and violated by Babel in the previous paragraph, where we are twice told that the maid had 'pointed breasts'. 'Debauchery had congealed in her gray, wide-open eyes,' Babel confides on one page, only to write on the facing page, 'turning away her eyes in which debauchery had congealed'.

Poetry was intended as a stay against the accusation of reportage, the lowest form of realism. In practice, for Babel, 'poetry' meant overwriting, flirtation with non-sense, exaggeration, deliberately chosen imprecision, anti-realism. And it is fatal for many of the stories. In an early story, 'Odessa', Babel complains that in Russian literature 'there haven't been so far any real, clear, cheerful descriptions of the sun.' His stories are, among other things, a sustained effort of reparation and overwriting. Here is a partial cull: the sun 'poured into the clouds like the blood of a gouged boar'; 'the sun soared up into the sky and spun like a red bowl on the tip of a spear'; 'the sky changes colour – tender blood pouring from an overturned bottle'; 'the dying sun in the sky, round and yellow as a pumpkin, breathed its last rosy breath'; 'a timid star flashed in the orange battles of the sunset'; 'we rode toward the sunset, its boiling rivers pouring over the embroidered napkins of the peasants' fields'; 'in his yard, the sun was tense and tortured with the blindness of its rays'; 'the cross-eyed lantern of the provincial sun'. Every one a dud. You can have too much of a bad thing.

Nor is the moon exactly ignored: 'the snaking moon'; 'only the window, lit up by the fire of the moon, shone like salvation'; the moon is twice described as 'a nagging splinter', which for once has a kind of precision. Otherwise, Babel seems bent on the widest gap possible between tenor and vehicle – as a guarantee of poesis. Now and then, success seems close. For instance, there is a kind of metaphoric counterpoint between the cool of evening and a mother tending a fevered child: 'The evening wrapped me in the soothing dampness of her twilight sheets, the evening placed her motherly palms on my burning brow.' Maybe it sounds less cluttered and more natural in Russian. In English, the nursing details, the dampened sheets to lower the temperature, simply overwhelm the cool crepuscular half of the comparison. Then there is the judiciously indecorous, anti-poetic comparison I associate with Pasternak: 'the sunset was boiling in the skies, a sunset thick as jam.' Again, the two-stage comparison with jam-making is unwieldy and faintly argumentative. I prefer the precisely Pasternakian comparison, 'the kerosene-coloured night of Baku', or the real oddity of the word 'implausible' in this figure: 'the fire of the sunset swept over him, as crimson and implausible as impending doom.'

But mostly the implausibility lies in the metaphors and similes themselves. 'Bullets unfurled like string along the road.' Bullets bring out the worst in Babel: 'the bullets plunge into the earth and writhe, *quaking with impatience*' (my italics). Any metaphor with an olfactory element is invariably solipsistic and inscrutable: 'her sponge cakes had the aroma of crucifixion'; 'a sour odor rose from the ground, as from a soldier's wife at dawn'; 'I stink like a slit udder'; 'a red-headed widow, who was drenched with the scent of widow's grief'; 'the cadaverous aroma of brocade'; 'Sashka's body, blossoming and reeking like the meat of a slaughtered cow'.

There is no single rationale for these overblown figures, rather a variety of contributing reasons. As well as the Russian tradition of the opaque, apparently unjustified comparison, there are two other causes to take into account: the potent example of the epic simile and the vernacular tradition. The vernacular tradition employs exaggeration as its stock in trade: think of Huckleberry Finn retailing (with an inflection of doubt) an image of his father's, when a man who has fallen from a high roof is buried not in a coffin but between two barn doors. It might be the *Beano*. You can identify this bent in Babel's imagery now and again. For instance, when Benya Krik fights his father, the favoured figure of speech is 'he shuffled his father's face like a fresh deck of cards.' In English pub argot, the equivalent euphemism would be 'to rearrange someone's features for the worse'. What makes these phrases both popular and vulgar is their artifice, their frank contrivance. Raymond Chandler's Marlowe is, like Babel, equally given to suave, original variations of this wise-cracking demotic.

'Konkin' subtly but self-consciously comments on the vernacular. In this story, a Cossack pursues a Polish officer whose dignity will not allow him to surrender to anyone other than the supreme commander, Budyonny. Exasperated, the Cossack declares his civilian identity and demonstrates it. He is a ventriloquist from Nizhny. And the whole story is ventriloquised by Babel, who is interested in the anecdotal method of the anonymous soldier. 'Konkin, the political commissar of the N Cavalry Brigade and three-time Knight of the Order of the Red Flag, told us this story *with his typical antics* during a rest stop one day' (my italics). The demotic style is antic. Doors don't simply open. They *burst* open. 'Barbara Stepanovna turned purple.' 'Her voice boomed like mountain thunder.' 'The snake of his peasant grin slithers across his rotten teeth.' Exaggeration is an implicit declaration of class solidarity.

Writing of the Red Cavalry, Babel was aware of his political duty to heroise, even as he unflinchingly and critically depicted the casual barbarities of his Cossack comrades. I believe that Babel was consistently subversive. 'And in a loud voice, like a triumphant deaf man, I read Lenin's speech to the [illiterate] Cossacks.' The speech is there for the political commissar. The 'triumphant deaf man' is there for the reader alert for irony. In 'Salt', another ventriloquised story, the narrator throws a female smuggler off a train, then shoots her. The story ends with this affirmation of Bolshevism: 'we will deal relentlessly with all the traitors who pull us into the pit and want to turn back the stream and cover Russia with corpses and dead grass.' The speaker, Nikita Balmashov, has just left the corpse of the woman by the side of the railway. This contradiction, that the revolution brings destruction indistinguishable from that of the former tyrants, is one to which Babel returns time and again.

The epic simile is part of the iron necessity to heroise, lest the ironies become transparent. And the epic simile carries the requirement of radical indirection. Where the normal simile insists on likeness, the epic simile prescribes differentiation. So Savitsky rises 'splitting the hut in two like a banner splitting the sky'. The commander's 'long legs looked like two girls wedged to their shoulders in riding boots'. In Babel's prose, the expansiveness of the epic simile proper is cognate with demotic hyperbole: 'he ran after [the prisoners] and gathered them under his arms, the way a hunter grips an armful of reeds and pushes them back to see a flock of birds flying to the river at dawn.' 'And Madame Gorobchik stood by her husband's bed like a mud-drenched crow on an autumn branch.' Only occasionally does Babel allow the epic simile its iota of irony: 'The damp mold of the ruins blossomed like a marble bench on an opera stage. And I waited with anxious soul for Romeo to descend from the clouds, a satin Romeo singing of love, while backstage a dejected technician waits with his finger on the button to turn off the moon.'

Yet, after all the allowances and explanations, much remains that is simply indigestible – confused, arbitrary, affected, contrived, arch and preening. 'My husband brings me firewood as wet as newly washed hair.' 'Blue roads flowed past me like rivulets of milk trickling from many breasts.' 'I rise from my bunk from which sleep had run like a wolf from a pack of depraved dogs.' 'You have laid impetuous rails across the rancid dough of Russian prose.' Babel's first Red Cavalry story, the two-page 'Crossing the River Zbrucz', has an ending that is not unforgettable but inescapable – the account of the dead Jew with his face 'hacked in two'. But almost equally inescapable is the melodrama of the sun 'rolling across the sky like a severed head', the 'snaking moon' – and the Jews who 'hop around in silence, like monkeys, like Japanese acrobats in a circus, *their necks swelling and twisting*'. My italics mark a physiological impossibility – an impossibility which is bound to mar the authenticity, the realism, on which Babel's uncertain claim to greatness is founded.

Derek Walcott's Poetry
(2000)

Plagiarism is, of course, the original sin. But a still more original version is copying yourself. There are many examples of self-plagiarism in Derek Walcott's extensive œuvre. On at least six occasions, Picasso is reported denouncing self-plagiarism as abject: 'copying others is necessary, but what a pity to copy yourself,' he told Dor de la Souchère.

Others first. Walcott's stated position on the anxiety of influence – that you could just as easily say 'the influence of anxiety' – is as unequivocally evasive as you might expect from a writer so clearly, lastingly and fatally touched by Dylan Thomas. '*The Bounty* makes clear Walcott's continuing relationship to Dylan Thomas's verse,' writes Bruce King, his sympathetic biographer. He must mean Walcott's 'snail-horned steeples' which owe so much – everything, in fact – to Thomas's 'Poem in October': 'the sea wet church the size of a snail / With its horns through mist.'

But Thomas's legacy to Walcott isn't simply the odd purloined image or two – or more – but also the considered embrace of fuddled syntax as a chosen poetic method. When T. S. Eliot said that the modern poet must 'dislocate if necessary, language into his meaning', Thomas evidently took Eliot too literally. There is in Thomas and Walcott a great deal of wilfully crippled language. Bruce King has this to say: 'some of [Howard] Moss's other comments point to difficulties that are so common to Walcott's writing that they are part of his style. There are words with uncertain reference which look forward and backward, there is a lack of verbs, the syntax may be erratic, punctuation is erratic in terms of clarifying meaning.' The amount of incompetent exposition in, say, *Omeros* is astonishing.

There are not only loose ends of plot. Hector loses his canoe in a storm on page 50, only to sell it on page 116 to buy his Comet car. Helen has stolen Maud's yellow frock on page 31, even though Maud Plunkett has altered it *for* Helen on page 29. On page 64 we are told (how reliably?) that the dress was a gift to Helen which Maud forgot. After all, Helen has definitely nicked towels from the Plunketts. There are also frequent passages where syntax and grammar seem designed to obstruct and occlude. Here are two related passages, dealing with

---

Bruce King, *Derek Walcott: A Caribbean Life* (Oxford, 2000).

Warwick Walcott, the poet's dead father: 'Out on the sidewalk the sunlight drained like a print / of a postcard flecked with its gnawing chemical / *in which* there was light, but with a sepia tint' (my italics). Walcott wants to say, I think, that the scene outside looks like a faded sepia postcard. This is Warwick Walcott in full fatherly spate: 'But before you return, you must enter cities / that open like *The World's Classics, in which* I dreamt / I saw my shadow on their flagstones, histories / that carried me over the bridge of self-contempt, / though I never stared in their rivers, great abbeys / soaring in net-webbed stone, when I felt diminished // even by a postcard' (my italics). The sense nearly survives its setting forth. Warwick Walcott prophesies his son will encounter at first hand the European culture the father only read about. He recalls his sense of inferiority and insularity, which could be exacerbated by a postcard of Europe, and yet was soothed by his reading. Reading his son, though, you start to dread the apparently helpful, but actually phantom connectives. *In which*. The syntax is purely gestural. It is no accident that my grammar-check – admittedly a crude instrument for assessing poetry – has underlined that entire quotation. It doesn't make sense.

Though Dylan Thomas ('past sleep-tight houses') is the main Other in Walcott, there is, via Thomas, Hopkins: 'in the indigo dark before dawn' is indebted to Hopkins's 'Moonrise'. Walcott is also touched by Auden, Yeats, Lowell, Heaney and Brodsky – less permanently, but so extensively that one is almost embarrassed by his lack of guile. The clichéd colonial paradigm of invasion and conquest has been fulfilled aesthetically. Odd, given that Walcott's pronouncements on the colonial past and its role in the present are so eminently sensible. Drawing on the Caribbean experience, he sees that no one and no race is without guilt – what happened, he asks, to the aboriginal Aurac people? Forget the past, then. Prepare, guiltlessly, to take advantage of English literature and all its language has to offer. In the event, though, English literature seems to have taken advantage of him – to have imposed its poetic practitioners successfully, absolutely.

Derek Walcott's reputation rests primarily on three works: *Another Life* (1973), 'The Schooner *Flight*' (1979) and *Omeros* (1990). The last, a work of over 300 pages, written over three years, published in 1990, is widely seen as the work that secured him the Nobel Prize in 1992. This review will concentrate therefore on *Omeros*. How good is it?

Walcott has always been a striking phrase-maker, and there are wonderful, memorable touches throughout *Omeros*. 'Then I heard patois again, as my ears unclogged' – whenever Walcott turns to dialect, 'then everything fit'. You are quenched and convinced by the authority, by the authenticity – 'Girl, I pregnant,/ but I don't know for who.' Now and then, of course, there are poetic flourishes rhetorically beyond the speakers. 'Their leaves start shaking / the minute the axe of sunlight hit[s] the cedars,' for example. This is a problem intrinsic to vernacular. How does the writer accommodate his linguistic gifts within the cramped, if fresh, givens of the vernacular? And unquestionably Walcott has those gifts: the egret's 'one *rusted* cry', the iguana's 'slit pods of its eyes', 'sunrise / *trickled* down its valleys', 'whales burst into flower', 'the wick of the cypress charred', 'the gold sea / flat as a credit card', 'and the only sound is the hot, lazy drum of the sea' (my italics). Walcott's metaphoric resource is widely celebrated – though a phrase like 'a bouquet of spume', if 200 pages away from 'whales burst into flower', still looks repetitious – parsimonious trope rotation.

In fact, surprisingly, the best Walcott is the plainest, those instances of straight observation, of unadorned directness: for Philoctete's perpetual shin-sore, 'like a radiant anemone', there is 'the usual medicine for him, a flask of white / acjou, and a jar of *yellow* Vaseline' (my italics). The colour is careful. That 'anemone' is fine, too, but weakened when, eleven pages later, we read that 'His knee was radiant iron' – an echo undiminished by the difference senses of 'radiant'. Walcott is good, also, on the way the erotic situates itself in the ordinary without being diminished – even perhaps enhanced. His St Lucian Helen of Troy, the *casus belli* between the fishermen Hector and Achille, is seen on several occasions, perhaps too many, 'swinging a plastic sandal' – a credible goddess, who, when she leaves Achille's exhausting jealousy for Hector, leaves 'a hair-pin / stuck in her soap dish'. Though there are fine phrases which, as it were, straddle the literal and the metaphoric – 'The reek of the beach / was rimmed with a white noise' – the more literal are the better. Walcott's much vaunted metaphoric facility has its negative side. Sometimes, he simply can't say things simply. In *Omeros*, there is precious little crying that isn't precious: 'Dew was filling my eyes', 'my dewy gaze', 'a coming rain hazing his pupils', 'both of them wept / the forgiving rain of those who have truly loved.' It could be *Enoch Arden*.

Then there are the stars. Plainly: 'From night-fishing he knew the necessary ones, / the one that sparkled at dusk, and at dawn, the other.' This is on a par with the flat effectiveness of 'she [Maud Plunkett] took off her damp gardening hat // and lay down on the *faded* couch, she loosed her bodice / *and blew down to her heart.*' This factuality has an irrefutability shared by the lover who *taps* Walcott's knuckles in the morning by way of goodbye – by way of affection, of acknowledgement, by way of saying how little need be said. Add to these the mourners who 'walk home / to their rusted villages, *good shoes in one hand*' (my italics), or the 'nut-littered troughs' of the sea, or bank tellers pausing to hear the Angelus – 'one wet fingertip / drying before it moved on to turn the next leaf'.

By comparison, the metaphors can seem contrived, muscle-bound, if powerful: in 'The Schooner *Flight*', we read 'nail holes of stars in the sky roof', conscious of the *i*'s in the comparison being dotted and the *t*'s being crossed. As we are in *Another Life*, where we read for the first time, 'the usual smoky twilight / blackened our galvanized roof with its nail holes of stars.' The latest sighting was in *The Bounty*: 'the stars that nail down their day'. You begin to wonder about Walcott's famous fecundity.

Which brings us to the subject of repetition in Walcott's poetry.

In *Omeros*, 'the corrugated iron / of the sea glittered with nailheads'. It is raining. In 'The Schooner *Flight*', it isn't raining, otherwise nothing has changed: 'the cold sea rippling like galvanize'. In *Omeros*, 'the sunrise was heating the ring of the horizon', whereas in 'The Schooner *Flight*' 'the sun / heat the horizon's ring.' In *The Arkansas Testament*, 'A Propertius Quartet', bafflingly, 'the sea's ring turned red with heat / under bubbling Colombian coffee.' Then there are the asphalt roads which produce a curiously persistent comparison: in *Omeros*, 'I smelt the drizzle / on the asphalt leaving the Morne, it was the smell // of an iron on damp cloth.' This Proustian equation had already been set down in 'The Schooner *Flight*': 'every hot road, smell like clothes she just press.' But even before that, *Another Life* spoke of 'The smell of drizzled asphalt / like a flat iron burning'. In the post-Nobel *The Bounty*, the trope recurs: 'a singed smell rose / from the drizzling asphalt'.

Omeros is an extraordinary anthology of repetition.

Initially, one is dazzled by the metaphoric brilliance of Walcott's comparison of the sway of the sea to the swoon of scales: 'the horizon's glittering scales'. Then you recall a prior, clumsier sighting, 240 pages previously: 'each brass basin / balanced on a horizon, but never equal'. And then it all comes back: in *Another Life*, 'the steel, silver scales of the sea'. It is possible, however, that these 'scales' are the more obvious fish scales, as they are in *The Bounty*: 'the sea shone / like its fish, the scales danced.' Nothing to do with weights and measures.

On pages 98 and 321, there are 'asterisks of rain'. On page 294, the starfish is an asterisk. On page 7, mosquitoes on his arms are 'flattened to asterisks' by Achille. On page 224, we meet 'asterisks of bulletholes'.

On page 38, the market discloses 'the iron tear of the weight' and on page 324 'the copper scales, swaying / were balanced by one iron tear'.

Then there are the Homeric lances, flung everywhere to create a spurious, overworked 'classicism': page 9 'the lances of oars', page 230 'with lances for oars', page 292 'lance of an oar'; page 15 'lances of rain', page 50 'lances of rain', page 149 'the rain's lances'; page 51 'the lances / of a flinging palm', page 31 'the palms' rusted lances', page 33 'copper spears of the palms'; page 35 'lances of sunlight', page 297 'a lance of sunlight'. Not to mention 'lances of yachts' or 'the feathered lances of cane'.

We could list all the comparisons of the sea to lace, or the heat haze as wires, but the list would be, well, epic … Instead, what about the comparison of rain to nails? Page 50: 'the crash / of thousands of iron nails poured in a basin // of rain on his tin roof'. Page 222: 'pouring tin nails on the roof'. The sea as parchment recurs on pages 3, 155 and 282. Of course, you can't have such egregious repetition without a built-in excuse – and *Omeros* duly supplies one. Page 96: 'and none noticed the Homeric repetition / of details, their prophecy.'

None noticed. Hold *on* a second there. Or do I mean a third, or a fourth.

Of course, the poem does have deliberate reprises: 'This was History. I had no power to change it. / *And yet I still felt that this had happened before.*' Often it has. There is a motif which links slavery to the work of ants. And when the slavers come to Achille's African village, the tableau of destruction depicts a mongrel and child in the street. Later in the poem, when the Sioux are raided, the child and mongrel motif is deliberately redeployed to make the link. But, equally obviously, this doesn't excuse the swarm of repetition in *Omeros* because many of those repeats are further repeated outside the poem. Repetition is a kind of disease in Walcott's work: in *Another Life* the narrator 'heard the grey, iron harbour / open on a seagull's rusty hinge' and a hundred pages later 'Day pivoted on a seagull's screeching hinge.' Is it indolence or inadvertence or pure incompetence?

Elizabeth Bishop, a peerlessly controlled, precise poet, memorably compared a basin to the moon in 'The Shampoo'. The whole stanza is memorable for its effortlessly sustained metaphor:

> The shooting stars in your black hair
> in bright formation
> are flocking where,
> so straight, so soon?
> – Come, let me wash it in this big tin basin,
> battered and shiny like the moon.

Walcott helplessly shoplifts her image and wears it out with overuse: page 12, 'stuck like a basin, / the rusting enamel image of the full moon'; page 235, 'the moon's cold basin'; on page 273, 'Moon-basins flashed in the riverbed.'

Clearly, there is a difference between Elizabeth Bishop's innate metaphoric tact and Walcott's unwieldy, wordy procedures. Where Bishop's analogy with the night sky is beautifully unforced, yet sustained, Walcott's extended metaphors arrive with the air of brazen, bald contrivance one associates with the cod

TV host Alan Partridge. A nudge too far. My italics in the following quotations: 'roosters, their cries screeching like red chalk / *drawing hills on a board*'; 'and a breaker arched with a sound like tearing cloth / *ripped down the stitched seam, a sound Mama make sewing // when, in disgust, she'd rip the stitches with her mouth*'; 'The lights stuttered in the windows // along the empty beach, red and green lights tossed on / the cold harbour, and beyond them, like dominoes / *with lights for holes*, the black skyscrapers of Boston.' The sound of Walcott painfully explaining. One last absurd unified *field* of agricultural imagery:

> he had counted the clustered berries on the nose,
> noted the eyebrows' haystacks, the dull canal gaze
> of his reflection, the forehead's deep-ploughed furrows,
>
> the bovine leisure with which he turned away eyes
> stupefied by distances ...

Could Walcott have a Dutch *farmer* in mind? Just a thought.

It is interesting to compare repeats in which the second version achieves a crispness denied the initial cluttered attempt. The hurricane in *Omeros*, Chapter IX provides instances of Walcott's writing at its worst:

> Lightning, his stilt-walking messenger, jiggers the sky
> with his forked stride, or he crackles over the troughs
> like a split electric wishbone. His wife, Ma Rain,
>
> hurls buckets from the balcony of her upstairs house.
> She shakes the sodden mops of the palms and once again
> changes her furniture, the cloud-sofas' grumbling casters
>
> not waking the Sun ...

This epic of plodding ingenuity, of deranged decorum, of laboured proliferation, leaves one longing for the brilliantly prosaic narration of Ma Kilman's cure of Philoctete, say, or the amusing, if irrelevant chapters about the political aspirations of Statics. How much more lightly the metaphors might be managed is demonstrated by Walcott himself: 'Lightning lifted his stilts over the last hill.' Similarly, there is the thumbsiness of 'in the grey vertical forest of the hurricane season' and the perfect economy of the later 'rain was an unshifting thicket'.

Some wordiness is forgivable. Heaney's brilliant comparison – 'fungus plump as a leather saddle' – waves aside the pedantic objection that, since all saddles are leather, 'leather' is tautological. The comparison is just, surprising, swift. It is self-explanatory and brilliant – obvious once it is pointed out. It requires no justification, no argumentation. Not that Heaney is entirely immune, though he is an infinitely more accomplished writer than Walcott. In *The Spirit Level* there is a terrible meddling moment of Walcottian over-insistence, a failure of tact: 'and the angler's motorbike / Deep in roadside flowers, like a fallen knight'. The image is perfect, did it stop there. Alas, it continues: 'Whose ghost we'd lately questioned: "Any luck?" ' The cause here seems to be the rhyme scheme, as much as anything else.

The rhyming in *Omeros* has been widely acclaimed, particularly by Brad Leithauser in the *New Yorker*. The currently high value placed on rhyme seems to me much exaggerated. Christopher Reid's poem 'Two Dogs on a Pub Roof' manages effortlessly to rhyme the same word exactly a hundred times. It is, I think, an ironic comment on the facility possible, given the latitude permitted. What was once a minor skill is now absurdly easy. Many of Walcott's rhymes are outrageous, following the example of Brodsky. *The Bounty* gives us 'even a', 'novena' and 'when a'. *Omeros* is an encyclopedia of brazen botches: 'jacket' / 'back, it'; 'tin-stealer' / 'Achille, the'; 'verandah' / 'Morne, the'; 'weather' / 'This year, the'; 'farmer' / 'uniform, a'; 'demeanour' / 'seen the'; 'savannah' / 'and the'; 'were the' / 'warrior'; 'Winchester' / 'was the'; 'flag-pole' / 'uphol-[stered]'. I could go on. The point is neither the ingenuity, nor the licence – though Hopkins and Browning have been scolded for greater ingenuity and less licence. The point is the continuous havoc Walcott's rhymes impose on his lines. *Omeros* is an epic of ugly lines, each one of which is individually allowable, but cumulatively disastrous:

> ... a fur monkey over the dashboard altar
> with its porcelain Virgin in flowers and one arm
> *uplifted like a traffic signal to halt. Her* [my italics]

Again:

> ... palm-fronds talking
>
> to each other. It was one of the mysteries
> of advancing age to like those tempestuous
> *gusts that hyphenated leaves on a railed walk, in-* [my italics]
>
> stead of keeping things in place and their proper use.

These two examples must stand for many where the integrity of the line is systematically violated.

In an interview for *New Letters*, Walcott said of *Omeros* that 'he had not had a plot in advance' and that 'his main aim as a writer was to give a clear picture of life in the Caribbean, especially its beauty.' Both these statements are fatal for the poem – which suffers from event-famine and an overdose of description. Who would have believed that all that lush landscape could be so monotonous, so relentless? *Omeros* is also without form. Anything goes in. Walcott goes to Lisbon in 1988 to attend a Wheatland Foundation conference, paid for by Anne Getty, and a touristic section finds its way into Walcott's epic. The slave trade is the slender link, the pretext for pages of picturesque watercolours in words.

There are three main narratives in *Omeros*: the love triangle of Helen, Hector and Achille; the Maud and Dennis Plunkett story which culminates in Maud's death; and the real but masked narrative of Walcott's own life. The last is potentially the most interesting, but the personal material, as opposed to the tourism of the international writer, is flinchingly unfrank. It seems to touch on Walcott's tormented relationship with his third wife, Norline Metivier. I deduce this from Bruce King's ultra-discreet life, which commendably guards the intimate detail of Walcott's biography, while disclosing the bare minimum of necessary facts. Walcott himself in *Omeros* mentions no names – and his insufferably coy treatment of sexuality is uniform with its treatment in the fictional narrative. Think of Larkin's tough candour in 'Love Again' – 'Love again: wanking at ten past three' – and compare Walcott's biblical, euphemised hand-job: 'House whose rooms echo with rain, / of wrinkled clouds with Onan's stain'. Sex throughout *Omeros* proves intractable for Walcott – especially masturbation. Helen, apparently to bring back Achille in some unexplained mystic fashion, masturbates in Chapter 29:

> … The hand was not hers
> that crawled like a crab, lower and lower down
>
> into the cave of her thighs, it was not Hector's
> but Achille's hand yesterday. She turns slowly round
> on her stomach and comes as soon as he enters.

The last line makes Walcott's cultural difficulty with masturbation clear. It isn't the real thing. Helen can come only with a man – he enters the room and enters her body too. But an innocent reader could be forgiven for not knowing *what* was going on precisely – given that crab and all that prestidigitation of hands. This is an early fuck in *Omeros*, with sperm – I think: 'we swayed together in that metamorphosis / that cannot tell one body from the other one, / where a barrier reef is vaulted by white horses.' I could easily be wrong. This is an even earlier fuck: 'She lay calm as a port, and a cloud covered her / with my shadow.' I could just as easily be wrong again. And this is Walcott *fantasising* a fuck with a Polish waitress in Toronto. He is reading at Greg Gatenby's Harbourfront. He is lonely and horny. It comes out as poetry: 'snow draped its bridal lace over the raven's-wing sheen. / Her name melted in mine like flakes on a river / or a black pond in which the wind shakes packets of milk.' Welcome back, *in which*. No wonder one of the three alleged charges of sexual harassment against Walcott has been so difficult to resolve. Walcott has never denied his words – only the meaning of what he said.

Bruce King has a brave try at unifying the *bricolage* and *brocante* of Walcott's epic – but he isn't convincing. The theme of Book I is 'that life consists of wounds' – of Philoctete's shin, of Dennis Plunkett's head wound, and of ... Apparently, the quarrel between the Plunketts is a kind of wound. As is, apparently, Helen quitting her job after being insulted by a tourist. Initially plausible, these 'themes' do not in fact engross the detailed narrative – where, in the words of Sinatra, anything goes. Including some appallingly twee poetic fictions – the bogus epic-ese of 'the surf abated / its sound, its fear cowering at the beach's rim' and the weeping porcelain Madonna on Hector's dashboard when he is killed in a road accident. Worse than these is the encounter in Ireland with the ghost of James Joyce – an ineffably vulgar copy of Heaney's Dante-influenced encounter with Joyce at the conclusion of *Station Island*. Where Heaney has Joyce hitting a litter basket with his ashplant, Walcott's account sinks under the weight of its clichés – the CNN version of the Troubles and the genial company of 'The Dead' singing along with their author, 'his voice like sun-drizzled Howth'. This isn't poetry at all. It is the Dante Experience Franchise trading at a loss.

Bruce King's biography is the first and probably the last full-length account of Walcott's life. It is unintrusive, well disposed, charitable to its subject – and finally, reluctantly, critical of the man and his work. It feels intermittently as if there are two books, not one – the authorised and the rebellious.

King is continuously interesting about Walcott's troubled relationship to his own blackness. He is authoritative and sometimes tedious on Walcott's drama, a subject he has already written about. His eagerness to praise Walcott – the biography's worth being grounded on his subject's artistic stature – means that his judgements begin to bite only in the second half. Before that, King's criticism is credulous and a bit budget – for example, the meaningless statement that 'long before he met Joseph Brodsky, Walcott was already at heart a Russian writer.' A Russian writer like whom? – Mayakovsky, Pasternak, Goncharov, Griboyedev, Pushkin?

Now and then, though, a piqued biographer lets slip judgements both subversive and true. We learn that bits of Walcott's prose autobiography went straight into *Another Life* and 'became *marvellous poetry*. Once Walcott moves beyond journalism his prose often becomes poetic – mood, impressionism, epiphanies, and *posturing*' (my italics). King proves to be rightly uneasy with Walcott's easy resort to 'large gestures' – 'running together slavery, imperialism, the attempted extermination of the Jews, the war in Vietnam, and personal sins, loses their specificity, their difference, the reality of what has been done.' History as simplification, then.

For King, the advent of Brodsky isn't an unqualified benign influence: 'this contempt of democratic levelling, *assertion of improbabilities*, and use of tangential replies was often Walcott's manner during these years. It is rather grand, probably influenced by Brodsky' (my italics). On Walcott's appalling critical prose – prose that can refer, hilariously, ignorantly, to 'Eliot and Pound in their Byronic romanticism' – King is divided. On the one hand, 'his best essays are unusually rich in style, in symbolism, in ellipses, epiphanies; they are, in fact, poetic, deep, rich.' On the other hand, 'as I look through fragments and drafts of Walcott's autobiographical pieces and essays, I am struck by the digressiveness, by the waffling about and the lack of economy.' I suggest that these two views are saying the same thing – politely, then truthfully.

Finally, before I forget – those 'slit pods' of the iguana that I praised. Compare 'crocodiles, slitting the pods of their eyes' on page 133. In *Omeros* there are seven instances of slitted eyes. At the last count.

Raymond Carver

(2009)

In 1967, Raymond Carver and his wife Maryann filed for bankruptcy protection. Carver was drinking heavily. He decided to train as a librarian and enrolled into the master's programme at the University of Iowa's School of Library Science. By June, he had abandoned this plan and was hired as a textbook editor at Science Research Associates in Palo Alto, California. It was Carver's first white-collar job. Carver's story 'Will You Please Be Quiet, Please' was selected for *Best American Stories 1967*. In 1968, *Near Klamath*, Carver's first book of poems, was published in the spring. So, literary achievement, if on a small scale.

But probably the most important thing in Carver's life had already happened. Late in 1967, he was introduced to Gordon Lish, the founder editor of *Genesis West*, an avant-garde magazine. Lish was also working for a textbook publisher in Palo Alto. In 1969, Lish became fiction editor at *Esquire* magazine and in November wrote to Carver asking for stories. (Lish's shift from avant-garde to mainstream was ironised in his 1971 essay 'How I Got to be a Big-Shot Editor and Other Worthwhile Self-Justifications' – that title, a boast and a knowing, wry disclaimer, gives you some idea of how clever Lish is.) In 1970, Lish line-edited Carver's story 'Neighbors' and accepted it for *Esquire*. Carver was grateful – for acceptance and editing.

By 1976, Lish's assiduous promotion of Carver paid off. McGraw-Hill, under the Gordon Lish imprint, published Carver's first book of fiction, *Will You Please Be Quiet, Please?* The twenty-two stories had all been previously published in periodicals and were further edited by Lish, with Carver's approval. In this year, Carver was hospitalised for acute alcoholism and wound up in Duffy's, a residential treatment centre in the Napa Valley. Did I mention that in 1974, Carver and his wife filed for bankruptcy protection a second time? Well, I did now.

In 1980, Carver, separated from Maryann, set up house with poet and Guggenheim Fellow Tess Gallagher in El Paso, then Syracuse in upstate New York. Carver gave a manuscript to Lish, now an editor at Knopf, and Lish edited the stories so intensively that the original was halved in length. On 8 July 1980, Carver wrote a despairing letter to Lish, insisting that, unless the original text was restored, publication of *What We Talk About When We Talk About Love* should

Raymond Carver: *Collected Stories*, edited by William Stull and Maureen Carroll (Library of America, 2009).

be cancelled. Part of Carver's problem was that several other writers, like Tobias Wolff and Stephen Dobyns, had seen the originals. They would know what Lish had done.

In the event, publication went ahead and Carver's name was made. Though thereafter Carver was confident enough to resist Lish's editing, ever since, there have been rumours that Gordon Lish was responsible for everything valuable in Carver's work. The editors of the Library of America *Collected Stories* (not complete) have chosen to publish Carver's original manuscript (*Beginners*) alongside Lish's edit (*What We Talk About When We Talk About Love*). They have done so at the urging of Carver's widow, Tess Gallagher, who feels the original manuscript is superior to Lish's edit. It isn't. It is manifestly inferior. Lish was an editor touched with genius.

But does this mean that Carver was untalented? Think of Ezra Pound's peerless and ferocious editing of *The Waste Land*. Every edit an improvement – and Eliot's reputation unaffected. Think of Charles Monteith's editing of the original typescript of *Lord of the Flies*: no one would wish back the thirty introductory descriptive pages of nuclear war cut by Monteith, who was Golding's editor at Faber. What remains is brilliant and all Golding's own work.

Is Carver a Golding or a T. S. Eliot? That is the fundamental question. We can test the hypothesis by examining Carver's work before-Lish and after-Lish. Before 1971 and after 1980. A related issue is the nature of the editing. Pound and Monteith cut. On occasion, Lish added and rearranged. He treated Carver's stories as rough drafts – which is what they were in reality after Lish had redesigned them, a bit like Picasso taking massive liberties with Velázquez's *Las Meninas*. Except that Carver was no Velázquez.

One of the things non-musicians find difficult is the attitude of serious composers to tunes. Stravinsky lifts the opening melody of *The Rite of Spring* from a collection of Russian folk tunes. Beethoven writes variations on the English National Anthem. Bartók and Kodály go out on the road, transcribing folk material. Tunes? They're for the birds. Messiaen notates birdsong. Carver thought of the tunes: the blue-collar drunks, the spaced-out infidelities, the bitter abruptnesses of alcoholic behaviour, those inexplicable aporias. Lish composed them, sometimes radically, sometimes delicately – but never mistakenly.

'So Much Water So Close to Home' in Carver's original was nineteen pages long. In Lish's edit it takes six pages. It is improved *beyond recognition*. 'I Could See the Smallest Things' is Lish's retitled version of Carver's 'Want to See Something?' The original is seven prolix pages, the edit four pages. It, too, is changed and improved beyond recognition.

An easy example. We have two versions of a Carver story where the tune is itself taken from the judgement of Solomon: offer each mother half the child and the true mother will give up her share. (As a topos of justice, this comes in for some searching, only apparently stupid, criticism from Jim in *Huckleberry Finn*.) Carver's version is the self-destructive alcoholic version, in which the two parents struggle for physical possession of a baby. It is all about the struggle of two wills. The object of the struggle, the baby, is merely the site of contention. Lish has added a brilliant, ironically affectless title, 'Popular Mechanics'. The original is called 'Mine'. It is a perfect, tiny touch, and it is Lish's. He has changed only one word and added two, but the effect is massive. It adds sardonic detachment, ironic contempt, to the palette of colours.

Lish has also taken out two clunks. Nothing 'major', you might think, but the short story depends on getting everything right. In Carver's original, as the two parents struggle for physical possession of the child, there is an over-explanatory, distracting sentence:

> She felt her fingers being forced open and the baby going from her. No, she said, just as her hands came loose. *She would have it, this baby whose chubby face gazed up at them from the picture on the table.* She grabbed for the baby's other arm. She caught the baby around the wrist and leaned back.
>
> He would not give. He felt the baby going out of his hands and he pulled back hard. He pulled back very hard.
>
> In this manner they decided the issue. (my italics)

There are several alterations to this passage, but the main one is the excision of the sentence in italics – a sentence that pulls focus somewhere else, disastrously. Lish also cuts the repetition of 'he pulled back hard. He pulled back very hard.' In the edit, it is 'he pulled back very hard'.

The opening paragraph is immeasurably improved by two slight, crucial alterations. Carver is a naturally repetitive writer – heavy on the gas, too reliant on the pedal. His version opens: 'During the day the sun had come out and the snow melted into dirty *water*. Streaks of *water* ran down from the little, shoulder-high window that faced the backyard. Cars slushed by on the street outside. *It was getting dark, outside and inside*' (my italics). This is Lish's version: 'Early that day the weather turned and the snow was melting into dirty water. Streaks of it ran down from the little shoulder-high window that faced the backyard. Cars slushed by on the street outside, where it was getting dark. But it was getting dark on the inside too.' You lose the repetition of 'water' and the apparent redundancy of Carver's 'outside and inside' is made quietly ominous.

Both Carver and Lish are copying Hemingway, but Lish is better at it. As the opening phrases show – 'During the day the sun had come out' and 'Early that day the weather turned'. Carver's awkward pluperfect is removed and the time-scale is clearer. It is nothing – nothing at all – and it is everything.

Carver, of course, was copying Hemingway before Lish happened along with his dark green eye-shield, his sharp, bloody pencil and his ample spike. Nothing wrong with imitating a great writer. Hemingway is no exception. This is the famous opening of 'Up in Michigan', in which Hemingway takes us inside Liz's amorous fixation on Jim: 'Liz liked Jim very much. She liked it the way he walked over from the shop and often went to the kitchen door to watch for him to start down the road. She liked it about his mustache. She liked it about how white his teeth were when he smiled …' The catalogue continues, all-inclusively. There isn't anything much she doesn't like. It ends: 'One day she found she liked it about the way the hair was black on his arms.' Hemingway repeats the trope in 'Cat in the Rain': 'The wife liked him. She liked the deadly serious way he received any complaints. She liked his dignity. She liked the way he wanted to serve her.' And so on. The addition in 'Up in Michigan' of 'liked it *about*' is only two words, but those extra words are lode-bearing.

The trope itself is taken directly from that great source work *Madame Bovary*. Charles is in undeclared love with Emma and visits her father to supervise the recovery of his broken leg: 'He liked to find himself riding into the farmyard and to feel the gate turning against his shoulder. He liked the cock crowing on the wall and the boys running to meet him. He liked the barn and the stables, he liked old Rouault, who patted him on the hand and called him saviour. He liked Mademoiselle Emma's little clogs on the scrubbed stones of the kitchen floor.'

Carver has noticed only Hemingway's notorious repetition – hence that 'water' twice at the beginning of 'Mine' ['Popular Mechanics']. And he knows that Hemingway's prose is a beady necklace of terse, declarative sentences. In actuality, Hemingway's prose can be deliberately prolix and is much more various and rhythmical in a way that escapes Carver. It can also be economical in a way Carver's prose hardly ever is.

On his own, without Lish, Carver leaves out very little. Try 'What Would You Like to See?' It recycles something cut by Lish from 'Want to See Something?' – a woman killed by a heart attack at the wheel, so her car crashes slowly into the carport – but is mainly remarkable for its mantra of unremarkable detail. Not technique, so much as obsessive-compulsive disorder. It reads more like a suspiciously circumstantial alibi than a short story.

The first story in this Library of America edition of Carver's stories is 'Fat'. It is pre-Lish. The opening story of *Cathedral* is (post-Lish) 'Feathers'. This is Carver trying to describe a fat baby in 'Feathers', admittedly protected from criticism (you could argue) by a characterised narrative voice:

> The baby stood in Olla's lap, looking around the table at us. Olla had moved her hands down to its middle so that the baby could rock back and forth on its fat legs. Bar none, it was the ugliest baby I'd ever seen. It was so ugly I couldn't say anything. No words would come out of my mouth. I don't mean it was diseased or disfigured. Nothing like that. It was just ugly. It had a big red face, pop eyes, a broad forehead, and these big fat lips. It had no neck to speak of, and it had three or four fat chins. Its chins rolled right up under its ears, and its ears stuck out from its bald head. Fat hung over its wrists. Its arms and fingers were fat. Even calling it ugly does it credit.

A not untypical failure. Carver's method, in essence, is painstaking notation, the prose of a Sunday painter, only one up from painting by numbers, while shielding the point of the story. Immense literalist clarity of detail paradoxically masking a narrative enigma. You see everything – except the point. The point usually proves to be allegorical.

In 'Feathers', the narrator takes his disaffected wife to supper with a work-colleague and his wife. They are the parents of the ugly baby. There is also a slightly alarming peacock in the story, the pet of the parents, which is allowed indoors because its presence soothes the ugly baby. The narrator and his wife leave – she unaccountably less disaffected and wanting her husband's 'seed'. As a result, she becomes pregnant and their life together enters a period of pro-longed drabness and discontent. The point of the peacock – the narrator's wife is given peacock feathers to take home – is that the maternal instinct is a mys-tery, a powerful biological imperative. When the narrator's wife plays with the ugly baby, we assume she is faking interest and affection. But the behaviour of the peacock sets us straight: 'The peacock walked quickly around the table and went for the baby. It ran its long neck across the baby's legs. It pushed its beak in under the baby's pajama top and shook its stiff head back and forth. The baby laughed and kicked its feet. Scooting onto its back, the baby worked its way over Fran's knees and down onto the floor. The peacock kept pushing against the baby, as if it were a game they were playing. Fran held the baby against her legs while the baby strained forward.'

It's the animal in us, you see.

There is one good piece of writing in this story: the peacock 'shook itself, and the sound was like a deck of cards being shuffled in the other room'.

In 'Fat', the narrator is a waitress, serving a very fat man. We know he is fat because, in this story of four and a half pages, the word 'fat' occurs twenty-five times. She is telling her friend Rita what the fat man ate in detail. More Sunday-painter literalism. Just before the end of the story, we reach a genuinely promising, anti-narrative point:

What else? Rita says, lighting one of my cigarets and pulling her chair close to the table. This story's getting interesting now, Rita says.

That's it. Nothing else. He eats his desserts, and then he leaves and then we go home, Rudy and me.

Rita, like most readers, wants closure and climax. Carver appears to resist, to deny the appetite for story, for point, purpose and narrative destination, the way Wordsworth does in *Lyrical Ballads*. In 'Simon Lee', Wordsworth snubs his readers with their yearning for 'outrageous stimulation': 'My gentle reader, I perceive / How patiently you've waited, / And I'm afraid that you expect / Some tale will be related ...'

Carver, though, succumbs – succumbs to the obvious – though he is careful to include Rita's bafflement: 'That's a funny story, Rita says, but I can see she doesn't know what to make of it.' This, of course, is an instruction to the reader: make something of it. It is a story about pregnancy, where 'fatness' is a synecdoche for pregnancy. First, the narrator wonders 'what would happen if I had children and one of them turned out to look like that, so fat'. (Compare, the identical topos of obese baby in 'Feathers'.) Then, when Rudy starts fucking her, 'here is the thing': 'When he gets on me, I suddenly feel I am fat. I feel I am terrifically fat, so fat that Rudy is a tiny thing and hardly there at all.' Pregnant with a foetus, in fact. O my homunculus.

I nearly forgot. The fat man, when he orders, uses the plural form to refer to himself. 'I think we will begin with a Caesar salad.' He's feeding for two, is all. This could almost be clever, were it not for the insistence on the plural and the unflagging account of the items on the menu and chosen from the menu. The food in 'Feathers' isn't stinted either in Carver's account. What you have here, in both stories, is an anecdotal twist, an O Henry ending, buried under a dumpster of dog-eared detail.

Carver is sometimes described as the American Chekhov – about as routinely as William Trevor is described as the Irish Chekhov. It's no surprise that, towards the end of his life, Carver should examine this parallel in a story, 'Errand'. Essentially, this story narrates Chekhov's death from TB in Badenweiler, a German spa town. Carver draws on Olga Knipper's memoir, Chekhov's sister's memoir, Chekhov's letters and journals. Carver is careful to mention that Chekhov and his friend and patron Souvorin both came from peasant stock – as Carver came from blue-collar, Bruce Springsteen-celebrated, working class. Another important part of the story touches on Chekhov's relations with *his* senior writer, Tolstoy. Tolstoy doesn't think much of Chekhov's plays, but he admires the stories, and likes Chekhov because he is 'modest and quiet, like a girl'. Carver's figure for himself in the story is equally modest. He is the servant who brings Chekhov, Olga and their doctor a bottle of champagne in the middle of the night – for a last drink before death. The servant, appropriately enough, is a shambles: 'the champagne was brought to the door by a tired-looking young man whose blond hair was standing up. The trousers of his uniform were wrinkled, the creases gone, and in his haste he'd missed a loop while buttoning his jacket. His appearance was that of someone who'd been resting (slumped in a chair, dozing a little) when off in the distance the phone had clamored.' (*'Clamored'*!)

His appearance was that of someone who has slept in his clothes – because Carver was a drunk. But the next morning, his appearance is sober: 'his uniform trousers were neatly pressed, with stiff creases in front, and every button on his snug green jacket was fastened.' He's been to AA, he's off the sauce and he's about to become the American Chekhov – modestly.

Which brings us to the champagne cork that is the point of the story. When the doctor opens the Moët, he works the cork carefully out of the bottle – 'to minimize, as much as possible, *the festive explosion*' (my italics). What is wrong with 'pop'? Or 'ring' for the telephone? Carver is writing in his suit and wearing a nineteenth-century tie.

Anyway, when he has poured three glasses, the good doctor, 'out of habit, pushed the cork back in the neck of the bottle'. An impossibility, of course. Or people wouldn't need to buy those chromium helmets that batten on the rim of the bottle-neck.

Why does Carver need the cork back in the bottle? Wouldn't it be enough for the serving boy to see the cork on the floor and close his hand on it surreptitiously. That way, the cork would be a figure for the servant, essential, ignored, peripheral, modest. It would also be a symbol of good writing – and the way it depends on seeing the importance of the detail, the irrelevant detail.

That, however, wouldn't have brought Carver's allegory home. The story isn't about the inadvertent killer detail. The story is about Carver inheriting Chekhov's spirit. The cork goes back in the bottle so it can leave it, pop out a second time, very shortly after Chekhov dies – like a soul leaving a body. The boy lays his hand on the soul of Anton Chekhov.

We think we know what Carver thought of Gordon Lish. This is from the famous letter of 8 July 1980: 'If the book were published as it is in its present edited form, I may never write another story, that's how closely, God Forbid, some of those stories are to my sense of regaining my health and mental well-being.' He felt ontologically in danger – as a writer and as a person. When he wrote this letter, Carver was already walking out with Tess Gallagher, whose opinion of Lish hasn't changed. Carver, I'd guess, was caught between a rock and a hard place – between Lish and Gallagher. Lish won the battle over *What*

We Talk About When We Talk About Love, but Gallagher has gone on fighting. Lish's position is that the matter is closed: 'a dead letter to me'. In 1991, Lish sold his archive to the Lily Library of Indiana University. The evidence is out there, then. Lish knows what the verdict will be. He doesn't need to fight. He only needs to wait. Gallagher may think publication of the original unedited manuscript in this Library of America edition will set matters right, support her version of the literary record – but she is wrong. It does exactly the opposite.

The title story of *Cathedral*, the first post-Lish volume, is about the visit of a blind man whose wife has died of cancer. It is narrated by a lush whose wife once worked for the blind man. They have kept in fairly close touch by exchanging tapes. The narrator's sensitivity has been permanently eroded by alcohol. The prolixity of the narrative is testing but perhaps excused by the narrator's impaired state. The Joyce story 'Counterparts' is written in style indirect libre for Farringdon, the drunken protagonist: 'He lifted up the counter and, passing by the clients, went out of the office with a heavy step. He went heavily upstairs until he came to the second landing.' 'Cathedral' has comparable passages: 'Once she asked me if I'd like to hear the latest tape from the blind man. This was a year ago. I was on the tape, she said. So I said okay, I'd listen to it. I got us drinks and we settled down in the living room. We made ready to listen. First she inserted the tape into the player and adjusted a couple of dials. Then she pushed a lever. The tape squeaked and someone began to talk in this loud voice.' Now you know how a cassette player works.

Would you like to know how people eat food?

When we sat down at the table for dinner, we had another drink. My wife heaped Robert's plate with cube steak, scalloped potatoes, green beans. I buttered him up two slices of bread. I said, 'Here's bread and butter for you.' [He's blind, see.] I swallowed some of my drink. 'Now let us pray,' I said, and the blind man lowered his head. My wife looked at me, her mouth agape. 'Pray the phone won't ring and the food doesn't get cold,' I said.

We dug in. We ate everything there was to eat on the table. We ate like there was no tomorrow. We didn't talk. We ate. We scarfed. We grazed that table. We were into serious eating. The blind man had right away located his foods, he knew just where everything was on his plate. I watched with admiration as he used his knife and fork on the meat. He'd cut two pieces of meat, fork the meat into his mouth, and then go all out for the scalloped potatoes, the beans next, and then he'd tear off a hunk of buttered bread and eat that. He'd follow this up with a big drink of milk. It didn't seem to bother him to use his fingers once in a while, either.

Genius.

After this epic meal, the wife and the blind man talk. The narrator is bored, switches on the TV (to his wife's annoyance) and rolls a joint. His wife takes a toke and is basically out of the action after that. The blind man and the narrator drink Scotch and smoke joint after joint. On TV there is a documentary about medieval cathedrals. The narrator asks the blind man what he knows about cathedrals. The answer is an amalgam of stuff from the TV. Then the blind man says he really knows nothing about cathedrals and he asks the narrator to describe a cathedral. It is a failure. ' "I'm sorry," I said, "but it looks like that's the best I can do for you. I'm just no good at it." '

The blind man makes a proposition: they will draw a cathedral together. 'He found my hand, the hand with the pen. He closed his hand over my hand. "Go ahead, bub, draw," he said. "Draw. You'll see. I'll follow along with you. It'll be okay. Just begin now like I'm telling you. You'll see. Draw," the blind man said.'

And they draw a cathedral. '"You didn't think you could. But you can, can't you? You're cooking with gas now. You know what I'm saying. We're going to really have us something here in a minute."'

We think we know what Carver thought of Gordon Lish. But this story is what Carver thought of Gordon Lish. It is a story about writing, a story about the editorial process – in which someone without talent is used by someone else to write. The major contributor is the blind man. He can't do it without the boobus, but it is clear who does the writing. It was brave of Carver to write the story. And it is odd that no one, I think, has seen what it is about – mainly because it tells us something we'd rather not know – that Carver had the courage to disclose the raw material, this kind of self-exposure, but Lish had the literary talent.

Elizabeth Bishop
(2008)

'Oh dear I do loathe explanations, explanations, etc.'
– ELIZABETH BISHOP to ROBERT LOWELL (17 June 1963)

Teachers are often piously told that they will learn things from their students. This has happened to me twice. Once when an undergraduate told me that Kipling's 'Mary Postgate' reminded him of a Maupassant story, 'Mère Sauvage', he'd read as a French A-level set text. It was Kipling's source. On the second occasion, a student to whom I was teaching Elizabeth Bishop's poem, 'Twelfth Morning; or What You Will', mentioned that one of the Three Kings was called Balthazár. He had no idea how this affected the poem and the boy named Balthazár at its close. But he was intelligent enough to know that he didn't know what the poem meant and also to feel (rightly) that my explanation was partial rather than definitive.

'Twelfth Morning' is an exemplary Bishop poem, well worth understanding for its own sake and for its representative status. The twelfth morning after Christmas is the Feast of the Epiphany, the 6 January, celebrating the manifestation of Christ's divinity to the Gentiles, the Gentiles who are represented by the Magi (the three wise men, sometimes vulgarly called the three kings). Elizabeth Bishop gives us a seaside scene and a secular allusion to King Balthazár – a black boy with a four-gallon can of water on his head.

In Michel Tournier's novel *The Four Wise Men*, Balthazár, the king of Nippur, says: 'black men put me off because, frankly, they raised a question I was incapable of answering.' He is white. His African brother, Gaspar, king of Meroë, is the black king traditionally depicted in paintings of the baby Jesus at Bethlehem. So Elizabeth Bishop's allusion might be no more than a gesture towards the three kings, rather than a specific insistence on names. Balthazár, though, is commonly depicted in Northern European paintings from the fifteenth century onward as a young African or Moor; while Gaspar, usually called Caspar, is an elderly oriental.

The star of Bethlehem has become the flash of sunlight on the can Balthazár carries. It 'keeps flashing that the world's a pearl' – of which the can is its

Elizabeth Bishop: Poems, Prose and Letters, edited by Robert Giroux and Lloyd Schwartz (Library of America, 2008).

highlight. *Pearl*, of course, is a medieval text, a dream vision about heaven. (The biblical source of the idea is the parable in which Jesus likens the kingdom of heaven to a pearl of great price, for which a merchant sells everything he has.) But Elizabeth Bishop's epiphanic revelation is ultimately secular – the black boy is celebrating his birthday – and the veiled but faintly visible spiritual world is earthed by one of Elizabeth Bishop's most characteristic conceits, brilliant and pedestrian: 'Like a first coat of whitewash when it's wet, / the thin gray mist lets everything show through.' What shows through isn't heaven but the world, unpromising, prosaic: 'a fence, a horse, a foundered house'. But the house alludes to the parable of the house that was built on sand (here, a dune), rather than on the rock of the Church. So, we have nostalgia for religion, a familiarity with its metaphoric topoi, its frame of reference, but no certainty, no given guide lines: 'The fence, three-strand, barbed-wire, all pure rust, / three dotted lines, comes forward hopefully / across the lots; thinks better of it; turns / a sort of corner ...' The horse, too, is a biblical reference (Revelation 19:11–14, Christ on a white horse) shared with T. S. Eliot's 'Journey of the Magi': 'And an old white horse galloped away in the meadow.' In Bishop's poem, its odd status is indicated by the fact that 'He's bigger than the house' – but whether this is the 'force of personality' or dozing perspective is hard to say. And the white horse is actually off-white – 'A pewter-colored horse, an ancient mixture, / tin, lead, and silver'.

So what we are left with is, as it were, the oxymoronic 'pure rust' – the promised land, the glimpse of Pisgah, but in decay, reduced to a few ruined references, dominated by the 'slap-slapping' of water in the can in all its irreducible reality.

There is something ragged always about Elizabeth Bishop's glimpses of the ineffable. She isn't a believer. She hasn't the courage of her convictions. Her affirmations are strictly tentative and temporary. Nothing is there for all time. Only, now and then, reality offers the after-image of a fleeting gesture – an empty outline she is tempted to fill. Nostalgia very nearly supplies the loss. 'The Moose', a poem from *Geography III*, approaches one kind of eternity – eternity as a final settlement, as accountancy – and displaces it with something insoluble. As if elementary arithmetic were ousted by Fermat's Last Theorem. The poem begins with a 36-line opening sentence whose subject, a bus, is postponed till line 32. It is a sentence which, by its epic deferment, summons the epic. The opening offers us a comprehensive, commanding overview – with local counter-intuitive surprises ('the long tides / where the bay leaves the sea / twice a day') – that is quasi-Godlike. It approaches omniscience. The epic invokes a topos of ancient tradition, of fixed ritual, of order. There is a pronounced inference of stability in this sure syntactical conduct through complication. There is a telos implied in the syntax, and we safely achieve it. Safe conduct as a sensation of syntax – much as it is in the majestic second sentence of *To the Lighthouse*. The clarity on offer is succeeded by fog and a narrower focus: 'cold, round crystals / form and slide and settle / in the white hens' feathers'; 'the sweet peas cling / to their wet white string'. The restricted view is reinforced by the sudden absence of syntactical amplitude: a woman shaking out a tablecloth is 'A pale flickering. Gone.' As the bus settles to sleep in the darkness, Bishop gives her readers 'a gentle, auditory, / slow hallucination'. It resembles the adult conversations overheard by a sleepy child: 'Grandparents' voices // uninterruptedly / talking, in Eternity.' In this eternity, 'things [are] cleared up finally': 'what he said, what she said, / who got pensioned'. Facts, memories, sifted, sorted, and solved.

Then the moose appears – not a figure for the Muse, Derek Mahon's glib guess – but as the representative of something 'grand, otherwordly'. The moose is also a moose in a Gertrude Steinian way: 'awful plain', 'a she', 'homely as a house'. But a moose with a pronounced noumenon marked by the count of repetitions: 'Why, why do we feel / (we all feel) this sweet / sensation of joy?'

Whereas before we were offered moral reckoning, settlements, justice, accountancy, now we encounter something unforeseen, unsettling and inexplicably wonderful – eternity shadowed forth and already fading, erased by the pressure of familiar things: 'a dim smell of moose, an acrid / smell of gasoline'. So finality is ousted by the quasi-mystical, whose mystery is in turn ousted by the insistent ordinary.

There are several poems in the Bishop canon that illustrate this approach to completion, which almost close on certainty, only to turn away at the last – principled and ruefully bereft. They are 'Sandpiper', 'The Fish', 'At the Fishhouses', 'A Miracle for Breakfast' and 'Over 2,000 Illustrations and a Complete Concordance'. In this last poem, the title promises us something definitive – far from niggardly, far from partial, something comprehensive. In fact, Bishop conflates the Bible with other old books, a procedure she was subsequently doubtful about: she wrote to her friends, U. T. and Joseph Summers (18 July 1955), 'Something wrong with the middle of "Over 2,000 Illustrations", and I really shouldn't have used that title if I wanted to drag in the old books we had with the Seven Wonders of the World in them, too.' This entails a certain local confusion, it is true, but the conflation serves the central argument. As the poem proceeds, place and milieu change. There is a quality of palimpsest, where we sometimes glimpse reality through biblical etchings, and sometimes in its own right. The second paragraph is actual travels – Mexico, Ireland, Rome, Marrakesh – an anthology of Bishop's itinerary across the world. At the end of this section, Bishop describes an actual encounter with 'what frightened [her] most of all'. It is a 'holy grave' in a 'pink desert' – a holy heathen grave. We have to infer what kind of a prophet is buried here – a Muslim, because the 'marble trough' is 'carved solid / with exhortation'. We also have to infer what it is that frightens her. The guide, Khadour, 'in a smart burnoose' is unafraid, 'amused' in a patronising way. At first, you think that Bishop is frightened by a direct encounter with a site still saturated with religious significance – however unpromising the signs seem to be. However, her fear is provoked by the very obliteration of significance – 'not looking particularly holy', 'an open, gritty, marble *trough*' (my italics), 'half-filled with dust, *not even the dust / of the poor prophet paynim who once lay there*' (my italics). She is frightened by the spectacle of the spiritually defunct – a deserted grave in a desert.

Her final section turns from the pagan to Christianity. Her travels – a synecdoche for our existence – are designated an accumulation: 'Everything only connected by "and" and "and" .' (How gravely witty to connect those two 'and's with 'and'.) There is no telos, no meaning, no argument, even of insidious intent. Just one not-even-damned thing after another. The 'and's also refer forward to biblical polysyndeton – not particularly hopefully. She opens the Bible, though, and the gilt 'pollinates' her fingertips. Or, rather, there are two imperatives: 'Open the book'; 'Open the heavy book.' The source of these imperatives? Both a voice, her own voice, from within – and a disembodied voice from outside the self. (Perhaps like the voice St Augustine tells us he heard in *The Confessions*, directing him to open the Bible.) There is an ambiguous aura of possibility. What Bishop sees is an illustration of the Nativity. Which she *imagines*. In brilliant detail – 'the dark *ajar*' (my italics), a flame which transcends physics, being 'undisturbed, unbreathing'. Yet, at the very moment we are half persuaded of transcendence, Bishop brings us down to earth: the Holy Family are 'a family with pets'. The final line is both a hyperbolic tribute to innocence and a concession to objective calculus. We observe the Nativity – 'and looked and looked our infant sight away'. We are so rapt that we continue to look for years. And / or we lose our innocence. The first is a pious hope. The second is reality. The ambiguity holds but then resolves itself.

In 'The Armadillo', Bishop is wrier. The poem describes illegal fire balloons and the fall of one from the sky – burning an owl's nest, disturbing an armadillo, and revealing a short-eared rabbit with fur intangible as ash and ignited eyes. The final stanza is in italics: '*Too pretty, dreamlike mimicry! / O falling fire and piercing cry / and panic, and a weak mailed fist / clenched ignorant against the sky!*' From amused notation to candid rhetoric, from the casual – 'the stars – / planets, that is', she corrects herself – to emphasis, to italics. What is the 'weak mailed fist' shaking itself at the sky? It is an emblem of how man reacts to natural catastrophe. We protest against intention, vindictiveness. We do not see that these things are merely contingent. We take them personally. And the mailed fist? It is, of course, the armadillo, in Spanish 'the little armoured one', as synecdoche. The ironic distance between the emblem of human behaviour and Bishop's sophisticated awareness marks out her position precisely. She can empathise, as it were, with Browning's Caliban, who sees lightning as a sign of Setebos's divine displeasure, but she herself understands the physics without the need for metaphysics.

'At the Fishhouses' is a kind of conversation poem like 'Tintern Abbey' – moving from description, through a transitional passage, to meditation, with a kind of anti-Benediction. Bishop's letters tell us the location is real, but that she dreamt most of the poem. This disclosure needn't concern us. The fisherman is real enough: 'The old man accepts a Lucky Strike.' 'He was a friend of my grandfather.' Yet he is also an emblematic figure, ironically beautiful ('There are sequins on his vest and on his thumb'), a pragmatist, an unsentimental survivor, who has scraped a living: 'He has scraped the scales, the principal beauty, / from unnumbered fish with that black old knife, / the blade of which is almost worn away.' He is emblematic of a Spartan existence, unable to afford beauty, the nearly last of a threatened line (that depleted blade): 'We talk of the decline in the population.' It is as if something less local, as if humanity itself, clinging, precarious, is represented by him.

There follows Bishop's meditation on the sea, the unpunctuated, continuous ocean: 'Cold dark deep and absolutely clear'. That unpunctuated extension represents infinity. It is 'bearable to no mortal'. Man's relationship with the inhospitable, inimical, as in 'The Armadillo', is examined. Religion here is the Baptist religion, with its ironic belief in 'total immersion' – something already said to be impossible. She sings Baptist hymns to a seal – a parody of conversion, of misplaced evangelism. The water remains itself: 'Cold dark deep and absolutely clear'. And there follows a passage of repetition reminiscent of Eliot's 'rocks and no water' sequence in *The Waste Land*: 'I have seen it over and over, the same sea, the same, / slightly, indifferently swinging above the stones, / icily free above the stones, / above the stones and then the world.' 'Over and over' ushers in a kind of infinity. As does the water, which is said to be above the stones and, therefore, above the world beneath those stones. In Bishop's coda, she examines the effect of contact between this inhuman, other-worldly element and the mortal. It is almost a version of hell fire: 'as if the water were a transmutation of fire'. But in fact it is simply the unbearable truth about the universal indifference surrounding us. Unbearable? Yes. Even as she articulates it, the truth is dressed, helplessly anthropomorphised: 'It is like what we imagine knowledge to be [objective, cold, neutral]: / dark, salt, clear, moving, utterly free, [note the advent of punctuation, of organisation, of making sense] / drawn from the cold hard mouth / of the world, derived from rocky breasts ...' The mouth may be hard and cold, the breasts hard and rocky, but the indifferent and inhuman has been humanised. We cannot not see in human terms. (It is like Wallace Stevens's 'In The Carolinas', where nature seems suddenly hospitable, and Stevens asks Mother Nature why her aspic nipples for once vent honey.) And the typically inconclusive conclusion? We know what we know only in time, which means our knowledge is temporary, provisional: 'and since / our knowledge is historical, [our knowledge is] flowing, and flown.' It is Bishop's 'Dover Beach'.

In 'Sandpiper' the key poetic predecessor isn't Arnold but Blake. But the end-point – uncertainty, inconclusion – is the same. This is partly a matter of Bishop's temperament as much as a worked-out system. In 'The Fish' we are given an inventory, exhaustive, comprehensive, poetically brilliant, of the fish. At its completion, Bishop lets the fish go. She stares and stares – 'until everything / was rainbow, rainbow, rainbow! / And I let the fish go.' The rainbow is her tears. Compare the first page of Golding's *The Spire*: 'The tears of laughter in his eyes made additional spokes and wheels and rainbows.' The rainbow is also the sign of the covenant between man and God in which man is granted dominion over birds and beasts – a covenant Elizabeth Bishop rejects. Her sandpiper is said to be 'a student of Blake' – seeking a world in a grain of sand, in other words, but here trapped by the fixed focal length designed for the micro-detail. The ocean again stands for the infinity on every side of us. And the bird is cognate with the armadillo – a solipsist with a short focus, deprived of the larger view. He is in search of meaning: 'looking for something, something, something'. Rather than a comprehensive overview, he is lost in beautiful detail: 'The millions of grains are black, white, tan, and gray, / mixed with quartz grains, rose and amethyst.' Any summation is a total that leaves out the working, the detail, the living.

How are we to take Elizabeth Bishop's sestina 'A Miracle for Breakfast'? She called it her Depression poem and there is a soup-kitchen element. But dimly discernible behind it also is Christ's miracle of the loaves and fishes. And there is the spectral presence of John 14:2: 'In my father's house are many mansions.' What is related is both not a miracle ('it was not a miracle') and a miracle ('my mansion, made for me by a miracle'). The charity on offer is nugatory (a single crumb and one drop of coffee) but is transformed momentarily by the imagination: 'I saw it [a white plaster mansion sumptuously supplied] with one eye close to the crumb.' The 'miracle' is intermittent, only temporarily a real presence – and the awaited miracle then appears to be working 'across the river' 'on the wrong balcony'. Revelation, miracle, then, is a bit like communism – an international failure that once, according to its adherents, worked perfectly somewhere, even if only in one soviet in 1919. What we have here is Elizabeth Bishop's ironic, playful take on the idea of the movable feast –

a holy day of celebration whose date migrates and which has no fixed address.

'In the Waiting Room' also describes a miracle, the miracle of human existence – and how horrifying a miracle that can seem. The miracle of life is a cliché we all unthinkingly assent to. In this poem, Bishop modifies the cliché significantly and gives us the *disconcerting* miracle of life. Her position – the instinct to opt out of humanity – is cognate with that of Stendhal, as summarised by Valéry in *Masters and Friends*: 'every pure, strong being feels that he is something other than a man; he refuses and in a naive way fears to recognise in himself one of the innumerable examples of a species or a type that repeats itself. In all profound minds some hidden virtue is perpetually at work creating a recluse. When brought in contact with or reminded from time to time of other people, they become conscious of a peculiar sensation that pierces with a sudden sharp pain, making them withdraw at once into some indefinable inward island. This is an attack of inhumanity.' This is so close to Bishop's poem – especially her aunt Consuelo's *oh!* of pain in the young Elizabeth's mouth – you wonder if perhaps Stendhal isn't somewhere in the mix.

Her last collection, *Geography III*, in 1976, pretends to the certainty of the primer. Presumably, *Geography IV, V* and *VI* would be more advanced. But even now, in the quotation from 'First Lessons in Geography', the initial simplicities and certainties – '*What is the shape of the Earth?* Round, like a ball' – quickly complicate themselves, and the extract ends with a welter of questions: *In what direction is the Volcano? The Cape? The Bay? The Lake? The Strait? The Mountains? The Isthmus? What is in the East? In the West? In the South? In the North? In the Northwest? In the Southeast? In the Northeast? In the Southwest?*' I think Elizabeth Bishop here is defining the limits of definition, its pseudo-clarity: compare, what is a novel? Answer, say: a composition of words. Actually, these 'answers' simply redescribe and defer the problem. What kind of a composition in words? What is a poem? An arrangement of words. These are the kind of illusory clarities, limited clarities, that Bishop rejects – preferring that welter of questions rather than a redescription of the question minus its interrogative tone.

'In the Waiting Room' is the first poem in *Geography III*. It is set on 5 February 1918, a strangely precise date. It takes place in a dentist's waiting room. The nearly seven-year-old Elizabeth Bishop is reading the *National Geographic*. Her aunt Consuelo is under the dentist in his surgery. In other words, the situation couldn't be more pedestrian, more unpromising. And yet Elizabeth Bishop manages to convey the absolute strangeness of the ordinary – the bizarreness of being human at all, of existing. It is not unlike Chekhov's deathbed assertion that life is as mysterious as a carrot. He was asked by Olga Knipper about the meaning of life and replied that her question was like asking what a carrot means: 'A carrot is a carrot and nothing more is known.' In literature, the strangeness of the ordinary – Nabokov's 'halo round the frying pan' in *The Real Life of Sebastian Knight* – is usually epiphanic, celebratory. Compare Derek Mahon's 'Ovid in Tomis': 'If so [no God], we can start / To ignore the silence / Of infinite spaces // And concentrate instead / On the infinity / Under our very noses – // The cry at the heart / Of the artichoke, / The gaiety of atoms.' In Bishop, though, the enigma of the ordinary is tainted with disgust and horror – oddly for a writer who lavished attention on details. As often in Bishop's poetry, we have 'cold, blue-black space' and the *unlikeliness* of human beings existing at all. The photographs in the *National Geographic* are there to show us how foreign the human species can be – 'black, naked women with necks / wound round and round with wire / like the necks of light bulbs' – but the rest of the poem makes us see how bizarre *everything* human is. The ordinary is implacably strange – as if seen, defamiliarised, by an anthropologist or a Martian (or even a Russian formalist). It is one of Bishop's best poems, I think, because its short lines are actually long conversational lines in disguise. For example, 'How had I come to be here, / like them, and overhear / a cry of pain that could have / got loud and worse but hadn't?' The breaks are there but the thrust has something of C. K. Williams's slightly breathless, looping momentum of a poem like 'Reading: The Cop': 'but still, today, when I noticed him back in the hallway reading what looked like a political pamphlet, / I was curious and thought I'd just stop, go back, peek in, but then I thought, no, not.'

It's important to emphasise that though Bishop's poetry may have this major theme – of recoil away from overarching explanation – it is also thrillingly various. 'Crusoe in England', for example, is a singular, intriguing poem, an allegory whose specifics are involving, deliberate distractions, concrete details disguising the central drift of meaning. 'Crusoe in England' is a poem about depression, a meditation on unhappiness, and, possibly, an enquiry into the essential singularity of same-sex relationships ('The island had one kind of everything'; 'Friday was nice, and we were friends. / If only he had been a woman! / I wanted to propagate my kind'). It is also a poem about loneliness, about being on an island, about being an island. It contradicts Donne's famous sermon. On his island, Crusoe is unhappy: 'My island seemed to be / a sort of cloud-dump.' The island's smallest industry is 'a miserable philosophy'.

Obviously, the speaker is someone else in addition to Crusoe: he tries to remember Wordsworth's much-later, anachronistic lines about the daffodils. The word that escapes him – 'The bliss of what?' – is *solitude*. However, once Crusoe is back in England, his existence is strangely depleted: 'The knife there on the shelf – / it reeked of meaning, like a crucifix' when he was on the island. His survival depended on it. 'Now it won't look at me at all.' In other words, unhappiness is an intrinsic condition, rather than conditional on circumstances.

He is unhappy on the island. He is unhappy back in England. This relates to Bishop's overarching theme: there are no solutions, no resolution.

Elizabeth Bishop was the least confessional of poets, but it is impossible not to read 'Crusoe in England' as an oblique account of her move back to the USA after the suicide of her lover, Lota de Macedo Soares. The poem, according to the extraordinarily useful chronology of the Library of America edition, tells us that 'Crusoe in England' was completed in 1971, four years after Lota's suicide in September 1967. The poem was begun in 1964, however – three years before her death. I don't believe the inception date completely rules out my idea that it was conditioned by Lota's death and a difficult year in San Francisco with her replacement, the woman known as 'R', who seems to have supplanted Lota as Bishop's lover and contributed to her suicide.

Bishop admired the primitive painter Gregorio Valdes but notes, with the shrewdness of a fellow-practitioner (she painted herself), that his work was very uneven. She was attracted to the primitive because it privileged the detail over the whole – as she does in an entirely deliberate, meaningful way. Bishop doesn't share the other fault of primitive painting and writing which she identifies in 'The USA School of Writing': 'There was also the same tendency in both primitive painting and writing to make it all right, or of real value to the world, by tacking on a grand, if ill-fitting, "moral", or allegorical interpretation.' Her own attempts at folk poetry, 'The Burglar of Babylon', 'Manuelzinho' and 'The Riverman', are highly sophisticated, discriminating attempts at the genre. She manages to preserve the unstable freshness, the irrefutable naivety, the intrinsic *conviction* – while dumping the moralising. 'The Riverman' is an extraordinary poem, the best of a brilliant bunch, spoken by an Amazonian native, who wants to be a *sacaca*, a 'witch doctor who works with water spirits'. She wrote it before she had been up the Amazon, but its narration is pitch perfect. The story unfolds in the only way it can. It is like the human body, any body, however peculiar, once all clothing is removed. It could only be like this. It could not be different, any other than the way it is. Despite the tone of simplicity, the pitch is downright. It has some of the fairy-tale authority that Yeats could muster in 'The Happy Townland': *'The little fox he murmured, / "O what of the world's bane?" / The sun was laughing sweetly, / The moon plucked at my rein.'* 'Riverman' starts: 'I got up in the night / for the Dolphin spoke to me …' The story begins *in medias res* in a special sense: the back-story, the background that might explain 'the Dolphin', is omitted, to wonderful effect.

The speaker follows the Dolphin ('a man like myself') into the river, while his wife is snoring. 'I went down to the river / and the moon was burning bright / as the gasoline-lamp mantle / with the flame turned up too high, / just before it begins to scorch. / I went down to the river …' The pedantry, the clumsiness, is beautifully judged, as is the inappropriateness of the quotidian image for a supernatural event. It is charming and authentically primitive. The repetition is divested of poetry. It is the speaker picking up his thread after the diversion of that comparison of the moon to a gas mantle. Once under water, the events are oneiric – bizarre and indisputable.

> They gave me a shell of cachaça
> and decorated cigars.
> The smoke rose like mist
> through the water, and our breaths
> didn't make any bubbles.
> We drank cachaça and smoked
> the green cheroots. The room
> filled with gray-green smoke
> and my head couldn't have been dizzier.
> Then a tall, beautiful serpent
> in elegant white satin,
> with her big eyes green and gold
> like the lights on the river-steamers –
> yes, Luandinha, none other –
> entered and greeted me.
> She complimented me
> in a language I didn't know;
> but when she blew cigar smoke
> into my ears and nostrils
> I understood, *like a dog*. [my italics]

It carries more conviction, this passage, than Miss Havisham's ruined wedding cake and dirty bridal train. Why? Because Elizabeth Bishop has managed to inhabit the primitive imagination with its strange literalness. The tone is bled of whimsy: he smells his comb and he knows his hair smells of river. Without saying so, this is evidence, proof that he has been under water. Further visits involve a party with Luandinha: 'Her rooms shine like silver [nothing unexpected there] / with the light from overhead, / a steady stream of light / *like at the cinema*' (my italics). There is a kind of repeat, deliberately clumsy, towards the end, when the speaker again describes the moon: 'When the moon burns white / and the river makes that sound / like a primus pumped up high …' The fantastic, as ever, has to be earthed.

Her last (or possibly penultimate) poem, 'Sonnet', envisages death (the 'broken thermometer') as release from uncertainty into a kind of freedom:

she becomes the 'rainbow-bird' produced by 'the narrow bevel / of the empty mirror' which no longer contains her image of 'a creature divided' (a possible reference to bi-sexuality). The rainbow-bird – a version of the soul – can fly 'wherever / it feels like, gay!' In the sestet, the problem for the 'undecided' self is direction: 'the compass needle / wobbling and wavering, / undecided'. In the octet, direction doesn't matter: 'flying wherever / it feels like'. It is a lovely, peculiar sonnet: it preserves the typical versus, necessarily in a poem about change, but the rhymes, appropriately, are rarely decided: 'level' / 'bevel'; 'divided' / 'undecided'; 'away' / 'gay'. Then 'bubble' / 'needle', 'mirror' / 'wherever'. Then unrhymed words: 'wavering', 'broken' (a lovely, simply mimetic line-break, followed by 'thermometer'), 'mercury', 'rainbow-bird'. The prized constraint of the sonnet – 'Nuns fret not at their convent's narrow rooms' – is loosened, relaxed.

She was a great poet, and it has been a gratifying experience to observe, in my own lifetime, this gifted writer, mysteriously slighted by critics, though prized by poets, come into her kingdom. This Library of America volume – with all her published (and some previously unpublished) prose and a generous selection of her letters, economically but illuminatingly annotated by Robert Giroux and Lloyd Schwartz – is a fitting monument to her extraordinary achievement. How the Library of America persuaded her publishers to forgo their commercial interests in such a profitable asset is itself a minor miracle. But perhaps the copyright holders and the publishers simply take a cut of the take, so, appropriately enough, it isn't a miracle after all.

William Golding
(2009)

William Golding began by wanting to be a poet. In *The Use of Poetry and the Use of Criticism*, T. S. Eliot quotes T. E. Hulme's *Speculations* with approval: 'There is a general tendency to think that verse means little else than the expression of unsatisfied emotion … The great aim is accurate, precise and definite description. The first thing is to realise how extraordinarily difficult this is … Language has its own special nature, its own conventions and communal ideas. It is only by a concentrated effort of mind that you can hold it fixed to your own purpose.' Accurate, precise and definite description. This is surely one of the main reasons for reading Golding the novelist, for thinking him a great writer. This modest, irreplaceable, central skill – like being able to draw if you are an artist, like being able to capture a likeness, the likeness of a person's features, the likeness of a fingernail, the likeness of tears.

This is Tennyson on tears in *The Princess*: 'The gracious dews / Began to glisten and to fall'; 'shook and fell, an erring pearl'; 'glittering drops'; 'the dew / Dwelt in her eyes'; 'down the streaming crystal dropt'; 'she fixt / A showery glance upon her aunt.'

Why does everything in this little anthology fail? Each example fails because Tennyson has not captured a likeness. He is like Mr Joyboy in *The Loved One* titivating a corpse. The poetic process here is one of idealisation and improvement. Tennyson isn't seeing the object as in itself it really is. He is seeing the tears as if they were items in a theatrical costumiers. The tears are in fancy dress, poetic Sunday best.

However, it doesn't follow that the great artist must capture a likeness photographically, like an academician trotting out meticulous sanguine portraits for Oxford Senior Common Rooms. Think of Brancusi's great drawing of James Joyce, set down with the inspired clumsiness, the bold shorthand, of a child eager to get on to the next drawing. Spontaneous, laconic, summary in its execution. A technique that transcends technique.

Here are some tears in Golding. First, *Lord of the Flies*. Ralph is alone and Samneric have gone over to the other side.

Inaugural William Golding Memorial Lecture, University of Exeter, 5 March 2009.

Memory of their new and shameful loyalty came to them. Eric was silent
but Sam tried to do his duty.

'You got to go, Ralph. You go away now –'

He wagged his spear and essayed fierceness.

'You shove off. See?'

Eric nodded agreement and jabbed his spear in the air. Ralph leaned on
his arms and did not go.

'I came to see you two.'

His voice was thick. His throat was hurting him now though it received
no wound.

'I came to see you two –'

Words could not express the dull pain of these things. He fell silent,
while the vivid stars were spilt and danced all ways …

Why is this passage so brilliant? The context, of course, feeds into the imagery. We need Ralph to repeat his simple statement as if it were a cul-de-sac, an
oubliette. An ordinary writer would say that Ralph's throat ached. Golding adds
'though it received no wound'. The negative comparison implies the degree
of pain. And how much better this is than the automatic phrase that is just
off-camera: Ralph's feelings were wounded; his wounded feelings. The nature
of the pain should be precise: it is dull, but it is inexplicable. Think how often
doctors ask you to describe what kind of a pain you are feeling. Pain isn't always
the same. Every pain has a likeness that has to be caught. And then the actual
tears are simply occluded and we are offered instead the effect they have on the
vision: 'the vivid stars were spilt and danced all ways.'

This is essentially a poetic procedure, a symbolist procedure. There is a
letter of Mallarmé to Henri Cazalis in which he writes that poetry should 'Pein-
dre, non la chose, mais l'effet qu'elle produit'. Don't paint the thing – tears – but the
effect it produces – astral instability. It follows for Mallarmé that the reading
process cannot be straightforward but must proceed by a series of decipherings,
'par une série de déchiffrements'. But of course this particular trope isn't restricted
to poetry. In Paper Men, Wilf meditates on Homer's portrayal of Helen of Troy;
'the way in which Homer gets his story across by describing not the woman but
her effect on others'.

Compare Conrad in Typhoon, where he describes not the storm but the
effect of the storm. 'The lamp wriggled in its gimbals, the barometer swung
in circles, the table altered its slant every moment; a pair of limp seaboots with
collapsed tops went sliding past the couch.'

Then compare Betty Flanders at the beginning of Jacob's Room. She is writing a letter, a grieving widow on the beach:

Slowly welling from the point of her gold nib, pale blue ink dissolved the full stop; for there her pen stuck; her eyes fixed, and tears slowly filled them. The entire bay quivered; the lighthouse wobbled; and she had the illusion that the mast of Mr Connor's yacht was bending like a wax candle in the sun. She winked quickly. Accidents were awful things. She winked again. The mast was straight; the waves were regular; the lighthouse was upright; but the blot had spread.

This is a famous passage – deservedly, when you watch Virginia Woolf fusing the pen with its lachrymose owner, tearful both; the pen sticks, the eyes fix. Famous, but not that familiar. The procession of details – the bay, then the light-house, and finally the mast – chart the progress of crying from inception to delivery. But they do so without any of Golding's lethal speed. We admire the treatment but we are not hurt by the moment. The bay, the lighthouse, the mast of the yacht process in a measured way and arrive like items in an inventory. And 'winked' isn't right, twice. So the technique is almost the same: we see the effect of tears, but in the Woolf the tears as well. The Woolf isn't bad, but the Golding is better. It is instantaneous and recognisable.

It is also subtle. I would single out the adjective 'vivid' as a crucial extra: this is the tropics; there is no light pollution. 'The stars were spilt and danced all ways' is good, but not as good as the *vivid* stars in Golding's account. Suppose the stars had been merely 'bright'. 'The bright stars were spilt and danced all ways.' Less good. *Vivid* implies precise points, a bright fixity, so the damage is the greater. An order is disrupted.

A few lines later, Ralph cries again and the stars 'spilled about the sky' again. There is a difference between 'were spilt' and 'spilled' and not just the differ-ence between passive and active. 'Spilt' and 'spilled' aren't the same thing. They don't sound the same, of course. But 'spilt' contains within it the word *split*, just as 'all ways' (all directions) contains 'always' (forever). Together, these subtle shifts suggest a permanent alteration to the cosmos. Something larger than a local effect created by crying. They are a spectral gesture towards the universal, beyond the local. (An abiding preoccupation in Golding, a characteristic shift in focus.)

Now tears in *The Spire*. This is Jocelin's aunt, 'the naughty one', the old king's mistress who has contrived Jocelin's preferment: 'Eyelids, dark and glis-tening, painted perhaps, eyelashes long and thick; water now caught among the lower ones ... The smile became a grimace, and the water fell.' Golding, unlike Tennyson, has seen that crying involves the entire face – not simply tears.

I turn now to *The Inheritors*. When Lok is utterly alone, Golding shifts his narrative perspective to the outside and Lok becomes 'the creature'. (It is a move as brilliant as the new focus on Jack at the close of *Lord of the Flies*: the monster reverts to a small boy again on the penultimate page: 'A little boy who wore the remains of an extraordinary black cap on his red hair and who carried the remains of a pair of spectacles at his waist, started forward, then changed his mind and stood still.' *Little*. We are looking at him from the new perspective of the naval officer.)

Lok's interior has now to be inferred. His foot finds by chance the child Liku's little Oa doll, a root that resembles 'the exaggerated contours of a female body'. For the first time, Lok realises Liku must be dead, something his mate Fa had already worked out. His grief is observed as a physical phenomenon, not as emotion. We see the physical signifiers of grief.

> The creature looked again towards the water. Both hands were full, the bar of its brow glistened in the moonlight, over the great caverns where the eyes were hidden. There was light poured down over the cheek-bones and the wide lips and there was a twist of light caught like a white hair in every curl. But the caverns were dark as though already the whole head was nothing but a skull.
>
> The water rat concluded from the creature's stillness that it was not dangerous. It came with a quick rush from under the bush and began to cross the open space, it forgot the silent figure and searched busily for something to eat.
>
> There was light now in each cavern, lights faint as the starlight reflected in the crystals of a granite cliff. The lights increased, acquired definition, brightened, lay each sparkling at the lower edge of a cavern. Suddenly, noiselessly, the lights became thin crescents, went out, and streaks glistened on each cheek. The lights appeared again, caught among the silvered curls of the beard. They hung, elongated, dropped from curl to curl and gathered at the lowest tip. The streaks on the cheeks pulsed as the drops swam down them, a great drop swelled at the end of a hair of the beard, shivering and bright. It detached itself and fell in a silver flash, striking a withered leaf with a sharp pat. The water rat scurried away and plopped into the river.

It is interesting to see what Golding has done to cause and effect here. Lok is grieving for the death of Liku. But Golding withholds the explicit significance of the doll. We have to work out what it means – and what it means is what it means to Lok – and we work that out gradually, slowly, as the tears make their way into our consciousness, gradually, slowly. The cause is hidden and the effect disguised. There is a pause between them that is mimicked by the meticulous indirection of Golding's description. There is a delay on our part which echoes the slowness in Lok's mind.

Why are these tears described as if for the first time? Because they are happening to Lok for the first time. The Neanderthalers do not cry. So, at the moment when the narrative makes Lok inhuman – the creature – Golding grants him the human gift of tears. Compassionately, ironically.

Let me quote Kipling's *Jungle Book* by way of explanation. Mowgli has been expelled from the Seeonee wolf pack: 'Then something began to hurt Mowgli inside him, as he had never been hurt in his life before, and he caught his breath and sobbed, and the tears ran down his face. "What is it? What is it?" he said. "I do not wish to leave the jungle and I do not know what this is. Am I dying, Bagheera?"' Bagheera replies: '"No, little brother. Those are only tears such as men use. Now I know thou art a man."'

In *The Spire*, Jocelin has a confrontation with Pangall. The caretaker is miserable because the builder's men mock him. Finally: 'There was a sharp tap on the instep of Jocelin's shoe; and as he looked he saw a wet star there with arms to it and tiny globes of water that slid off the dubbin into the yard.' Another great tear singled out by a great writer. I will come back to it.

Now I want (a bit more briefly) to look at fires in Golding. Whereas tears are human, fire is not, though the Neanderthalers naturally assimilate it to themselves:

> She knelt in the overhang and laid the ball of clay in the centre of it. She opened the clay, smoothing and patting it over the old patch that lay there already. She put her face to the clay and breathed on it. In the very depth of the overhang there were recesses on either side of a pillar of rock and these were filled with sticks and twigs and thicker branches. She went quickly to the piles and came again with twigs and leaves and a log that was fallen almost to powder. She arranged this over the opened clay and breathed till a trickle of smoke appeared and a single spark shot into the air. The branch cracked and a flame of amethyst and red coiled up and straightened so that the side of her face away from the sun was glowing and her eyes gleamed. She came again from the recesses and put on more wood so that the fire gave them a brilliant display of flame and sparks. She began to work the wet clay with her fingers, tidying the edges so that now the fire sat in the middle of a shallow dish. Then she stood up and spoke to them. 'The fire is awake again.'

How important that last sentence is. Without it, what we have is almost a witness statement, almost flatly factual, with gradual touches of art: the single spark; then the quasi-fireworks display; then the climactic poetry of that final sentence which transforms the fact into poetry and ignites the prose.

Here are some fires in *Lord of the Flies* that assess Golding's ability to render the inanimate, the non-human. A lovely poetic paradox: 'The branches grew a brief foliage of fire.' Then there is Nabokov's pale fire, imperceptible in sunlight. 'The flame, nearly invisible at first in that bright sunlight, enveloped a small twig, grew, was enriched with colour, and reached up a branch which exploded with a sharp crack.' At the novel's end, the boys set the island on fire in their pursuit of Ralph. It is Golding's great descriptive opportunity and he excels himself: 'He heard a curious trickling sound and then a louder crepitation as if someone were unwrapping great sheets of cellophane.' (The poet Robin Robertson has a fire that unwraps sweetie papers, 'the sound of coals / Unwrapping themselves like sweets': good, but belated.) Finally, the flames reach the beach: 'the fire reached the coconut palms by the beach and swallowed them noisily. A flame, seemingly detached, swung like an acrobat and licked up the palm heads on the platform.' *Swung like an acrobat.* And look what Golding has done with those old stagers, tongues of fire. They are there, renewed, in the orality of 'swallowed' and 'licked'.

Unless writers can do this – describe the human and the non-human – their themes could not matter less. The academy, though, likes to pretend that it is the seriousness of the subject that lends importance to a writer. And actually Golding has very profound themes, great themes, though they are not, in themselves, what make him a great writer. For many writers – Dickens, for one; Joyce for another – their themes are ways of organising and provoking their invention, their imagery and the sentences that constitute their work. Golding is a different kind of writer from either Joyce or Dickens. His subjects are not there to excite creation. The writing serves the subject. But unless it was great writing, we wouldn't care about the subject, those themes that Golding returns to, compellingly, compulsively, from first to last.

When I was speaking about tears, I said I would return to the tear of Pangall that falls on Jocelin's dubbined boot in *The Spire*. 'There was a sharp tap on the instep of Jocelin's shoe; and as he looked he saw a wet star there with arms to it and tiny globes of water that slid off the dubbin into the yard.' I want to return to it because Golding himself returns to it in his last novel *The Double Tongue*, where we read about the first period of Areika, the Pythia: 'I heard a faint but positive *tap* and, by some instinct looking down, I saw the first drop of my blood starred on the strap of my right sandal.' A tap followed by a star, in both cases, separated by 31 years. And in *The Inheritors*, the tear falls backwards, as it were, with a *pat* on a withered leaf. Why does Golding repeat that topos of a tap followed by a star? Probably because he remembered the original but couldn't find it – it took me some time before I found it – and therefore decided that he hadn't already used it after all.

(By the way, this star of first menstrual blood is a masculine mistake: there is no bright blood in the first instance of menstruation, only a brown viscous discharge that commonly makes young women think they must be ill in some way they don't understand. The discharge could not fall.)

And now to the repeated theme in Golding's work of the mystical and the medical. In *The Double Tongue*, Arieka, when she becomes the Pythia and enters the oracle for the first time, feels that she has been raped by Apollo (or just possibly Dionysus) – or possessed by a god. But she is uncertain: 'Perhaps the first time I went shrouded down the steps as into my own grave I became hysterical. A medical condition. Or possessed by a god. By Him. Him. It was something I brooded over.' This is Arieka's recollection and meditation. Golding also gives us the actual event in all its confusion: she is first possessed by laughter, the god's laughter issuing from her own mouth. Then she uses her mouth to beg for mercy in her own voice: 'it was so strange to feel that same mouth which had opened and bled at the passage of the god's voice could now make words for a poor woman on her knees.' Her mouth has a double function, then – and the answers it gives as the oracle are always double, capable of two interpretations. So, on the one hand, a rape by Apollo: 'the god would have me there in the holy seat whether I would or no, oh yes, it was a rape, this was Apollo who fitted me into the seat, twisted me any way he would, then left me.' She shouts out with her own voice: 'One mouth or the other!' Meaning that the god should choose whether the mouth was hers or his – and further between her proper mouth and the lips of her vagina. So, she is used, possessed, and feels it as a rape. On the other hand, it is a hysterical episode and there is a medical explanation. *The Double Tongue* is Golding's posthumously published novel.

In Golding's first book, *Lord of the Flies*, Simon is a mystic with clairvoyant powers. 'Passions beat about Simon on the mountain-top with awful wings' is Golding's gloss when Simon retrieves Piggy's specs after Jack has smacked them off. We don't feel disproportion, or exaggeration in this evocation of Simon's emotional turbulence. We feel Simon is on the side of the angels – literally. Simon is also Golding's mouthpiece in the novel, perhaps a trifle too conveniently: he thinks maybe there is a beast, but 'maybe it's only us.' Later, after Samneric have fled, he thinks usefully and logically, feeling 'a flicker of incredulity – a beast with claws that scratched, that sat on a mountain-top, that left no tracks and yet was not fast enough to catch Samneric'. This is plausible, but Golding then issues a press release through Simon, who is briefly an author surrogate: 'However Simon thought of the beast, there rose before his inward sight the picture of a human at once heroic and sick.' This is over-articulate and it was better earlier when Golding disguised his message: 'Simon became inarticulate in his effort to express mankind's essential illness.' When Simon has his confrontation with the Lord of the Flies, he learns that 'I'm part of you' – but the gift of a schoolmaster's voice to the pig's head saves the section from being over-expository. It is a near thing. But great art is full of near things.

Golding attempts to offset Simon's authority by making it clear that he is suffering from a form of epilepsy. Right at the beginning of the novel, Simon 'faints': ' " He's always throwing a faint," said Merridew. "He did in Gib; and Addis; and at Matins over the precentor." ' The medical versus the mystical, again, for the first time in his œuvre. Karen Armstrong's 1982 book *Through the Narrow Gate* is an account of her religious experiences as a nun – and their origin in her undiagnosed epilepsy. My own father frequently described a mystical experience of being taken over bodily by his Negro spirit guide, Massa. This involved physical gigantification – or a sense of physical gigantification – and I am sure was a form of epileptic seizure.

In *The Paper Men*, Wilf Barclay's vision of a vindictive God, an unforgiving Intolerance, is also perhaps the result of what the Sicilian doctor calls a 'leedle estrook' – a stroke. A stroke, thinks Wilf, or a universal flail. Likewise, Wilf's ironic stigmata in his hands and feet could be explained by acute gout. He experiences relief from pain when he moderates his drinking. The final stigma, the missing wound in his side, will be supplied by his thwarted and deranged biographer, Rick Tucker, when he pulls the trigger of Capstone-Bowers's Bisley gun.

In *The Spire*, Jocelin has an angel that sometimes warms his back and sometimes thrashes it. There is also a medical explanation: 'So in the end Jocelin felt nothing but the pain of his back (and the sick fire when they turned him over to pack it with lamb's wool).' Jocelin has TB of the spine: 'a wasting, a consumption of the back and spine'. Just before his death, he escapes the sickroom and encounters an apple tree outside – 'a cloud of angels flashing in the sunlight'.

Nothing is simply one thing.

That phrase, nothing is simply one thing, is a quotation from Virginia Woolf's *To the Lighthouse*. When James Ramsay goes with Mr Ramsay to the lighthouse, James reflects: as a young boy,

> The Lighthouse was then a silvery, misty-looking tower with a yellow eye that opened suddenly and softly in the evening. Now –
>
> James looked at the Lighthouse. He could see that it was barred with black and white; he could see windows in it; he could even see washing spread on the rocks to dry. So that was the Lighthouse, was it?
>
> No, the other was also the Lighthouse. For nothing was simply one thing.

In the context of Virginia Woolf's novel, the Lighthouse shares the characteristics of both his parents. His mother's transfigurative imaginative warmth, his philosopher father's insistence on empirical reality. Virginia Woolf's implicit thesis throughout her great novel is that there is fact and there is the possibility of transcendence. That is why we never learn the Christian names of either parent. They exist as a permanent polarity, meaningful only as a relationship, as a union of both possibilities.

There is a moment earlier when Lily Briscoe, the artist, the abstract painter, observes Mr and Mrs Ramsay observing their children Prue and Jasper throwing catches.

> So that is marriage, Lily thought, a man and a woman looking at a girl throwing a ball ... And suddenly the meaning which, for no reason at all, as perhaps they are stepping out of the tube or ringing a doorbell, descends on people, making them symbolical, making them representative, came upon them, and made them in the dusk standing, looking, the symbols of marriage, husband and wife. Then, after an instant, the symbolical outline which transcended the real figures sank down again, and they became, as they met them, Mr and Mrs Ramsay watching the children throwing catches.

The symbolical outline which transcended the real figures ... As readers, we are in the presence of a home-made Platonism, however briefly. Mr and Mrs Ramsay are eternal archetypes. How like the Platonism of *The Double Tongue* this is. In Section VI, Ionides explains that the gifts of suppliants to the oracle belong 'not to the Pythia but to the IDEA of the Pythia of which, my dear, you are an individual copy'. Immediately before this explanation, Ionides and Arieka are opening the chests of the previous, now dead, Pythia. They encounter 'some bricks': 'They had queer signs on them which made Ionides cry out. They were the same as the Cretans had used in old times.' The slave Perseus, the librarian, translates the cuneiform signs: they are a list of what the chests once contained. Gold ingots, images and a censer. Arieka comments: 'it was quaint to see how the words written on the bricks had made him feel for a moment that the gold was really still there!' It is an emblem of transcendence. The sign, the IDEA, suggests the lost reality. 'I had never seen our friend Perseus so elevated. It was touching, for indeed there was no gold to be seen, but what Plato, perhaps, would call the IDEA of gold.'

In *Darkness Visible*, there is another version of this topos – the allegorical aerial cash payment apparatus at Frankley's, the ironmonger's where Matty goes to work after leaving school. 'After the convulsion of the First World War the place grew a spider's web of wires along which the money trundled in small, wooden jars. For people of all ages, from babies to pensioners, this was entranc- ing. Some assistant would fire the jar – clang! – from his counter and when the flying jar reached the till it would ring a bell.' I don't think that phrase is acci- dental. Does this overhead railway ring any bells? Make you think of prayer? (Of Herbert's 'church bells beyond the sky heard' in his 'Prayer'?) Make you think of religion? – especially when, long after it has fallen into disuse, it is still a lingering spectral reality: the shop assistants reach up automatically. Golding's language hereabouts is saturated in the spiritual: 'Since young Mr Arthur was devout, by one of the spiritual mysteries of the human condition it is undeni- able that during his reign the assistants became more and more holy.' In secular terms, this means only that Mr Arthur reverences the old customs and that his assistants are barely employed. They are functionaries without a function. They toil not, neither do they spin. The language is metaphorical, not literal – but it is suggestive, too, of something beyond the literal, the faint aroma of incense, of afterlife, of otherlife.

I want now to come to my next argument. Golding is a great writer because he can describe, as I have said. Is he also a great writer because he voices and ventilates the great issues of the twentieth century? Is the great writer, is Gold- ing, a pythia – someone who speaks more than he knows, someone with access to a larger reality? A pythia, but a flawed pythia, knowing how mundane and ordinary the pythia can be. A pythia even as he is the same Bill Golding whom I met in Tesco in Truro buying two kinds of tinned spaghetti for my children when we visited him in Cornwall. Do they prefer Alphabetti? he asked, or do they prefer Haunted House spaghetti?

Heinz *Haunted House* spaghetti.

Even in Tesco the issue came up, accidentally. Nothing is simply one thing.

In his essay 'Shakespeare and the Stoicism of Seneca', T. S. Eliot wrote: 'Shakespeare, too, was occupied with the struggle – which alone constitutes life for a poet – to transmute his personal and private agonies into something rich and strange, something universal and impersonal ... The great poet, in writing himself, writes his time. Thus Dante, hardly knowing it, became the voice of the thirteenth century; Shakespeare, hardly knowing it, became the representative of the end of the sixteenth century, of a turning point in history.' *The great poet, in writing himself, writes his time.* Is this true? How would you test it?

Is the great poet expressing the zeitgeist? Or is the great poet creating the zeitgeist? It is obvious to me that any historical period will have two zeitgeists, not one. At the time, there is the consensus, what everybody thinks. And that is the zeitgeist, the contemporary orthodoxy. Then there are the great writers and thinkers who oppose the zeitgeist – who, because they are great writers and thinkers, become the alternative zeitgeist for posterity. Let us call these two zeitgeists by two different names – zeitgeist regular and zeitgeist super.

Does Eliot's formulation – the great poet, in writing himself, writes his time – actually only mean that the best writers have the last word? Inferior writers are forgotten. Eliot clarifies for us: 'it was his [Shakespeare's] business to express the greatest emotional intensity of his time, based on whatever his time happened to think.' No ambiguity there. The writer takes the thought of his time and expresses it with great emotional intensity. (So much for my own theory of two zeitgeists, regular and super, you might think – except that Eliot is proposing a regular zeitgeist, 'whatever his time happened to think', plus added vitamins, 'the greatest emotional intensity'.)

Ted Hughes, in 'A Dancer to God', one of his essays on T. S. Eliot, written for the unveiling of a plaque to T.S.E. outside 3 Kensington Court Gardens, distinguishes between Eliot and Yeats, between the truly great and the merely great. Eliot, Hughes says, 'stands in the centre of the cyclone of our modern apocalypse. And he speaks from that centre, as a unique, still point of awareness and eloquence, in our time comparable perhaps only to such a figure as Einstein. In other words, while Yeats, in all the greatness and great beauty of his work, stays confined within English, Eliot moves at large throughout all variations of language and culture, claimed by all, as they became aware of him, and needed by all.' Eliot, as Hughes envisions him, expresses the cultural calamity of our time, 'the overwhelming desacralisation of the Western world', 'a loss of contact with the divine source and a loss of all meaning which the divine source gave'. Hughes's Eliot, then, is a shaman – speaking the ill of all the world, transcending language.

What is Golding's central idea? It is surely the fusion of infinite and the limited – denying neither – the fusion of the sublime with the sometimes ridiculous. Think of the séance at the end of *Darkness Visible* and its mixture of the genuinely mystical with the desire to scratch one's nose. And this sense of a fugitive spiritual grandeur, something half seen in the tail of the eye, an innuendo at the back of one's mind, makes Golding one with a great many writers in the twentieth century. Ted Hughes, for example, who was determined to open negotiations with whatever was out there, as he explained to Egbert Faas in a famous interview. George Steiner has said that it is possible for humanity to live without God, but not without a sense of the absence of God – of something missing, the absent presence. God, for many twentieth-century writers, is conspicuous by His absence – and Golding is one of these writers.

In *The Double Tongue*, Arieka cannot think of ants as living things: 'my mind could go down as far as fish but no farther.' The same thought occurs in E. M. Forster's *A Passage to India*: in Chapter 4, Mr Sorley, a missionary, wonders whether God's infinite mercy can embrace the wasp. Mammals, yes, but not the wasp. It isn't an exact match, but it shows a similar disposition, perhaps even a zeitgeist. I am normally very suspicious of the idea of intertextuality – which often seems an excuse for assuming relationships between authors without the burden of proof. But if you consider Forster's treatment of the punkah wallah outside the court where Adela Quested is testifying against Aziz, you can see exactly the same combination of the mystic with recalcitrant factuality that we find in Golding's fiction. When Miss Quested withdraws her accusations, the credit is given to the punkah wallah, who is both indifferent to the proceedings and instrumental in changing them – an Indian of low birth and a god 'winnowing souls'. 'Before long no one remained on the scene of the fantasy but the beautiful naked god. Unaware that anything unusual had occurred, he continued to pull the chord of his punkah, to gaze at the empty dais and the overturned special chairs, and rhythmically to agitate the clouds of descending dust.'

In Coleridge's *Biographia Literaria*, he writes about the natural, organic world, and how, if we identify its physical laws, the husk of reality drops off and we see its spiritual essence. Golding is one of many major twentieth-century writers to experience wary nostalgia for an elusive spiritual essence. Elizabeth Bishop is another, Ted Hughes yet another. And Eliot, of course. You can find the same hybridity of secular and sacred in a populist, triter form in Peter Shaffer's *Yonadab* and *Amadeus* – where the farting, foul-mouthed, loud-mouthed Mozart is also the vessel through whose music God makes his presence felt. Where the nihilistic voyeur, Yonadab, uncovers a religious need in himself, succumbs, with alert surprise, to his own cynical fabrication and discovers an unappeasable, ineradicable yearning for immortality. In John Updike's 1997 novel, *Toward the End of Time*, Turnbull the 'hero', experiences sudden branches of time – in which, arbitrarily, he becomes, for example, an Egyptian grave-robber, or a lay gardener at Lindisfarne when the murderous Viking hoards descend. In all these writers, great and lesser, nothing is simply one thing.

William Golding's *The Spire*
(2011)

The Spire was published in 1964. The dean of a cathedral, Jocelin, wants to add a spire to the building, which has no foundations and is therefore a kind of miracle already. The novel is about the second, highly imperfect miracle, the erection of the spire – and the cost, which is financial, physical and spiritual. And it is about creative realisation, bringing the impossible into being. Golding wrote the first draft of *The Spire* in fourteen days – itself a kind of miracle.

In 1978, the great American poet Elizabeth Bishop gave an interview to the *Christian Science Monitor*. At this time, a year before her death, she was an unregarded, marginalised figure. She was responding to a criticism sometimes levelled at her work. She said: 'Observation is a great joy. Some critics charge that I'm merely a descriptive poet which I don't think is such a bad thing at all if you've done it well.' It isn't the most robust defence – 'which I don't think is such a bad thing at all' – but it's robust enough in its modestly assertive way. A defence of description.

Literary critics often judge writers – favourably and unfavourably – by their doctrine. Dr Leavis invariably asked if writers were 'life-enhancing', on the side of life. Being 'on the side of life' meant agreeing with Dr Leavis agreeing with D. H. Lawrence. Its opposite – 'doing dirt on life' – meant not agreeing with Dr Leavis agreeing with D. H. Lawrence. It is the difference between being basically joyful or basically jaundiced in your attitude to life. *Basically. Overall. On the whole. By and large.* But literature is about particulars. It isn't about life, or the universe either. It lives in particulars – or it is lifeless. Without particulars, there won't be any life to be on the side of, or do dirt on. These are a few particulars I discovered for the first time in John Carey's biography of Golding.* They are taken from various unpublished works, including Golding's journal. An anchor is 'a chrysanthemum of phosphorescence'; a boat has 'the clumsy beauty of a double bass'; at war, he sees 'a Christmas tree of exploding ammunition'; this is a close-up of a woman reaching her orgasm, 'eyes shut, forehead lined, a kind of anguish, concentrated on reaching through her slow rhythms, a far, deep spot, dark and wicked'. This is a huge spider on his pillow: 'the dry tap and scramble'. He was afraid of spiders.

The Essay: Golding Remembered, first broadcast on Radio 3 on 22 September 2011.

* John Carey, *William Golding: The Man Who Wrote Lord of the Flies* (Faber and Faber, 2009).

My point is a simple one. Golding could describe things. Incomparably. And he could describe *anything*, judging by the range of subjects in those quotations. So could James Joyce and John Updike. Vladimir Nabokov and Saul Bellow. And Elizabeth Bishop. Of course, D. J. Taylor thinks that in the case of Bellow, the good writing is only there to show us all 'how good a writer he is' – being, in a word, 'literary'. And D. J. Taylor piously hopes that 'the first casualty of the next ten years of novel-writing will be literariness'. No more writing. Especially no more great writing. Because that is just showing off. Eccentrically enough, I daresay, I find myself out of sympathy with Taylor's position. Call me naive, call me wilful, I hold a different position. I like great writing.

This is Golding describing dust. The cathedral of stone is being dismantled and added to – creating a cathedral of dust, a phantom, a twin. In *Seeing Things*, Seamus Heaney evokes 'a pillar of radiant house-dust'. Here is Golding's creation of not one pillar but several:

> Everywhere, fine dust gave these rods and trunks of light the importance of a dimension. He blinked at them again, seeing, near at hand, how the individual grains of dust turned over each other, or bounced all together, like mayfly in a breath of wind. He saw how further away they drifted cloudily, coiled, or hung in a moment of pause, becoming, in the most distant rods and trunks, nothing but colour, honey-colour slashed across the body of the cathedral … He shook his head in rueful wonder at the solid sunlight.

So, as temporary as a mayfly *and* a serious rival and replacement. *Solid* sunlight. A vision valid as vision, as something definitely seen. Dust definitively described by a master. Dust described, dust done and dusted.

This is Golding describing the application of a steel tourniquet to hold the spire together: 'there was a band of steel, a foot wide and two inches thick, studded with blue rivets. Everywhere it lay close against the stone that was scarred and broken. But the band was alive and talking. It cried, wangle-angle-bangle-clang! It mouthed, and in the pauses of the mouthing, settled to a steady ringing.' *A foot wide. Two inches thick.* The dull dimensions give you a vivid idea of the forces at work.

Golding can scorch us by the immediate heat of his sentences. But sometimes he chooses the slower narrative burn. In this talk, I want to see what Golding does in the first chapter of *The Spire*, the first twenty-nine pages.

He begins with Jocelin holding the model of the spire and laughing.

'He was laughing, chin up, and shaking his head. God the father was exploding in his face with a glory of sunlight through painted glass, a glory that moved with his movements to consume and exalt Abraham and Isaac and then God again. The tears of laughter in his eyes made additional spokes and wheels and rainbows. / / Chin up, hands holding the model spire before him, eyes half closed; joy – "I've waited half my life for this day!"'

It doesn't quite make sense, or it doesn't make immediate sense. It is like Hopkins's opening trump, 'As kingfishers catch fire ...' Kingfishers don't catch fire. Hopkins is using a metaphor to capture the burst of colours given off by the kingfisher. Ted Hughes uses the same idea of combustion for bold colours in 'Macaw and Little Miss', a poem from his first book, *The Hawk in the Rain*: 'the macaw bristles in a staring / combustion ...' The brilliant extra touch is that adjective 'staring' appended to 'combustion'. All the indignation peculiar to the macaw is there.

In Golding's opening sentence we read 'God the Father was exploding in his face', which is initially as enigmatic as it is dramatic – until it is resolved as a metaphorical description of sunlight streaming through a stained-glass window. The semantic delay is important. There is a semantic lag, a slight, postponed understanding, throughout *The Spire*.

'He was laughing, chin up, and shaking his head.' It reads at first like third-person impersonal, authorial prose, but, as the paragraph proceeds, we become aware that the narrative isn't impersonal: it is focalised for Jocelin. It emanates from his point of view. It is coloured by his consciousness. It isn't free indirect speech – a clearer indicator that we are privy to a character's thoughts. An example from Jane Austen: 'The comfort of such a friend at that moment as Colonel Brandon – of such a companion for her mother – how gratefully was it felt!' You can hear Elinor Dashwood's voice, her emotion. Focalisation gives us not the character's voice, but the timbre of their thought. And this is crucial to *The Spire* because, for most of the narrative, the reader is trapped in Jocelin's subjectivity, in Jocelin's solipsism. We find it difficult to judge him – his motives, his purity, his corruption, his ambition, his vanity – because the view of him is restricted. As in a theatre, where the seats are cheaper because a pillar interferes with the view of the stage.

In this case, not a pillar, exactly, but a nose. Three examples. 'He stood, smiling round his nose, head up.' Second example: 'so Jocelin felt a smile bend the seams of his own face as he looked round his nose at him.' Third example (from Chapter 2): 'Jocelin laughed down over his nose delightedly.' The nose stands for the obstacle of the self.

Golding knew exactly what he was doing. Later, he describes Jocelin's fractured memories in terms of narrative: 'they were like sentences from a story, which, though they left great gaps, still told enough.' Clearly self-referential. True, we are afforded glimpses, dispatches, outsights, as it were, from the outside world. Two young deacons are overheard by Jocelin, denigrating someone unspecified: 'Say what you like; he's proud.' Second deacon: 'And ignorant.' First deacon: 'Do you know what? He thinks he is a saint! A man like that!'

We can't be sure they are referring to Jocelin, except for the word 'but' which begins this sentence: 'But when the two deacons saw the dean looming over them, they fell to their knees.'

However, the criticism of Jocelin is obliterated by Jocelin's subjectivity, his overriding joy at having held in his hand the model of the spire that is to be built. 'He looked down, loving them in his joy.' And he refuses to accept explicitly that they are talking about him. He says: 'Now, now, my children! What's this? Backbiting? Scandal? Denigration?'

'They bent their heads and said nothing.'

Jocelin: 'Who is this poor fellow? You should pray for him rather.' He refuses to accept delivery of the insult he has overheard – and so we cannot be completely sure what he knows and what he doesn't know. *The Spire* confines us to Jocelin's consciousness – not absolutely, not forever, not ultimately, but for most of the novel's length. We can't be certain.

There is in the opening pages a dumb mason who is sculpting Jocelin's head for a gargoyle to be built into the spire. He carves while Jocelin loses himself in prayer. It is an objective record. Yet Jocelin disputes it: 'Oh no, no, no! I'm not as beaky as that! Not half as beaky!' Then he contemplates the gaunt stone portrait head and reinterprets its bony features as the portrait of spirituality: 'Nose, like an eagle's beak. Mouth wide open, lined cheeks, hollow deep under the cheekbone, eyes deep in their hollows; he put up a hand to the corner of his mouth and pulled at the parallel ridges of flesh and skin. He opened his mouth to feel how that action stretched them, striking his teeth together three times as he did so.' The dumb man makes a gesture that Jocelin interprets to mean bird flight. And from that supposition it is only a step to identifying with angels: 'Rushing on with the angels, the infinite speed that is stillness, hair blown, torn back, straightened with the wind of the spirit, mouth open, not for uttering rain-water, but hosannas and hallelujahs.'

The function of the gargoyle is overridden, written over. By Jocelin, primarily, though he is conscious of his hubris. A hubris he attributes to the sculptor. 'Don't you think you might strain my humility, by making an angel of me?'

And what is the answer to this question? A negative. The sculptor shakes his head. 'Humming in the throat, headshake, doglike, eager eyes.' Negative certainly, but what kind of a negative? Is the dumb sculptor denying that Jocelin's humility is vulnerable? Or is he denying that he ever thought of portraying Jocelin as an angel in the first place? Jocelin's extrapolation is, after all, based on a gesture.

What is the dumb sculptor doing in the novel? He represents the muted objective narrative voice. Which we hear only as William James's description of consciousness: 'one great blooming buzzing confusion'.

'For a long time, they were both still and silent, while Jocelin looked at the gaunt, lifted cheekbones, the open mouth, the nostrils strained wide as if they were giving lift to the beak, like a pair of wings, the wide, blind eyes.' And then Golding gives us Jocelin's thought in free indirect speech: 'It is true. At the moment of vision, the eyes see nothing.' The wings of the nostrils made into actual wings. And the blind stone eyes, those familiar blanched almonds, interpreted as visionary, as Yeats interprets them in his half-crazy occult amalgam of arcana, *A Vision*. T. S. Eliot has a more double-edged take on the visionary moment in *The Waste Land* and it is one, I think, that Golding borrows here: 'I could not / Speak, and my eyes failed, I was neither / Living nor dead, and I knew nothing, / Looking into the heart of light, the silence.' *My eyes failed*. In the Golding: 'the eyes see nothing' at the moment of vision.

It is Golding's task as a novelist to keep this ambiguity alive for the length of his novel. Let me return to the very beginning of *The Spire* and ask a question. Why is Jocelin laughing? Well, the obvious reason is that he is laughing because he is happy. He has the model of the spire in his hands. But is that all? In the stained glass there are two images. God the Father exploding in his face – exploding in his face, blowing up in his face, a phrase that suggests a disaster brought on the self by the self. It blew up in his face. The other image in the stained glass is Abraham and Isaac. In Hebrew, the name 'Isaac' means 'she laughed'. *She* is Sarah, the wife of Abraham. When Abraham was over 100 and Sarah well beyond child-bearing age, Sarah was promised a son – and she laughed. But the promise comes to pass. Miracles are possible. The spire might also come to pass – and does, at an extraordinary cost. After extraordinary sacrifices. Sacrifices: again we think of Abraham agreeing to sacrifice the boy Isaac and thus demonstrate obedience to a relentless deity – to 'consume and exalt.' And those rainbows created by Jocelin's tears of laughter are naturalistic, brilliantly naturalistic, but they also nod to the rainbow of the covenant between God and man after the Flood, giving man dominion over the earth and its animals. Power. Like the imperfect power Jocelin wields.

And there is another reason why Jocelin is laughing. He is laughing because *The Spire* is a divine comedy. In Dante, the word *commedia* doesn't mean the Comedy Store. It means a happy ending – paradiso, after the inferno and purgatory. In Golding's novel, comedy means something dark, and bitterly ironic. Is Jocelin's angel an angel? Or is the angel an hallucination caused by Jocelin's tubercular spine? There are two explanations. It is not until the final pages that we know for a certainty that we can never know.

There are two explanations just as there are two cathedrals – one of stone, one of dust – in the first chapter. At the end of *The Spire*, Golding returns to the idea of dust. The dying Jocelin examines a patch by a mounting block. 'But for all the feet that had trodden it, it remained ordinary dust.' Not a cathedral of individual motes shot through by the sunlight of genius.

Updike: *Just Looking*
(1990)

As a title for this gathering of essays, *Just Looking* is as engagingly unpretentious as its contents, and yet misleading. Lavishly illustrated, sometimes with pictures that aren't actually discussed (by Hopkins, Poe and Oscar Wilde), apparently effortless, occasional, these pieces are freighted with the chronic preoccupations evident since the beginning of this intelligent writer's long career. They are not the innocent reports they seem to be. Witness Updike's comment that Sargent derives from 'the darting, flippant brushwork of Frans Hals'. On the other hand, neither are they as knowledgeable as, in their casual way, they half take for granted. Sometimes, too, they are not even the accurate reports one might expect from this vigilant novelist. Discussing Jean-Robert Ipoustéguy's sculpture *La Naissance*, Updike finds it 'as polished and iconic as one of Brancusi's "eggs" and yet as anatomical as a medical book'. Since he was born in 1932, Updike quite possibly belongs to that generation of fathers banned from the delivery suite. This would account for his failure to perceive the discrepancy between Ipoustéguy's mislocated vulva and placid anus and the tormented bloodiness of childbirth in the flesh, as opposed to the marble and bronze.

Occasionally, Updike's description is inspired, as when he hits off a tight grouping of figures in Degas's *Semiramis Building Babylon* as 'people in a transparent elevator', or when he flippantly notes that Degas's young spartans 'crouch and stretch purely for the benefit of the artist'. Such moments are surprisingly rare. More often one finds oneself in niggling disagreement.

For instance, at the apex of Juan Gris's collage *Breakfast* (1914), he discovers 'a packet of mail' where I see a wrapped brie or camembert with the maker's name, Eugene Martin, prominently displayed. It may be a parcel, of course. Without looking at the original, it is impossible to be certain, though even in reproduction the label looks printed rather than hand-printed like an address. At any rate, a parcel wouldn't make quite the cubist point that Gris is angling for – the imposition of the square on the circle, the subdued natural curve of the cheese. Be that as it may, it is revealing that Updike once preferred Gris to Picasso, the processed cheese to the reeking original: 'Picasso seemed a bit too noisy, too bustling and carnal for my hagiography.' This preference points to a generally apparent weakness in Updike's artistic taste and disposition: he is

---

John Updike: *Just Looking: Essays on Art* (André Deutsch, 1989).

impatient to be pleased, made irritable by difficulty and uneasy by art that is chary of the beautiful. In this frame of mind, he can be pettish and imperious: of a Degas exhibition at the Metropolitan Museum of Art in New York, he complains that the visitor 'will have a long slog before he comes to something easy to love'. Updike knows what he likes.

And yet he is sophisticated enough to mistrust his undisclosed demands when they are gratified too easily. He is irked by Renoir's prettiness, though not by Matisse's equally determined charm. In this, he is like many 'sophisticated' art lovers for whom grace and lucidity are disqualifications. Dufy has few defenders in this 'sophisticated' class – reminding one of Nabokov's sharp observation that 'people who denounce the sentimental are generally unaware of what sentiment is.' The paintings of Fairfield Porter, traditional, carried out in the teeth of abstract expressionism, are subjected to a stern interrogation, during which any number of flaws are stigmatised (like Porter's difficulty with faces) before Updike can allow himself the ludicrously indulgent comparison of *Interior with a Dress Pattern* to 'the sumptuous calm of Matisse's *Red Studio* and Piero della Francesca's stately explorations of perspective'.

Similarly, faced with Andrew Wyeth's frequently nude sequence of Helga Testorf, Updike resists his inclination to the obvious. He notes Wyeth's 'glamorizing touch' and his bogus claims to be an abstractionist, then he caves in. But before he is prepared to admit that he prefers the nudes, he goes out of his way to claim 'an expressionistic strangeness' for Wyeth's *Farm Road*, a picture in which Wyeth practises an ordinance of self-denial – and is followed by Updike. In *Farm Road*, the fully clothed Helga is a different kind of bust, a head and shoulders seen from behind. Her plaited and parted hair is echoed by a clump of trees on the top of a steep hill. Her coat and the hill are the colour of burnt caramel. The expressionist element is created by the steep pitch of the hill, whose alarming gradient almost reads as flatness, as sheerness – so that Helga might have her face pressed against a canvas and not merely turned towards a hill. It is an interesting painting, but one feels the strain of Updike's admiration here – as one doesn't feel it in his final paragraph, which arrives like a long-deferred orgasm. 'The nudes are what make the show sensational, and also what make it worthwhile.' Here we have the Updike taste – relaxed, unbuttoned, satisfied.

But the tussle is typical. In Updike's work, wonder is always dogged by disillusionment and guilt. Discussing a double portrait of Adam and Eve by Cranach the Elder, he concludes with two sentences couched in his characteristic rueful eloquence: 'Lost Eden still hangs above their heads; the stony earth of the future lies at their feet. Between, the naked present shines.' This is the Updike vision – far removed from the innocent pastime of 'just looking'. No one is fooled by the formula 'I'm just looking.' In Updike's world there is always a price to be paid. Like the nameless speaker of Browning's 'Pictor Ignotus', Updike knows that perfection can never be perfect, that there is a question which must be answered: 'Tastes sweet the water with such specks of earth?' In *Of the Farm*, for instance, Joey identifies his new wife with the field he is mowing, and thus with the farm he has always loved. The idea of husbandry is implicit in Updike's conceit, which, though initially implausible, is brought to a successful, hazy yet blunt erotic conclusion:

> Black-eyed susans, daisy fleabane, chicory, goldenrod, butter-and-eggs each flower of which was like a tiny dancer leaping, legs together, scudded past the tractor wheels. Stretched scatterings of flowers moved in a piece, like the heavens, constellated by my wheels' revolution, on my right; and lay as drying fodder on my left. Midges existed in stationary clouds that, though agitated by my interruption, did not follow me, but resumed their self-encircling conversation. Crickets sprang away, crackling, from the wheels; butterflies loped through their tumbling universe and bobbed above the flattened grass as the hands of a mute concubine would examine, flutteringly, the corpse of her giant lover. The sun grew higher. The metal hood acquired a nimbus of heat waves that visually warped each stalk. The tractor body was fleeced with foam and I, rocked back and forth on the iron seat shaped like a woman's hips, alone in nature, as hidden under the glaring sky as at midnight, excited by destruction, weightless, discovered in myself a swelling which I idly permitted to stand, thinking of Peggy. My wife is a field.

The equation is achieved – despite that lurch in the prose at 'mute concubine' when Updike modulates from the literal to the figurative; despite, too, the ominous sexual undertow present in the phrase 'excited by destruction'. Yet this desired and desirable identification is set about with qualifications. The beloved farm gives Joey hay fever. On either side of this fusion of woman and landscape there are examples of poor husbandry: Joey's 'weak response' to his mother's verdict on the second wife's intellectual shortcomings; her further pronouncement, 'You've taken a vulgar woman to be your wife.' Tastes sweet the water with such specks of earth?

For Updike, the Museum of Modern Art in New York once acted as a 'steepleless cathedral of artistic faith', the church of another religion. But on visits there now, he finds money-changers in the temple: 'it has opted, instead, for a greedy open-endedness and a bigger souvenir shop; it has led the transformation of museums into gorgeous tourist traps.' Anyone a modicum more robust might ignore the postcard counter and the vending area and pass on to the pictures, old favourites if necessary, without offence. Updike is a connoisseur of disappointment. The early story 'You'll Never Know, Dear, How Much I Love You' is closely modelled on Joyce's 'Araby': in both, the early romantic impulse is disappointed by the tawdry reality of the bazaar and carnival. Joyce ends: 'Gazing up into the darkness I saw myself as a creature driven and derided by vanity; and my eyes burned with anguish and anger.' The young Updike mimics this absurdly rhetorical interior monologue: 'Thus the world, like a bitter coquette, spurns our attempts to give ourselves to her wholly.' Two other early stories, 'Wife-Wooing' and the one-and-a-half-page masterpiece 'Archangel', return to this theme of the spurned romantic impulse. In 'Wife-Wooing', the egoist husband (surely not unrelated to Gabriel Conroy in 'The Dead') fails to bring his erotic impulse to fruition, and his delight in his wife's Joycean 'smackwarm' thighs has faded by morning to its opposite, disgust at her 'sallow décolletage'. Not only the use of Homeric parallels in *The Centaur*, or the presence of Leopold Bloom, advertisement canvasser, standing father to Harry Angstrom and his Toyota concession, persuade one that Joyce is a crucial, parental novelist for Updike. The very givens of Updike's romantic-realist axis are provided by Joyce: 'Wife-Wooing' would not be possible without the enabling example of Joyce's even-handed balance of 'fishgluey slime' with 'yes so we are flowers all a womans body yes that was one true thing he said in his life.' Updike's version is, of course, less bustling, less noisy, less carnal. And mostly, beside Joyce, he looks somewhat processed and homogenised. 'Archangel' is an exception, and it signifies the point at which Updike's way of seeing diverges from that of Joyce.

'Archangel' is a list of things which Updike loves – including three items he writes about in *Just Looking*, namely 'the Brancusi room, silent; *Pines and Rocks*, by Cézanne; and *The Lace-Maker* in the Louvre hardly bigger than your spread hand'. When the enumeration is complete, the wooing is seen to fail: 'My arms are heaped with apples and ancient books; there is no harm in me; no. Stay. Praise me. Your praise of me is praise of yourself; wait. Listen. I will begin again.' Whereas Joyce is content to accept a radically unstable reality, oscillating between the woman and the world as 'mountain flower' and 'armpits' oniony sweat', Updike is bent on retrieval and redemption: 'Listen. I will begin again.' This is not a Poundian case of 'error is all in the not done, / all in the diffidence that faltered.'

When Updike writes of the super-realist Richard Estes, he might be speaking of the redeemer in himself: 'Nobody loves our hideous city streets as Richard Estes does.' There is in him a strenuous determination to reclaim the merely factual and mundane, as he does brilliantly in 'Plumbing', an early story (I'd guess) which has fetched up somewhat inappropriately in the Maple saga of coupling and uncoupling, *Your Lover Just Called*. What Estes does for public phone booths,

Updike does for the plumber's 'magnificent, ironical bills' in which '1 1¼" × 1" galv bushing' costs 58¢, as against $550 for labour. Threaded in this notation is a meditation on memory and death.

Temperamentally inclined to the humble as he is, you might expect Updike to warm rather more than he does to Degas, the Muybridge of dancers, laundresses and bathing women. Of course, he admires Degas, but there is a detectable prickliness, all the same. It may derive from Updike's own experience as a practitioner. He studied at the Ruskin in Oxford and is therefore expert enough to set down a splendidly thorough account of artistic ineptitude: 'As those who have both drawn and written know, the problems of definition differ radically. A table or a person becomes in graphic representation a maze of angles, of half-hidden bulges, of second and third and fourth looks adding up to an illusion of thereness. When colour is added to line, the decisions and discriminations freighted into each square inch approach the infinite; one's eyes begin to hurt, to water, and colours on the palette converge towards gray mud.' This insider's knowledge, tainted with mediocrity, makes Updike more than charitable to third-rate illustrators and commercial artists of any stripe, yet less than generous to the great, to whom he brings some of the pernickety professional standards of the rank amateur. Eliot's preface to an unwritten book, *Four Elizabethan Dramatists*, contains a passage germane here: 'A play of Shakespeare's and a play of Henry Arthur Jones's are essentially of the same type, the difference being that Shakespeare is very much greater and Mr Jones very much more skilful.' This explains a lot when Updike criticises Degas's 'unevenness of rendering': the woman's dress in *Woman Leaning Near a Vase of Flowers* is less finished than the flowers; Giulia Bellelli's face 'exists on a much ghostlier plane than Giovanna'. Updike puts it all down to Degas's tendency to improvise with his materials, to be a handyman, a bricoleur. I can't help wondering what Updike made of the more extreme technical violations in, say, Degas's portrait *Mary Cassat with Small Dog* (1890), or his 1861 portrait of Princesse Pauline de Metternich, which was done from a still extant photograph. The photograph shows a woman not unlike the late Marghanita Laski, with full lips gathered over a generous helping of teeth. Degas's portrait, on the other hand, gives us a smudged face, as if a tremor is passing through the picture as we watch. It is difficult to describe the effect on the viewer of such a picture without sounding like Pater on La Gioconda, when one would prefer to sound like Henry James on Milly Theale and the Bronzino in *The Wings of the Dove*. Nevertheless, one has to be open to the picture's suggestion. We see it, so to speak, through a veil of tears – hers and our own. The physical movement, the smear, the smudge, translates until it is emotional and we are moved ourselves. It is more interesting than the photograph, and Degas has accomplished his transfiguration by an amateur's trick which an amateur would never stoop to. Amateurs conceal their mistakes by smudging. Professionals get it right and do not resort to deception – unless they happen to be Degas, a genius who can see that the correct can be improved, given greater suggestiveness, by a trick employed only by the incompetent. Great artists never care about whom they learn from. And, of course, even great artists make mistakes, genuine mistakes, where we would think them least capable of blundering: Degas is a great anatomist, but he is not a perfect anatomist. *Woman Drying Her Neck* and *Woman Resting Her Leg* (1898 and 1880–85 respectively) can now be seen in the Musée d'Orsay, where particular attention should be paid to the extraordinary shoulder blades of the former and the astonishing upper arm of the latter. Given his gullibility with Ipoustéguy's *La Naissance*, I wouldn't expect Updike to notice, though he can see the anatomical improbability of Modigliani's *Reclining Nude* in MoMA.

Increasingly, I came to feel that, as a writer on art, Updike simply does not know enough. Little though I know myself, I found myself finding mistakes you might not expect. In the piece on Fairfield Porter, Updike epitomises Porter's art as 'a colour-drunk hymn to (in his phrase) "things as they are" '. But the phrase is from Wallace Stevens's 'The Man with the Blue Guitar': 'They said, "You have a blue guitar, / You do not play things as they are." ' Updike might have guessed as much from the recognisable, if blurred, cover of the *Collected Poems* in the foreground of Porter's *Lizzie at the Table* (1958). After Ian Dunlop's study, it is strange to find Updike still describing Degas as an impressionist. The first Impressionist exhibition was actually called the *Société anonyme des artistes, peintres, sculpteurs, graveurs, etc.* Degas was out of sympathy with the artistic ideas of Monet and Pissaro, but he felt the need for an alternative to the official Salon – a place where the realist school to which he felt he belonged might exhibit. Discussing Monet's *La Japonaise*, Updike notes that the head seems to come from Renoir, the 'studio-lit staginess from Manet' and the general atmosphere from Whistler. He prefaces the catalogue of debt with this testimonial: 'Monet, who imitated almost no one but Nature herself'. In the Metropolitan Museum of Art in New York, to the right of Monet's *The Green Wave '65*, is a note which states that 'even before painting the *Green Wave*, Monet had made two seascapes so dependent on the style of Manet that the older artist had complained of plagiarism.' My memory, which may be faulty, is that Manet actually threatened to sue. Updike's analysis of the picture isn't his happiest essay, either. He seems to have missed a great deal. The painting shows Madame Monet in a long Japanese robe, with a samurai drawing his sword on the back. He isn't, therefore, 'poised to kill', as Updike maintains. He really represents a technical challenge to Monet: the samurai is grotesque, but the distortion is magnified by the fall of the garment. How do you paint the distorted distortion without its looking like a mistake?

Monet emerges with full marks. Updike doesn't even see the difficulty which has been surmounted. Neither does he ask the obvious and pressing question about Monet's background – a haphazard arrangement of fans on the wall, of which two have fallen at her feet. Why the uprush and clutter of fans? Wind is the answer, I would hazard – because her Japanese gown is waisted not at the waist but just above the knee, so that it forms a twister or tornado, wide at the hem in the foreground. Madame Monet holds a fan in her hand to symbolise the turbulence which the passage of her beauty makes. The artistic vision here is shrewd and cunning and carefully calculated – calculated, too, to make nonsense out of Updike's pious concluding sentence: 'Monet's work continuously celebrates the innocence of vision.' Just looking. I prefer Degas's cynical aphorism: 'a picture is something which calls for as much cunning, trickery and vice as the perpetration of a crime.'

Updike Tribute
(2009)

In his introduction to *The Early Stories: 1953–1975*,* John Updike cites various influences on his stories – including Chekhov. I think Updike, the escapee from literary New York, has in mind their shared predilection for the provincial. Actually, he and Chekhov are very different short-story writers. Though he has a style – hence the epithet 'Chekhovian' – Chekhov isn't a stylist. He is stylistically invisible, as Nabokov and Updike are candid conjurors. Chekhov's art is all in the conception, the situation, and his treatment is all in the tone – a benign, genial, understated narrative manner masking implacability, and an inevitable irony. A young girl from a village is unhappily married to a husband who terrorises her. Her aged, illiterate parents write to her at Christmas, using the village letter-writer, who sets down army regulations instead of their dictation. The story is all about being at the mercy of others – a brutal husband, a scribe of motiveless perversity. When the letter is in her hands, however, the girl doesn't read it. She knows who it must be from. She knows *where* it is from. And she remembers a time of great happiness, before her marriage – the catkins, the hares jinking through the flooded fields of her childhood. Chekhov is a great quartermaster of unadorned eloquent detail.

The same introduction ends with Updike's up-front credo: 'to give the mundane its beautiful due'. This is also un-Chekhovian, this willingness to announce a conclusion. Typically, a Chekhov story will end in indirection, deflection. 'It began to spit with rain.' 'It was only afterwards she noticed she'd broken a button on her overcoat.'

Whereas Updike is fearlessly, unfashionably direct. His stories sometimes end, like movies, with a big-screen clinch. The last sentences of 'The City' – a story in which a computer-software salesman falls ill with a complex appendicitis and is hospitalised – let us glimpse the anonymous, provincial city, in all its unguarded, off-duty aspect. A bicycle lying on its side is part of the recovered man's paean to life itself. Then there is a surprising, beautifully counter-intuitive inflection. What he likes – and what Updike likes, too – is the way the city offers itself, its intimate details, with the matter-of-factness, the unbothered pragmatism, of a working prostitute.

This is the last paragraph of 'Transaction', an account of a drunk business-

* John Updike: *The Early Stories: 1953–1975* (Hamish Hamilton, 2004).

man sleeping for the first time with a prostitute. Afterwards, he wonders if he has given her a baby, or if she has given him a venereal disease. He fills the condom with water to test it. It is sound:

> What she had given him, delicately, was death. She had made sex finite. Always, until now, it had been too much, bigger than all systems, an empyrean as absolute as those first boyish orgasms, when his hand would make his soul pass through a bliss as dense as an ingot of gold. Now, at last, in the prime of life, he saw through it, into the spaces between the stars. He emptied the condom of water and brought it with him out of the bathroom and in the morning found it, dry as a husk, where he had set it, on the glass bureau top among the other Christmas presents.

Nothing Chekhovian there, not even the subtle, yet tart, finely focused irony of 'other' in the final sentence. Nor that essential, muted adverb 'delicately', which blunts the otherwise blunt statement, as if Updike were playing a Beethoven concerto on a dummy keyboard, but overwhelmed by the interior music: 'What she had given him, delicately, was death.'

Updike shows us there are other ways of finishing off than the Chekhovian *niente* ending, trailing off into silence. The crescendo, for example. Of course, this isn't always true. 'Who Made Yellow Roses Yellow?' is about a Trust Fund wastrel and a college friend of lower social status. At their Ivy League university, the wastrel has advanced the interest of the other, while patronising him. Now the rich wastrel, newly returned from a sojourn in France, wants an entrée into advertising, a reciprocal favour, from the now successful *Untermensch*. It is not forthcoming, nor is it directly requested. The story ends with a concealed punchline. The wastrel demonstrates his enviable mastery of French to the admiring other by telling him to 'kiss my arse' – in French. '*Baisez mes douces fesses.*' The implied social *cachet* is no longer powerful, however. The *sans-culotte* is wearing the trousers.

Actually, the story's real interests lie elsewhere. Updike the craftsman is primarily interested in the telephone conversation as a thing to be captured. He is captivated by the essential one-sidedness of the exchange in any telephone conversation. The caller calls the shots. (Think how disconcerting it is to be phoned by someone who then behaves like the laconic recipient of the call.) The writer is listening hard to trap this special effect. He begins (brilliantly) with a secretary picking up the incoming call with its interruption to another narrative: 'the receiver was picked up, exposing the tail end of a girl's giggle. Still tittery, she enunciated, "Carson Chem-i-cal".' There follows on that Salinger-like notation of phone-ese ('of-fice'), a virtuoso rendition of a comic telephone riff, fluent spiel, interrupted by baffled questions. The wastrel is pretending to be a motor-mouth salesman – ostensibly for ebullient comedy, but also to wrong-foot the recipient of the call, poor Clayton Clayton (a literary relative of Nabokov's Humbert Humbert). There is a lovely, accurate repetition caught in Updike's butterfly net: 'Then I'll see you then.' I thought of Frost's *poetic* first: the phone conversation in 'Snow': 'I thought I would. – I know, but, Lett – I know – / I could, but what's the sense?' (A poetic first, well before T. S. Eliot's *Sweeney Agonistes*. And even before Joyce's fascination with the instrument, evident in Blazes Boylan's '– May I say a word to your telephone, missy? he asked roguishly.') All phone conversations are one-sided, but, while we are familiar with the trope of hearing only one half of the conversation, it is more difficult to give both halves of the conversation, as Updike does, and still preserve the unequal, one-sided essence.

Updike's ear for actual conversation, for *dialogue* and its proportions, its inequalities, is acute and spot-on when the two men meet later for lunch. 'You don't sound too enthusiastic.' This is followed by the marvellously, authentically awkward, 'I hadn't meant to. I mean I hadn't meant not to ...' The young writer beautifully giving the mundane its ugly, inept, accurate due.

Elsewhere, the stories are freighted with weighty, if muted, significance. 'Dentistry and Doubt' concerns the visit to an English dentist of a young Pennsylvanian theologian, studying Hooker in Oxford. Updike's notation is splendidly unhurried. The young man owns up to inferior, 'indifferent' teeth. After three pages, the prose suddenly lifts as the injection becomes imminent: '*Burton's heart beat like a wasp in a jar.*' Seldom, if ever, has an injection been more meticulously described, in its administration and its effect. It is Joycean: '*The sharp prick and the consequent slow, filling ache* drove Burton's eyes up, and he saw the tops of the bare willow trees, the *frightened* white sky, and the black birds. As he watched, one bird joined another on the topmost twig, and then a third joined these two and the twig became radically crescent, and all three birds flapped off to where his eyes could not follow them' (my italics, Updike's genius). The starlings are important. They represent the competitiveness of evolution: as he listens to the 'squeaking' of the silver amalgam, Burton reflects on this alternative amoral, godless narrative. But by the time the dentistry is over, he concludes, 'Outside the window, the wrens and the starlings, mixed indistinguishably, engaged in manoeuvres that seemed essentially playful.' Somehow, the theologically ignorant dentist, ministering to decay, has assumed a godlike, beneficent noumenon, while never ceasing for a second to be simply a dentist. The religious debate is out in the open, only the dentist's significance is screened.

The same technique, in which the micro becomes macro, occurs in

'Plumbing', where an itemised plumber's bill is the starting point for a meditation on decay and mortality. The ordinary is neither slighted – Updike does it full justice – nor is it dragooned into allegory. The significance is simply there like a watermark held to the light. It ends with beautiful, confident explicitness:

> the plumber sighs, as poets do, with an eye on the audience. 'See, keep on with it like this, you'll burn out your new pump. It has to work too hard to draw the water. Replace it now, you'll never have to worry with it again. It'll outlast your time here.'
>
> My time, his time. His eyes open wide in the unspeaking presences of corrosion and flow. We push out through the bulkhead; a blinding piece of sky slides into place above us, fitted with temporary, timeless clouds. All around us, we are outlasted.

It is difficult to do justice to this perfect writing – the shift, the modulation from 'It'll outlast your time here', meaning this house, to the larger issue; the plumber's exactly rendered vernacular; the intelligent, paradoxical adjectives attached to those clouds, 'temporary, timeless'; the risk of 'All around us, we are outlasted.' Nothing could be less Chekhovian.

Except, perhaps, my favourite Updike story, a great list which is only a page and a half long, 'Archangel'. It is written in a quasi-biblical high style. There is an element of pastiche, a touch of the Song of Songs in this annunciation – at once angelic and also the eloquence of a writer trying to seduce a woman with his literary gifts, his verbal fecundity. He writes like an angel, we say ... The sacred and the profane are not confused, but fused – as they are in the finale of 'Transaction', where masturbation manages to deliver up the soul. Each image is a libation, a sacrifice, a tribute laid before something worshipped – a goddess and a woman, the exalted woman morphing, mysteriously, untraceably, into Gaia. The story isn't a story. It is a proposition and an act of worship. It tells us what love means when it is unattainable – plenitude, prodigality, generosity, afflatus. 'Onyx and split cedar and bronze vessels lowered into still water: these things I offer. Porphyry, teakwood, jasmine, and myrrh: these gifts I bring. The sheen of my sandals is dulled by the dust of cloves. My wings are waxed with nectar ...' These things are – how can I put it? – from the classical repertoire. 'Thick-lipped urns will sweat in the fragrant cellars.' (Compare the 'thick-lipped undersides' of basins seen by the appendicitis case lying on the bathroom floor in 'The City'.) To these properties, Updike contrives to add the contemporary: 'the sliced edges of a fresh ream of laid paper, cream, stiff, rag-rich'; 'the ball diminishing well down the broad green throat of the first at Cape Ann'. Golf! Golf immediately succeeded by unpunctuated lyricism: 'The white arms of girls dancing, taffeta, white arms violet in the hollows music its ecstasies praise the white wrists of praise the white arms and the white paper trimmed the Euclidean proof of Pythagoras's theorem its tightening beauty the iridescence of an old copper found in the salt sand.' Those ecstatic interruptions – 'praise' – could almost be taken from Catullus's hymn to Hymen. The lover can hardly keep up with himself – knowing there is too much to say.

The story ends: 'Stay. Praise me. Your praise of me is praise of yourself; wait. Listen. I will begin again.' The writer has failed and must begin again – wooing the world itself, not just a woman, giving the mundane its beautiful due. Wanting and waiting for the world to surrender.

When Updike was correcting the proofs of his (last) interview with Mark Lawson, an interview published in *Areté* (Issue 27, Winter 2008), I learned that Updike was dying. I reviewed him twice – *The Witches of Eastwick* and *Just Looking* – both times quite severely, by his own high standards. In my introduction to *Ulysses*, I placed him a definite second to his beloved Joyce, to whom, with Nabokov, he owed most. Who doesn't come second to Joyce? I wanted to tell him how much he had meant to me as a writer, without acknowledging I knew he was dying. I wrote this letter.

Dear Mr Updike,

Thank you for returning the interview proofs so promptly – the issue, with your corrections, goes to the printers on Monday – and apologies for this tardy acknowledgement.

I didn't expect you to fly all the way from the US to be at the *Areté* Contributors' Party last Saturday, but you were in my thoughts. I never quite realised when I started *Areté* that – with unforeseen, unguessed-at luck – it might mean publishing my heroes. Of which you are one. I read *Pigeon Feathers* when I was an undergraduate over 40 years ago. One of my poems, written 20 years later, is indebted to 'Archangel' with its lovely fusion of the sacred and the profane. Two pages of ordinary miracles and faultless prose – poetry, actually. I remember being stirred by a sex scene in *Rabbit, Run*. (More than once!) I wrote in my earlier letter that you are an old admiration. You are. You have been part of my mind, actually, for as long as it has been thinking about literature. Thank you. And thank you for the interview.

With All Good Wishes

Updike died less than a week later, before this letter could have reached him. That is a Chekhovian ending.

But I want to end like Updike, a writer who was true to the tarnish of things and their sudden transcendence, who knew that the profane was the perfect place in which to find the spiritual, whose prose knew that the brightness of polished brass depends on the brief dirt, the beloved dinginess of Duraglit.

Memory in Literature
(2005)

In *À la recherche du temps perdu*, Proust says many acute things about memory – about physical memory in the body, for instance, in *Du côté de chez Swann*. One assents and thinks of Robert Frost's 'After Apple-Picking': 'My instep arch not only keeps the ache, / It keeps the pressure of a ladder-*round*' (my italics).

Proust is good, too, on memory's inaccuracy and its arbitrariness. Think of Albertine's wandering beauty spot in *À l'ombre des jeunes filles en fleurs* or Marcel's observation in *Le Temps retrouvé* that one forgets the duel one nearly fought but remembers the yellow gaiters one's opponent wore as a child in the Champs-Elysées. A strikingly dramatic but implausible illustration, this, almost worthy of Henry Carr's slippage and distortion in Stoppard's *Travesties* – where sartorial details, reveres, and darts and flares are given a Wodehousian precedence over world events. Less good, though, than Henry V's prediction that soldiers at Agincourt will remember their part in the battle 'with advantages'.

I prefer, too, T. S. Eliot's more sober sense of arbitrariness in the 'Conclusion' to *The Use of Poetry and the Use of Criticism*:

> Why, for all of us, out of all we have heard, seen, felt, in a lifetime, do certain images recur, charged with emotion, rather than others? The song of one bird, the leap of one fish, at a particular place and time, the scent of one flower, an old woman on a German mountain path, six ruffians seen through an open window playing cards at night at a small French railway junction, where there was a water-mill: such memories may have symbolic value, but of what we cannot tell, for they come to represent the depths of feeling into which we cannot peer.

They are, then, these memories, super-charged with sensation – sensation which is powerful, but indescribable. This sensation – of significance, of occluded feeling – is the subject of this essay. Can we describe it? Can we say what it means?

Proust is interested in the particular sensation that accompanies remembering. The tea-soaked madeleine loses its force when it is repeatedly tasted. Tom Stoppard recorded something similar in the first issue of *Talk* magazine when he

---

All references to *À la recherche du temps perdu* are from the edition translated by C. K. Scott Moncrieff and Terence Kilmartin, revised by D. J. Enright (Chatto & Windus, 1992).

wrote 'On Turning Out to be Jewish' (September 1999). He meets in Czechoslovakia a woman whose cut had been stitched decades before by doctor Straussler, the father he never knew: 'Zaria holds out her hand, which still shows the mark. I touch it. In that moment I am surprised by grief, a small catching-up of all the grief I owe. I have nothing that came from my father, nothing he owned or touched, but here is his trace, a small scar.' A moving moment. But Stoppard has recorded unsentimentally that its power to move diminishes every time he tells the story.

Is the sensation simply nostalgia – like the nostalgic regret of Nicholas Bulstrode in *Middlemarch* for the time when he was an effective Calvinist dissenting preacher in Islington's Upper Row with an ambition to be a missionary? Or is it something more profound – like Proust's meditation, in *À l'ombre des jeunes filles en fleurs*, on his Aunt Léonie's sofa in the brothel. On that same sofa, Marcel has first experienced love with a girl cousin. Proust gives us a stereoscopic irony as the seedy and the pre-sexual amalgamate. There seems to be a hidden message in the coincidence. Is the coincidence merely a coincidence? Or has the coincidence been arranged? Elements of this supernatural innuendo emerge repeatedly in Nabokov's *Speak, Memory*. General Kuropatkin is showing the young Nabokov tricks with matches on a sofa, when he is summoned away: 'the loose matches jumping up on the divan as his weight left it'. Fifteen years later, the disguised, fugitive general asks Nabokov's father for a light ... Nabokov says the true purpose of autobiography is 'the following of such thematic designs through one's life'.

In Book XI of *The Prelude*, Wordsworth writes about significant yet insignificant memories as 'spots of time':

> There are in our existence spots of time
> Which with distinct pre-eminence retain
> A vivifying Virtue, whence, depress'd
> By false opinion and contentious thought,
> Or aught of heavier or more deadly weight,
> In trivial occupations, and the round
> Of ordinary intercourse, our minds
> Are nourished and invisibly repair'd ...

This explanation isn't an explanation at all. It is a statement of intrigued bafflement: 'the hiding places of my power / Seem open; I approach and then they close.' And the example that Wordsworth gives is interestingly drab. It has a few meagre components – a 'naked Pool, / The Beacon on the lonely Eminence, / The Woman, and her garments vex'd and toss'd' – and its power is largely retrospective. It is 'in truth, / An ordinary sight'. Looked back on, though, the dreariness becomes a 'visionary dreariness' that Wordsworth would need colours and words unknown to man to paint. The discrepancy here, in Eliot, and in Proust, is between the original experience and that experience when it is hallowed by remembrance.

The effect is something like cropping in photography. Though each of these writers professes to be *bouleversé* by the detail of the experience, actually the experiences are vital because they exist cropped of context, shorn of explanation. At the beginning of *The Waves*, Virginia Woolf gives us the childhood memories of Rhoda, Louis, Bernard, Susan, Jinny and Neville as highlights, ordinary epiphanies: Mrs Constable pulling up her black stockings; a flash of birds like a handful of broadcast seed; bubbles forming a silver chain at the bottom of a saucepan; air warping over a chimney; light going blue in the morning window. These mnemonic pungencies are different from the *Bildungsroman* of Joyce's *A Portrait of the Artist as a Young Man* as that novel gets into its stride. They resemble rather the unforgettable anthology of snapshots Joyce gives us at the novel's beginning – a snatch of baby-talk; the sensation of wetting the bed; covering and uncovering your ears at refectory. Or Bellow's *Augie March*, when Augie is a kind of shipboard unofficial counsellor, the recipient of emotional swarf: 'Now this girl, who was a cripple in one leg, she worked in the paint lab of the stove factory'; 'He was a Rumania-box type of swindler, where you put in a buck and it comes out a fiver.' Cropped for charisma.

Of course, memory itself is naturally cropped, as Stendhal records in Chapter 13 of *Vie de Henry Brulard*, where he notes that some memories are undated, vivid as fragmented frescoes, but surrounded by the blank brickwork of oblivion.

Actually, *anything* fragmented, as the romantics knew from Percy's *Reliques*, is granted a penumbra of suggestion that we mistake and read as vividness of outline. A perfect example is Auden's 'Journey to Iceland':

> the site of a church where a bishop was put in a bag,
> the bath of a great historian, the fort where
>   an outlaw dreaded the dark,
>
> remember the doomed man thrown by his horse and crying
> *Beautiful is the hillside. I will not go,*
> the old woman confessing *He that I loved the*
>   *best, to him was I worst.*

Memories are more effective than memoirs. Isolation counts for more than continuity. The Paris of Hemingway's *A Moveable Feast* is less vivid than the same material telescoped in 'The Snows of Kilimanjaro'.

This is *A Moveable Feast*: 'All of the sadness of the city came suddenly with first cold rains of winter, and there were no more tops to the white houses as you walked but only the wet blackness of the street and the closed doors of the small shops, the herb sellers, the stationery and the newspaper shops, the midwife – second class – and the hotel where Verlaine had died, where I had a room on the top floor where I worked.' It isn't just the clumsiness of the three 'where's. It's the automatic, sentimental cliché that poisons *A Moveable Feast* – the *flyblown* yellowed poster, the unknown girl at the café 'with a face fresh as a newly minted coin if they minted coins in smooth flesh with rain-freshened skin, and her hair was black as a crow's wing and cut sharply and diagonally across her cheek.'

Nostalgia, as Kundera redefines it in *Ignorance*, is 'the suffering caused by an unappeased yearning to return'. In *A Moveable Feast*, Hemingway fails to return to his past – he is exiled from his memories, because his prose is writing itself and he is having a hard time keeping up.

In 'The Snows of Kilimanjaro', on the other hand, the detail is seen and hand-picked: 'There never was another part of Paris that he loved like that, the sprawling trees, the old white plastered houses painted brown below, the long green of the autobus in that round square, the purple flower dye upon the paving, the sudden drop down the hill of the rue Cardinal Lemoine to the River, and the other way the narrow crowded world of the rue Mouffetard. The street that ran up toward the Pantheon and the other that he always took with the bicycle, the only asphalted street in all that quarter, smooth under the tires, with the high narrow houses and the cheap tall hotel where Paul Verlaine had died.' By 1964, Hemingway has forgotten the flower dye and the round square. His memory fails. So his memories fail.

Nostalgia, of course, has a non-Kunderan meaning, less connected with suffering and more with emotional indulgence. As in, 'they wallowed in nostalgia.' Here the territory is thick with shared memories, with mnemonic solidarity. For example, Ursula in *Women in Love* remembers 'the servant Tilly, who used to give her bread and butter sprinkled with brown sugar'. In one of Edna O'Brien's novels, the heroine sits on the step of the back door, eating sugar on bread.

In *Le Temps retrouvé*, Marcel floats a theory of involuntary memory which he opposes to the willed act of memory. The theory is founded on three rapidly consecutive examples less famous than the madeleine in *Du côté de chez Swann*.

They are as follows. Two uneven paving stones outside the Princesse de Guermantes's mansion recall two particular paving stones in the baptistry of San Marco in Venice. The *ting* of a teaspoon against a plate recalls the noise of a railway man's hammer testing the wheels of the Paris train as it stood outside a wood – when Marcel (page 202, twenty pages earlier) reflected on his lack of talent for literature, a verdict based on his apparent indifference to nature. 'I am in the midst of nature. Well, it is with indifference, with boredom that my eyes register the line which separates your radiant foreheads from your shadowy trunks.' Now the formerly tedious scene dazes Marcel with its previously unmentioned specifics – opening a bottle of beer, hearing the tapped wheels. It is radiant with recall. The experience is experienced with its accessories. And, lastly, the texture of a napkin brings back the very texture of Marcel's bathing towel at Balbec. The napkin contains the towel, which contains an ocean green and blue as a peacock's tail – *the* ocean, since involuntary memory never recalls the indefinite article.

Involuntary memory, in this account, restores reality in its entirety, with all its *qualia* intact, and is therefore a form of resurrection. It is, further, a kind of 'immortality'. Marcel, accordingly, feels joy that makes death a matter of indifference to him. His faith in his literary talent is restored by the intensity with which he recalls these essentially banal experiences.

The idea is shared, or perhaps borrowed, by Nabokov, a much greater writer, in Chapter 3 of *Speak, Memory* (Part VI): 'I see again my class-room, the blue roses of the wall-paper, the open window. Its reflection fills the oval mirror above the leathern couch where my uncle sits, gloating over a tattered book. A sense of security, of well-being, of summer warmth pervades my memory. That robust reality makes a ghost of the present. The mirror brims with brightness; a bumblebee has entered the room and bumps against the ceiling. Everything is as it should be, nothing will ever change, nobody will ever die.' In Nabokov's account, memory is complete, beyond process, exempt from change. The reasoning here is coherent.

Proust's exposition of 'fragments of existence withdrawn from Time' is somewhat muzzy by comparison: 'the truth surely was that the being within me which had enjoyed these impressions had enjoyed them because they had in them something that was common to a day long past and to the present, because in some way they were extra-temporal, and this being made its appearance only when, through one of these identifications of the present with the past, it was likely to find itself in the one and only medium in which it could exist and enjoy the essence of things, that is to say: outside time.'

In any case, Proust's laborious explanation is partial. He has not elucidated the mechanism of memory properly. The mystery that needs explanation is why the recalled experience should bring such acute pleasure when the actual, original experience was 'tedious', and therefore unapprehended.

Proust's 'answer' is that we experience intimations of immortality. It is possible, though, that we simply enjoy the act of remembrance – and that this requires no explanation. It is a fact, the way we are, part of any human being's hard-wiring.

On the other hand, the pleasure is extraordinary. It is comparable to 'the constant readiness to discern the halo round the frying pan or the likeness between a weeping-willow and a Skye terrier'. That simile from Nabokov's *The Real Life of Sebastian Knight* is a clue to the true nature of memory's mechanism, as I hope to explain.

Memory is like metaphor in its operations.

Memory is sexual in its operations.

In English we speak of 'coming' when we speak of orgasm. 'I'm coming' means that the sexual partner is arriving at the predestined place, the site of pleasure. The journey can be long or short but the elusive destination is known in advance.

The words Marcel uses to describe the pleasure that accompanies his three involuntary memories are 'a shudder of happiness', '*avec un tel frémissement de bonheur*'. Not that this is explicitly or exclusively sexual. The word *frémissement* can be applied to fear or anger, as well as to pleasure. It is, too, according to my *Petit Robert*, a light (*léger*) sensation, rather than Eliot's 'blood shaking the heart'. The other word Marcel uses is '*une joie*'. In French, another word for joy, *jouissance*, is also the word for coming, for *plaisir sexuel*. *Jouissance* seems less pedestrian than 'coming'. But having an orgasm – or *orgasme* – is '*parvenir à la jouissance*'. And *parvenir* means to arrive at a predetermined point.

I suggest that the pleasure, the joy *really* experienced by Marcel, and by the rest of us, is bound up with the sensation of imminence, suspense and arrival – common to sex and simile.

Memory is metaphorical in its operations. The pleasure experienced by Marcel is primarily the actual act of remembrance, and only secondarily in the recovered detail of what is remembered. In each of these three involuntary memories, Marcel experiences a delay. The paving stones are like ... what? The teaspoon is like ... what? The texture of the napkin is exactly like ... what? Marcel claims the recall is instant, but it isn't. As he tests the uneven paving stones, he has to repeat the initial movement exactly: 'Every time that I merely repeated this physical movement, I achieved nothing; but if I succeeded, forgetting the Guermantes party, in recapturing what I had felt when I first placed my feet on the ground in this way, again the dazzling and *indistinct* [my italics] vision fluttered near me, as to say: "Seize me as I pass if you can, and try to solve the *riddle* [my italics] of happiness I set you."'

The pleasure of memory is the pleasure we experience when we read a good simile – the pleasure of difference between the two things being compared, the pleasure we take in the justice of the comparison and the sensation of comprehension. Every good simile is a kind of riddle. X is like Y. Why is X like Y? The mind sifts the evidence for and against, seeking the evidence for. Why is a Bang & Olufsen television set like Darth Vadar? Because it has a dark screen, unlike most conventional television sets. There are a million ways in which a B & O television set *isn't* like Darth Vadar. The fractional delay in any simile occurs while the mind works out the way in which the B & O television *is* like Darth Vadar. Marcel solves the riddle of what the paving stones remind him of. He arrives at a solution, he *comes* to the obscure destination, to the only conclusion retrospectively possible.

At its most banal, this process is what Bloom experiences in the 'Lestrygonians' episode of *Ulysses*, when he tries to remember a name across twenty odd pages. Finally, it comes to him: 'Pen. Pen. Penrose.' The itch is scratched. The search has come to a conclusion.

At its most complex, it is Molly's recollection at the end of *Ulysses* of losing her virginity to Bloom on Howth Head. Whereas in Proust, the present provokes a specific memory of the past, Molly's memory of Howth is underlaid with an earlier memory, and, surrendering to Bloom, she surrenders also to an earlier lover: 'yes when I put the rose in my hair like the Andalusian girls used or shall I wear a red yes and how he kissed me under the Moorish wall and I thought well as well him as another'. Molly's first proper kiss and her first full act of intercourse are conflated. Lieutenant Jack or Joe or Harry Mulvey (Molly can't remember his Christian name) is twinned with Leopold Bloom. Memory as multiple orgasm, so to speak.

In 1948, Vladimir Nabokov began *Speak, Memory* with a phrase that was later lifted by Samuel Beckett and vulgarised in *Waiting for Godot*: 'the cradle rocks above the abyss.' (In Beckett, 'they give birth astride the grave.' Twice.) The word 'remember' is itself an implicit rejoinder to death. Its etymology counters dismemberment. It is very rare therefore to encounter a flat rejection of memory like Ursula Brangwen's in *Women in Love*: 'She wanted to have no past. She wanted to have come down from the slopes of heaven to this place, with Birkin, not to have rolled out of the murk of her childhood and her upbringing, slowly, all soiled. She felt that memory was a dirty trick played upon her. What was this decree, that she should "remember"! Why not a bath of pure oblivion, a new birth, without any recollection or blemish of past life.'

Of course, Lawrence had a low opinion of Proust: 'too much jelly-water: I can't read him.' As did Evelyn Waugh, who wrote to Nancy Mitford (16 March 1948): 'I am reading Proust for the first time – in English of course – and am surprised to find him a mental defective. No one warned me of that. He has absolutely no sense of time. He can't remember anyone's age. In the same summer as Gilberte gives him a marble & Françoise takes him to a public lavatory in the Champs-Elysées, Bloch takes him to a brothel.' Nor was Joyce keen to be matched against Proust. On 24 October 1920, Joyce wrote to Frank Budgen: 'I observe a furtive attempt to run a certain M Marcel Proust of here against the signatory of this letter. I have read some pages of his. I cannot see any special talent but I am a bad critic.'

On the whole, though, Proust's influence makes itself felt wherever memory is important.

In spite of his confession in 1948 that he hadn't read À la recherche, Waugh's Brideshead Revisited (1945) is clearly influenced by an idea of Proust's novel. Not only is there a reference to Charlus – the toady don Mr Samgrass spends 'a cosy afternoon with the incomparable Charlus' – but there are several uncharacteristic extended metaphors stretching for a paragraph at a time. Uncharacteristic of Waugh – and, though a famously Proustian trope, one less frequent, it is my impression, in the later volumes of À la recherche, where the sentences themselves are pithier, more Waugh-like. And Charles Ryder, Waugh's narrator, encapsulates his theme at the beginning of Book III: 'My theme is memory ... These memories, which are my life – for we possess nothing certainly except the past – were always with me. Like the pigeons of St Mark's.' An extended metaphor ensues. Is it a coincidence or a Freudian slip that the pigeons are situated in San Marco, a locus central to Le Temps retrouvé?

I should say, too, that Virginia Woolf's The Years – with its time range from 1880 to 1937, its repeated motifs, its chronological gaps during which characters alter dramatically – was an attempt to emulate Proust in English. Delia's party at the end of The Years gathers all the narrative's aged survivors in one place, just as Proust assembles his survivors at the Princesse de Guermantes's, where their aged appearances are ironically and famously described as fancy dress – an extended conceit that begins brilliantly but soon shows signs of strain, like a man with asthma holding his breath.

Of course, Virginia Woolf idolised Proust: on 6 May 1922 she wrote to Roger Fry, 'Proust so titillates my own desire for expression that I can hardly get out a sentence. Oh if I could write like that! I cry. And at the moment such is the astonishing vibration and saturation and intensification he procures – theres [sic] something sexual in it – that I feel I can write like that and seize my pen and then I can't write like that. Scarcely anyone so stimulates the nerves of language in me: it becomes an obsession. But I must return to Swann.' Fulsome praise, though in October she is still on volume one. Three years later, on 9 February 1925, Woolf tells Margaret Llewelyn Davies that she's only read three volumes. No obstacle to her claim on 21 April 1927 to her sister Vanessa that Proust is 'far the greatest novelist'.

She seems, however, never to have actually finished reading À la recherche. In a 1928 newspaper piece, 'Preferences', she writes 'I have also bought and propose to read should my life last long enough the final volumes of Proust's masterpiece.' (Le Temps retrouvé was published in 1927.) On 27 April 1934, she tells Ethel Smyth she's reading Sodom et Gomorrhe. And on 21 May 1934, again to Ethel Smyth: 'I cant [sic] write myself within its arc; that's true; for years I've put off finishing it.'

And yet in April, May, June of 1929, her three-part essay, 'Phases of Fiction',* claims that Proustian psychology is an advance on Henry James, while adding the qualification that the 'expansion of sympathy' is almost self-defeating. Everything in Proust, however trivial, provokes an extended meditation. 'Proust is determined to bring before the reader every piece of evidence upon which any state of mind is founded.' The risk is that the commentary is surplus to requirements, that there is no hierarchy of importance – that the footnotes bury the trickle of text, as it were. 'We lose the sense of outline.'

How do we account for Virginia Woolf's high opinion of Proust if it is so precariously founded? It is partially explained by this hyperventilating assessment to Roger Fry on 3 October 1922: 'One has to put the book down with a gasp. The pleasure becomes physical – like sun and wine and grapes and perfect serenity and intense vitality combined. *Far otherwise is it with* Ulysses: *to which I bind myself like a martyr to a stake, and have thank God, now finished – My martyrdom is over. I hope to sell it for £4.10.*' (my italics).† Joyce was right when he told Budgen there was a Proust special promotion in train. For Virginia Woolf, Proust was a way of putting her rival Joyce in his place – and a way, too, of acceding easily to the preferential judgements of homosexual Bloomsbury.

One is queasy, however, at her little litany of praise – grapes, Evian water, pinot noir and the seafront at Cannes! – because its blowsy imprecision suggests impeccable ignorance. And, although her essays refer often to Proust, one sometimes wonders if she had read as little as Evelyn Waugh.

Her essay 'Pictures' invokes a Proustian scene in a theatre, in which 'we have to understand the emotions of a young man for a lady in the box below'. Andrew McNeillie, the editor of the essays, does not identify this minutely, yet vaguely, invoked incident. Nor can I find it. (When Marcel goes to see Berma in

---

* The only two specific citations in 'Phases of Fiction' are both to Vol. III, Le Coté de Guermantes – to page 385 (Marcel saying he is not asleep as he is woken by his mother to go to his grandmother's death-bed) and to page 688 (Swann telling the Duchesse de Guermantes that he will be dead in three or four months as she gets into her carriage to go out to dinner).
† Very different from her public assessment in the Times Literary Supplement (23 May 1918), where she lauded the spirituality of Ulysses.

Le Coté de Guermantes, he is in the stalls looking *up* at the boxes.) It is, in any case, dangerously close to nonsense:

> At the same time our senses drink in all this our minds are tunnelling, logically and intellectually, into the obscurity of the young man's emotions, which, as they ramify and modulate and stretch further and further, at last penetrate so far, peter out into such a shred of meaning, *that we can scarcely follow any more* [my italics] were it not that suddenly, in flash after flash, metaphor after metaphor, the eye lights up that cave of darkness, and we are shown the hard, tangible, material shapes of bodiless thoughts hanging like bats in the primeval darkness where light never visited them before.

As I type this out, I am hardly surprised it corresponds exactly to nothing factual in Proust. It is an hommage to Proust's obscurity.

Beckett wrote a brief (and intermittently unreadable) monograph about Proust, and *Krapp's Last Tape* is a kind of dwarf À *la recherche*, shrunk in the wash. On the one hand, there is the unforgettable (but ironically forgotten) physical memory of the black ball in the dog's mouth: 'a small, old, black, hard. Solid rubber ball. (*Pause.*) I shall feel it, in my hand, until my dying day.' On the other hand, there is the hypnotic memory of the punt and the girl. Ruth Miller, an early Bellow biographer, remembered Bellow reading to her the passage in *Le Temps retrouvé* when Marcel is stuck in his train in a field. In *Herzog*, Herzog persecutes his friend Nachman with 'the engine of his memory'. And Bellow's *The Adventures of Augie March* owes a debt to Proust as well as a more obvious debt to Twain's *The Adventures of Huckleberry Finn* and the American vernacular. When Augie announces that he 'will go at things' in his 'own way', 'free-style', and that his memories will be set down as they arrive, 'first to knock, first admitted', he is not in fact going at things entirely in his own way. It is also the Guermantes' way, Swann's way and Proust's way – the way of involuntary memory.

Kipling and Racism (1999)

Was Kipling a racist? His poem 'We and They' is an impeccable statement of cultural relativism:

> All good people agree,
>   And all good people say,
> All nice people, like Us, are We
>   And every one else is They:
> But if you cross over the sea,
>   Instead of over the way,
> You may end by (think of it!) looking on We
>   As only a sort of They'

You couldn't have a more complete and enlightened statement of the case for cultural relativity if the poem had been written by Edward Said.

I want to look at Kipling's racism and its complications. I think that even Kipling's admirers are prejudiced against him. We *know* he must be a racist – patronising and condescending at his least obnoxious; loathsome and ugly at his worst. I want to complicate this caricature. Part of me thinks the caricature exists because it is easier for advocates to concede the worst and move on than it is to haggle over detail.

For example, in his introduction to his Oxford Authors selection of Kipling, Daniel Karlin resumes two central mitigating arguments. First, retrospective justice – the *injustice* of retrospective justice – the sense that Kipling must be seen in his historical context and not judged anachronistically by contemporary standards. And, second, the ransom argument – that positive racial portraits sometimes balance negative ones. The example Karlin gives is Hurree Chunder Mookerjee, the Babu in *Kim*, who can be weighed against Kipling's incessant libels of the Bengali Babu.

Karlin then rejects both arguments completely. For him, the nuances never eliminate the uglinesses, *cannot* eliminate the uglinesses.

And it is true that Kipling's stories constantly place before us observations which are morally unpalatable. Think of 'An Habitation Enforced', where the obnoxious pushiness of the nouveau riche Mr Sangres is heightened by the pigment of his skin. Mr Sangres is Brazilian and therefore 'dusky' as well as pushy.

Lecture given to the Kipling Society, Magdalene College, Cambridge, September 2001.

Finally, one of the peasants refers to him as 'that nigger Sangres'.

At junctures like these, it *does* seem appealing simply to concede Kipling's racism – so that one can get on and quote the writing.

But we need, for accurate justice, to consider each case. Which is impossible. I propose to avoid the usual instances, 'Beyond the Pale', 'Lispeth', 'Without Benefit of Clergy'. 'Loot' I have already defended in my 1993 Channel 4 programme, *J'adore Rudyard Kipling*. What about the letters? What about the private man in the secrecy of his correspondence? What about the travel writings? I want to concentrate on these two aspects of Kipling. So far, I think neither has been read well by critics. It is partly that, because there is so much of Kipling to read, the travel writings tend to be read once and once only, leaving the biographer with misleading index cards.

This is the only way I can account for the misreading by Harry Ricketts and Andrew Lycett of a passage in *From Sea to Sea*, Vol. I, Chapter 24, page 489.[*]This is Kipling. He's describing a murder in a Chinese gambling den in San Francisco: 'Mark how purely man is a creature of instinct. Rarely introduced to the pistol, I saw the Mexican half rise in his chair and at the same instant found myself full length on the floor.' While dropping to the floor, Kipling hears 'an intolerable clamour like the discharge of a cannon'. In the great silence following, Kipling gets to his knees. And from there gives us an unforgettably downbeat description of a death.

> The Chinaman was gripping the table with both hands and staring in front of him at an empty chair. The Mexican had gone, and a little whirl of smoke was floating near the roof. Still gripping the table, the Chinaman said 'Ah!' in the tone a man would use when, looking up from his work suddenly, he sees a well-known friend in the doorway. Then he coughed and fell over to his own right, and I saw that he had been shot in the stomach.
>
> I became aware that, save for two men leaning over the stricken one, the room was empty …

And Kipling flees.

Who could possibly forget this?

Well, anyone who has read the whole of Kipling. Certainly Andrew Lycett and Harry Ricketts.

---

[*] Harry Ricketts, *The Unforgiving Minute: A Life of Rudyard Kipling* (Pimlico, 2000); Andrew Lycett, *Rudyard Kipling* (Weidenfeld & Nicolson, 1999). All references to *From Sea to Sea* are from the Macmillan two-volume edition of 1914.

This is Andrew Lycett getting it wrong: 'when he picked himself up from the floor, Rudyard found that everyone had fled the room.'

This is Harry Ricketts getting it wrong: 'a sortie to a gambling den in Chinatown produced a dead Mexican, shot before his eyes over a poker game.'

And these are uncontroversial facts. Think of the scope for misreading and inaccurate transcription when interpretation is involved – interpretation of controversial questions.

In what follows, I propose to sift the evidence for and against Kipling – taking in sequence his attitude to Indians, Blacks, Irish, Chinese, Japanese, Jews and Germans. I do not expect to exonerate Kipling in every instance, but the evidence is more intricate than our initial inclinations might suggest. Our contemporary condemnations are blanket – like our terminology. Our terminology has evolved. Though 'African-American', like 'Asian-American', is precise enough, ethical purity has, on the whole, entailed terminological vagueness. The Negro was first 'coloured', briefly 'Nation', and then 'black' in an apparently courageous embrace of racial insult – except that 'black' now applies to any 'person of colour'. Some Asians prefer to be called 'black', though Salman Rushdie recently described himself as 'brown'. Arabs are usually called Arabs. 'Person of colour' is the currently favoured overall term – an ethical strategy to neutralise all those petty distinctions of colour so prized by racists of all complexions. But it is a strategy not particularly helpful in this context.

Indians

Kipling's story 'The Head of the District' is sometimes read as racist and patronising. It was written in 1890, seven years after the Ibert Bill, which is its ultimate subject. The bill was liberal in orientation and supported by the viceroy, Lord Ripon. One of its revisions to the Criminal Procedure Code was to invest native magistrates with jurisdiction over British subjects – including, most controversially, the power to try white women. Kipling was hissed in his club when the seventeen-year-old's paper, *The Civil and Military Gazette*, 'ratted on the bill', supporting it after initial opposition. 'The Head of the District' is usually read as Kipling's mordant comment on native Indian inability to govern and administer state affairs competently.

When Yardley-Orde, the white head of the district dies, the government in its liberal wisdom appoints a Bengali as his replacement, one Grish Chunder Dé, MA. The new deputy commissioner's Afghan subjects are unimpressed, indeed insulted by the appointment. They revolt, and the Bengali panics. 'I have not yet assumed charge of the district' is his cowardly response to the crisis. His brother,

Debendra Nath Dé, is beheaded in the rebellion.

So far, this reads like a narrative of higher administrative incompetence told by the complacent voice of Anglo-India, chortling with racist condescension. No backbone, these natives. In fact, the story can be read in this way only if the reader is as prejudiced against Kipling as he believes Kipling to be prejudiced against Indians.

The rebellion is really put down by Khoda Dad Khan, an Afghan warrior loyal to the Bengali's white predecessor, Orde, and to Orde's second-in-command, Tallentire. It is Khoda Dad Khan who kills the mullah behind the uprising. In other words, it is *he*, Khoda Dad Khan, who is effectively the Head of the District. It is he who realises that revolt against the British is futile – a drain on human resource – and it is Kipling who realises that the British can govern only with the consent of the indigenous population. Without consent, there can only be conquest – not the same thing as government by any means. Kipling knows that the Afghans rule themselves. What is more, they know it, too, and it is marked in the story by a single subtle shift. When Orde dies, he speaks affectionately to the Afghans as children. 'For though ye be strong men, ye are children' is his almost final word. *Children* – the great, standard patronising Imperialist epithet, designed to demean the dignity of another race.

Kipling is careful, though, in his coda, to mark and salve this sensitivity. Tallentire and Khoda Dad Khan are discussing the Bengali's successor. Fully aware of where power really lies, both men connive at the myth of British rule. Tallentire 'thunders' at Khoda Dad Khan that his people are 'children and fools', that 'the Government will send you a *man*' to rule the district. To which Khoda Dad Khan, momentarily lapsing from his part in the Imperialist charade, lets slip the truth: 'Ay ... for we also be men.'

The moral of 'The Head of the District' for literary critics is that there is no such thing as 'the Indian' or 'the native'. In this story there is the Afghan (or the Pathan) and there is the Bengali. Kipling distinguishes between them.

Two crucial letters maintain this distinction and complicate it. They were written to Margaret Burne-Jones when Kipling was still working at the *Civil and Military Gazette*. They are dated 27 September 1885, and 28 November 1885 to 11 January 1886. I want to discuss the second in detail because I think it seriously misrepresented in Andrew Lycett's account (pages 119ff.).

Kipling's second letter first of all attacks the concept of 'the native' – 'When you write "native" who do you mean? The Mahommedan who hates the Hindu; the Hindu who hates the Mahommedan; the Sikh who loathes both; or the semi-anglicised product of our Indian colleges who is hated and despised by Sikh, Hindu and Mahommedan.'

Kipling recorded these distinctions. He didn't invent them. And they still exist. In the aftermath of the 2001 race riots in Oldham, the *Today* radio programme had an interview in which a Hindu woman complained about the blanket label 'Asians' – and blamed the riots on sections of the Muslim community.

You might maintain that, nevertheless, Kipling despised the Bengali Babu, whom he makes his target in 'The Head of the District'. It is true that, on the whole, Bengalis get poor press from Kipling. The panic of Grish Chunder Dé is reproduced in *From Sea to Sea* (Vol. II, 'The Giridih Coal-Fields'), where Kipling sketches an *imagined* mining accident in which the Bengali Babu panics and blames everything on the sirdar of the gang. Kipling's verdict is 'The best of accountants, but the poorest of coroners is he.'

'The best of accountants'. Kipling does pay tribute to this specific quality, this aptitude, in the Bengali Babu. In 'Among the Railway Folk' (Vol. II, page 281), he closes with this paean: 'The Babus make beautiful accountants, and if we could only see it, a merciful providence has made the Babu for figures and detail. Without him, the dividends of any company would be eaten up by the expenses of English or city-bred clerks. The Babu is a great man, and, to respect him, you must see five score or so of him in a room a hundred yards long, bending over ledgers, ledgers, and yet more ledgers – silent as the Sphinx and busy as a bee.'

Of course, there is an ironic tinge in that Sphinx-like silence, given the Bengali Babu's legendary loquacity – 'celebrated' in 'City of Dreadful Night' (Vol. II, page 219), where Sir Steuart Bayley endures Bengali bombast by the hour – but nevertheless Kipling's final, judiciously particular verdict is clear. '*The Babu is a great man*' – when he is a clerk.

A verdict which is, of course, sufficient reason now to convict Kipling of racism. He is well disposed to the Indian, the indictment goes, only so long as the Indian knows his place. So the Babu is a great man if he sticks to clerical work. The Indian, though, isn't interested in Kipling's benevolent disposition. It is irrelevant. The Indian rather wants justice. Ergo, Kipling is essentially racist.

I want to argue strongly against this. For several reasons. First, compared to the worst Imperialist racists, Kipling is indeed benevolent and enlightened. There are degrees of racism. Hitler's anti-Semitism is clearly far worse than that of T. S. Eliot, supposing you happen to believe Eliot *was* anti-Semitic. Which I incline to disbelieve. Secondly, there is an injustice inherent in the retrospective application of the standards of 2002. No one at the time would have recognised them as valid. In fact, the application of racial and class categories was universal until the end of the Second World War. The war completely broke down accepted ways of categorisation. Up to that date, working-class men and women would have described themselves as working class, the middle class as middle class. And so on. Categorisation, however deplorable, was then a matter of fact and a fact of life.

In his second letter to Margaret Burne-Jones, Kipling addresses her central question. She had asked if the English and the natives had interests in common: 'd—d few', Kipling replies – adding:

> faith if you knew in what inconceivable filth of mind the peoples of India were brought up from their cradle; if you realised the views – or one tenth of the views – they hold about women and their absolute incapacity for speaking the truth as we understand it – the immeasurable gulf that lies between the two races in all things, you would see how it comes to pass that the Englishman is prone to despise the natives – (I must use that mis-leading term for brevity's sake) – and how, except in the matter of trade, to have little or nothing in common with him.

And that is where Andrew Lycett leaves the quotation and the question of Kipling's attitude to Indians.

At which point, Kipling sounds like an authentic pukka sahib. But Andrew Lycett has reversed the order of Kipling's letter to make this *beginning* Kipling's conclusion. Lycett writes: '*At the end of the day,* he admitted that the British in India had very little in common with their subjects' (my italics). True, but mis-leading. Because Kipling goes on, amazingly, to *deplore* this gulf and to show his ambition to penetrate Indian society.

The letter *continues*: '*Now this is a wholly wrong attitude of mind* [my italics] but it's one that a Briton who washes, and don't take bribes, and who thinks of other things besides intrigue and seduction most naturally falls into.'

'*When he does* [fall into this wrong attitude of mind] [Kipling's italics] – good-bye to his chances of attempting to understand the people of the land.' Kipling then describes his novel *Mother Maturin* as an attempt to penetrate the authentic native life, which is unaffected by British rule. 'The result has been to interest me immensely and keenly in the people and to show me how little an English-man can hope to understand 'em.' Of this life, Kipling avers that 'our rule, so long as no one steals too flagrantly or murders too openly, affects it in no way whatever' – which could be a gloss on Kipling's 'The Head of the District'. The letter continues with a remark often quoted against him – that the Indians are a cross between children and men, 'touchy as children, obstinate as men'.

But Kipling goes on:

the proper way to handle 'em is not by looking on 'em 'as excitable masses of barbarism' (I speak for the Punjab only) or the 'down trodden millions

of Ind groaning under the heel of an alien and unsympathetic despotism',
but as *men with a language of their own which it is your business to understand*;
and proverbs which it is your business to quote (this is a land of proverbs)
and byewords and allusions which it is your business to master; **and feelings which it is your business to enter into and sympathise with**. [my
italics and bold]

This scarcely sounds like a racist to me.

Later in the same letter, discussing Ram Dass, his printer, Kipling again
writes something frequently quoted against him: 'Remember Wop in spite of
what good lies in the native he is uttterly unable to do anything finished or
clean, or neat unless he has the Englishman at his elbow to guide and direct and
put straight.' Here, importantly, we should note that, writing to W. E. Henley
(18–19 January 1893), Kipling makes the identical criticism of white Americans.
He says that, in America, 'a certain defect runs through everything – workmanship, roads, bridges, contracts, barter and sale and so forth – all inaccurate, all
slovenly, all out of plumb and untrue. So far the immense natural wealth of the
land holds this ineptitude up; and the slovenly plenty hides their sins unless you
look for them. Au fond it's barbarism – barbarism plus telephone, electric light,
rail and suffrage but all the more terrible for that very reason.'

Odd, isn't it, that Kipling should equate native Indians and white Americans as essentially barbarous? However eccentric, the judgement begins to look
impartial rather than racist. And one finds the same kind of cross-racial equation made in *Letters of Travel (1892–1913)*, where Kipling notes the slovenliness
of New York's streets and declares them 'first cousins to a Zanzibar foreshore,
or kin to the approaches of a Zulu kraal'. Kipling's comparison is intended to
shock by its initial unlikeliness. The barbarity of the Zulu is taken for granted,
as the barbarity of the American is not. But this could be described as racist only
if one were not prepared to concede that there might be something primitive
in a Zulu kraal.

Given his reputation as a racist, it is equally odd to find Kipling rebuking a
clergyman for ethnic insensitivity (16 October 1895):

it is my fortune to have been born and to a large extent brought up among
those whom white men call 'heathen'; and while I recognise the para-
mount duty of every white man to follow the teachings of his creed and
conscience as 'a debtor to do the whole law', it seems to me cruel that
white men, whose governments are armed with the most murderous
weapons known to science, should amaze and confound their fellow creatures with a doctrine of salvation imperfectly understood by themselves

and a code of ethics foreign to the climate and instincts of those races whose most cherished customs they outrage and whose gods they insult.

Kipling returns to this idea in *From Sea to Sea* (Vol. II, page 61): 'Very many Americans have an offensive habit of referring to natives as "heathen". Mahometans and Hindus are heathen alike in their eyes.'

Which seems almost enlightened – were not the protester Kipling.

Nevertheless, Kipling's idea of the White Man's Burden is predicated on a self-pitying gloss on Imperialism – seen not as economic exploitation but as the fatiguing exercise of authority and enlightenment. It also seems to be predicated on the idea of 'lower races', however much sympathy Kipling would like to bring to their administration.

But even this is complicated. The poem 'The White Man's Burden' has been widely misread. In effect, critics have stopped, affronted, at the first stanza: 'Your new-caught, sullen peoples, / Half-devil and half child.' It is the imputation of childishness that lodges in the throat – and, alas, in the brain. Has anyone, I wonder, read to the end of the poem and understood it?

The reward for taking up the White Man's Burden is stated in the last line: 'The judgment of your peers!' Who are those 'peers', those equals? Since the poem is addressed to the USA, you might think that 'peers' refers to British Imperialists. But you would be wrong. The 'peers' in question are the 'new-caught, sullen peoples' – raised to equality. As the previous three stanzas make clear (my italics throughout):

> Take up the White Man's burden –
> And reap his old reward:
> The blame of those ye better,
> The hate of those ye guard –
> The cry of hosts ye humour
> (Ah, slowly!) *toward the light*: –
> 'Why brought ye us from bondage,
> Our loved Egyptian night?'
>
> Take up the White Man's burden –
> Ye dare not stoop to less –
> Nor call too loud on Freedom
> To cloke your weariness;
> By all ye cry or whisper,
> By all ye leave or do,
> The silent, sullen peoples

Shall weigh your Gods and you.

Take up the White Man's burden –
Have done with childish days –
The lightly proffered laurel,
The easy, ungrudged praise.
Comes now, to search your manhood
Through all the thankless years,
Cold, edged with dear-bought wisdom,
The judgment of your peers!

In this account, the Imperialist aim, which mustn't be rushed, is eventual independence: 'Nor call too loud on Freedom / To cloak your weariness.' In other words, grant Freedom at the proper juncture, when the moment is ripe – and not because fatigue makes you want to rest.

Kipling's penultimate stanza ends explicitly with the judgement of the colonised on the colonisers: 'The silent, sullen peoples / Shall weigh your Gods and you.' But Kipling waits until the last line of the poem to spring his surprise – a surprise marked by an exclamation mark. There he makes it clear that, in the end, the judgement of the colonised on the colonisers will be the judgement of equals, 'the judgment of your peers'.

The aim, then, is not subjection and exploitation in perpetuity, but 'Freedom' with a capital *f* and elevation to equality.

Ah yes. Those 'lower races' … As we shall see, Kipling was capable on occasion of seeing Oriental races – the Japanese, the Chinese – as racially superior.

While Kipling can respect another race, he seems to reserve a special dislike / distaste for the half-breed. In a letter to Andrew Macphail (20 November to 7 December 1908), he refers to the Afrikaner – post-Boer War, of course – as 'a race largely tainted with native blood'.

Yet consider Kipling's humane comment on Eurasians in Chapter 8 of 'The City of Dreadful Night' (Vol. II, pages 262ff.): 'we know nothing about their life which touches so intimately the White on the one hand and the Black on the other … Wanted, therefore, a writer from among the Eurasians, who shall write so that men shall be pleased to read a story of Eurasian life; then outsiders will be interested in the People of India, and will admit that the race has possibilities.'

It could almost be George Eliot, who believed the novel's moral purpose was to extend our moral sympathies, who wrote of those hidden lives and 'that roar which lies on the other side of silence'.

Negroes

Margaret Peller Feeley, in 'The *Kim* that Nobody Reads', has shown how Kipling altered the drafts of his novel to tone down the glamour of the English and eliminate casual racist remarks. Of course, there will always be criminographers for whom the most damning interpretation of evidence is the truth – here, that Kipling's first thoughts were his true thoughts. Casual racist remarks, then, are what came naturally to Kipling.

But it is surely the case that what is considered – those alterations, those tonings-down – should itself be taken into consideration.

The letters yield a further example. On 11 January 1904, Kipling composes an inscription for the Shanghai Memorial and sends it to Sir Lewis Mitchell – Mitchell objected to the phrase 'in fight against savages', 'as likely to hurt Native feeling a century hence. Kipling at once agreed to my substituted words "the Matabele".'

If this is evidence of Kipling's insensitivity, it is equally evidence of his sensitivity.

But consider this difficult, unpleasant passage in *From Sea to Sea* (Vol. II, pages 9ff.): 'Now let me draw breath and curse the negro waiter and through him the negro in service generally. He has been made a citizen with a vote; consequently both political parties play with him. But that is neither here nor there. He will commit in one meal every *bétise* that a scullion fresh from the plough-tail is capable of, and he will continue to repeat those faults.'

Kipling's target here isn't simply 'the negro in service', though he continues in this irritated-diner-vein for a few more sentences, until he is flagrantly, unforgivably racist: 'Now God and his father's Kismet made him intellectually inferior to the oriental.'

And here Kipling has no excuse.

He cannot hide behind the persona of the brash Globe-Trotter, as he does successfully elsewhere. The person opining is unmistakably Kipling himself, *in propria persona*. And if he isn't asserting *white* racial superiority, but *oriental* racial superiority, he *is* insisting on black racial inferiority.

He is a big, black, vain baby and a man rolled into one. A coloured gentleman who insisted on getting me pie when I wanted something else, demanded information about India. I gave him some facts about wages. 'Oh hell,' said he cheerfully, 'that wouldn't keep me in cigars for a month.' Then he fawned on me for a ten-cent piece. Later he took it on himself to pity the natives of India – 'heathen' he called them, this Woolly One whose race has been the butt of every comedy on the Asiatic stage since the beginning.

It doesn't help that Kipling is offended on behalf of the Indian, nor that he shares an Indian race prejudice.

He identifies the Negro's head as Yoruba: 'He did his thinking in English, but he was a Yoruba negro, and the race type had remained the same throughout his generations. And the room was full of other races – some that looked exactly like Gallas (but the trade was never recruited from that side of Africa), some duplicates of Cameroon heads, and some Kroomen, if ever Kroomen wore evening dress.'

So what is Kipling's message here? It is this. The persistence of racial type will survive evening dress and 'thinking in English'. That is the message.

And the type is inferior in perpetuity:

The American does not consider little matters of descent, though by this time he ought to know all about 'damnable heredity'. As a general rule he keeps himself pretty far from the negro and says unpretty things about him. There are six million negroes more or less in the States, and they are increasing. The Americans once having made them citizens cannot unmake them. He says, in his newspapers, they ought to be elevated by education. He is trying this: but it is like to be a long job, because black blood is much more adhesive than white, and throws back with annoying persistence. When the negro gets a religion, he returns, directly as a hiving bee, to the first instincts of his people.

And Kipling then describes his attendance at an African-American church:

The congregation were moved by the spirit to groans and tears, and one of them danced up the aisle to the mourners' bench. The motive may have been genuine. The movements of the shaken body were those of a Zanzibar stick-dance, such as you see at Aden on the coal-boats; and even as I watched the people, the links that bound them to the white man snapped one by one and I saw before me – the *hubshi* (the Woolly One) praying to a God he did not understand. Those neatly dressed folk on the benches, the grey-headed elder by the window, were savages – neither more nor less.

Phew. 'The *hubshi* … praying to a God he did not understand.'

And Kipling concludes with a question and a dire prediction, which has proved lamentable but not inaccurate: 'What will the American do with the negro? The South will not consort with him. In some States miscegenation is a penal offence. The North is every year less and less in need of his services. And he will not disappear. He will continue as a problem. His friends will urge that he is as good as the white man. His enemies … it is not good to be a negro in the land of the free and the home of the brave.'

My quotation here comes from the 1914 edition of *From Sea to Sea*. The earlier edition of 1900 has no ellipsis at 'His enemies'. The text runs thus:

> His enemies – well, you can guess what his enemies will do from a little incident that followed on a recent appointment by the President. He made a negro an assistant in a post office where – think of it! – he had to work at the next desk to a white girl, the daughter of a colonel, one of the first families of Georgia's modern chivalry, *and all the weary, weary rest of it* [my italics]. The Southern chivalry howled, and hanged or burned someone in effigy. Perhaps it was the President, and perhaps it was the negro – but the principle remains the same. They said it was an insult. It is not good to be a negro in the land of the free and the home of the brave.

We don't know why Kipling excised this passage. Perhaps because it proved apocryphal. Whatever the factual status of Kipling's reported anecdote, his sympathies are clearly against the wearisome bogus chivalry, against segregation, and with the Negro. His ironic parenthesis, 'think of it!', is incredulous. He had no time for segregationist cant. There were limits to his prejudice.

Kipling's personal relations are germane to the question of his racism – or rather the gap between the reflex assumptions of his class and his considered experiential views. In September 1907, Kipling and Carrie went on a tour of Canada, from Montreal to Vancouver, and were given the use of their own railway car, with their own attendant – initially designated 'the Noble Nigger' in letters to the Kipling children – who 'would be our guide, philosopher and friend'. In the next letter, Kipling reports that 'our porter William (a negro) became a friend of the family'. He is 'William (our William)' by the end of the letter, telling Kipling touching anecdotes. In a letter to a friend, William is 'the Negro Potentate in charge' and 'negro King' who 'entertains us with stories'.

In my audited account of Kipling's racism, I should like to place this account of the Negro railway conductor in service in the credit column, directly opposite the irritated debit account of the Negro waiter in service of *From Sea to Sea*.

In *Something of Myself*, Kipling gives a more decided, less gradualist account of his relationship with William. William isn't *ever* 'the Noble Nigger'. He is 'coloured porter, our Nurse, Valet, Seneschal, and Master of Ceremonies'. Here Kipling is mostly interested in William's vernacular: 'bekase' for 'because', 'haow' for 'how', 'dey' for 'they', etc. To this end, Kipling recounts one of William's anecdotes – about a friend who wants to be a conductor, but thinks he can succeed simply by copying William. He fails dismally, of course, and cries in a cupboard. William has to do the work for him.

Why does Kipling tell this parable, as he calls it? That it *happened* isn't a reason for inclusion. I think the reason is unconscious. The anecdote is an act of unconscious discrimination on Kipling's part – he is discriminating between his prejudice and his experience. Prejudice requires Negro incompetence, the caricature crying in the cupboard. Experience requires tribute to the omni-competence of William.

The Irish

Kipling is undoubtedly prejudiced against the Irish (and, incidentally, the Welsh) – largely because they resist British rule and insist on their national language.

This is a letter to Andrew Macphail (5 October 1913):

> I had a man the other day from the interior of Wales poisonous-full of his own 'nationality' and its tongue and the teaching thereof. But I entirely agreed with him and was prepared to help in giving funds for the teaching of Cymric and Ogham and all the rest – compulsory if need be. Says he gratefully: – 'But I shouldn't have expected this of you Mr Kipling.' 'Man' says I, 'anything that cripples and diverts and renders more unintelligible the inferior and crippled breeds of the earth has my blessing and support.'

In *Something of Myself*, Kipling candidly disparages the Irish: '[They] had passed out of the market into "politics" which suited their instincts of secrecy, plunder and anonymous denunciation.' This, and other disparaging anti-Irish remarks scattered through Kipling's correspondence, looks racist – and it is, but the racism is an emphasis given to political disagreement. Vis-à-vis the Irish, we can see the absence of true racism in a letter to Andrew Macphail (21 October 1911): there, Kipling excoriates the Irish for their diminished aesthetic sense, their clinging to 'Erse', their gobbing (like US citizens), the manure pit of the station, etc. Then: 'we got into the North and the car literally bumped into a new country of decent folk.' Decent folk who are, of course, Irish – but Irish who wish to be part of the United Kingdom.

In *From Sea to Sea*, a variety of verdicts on the Irish are handed down. On a train (Vol. II, page 139), a drunken actress weeps because the conductor has taken her five-dollar bill to look for change. She fears he will not return. Kipling writes: 'He was an Irishman, so I knew he couldn't steal.' Eventually, the conductor reappears, 'the five-dollar bill honestly changed'.

At the end of Vol. I, though, Kipling denounces Irish politics, as usual for being anti-English: 'the Irish vote is more important [than the Italian vote]. For this reason the Irishman does not kill himself with overwork. He is made for the cheery dispensing of liquors, for everlasting blarney, and possesses a wonderfully keen appreciation of the weaknesses of lesser human nature. Also he has no sort of conscience, and only one strong conviction – that of deep-rooted hatred toward England.'

The Yellow Peril

From Sea to Sea contains ostensibly virulent anti-Chinese remarks, but these are in the persona of the despised globetrotter. The letters have one reference to 'the Yellow Peril'. A postscript to Jules Huret (31 August 1905) asks 'Who launched the phrase?' The answer is Kaiser Wilhelm II of Germany.

In his recent biography, Harry Ricketts discusses Kipling's racism in the context of the letters of travel in *From Sea to Sea*. He quotes several examples of Kipling's Sinophobia but is curiously equivocal about their status: on the one hand, Kipling is 'flagrantly racist'; on the other hand, 'the uneasy phrasing and tone suggested that he did not entirely believe in the opinions he was voicing.' Again, Ricketts says, he was 'careful while he sent up the Europeanised Japanese to point out his own ignorance and presumption'. Exactly.

In India, Kipling unaffectedly despised the globetrotter whose confidence was matched only by his superficiality. Leaving the known Indian subcontinent, Kipling is explicit in his identification with the contemptible globetrotter: if the globetrotter libelled India, it was Kipling's comic role to revenge India by libelling other countries. 'It was my destiny to avenge India upon nothing less than three-quarters of the world. The idea necessitated sacrifices – painful sacrifices – for I had to become a Globe-trotter, with a helmet and deck-shoes. In the interests of our little world I would endure these things and more. I would deliver "brawling judgements all day long; on all things unashamed".' (Vol. I, page 208). And this is the persona Kipling adopts for his opinions.

Since the question of the globetrotter persona has been presented by recent biographers as problematic, I propose to cite the evidence at some length. The globetrotter is 'the man who "does" kingdoms in days and writes books upon them in weeks' (*From Sea to Sea*, Vol. I, pages 1–2). A page or two later: 'Once or twice in my life I have seen a Globe-trotter literally gasping with jealous emotion because India was so much larger and more lovely that he had ever dreamed, and because he had only set aside three months to explore it in. *My own sojourn in Rangoon was countable by hours, so I may be forgiven when I pranced with impatience because I could not at once secure a full, complete, and accurate idea of everything that was to be seen'* (my italics).

Then Vol. I, page 241: 'I put my twelve-inch rule in my pocket to measure all the world by.' Compare Vol. I, page 275: 'It grieves me that I cannot account for the ideas of a few hundred million men in a few hours.' A hundred pages later, he is undeterred (page 361): 'Thus we talked of the natures and dispositions of men *we knew nothing about* till we had decided [six generalisations]' (my italics).

In Vol. I, on page 245, Kipling notes uneasily that the Chinese work hard despite the climate. Feigning comprehension of the racial hatred of 'the lower-caste Anglo-Saxon' for the Chinaman, Kipling adds to the crucial parenthetical signal of irony: viz. '(this has the true Globe-trotter twang to it)'.

Elsewhere, Kipling's irony relies on the auto-destructive excess of his comments. Extremism signals irony.

He accuses the Chinese of cannibalism: '[the Chinese baby] isn't as pretty as the pig that Alice nursed in Wonderland, and he lies quite still and never cries. This is because he is afraid of being boiled and eaten. I saw cold boiled babies on a plate being carried through the heart of the town. They said it was only sucking-pig, but I knew better. Dead sucking-pigs don't grin with their eyes open.'

The ironic undertow to all Kipling's 'hatred' of the Chinese is an awareness of their possible racial superiority. In Hong Kong, Kipling and his Professor-companion are impressed by Chinese art and agree that its accuracy makes it superior to Indian art. The Professor thinks (page 275) 'they will overwhelm the world.' The globetrotter Kipling says he hasn't seen 'a single Chinaman asleep while daylight lasted'. And it is this ability to work which evinces his fear and admiration.

In Canton, Kipling twice says he hates the Chinaman. And on page 306 he says: 'it is justifiable to kill him. It would be quite right to wipe the city of Canton off the face of the earth, and to exterminate all the people who ran away from the shelling. The Chinaman ought not to count.' It is astonishing to me that anyone could read this straight, especially when the Professor immediately visits deflation on the callow Kipling (page 306): 'Why on earth can't you look at the lions and enjoy yourself, and leave politics to the men who pretend to understand 'em?' And later Kipling underlines the criticism of his globetrotter side (page 311): 'The Professor says that I have completely spoiled the foregoing account by what he calls "intemperate libels on a hard-working nation".'

It is this persona who, in Japan, comes in for frequent strictures from his Professor-companion: 'if you think you can understand Japan from watching it at a railway station you are much mistaken.' And this is Kipling's rueful, implicit opinion also.

Underneath the comic globetrotter-ese, there is a recognition that the Chinese are *workers*, unquelled by the climate. They are a force to be reckoned with. And they know it: 'they stand high above the crowd and they swagger, unconsciously parting the crowd before them *as an Englishman parts the crowd in a native city*. There was something in their faces which I could not understand, though it was familiar enough' (my italics). The adopted globetrotter persona may not know more than 'I do not like Chinamen', but Kipling is aware they are rivals, they are Sahibs, as my italics show. He isn't a simpleton. He's a subtle and extraordinarily intelligent ironist.

The Japanese

By the time Kipling has reached Nagasaki, his globetrotter's assumed confident racial superiority is succumbing to a sense of plurality (page 322): 'it's due to the extraordinary fact that we are not the only people in the world. I began to realise it at Hong Kong. It's getting plainer now. I shouldn't be surprised if we turned out to be ordinary human beings, after all.' So much for the English master race.

It is quite clear that, in *From Sea to Sea*, Kipling adores the Japanese – for their natural artistry, for their demonstrative love of children and for their physical smallness. He was a small man himself – but larger than the Japanese. 'Japan is a soothing place for a small man. Nobody comes to tower over him, and he looks down upon all the women, as is right and proper.'

Most of all, though, Kipling admires the Japanese for their Otherness (Vol. I, page 319): 'Then I fell to admiring ... the surpassing "otherness" of everything around me.'

The one thing he deplores is their attempts to ape European civilisation, which he regards as misguided and faintly comic. For instance, Vol. I, page 447: 'It's enough to make you weep to watch this misdirected effort – this wallowing in unloveliness for the sake of recognition at the hands of men who paint their ceilings white, their grates black, their mantelpieces French grey, and their carriages yellow and red ... And in the face of all these things the country wants to progress towards civilisation!' And here Kipling adds an ironic, exasperated exclamation mark to evaluate the worth of that 'civilisation'. (See Vol. 1, page 335 also.)

There are even two expressions of Kipling's racial inferiority to the Japanese.

The first (Vol. I, page 376) is: 'Japan is a great people. Her masons play with stone, her carpenters with wood, her smiths with iron, and her artists with life, death, and all the eyes can take in. Mercifully she has been denied the last touch of firmness in her character which would enable her to play with the whole round world. We possess that – We, the nation of the glass flower-shade, the pink worsted mat, the red and green china puppy dog, and the poisonous Brussels carpet. It is our compensation.' You'd have to be unrelentingly obtuse to take that quotation as triumphalist Imperialism.

Now the second example (Vol. I, page 320): 'What I wanted to say was, "Look here, you person. You're much too clean and refined for this life here below, and your house is unfit for a man to live in until he has been taught a lot of things which I have never learned. Consequently I hate you because I feel myself your inferior, and you despise me and my boots because you know me for a savage.'

The Jews

Here Kipling cannot be defended. His remarks are mostly hostile, if unexcited. Because his correspondents so evidently share his views, agreement is taken for granted. On 14 November 1913, discussing the Marconi scandal and his unprintable poem 'Gehazi', Kipling writes to Max Aitken: 'I can't "garble" my "Gehazi".' It's meant to be for that Jew boy on the Bench.' This is on a par with his disparaging remarks about Hebrew millionaires and Jewish takeovers of the theatre.

And yet. In 'The House Surgeon', Kipling gives us an entirely amiable portrait of the Jewish furrier L. Maxwell M'Leod – whose unlikely name is the only possible ironic touch in the characterisation. His Jewishness is a fact only, quite unremarkable.

In *From Sea to Sea*, however, we find another surprising complication. On the one hand, there *is* the anticipated candid anti-Semitism, an unpleasant offshoot of anti-Americanism (Vol. I, page 262): 'But the real reason of my wish to return [to India] is because I have met a lump of Chicago Jews and am afraid that I shall meet many more. The ship is full of Americans, but the American-German-Jew boy is the most awful of all.'

In America, on Independence Day, Kipling meets a German boy whose return to Europe for schooling has lost him his American accent. Kipling comments (Vol. II, page 73): 'but no continental schooling writes German Jew all over a man's face and nose.'

And nose. A facial feature evidently so large that Kipling grants it independence. The nose secedes from the otherwise united features of the face. It sets up on its own. It refuses to assimilate. Anti-Semitism seldom presents itself in so pure a form.

And yet this is Kipling sixty pages later (Vol. II, page 131). He is sweetening particular prior criticisms with an overarching declaration of affection for Americans: 'I love this People, and if any contemptuous criticism has to be done, I will do it myself.' He imagines the Man of the Future.

What racial ingredients would you predict?

Wait till the Anglo-American-German-Jew – the Man of the Future – is properly equipped. He'll have the least little kink in his hair now and again; he'll carry the English lungs above the Teuton feet that can walk for ever; and he will wave long, thin, bony Yankee hands with the big blue veins on the wrist, from one end of the earth to the other. He'll be the finest writer, poet, dramatist, 'specially dramatist, that the world as it recollects itself has ever seen. By virtue of his Jew blood – just a little, little drop – he'll be a musician and a painter too.

As a footnote to this look at Kipling and the Jews, I'd like to draw your attention to 'The Burden of Jerusalem' – one of two unpublished Kipling poems discovered in April 1988 by Christopher Hitchens in the Roosevelt Library at Hyde Park, New York.

The poems had been sent to Roosevelt by Churchill on 17 October 1943. They are not included in the published correspondence (three volumes). Let Churchill explain why: 'Similar copies were given to me by the President of the Royal College of Surgeons of England on the occasion of my admission as an Honorary Fellow of the College ... I understand that Mrs Kipling decided not to publish them in case they should lead to controversy and it is therefore important that their existence should not become known and that there should be no public reference to this gift.'

The second poem, 'A Chapter of Proverbs', needn't concern us here. You can find it reprinted in full in Christopher Hitchens's strangely neglected essay in *Grand Street*, (Spring 1990).

'The Burden of Jerusalem' is a title with two applications. It is a reference to the repeated refrain of Zionists, the *burden* of Zionists ('Next year in Jerusalem'). And it is a reference to the political burden of Jerusalem on British Imperial shoulders, given the British Mandate in Palestine.

In the penultimate stanza, there is an oblique reference to the Balfour Declaration (1917) – which pledged British support to the Zionist hope for a Jewish national home in Palestine, with the proviso that the rights of non-Jewish communities should be respected. 'And burdened Gentile o'er the main, / Must bear the weight of Israel's hate / Because he is not brought again / In triumph to Jerusalem.' Israel, of course, meaning the Jews of the Diaspora.

The poem's argument is that Islam and Judaism are battling and have battled for Jerusalem, Zion, ever since the fatal split between Abraham's offspring. This is the biblical story from Genesis which Kipling's poem draws on. Hagar was the Egyptian handmaid of Sarah, Abraham's legitimate wife. When Sarah was no longer able to bear children, she begged Abraham to lie with Hagar, so that she, Sarah, might 'obtain children by her'. Ishmael was the son of Hagar.

It is the first recorded example of surrogacy.

When Hagar conceives, Sarah decides that she, the barren wife, is held in contempt by her maid. She asks Abraham to intervene. He shifts the responsibility to Sarah – arguing that Hagar is *her* maid.

Sarah deals harshly with Hagar, who then flees. Only to be accosted by an angel of the Lord – who persuades her to return, to submit to Sarah, with the promise of this reward: her seed will be so multiplied 'that it shall not be numbered for multitude'. This is Islam.

Isaac is the legitimate son of Abraham born to Sarah by special dispensation – she was then aged 90. Hagar and Ishmael are then cast out – Sarah's preference, which Abraham is advised by God to follow. Ishmael is preserved, however, because he is the son of Abraham and God promises Ishmael that he will be the founder of a great nation, i.e. Arab Islam.

The *burden* of Kipling's poem is the Jewish Diaspora: 'Then they were scattered North and West.' Pogroms and persecution follow: 'And every realm they wandered through / Rose, far or near, / And robbed and tortured, chased and slew, / The outcasts of Jerusalem.'

The further burden is Kipling's sense of the triumphant survival of Zionist aspiration over every oppressor and tyrant: 'So ran their doom – half seer, half slave – / And ages past, and at the last / They stood beside each tyrant's grave, / And whispered of Jerusalem.'

What follows might appear to be tinged with prejudice. It refers to Jewish financial acumen. It forgivably caricatures Jewish movie moguls. But it is replete with respect for Jewish tenacity and the refusal of the Jews to intermarry and assimilate.

> We do not know what God attends
> The Unloved Race in every place
> Where they amass their dividends
> From Riga to Jerusalem.

> But all the course of Time makes clear
> To everyone (except the Hun)
> It does not pay to interfere
> With Cohen from Jerusalem.

> For 'neath the Rabbi's curls and fur
> (Or scents and rings of movie-kings)
> The aloof, unleavened blood of Ur,
> Broods steadfast on Jerusalem.

Ur was ruled by Chaldeans, so the line means that Jewish blood was kept pure even when Abraham lived in Ur.

The moral of Kipling's poem, as opposed to its burden, is in the last stanza: 'Yet he who bred the unending strife, / And was not brave enough to save / The Bondsmaid from the furious wife, / *He* wrought thy woe, Jerusalem.'

Kipling *isn't* blaming Sarah, the fierce wife. He's blaming Abraham for cowardice, for the failure to exercise the authority invested in him. He should have been the arbitrator. So the allegory is an allegory of rule – justice should be impartially exercised rather than being left to the disputants. The White Man's Burden.

The Germans

Kipling is rabidly anti-German. On 31 August 1905, he writes to Jules Huret, who had interviewed him for *Le Figaro*. Pinney's note tells us that Kipling deleted from the proofs conversational, off-the-cuff remarks that were exaggerated and indefensible: viz. that the Germans had done nothing special in commerce, industry or science; that he, Kipling, owed nothing to German literature (his letter says 'in literature I know that I owe much to Heine'), that German troops had done nothing effective in south-west Africa.

Clearly Kipling's considered views weren't just snow jobs but more closely approximate to the truth of his views.

After this admission to Huret in August 1905 that he owed something to (the Jewish) Heine and that the German contribution to science, etc., wasn't completely negligible, Kipling went rapidly and insanely anti-German – because England was at war and because his son was killed by the Germans and because Kipling believed all reports of German atrocities (some of which were true, of course). Kipling sees the war aim not as victory 'but a war of extermination for their race'. At first, there is a hint of defensiveness: he denies 'hatred', denies 'something our friends might take for brutality, but which isn't'.

To Theodore Roosevelt (21 April 1918), he recommends reprisals on the American Hun 'citizens'. To Frank Doubleday (21 August 1918) he suggests that Germans should always be referred to by the pronoun 'it' in Doubleday books; he recounts how a woman went to a crashed Zeppelin to savour the smell of burnt Hun. To Sir Almroth Wright he suggested that Germans exploit sexual perversion in their politics and that their sadism attracts the masochism of pacifists and conscientious objectors.

When he hears that the Germans are melting corpses for pig feed, Kipling writes a poem in which a German woman spreads a dead rendered German on her bread as fat. Of course, it was never printed, but it is there in a letter sent to Andrew Macphail (21–2 April 1917).

On 14 January 1919, he mounts a theory that the Germans have been systematically undermining his literary reputation since the Boer War. He even blames Hun prisoners of war for an outbreak of foot and mouth disease – caused, he alleges, by their throwing away scraps of infected Hun meat (14 December 1919). He finds them a sort of 'were-wolf people', in fact – subhuman, animal, 'the baser side of humanity'. As for a railway strike, nominally 'It is the railway men and the Trades Unions who are doing it. Actually, it is the Hun, the Bolshevik and the Jew of Poleland chiefly. In spite of their best efforts to speak and act like white men, one sees in the cruelty practised on the railway horses, the hand of the Hun.'

In November 1919, Kipling is denouncing Einstein's theory of relativity:

Do you notice how their insane psychology attempts to infect the Universe? There is one Einstein, nominally a Swiss, certainly a Hebrew, who … comes forward, scientifically to show that, under certain conditions Space itself is warped and the instruments that measure it are warped also … The more I see of the Boche's mental workings the more sure I am that he is Evil Incarnate, and, like all evil, a pathetic Beast. Einstein's pronouncement is only another little contribution to assisting the world towards flux and disintegration.

What are we to make of this? On 15 July 1919, Kipling writes that 'Nothing matters much really when one has lost one's only son.' To Sir Hugh Clifford, another bereaved father, Kipling writes on 18 November 1918: 'Glad you escaped the peace celebrations. I bolted home from town and had my dark hour alone.' Kipling never allowed himself public expression of his grief. His letters insist that his son's death was a noble sacrifice. Kipling believed this. He could not believe anything else. And it drove him mad. The recurrent accusation that the Hun is deranged is a reflection of his own derangement. Kipling wasn't a racist. Poor Kipling. He was a father driven mad with grief.

Just So Stories
(2001)

The *Just So Stories* were published in 1902. But Kipling had test-told them to children for at least five or six years before. He loved children. There is a photograph of him in a straw boater, sitting cross-legged, surrounded by a semicircle of children on the deck of a ship going to Cape Town. He is telling the *Just So Stories*. Two boys in sailor suits on the left are listening attentively. Lost in the story, they are looking, not at the famous author, but at the planks of the deck. The written versions are still intensely oral. They are written to be read out loud, to be performed: 'All the fishes he could find in all the sea he ate with his mouth – so!' Or: '"I think," said the Crocodile – and he said it between his teeth, like this.'

Where does the wind come from? Children want to know *why*. And the *Just So Stories* speak to the desire for explanation which is central to the childish consciousness. And they speak with affectionate irony.

Kipling's language exhibits a lively dynamic. There is the caricature adult voice, sounding ever so like Henry James: 'noble and generous Cetacean', 'infinite-resource-and-sagacity', 'can you tell me the present habitat of the aboriginal Fauna', 'will permanently vitiate your future'. Then there is the caricature child's voice with its breathless abbreviations and mispronunciations: ''satiable curtiosity'. These two registers represent the conventional gap between adult sophistication and childish naivety, between 'know-how' and 'how?' and 'why?' To these Kipling adds a third register in which the writer emulates the language improvisations of children – improvisations that are often brilliant and accurate. Kipling becomes a child for his childish readers: the 'ooshy-skooshy' sea, the 'nubbly' taste of man. Not to mention all the wonderful words for shadows in 'How the Leopard Got His Spots': 'speckly', 'patchy-blatchy', 'slippery-slidy', 'speckly-spickly', 'sprottled', 'spottled'.

Kipling knows his young reader – who revels in narrative ritual ('O best Beloved') and formulaic repetition ('you must *not* forget the suspenders') and the rap of pure sound: 'he stumped and he jumped and he thumped and he bumped, and he pranced and he danced, and he banged and he clanged.' To these essentials, Kipling adds the pleasure of accuracy: the 'shiny' grass of the veldt, the crocodile's 'musky, tusky mouth'. The Ethiopian's 'black' skin seen in all its particularity: 'a nice working blackish-brownish colour, with a little purple in it, and touches of slaty-blue'. Finally, magnificently, Kipling adds his invented, ingenious and beautiful creation myths: 'sometimes the fingers slipped and the marks got a little blurred; but if you look closely at any Leopard now you will see that there are always five spots – off five fat black finger-tips.'

Stoppard's Trilogy
(2002)

Tom Stoppard's trilogy *The Coast of Utopia* is absorbing and addictive. A sad, rueful, ironic comedy, it distinguishes perfectly between sentiment and sentimentality – and shows how imperceptibly, how inevitably, the first coarsens into the latter, in both the public and the private sphere. For Stoppard, human experience is essentially impure and his trilogy courageously follows the arc of actual experience – so there is no synthetic climax, plenty of shapelessness, but no obviously *dramatic* shape. After nine hours, it concludes in anti-climax – with the disappointed, marginalised Herzen, two years away from his death in Switzerland.

Salvage (Part III) begins and ends with Herzen asleep and dreaming. Why? Because the Utopian idea is a dream, but an unrealisable dream. Natalie Ogarev voices its optimism when she first re-encounters Herzen: '(*gazing raptly at Herzen*) To dream men's dreams ...!' In *Salvage*, both Herzen's dreams are bad dreams – of bickering exiles at the beginning of Part III and, at the end, the dream of a dogmatic Marx issuing his 'incontrovertible' *obiter dicta*. Whereas 'the best lack all conviction' – humanist Herzen and the tentative Turgenev.

Predictably, perhaps, some critics have reported a drama in which ideas dominate the human histories. Peter Kemp in the *TLS* found the trilogy structureless, rambling, repetitive, digressive and buried under its author's research: 'Having spent years immersing himself in research for this epic project, Stoppard seems unwilling to leave anything he garnered behind in his notebooks. A plethora of political and intellectual history is unloaded into a trilogy which zigzags around to accommodate his findings.' What is wrong with this picture?
Everything.

The private is squeezed, in this account, until the characters are Giacometti figures, withered like spent matchsticks under the weight of their thought balloons. Except for the programme, which is replete with po-faced, thumbnail exegesis, this is completely untrue. The prevailing tone is wryly comic. The private dominates throughout. The National stage isn't a foot deep in leaflets summarising Schelling, Fichte, Kant, Hegel, Proudhon, Saint-Simon, Rousseau, Fourier and Marx. That list of names is taken from *Salvage*, where Alexander

The Coast of Utopia trilogy was first performed in the Olivier auditorium of the National Theatre in 2002.

Herzen is summarising his ideological development – a decidedly sentimental education in this version – for the benefit of his son Sasha. His friend Ogarev interrupts impatiently: 'Stop boring the poor boy, he's going to be a doctor.' But in fact Herzen's exposition has been ironically punctuated throughout by the undercutting banalities of ordinary existence. Herzen mentions Proudhon's 'abolition of authority' and this is ironically paralleled in the private domestic sphere by its opposite, the assertion of authority: 'Stop crying or I'll give you an enema.' The inversion is as blunt as Flaubert's ironic counterpoint in *Madame Bovary* of Rodolphe's seduction and the auction of farm animals.

In *Shipwreck* (Part II) there is an exquisitely crafted scene ('November 1851') which will serve to show how the private and the public constantly echo each other. In Nice, Herzen is visited by the Russian Consul, who bears a message from Count Orlov, the servant of His Imperial Majesty, ordering Herzen to return to Russia. Herzen refuses – incomprehensibly to the Consul, since the message carries the authority of the Tsar. Incomprehensibly, and also danger-ously – *for the Consul*, who will be the bearer of bad news: 'it would call attention to my name in a most unfavourable context.' Herzen points out that, in fact, Count Orlov would be the recipient of the Consul's news – not the Tsar.

> CONSUL: It's the same thing. Count Orlov would never forget my name.
> HERZEN: But you're only the messenger.
> CONSUL: There's a streak of Cleopatra in him.

The scene is at once farcical – the Consul rises and inclines his head obsequiously at every mention of the Tsar – and indicative of the ethos of despotism. The solution is for Herzen to write a sealed reply to Count Orlov. The endangered messenger motif is continued later, after a transition in the scene, when Herzen returns to tell his wife that their beloved deaf son, Kolya, has been drowned at sea, with his grandmother, tutor and maid. The disclosure, like Nabokov's story 'Breaking the News', is in stages:

> HERZEN: They're not coming. The boat from Marseilles … isn't coming.
> *Herzen embraces her, weeping.*
> NATALIE (*bewildered*): They're not coming at all?
> HERZEN: No. There was an accident at sea … Oh, Natalie!
> NATALIE: When is Kolya coming?
> HERZEN: He's never coming. I'm sorry.
> *Natalie fights out of his embrace and pummels him.*
> NATALIE: Don't you dare tell me that! (*She runs inside.*)

The medium is the message – Cleopatra's confusion of the bearer with the bad news. Here, the parallel between public and private is clear, but subtle enough not to impair the immediate shock of the tragedy. The literary precedent, the citation of Cleopatra, is far enough away to be usefully pre-emptive without being obtrusive. The symmetry between the Consul and Herzen is understated and tactful. Rather than crying 'snap', Stoppard breaks your heart instead. The swiftly permeable, shared border between comedy to tragedy is Chekhovian.

More often, it works the other way, ironically undercutting: 'You have broken your father's heart! When you get to Moscow go to Pliva's and tell them to send another metre of the grey silk – will you remember? – the grey silk!' More often because bathos is easier. Modulating from comedy to pathos is tougher to bring off.

And here it almost doesn't work because there is another *unintended* precedent unhelpfully present in the staging of this tragic exchange between Herzen and his wife. Trevor Nunn's direction of this key moment inadvertently summons up a stock Hollywood topos – of a woman fighting *into* the embrace of a strong man, anger overtaken by love and submission. Stoppard's text – where Herzen's wife isn't simply attacking the messenger, but fighting *'out of* his embrace' – is not responsible. Perhaps the cliché is in the pummelling of Herzen's chest – the favoured token site. Had Eve Best, who played Natalie, hit him in the face, the scene would have shed all trace of inferior models.

The echoic structure of public and private is clear but understated throughout: in *Salvage*, the quarrelsome political exiles are mirrored in the struggle between the strict pedagogic methods of the German governess and the English maid's combination of laxity and corporal punishment. Both are subsequently displaced by the erratic Natalie Ogarev, who brings warmth, irritability and inconsistency to child-rearing. (The trouble here is that the primary domestic conflict can be boring: 'MARIA: Coffee in the morning keeps a body regular. MALWIDA: And excitable.') In *Shipwreck*, the failure of the French Republic has a private parallel – the failure of the friendship between the Herzens and the Herweghs. 'We, too, will look to our faults – our passions and vices – and prepare ourselves by living by our ideals in a republic of our own,' says the deluded Herzen.

His conviction – that in private life 'fidelity is admirable, but proprietorship disgusting' – is tempered by his sense of the limits of tolerance: 'What is the largest number of individuals who can pull this trick off? I would say it's smaller than a nation, smaller than the ideal communities of Cabet or Fourier. I would say the larger number is smaller than three. Two is possible, if there is love, but two is not a guarantee.' Herzen is about to discover exactly how difficult the balance between self-interest and self-abnegation is – when his wife embarks on an affair with the German revolutionary poet George Herwegh. All this parallels the public debate about freedom. Limitations on individual freedom are necessary but should be imposed by the individual himself, acting freely: 'What freedom means is being allowed to sing in my bath as loudly as will not interfere with my neighbour's freedom to sing a different tune in his.'

We have already encountered these commonsensical libertarian sentiments in *Voyage* (Part I), where they are voiced, somewhat surprisingly, by Alexander Bakunin – the owner of several thousand serfs. 'Philosophy consists in moderating each life so that many lives will fit together with as much liberty and justice as will keep them together – and not as much as will make them fly apart, when the harm will be greater.' These unimpeachable sentiments issue from a man accused by his son Michael of being a domestic despot. It is an accusation impossible to sustain in the face of his benign, pragmatic, imperfect paternalism, and an accusation which returns on that same 'enlightened' son, who jealously tyrannises over his sisters' private lives, issuing fiats and destructive directives. Paradoxically, Michael, not his father, is the despot – giving us a preview of revolutionary authoritarianism based on complacent self-certainty. Bakunin *fils* is a stranger to self-doubt and self-irony. In Stoppard's account, he is a richly comic figure, like the majority of the revolutionaries – Herzen excepted. In reality, Bakunin left the army as a protest against the Tsar. Here, he leaves on a whim – 'on the grounds of ill health, Papa. I'm sick of the army.' His ideas are a joke and a convenience, the ideological armature of his egotism: 'Whatever I want, that's what *God* wants.' He has no sooner proclaimed that 'the outer world of material existence is mere illusion' than he is exclaiming, 'God, I'm *starving!*' – and stuffing his face.

The exposition of ideas, then, presents no difficulty for Stoppard because he ignores their purported 'difficulty' and instead shows their fatuity. Stankevich may say that 'the laughter of women is like the spiritual communion of angels. Women are holy beings. For me, love is a religious experience.' We know the laughter that provoked these reflections is caused by a comparison of human copulation to 'the tinker's jackass' when it 'got into Betsy's paddock'. Stankevich's ideas are absurd and connive with his sickly libido. On Hamlet: 'She was the wrong woman for him. The duel was between knowledge and denial, the dialectic dramatised, it's all there in Hegel.' These days, he could get a job in most university English departments.

Stankevich's death from TB – off-stage, in Italy, in the arms of Varenka, the married sister of Liubov Bakunin, the woman he shyly, ineffectually loves for most of *Voyage* (Part I), is tantalisingly reported, without elaboration. A great (parenthetical) surprise – which, on reflection, isn't a surprise. Nor is it a loose end, I think, but a laconically poignant indication that approaching death concentrates the highest mind – philosophy succumbs to more earthly imperatives.

John Peter (*Sunday Times*) and John Gross (*Sunday Telegraph*) are impatient with Stoppard's impatience with ideas. Stoppard is, they argue, our great play-wright of ideas. He isn't. He is nimble, down-to-earth, *really* intelligent – and, therefore, swift to let the hot air out of many a time-honoured profundity. He has said as much in interview: 'something which has preoccupied me for a long time is the desire to simplify questions and take the sophistication out.' For John Peter, Stankevich is low entertainment, a soft target, a distraction from the pre-scribed task – to expound the history of ideas. For me, and, I think, for Stoppard, these great seminal ideas are like photographs without people in them.

In *Squaring the Circle*, his 1984 TV film about Solidarity and Walesa, ideas are put in their place by the truth-telling Witness: '*Theories don't guarantee social justice, social justice tells you if a theory is any good.* Right and wrong are not com-plicated – when a child cries, "That's not fair!" the child can be believed' (my italics). We can deduce Stoppard believes this himself, because it is repeated from *Professional Foul* (1977): 'A small child who cries "that's not fair" when punished for something done by his brother or sister is apparently appealing to an idea of justice which is, for want of a better word, natural.' The crucial point for my argument here – in addition to *his* point about justice – is that Stoppard doesn't give a damn about theories. He cares about people. Or rather he does give a damn about theories – because he knows how dangerous and stupid ideas can be when they are put into practice by infatuated ideologues. Hence his attrac-tion to the sceptical figure of Herzen, who subscribes to the Joycean mistrust of 'those big words that make us so unhappy': 'we're asking people to spill their blood – at least spare them your conceit that they're acting out the biography of an abstract noun.' So it is perverse to require of Stoppard a reverential treatment of Nikolai Chernychevsky, or of Marx – here a social climber and a theorist utterly ignorant of the working class. As is Bakunin: (*Shipwreck*, March 1848):

BAKUNIN: I've been living in barracks with the Republican Guard. You won't believe this but it's the first time I've actually met anyone from the working class.
MARX: Really? What are they like?

Bakunin's answer is a lovely, slow burn: 'I've never come across such nobil-ity.' This chimes with another excellent running joke – the imperious servants in the Herzen household, who patronise their patrons. When the French Republic is declared, Herzen proposes the toast '*Vive le prolétariat!*' – and immediately adds for the pained servant's benefit, '*Mille pardons, Benoit.*'

How plausible this is. How shrewd of Stoppard to pick at the reputation and discover the flawed human being beneath. John Gross and John Peter flinch from the human figure, genital warts and all. They would prefer a full-length portrait of the big idea – an abstraction in a toga. Accordingly, they mistake satire for caricature. In one instance, John Gross is half right. Aksakov, the Slavist – all belted *rubashka* and baggy trousers tucked in his boots – *is* played as a buffoon by Sam Troughton. But this is the fault of Trevor Nunn's bustling, overstated, 'orange-sellers-aplenty' Peter Hall production style. Stoppard's text gives Aksakov credit where it is due. Even Herzen concedes: 'Aksakov is right – I don't know the next step.' Granovsky: 'He's right about us having no ideas of our own, that's all.' Granovsky again: 'The Slavophiles are not entirely wrong about the West, you know.' To which Herzen concedes: 'I'm sure they're entirely right.'

But Vissarion Belinsky, the literary critic, is Stoppard's great creation – the perfect mix of satire and sympathy. Belinsky is brilliantly played by Will Keen. His cough – an impossibly extended aria of barks and wheezing – is in a way the key to his character. Belinsky's galloping consumption is itself consumed by comedy – and the man is both ridiculous and touching. In *Voyage* (Part I), Tatiana Bakunin, who hero-worships Belinsky, summarises his current position: 'Russia is stuck between dried-up old French reasoning and the new German thought which explains everything.' An accurate epitome. The trouble is Belinsky reads neither French nor German. As for Russian literature: 'We have no Russian literature.' It is derivative: 'it's like a fancy dress party where everyone has to come dressed up as somebody else – Byron, Voltaire, Goethe, Schiller, Shakespeare and the rest.' A fierce critic of Russian literature, then, he is also sentimental about its potential. In *Voyage*, art is an engine of social change only in a mystical way: 'Let social purpose hang itself.' Belinsky's 'idea' is that art will 'replace' reality.

Stoppard has said that his dialogue is literary rather than realistic – that 'all my people speak the same way, with the same cadences and sentence structures. They speak as I do.' Some of Stoppard's expository dialogue for Herzen is clunky: 'It was as if I'd come to the end of a long journey that started when I left Moscow more than six years ago with Natalie and the children and my mother, packed into a carriage hung with furs against the January cold.' You wouldn't want to be an actor with that in your mouth. Some of Herzen's literary dialogue is over-literary: 'Cynicism fills the air like ash and blights the leaves on the freedom trees.' It might be Yeats chilling a drawing room with this conversational opener, reported by Lord David Cecil: 'There is a clashing of swords on the floor of heaven.' However, the *incoherence* of Belinsky's ideas produces some of Stoppard's best dialogue, dialogue to rival Mamet's: 'But a great artist can change all that, make it irrelevant, well, not one, but even one, even Pushkin for a start, I mean Pushkin up to, say, *Boris Gudonov*, he's finished now, he hasn't written a *great* poem for years, but even Pushkin, or Gogol's new stories, definitely Gogol, and there's more to come, I know they're coming and soon, here things are growing not by the year but by the *hour* … You see what I'm saying?' Not quite. But that is Stoppard's point – Belinsky's passion for literature is striking, moving even, but it isn't orderly, it isn't even articulate. Nor does it make sense.

By Part II, *Shipwreck*, Belinsky has rejected the idea of art for art's sake. Literature is now a tool for social change: 'In Russia, there's no division of labour, literature has to do it all. That was a hard lesson for me, boy. When I started off, I thought art was aimless, pure spirit.' Belinsky's character is a paradox – social shyness, downright dogmatism and intellectual promiscuity: 'How is it that everybody knows what he thinks and sticks to it!' Belinsky is the inconsistent dogmatist:

> BELINSKY: … You're going to be one of our great writers, one of the few – I'm never wrong.
> TURGENEV (*moved*): Oh … (*lightly*) You said Fenimore Cooper was as great as Shakespeare.
> BELINSKY: That wasn't wrong, it was only ridiculous.

The relatively peripheral Turgenev – humane, clear-sighted, private, undogmatic – is the figure nearest to Stoppard in *The Coast of Utopia*. Herzen is central to the piece, superior in intelligence and in humanity to the other revolutionaries, but Stoppard observes him shrewdly and critically. When Belinsky takes his (final) leave of the Russian community in Paris, he makes a last speech about Russian literature, a phenomenon he has spent his life denying the existence of. The received scholarly view of Belinsky is a cross between a midwife and Ezra Pound – trouncing the derivative and the dated, but assisting the birth of the original, the innovative, the Russian. This outline is discernible in Stoppard's portrait, but we are given a more magnificently confused, inconsistent, comic and, it has to be said, *plausible* figure. Bakunin asks him to stay where he can be published uncensored. He prefers to return to Russia: 'At home the public look to writers as their real leaders. The title of poet or novelist really counts with us. Writers here, they think they're enjoying success. They don't know what success is. You have to be a writer in Russia, even one without much talent, *even a critic*' (my italics). The sentimental chauvinism and egotism of a critic who still doesn't read French. However, the interesting thing to note is Stoppard's crucial stage direction – '*Herzen, mopping his eyes.*' An SD never staged in Trevor Nunn's production, where Stephen Dillane was dry, contained, slightly self-regarding, the very opposite of lachrymose – delivering his lines, barring the odd fluff, evenly, audibly, monotonously within a limited vocal dynamic. And fatally for a play which turns out to be about sentimentality. No one saw it – well, *I* didn't see it – because it wasn't staged. It wasn't *performed* by Dillane because the director didn't understand it.

Stoppard, of course, attended rehearsals. He understands perfectly why this is necessary: 'with the most intelligent and sympathetic director possible and the most accomplished and intelligent actors available you will only get about 70 per cent of what you meant, because a script turns out to be a great deal more obscure in its intentions than one could possibly imagine oneself.' But there is still a snag. It is a strange thing to watch your own work in rehearsal. You *know* what it is supposed to mean. So that is what it means. The words are there. The actors speak them. You think the audience will get your meaning, therefore. You are unworried as long as the transmitters are transmitting.

The director is there, among other things, to tell the playwright what seems pointless – so it can be cut, or so the point can be brought out. Stoppard acknowledges a debt to Trevor Nunn in a prefatory note – 'for encouraging me towards some additions and subtractions'. And I am sure there are many other debts. However, I doubt if Nunn had the courage to tell Stoppard that *Salvage* (Part III) *in this production*, seems a long *niente* ending. There is any amount of local tweaking and burnishing, but Part III needs a vision of *Salvage* as tinged with an almost imperceptible failure of spirit. Herzen is not defeated by circumstances. Stoppard shows us in *Salvage* a man who is broken by the deaths of his wife and child, but continues as if he were whole. Almost out of habit. So it is not tragedy's pity and terror – it is too gradual for that – but self-pity, sentimentality, resignation and a terrible sadness. Events fail Herzen. Of course they do. But, partly because events fail him, Herzen, more importantly, learns to inhabit the failure of himself.

When *Talk* magazine appeared in September 1999, Stoppard contributed a wonderful piece, 'On Turning Out to be Jewish'. Obliquely, implicitly, it was also a piece about sentimentality – an object lesson in its refusal to entertain the usual limited menu of emotions suggested by interviewers asking about his past. It is moving – because it is calmly accurate at every turn. 'In my mind I always knew what my father looked like, and my memory of him is supported by (or perhaps consists in) a few tiny snapshots.' The quasi-corrective parenthesis is why Stoppard is a great writer. When the young Tom is told of his father's death, he sets down his reaction: 'For my part, I took it well, or not well, depending on how you look at it. I felt almost nothing. I felt the significance of the occasion but not the loss.' At one point in the memoir, Stoppard records touching a small scar on a woman's wrist – a wound which had been stitched by his father. 'In that moment I am surprised by grief.' The writing places it as an imaginative impulse. As he touches the scar, he is touched – so it's a verbal and physical reaction to his father's death. Somewhere else, not in the *Talk* piece, Stoppard has scrupulously recorded the diminishing power of this moment every time he tells it. Here he simply says it has 'the power to move, but not to reclaim'.

Why am I telling you this? Because there is a recurrent motif in Stoppard's trilogy, a motif usually attached in the plays to George Sand, 'the philosopher of love', the nineteenth-century touchstone for powerful feeling. In her novels, love is indivisible, an irresistible force. In Stoppard's trilogy, it isn't. It changes. Passion is touched with comedy, with self-deception as well as subterfuge. Part II, *Shipwreck*, begins with Herzen's wife expressing her nostalgia for their grand passion, for their elopement – before Herzen had a brief bonk with a servant. This nostalgia finds an outlet first with another woman, a pash – harmless enough. Harmless enough for it to be confessed to another more worldly woman, who asks, 'You were lovers?' And is answered directly, 'No. What do you mean?'

Stoppard revisits this territory when Natalie Herzen embarks on an affair with George Herwegh. A whole scene, brilliantly written, genuinely painful, verging on the ludicrous, is devoted to the confession Herzen has to wring out of her. 'Plain speech for God's sake! Has Herwegh – known you?' The very question she was previously able to answer swiftly in the negative. 'Is Herwegh your lover?' Her answers are a kind of moral chess, a great defensive campaign – devious and delivered in tones of affront and wronged reproach:

HERZEN: Christ! Just tell me without the doubletalk! – Is Herwegh your lover?!

NATALIE: He loves me, yes – he loves me –

HERZEN: Is he your lover? Have you been to his bed?

NATALIE: Oh – I see. You have no objection if I take him to my heart, only to my bed –

HERZEN: Precisely. Or his bed, or a flowerbed, or up against the back of the town hall –

NATALIE: Alexander, Alexander, this is not you, this is not the great-hearted soul I gave my tender innocent heart to when I –

Her justification, as she sees it, is the George Sand ideal: 'the ideal of a love which is greater the more it includes.' With Natalie, all that phoney 'love' stuff is for real. And it becomes real for Herzen in Part III, *Salvage*, after her death and the death of his deaf son, Kolya. *Shipwreck* ends with Herzen on board ship with Bakunin by chance. Herzen brings him up to date. He imagines, accurately, almost unbearably, the drowning of his son: 'I just wish it hadn't happened at night. He couldn't hear in the dark. He couldn't see your lips.' And he stems

Bakunin's sentimentality: 'No, no, not at all! His life was what it was. Because children grow up, we think a child's purpose is to grow up. But a child's purpose is to be a child ... The death of a child has no more meaning than the death of armies, of nations. Was the child happy while he lived? That is a proper question, the only question.' This is noble and fearlessly clear-sighted.

Salvage (Part III) shows us the corrosion of sentimentality. Herzen's own version of Kolya's end is replaced by his dead wife's whimsical, melodramatic account: 'Natalie said over and over, "He must have been so cold, so frightened, seeing the fishes and the lobsters!" ' Herzen's children are commendably matter-of-fact, bluntly refusing the sentimental recourse to the past:

HERZEN: It's good to be talking Russian together. We must always ... Mummy was teaching Kolya Russian words, do you –?
TATA: They're both dead, and that's all. Well, they are. We can't help it.

Tata's brisk intervention adumbrates many previous episodes of parental morbidity – though they coexist with real sentiment, best seen in Herzen carrying a child's glove, Kolya's recovered from the wreck. At this point, early in *Salvage*, Herzen's intelligence hasn't entirely succumbed. He knows what the reality of his marriage was: 'I want her back so that I can take her for granted again.'

Later in the play, he accepts Natalie Ogarev's hagiographic version of his dead wife – a version in which the very greatness of her soul caused the affair with the unprincipled Herwegh: 'Your wife was a saint, Alexander. It was because she was a saint that she was defenceless against evil.' Thus primed, Herzen embraces this bogus portrait: 'Her devotion to me, her remorse, *her courage* when she faced the madness that man infected her mind with' (my italics).

No wonder he is nonplussed later when Natalie Ogarev, with whom he has begun an affair, suddenly rescinds this hagiographic description, provoked by jealousy of Natalie 1, the dead wife: 'Oh, Natalie was all right, she was just silly for a poke, and Herwegh was kingdom come.' So much for the authorised version.

The affair with Natalie 2, the wife of his best friend, Nick Ogarev, puts Herzen in exactly the same position as 'that man', the treacherous Herwegh. Herzen has cuckolded Ogarev, just as Herwegh cuckolded him. Sentimentally enough, neither Herzen nor Natalie 2 makes the obvious comparison. And there is a difference – Herzen minded; Nick Ogarev appears not to mind, despite his wife's best efforts to ratchet up the emotions of everyone concerned: 'He's in pain. We've broken his heart.' Manifestly, though, they haven't. What was painful for Herzen is possibly a relief for Ogarev. Natalie 2 has gypsy temperament and is the wearisome, changeable type a husband might easily want to shed. Minutes after her assertion that their adultery has broken his heart, she says: 'Nick, who's truly in the right, is the only one of us who makes no fuss about this.' Her egotism makes even the death of her and Herzen's twins an occasion not for grief so much as self-dramatisation: 'I murdered my two little ones, you know.' They died of diphtheria in Paris. Against this, one sets Nick's earlier, but still resonant, gibe against sentimentality: he tells a story about his sled being pursued by wolves. One by one he has to throw his children to the wolves to buy a respite ...

In politics, there is the same admixture of sentimentality. One revolutionary sneers at another's ill-attended lecture – and Herzen is suddenly 'near tears' (though not at the National Theatre). The tears are for all the failed revolutionaries: 'men who walk across London to give a piano lesson redrawing the frontiers of Europe on the oilskin table-tops of back-street restaurants, toppling emperors like so many sauce bottles'. It is affecting and it is tainted by self-pity. Likewise the initially inspiring account of Herzen and Ogarev vowing as schoolboys to revenge the Decembrists – an evocation that becomes thinner every time it is invoked. Turgenev is crucial here. Herzen's magazine *The Bell* is mainly critical of others, but it, too, has a programme: 'it's the Russian peasant! ... Personally, I only denounce you as *sentimental fantasists* [my italics]. You're talking to a man who's made a literary reputation out of the Russian peasantry, and they're no different from Italian, French or German peasants. Conservatives *par excellence.*' And yet, when the nihilists and brutalists take over the political scene and denounce Herzen's sentimentality ('your tedious, hackneyed, sentimental addiction to reminiscence'), we prefer Herzen to these self-styled realists and the cruelty they are about to visit on the Russian people. And we remember the warning of Polevoy in Part I: 'Well, it will happen to you one day ... some young man with a smile on his face, telling you, "Be off with you, you're behind the times!"'

The Coast of Utopia is, I think, a great play – though I'm not sure I've seen it staged yet. That may be because I am misreading Stoppard's text. The memorably painful spectacle of Daniel Mendelson – in the *New York Review of Books*, loftily explaining to Stoppard what the playwright meant by *The Invention of Love* – is a caution to critics. Nevertheless, it has faults. The main one is that Stoppard, whose great strength is that he unsummarises history, has a corresponding weakness. He cannot handle milieu, the minor characters, of which there are a great many in this trilogy. Sazonov is there to illustrate the prevalent danger of sentimentality, but the Polish plot he is engineering is barely intelligible on the page. Staged it is completely opaque. *The Invention of Love* faced the same problem, and *Squaring the Circle* was a dramatist's nightmare of complicated documentary detail – which Stoppard 'solved' by having a narrator and a text that was a lecture with slides. A tricksy lecture, with good slides and great jokes – but a lecture with slides.

But who *can* stage milieu? Chekhov's minor characters are given a line apiece which they repeat like a radio call-sign. Manifestly, they don't matter. They are interchangeable, expendable – like Rosencrantz and Guildenstern. The irony is that the perfect example is so near to hand. If minor characters matter, the solution is to make them central. Here, the dream sequence that begins Part III is a mistake. The audience has no idea it *is* a dream until it is over – and so we begin with incomprehensible chaos and the simultaneous introduction of *twelve* characters. The final dream of Part III wasn't obviously a dream, either – but this was the fault of Trevor Nunn.

Nunn also muffed the overlap of two simultaneous scenes in *Shipwreck* – simultaneous but in different locations. Together, they make a tableau of Manet's *Déjeuner sur l'herbe*. It was impossible not to read them as a single scene happening in the same place – because they were both in the same, undifferentiated stage space. But this would have tested any director.

A few other minor cavils. Kolya and his deafness – suddenly, brilliantly staged for us, as the action continues in silence – is so affecting it seems a pity to make him a symbol of Russia failing to hear the noises of civilisation. Some of the short scenes are set up only to convey a morsel of information – for example, that Natalie has given birth in *Shipwreck*, though I suppose there may be an irony that Herwegh, offering his congratulations to Herzen, is actually the father. The whipping of the serfs in Part I was a nudge too far – but again the director's fault. Turgenev quoting from his memoir sounded, well, like a man reciting a piece of prose. And it is impossible to believe that Herwegh would sit at Herzen's wife's feet, in Herzen's presence, with his arm across her lap. Earlier in *Shipwreck*, the stage directions say '*she embraces Herzen as warmly as decorum allows her*' – and that is husband and wife. Coarse direction again, lest we miss the point.

In spite of all these criticisms, this is theatre for adults – nine hours and it could have been longer.

Stoppard: A Speech
(2004)

Sir Tom Stoppard. It would take more than my allotted five minutes even to list his achievements. You see, as well as the stage plays, there are the radio plays, the TV plays, the film scripts, the novel, the lectures, the interview as an art form. Maybe I can give you the general idea by a kind of simile. Last week I went to the annual Hussey Lecture on the Church and the Arts. It was given by the great art historian Rosemary Hill and was about Pugin. Between 1838 and 1841 Pugin built twenty-two churches, three cathedrals, three convents, six houses, several schools and a Cistercian monastery. The Houses of Parliament were still to come. He was the Stoppard of his day. Fecund, brilliant, for all time. In the architectural field, of course.

Sir Tom Stoppard. Talking to Joan Bakewell on TV about his knighthood, he told an anecdote about Freddy Ayer and Isaiah Berlin. Ayer told Berlin that he had accepted his knighthood for philosophy. Berlin said: that is absolutely the wrong reason: I accepted mine for my mother. Tom said that *he* had accepted for his mother. Modest and true.

In this Tom reminds me of another Tom, another modest genius – T. S. Eliot, Tom Eliot. Who described himself in one of his essays as 'a minor poet' accustomed to having unintended cosmic significances extracted from his work 'such as it is'. It's typical of Eliot's modesty, too, that he should work a sly self-ironic variation on Pater's famous formulation that all art aspires to the condition of music. Eliot's version of this – he's talking about popularity – is this: 'From one point of view, the poet aspires to the condition of the music-hall comedian.'

Modesty. Of course, if you are as brilliant as Tom Stoppard, modesty involves you in a good deal of straightforward lying. Here are a couple of lies. Both taken from a single interview. 'I can't do plots and have no interest in plots.' Well, the marvellous plot of *Night and Day* disposes of that fib. OK, here's another. 'Alan Bennett is one of the best playwrights we've had this century [that's *not* a lie] and he does exactly what I don't do and can't do; he makes drama out of character study.' That's not true, either. Just think about Galileo, Housman, Anderson in *Professional Foul*. Just think about Flora Crewe in *In the Native State*, Ruth in *Night and Day* – two marvellous parts for women – parts for women, something

Speech given on the awarding of the Bodley Medal to Tom Stoppard, Oxford, 22 November 2004.

else he's not supposed to be able to do. Or think about Vissarion Belinsky or, better, Alexander Herzen as he shifts from sentiment to sentimentality in Tom's great masterpiece *The Coast of Utopia*.

But Tom's greatness (I think) lies in an area sometimes seen as a weakness – in his treatment of emotion. He can be very moving. I was in tears at my kitchen table only ten days ago. It was 6 a.m. I was rereading *In the Native State* for a tutorial and had reached the moment when Flora's sister Eleanor is standing by her grave in India. There is a brilliant evocation of fallen blossom on the grave stone: 'And I have never seen such blossom, it blew everywhere, there were drifts of snow-white flowers piled up against the walls of the graveyard. I had to kneel on the ground and sweep the petals off the stone to read her name.' But what really wiped me out were three ordinary words: Bye bye darling. That did it. That understatement, that simplicity.

In the first issue of *Talk* magazine, he wrote about his Jewishness. I was struck by many things but in particular by his account of being told that his father, whom he hadn't seen for four years, had died. He must have been six or seven. 'For my part, I took it well, or not well, depending on how you look at it. I felt almost nothing. I felt the significance of the occasion but not the loss.' Not nothing. *Almost* nothing. And then that *almost* nothing accurately, honestly described. We like our emotions big. Or we think we do. In reality, we don't display our emotion, we try to control it – like Henry in *The Real Thing*. We gauge Housman's love for Moses Jackson by the way he deliberately ploughs in finals, sacrifices scholarship on the altar of love. He fails deliberately – so he can work in the Patent Office with Jackson. There is no display.

In Olivier's autobiography, he writes about a note given to him by his wife Joan Plowright when he's playing Othello. She says that Brenda de Banzie – playing Emilia – looks as though she is trying to cry. Whereas we try *not* to cry. Stoppard understands this truth. That we are modest about our emotions. And it is one reason – as well as his verbal and intellectual dexterity – why his work will last.

My role is as a sponsor tonight. Which seems an impertinence. I really think I'm a eulogist. The trouble with eulogies is that they can look immodest. When I was Seamus Heaney's editor at Fabers, he insisted that we never use a famous quotation on any of his books. It was by Robert Lowell and it said that *North* was a new kind of political poetry by the best Irish poet since Yeats. You can see why an editor might want this on a dust jacket – laudatory and true. Seamus would have none of it.

At the dinner for Tom Stoppard after his Isaiah Berlin Memorial Lecture, my wife, Li, sat on his right. Afterwards, she said that she regretted very much not telling Tom that he was the best playwright since Shakespeare. I wrote to him a bit later, about something else, and mentioned this – saying it was true, but I was relieved for him that my wife *hadn't* said it, adept as he undoubtedly must be by now in receiving compliments. Well, he is adept and slipped out of it beautifully. When he replied, there was a marvellous laconic joke: 'Surely Li meant "since Aeschlylus".'

Ladies and Gentlemen: Tom Stoppard. The most modest dramatist since Shakespeare.

Life Studies
(2003)

In *To Jerusalem and Back*, Saul Bellow remarks that 'in every generation we recognize a leader race of masterminds whose ideas ("class-struggle", "Oedipus complex", "identity crisis") come down over us like butterfly nets.' Marx, then. Freud. Bellow's particular target for his faux-reluctant scepticism is Sartre. His choice of words is revealing. 'A leader *race* of *master*minds' is a near rhetorical relative of 'the master race', and those metaphorical nets deprive us of liberty. We are really talking about intellectual dictatorship. Tendentiousness shading into tyranny.

I want to consider a special case of this proposition. It is that a *misinterpretation* of T. S. Eliot's essay 'Tradition and the Individual Talent' has been seminal in the twentieth century – as if an impostor had exercised power illegitimately for the best part of 80 years. Briefly, the rogue proposition is this: that the idea of artistic impersonality entailed the rejection of the personal in art. It all depends on what Eliot meant by 'impersonality'. The author of *Ash-Wednesday* ('Because I do not hope …') can hardly have meant to rule out the personal. Eliot's 'impersonality' addresses and describes 'the artistic process', the artistic *treatment* of the personal.

In 1958, Robert Lowell wrote to Randall Jarrell that *Life Studies* was 'all very direct and personal'. So much so that Allen Tate's response to the manuscript was also direct and personal: '*all* the poems about your family, including the one about you and Elizabeth, are definitely *bad* … the poems are composed of unassimilated details, terribly intimate, and coldly noted.' Of course, there *were* moments of brilliance, Tate conceded, but 'there is an imaginative thrust towards a symbolic order which these new poems seem to lack.' It is easy to laugh at Tate. It is less easy to see that his parsonical and prim judgements derive from T. S. Eliot, with his 'features of clerical cut' – the eventual first publisher of *Life Studies*. As well as moral affront, Tate's reservations embody an aesthetic position inherited, unquestioned, from Eliot.

Eliot's essay was classicist – an aesthetic whose thrust was essentially negative, defined in opposition to 'romantic'. The romantic position values strong

Virginia Hamilton Adair, *Ants on the Melon* (Random House, 1999); Michael Rosen, *Carrying the Elephant* (Penguin, 2002); Hugo Williams, *Collected Poems* (Faber and Faber, 2002); Robin Robertson, *Slow Air* (Picador, 2002); D. Nurkse, *The Fall* (Knopf, 2002).

emotions, makes them central to the achievement of art. It was a mistake Eliot was determined to overturn: in art, he wrote, 'it is not the "greatness", the intensity, of the emotions, the components, but the intensity of the artistic process, the pressure, so to speak, under which the fusion takes place, that counts.' Instead, he argued for the impersonality of great art. By 'impersonality' Eliot understood objectivity, impartiality, disinterestedness, distance – the control of accidentals, of subjectivity, of mere contingencies. Hence the idea of the objective correlative and its implied contract between writer and reader – that the impenetrably private is inadmissible as art.

But this does not mean, could not mean, that art should be purged of anything personal – as Tate and others wrongly believed. On the contrary, Eliot maintains the emotions are what we make art from. Look at that quotation again: 'it is not the "greatness", the intensity, of the emotions, *the components*' (my italics). The emotions are 'the components', but they have to be made into something. 'Tradition and the Individual Talent' *is*, though, a denunciation of unreconstructed subjectivity in art. Feeling strongly cannot make you a poet. Otherwise, every sentimental drunk, every football fan, every religious bigot, would qualify. Creativity means creating something.

What, though, are we to make of this famous epitome? 'Poetry is not a turning loose of emotion, but an escape from emotion; it is not an expression of personality, but an escape from personality.' Surely this suggests revulsion from the personal? 'Escape' is the difficult word here. Like 'turning loose' it means 'freedom' – but in a different sense, an opposed sense. 'Turning loose' suggests self-indulgence, licence, 'freeing up'. Whereas what Eliot means by 'escape' is 'freedom from' – getting outside something, no longer being trapped inside it.

The very simplicity of this central idea – that being a poet means more than feeling like a poet – works against it. Can Eliot have expounded something so obvious? Selective quotation can encourage us to misconstrue Eliot's argument. For example: 'the more perfect the artist, the more completely separate in him will be the man who suffers and the mind which creates.' Eliot is arguing for the black-box theory of art, the flight recorder in the flaming aircraft – for objectivity over subjectivity. But it *sounds* like divorce, like a decree absolute, after which the artist and his personal experience go their separate ways. That is why Allen Tate felt able to condemn *Life Studies*. He believed he had the authority of the century's greatest poet on his side. He was wrong. But he was not alone. Lowell himself probably felt *Life Studies* was subversive, that it transgressed Eliotean fundamentals – that it was flagrantly personal in the teeth of Eliot's 'Impersonal theory of poetry'.

Perhaps ten years later, Ian Hamilton demonstrated the continuing power of Eliot's authority by mounting a rival aesthetic. An intensification of Lowell's example, it was consciously, defiantly defined against Eliot – even as Hamilton, like nearly everyone, misconstrued Eliot's argument. For Hamilton, poetry *was* the personal. But only up to a point. There were large areas of exclusion. Poetry was such a high calling that only deeply personal experience could be admitted as subject matter – the death of a father, the madness of a wife, the onset of love, the failure of love. Only on these terms – fatally narrow terms, skirting the precious – could Eliot be opposed. Anything lesser was inadmissible, trivial, unworthy of poetry. It meant that Hamilton's humour played no part in his poetry – one of many impoverishments mistakenly embraced. Admirers call his poetry 'lyric'. The alternative is to think of it as a simplification, threatened by sentimentality. As I do. Later in his writing career, Hamilton ventured into more ordinary territory, but gave these poems self-ironising titles like 'Larkiniana' that effectively disowned them.

At the same time, there were in Hamilton concurrent assumptions at odds with the idea of poetry as a high calling, as the exercise of sincerity – for instance, the idea that poetry was 'art', often artificial, therefore. More importantly, poetry was necessarily public. It publicised the intensely private – and was liable to be touched by the tawdry, unless this intimate material was treated with exemplary restraint.

Eliot's presence, then, declared itself in three ways. First, Hamilton insisted on the personal, thus opposing the 'Eliot' who allegedly rejects the personal. Second, he opposed Eliot's idea – genuine in this case – that strength of feeling is peripheral to artistic success. For Hamilton, sincerity is central. Thirdly, the combination of deep feeling and artistic restraint was a version of Eliot's separation of the suffering man from the creative artist.

The misinterpretation of Eliot's 'Tradition and the Individual Talent' reflects a deep-seated, more general unease – with the *à clef* approach to literature – that precedes the essay. For example, Henry James's letters frequently touch on the queasy area between life and art. On 15 February 1885, writing to his brother William, James touches on the accusation that Miss Birdseye in *The Bostonians* is taken from the real-life figure of a Miss Peabody. James is in denial: his portrait is tender in its broad lines, 'even if Miss Peabody *should* think I meant to portray her (which, however, heaven forfend!)'. James insists: 'As I told you yesterday I never wished or attempted to represent her *at all.*' All this protestation might be more convincing did not the same letter refer to another novelistic intrusion and appropriation: 'I am told, on all sides, that my *Author of Belltraffio* is a living and scandalous portrait of J. A. Symonds & his wife, whom I have never seen.' This is disingenuous. James may not have seen husband or wife, but he certainly knew about them. In a letter dated 26 March 1884, only a year earlier, he writes: 'Edmund Gosse mentioned … a possible *donnée*. He was speaking of J. A. S. (from whom, in Paris, the other day I got a letter).' James can't have forgotten. Apart from considerations of libel, the unease seems to stem from a misplaced scruple – not a moral scruple about privacy and appropriation, but a scruple about artistry and reportage. Fiction was supposed to be creation *ex nihilo* – this was the fiction about fiction – not the novelist eavesdropping on life and taking notes in shorthand. A misconception that is surprisingly durable. Here is hypocritical Hemingway reproaching Scott Fitzgerald for using Sara and Gerald Murphy in *Tender is the Night*: 'you took liberties with people's pasts and futures that produced not people but damned marvelously faked case histories.'

Some of the same unease is still visible in Seamus Heaney's 'Whatever You Say, Say Nothing': 'media-men and stringers sniff and point, / Where zoom lenses, recorders and coiled leads / Litter the hotels.' The results of this journalism are empty pieties and the newspaper clichés carefully listed by Heaney. It took P. V. Glob's *The Bog People* to release and validate Heaney's portrayal of the Troubles. Glob's study of Iron Age sacrificial victims poetically legitimised Heaney's primary material – which was also fodder for the front pages – by distancing it, by providing an Eliotean objective correlative.

Actually, the fear of reportage is misplaced. In itself, documentary does not necessarily entail sensationalism, cliché, ready-made thinking, conventional piety. Of course, it can be done badly. But 'journalism' need not inevitably mean something slipshod, inaccurate and superficial. In the same way, the personal need not mean self-indulgent display or self-indulgent solipsism. All the books under review use personal material. All use it slightly differently.

Virginia Hamilton Adair's *Ants on the Melon*, her only book, appeared in America in 1996 to general acclaim, but failed to find a publisher in England. She was 83 and going blind. Her husband, an historian, had committed suicide in 1968 after 35 years of marriage. He shot himself in their bedroom, without leaving a note. Her poetry has the sole advantage of age – not wisdom, but experience, endurance, which can produce lines like 'The August of my hysterectomy ...' The poems are sometimes less than competent technically. This is from 'Exit Amor', one of several poems about her husband's suicide: 'But forever across the bed you sprawl.' 'Savage our exultation' is another inversion. These are a couple of her maladroit couplets celebrating Borges: 'Your visions and voice a stirring music start / With answering drumbeats from the hearer's heart. // I could not know how soul in Spanish sings / (heard only on the radio selling things).' The book, however, contains a masterpiece, which accounts for the acclaim. It is called 'One Ordinary Evening'. About her husband's suicide, it perfectly illustrates how the personal becomes the impersonal in poetry.

Lying entwined with you
on the long sofa

the hi-fi helping
Isolde to her climax

I was clipping
the coarse hairs

from your ears
and ruby nostrils

when you said, 'Music
for cutting nose wires'

and we shook so
the nailscissors nicked

your gentle neck
blood your blood

I cleansed the place
with my tongue

and we clung tight
pelted with Teutonic cries

till the player
lifted its little prick

from the groove
all arias over

leaving us
in post-Wagnerian sadness

later that year
you were dead

by your own hand
blood your blood

I have never understood
I will never understand

This is a poem of great aesthetic courage. It dares to juxtapose the banality of
nostril hairs with the fact of suicide. It is drily ironic about Wagner: 'the hi-fi

helping / Isolde to her climax'. It flinches at nothing. A more knowing poet, a poet like Ian Hamilton, say, might have edited out these unworthy elements, as low, as touched with comedy. The weighting of words, the balance of lines, but especially the intuitive decision not to punctuate, to let the elements bleed into each other, to create the crucial sense of suddenness – everything in this poem is perfect. It is also enviably simple and direct. Which enshrines the central irony – the plain fact of suicide and its unintelligibility. 'I will never understand.'

We readers, however, understand only too well. Virginia Hamilton Adair tells us more than she knows, simply by setting things down simply. In his essay on Massinger, Eliot has this to say about the dramatist: 'What the creator of character needs is not so much knowledge of motives as keen sensibility; the dramatist need not understand people; but he must be exceptionally aware of them.' Something like this happens in 'One Ordinary Evening'. Hamilton Adair is a naive poet as some painters are naive painters. Her great poem tells us everything we need to know about the failure of the body – those ruby nostrils, those nostril hairs, the body's laughable charade, the delusion of sexuality. Middle age is poised where comic realism tips into tragedy. The comic discrepancy between our Wagnerian pretensions of sexuality and our frail physical means to ecstasy are enacted by the hi-fi – 'the player / lifted its little prick / / from the groove / all arias over.' Everyone's failing sexual powers are here. As Dencombe says in Henry James's *The Middle Years*, 'The infinite of life had gone, and what was left of the dose was a small glass engraved like a thermometer by the apothecary.' What at first seems funny becomes fearful as its true force is felt.

Michael Rosen isn't a naive writer like Virginia Hamilton Adair, but a deliberately artless writer, whose strengths are honesty, alertness to comic incongruities and a notable lack of sentimentality. *Carrying the Elephant* is an autobiography in anecdote form. It is also freighted first with sadness – a failed marriage – then tragedy, when his eighteen-year-old son dies of meningitis. You want to like the book, for obvious reasons. The sections are said to be prose poems, but they are mostly reminiscence without shape. Some of them will be gnomic to the general reader – who may not know who Dame Helen Gardner was, or what a *viva* was. Those who do know, may lament the linguistic poverty of *Carrying the Elephant*. Where the prose anecdotes aspire to form, the shapes are trite: for example, Rosen's failing marriage is implicit in the house with the paradoxically well-kept outside and the chaotic inside. Some of the language is pointlessly ugly, even for prose. This is a neighbours' marital break-up, where the wife walks out: 'Did that for a couple of weeks then left with the baby leaving David with the three boys.' It's as if Rosen had left his Uher on by accident in the pub. Because his strength is candour, the sexual material here is all the more authentic for the offhand presentation: 'they also said that they met up with Old Man Harris in the woods and they wanked him off *into a bucket'* (my italics). The trouble is, he isn't a writer. In Eliotean terms, *Carrying the Elephant* is all components and no process. Rosen doesn't *want* to be a writer. He wants poetry without the poetry.

So does Hugo Williams, who dislikes metaphor, simile, metre, rhythm; in fact, *all* the paraphernalia of poetry – preferring to locate his strengths elsewhere. His *Collected Poems* allow us to see why he looks askance at metaphor. He is no good at it: 'Both know they walk / Tightropes like duellists and to gore / / The enemy is to fall on one's sword.' This, 'The Pick-up', is from his earliest book, when Thom Gunn was the new hipster on the block to imitate, and Ian Hamilton had yet to make his influence felt. 'The Cripple', also from *Symptoms of Loss* (1965), is an anthology of equally inept similes, including 'someone leaning from a window, *like a dove*' (my italics). The *refusenik* list at the head of this paragraph might not seem to leave *that* much to work with, but Williams is one of our best serio-comic poets.

Which, on the face of it, is surprising, since he began as an epigone of Ian Hamilton and the school of High Confessionalism – 'madhouse and the whole thing there', as Empson put it. His *Collected Poems* is still confessional, but it is consciously pedestrian, its poetic economy founded on humorous bathos and a deadpan manner:

> I know all about my little game
> of declaring more than I earn
> to the Inland Revenue – or was it less?
> I'm guilty as hell,
> or I wouldn't be sitting here like this
> playing footy-footy with my desk
> I'd be upstairs in bed with my bed.

This is almost equal to the comic Eliot of 'The Boston Evening Transcript'. Angst is treated wryly, ironically. In *Billy's Rain*, for example, when the love affair is over, the unhappy Williams meticulously records the shamefully swift return of normality: 'I don't feel so bad any more. / I think to myself, / "I'll soon put a stop to that!"' ('Everyone Knows This') The best poem is called 'Her News': in it, the ex-lover telephones with news of her pregnancy. Before he realises the baby cannot possibly be his, Williams panics at the idea of a new relationship, in theory the thing he most wants: 'But no, I couldn't go through all that again, / not without my own wife being there, / not without her getting cross about everything.' To high confessionalism, Williams has added the ludicrous, the embarrassing, the outflanked, the trivial, the inconveniently honest, the unexpectedly true. 'The mildewed hipsters / have purple paisley inserts, patch pockets, studs / and novelty exterior fly buttons with cannabis leaves. / Jim's eyes shine to see the switched-on funky gear. / He lies down on his back to get into them.' Well, we've all been there. Where his hero Ian Hamilton edited out, Hugo Williams edits in – and is the better poet.

The weaknesses of the Williams method – or lack of method – occur when the rhythm has been so successfully repressed that what remains is chopped-up prose – a category that is usually invoked by reviewers with only a primitive rhythm section themselves. But I don't see how else you could describe this passage from 'Ireland Swings': 'As everyone knows by now, / Dickie and Rowland Soper / are travelling together / to Luxembourg, / where Dickie will be singing / Ireland's entry / in the Eurovision Song Contest, / with brother Rowland producing.' It isn't as inept overall as E. J. Thribb, but 'to Luxembourg' and 'Ireland's entry' are daunting lines of implausible terseness. And this is how 'Self-Portrait with a Space Crash Helmet' begins: ' "Are you a member, sir?" / Of course I'm not, so I have to pay in full / for the pleasure of entering some former gents / where even I can tell / fulfilment isn't waiting / in the smell of beer and men.' And this is the beginning of 'No Particular Place to Go': 'O'Sullivan's Record Exchange / in the Peskett Street Market / was out of bounds to Lower Boys / on account of Miss O'Sullivan's taste / in music.' The line-break in line four is fatal, leaving 'in music' to make its living in the next line without much in the way of capital.

In a general way, as a matter of policy, Williams leaves out the music in poetry. Does this matter? Eliot said of Kipling: 'what fundamentally distinguishes his "verse" from "poetry" is the subordination of musical interest ... There is a harmonics of poetry which is not merely beyond the range of [Kipling's] poems – it would interfere with the intention.' I think this is unjust to Kipling's under-rated ear, but a useful general principle – and one that clearly applies to Hugo Williams's verse, which, even in its earliest rhyming manifestations, was always aurally pedestrian. On the other hand, consider Auden's rejoinder to Eliot's strictures on Kipling's lack of music. The same strictures, he argued, would apply to 'Ben Jonson, for instance, who wrote out a prose draft which he then versified, Dunbar, Butler's *Hudibras*, most of Burns, Byron's *Don Juan*, etc.' The problem isn't solved by Auden's intervention, sharp though it is. We go to neither Burns, nor *Don Juan*, nor *Hudibras* for the singing line of inexplicably unique music. If we did, we should be disappointed by the discovery of something coarser. Aurally, it is here that Williams belongs.

In fact, his poetry works best when it deploys some obvious rhetorical device like repetition. For example, 'When I Grow Up' uses its title as a refrain. This is one of Williams's best poems – an hilariously tasteless meditation on old age, which advances the proposition that age and decay are desirable, on the analogy of children looking forward to the time when they are grown up. 'I think it's only fair that I should be allowed / to cough up a bit of blood when I feel like it.' Another favoured, indeed overused device is the repeated 'Now that ...' construction. In 'Death of an Actor' it is the central rhetorical device: 'Now that I am cold / Now that I look like him ...'; 'Now that I'm alone / Now that I have come to this nice / Indifference ...'; 'Now that he is dead / Now that he is remembered ...'; 'Now that it is late / Now that it is too late ...' You can find the figure in 'Now That I Hear Trains', too: 'Now that I hear trains ...'; 'Now that I look unlike ...' Then there is 'The Spell': 'Now you are far away ...' And 'Self-Portrait with a Map of Ireland' revisits the tic in Section 6: 'Now the girls are coming home ...' Then there is 'Self-Portrait with a Slide': 'Now every-thing is slipping through my fingers ...' Now that the poet is stuck in a rut ... It doesn't help either that the mannerism seems to have originated in Muldoon's '*From* Last Poems': 'Not that I care who's sleeping with whom / now that she's had her womb / removed, now it lies in its own glar / like the last beetroot in the pickle jar.'

Robin Robertson has an exacting ear, an ear able to register shifts in the folds of silk. Sinatra's phrasing, his deliberate mastery of the spontaneous pause, is the nearest equivalent:

> In the flickering room
> the fire
>
> finds the whisky, lit
> in its gold slot,
>
> in the warm
> heel of the glass.

Finds! It is easy to understand why, as the newly appointed poetry editor at Secker & Warburg, he decided, two decades ago, to axe virtually all the intel-lectually addled, tone-deaf mediocrities – a decision subsequently reversed when the 'poetry world' vented its whingeing displeasure. There are some good similes in *Slow Air*, too – three of them in 'The Long Home': 'The firewood's sap / buzzing like a trapped fly'; 'the sound of the coals / unwrapping them-selves like sweets'; 'a bucketful of ice / into the sink, like a tremendous / burst of applause'. As for metaphor, what about Rilke's gazelle 'ready / to recoil and ricochet away // but waiting, listening'?

Robertson's marvellous addition to Rilke's panther – 'he seems to pass through his own body – like whisky / swilled to the neck of the bottle then back on itself' – tells us we are reading the poetry of a drinker, a student of the malt that wounds ('I liked a drink too, / but would always leave before him, / walking home, as if on a wire'). And the poems in *Slow Air* centre on a few personal events – drinking, the failure of a marriage, the death of the poet's father. Ian Hamilton territory, in fact. The governing theme is self-destruction, its irresistible vertigo. Robertson is a *poète maudit*, whose strength is a saving self-irony: 'the legend // of myself: self-exiled, / world-wounded, god'. 'The Oven Man' is unsentimentally acute about the high of self-destruction. Using an air-balloon metaphor, it concludes: 'During all this commotion / I am inside, in expansive mood, // relaxing / like a Sunday roast // in my juices, / my puddle of blood.' 'Break' is equally calm, equally detached, about the end of his marriage: a glass breaks in the washing up, 'she could see blood / smoking from the flap of skin', and she stands 'feeling nothing'.

Robertson's weakness is self-pity: 'I am far from home, / remembering how to live, remembering / I have no home.' He can lean to melodrama. When his father dies, he blames himself: 'He was uncomfortable, / so I asked the nurse / if we could lift him higher. / He died an hour later. / Usually happens, she explained, / after you move them. / Forgive me, I say, at his feet, / through a mouthful of nails.' Just so, the crucifixion. To be sure.

If he blames himself unreasonably here, elsewhere Robertson can be quietly self-exculpating. 'March, Lewisboro' offers its reader a contrast, between the sensitive bird-watching early-riser, observing with enviable precision 'the oiled rook' as it 'strides / into the wind's current', and the grouchy female egotist issuing italicised imperatives from the sack. *'What's wrong with you / that you can never sleep?'*; *'And check the mail! / I'm expecting a letter.'* On the one hand, the magical 'white and walk of the morning'; on the other, coarse daylight with cars and glossy magazines. I can't help sensing something self-serving here. It is too easy, given the other poems, to imagine a sleep-starved wife at the end of her tether, persecuted by unreasonable, arbitrary behaviour. The poem is haunted by a subversive, phantom narrative. Perhaps one senses it because the writing here is less good. For instance, that 'oiled rook' 'bundles herself into the air' – exactly as she did in Ted Hughes's 'Ravens': 'A raven bundled itself into air from midfield.' There are other moments of tired writing, too: 'A salting of snow, blown / across the white table of the lake.' It might be Derek Walcott elaborating and extending that dull equation of 'snow' and 'salt', a substandard metaphor argued into conviction. Equally, it is the James Joyce of 'The Dead' (rather than Rilke, who is acknowledged) who is responsible for the cadences of the final poem, 'Fall', which ends with a direct quotation: 'softly falling'.

Another weakness of this kind of lyric poetry is its reluctance to take on the more intractable facts – like the facts of life. Sex is a problem in *Slow Air*. Masturbation: 'Poor monster, pulling at himself, / the DNA unspooling from his

hand: / white butterflies / spill into the dark.' First orgasm: 'my first liquefac-
tion'. Either impotence, or post-coital detumescense: 'the slashed fetlock, / the
buckling under; // I wake in her body / broken, like a gun.' The terse lyric is
easiest with nature, bird-watching, landscape. Sometimes it is positively glib.
This is the summation of Robertson's father's death: 'The dam he built / in the
stream is finally broken: / cold Highland water / rushing to the sea.' What an
exhausted topos this is, worn out with visitors. How much less eloquent it is,
with its straining for eloquence, than the flat notation of 'The ward-plan wiped
clean for another name.'

But I don't want to end on a negative note. This is 'Raising the Paint', a poem
of frightening calm, which numbly, methodically, demonstrates the power of
alcohol to inspire clarity and detachment:

> Pleased by the ruined bed,
> the full ashtray,
> I checked my glass for finger-marks,
> turning it, over and over.
> As I left the house
> I ran the key
> along the panels of the door,
> raising the paint.
> The tide was out,
> and each step whitened the sand
> like pressed skin.
> Behind me, all this evidence:
> an almost straight line
> of footprints,
> clothes, credit cards,
> proving I exist.

In 'Skunk Hour', Lowell experienced the same impalpability, the same imperative to leave a trace – only to be confronted by a skunk for whom he did not
exist. When you have destroyed yourself, Robertson's poem argues, the psychic
vacuum left searches for traces, any traces, of what it once was. This is personal
poetry with impersonality stamped all over it. It explains how the two apparently opposed postures are possible in the same poem, in the same Eliotean
theory of poetry.

Madness is a difficult subject for literature, but a particularly difficult subject
for poetry, because it is, by definition, ultra-personal. So solipsistic, in fact, that
it divides the sufferer from other people with their shared standards. It is a great

deal more personal than, say, alcoholic despair. In D. Nurkse, madness has found its greatest poet. He writes brilliantly, truthfully, about being a child ('the huge hour until sunset'), growing up ('her tongue / talkative in my mouth'), love, sex ('That room was so tiny / everything we touched was us'), the failure of love ('If loneliness were a taxi, / I'd give it our old address') – but he writes about madness with the precision of genius, setting down the most intensely personal states with the coolest impersonality.

The literary failures in this problematic area are legion. Think of Dosto-evsky's *Notes from Underground* – a transcript of tediously authentic loquacity and egotism. On the other hand, there are great prose portrayals of madness. I would cite Salinger, Plath and Hemingway – Holden Caulfield, Seymour Glass, Esther Greenwood and the Nick Adams of 'A Way You'll Never Be'. All these characters are profoundly disturbed. One of them kills himself, one attempts suicide several times. They are, in Berryman's words, 'severely damaged, but functioning'. In fact, the severity of the damage is masked. Seymour Glass is perfectly capable of entertaining the little girl, Sybil, with the fantasy of banana-fish – an idea suggested by the recipe of fish with bananas – before shooting himself. These authors succeed in part by concentrating on behaviour rather than on feelings. We watch Esther Greenwood feeding her wardrobe to the night wind, or burying a hotdog in the sand. Plath reports on her feelings, too. So there *are* coordinates, but they are minimal because the feelings are unintel-ligible: 'I couldn't understand why I was crying so hard.' Sometimes they are more specific – but unintelligible. Esther contemplates the hundred-letter word in *Finnegans Wake*: 'it sounded like a heavy wooden object falling downstairs, boomp boomp boomp, step after step.' (Plath is borrowing Huckleberry Finn's evocation of thunder: 'like rolling empty barrels down stairs, where it's long stairs and they bounce a good deal, you know.')

Nick Adams is shell-shocked, yet capable of sane discriminations. His mad-ness is lucidly reported. He is terrified by the 'memory' of something ostensibly ordinary and unthreatening: 'He never dreamed about the front now any more but what frightened him so that he could not get rid of it was that long yellow house and the different width of the river.' There is also 'a long stable and a canal', equally ordinary, equally terrifying. The conviction of Hemingway's por-trait stems partly from this paradox and partly from the physical manifestation of Nick's derangement: he feels suddenly overpowered by words. 'He felt it coming on again.' 'He was trying to hold it in.' When it comes, it comes like a Pinter riff, uncontrollably associative. Asked about his American uniform, Nick finds himself delivering a lecture on locusts: 'It is a little tight in the collar but soon you will see untold millions wearing this uniform swarming like locusts. The grasshopper, you know, what we call the grasshopper in America, is really a locust. The true grasshopper is small and green and comparatively feeble …'

From the outside, if someone is mad, degrees of madness seem irrelevant. Derangement is, by definition, a species of nonsense – as unavailable to others as our dreams. And yet at least two writers, Lewis Carroll and Kafka, have managed to convey the quiddity of the world of sleep. They have done it by a literary act of patient notation and, *crucially*, by assuming normality in the abnormal. When we dream we are the slaves of an apparent logic. Often, the same is true of madness. And, in fact, madness often seems normal to the outsider. Madness isn't obvious or monolithic – as Salinger, Plath and Hemingway clearly realise – though it frequently is in poetry.

This is Lowell's 'Man and Wife': 'All night I've held your hand, / as if you had / a fourth time faced the kingdom of the mad – / *its hackneyed speech, its homicidal eye* ' (my italics). These are lines you might expect from a poet who had to be flown home in a straitjacket from Buenos Aires – after mounting equestrian statues naked and declaring himself the Caesar of Argentina. The behaviour is spectacularly aberrant, but identifiably so – in a way that explains that phrase, 'its hackneyed speech'. On the other hand, Lowell once went mad and threw a huge party – at which the guests noticed nothing. Dido Merwin was there: 'The extraordinary thing was that nobody seemed to realise he was mad.' The next day he was committed. Most madness is like this, less conspicuous than you might expect.

D. Nurkse has had a strange publishing record – Poet Laureate of Brooklyn, and five books from publishers like Four Way Press, Hanging Loose Press, State Street Press, Owl Creek Press. At last he's found a mainstream publisher. His background is Estonian. Nurkse's poetry is exceptional because of the accuracy he brings to the description of extreme mental states *and* the surrounding physical circumstances. The very first poem of this brilliant new collection is called 'The Threshold'. It is about being over the edge of madness, while you believe you are only on the edge. This is how it opens:

> As I waited for the doctor
> I realised nothing was wrong with me,
> just a voice whispering the word
> triage, a few sleepless nights,
> a change in the weather, great winds
> visible in the crests of trees
> I could glimpse through a vent
> at the far end of the corridor,
> the immense power of dreams
> unchecked by waking …

What could be more normal? On the presumption of normality, we translate the cliché of hearing voices into worrying away at the meaning of a word ('triage' is the action of sorting according to quality). Then there is lack of sleep and a change in the weather.

The spell of normality is broken by the vision of natural turmoil – 'great winds / visible in the crests of trees' – seen through 'a vent / at the far end of the corridor'. Not a window. *A vent.* The presumption of normality vanishes. Then Nurkse transports us into madness itself, dreams from which one cannot wake up – even though the nights are sleepless. There is no melodrama here, only the irresistible morph whose sudden momentum takes us with it. We are like the young Nurkse, who focuses the sun on his hand through a magnifying glass: 'I aimed at my hand / and sensed that fire / infinitely distant, close, / then inside me …'

Nurkse's poetry exhibits a calm fidelity to feelings, however strange, and a parallel responsibility to external facts. In 'The Part', Nurkse gives us the barber's shop: 'Three combs on a frayed towel – / one tortoiseshell, one transparent, / one clogged with white hair – / and a bottle of Cutler's Bay rum sealed with a foil wisp.' And he gives us himself, hearing the barber say: '*you are my long lost son / returned to me from the grave.*' Then he distinguishes between 'my voice' – in his head – and the barber's '*a little more off the ears* '.

It is this combination which makes his poetry so irresistible in spite of its strangeness – a strangeness which again reminds me of T. S. Eliot on Kipling: 'part of the fascination of this subject is in the exploration of a mind so different from one's own.' Nurkse's music isn't as immediate, as *obvious*, as Robertson's, but it is there for anyone with an ear – sounding itself uniquely. Unlike Robertson, Nurkse is unembarrassable by the world of things: 'only the walnut cheese log remained, / stoved-in in the spun-glass chafing dish.' The calculated mimetic clumsiness of that repeated 'in' is a bravura sound effect.

This is 'Cat's-Eye', one of several poems about his father's death. It records, unflinchingly, the unconquerable egotism of the child:

> My father waved good-bye.
> I didn't wave back,
> scared I might drop
> my new cold smoky marble.
>
> At the core a spiral
> glinted and coiled
> like a small windy flame
> turning in on itself.

That night my mother
shook me from a dream,
whispering he was dead,
he was dead, he was dead,
as if to teach a language
and I answered: he is dead.

Even in sleep
my hands had not opened.

The simplicity here – the marble as the candid emblem of the self – is the simplicity of a poet completely confident in his gift. And rightly so. The art is there in the mother's despair, the triple repetition of 'he was dead' – and the child's detached, unsentimental simile, 'as if to teach a language'.

Only a world-class writer would risk it. But Nurkse is a world-class writer.

Robert Lowell's *Collected Poems*
(2004)

In 1962, the British publication of Robert Lowell's *Imitations* was preceded by extracts in the *Observer* that took up the entire broadsheet review front. It was a measure of Lowell's extraordinary prestige. The only comparable occasion was the *Observer*'s 1966 publication of 'Thanksgiving for a Habitat', a sequence from Auden's *About the House*, which came with a huge photograph of that iconic, roughly repaired, fractured face. Lowell's imitations were accompanied by woodcuts. The writing, not the writer, was the celebrity.

Or so it seemed. *Imitations* was full of celebrities – in translation and sometimes so morphed by the process of imitation that their poems took on Lowellian tics of style. The idea of the book explains part of Lowell's cultural heft. Pound, his high modernist predecessor, had imitated Li Po, the *Seafarer* poet, Sextus Propertius, the troubadour poets, Ovid. He was saturated in world culture from Confucius to Firdausi. Lowell's emulative range of reference was comparable – Villon, Sappho, Leopardi, Hebel, Saba, Ungaretti, Annensky, Pasternak, Heine and Montale. It was a performance confident enough – in its assumption of equal poetic status – to take liberties with its originals, knowing its licence would not be mistaken for inadvertency. Lowell's range sought to rival T. S. Eliot's legendary literary reach – which allowed Eliot, for example, to discriminate learnedly between the sermonising styles of the deliberately dazzling Donne and the subtler Lancelot Andrewes.

The great Swift biographer, Irvin Ehrenpreis, once told me that conversation with Lowell was a competitive affair – recondite, wide-ranging, professional, a million miles away from social chit-chat. And Michael Longley, persecuted by the indefatigably academic Lowell, arose at 6 a.m. for a moment or two of peace from poetry, only to find that his house-guest had followed him downstairs in stockinged-feet to pursue the previous evening's conversation about Sir Philip Sidney ...

Notebook gossips about the great. Learned still, it carries its learning anecdotally – a fusion of Vasari, Yeats's *The Trembling of the Veil*, Stephen Spender's anecdotal poems (which themselves depend on Yeats's prior example) and Aubrey's *Brief Lives*. The poems scrape an intimacy with everyone who is anyone – with the odd nobody thrown in for plausibility. As he tells it, Lowell

---

The Collected Poems, edited by Frank Bidart and David Gewanter (Faber and Faber, 2003).

has heard the chimes at midnight with Clytemnestra, Sir Thomas More, Cheops, Saint-Just, Cranach, Frost, the Eliots (Thomas Stearns and Mrs Lewes), Jackie Kennedy, Bobby Kennedy, Mary Stuart, Marcus Cato, Pound, Flaubert, Eugene McCarthy, Berryman and many more. In no particular chronological or hierarchical order. Of course, Lowell *had* met some of these historical figures – according to Peter Taylor, Ford Madox Ford feared 'that boy will write something terrible about me one day' – but all of them contributed to Lowell's own glamour. No one ever suggested that Lowell was a kind of Zelig. Woody Allen's rubbernecking wannabee was the opposite of patrician, self-confident Lowell. Lowell knew all these figures, it seemed, by their first names – and if he didn't always use their first names, it was out of pure consideration for his readers, who would know them best by their surnames. I don't want to seem priggish about these poems. Gossip is part of ordinary life and therefore should find a place in poetry. Nevertheless, there is something in *Notebook* that reminds me of Saul Bellow's account (in *To Jerusalem and Back*) of celebrities at the White House – 'gripped by an all but demonic desire for the optimum encounter'.

Fairness requires me to record that, famously, Lowell turned down Lyndon Johnson's invitation to the White House, for political reasons, after having initially accepted – and became a front-page celebrity as a result. Actually, Lowell's excellent letter to Johnson rather disarms our snide scepticism by its charming admission of Lowell's human enough susceptibility to social blandishments – 'I am afraid I accepted somewhat rapidly and greedily.' As we all might.

After a reading at the Oxford Union in 1974, Lowell was asked which English poets he admired. He smiled a little ruefully and began. 'I like Ted Hughes, I like Philip Larkin, I like Geoffrey Hill, I like Peter Porter, I like Edwin Brock, I like Anthony Thwaite ...' He recited a list of at least thirty names of living poets, perhaps more – finishing with, after a perfectly timed pause, 'I hope I didn't leave anyone out.' This said with a seductively wicked glance around the hall. His audience was completely charmed. As a performance, it was winningly mischievous, a send-up – the literary log-roller picked out by Norman Mailer in *The Armies of the Night* giving a baroque, bravura display of ironic name-dropping.

The next day, Christopher Reid and I saw Lowell in the Paperback Shop in Broad Street. We were looking for Borges, who, we'd heard, was in Oxford – perhaps to receive an honorary degree. With beautiful manners, Lowell shook both our hands and listened politely as we explained our mission. 'Well,' he said, 'I had dinner with him last night in All Souls, but I couldn't say where he is right now.' The Duc de Nemours was probably at dinner, too.

It was this glamorous figure who presented Seamus Heaney with the Duff Cooper Memorial prize for *North*, having altered the perception of that book, after indifferent reviews, by one intervention in the *Observer* 'Books of the Year'.

The Duff Cooper Prize is worth very little financially. Its prestige depends crucially on who presents the prize – as its recipient once explained to me. At that time, you couldn't do better than Robert Lowell.

And his influence was everywhere. For a start, in Heaney's 1979 *Field Work*. My copy is marked with several laconic, marginal L's: 'Who's sorry for our trouble?', 'Basalt, blood, water, headstones, leeches' (from 'After a Killing'); 'O charioteers, above your dormant guns' ('The Toome Road'); 'The way we are living, / timorous or bold, / will have been our life. / Robert Lowell …' ('Elegy': in fact, the whole of this elegy for Lowell, not just its deliberate allusions, is gravid with Lowell's plangency, with Lowell's line-breaks, sedulously imitative without being intentional – and rhetorically over the top). As this example shows, there was something utterly distinctive in Lowell's language, something patented and impossible to steal without looking derivative.

In Derek Walcott's *Midsummer*, if Lowell isn't quite omnipresent, it is only because Larkin and Elizabeth Bishop are also making inroads on Walcott's style. For a longish time, Lowell displaces Dylan Thomas: 'Ah, to have / a tone colloquial and stiff, / the brevity of that short syllable, God, / like Li Po or a Chinese laundry mark.' I have written already in *Areté* (Issue 3, Autumn 2000) about Walcott's Xeroxes of Lowell, his undisguised lifts. Here I want to point out Lowell's influence – in number L's enigmatic aphoristic closure, for example, 'Youth is stronger than fiction'. And in XVII's indebtedness to two Lowell poems, 'Obit' from *Notebook* and 'Epilogue' from *Day by Day*. 'Obit': 'I'm for and with myself in my otherness, / in the eternal return of earth's fairer children, / the lily, the rose, the sun on dusk and brick, / the loved, the lover, and their fear of life.' 'Epilogue': 'Pray for the grace of accuracy / Vermeer gave to the sun's illumination / stealing like the tide across a map / to his girl solid with yearning.' Now Walcott's XVII: 'What work lies ahead of us, what sunlight for generations! – / The lemon-rind light in Vermeer, to know it will wait / there for others, the broken eucalyptus / leaf, still sharply smelling of turpentine, / the breadfruit's foliage, rust-edged like van Ruysdael.' It almost fools you, but it's a fake – like Van Meegeren. Lowell's tutelary presence in Walcott was eventually supplanted, first by Heaney, then finally, disastrously, by Brodsky – who, by a commodius vicus of recirculation, has his own skewed debts to Lowell.

Even the wary Ian Hamilton succumbed – consciously following the poetic programme initiated by *Life Studies*, with its embrace of the private and of psychic extremities, but also unconsciously aping particular lines. Lowell's 'Waking in the Blue' is set in McLean's, a private upper-class asylum, populated by 'These victorious figures of bravado ossified young'. In Hamilton's 'Now and Then', the scene is again an asylum: 'A gentle sun / Smiles on the dark, afflicted heads / Of young men who have come to nothing.' Characteristically, Hamilton opts for a slightly sentimentalised, generalised version of insanity, where Lowell's poem is humorous, accurate, hard and particular.

The great final sequence of Michael Hofmann's Oedipal *Acrimony* is unthinkable without the prior example of Lowell's *Life Studies*. Brilliant with betrayal, riven with resentment, tender with hatred, fixated by Gert Hofmann, his writer-father, devastatingly truthful, obsessed in a way that makes the word 'love' look like the feeble shorthand it is, *Acrimony*'s 'In My Father's House' surpasses its source. Hofmann's first book, *Nights in the Iron Hotel*, written while he was failing to finish a Ph.D. thesis on Lowell, is another matter. It is promising, even talented, but studiously indebted to Lowell's *Notebook* and slavish to the master's aposiopeses, which perforate *Nights in the Iron Hotel*, from breakfast in bed to the bill at reception. Nor has Hofmann written anything of interest since *Acrimony*. Which tells us something important about artistic example and genuine innovation. For that, two things are necessary: the discovery of new subject matter and the ability to bring it to book, to *write* it for the first time. Great poets initiate. Talent improves, refines, sometimes surpasses its source – and stops.

But was Lowell a great writer? Was he a flawed genius? Was he even a good writer? With this spottily annotated, £40, thousand-page *Collected* – lacking *Notebook*, including some early drafts – will we be able to decide whether he was charismatically *maudit* or merely *manqué*?

In March 1954, after the burial of his mother, Robert Lowell resumed his Cincinnati lecturing job. In days he was informing friends that his marriage to Elizabeth Hardwick was over. He planned to marry Giovanna Madonia, a woman he'd met two years before in Salzburg. Hardwick realised Lowell had entered a manic phase, but she found no one on the English faculty who would believe her. Two complementary clichés conspired against her: the idea of the dumped, duplicitous spouse who couldn't take the truth, and the idea of the poetic genius, absolved of quotidian responsibilities, in the grip of his gift, talking a mile a minute and living life to the hilt. For the faculty, Lowell wasn't *mad* – he was rather a *monstre sacré* whose categorical imperatives were in a category of their own. It was some time before they realised that Lowell wasn't making sense. Or perhaps they thought that poets, if they were full-on poets, just didn't make ordinary sense – that, to adapt Frost's famous dictum, the 'sound of sense' was somehow superior to *common* sense – which was the trivial prerogative of all.

These things are a parable – as I will explain – of obscurity and the impressiveness of obscurity. (And, incidentally, of academic gullibility.)

In 'Eating Out Alone', a dullish, crepuscular unrhymed sonnet from *History* (1973), Lowell ruminates on his solitary eater's tendency to elevate the marginal interest of the occupants of other tables – to impose on them fantasies of sex and *outré* opinions. Thus far, Lowell might be doodling on the tablecloth – with none of Picasso's authority or flair. The poem is a nothing. Until, suddenly, we confront a line out of Picasso's *Vollard Suite*: 'The minotaur steaming in a maze of eloquence'.

This line – on its own – is sufficient to explain Lowell's extraordinarily compelling charisma for other poets. He was a phrase-maker's phrase-maker – with a feel for alliteration and frequent recourse to a pronounced iambic pulse. This combination, this formula, was Lowell's helpless resource again and again, without ever becoming routine – an addiction that escaped the automatic. An anthology, taken from memory. Of Bobby Delano, 'cousin of Franklin Delano Roosevelt': 'My freshman year, he shot himself in Rio, / odious, unknowable, inspired as Ajax.' Of Elizabeth Hardwick: 'After loving you so much, can I forget / you for eternity, and have no other choice?' From 'White': 'the clam-shell cunted in the ground of being'. Of Bobby Kennedy's assassin: 'No Name can judge their killer, / his guiltless liver, kidneys, fingertips and phallus.' Of T. S. Eliot: 'lost in the dark night of the brilliant talkers, / humour and honour from the everlasting dross'. From 'Waking Early Sunday Morning': 'when that kingdom hit the crash: / a million foreskins stacked like trash' and 'like old white china doorknobs, sad, / slight, useless things to calm the mad'. Or the line singled out, in his commemorative 1984 *New York Review of Books* essay, by Derek Walcott as *echt* Lowell – 'her breasts spread apart like ox-horns.' [Slightly misquoted by Walcott. It should be 'the breasts / spread like ox-horns.'] This inimitably Lowellian phrase – one of many flashed by the breast-fixated Lowell – is from 'A Roman Sarcophagus', Lowell's imitation of Rilke, ironically enough. With Lowell, imitation was closer, not to conquest – which would aggrandise the process – but to cohabitation .

'The minotaur steaming in a maze of eloquence': this line will also account for a fatal deficiency which derives directly from that gift. Lowell was in the grip of his gift. It wasn't always, or often, under his control. The minotaur, as Lowell knew, was trapped in the maze – constructed by Daedalus to conceal the minotaur's deformity. The minotaur wasn't the maze's architect. Eloquence, then – if we follow the metaphor's logic – is a maze in which the poet is lost. Snorting, impressive, powerfully verbal – and pathetically, *semantically* confused and irresolute. Dazzling and dim, forthright, unfocused, at the same time. 'Pity the monsters.'

Pity Lowell, who was possessed of a gift that possessed him. No wonder the B.U. sophomore in 'Waking in the Blue' falls asleep over *The Meaning of Meaning*. The academic background that encouraged this trait in Lowell is, of course, the New Criticism – whose practitioners, men like Cleanth Brooks and R. P. Blackmur, made ambiguity the central, defining characteristic of poetry.

(A risible 'definition' notably remote from the poetry of Pope, Byron and Matthew Arnold but which nevertheless flourished fashionably for 30 years. Eventually, as we know, it was supplanted by Deconstruction, which broadened the field to make radical indeterminacy the central, defining characteristic of all *language*.)

Critics provoked several Lowell poems, including 'Playing Ball with the Critic' – a bruising experience in Lowell's account, an account which begins with American football and ends not with the minotaur, but with the bullring: 'it's a privilege to earn the bullring.'

There is a faculty photograph at Kenyon College, in which Lowell keeps company with Kenneth Burke, John Crowe Ransom, L. C. Knights (the author of the ironically titled essay 'How Many Children Had Lady Macbeth?') and the Crown Prince of Ambiguity, William Empson. However, the ultimate source and sanction for this poetic 'method' was probably the unwitting T. S. Eliot. In his essay 'The Metaphysical Poets' (1921), Eliot mooted that, on occasion, of necessity, language might have to be dislocated into meaning. Dylan Thomas certainly took the prescription much too literally and, I think, we can find here the justification for Lowell's 'bent generalizations' – as he called them in the 'Afterthought' to *Notebook* – and of much else skewed and bent besides.

Consider the last lines of 'For George Santayana' in *Life Studies*: the atheist, Catholic apostate Santayana is correcting his galley-proofs, using a magnifying glass whose amphitheatre becomes a Roman circus. The metaphor invites us to see a secular miracle, the salvation of work, an alchemy in illness and suffering:

> under your throbbing magnifying glass,
> that worn arena, where the whirling sand
> and broken-hearted lions lick your hand
> refined by bile as yellow as a lump of gold.

The *throbbing* magnifying glass is incomparable – and the doubled present participles are for once aptly repetitive. [In fact, it isn't incomparable. It is dependent on Eliot's prior, enabling example in *The Waste Land*: 'like a taxi *throbbing* waiting'.] The iambic pulse arrives – like cavalry in the last reel – with undeniable, obvious afflatus. But there is ineptitude in the syntactical implication that 'the whirling sand' also licks Santayana's jaundiced hand. 'Whirling sand' may touch the hand, sting it even, but *licking* isn't what sand does. It doesn't help either that the final line might, at a stretch, qualify the tawny lions, rather than the hand. It wouldn't take much to improve the syntax:

> under your throbbing magnifying glass,
> that worn arena's whirling sand
> where broken-hearted lions lick your hand,
> refined by bile as yellow as a lump of gold.

Given the regular glitches in Lowell's sense, his admirers needed to have their alibis in place – even the undeceived, habitually unimpressed and tersely impatient biographer, Ian Hamilton, in whose life of Lowell can be heard the sound of one hand clapping. Hamilton is critical, but compromised by his biographical project. Finally, you feel, he admires only *Life Studies* – and even there attempts some excluding distinctions and discriminations. Yet he, too, succumbs. Quoting the final couplet of 'Beyond the Alps', Hamilton writes: 'The poem's final image is one of Lowell's most perfect and impenetrable':

> Now Paris, our black classic, breaking up
> Like killer kings on an Etruscan cup.

'Most perfect *and* impenetrable.' Hamilton quotes an explication, 'but the image continues to resist simple exegesis.' Resistance here isn't obscurity, isn't a flaw, but a strain of perfection, quite clearly. And this is Hamilton on Randall Jarrell (Lowell's earliest cheer-leader) and the line 'The Lord survives the rainbow of His will.' Again, Hamilton is uninterested in exegesis: 'Many a learned paper has been written on that final line of Lowell's "The Quaker Graveyard in Nantucket", yet it is no "clearer", no less haunting, than it ever was: it was lines like this (and there are perhaps thirty of them in *Lord Weary's Castle*) that reduced even a proudly analytical reviewer like Jarrell to using words like "magic".' (This is a minor travesty of Jarrell, who never uses the word 'magic', and whose splashy generalised enthusiasm for Lowell is always tempered by specific reservations.)

I think we are being assimilated into the credulous English Faculty of Cincinnati by Hamilton's 'account' of this line – which, after all, has a perfectly available meaning to anyone familiar with, say, Hopkins's God and His duality. In this case, God drowns the world, then establishes a covenant with humanity – symbolised by the rainbow – and then proceeds to preside over a universe replete with further drownings and natural disasters. We may envisage a privileged relationship with God – God Himself may envisage such a relationship – but experience contradicts the theory every time. 'The Lord survives the rainbow of His will.' Feel the power of the pentameter.

In the 1986 lecture 'Lowell's Command', Heaney's strategy is to bypass any local difficulties by co-opting Lowell's poetry to a larger theory of poetry – in essence, the idea that poetry isn't ultimately about anything. Rather it is about itself. Hopkins's notebooks provide a less inflated version of the same theory – that the central pleasure of poetry is not its ostensible subjects, those balsa-wood ideas that so irritated Nabokov, but its verbal textures, 'the inscape of speech for the inscape's sake'. Heaney calls this 'the jurisdiction and vigour of [the poem's] own artistic means' – the government of the tongue, in other words. Authority lies in the poet's tongue, 'in the conviction of the tongue's right to speak freely and soundingly'. Though this is true in a sense – a sense which is fundamentally sentimental, because it is a version of poetry edited for simplicity – it quickly leads Heaney into simple-minded pietas. He asks us to believe that, in *Life Studies*, *For the Union Dead* and *Near the Ocean*, Lowell's subject matter is a pretext for the voice. I put it more crudely than Heaney, of course. This is Heaney trying to have it both ways, as far as possible: 'while these books often tangle with a great heavy web of subject matter, autobiographical, cultural and political, they are not primarily interested in commentary or opinion about such subject matter.'

Nothing could be further from the truth. This is Lowell in 1957 on what poetry could learn from prose: 'In prose you have to be interested in *what* is being said.' He likes Larkin and W. D. Snodgrass because each of them 'says something'.

Heaney's consistently eloquent and conveniently lax theory works like vanishing cream. It soothes away all traces of difficulty. Writing about 'The Quaker Graveyard at Nantucket', Heaney characterises it contradictorily as 'a gale-force of expressionism' yet includes it in a generalisation covering the early work – 'the robust Symbolist opacity of the first books'. The theory then allows him to describe the sound-world of the poem – in a lush, expert, extended orchestral metaphor – and leave it at that, having evoked 'the purely literary resources of the medium itself'.

Turning to Section VI, 'Our Lady of Walsingham', we can see Heaney's strategy for dealing with Lowell's difficulty is identical to Hamilton's. 'Why this figure of the Virgin should enter the poem could be explained intellectually by contrasting her with the predatory, Calvinist, blood-spilling whalers.' So much for the intellect. Then we're back to intuition, to 'magic', in effect to blarney: 'poetically speaking, however, we sense its rightness as a matter of emotional effect, a result of its timing and placing.' In other words, Heaney hasn't a clue. As his perfunctory explication makes clear. In fact, the Virgin of Walsingham shares God's fathomless mystery – as if the myth of Christ, suffering crucifixion, being born in a manger, were the thinnest of fictions, the flimsiest attempt to humanise something fundamentally inhuman, non-human:

> ... There's no comeliness
> At all or charm in that expressionless
> Face with its heavy eyelids. As before,

This face, for centuries a memory,
Non est species, neque decor,
Expressionless, expresses God: it goes
Past castled Sion. She knows what God knows,
Not Calvary's Cross nor crib at Bethlehem
Now, and the world shall come to Walsingham.

Of course, a great proportion of 'The Quaker Graveyard' *is* only loosely in touch with sense. True, the poem flaunts the body language of the grand style. It is all swagger and majesty from the first line – which doesn't make sense. 'A brackish reach of shoal off Madaket' sounds authoritative, nautical, like something out of the ship's log, as if the Ancient Mariner were giving technical evidence to a court martial. But it's a fraud. In these waters the North Atlantic Fleet fishes out the body of a drowned sailor. What is the North Atlantic Fleet doing in shallow waters, the 'shoal' of the line? If the North Atlantic Fleet is at sea, then surely the adjective 'brackish', meaning 'salty', is redundant?

Now visualise a seagull. 'Sea-gulls blink their heavy lids / Seaward.' Conceivably Lowell wants to assimilate the seagulls to Our Lady of Walsingham, but he does so at the cost of violating ornithological reality. Why not lashings of mascara while we're about it?

Section II opens thus: 'Whenever winds are moving and their breath / Heaves at the roped-in bulwarks of this pier, / The terns and sea-gulls tremble at your death / In these home waters.' Manifestly we are in the hyperbolic world of the pastoral, where all of nature commonly mourns the dead person – who is the pretext for an extended poetic fiction. Anthony Hecht pointed out that, in its earliest version, 'The Quaker Graveyard at Nantucket' had exactly the same number of lines as 'Lycidas'. No point, therefore, in appeals to strict empirical reality. But it is one thing to assert, in the pastoral tradition, that the sea-birds 'tremble' at Warren Winslow's death. It is quite another to suggest this only happens 'whenever winds are moving'. If you're going to have universal mourning then have universal mourning – and don't restrict it to months with an *r* in them, or in this case to periods when it is windy. Drop 'whenever', the specious syntactical link between these three lines.

It isn't, I think, that Lowell couldn't be bothered. Or didn't know what he was doing. He was neither careless nor incompetent, though he could often seem both. Take the second paragraph of 'The Mills of the Kavanaughs': it is a single, sixteen-line, rambling, rhyme-led sentence containing eleven clauses. It is hard to believe a fifth-rate poet could write *so* badly, let alone a serious poet. As exposition it is a complete failure – like watching an escapologist tie himself up yet more tightly in yet more knots.

I hesitate to quote. I want you to finish this review, rather than get lost in Lowell's maze of inelegance till the steam comes out of your ears. Here it is, though, with the clauses numbered:

> Our people had kept up their herring weirs,
> Their rum and logging grants two hundred years,
> [2] When Cousin Franklin Pierce was President –
> [3] Almost three hundred, Harry, when you sent
> His signed engraving sailing on your kite
> Above the gable, [4] where your mother's light,
> [5] A daylight bulb with tortoise talons, [4 continued] pipped
> The bull-mad june-bugs on the manuscript
> [6] That she was typing to redeem our mills
> From Harding's taxes, [7] and we lost our means
> Of drawing pulp and water from those hills
> Above the Saco, [8] where our tenants drilled
> Abnaki partisans for Charles the First,
> [9] And seated our Republicans, [10] while Hearst
> And yellow paper fed the moose [11] that swilled
> Our spawning ponds for weeds like spinach greens.

Despite every indication, this is not straightforwardly incompetent. This was written for a literary culture which prized and praised difficulty. Obscurity, impenetrability, was a guarantee of ambiguity. Lowell was rewarded – with Pulitzer prizes, with rave reviews – for writing like this. 'Like this' meant knowing that he shouldn't quite know how he was doing it. Not incompetence, then, but anti-competence.

All Lowell's early bad writing is of its time. As well as ambiguity, weightiness was required of poets. Poetry in this period was on steroids. Like Will Carling, the ex-English rugby captain, poetry was so muscle-bound it couldn't manage anything simple like crossing its legs. This is Lowell's 'In Memory of Arthur Winslow', who died from cancer:

> This Easter, Arthur Winslow, less than dead,
> Your people set you up in Phillips' House
> To settle off your wrestling with the crab –
> The claws drop flesh upon your yachting blouse
> Until longshoreman Charon come and stab
> Through your adjusted bed
> And crush the crab.

Only one word of this primped and gussied 'classical' opening isn't bogus – that *adjusted* bed. The rest is period, period.

This was a time – hard to believe now – in which religious belief was intellectually chic. Think of Eliot, Auden, Evelyn Waugh, Graham Greene, Charles Williams. Lowell's early beliefs initially seem fashionable features of the period, too – Catholic with undertones of Calvinist Klein. And, of course, Lowell had shed them smartly enough by 1948, having converted in 1940–41. But the preoccupations remain – and animate, for instance, 'Waking Early Sunday Morning', the opening poem of *Near the Ocean*. This is a poem about an atheist's longing for transcendence – in a world where the Church is suddenly bereft of majesty and power, where Jehovah no longer survives the rainbow of His will:

> When will we see Him face to face?
> Each day, He shines through darker glass.
> In this small town where everything
> is known, I see His vanishing
> emblems, His white spire and flag-
> pole sticking out above the fog,
> like old white china doorknobs, sad,
> slight, useless things to calm the mad.

It is surprising to see Ian Hamilton describing 'Waking Early Sunday Morning' as 'a key "political poem" of the 1960s'. It is *Sunday* morning, after all, and Lowell consistently deplores the lite religion on offer – 'the new electric bells', the 'Bible chopped and crucified'. Whereas, in the old days, when Jehovah smote Philistia, it stayed smitten:

> Hammering military splendor,
> top-heavy Goliath in full armor –
> little redemption in the mass
> liquidations of their brass,
> elephant and phalanx moving
> with the times and still improving,
> when that kingdom hit the crash:
> a million foreskins stacked like trash ...

Even here, however, we see Lowell's besetting fault. The last line couldn't be clearer – or more memorable. But what precedes it is impressive, ungainly and unfocused. That 'hammering' – what is its grammatical status? Is Jehovah to be understood as the subject of the verb? Or the military splendour 'hammering' itself – noisy, clangorous? Look at the phrase 'little redemption'. What does it mean? It means – in its impacted way – that this isn't the God of the New Testament, redeeming sinners; this is the Old Testament Yahweh blowing away the uncircumcised goyim.

Hamilton's reading is idle and perfunctory, as well as wrong. But it isn't *entirely* his fault because 'Waking Early Sunday Morning' begins with two misguided metaphors – full of sound and fury and signifying opposites. Lowell's image for untrammelled transcendence, for *escaping* the confining physical element – for spiritual *freedom*, for 'breaking loose' – is the chinook salmon leaping out of the water. But Lowell actually describes the salmon going against the current of the waterfall – with pain and enormous difficulty. It doesn't seem a desirable condition to be 'raw-jawed', 'weak-fleshed' and exhausted. Nor does the idea of transcendent spirituality seem well served by the image of the salmon managing to fit in a fuck before it dies: 'alive enough to spawn and die'. The same stricture applies to the second stanza, where Lowell's joy is compared to the joy of a trout 'smashing a dry fly': 'no rainbow smashing a dry fly / in the white run is free as I'. But if the trout has taken the dry fly, it has also taken the hook and is no longer free, whatever its initial exuberance.

I am equally puzzled by these lines in Stanza 6: 'O that the spirit could remain / tinged but untarnished by its strain!' Might these lines be a reference to Lowell's recurring mania? Being out of your mind is, of course, a form of transcendence. In other words, Lowell would like to retain a smidgeon of the exaltation that comes with madness, without the other negative symptoms.

Present the reader with enough of these difficulties and Stanza 12's reference to the President skinny-dipping with his staff might look, in its clarity, like the poem's telos. And it becomes a key political poem of the 1960s.

The nostalgic religious theme is present, too, in 'Beyond the Alps' – another notoriously difficult poem. It exists in several inspissated versions and was worked over by Lowell without achieving even the rudiments of clarity. In general terms, 'Beyond the Alps' is an expression of Lowell's nostalgia for religious mystery. 'Much against my will, / I left the City of God where it belongs': Lowell was writing two years after ceasing to be a Catholic. But this doesn't rule out a fierce nostalgia for religious mystery: 'Much against my will ...' The ungraspable, the papal dogma of Mary's Assumption, still exerts a mesmeric pull: 'The lights of science couldn't hold a candle / to Mary risen – at one miraculous stroke, / angel-wing'd, gorgeous as a jungle bird!'

And Lowell is similarly attracted by untamed nature. On the one hand, a pullman crosses the Alps, with stewards banging their gongs. On the other hand, Everest remains gratifyingly unconquered.

Enter ambiguity.

Lowell is also attracted to the cultivated complacency of the rich Victorian tourists who simply 'accepted the universe'. The voice of religious nostalgia coexists with the voice of the rationalist and apostate, the iconoclast who identifies with all the other critics of Rome: Lucan, Juvenal, Tacitus, Ovid.

Thesis: religious nostalgia. Anti-thesis: rationalism. Synthesis?

Once, in the case of Minerva, Goddess of Wisdom, the miraculous and the rational were unified. But 'There are no tickets for that altitude' – unlike the pullman crossing the Alps. It is a myth.

But so is the idea of the perfected *polis*. The final couplet – 'perfect and impenetrable', according to Ian Hamilton – is perhaps Lowell's comment on the durability of any civilisation: 'Now Paris, our black classic, breaking up / like killer kings on an Etruscan cup.' We may think of Paris as an enduring classic, but it is as fragile as the painted clay representing a lost civilisation.

'Beyond the Alps' is, as it were, the last of early Lowell. With Part Four, 'Life Studies', Lowell suddenly, temporarily, sheds complication. And it is here that his reputation rests – as an achievement in itself and as a seminal example for subsequent writers. In *Four Quartets*, Eliot writes of simplicity as a condition 'costing nothing less than everything'. What simplicity cost Lowell can be gauged by the prose section of *Life Studies*, '91 Revere Street'. It wasn't easy. He had made up his mind – and now he had to unmake his habits of thought, his tic of creative, suggestive disorder. And he couldn't quite.

Lowell credited the influence of prose – 'in prose you have to be interested in *what* is being said' – with the transfiguration of his poetic style. And the prose in *Life Studies* is justly celebrated, though not often accurately described. It operates out of a characteristic confusion, a pell-mell Whitmanian, Bellovian response to memory. 'First to knock, first admitted,' as Augie March says. This is Ledyard Atkinson's much younger wife: 'She was a radiant Christian scientist, darted about in smart serge suits and blouses frothing with lace.' The second half of this sentence has little or nothing to do with the first half. The passage continues about Christian Science.

More radically disjunct is this sentence about her husband, which begins with Ledyard's personal appearance, moves on to his predilection for social grandeur, and concludes with a mini-inventory of his cabin: 'Serene, silver-maned, and Spanish-looking, Cousin Ledyard liked full-dress receptions and crowed like a rooster in his cabin crowded with liveried Filipinos, Cuban trophies, and racks of experimental firearms, such as pepper-box pistols and a machine gun worked by electric batteries.' Vivid and detailed, fascinating but faintly manic in its disarray.

Sometimes whole paragraphs arrive with a pastiche of organisation. This is about Lowell's Aunt Sarah, the failed pianist. The paragraph is built around two ideas – beauty and luxury – but it doesn't actually make sense:

> Mother's comfort was chic, romantic, impulsive. If her silver service shone, it shone with hectic perfection to rebuke the functional domesticity of naval wives. She had determined to make her *ambiance* beautiful and luxurious, but wanted neither her beauty nor her luxury unaccompanied. Beauty pursued too exclusively meant artistic fatuity of a kind made farcical by her Aunt Sarah Stark Winslow, a beauty too lofty and original ever to marry, a *prima donna* on the piano, too high strung ever to give a public recital. Beauty alone meant the maudlin ignominy of having one's investments managed by interfering relatives. Luxury alone, on the other hand, meant for Mother the 'paste and fool's-gold polish' that one met with in the foyer of the new Statler Hotel.

Though prose, this is no easier to follow than that eleven-clause second paragraph of 'The Mills of the Kavanaughs'.

And throughout '91 Revere Street' there are little local enigmas – enigmas often overlooked in the gossipy excitement of reading Lowell's prose memoir, but which are strangely reminiscent of similar off-key enigmas in 'The Mills of the Kavanaughs'. For example, compare the '*lethal* ferns' of the Burckhard 'hall-drawing room' in '91 Revere Street' with the '*callow* pollen' in 'The Mills of the Kavanaughs' (my italics).

Sometimes one can discern Lowell's wonky logic, as when Mrs Atkinson is wittily credited with 'the memory of a mastodon' – even longer therefore than the proverbial elephant. More often, not. What is one to make of the young Lowell's reaction to the diminished charisma of Elie Norton once she has peed herself in class, 'seldom meeting her eyes now, I felt rich and raw in her nearness'? What does this mean? Lowell's account of his emotions hereabouts begins to flounder. He has already confessed to feeling 'manic with superiority', which is logical, if cruel. Why, then, does he experience *in himself* 'something caved in, something crippled in the way I stood up to her'? Is this related to the utterly baffling emotion he records as existing in tandem with his manic superiority, 'a feeling of goaded hollowness'? Now how would *that* feel? It seems precise but is in fact approximate at best. Rather like the accent of Eric Burckhard – 'an enthusiastic Mont Blanc chirp' – where Mont Blanc seems to be standing in for Switzerdeutsch, or a general German quality. A few sentences later, Lowell is more precise: 'child and nurse spoke no English but only a guttural, British-sounding, Swiss German.' This helps – except that 'British-sounding' *doesn't*, any more than 'French-sounding' would have helped.

Mrs Burckhard, Eric's mother, is given 'dramatic, dulling blonde braids'.

The contradiction here, between dramatic and dull, can be resolved. The young Lowell has never seen Brünnhilde braids before, so they are 'dramatic'. They are also 'dulling' because they are modulating to grey. Here, the New Critical reflex – to seize even the shadow of ambiguity – is clear.

Sometimes, though, there seems to be no reason beyond a manic exuberance. This is Lowell comparing a Tibetan screen to a water buffalo: 'Colonel Myers' monumental Tibetan screen had been impiously shortened to fit it for a low Yankee ceiling. And now, rough and gawky, like some Hindu water buffalo killed in mid-rush but still alive with mad momentum, the screen hulked over us ... and hid the pantry sink.' Conceivably, the screen depicts a Hindu water buffalo, but that is not what Lowell says – and the delicious bathos of his comic conclusion only just manages to mask his strenuous but implausible conceit. Somehow, he's taken his reader into a Looking Glass world of nonsense. Why is a screen like a water buffalo? Why is a raven like a writing desk? There's no answer to that.

'Skunk Hour' is probably the most celebrated of Lowell's poems. 'For the Union Dead' is a rival – a great poem which lucidly contrasts the idealistic self-sacrifice of Colonel Shaw, dying for a cause, with the base instinct for self-preservation embodied in the indestructible Mosler Safe – Lowell's symbol of materialism, of capitalism. 'For the Union Dead' is not in the least harmed by its clarity. 'Skunk Hour' is another lucid poem, as it happens, but one which has been almost 'explicated' out of existence. Lowell has contributed his own misleading commentary. You might think that 'Skunk Hour', on the face of it, was likely to be the opposite of Happy Hour. After all, 'I hear my ill-spirit sob[s] in each blood cell.' Nevertheless, in the interests of New Critical ambiguity, Lowell tells one correspondent in 1958 that the skunks are a 'healthy, joyful apparition'.

Pull the other one.

And of course Lowell does. By 1962, his corrective gloss itself needs correction – or the required ambiguity will evaporate. He tells Berryman: 'Most people take the skunks as cheerful [but] they are horrible blind energy, *at the same time* ... a wish and a fear of annihilation' (my italics).

Among the ploys, that last phrase happens to be true. 'Skunk Hour' is organised around the theme of effacement. It looks desultory, perhaps, as it rambles from subject to subject, from person to person, before focusing on Lowell himself and his encounter with the skunks. However, the 'hermit heiress', the 'summer millionaire' and 'our fairy decorator' share degrees of invisibility – they are hidden, disappeared, or about to disappear. When Lowell confronts the mother skunk, it is as if he too is invisible. She 'will not scare'. 'Skunk Hour' is a poem about madness – 'My mind's not right' – but Lowell is also playing with the colloquialism of not being all there. It is an idea already touched on in

'Waking in the Blue': 'Absence! My heart grows tense ...'

'Skunk Hour' is celebrated partly because it is sensational. It is as confessional as anything Anne Sexton ever wrote. Here we have the poet as Peeping Tom: 'I watched for love-cars.' But its opening is pedestrian and plagued with arbitrary line-breaks before it suddenly takes a leap into full-blooded melodrama and a misjudged allusion to the Satan of *Paradise Lost*: 'I myself am hell.' Every thing depends on the skunks. And the skunks are marching up Elm Street, not Main Street, with Freddie Kruger eyes: 'white stripes, moonstruck eyes' red fire'. The skunks are a failure.

In my inventory of writers influenced by Lowell, I omitted to mention myself. Two of my published poems, 'The Onion, Memory' and 'Gethsemane', are indebted to Lowell. 'Gethsemane' is specifically in hock to 'Skunk Hour'. Many more early unpublished poems were even more indebted.

What was so difficult to resist then seems uncompelling now.

But as I search for some clinching phrase to express this undeceived conclusion, I find myself finding it in Lowell's own lines: 'The erotic terror / of her helpless, big bosomed body / lay like slop.'

This unforgiving, unforgettable phrase – and other phrases just as memorable – explains why so many writers were once so infatuated with Robert Lowell.

Lowell's Letters
(2005)

Perfection of the life or art? In Robert Lowell's *Notebook* (1970), we read in 'The Literary Life, a Scrapbook': 'Who wouldn't rather be his indexed correspondents / than the boy Keats spitting out blood for time to breathe?' Three years later, in *History* (1973), this has been reconsidered, revised and inverted: 'Who would rather be his indexed correspondents / than the boy Keats spitting out blood for time to breathe?' No surprise.

The change turns on the relative weighting of literary fame and longevity. On reflection, Lowell chooses literary achievement. His highly developed sense of vocation is apparent from the early pages of these letters. The first is to Ezra Pound, offering himself as disciple–pupil: 'Your *Cantos* have re-created what I have imagined to be the blood of Homer. Again I ask you to have me [as an apprentice].' Not long after, the emulative Lowell responds with reservations to Pound's (understandable) reserve: 'Your *Cantos* practically ignore hard narrative and motion', 'Can the main current of English literature float such a vast quantity of spondées and compound nouns?' After pausing to praise the skill of Eliot's 'Ariel' poems – but deplore their depleted vitality – the tyro Lowell vauntingly concludes: 'I would like to bring back momentum and movement in poetry on a grand scale, to master your tremendous machinery and *to carry your standard further into the century*' (my italics). If Pound experienced a frisson of obsolescence, who could blame him? As late as 1948, the 32-year-old Lowell is writing to Santayana: 'Chaucer and Homer are models of all that I would desire.' (Midgets need not apply.) And to Elizabeth Bishop (2 July 1948) he admits: 'sometimes nothing is so solid to me as writing – I suppose that's what vocation means.' In 1957, the 40-year-old Lowell reiterates: 'I've never thought there was any choice for me about writing poetry.'

In Lowell's case, though, the comparison with Keats isn't a perfect fit. The trouble is the implied unbridgeable distance between top-honcho Keats and his lowly, undistinguished correspondents, herded in the ghetto of the index. Not true of Lowell's index. Elizabeth Bishop is a much better poet and letter-writer. Larkin's letters are funnier: he inscribes *High Windows*, 'From a Drought to a Deluge'. Hughes's letters more original and energetic. Pound's quirkier.

Lowell corresponds with all four, though most extensively, candidly and

---

The Letters of Robert Lowell, edited by Saskia Hamilton (Faber and Faber, 2005).

unguardedly with Elizabeth Bishop. Their relationship is intimate and mutually supportive – until, right at the end of his short life, suddenly Lowell's patience is, if not exhausted, certainly chafed: 'Elizabeth Bishop is about to visit here for two days,' he writes to his ex-wife Elizabeth Hardwick (8 June 1976),

> an informal visit but not one to take lightly. The dog must be sent away because of her asthma but will that be enough? Half our chairs are tainted with dog hairs. Then so many things she can criticize, the disheveled garden, the carefree garden man, our care of Sheridan [Lowell's small son]. Should he be sent away too? So many things down to [i.e. including] my not writing meter, making errors in description. Of course no one is more wonderful, but so fussy and hazardous now. Her set subject in person and letters is scolding with affectionate fury over Frank Bidart (whom she half depends on) a safe thing though grating.'

Keats, by general consent, is the great poetic letter-writer. This is Eliot in *The Use of Poetry and the Use of Criticism*: 'The Letters are certainly the most notable and the most important ever written by any English poet … There is hardly one statement of Keats about poetry, which, when considered carefully and with due allowance for the difficulties of communication, will not be found to be true; and what is more, true for greater and more mature poetry than anything that Keats ever wrote.' And this is Robert Lowell self-deprecatingly writing to Elizabeth Bishop (7 April 1959): 'Keats – I read the letters fall [in the autumn] a year ago. Better than anything except Laforgue's. I think his bold opinions on his friends impressed me more than anything. I wouldn't be that mature, if I lived to ninety, and memorised Montaigne and had hallucinations that I was Santayana.' After reading this volume's 852 pages you have to agree. Even though 852 pages is only a sliver. For example, there are only eighteen letters here for 1963. The average chosen for 1936 to 1977 is seventeen a year. Even on this selective basis, Lowell isn't a great letter-writer and these letters are only mildly absorbing. It is possible, though, to make a selection of the selection that is entertaining but a subtle misrepresentation of the duller truth.

There are marvellous phrases, of course: African masks are 'all grass and grimace'. Lowell is always good with his daughter Harriet. At her birth, he writes: 'Five minutes old, little H looked strangely like both her parents and like you [Harriet Winslow, Lowell's cousin] but also more like Dylan Thomas than say, Audrey Hepburn. Staring with glossy, bulging little eyes, she is withering with contempt some importunate bystander trying to make conversation by asking her if she accepts the universe.' This is the daughter of intellectuals, a prodigy, whose first words Lowell imagines will be '*Partisan Review*'.

Famous for taking himself seriously – the man who, according to Berry-man, was not amused by Randall Jarrell's improvised parodies of Lowell poetic effects – he emerges here as a winning self-ironist. When his play *The Old Glory* is performed, it takes three and a half hours, 'plus a stupefying hour and a quarter dinner break', after which 'the chief actor looked out into the audience with his captain's telescope and saw five people snoring. I had to squirm and shift horrifyingly like an arterial-sclerotic to stay awake.' He repeats this charming, self-deprecatory riff in another letter. His musical knowledge comes in for a certain amount of ribbing, too: 'I have been listening furiously to music from Gesualdo to Webern and have even, like Bouvard and Pécuchet, absorbed ter-minology. I drive Elizabeth almost livid and speechless now by suddenly saying, "isn't that an augmented canon in cancrizans reversed?"' This to Natasha Spender in 1956, a comic routine elaborated from a letter of 24 April 1952 to Elizabeth Bishop: 'I know all about the sonata form (a misnomer according to Tovey) canons, and modulations, but have difficulty distinguishing them when heard, and have so far failed to convince the cynical and skeptical Eliz. H. Lowell that I am not tone-deaf.'

The main charm of this correspondence is hinted at in Lowell's admiration for Keats's 'bold opinions on his friends'. Gossip, anecdote and affectionately malicious epitome intermittently animate this correspondence. In a letter to Peter Taylor (3 April 1948), reporting a visit to Ezra Pound in St Elizabeth's, Lowell touches on this propensity: 'Pound: "I must give a vignette. Lowell likes anecdotes some of the time." Randall: "What do you mean *some* of the time?"' When he's reading Bertrand Russell's *History of Western Philosophy*, he tells San-tayana (10 March 1952) it is pleasingly anecdotal: 'It's delightful just as a series of opinions, character sketches etc.' Writing to Blair Clark (21 March 1954), Lowell capitalises on this preference: 'I have found a line of talking in anecdotes that both my Cincinnati audience and I can follow.' Sometimes we are treated to a tiny flash of unexpected exuberance: when T. S. Eliot dances with his new bride, 'they danced so dashingly at the Charles River boatclub brawl that he was called "Elbows Eliot".' Or another flash of Terpsichorean eccentricity: 'An evening with Dwight Macdonald during which he was more than usual genial – we'd said goodbye to Macdonald and separated about ten feet when Randall began doing gigantic ballet leaps in the air and giggling.' Though Lowell doesn't say so, we can assume drink plays its part in Jarrell's jumps. After all, Lowell can imagine no one telling off either the severe Jarrell or the equally severe Mary McCarthy – as he confesses to Elizabeth Bishop (24 April 1952).

A good deal of alcohol is consumed in the course of these letters. This is Dylan Thomas drinking (30 March 1950): 'Somehow he was kept on beer most of the time, but he'd begin at 7 in the morning and end at 12 – no meals except breakfast. About the best and dirtiest stories I've ever heard – dumpy, absurd body, hair combed by a salad spoon, brown-button Welsh eyes always moving suspiciously or fixing on the most modest person in the room ... a great explosion of life, and hell to handle.' Allen Tate is often intoxicated in these letters: 'Incredible dinner at the Eberharts with the Tates, Madame Perkins, K. A. Porter, Auden, Ted Spencer's sister and Betty Eberhart's German cousin. Allen very tight gave two identical very formal toasts to the memory of Ted Spencer, and Auden helpfully took out all our plates, still unfinished, to the pantry, and Katherine Anne announced she was seventy.'

Age brings out the best in Lowell. This to Elizabeth Bishop (3 April 1964):

The old get older, I've seen Marianne Moore a couple of times, once introducing Auden very wittily calling him a 'fantast who was also a sage', and ending with a humorous quote from Auden that all ills of the body were ills of the soul, and 'I give you Mr Auden'. Then later at a small poets party for Vernon Watkins, where for all her fragility she stayed with us 7 hours talking. Her baseball is way over my head. So is John Ransome's aesthetics and philosophy. He came here for the National Book Award with his post box key instead of his suitcase key, no money except his ticket, and hardly knew his hotel, yet talked with fascinating merry complexity on Kant, Valéry and Stevens. Eliot too is apparently very weak and old and fearful to be far from his wife, yet sang me a humorous song called Mr Caruso on the phone.

He notices what people are wearing, too: (24 October 1956) 'Marianne Moore was sprawled like some Boucher goddess in a print dress and black cartwheel hat on the huge marble disc of the huge marble bannister.' Allen Tate's deliberate wardrobe is invoked with inflections of satire: 'Allen Tate, who arrived at our house for the occasion [an e e cummings reading] dressed in a very pale, very delicately made khaki coat, a khaki hat with a plaid hat-band, loafers that shone like armour in a Rembrandt painting'. Nonentities are vividly boring: '["Piggy" Warburg's] voice was terrible in the little space and made one feel as though it were an airplane descending forever from a great altitude.' In 1948, Lowell takes a Mrs Longworth to see Pound at St Elizabeth's: 'she chattered for half an hour about everything under the sun ending with a synopsis of two 1880 novels she'd read as a girl. Pound (restless, silent, but not motionless misery) "You like reading more than I do".'

Pound is a recurrent focus. One particularly revealing letter (10 February 1963) is a shorthand report of Lowell's meeting with his daughter, Mary de Rachewiltz, after Pound's death. She reports her transition from disciple to daughter and the steady eclipse of awe [Lowell's ellipses]: 'Until six years ago I never questioned one of his thoughts ... Of course I wasn't prepared to be impressed by T. S. Eliot ... When he came back [to Italy after his release from St Elizabeth's], we didn't know that even he couldn't do anything ... two years of sitting hardly raising an arm and thinking all his contemporaries' careers had gone better than his ... stopped me from translating the *Cantos*, saying they were no good. Do people in such a state really feel the terrible things they say? ... at first it was *Cantos* at every meal.' Six statements that take us to the heart of Pound's depression and his final silence – which has less to do with remorse for his anti-Semitism and more to do with regret for his blighted career; coming last to Eliot and Joyce, as he saw it, rather than culpability and penance.

Lowell understood the element of competition in the arts and referred to it openly. On 10 July 1963, he writes to Roethke: 'I remember Edwin Muir arguing with me that there is no rivalry in poetry. Well, there is.' Writing to Jerome Mazzaro (26 May 1969), he sounds like Hemingway getting on the gloves to spar with Shakespeare: 'A graver matter is the competition, the boxing match. Without it, I think we miss some of the pleasure of writing: part of it is rather like a tennis match. Who would play without scoring?' Elizabeth Bishop would be my answer. Art is the spur, art for the art's sake, not fame. But perhaps not for Lowell, or, finally, poignantly, for Pound – Pound the great enabler, selfless midwife not only to *The Waste Land*, but 'Whispers of Immortality' and of *Ulysses*, suddenly succumbing to self-doubt and the poison of the market-place.

For such an openly emulous writer, however, Lowell was a notably generous mentor, assiduously pushing his friends, fuelled by genuine admiration. He recommends Elizabeth Bishop and Randall Jarrell to the anthologist Louis Untermeyer. To F. S. Flint in 1948, he advises that 'E. Bishop is genuine ... a touch-stone, except for Jarrell, her contemporaries seem pretentious, faked, empty etc. Randall has a better mind than I have.' This dual recommendation is repeated to Santayana on 20 May 1948 as 'the best new poets in my judgment'. And, again, to Eliot, 18 January 1949: 'Wish Eliot the Poet and Eliot the Editor would take a look at Jarrell and Bishop (Elizabeth).' It may be more significant, oddly enough, that he tells Bishop (8 December 1947) that Jarrell 'has written a wonderful poem on the death of a colored child'. He recommends John Berryman to Paul Engle at Iowa for a post he, Lowell, cannot take up: 'He is a wonderful person, a good poet and probably fifty times as good a teacher as I would have been.' All the same, we can see Lowell succumb to a calculus of competition when Berryman gets going on the *Dream Songs* and becomes a serious rival. *Notebook* is an act of supplanting and rivalry. Lowell wants to engross the quotidian, to soar from the minuscule to the majestic in the manner of Berryman. (And in the manner of Philip Larkin, another poet for whom Lowell has nothing but praise – an admiration unreciprocated by Larkin, who takes a swipe at *Lord Weary's Castle* in a letter to Robert Conquest: 'old R. L. who's never looked like being a single iota of good in all his born days. Lord Hairy's Arsehole. Gibber gibber.') For most of the time, Berryman wasn't a threat. There is a quietly terrible letter to Elizabeth Bishop (14 April 1962) that seems complacent and culpably unaware of the contrast between Berryman's straitened circumstances and his own good fortune, mingling with Mrs Mellon, Jackie Kennedy, Bobby Kennedy, Robert McNamara et al. First there is Berryman: 'utterly spooky, teaching brilliant classes, spending week-ends in the sanitarium [*sic*]. Drinking, seedy a little bald, often drunk, married to a girl of twenty-one from a Catholic parochial college, white, innocent beyond belief, just pregnant. They live in two rooms – in one Kate is asleep, getting through the first child pains, in the other, a thousand books, and John going into the 7th year on a long poem that fills a suitcase and is all spoken by John, first son (seven) from his second marriage. The poem is spooky, a maddening work of genius, or half genius, in John's later obscure, tortured, wandering style, full of parentheses, slang no one ever spoke, jagged haunting lyrical moments etc.'

The mistake here about the narration / narrator is like the mistake (later corrected) about Mr Bones in Lowell's *New York Review of Books* essay on the *Dream Songs*. Lowell unaccountably thought Mr Bones was another character addressing the 'hero' Henry, whereas Mr Bones *is* Henry, the name being a *memento mori* (a phrase consistently misspelled throughout these letters as *momento mori*, even though Lowell was a Latinist). Lowell also manages to call Henry 'Harry' in one of these letters (19 September 1959) – an index of indifference, not just carelessness.

After an interval of this and that, Lowell's letter forgets Berryman's two rooms: 'Where am I? ... Oh the White House – we are going there to dinner sometime next month to meet Malraux; Edmund [Wilson] and Allen [Tate] are going and I suppose legions of others. Only black tie, not white.' One doesn't want to be stonily censorious. Who, after all, wouldn't be pleased with themselves at such an invitation? And Lowell is doing his best to play it down – cast of thousands, only black tie ... Nevertheless, one is gratified by Lowell's perturbation some six years later (22 September 1968) when he is compelled to a little poetic accountancy by Berryman's unaccountable if brief success. The measuring tape is out:

> I'm dumbfounded at how many of the same things we have: rough iambic lines, often pentameter (for me mostly), short sections that are not stanzas; wife, wives, child, old flames, new ones, sex, love, loves, portraits of writers (I have Frost, Jarrell and Williams too), landscape (I have more of

this) portraits of the dead, full middle age, humor, death etc. Well, you have a hundred things I don't: rhymes, Henry, more jokes, Delmore [Delmore Schwartz, a want soon to be remedied], Ireland; and you must be the best Irish poet since Yeats [a joke Lowell was to recycle seriously for Seamus Heaney in 1974]. What I like is your ease in getting out everything – I mean everything in your experience, learning, thought, personality etc. mills thru the poetry.'

Notebook and its subtle, allowable larceny – or attempted annexation – follows from this, as much as from the prior impulse behind *Life Studies*, of which Lowell said (13 March 1960): 'they are meant to give a sort of notebook effect, an impression of truth and fragmentary naturalness.' As does the fatally diluted verbal texture of *The Dolphin*, where the music of what happens has some of the thin, unformed, aleatoric quality of Luciano Berio's 'quotations' from unmusical reality. The quoted letters of Lizzie Hardwick, a moral *cause célèbre* at the time, now read as artless, flaccid happenstance rather than poetry. They are letters, not literature. That is the crucial, fatal difference. The morality of quoting private material, doctored or semi-verbatim, now seems beside the point. Of course, Lowell had the example of William Carlos Williams's *Paterson*. In fact, there is a letter here attempting to mollify Marcia Nardi, whose letters were used by Williams without her permission. More, Lowell encouraged Lizzie Hardwick (30 January 1965) to 'write anything you want. I want to see out of curiosity, but won't censor.' Years before, however, in 1944, he asked Eberhart not to publish his play *The Crystal Sepulcher*, in which Lowell featured, unflatteringly and only lightly disguised: 'it is personal with a vengeance, in about a thousand details. It will be recognized by everyone and, of course, I am not crazy about that kind of free advertising ... So far as I'm concerned don't print it.' Twenty-nine years later, in 1973, he felt differently. In the interval, he had written *Life Studies* and braved the disapproval of those disturbed and discomfited by the nakedness alluded to in the volume's title.

Saskia Hamilton's introduction attempts to conflate poetry and the letter, to collapse the two categories. There is a single sentence she analyses cleverly, subtly, nimbly, as if it were poetry: 'Still one has to grunt and sweat a bit to get the talk going.' The stillness at the sentence's beginning is contrasted with the motion at the sentence's end. The under-echo of *Hamlet* – 'To grunt and sweat under a weary life' – is noted. One is momentarily impressed. Thereafter, though, the letters resist this fancification and falsification. There is one moment in this volume when Lowell notices that his paragraph begins and ends with the same word – 'anyway'. Otherwise, all is spontaneity and artlessness, the words Lowell chooses to characterise the letter, in a letter (10 April 1959) to Allen

Ginsberg: 'I think letters ought to be written the way you think poetry ought to be. So let this be breezy, brief, incomplete, but spontaneous and not dishonestly holding back.' Manifestly, Lowell doesn't think much of Beat poetry – 'They are phony in [a] way because they have made a lot of publicity out of very little talent'; 'reciting so-so verse'; 'they are fairly easy to listen to.' It follows logically, therefore, that Lowell doesn't think much of this method of writing poetry – where it is 'incomplete, but spontaneous'.

Except, of course, that in *The Dolphin* letters are incorporated wholesale. With fatal consequences for the poetry, I would argue. But the whole volume is under-powered, largely because Lowell feels the intrinsic force of his subject as irrefutable – a man in love with two women. Its autobiographical importance is so clear to him that he feels no need to *write* it. A poem like 'Volverán' in *Notebook*, on the other hand, based on the Spanish original of Gustavo Adolfo Bécquer, is rapt in the toils of its passionate repetition. It risks *writing*:

> Dark swallows will doubtless come back killing
> the injudicious nightflies with a clack of the beak;
> but these that stopped full flight to see your beauty
> and my good fortune … as if they knew our names –
> they'll not come back. The thick lemony honeysuckle,
> climbing from the earthroot to your window,
> will open more beautiful blossoms to the evening;
> but these … like dewdrops, trembling, shining, falling,
> the tears of the day – they'll not come back …
> Some other love will sound his fireword for you
> and wake your heart, perhaps, from its cool sleep;
> but silent, absorbed, and on his knees,
> as men adore God at the altar, as I love you –
> don't blind yourself, you'll not be loved like that.

> [I'm quoting the revise, 'Will Not Come Back', from *History*
> because it is clearer.]

The hyperbole, the passion coexists with the unsentimental possibility (denied) of replacement, of subsequent love. But the passion is there in the insistent repetition – and the single, carefully chosen, counter-intuitive, unexpected, un-clichéd, quietly brilliant word, *absorbed*. Nothing in *The Dolphin* approaches this conviction.

Can the two categories be legitimately collapsed into each other? Before *The Dolphin*, in *Notebook*, we have a measure to judge between prose and poetic versions because several of the poems about writers there reproduce material in these letters and in prose essays. What is the difference? Where, if anywhere, is the poetic art? What distinguishes the poems from their prose counterparts? In some cases, it is the sense of closure. This is from the end of Lowell's prose reminiscence of Eliot: 'When I was about twenty-five, I met him for the second time. Behind us, Harvard's Memorial Hall with its wasteful, irreplaceable Victorian architecture and scrolls of the Civil War dead. Before us, the rush-hour traffic. As we got stuck on the sidewalk, looking for an opening, Eliot out of a blue sky said, "Don't you loathe being compared with your relatives?" Pause, as I put the question to myself, groping for what I really felt, for what I should decently feel and what I should indecently feel. Eliot: "I do." Pause again, then the changed lifting voice of delight. "I was reading Poe's reviews the other day. He took up two of my family and wiped the floor with them." Pause, "I was delighted."'

It's good, well told. Five years later, however, the poem 'T. S. Eliot' is swifter, less stagily directed, more economical and comes with two eloquently paradoxical final lines:

> Caught between two streams of traffic, in the gloom
> of Memorial Hall and Harvard's war-dead ... And he:
> 'Don't you loathe to be compared to your relatives?
> I do. I've just found two of mine reviewed by Poe.
> He wiped the floor with them ... and I was delighted.'
> Then on with warden's pace across the Yard,
> talking of Pound, 'It's balls to say he only
> pretends to be like Ezra ... He's better though. This year
> he no longer wants to rebuild the Temple at Jerusalem.
> Yes, he's better. "You speak," he said, when he talked two hours.
> By then I had absolutely nothing to say.'
> Ah Tom, one muse, one music, had one the luck –
> lost in the dark night of the brilliant talkers,
> humor and honor from the everlasting dross!

The companion poem about Ezra Pound has its genesis in a letter to James Laughlin (31 August 1966):

The visit to Ezra was awesome and rather shattering, like meeting Oedipus – he said, 'I began with a swelled head and am ending with swelled feet'. And many other things, then long stretches of silence. He is very worried that he is using up Olga's money. He has a nobility I've never seen before, the nobility of someone, not a sinner, but who has gone far astray and learned at last too much. I told him he was one of the few men alive who had the courage to go through Purgatory. He answered, 'Didn't Frost say you'd say anything once?' I felt I was talking cant, when I tried to cheer him. No self-pity, but more knowledge of his fate than any man should have.

In an earlier letter (6 May 1966) to Olga Rudge, the purgatory trope is finessed: 'the only man alive who had lived through Purgatory, and come through white with a kind of honesty and humility'. It cut no ice with Olga Rudge. Stephen Spender: 'Olga Rudge was there and I told her the news of Robert's death. "The best thing that could have happened to him," she said, "after what he wrote about Ezra."' Saskia Hamilton's notes cite unpublished papers and Lowell's *Paris Review* interview. But Olga Rudge would not have had access to the former and the interview merely says that the *Pisan Cantos* is 'a very mixed book'. Lowell argues, too, that Pound's mad, odd beliefs 'were a tremendous gain to him; he'd be a very Parnassan [*sic*] poet without them.' Maybe Olga Rudge's quarrel was really with her rival Dorothy Pound – the mistress's loyalty competing with the wife's less absolute fidelity. Writing to J. F. Powers (1 December 1947), Lowell reported 'Mrs P took me to dinner and confessed that Ezra's economics bore her to death, but she has faith.' Even Pound's intimates, then, could waver. My guess is that Lowell's offence wasn't his mild scepticism about the Poundian agenda, but his *Notebook* poem 'Ezra Pound', which ends with the swelled feet *mot* and uses the purgatory idea. It begins unfortunately: 'Horizontal in a deckchair on the bleak ward, / some feeble-minded felon in pajamas, clawing / a Social Credit broadside from your table …' Olga Rudge probably thought that Lowell intended Pound in the description 'some feeble-minded felon in pajamas'. In the revise for *History*, Lowell is at pains to effect a separation: 'Horizontal on a deckchair in the ward / of the criminal mad … A man without shoestrings clawing / the Social Credit broadside from your table, you saying …' Too late to erase the perceived insult.

Actually, the original version is neat but essentially an act of reparation: in it, Pound is made to be generous to Eliot and repentant about the Jews. As a poem, it is interesting, anecdotal, but a mite doctored and sanitised – with a punch line rather than a final line. Lowell's comment on *Life Studies* applies here: 'a poem could stop, when its lifeline ended and didn't have to break its back to be a poem.' If, then, letters and poetry are here collapsed into each other, it isn't because the letter is literature, but because the poem is less than a poem, deliberately.

'To Allen Tate II' condenses material from a letter to Peter Taylor (13 January 1962). In the letter, Tate is 'fixed and transfixed by Bourbon', a phrase superior to anything in the poem – but unusable in public. The private prose material describing the encounter between Tate and Lowell's daughter Harriet is clearer and nastier. In the poem, the drinking is airbrushed away. The innuendo about Tate's philandering has also been edited out in the poem: Tate says that Harriet 'will be dear to me' when she is older and Lowell adds in brackets 'One had a feeling that she would be much more dear to him then.' The conclusion is not therefore that letters and poems are equally literature, but that the cosmetic poem isn't much good.

There are several excellent notes in this edition – for example, a good note on Lincoln Steffens (for page 260) and a definitive note (for page 247) on a 300-page play by an Englishman at the Harvard Summer School symposium on drama. However, this edition is seriously under-annotated. On the one hand, typos are noted. On the other hand, Aline Berlin, the wife of Isaiah Berlin, isn't identified in a letter to Lizzie Hardwick (31 May 1970). Enid Starkie is identified as an 'Irish literary scholar' rather than a Professor of French. Alger Hiss is mentioned twice, identified nowhere and excluded from the unreliable index, along with many other things. Vice-President Spiro Agnew isn't thought worthy of a note. When, at the height of his infatuation with Giovanna Madonia Erba, Lowell writes 'O my Giovana, my Giovana! I cannot live without thee!', Saskia Hamilton notes the misspelled name but not the allusion to Gluck's *Orfeo ed Euridice*. When Lowell writes to Elizabeth Bishop (10 April 1948) 'There are no bears, or cats or dogs among the roses at Mrs Dawson's, only a negress named Florence', we need to know that this is an allusion to Wallace Stevens's 'The Virgin Carrying a Lantern': 'There are no bears among the roses, / Only a negress who supposes …' We also need to know that Lizzie Hardwick's piece in the *New York Review of Books* on Mary McCarthy's novel *The Group* was a parody, not a review. The review was by Norman Mailer. At present, the note doesn't distinguish, but merely records Hardwick's pseudonym, Xavier Prynne, without explanation. For the letter on page 275, there are no notes. The letter includes this: 'William James once gave his classes this example of understatement: "Marlboro Street is hardly a passionate street".' Which should be cross-referenced to page 521, where Lowell writes: 'The man who said "hardly passionate" about Marlboro St. was either Henry or William James, but I don't know the source.' The reference to William James on page 275 isn't in the index.

The chronology tells us that Lowell had affairs with Gertrude Buckman and Carley Dawson, but the notes to the text are almost coy: Lowell writes to Carley Dawson, 'well, we shall hear Rubenstein' and the notes tell us 'Lowell soon started to attend concerts with her.' The letters themselves are more fulsome. I don't want to labour these deficiencies. Two last points. In my son's school edition of T. S. Eliot's *Selected Poems*, against the line 'To Carthage then I came', a scholiast had written 'reference to Carthage'. Many of these notes are like that marginalium. They refer but they do not illuminate. For example, Lowell mentions (5 January 1949) Stendhal's 'four kinds' of love. Saskia Hamilton's note refers us to 'Stendhal, *De L'Amour* (1822)'. This is like the note to Letter 268 to William Carlos Williams: '*Journey to Love*: Williams, *Journey to Love* (1955)'.

Why do we read poets' letters? Primarily for the light they throw on the poetry, you might have thought. It is odd, therefore, that Saskia Hamilton should specifically exclude this kind of annotation: 'From the first letter, Lowell's correspondence is saturated with events, images, and phrases that occur in his poetry; to mark each instance would require an extra volume of notes. I have therefore identified only direct references to Lowell's poems and prose.' This seems misguided. So, when Lowell says of Pound (letter to Laughlin, 20 November 1963) 'I've just read the *Pisan Cantos* again, and feel that no poetry since Thomas Hardy so moves the heart', might not a cross-reference to Ian Hamilton's interview in *Collected Prose* be appropriate? 'With Pound – I think of the *Pisan Cantos* – a hard, angular, in some ways shrill and artificial man by courage let the heart break through the iron rib ... more heart than any poet since Hardy.'

Remember that reference to Allen Tate's loafers, shining 'like armour in a Rembrandt painting'? Not unlike the loafers of 'William Carlos Williams': 'and loafers polished like the rosewood on yachts'. Worth a mention in the notes perhaps.

Twice in this correspondence, Lowell shrugs at the futility, the *impossibility*, of re-creating the gestalt of his madness: 'talking about the past is like a cat's trying to explain climbing down a ladder' (15 March 1958). In *Notebook*'s 'Eight Months Later', the last line is 'Who will live this year back, cat on the ladder?' Also worth a mention in the notes?

Finally, finally, a less docile editor might have scrutinised Lowell's response (20 September 1973) to an *Agenda* questionnaire in which he idiosyncratically conflates free verse and syllabics: 'no one wrote better free verse than Marianne Moore's measured, unscannable run-on syllabic stanza.' He defines free verse as 'unscanned' and says it 'seems as free as prose' – which is contrary to Eliot's definition that there is no such thing as free verse 'to the man who wants to do a good job', and that free verse always exists in relationship to a fixed metre, coinciding and diverging. Certainly good free verse will have a rhythmic pulse. Most people defining syllabics would say, like Roy Fuller, that syllabics, *not* free verse, is the occasion for avoiding *all* scansion – actually quite a testing requirement for poetry in English. Perhaps this is also the occasion to point out that Lowell's 'unrhymed blank verse sonnets' are only intermittently in blank verse. For example, *Notebook*'s 'The River God' begins with a pentameter – 'The Aztecs gave the human sacrifice' – but the rest of the sonnet is more irregular than regular: 'the river god caught them in his arms when they drowned' has twelve unpatterned syllables.

The Lowell–Bishop Letters
(2008)

Poor Stephen Spender. A genuine, funny, diffident, self-deprecating figure who became – unjustly, unalterably – a byword for cultural fraudulence. Evelyn Waugh thought that his use of the English language was like watching a chimpanzee with a precious Ming vase. George Orwell was dismayed to find that the butt of his journalism was charming in person. In 1950, Robert Lowell acknowledges the same dividedness between automatic scorn and radical, rueful revision: 'Spender was all over the place and, I'm sorry to say, very pleasant and intelligent.' In 1955, Elizabeth Bishop dreams she is Stephen Spender, reciting 'In the beautiful morning / a beautiful poem fell to the ground / from the beautiful lips of the poet ...' – which 'seemed to be very funny at the time'.

Why? It was partly the personal beauty that Bishop homes in on. It was partly the networking that Lowell picks out. There is an irony here. Lowell was a very beautiful young poet, in the Spender way, as Elizabeth Bishop recalled: 'he needed a hair cut, and he was very handsome and handsome in an almost old-fashioned poetic way.' Lowell described himself as 'trying to play the role of the hesitant, muddled, intuitive poet'.

And he was the friend of all the world from the very beginning – plugged into the cultural grid of the *New York Review of Books*, part of the poetic and critical circle at Kenyon College, visiting Ezra Pound at St Elizabeth's, being sung to by T. S. Eliot over the transatlantic telephone, meeting André Malraux at the White House. One sentence says it all: 'After a while, Jackie [Kennedy] suddenly present and talking to Mike Nichols [film director], Hellman group [Lillian, the playwright, not the mayonnaise heiress] there, both Senator Kennedys [Bobby and Teddy], McNamara [Secretary of State for Defense].' But let's have another more literary grandee: 'Caroline and I may go to Moscow to see Madame Mandelstam who has begged me to come "before it's too late – life is not imagination".' You see?

The other irony is that Lowell's poems, as you might expect, are famously gossipy. Some of them are even about gossip. This of T. S. Eliot: 'Ah Tom, one muse, one music, had one the luck – / Lost in the dark night of the brilliant talkers, / Humour and honour from the everlasting dross!' Lowell's *Notebook* is

---

Words in Air: The Complete Correspondence between Elizabeth Bishop and Robert Lowell, edited by Thomas Travisano with Saskia Hamilton (Faber and Faber, 2008).

a kind of *Who's Who*, amongst other things. And Spender's best work is anecdotal, too – his autobiography, *World within Worlds*, and the poems 'Port Bou' and 'To Manuel Altolaguirre'. Spender's models are Yeats's *Autobiographies* and poems of reminiscence like 'Beautiful Lofty Things' and 'In Memory of Major Robert Gregory'. It is an honourable tradition.

But it is a tradition that Elizabeth Bishop stands athwart. She avoided knowing people, it seems. When she plans a trip to Italy, in 1964, Lowell recommends her to visit Ungaretti and Montale. She replies: 'you know I never dream of calling on anybody!' And it is the salvation of her as a poet, the source of her greatness. She is self-centred in the very best sense. And, luckily, she was avoided by success. The great difference between her letters and those of Lowell is that his have only two topics – poetry and gossip. They are fatally restricted in subject matter, however glamorous initially, to what you might call the official world of literature and letters. Bishop's gossip is unofficial and typified by her poem 'Under the Window: Ouro Preto' (Ouro Preto was the remote Brazilian village where she lived): 'The conversations are simple: about food / or, "When my mother combs my hair it hurts." / "Women." "*Women!*" '

All the great things in this volume are small and they are Elizabeth Bishop's: 'The little boy, age three, has a horse – a length of yellow string that is getting dirtier every day. He drags it between his legs, galloping everywhere with it – and it has to be taken into our Volkswagen bus – or into his bed – with great care. His sisters actually go for rides on our donkey, Mimoso – but he prefers the piece of string.'

This reminds me of Mr Wodehouse in *Emma* talking about his grandchildren: 'They are all remarkably clever; and they have so many pretty ways. They will come and stand by my chair and say, "Grandpa, can you give me a bit of string?"' Sir Walter Scott said that Jane Austen couldn't do the 'big Bowwow' – Lowell's forte, as it were. But she was incomparable as the recording angel of muddy pattens and missing spectacle rivets. So is Elizabeth Bishop the notary of, for instance, false teeth: going by boat to Brazil in 1957, she records 'the captain kept scolding the steward for not wearing his new teeth.' In 1963, an old aristocrat is instructed to wear her jewels. 'When the old lady arrived she said, "See – my jewels", and showed that she had her *teeth in* for the occasion.'

While Lowell is at the White House, Bishop is (typically) otherwise engaged: 'Did I tell you that when we flew back the last time we brought four quarts of homogenized milk with us, in the refrigerator on the plane, and gave a cornflake party immediately upon arrival. It was a great success, too.' She can even tame a revolution: 'she [Lota, Bishop's partner] had a safe-conduct from one of the generals and went in and out, through the President's troops, which surrounded the palace. *All the men inside showing each other their guns etc.*' (my italics).

While Lowell is reporting the failure of the Rhavs' marriage – who will remember Philip Rhav in 50 years? – Elizabeth Bishop, saved from success, is looking out of the window, as it were, and seeing, unforgettably, that 'nuns & priests are playing tennis.'

Double Exposures: Ted Hughes
(2006)

I first met Ted 40 years ago, in late 1963, or early 1964, when he read at the Oxford University Poetry Society. Afterwards, everyone retired from St Anne's JCR to the Lamb and Flag in St Giles. There Ted drank two modest half-pints of beer and answered questions from tyro poets. I remember he told one earnest undergraduate – who had been boring about the number of revisions he made to his poems – that it was as Keats said, poetry should be natural and should come as easily as leaves to the tree.

I had been given *Hawk in the Rain* and *Lupercal* in 1962 by a history master, who bought both in Bowes & Bowes in Cambridge. These were exemplary books for me. Ted was a major influence. If it doesn't show, that's just because I was canny enough to steer clear of animals. I also had seen Al Alvarez's memorial note about Sylvia in the *Observer* – lamenting the incalculable loss to poetry, reprinting 'Edge' and 'Contusion' – so I'd bought *Ariel* and read it with difficulty. Ted's poetry was easier, I thought.

Afterwards I walked Ted back to his hotel, the Eastgate, on the High Street, and we talked. When I asked him how he got published, he said he'd had a very ambitious and industrious American wife who sent out the poems regularly and kept a card index of their progress. He asked me, knowing I was a fellow-Northerner, if I was happy at Oxford. I wasn't. I was reading PPE. Symbolic logic was beyond me. Economic theory was a mixture of graphs and terror. I still remember that my economics tutorials were on Thursdays at 5. By 4 o'clock my shirts were drenched in sweat down to the cuffs. (At the end of the year, I changed to read English and was happier.) Ted, who'd changed from the English tripos at Cambridge to Archaeology and Anthropology, advised me to leave Oxford if I wanted to write. The next time I met him, in 1976, fourteen years later, he remembered our talk – and said reproachfully that, counter to his advice, I'd stayed on in Oxford ever since.

Lots of things are typical of Ted in this little reminiscence. The careful attention he paid to my end of the conversation. The radical advice. He once recklessly urged Seamus Heaney to give up academe and become an eel-fisherman. (Interestingly, Seamus did give up his job and leave Northern Ireland for the Republic and life as a full-time writer.) Thirdly, he remembered the conver-

Lecture given to the Ted Hughes Conference, Emory University, 5 October 2005.

sation fourteen, fifteen years later. Ted had more charisma than anyone I've ever met. A lot of Ted's charisma came from the quiet intensity that he directed outwards. He wasn't self-absorbed, he was attentive. In this way, the poems were extensions of his natural personality. Sylvia seems to me to be an example of the egotistical sublime. Her subject is herself, her predicament, her violent romantic emotions. She is a capital 'I', whereas Ted is an eye, a seeing eye, something looking at what is outside. He's Keatsian. Keats said that when he saw sparrows he was there with them pecking in the gravel.

But I don't want to suggest that he simply sat there radioactive with taciturn charisma. My experience of him was that he was a great talker, a spellbinding talker, after an initial statutory Yorkshire reluctance. He always seemed a man who weighed his words, unexcitable, calm, measured, but in fact he was a fluent and brilliant talker. The best account of this charisma is Ben Sonnenberg's in his memoir *Lost Property*. Sonnenberg was the founding editor of *Grand Street*. He met Ted at Bill and Dido Merwin's in London: 'Ted Hughes was tall and rough-featured and dark, with a dark baritone voice. I never met anyone I admired so much who was at the same time so approachable. I wrote in my notebook that meeting him I felt like Hazlitt meeting Coleridge for the first time: bowled over by his warmth and energy. Listening to him, I did in fact fall off my chair. When he helped me up from the floor, I wrote in my notebook, "He didn't stop talking and I felt the vibration of his voice running down his arm."'

When he was with friends, he was very unbuttoned, very unguarded, for a man hounded all his life by the press. He once told me that, going to visit Carol, before they were married and when she was living in a nurses' hostel, he was arrested as a suspected rapist and bundled into a police car, where he was subjected to a spate of abuse and taken to the police station. When I told him that I couldn't drive – 'like all great poets' – he was suddenly serious, revealingly serious. 'Don't ever learn.' 'Why not?' I asked. 'Because you can always drive away from *anything*.'

He told me about pheromones. In the profile of Ted that I wrote for the *Sunday Times* when he was appointed Poet Laureate, I mentioned 'pheromones' and 'foot boards' rather cryptically as subjects on which Ted had interesting things to say. The profile is reprinted in my essay collection *Haydn and the Valve Trumpet*. I think I was then being more discreet, more hyper-protective, than I need to be now. This is what he had to say. If you had an aerosol of pig pheromones, it worked with human beings. If you sprayed one seat in, say, the Festival Hall and asked a woman to choose any seat in the house, she would choose the seat sprayed with pheromones. Ted knew a furrier who used the spray to make women buy the most expensive coats. The pheromones had been developed for artificial insemination. The sow's muzzle was sprayed and she was inseminated while blissed-out in a cloud of unknowing. Ted acquired an aerosol can by mail order. One night at Court Green, at the close of an edgy dinner party to which the Baskins had arrived late after a quarrel, he went into the drawing room, where there would be coffee – and let rip with the aerosol. The conversation became livelier, intense, competitive, as the males fought for attention.

Ted was always interesting about sex. He once told me that the majority of back problems were caused by the lack of a foot board on the modern bed – which meant that there was nothing to push against and give you proper purchase. I remember, too, saying that his title *Some Insects, Some Beasts, Some Flowers* was ungainly. Somehow, I said, the title implied a mechanical progress through an index of possible subjects. What next? Some Amphibia? He simplified it – to *Flowers and Insects*. But *en passant* he said that he thought poetic subjects were like women: you saturated them with attention – and then moved on. I also remember that Fabers was offered the UK rights to Tomi Ungerer's *Fornicon* for possible publication. It's a brilliant, stirring, filthy, funny version of sex – all done in cool drawings of mechanised dildos, for instance, powered by bicycle pedals and chains. The humour took in, for example, a cat with a rubber bondage mask, making itself available over a mechanical dildo. I wanted to publish it, but I knew it would need an introduction from someone with literary and intellectual heft. My first (cynical) choice was Angela Carter – a feminist *and* a woman deeply interested in unconventional sex. She turned me down. I thought Ted might be persuaded. I told him about the book as he drove me in a van around the lanes of Devon. Have you got a copy? he asked. Yes, I said, I brought a copy so you could have a look. He took the book there and then, opening it across the steering wheel, and skimming through the text as he drove. I never saw it again. He didn't write an introduction, either.

There was one exception, one moment of curious pudeur. When Jacqueline Rose wrote her terrible book, *The Haunting of Sylvia Plath*, Ted was very agitated by her interpretation – her very stupid interpretation – of 'The Rabbit Catcher', which she claimed described an act of oral sex. It doesn't, in fact. But I couldn't understand why Ted was so upset. After all, as I said, acts of oral sex are not unknown among couples who have been married for quite a long time. In fact, 'The Rabbit Catcher' isn't about Ted and Sylvia *at all*, let alone the details of their sex life. It is squarely about Sylvia's fascinated relationship with death – who is here the rabbit catcher.

He told me about getting the Queen's Gold Medal for Poetry. At 10 or 10.30 a.m. he and Carol met Sir John Betjeman at a hotel near Buckingham Palace. They drank quite a lot of vodka tonics before setting off for the palace in a cab. There, they drove into the inner courtyard – where there was an awning and a red carpet. Betjeman at that time was suffering from Parkinson's Disease and had drunk a fair bit. He emerged from the cab on his hands and knees and, playing it for laughs, began to crawl up the red carpet, hooting with laughter. Carol was stopped by an equerry from taking photographs. Inside the palace proper, they drank sherry because everything was behind schedule. The Queen was delayed, having sherry with a Commonwealth prime minister. More sherry was pressed on Ted and Sir John. Finally, more than a little tipsy, they left Carol behind and ascended in a small golden lift to Her Majesty's chambers. Betjeman comically scratched the gold of the lift and wondered if it were twenty-four carat. Then the double doors opened on the Queen. She, too, was merry by this time. She was also very small. Ted: 'You know she's small, but this was like meeting Alice in Wonderland. She's *this* big.' And he measured an inch between his finger and thumb. Ted planned to engage the Queen in conversation about farming and fishing, but she was well briefed and kept bringing the conversation back to his poetry. Then the interview was over. Ted and Sir John retreated backwards from the royal presence and closed the double doors behind them. At which point, they remembered that the Queen had not given Ted the medal for poetry. They tapped and re-entered. The Queen laughed and went to take the medal from a mantelpiece. It fell and rolled under the grand piano. Ted, Betjeman and the Queen all crawled under the piano to retrieve the medal …

According to Carol, this colourful conclusion has been enhanced in the telling. 'I acknowledge that Ted himself could amplify and sometimes exaggerate an event according to his audience.' They didn't leave the room. The medal was dropped by the Queen – who was as sober as one of her own judges – and retrieved by Ted. In his account written to his daughter Frieda, which is part of the Hughes archive at Emory, there is great comedy at the Moss Bros fitting *on the very morning of the presentation*, the lift is described as a little palace in itself, the bow from the neck is practised, Ted is smitten by the Queen – and the medal isn't dropped at all.

(I had already found myself wondering about the artistic structure of this anecdote – the conjoined motifs of crawling and alcohol suggest the controlling innuendo of the phrase a 'pub crawl'.)

But what I really want to talk about is Ted as a letter-writer. He was incapable of writing a dull letter, and the *Collected Letters* will be like immersing yourself into a fully functional eco-system – if we ever get to see them in their entirety. It isn't a conventional commercial publishing project. There are too many letters for that. Nearly as many as the unpublished letters of Stanley Spencer – who wrote miles and miles of toilet paper to his first wife, Hilda, before and after her death. Of course, we are all looking forward to Christopher Reid's *Selected Letters*. But a proper *Collected* will need funding from a foundation – perhaps by Bollingen, or Drue Heinz, or the Paul Getty Foundation. Even Paul Keegan's marvellous *Collected Poems*, for all its inclusion of previously uncollected poems, isn't a proper *Collected* because it omits, without explanation, the main body text of *Gaudete*. I assume the constraints were financial, though Paul never replied to my email asking about the omission. (Carol tells me that Paul was following Ted's own example in *New Selected Poems 1957–1994*, where he excluded the narrative and published only the poems in the appendix. I don't really accept that the narrative can be separated from the poems, since the narrative is itself poetry. Paul Keegan and Carol Hughes both think that the hybridity of the core narrative – mostly poetry, but spliced with prose – justifies its omission from the *Collected*.) (Paul Keegan eventually did reply. The burden of his argument was as follows: *Gaudete* began life as a film script and was later 'transcribed' by Ted. Keegan distinguishes between composition and transcription – and firmly insists on a distinction between the poems in the 'Epilogue' and the 'poetry' of the main text, which is anyway leavened with prose. It is obvious to me that, if it is possible to distinguish the prose from the poetry in the main narrative, then the 'poetry' is therefore poetry, not prose, and not some *tertium aliquid*. Clearly, it is different from the lyrics in the 'Epilogue', but it is still poetry – vigorous narrative poetry. The argument that Ted excluded the main text from two *Selected Poems* carries no weight with me. I think he was persuaded, perhaps by Carol, that the main priapic narrative was likely to be interpreted autobiographically.)

A *Collected Letters* will be magnificent and magnificently unbuttoned and visionary. By visionary I mean an unsleeping consciousness of the metaphysical shadow cast by even ordinary events. Ted was always interested in the shared border between the ordinary and the extraordinary, between the physical and the metaphysical. In 1979, I wrote to him about the birth of my son Isaac. 'Isaac is a fine name. I expect he's looking human by now. Congratulations to all three of you. [And then he changes up a gear, looks at the bigger picture.] Interesting business, being a father – but very ageing. And it gets more so. Definite sense of replacement. The old insect inside the cell – "OK reproduction complete, death now permissible." Paternity's always felt to me just slightly posthumous. // My son's just grown past me, + he's just demonstrated how he can throw a surveying pole about three yards further.'

For Ted, conventional reality overlaid something else, something larger. It was like wallpaper – and he was interested in lifting a corner, making a tear, to discover what was hidden underneath. He 'rent the veil of the usual' – a phrase Seamus Heaney supplied me, as his editor, for a blurb to *Station Island*, but a phrase that applies more exactly to Ted's poetry. Ted saw through a glass darkly. When he was interviewed by Clive Wilmer for a BBC Radio 3 programme *Poets Talking*, in 1992, he expatiated on the role of myth in his poetry:

Looking back now at my first books, I can trace odd leading images directly back to certain mythical things that interested me. For instance, the 'Hawk Roosting'. He's a straight monologue for a notion of the Egyptian hawk, Horus: the immortal hawk who is the eye of the sun, who flies through all hawks, or who absorbs all hawks. In a sense I was trying to raise the creatures that I'd encountered in my boyhood in South Yorkshire and West Yorkshire. I was trying to raise them into some mythic frieze. I was thinking of them as a sort of mural. The pike, for instance: they were to be angels hanging in the aura of the Creator. So they were just hanging in the great ball of light, just pulsing away there, very still, because they were originally angels. My model, I remember, was Blake's 'Tyger'. I was thinking, if I could raise my pike to that kind of intensity and generality! That was the ideal. There were much more obvious efforts to do that in the original draft, but I cut them out and left myself with the old South Yorkshire fish. But that was the original purpose and motivation behind the poem itself, and so, too, with the hawk. So, too, with some others.

So the bull Moses isn't idly named. Two things about the biblical Moses are relevant: one is the encounter with God in the burning bush, the ordinary object from which divinity blazes forth. The other is the element of Tantalus in the Moses story. He leads the Israelites through the Sinai Desert but cannot himself enter the Promised Land, merely view it from the top of Mount Pisgah. He is a liminal figure – like T. S. Eliot's Magi or Simeon. He is poised on the brink of something larger. His brinkmanship is something he holds in common with Ted. In a famous interview with Egbert Faas in the *London Magazine* (January 1971), Ted said: 'I was all for opening negotiations with whatever happened to be out there.'

So naturally he is interested in any potential intermediary. In 'The Bull Moses', the bull belongs to another world, another order of existence: 'nothing of our light / Found any reflection in him.' He is a captive in our universe: 'The weight of the sun and the moon and the world hammered / To a ring of brass through his nostrils.' We sense 'the locked black of his powers' – and the emphasis is on 'locked'. The poem closes with the boy Hughes closing and bolting the bull's pen. The paradox is the tension between the torpor of the bull and the untold potential of its power. It is, then, paradigmatic: it stands for the world of ordinary experience, the unremarkable passage of time, and the potential explosion of power, of nuclear fission.

I invoke nuclear fission deliberately because Ted evokes it, too, in his brilliant parable poem 'Football at Slack' in *Remains of Elmet*. Football is a deliberately unpromising starting point for an inquiry into the metaphysical, the hidden divine. So is the place name – Slack. In a sense, 'Football at Slack' is part of a generalised topos shared by many twentieth-century poets living in a predominantly secular world: it is the movement from the deliberately flat, the calculatedly banal, to the enhanced acoustic of the sacred, sounding itself like a massed choir. Think of Larkin's 'High Windows', which begins 'When I see a couple of kids / And guess he's fucking her and she's / Taking pills' – and ends 'and is nowhere, and is endless'. Seamus Heaney exploits this method throughout *Seeing Things* and it is Eliot's stock in trade in 'The Journey of the Magi'. In Eliot's poem, we start with Lancelot Andrewes's insistence on the mundane starting point – crucially elaborated by Eliot into sherbet, camels refractory and sore-footed, plus proleptic symbols of soldiers dicing – and eventually reach the final, baffling confrontation with the divine and its accompanying sensation of fear and diminishment. In 'Football at Slack', Ted begins, very cleverly, I think, with a kind of comedy, a disguised Hopkinsian rodeo: 'Between plunging valleys, on a bareback of hill / Men in bunting colours / Bounced, and their blown ball bounced.' It's hard not to think of Henri Douanier-Rousseau's striped Victorian footballers with their cloned moustaches and their eyes off the ball as if they were really a *corps de ballet*. There is something verging on the farcical. The fusion of farce and the frightening is something Ted understood very well. In a letter to me in 1979, he devotes a paragraph to my second book, *A Martian Sends a Postcard Home*: 'That double exposure of comic and seriously horrible is very real.' Spot on for my poetry, but spot on for Ted's poetry also. Double exposure is exactly what a lot of Ted's poems are about. The hawk and Horus. The pike as angels. And, here, drenched footballers as a type of religious Dervish seeking entrancement through the physical. The 'rain lowered a steel press' but 'their shouts bobbed up / Coming fine and thin, washed and happy // While the humped world sank foundering'. So the world we know is a sinking ship, about to go to the bottom; the footballers, however, are survivors. They have a life after death, which Ted describes in visionary, surreal, yet at the same time realistic and recognisable terms as 'But the wingers leapt, they bicycled in air / And the goalie flew horizontal // And once again a golden holocaust / Lifted the cloud's edge, to watch them.' So, the sun reappears around a cloud, the goalkeeper dives to make a save, and working their legs for extra height the wingers attempt to head a high crossed ball. That is the cover story, the realistic alibi. But what we have read is the destruction of the world, the saved suddenly freed from the laws of physics and watched by the burning presence of divinity.

The next poem in *Remains of Elmet*, 'Sunstruck', is a companion piece, another parable, another double exposure – this time about cricket. Ted uses the idea of the boundary and the pitch between the two wickets as a metonymy for all the limitations of the conventional world that prevent transcendence. 'And the legs running for dear life, twinkling white / In the cage of wickets / Were cornered again by the ball, pinned to the crease, / Tethered to the green and white pavilion.' The idea is that the excitement of the game might release us from these limitations, enable us to cross some frontier into a different spiritual dimension: 'Fleeing after the ball, stampeding / Through that sudden hole in Saturday ...' I never read these lines without a wry reminiscence of the Monty Python film, *Time Bandits*.

It is part of Ted's genius that he should marry this craving for transcendence to something humanly recognisable – the craving for a weekend free of work. Here he invokes the threat of the working week and contrasts the sense of liberty at the weekend: failure to escape means returning to 'the wage-mirage sparkle of mills / Toward Lord Savile's heather [as a keeper or a beater] / Toward the veto of the poisonous Calder [the river ruined by work, by industrial pollution]'. The poem ends with the idea of a futile life lived unsuccessfully, a sense of the transcendence unfulfilled. At the end of the day, the home the cricketers return to isn't simply home. Or, rather, it is also the long home, the final resting-place. And Ted ends with a double exposure: 'the cool sheet and the black slot of home'. That cool sheet is also a winding sheet and the black slot is also the grave.

This double exposure, in which something is simultaneously itself and also something else, occurs at the end of 'Full Moon and Little Frieda', when Frieda suddenly sees the risen moon: '"Moon!" you cry suddenly, "Moon! Moon!" // The moon has stepped back like an artist gazing amazed at a work // That points at him amazed.' The conceit is the idea of art holding up a mirror to life. So the artist is the amazed moon reflected in the amazed face of little Frieda. The artist, then, is in two places at once – not a classic overlaid double exposure, but in two places simultaneously, both in space and aggrandised, as well as on *terra firma* and smaller. But, as always in Ted's poetry, the microcosm and the macrocosm are in a two-way relationship.

The concept of double exposure is useful, too, when we consider Ted and his writings on metre, his critique of Emily Dickinson, his account of Sylvia Plath, his take on T. S. Eliot and of course his take on Shakespeare. I'll deal with all of these but I want to come at them via a reminiscence. When William Golding died, there was a memorial service at Salisbury Cathedral, Golding's model for *The Spire*. Ted read from *The Inheritors* – the passage where Fa is sent to the ice women to intercede with Oa, the earth goddess, for the life of Mal, who is dying of old age. 'Without help Mal will die. Fa must take a present to the ice women and speak for him to Oa.' It's easy to see why Ted chose this passage, rather than, say, the very poignant description of Mal's death. It is a passage which embodies a belief in the Goddess of Complete Being, or Mother Nature. For Golding, such a belief is primitive and imaginatively necessary, imaginatively plausible. He is a novelist, practising his craft. For Ted, it is fundamental rather than primitive, part of his bedrock belief system. The passage goes like this:

> The place was huge and open. It was walled with rock; and everywhere ice-ivy plants reached upwards until they were spread out high above his head on the rock ... [It is a kind of natural Gothic cathedral] Their high branches vanished into caverns of ice. Lok [the male Neanderthaler, who has blundered after Fa] stood back and looked up at Fa who had gone higher towards the other end of the sanctuary. She crouched on the stones and lifted up the parcel of meat. There was no sound, not even the noise of the fall. Fa began to speak in little more than a whisper. At first he could hear individual words, 'Oa' and 'Mal': but the walls rejected the words so that they bounded back and were thrown again. 'Oa' said the wall and the great ivy, and the wall behind Lok sang 'Oa Oa Oa'.

When Ted read this in the Cathedral, he threw his voice upwards – and it was electrifying, as if some great creature of sound, at once a bird and a beast, was panicking and crashing around the stone, trapped and desperate to escape. Sound effects aside, here was a great collision of pagan and Christian belief – but also a celebration of the sacred that transcended both. It was a double exposure.

My implication here is that Ted the critic is often acute but often the helpless hijacker. He was a systematiser who engrossed into his pattern of thought nearly everything that crossed his consciousness. And always, instinctively, he sought out the larger pattern, the transcendent shape. In this, he is a little like Virginia Woolf in *To the Lighthouse*. The hybridity of experience, the second sense of Platonic shapes, is most famously embodied in this sentence describing the dinner with the *bœuf en daube*: 'It partook, she felt, carefully helping Mr Bankes to a specially tender piece, of eternity.' The same admixture, the same fusion of the permanent and godlike with the ordinary, is to be found also in Yeats's 'Beautiful Lofty Things'. Which ends with Maude Gonne 'waiting a train' at Howth Station – like anyone else, you might think, until Yeats adds 'Pallas Athene in that straight back and arrogant head'. The duality here, between Olympus and Howth railway station, is exactly paralleled in *To the Lighthouse*, where Mr Bankes imagines Mrs Ramsay at the other end of the phone: 'He saw her at the end of the line, Greek, blue-eyed, straight-nosed. The Graces assembling seemed to have joined hands in meadows to compose that face. Yes, he would catch the 10.30 at Euston.'

Ted shares this propensity to see the symbolical, transcendent outline around the ordinary. And he often identifies it in other writers, sometimes too readily. He makes Eliot a shaman, for example, in his essay 'The Poetic Self: A Centenary Tribute to T. S. Eliot'. Ted was very open to apparently heterodox ideas. He wrote me a letter praising my interpretation of *The Waste Land* as a Buddhist poem – wondering what the academic world would make of it. Not much, I can tell you. *He* was persuaded, however, and I'm going to quote a bit of his letter, not because I'm praised, but because it shows Ted's gift for analogy and metaphor:

> It [my essay] reminded me a little of a QC I watched at a Public Enquiry in North Devon. His evidence wasn't to be questioned. But the way he delivered it was the surprising thing. He didn't orate, or ingratiate or solemnly browbeat or morally orchestrate or flood us with the usual courtly cant. He simply gave each piece of evidence, one piece at a time, each piece in a great silence. He would lay the piece out, without any interpretation, in a clean sentence, and then wait. He'd wait about ten or fifteen seconds – a very long time in an electrified court. The effect, the real dramatic kinetic impact of each piece, was quite stunning. And the argument that rose out of the whole sequence was irresistible.

Then Ted adds in ink: 'This struck me – because I was on the opposite side.'

In the case of Eliot and Buddhism, though, we were sort of on the same side – that is, well away from the centres of academic orthodoxy. Ted had already drafted, if not finished, 'The Poetic Self: A Centenary Tribute to T. S. Eliot' by 1988. His letter to me is dated January 1989. I think I must have sent him my essay because he'd been airing his ideas about Eliot and I'd been struck by our directional similarities. In his letter, typically, Ted is interested in the general role played by Buddhism in twentieth-century poetry. He is particularly alert to the irony that academic Eliot should make hippy Buddhist Ginsberg and his followers look so belated. 'Did anybody in those days point out that the great Western Buddhist poem had already been written – by the one they regarded as on the whole a figurehead of the enemy and the "academics"? Or that there must be some level on which those Beats were Eliot's epigoni – and that W. C. Williams was, by comparison, the "academic"[?]'

Ted's thesis about Eliot is an idiosyncratic remodelling of the relatively familiar, but arguable idea that great poets are great because they express the zeitgeist. I have a problem with the idea of the zeitgeist itself. First, because I agree with Dickens's opening paragraph to *A Tale of Two Cities*: 'It was the best of times, it was the worst of times …' In other words, there is always sufficient historical evidence to support plausible but opposing views of any historical period. Should you want to show an age of progress and self-confidence, nothing is easier. Should you want to show an era of conservatism and prudence, nothing is easier. Second, each era has tendencies which are *opposed* by its best writers. Arnold is a great critic of Victorian values; so is Dickens; so is Wilde. They constitute an alternative, oppositional zeitgeist, which is more successful than the original zeitgeist they opposed – whose features and characteristics we must deduce from the arguments put by great writers against them.

When Ted comes to identify the zeitgeist flowing through his favourite writers, it tends to be the crisis he himself is preoccupied by. So Eliot, like Yeats, is a shaman who takes on the flaws, the illnesses, the diseases of his time – and cures them. And what would you expect those illnesses to be, given Ted's predilections and propensities? Exactly:

> The undertow of Eliot's early tortured self-examination was the knowledge that this had irreversibly happened, that religious institutions and rituals had ceased to be real in the old sense, and that they continued to exist only as forms of "make-believe", ways of behaviour rather than of belief. A new kind of reality had supplanted them. In the twinkling of an eye, as Nostradamus would say [or I Corinthians 15:52], the whole metaphysical universe centred on God had vanished from its place. It had evaporated, with all its meanings. This emptiness was Eliot's starting point.

Ted's essay continues: 'We see now that Eliot was the poet who brought the full implication of that moment into consciousness. It formed the features of his genius. It determined the novelty and scope and import of his greatness. And it decided his unique position in the history of poetry. That desacralised landscape had never been seen before. Or if it had been glimpsed, it had never before been real.'

My problem with this eloquent and ingenious overview of Eliot is that he isn't converted until 1927, and he doesn't begin as a spiritual poet *manqué*. Although *The Waste Land* does address the condition of spiritual aridity, with the desert as a spiritual emblem, much of the early poetry is social, ironic, comic, with a completely different focus – a focus, a preoccupation, which turns on a fruitful contradiction in Eliot, whose early poetry is both an attack on sentimental exaggeration of feeling *and* a resolve to feel to the full. I do not think 'The Love Song of J. Alfred Prufrock' is about the 'convulsive desacralisation of the spirit of the West'. I think it is a poem about a man who is too timid to proposition or propose to a woman who is his social superior.

I think the same reservation will apply to Ted's introduction to his selection of Emily Dickinson's poetry. Emily Dickinson is the author of several orthodox Christian poems and many more poems that are sarcastic critiques of Christianity. She was an atheist, as she explained to T. W. Higginson: 'they [the rest of the family] are religious – except me – and address an Eclipse, every morning – whom they call their "Father".' It couldn't be clearer. The orthodox Christian poems are written specifically for orthodox Christian recipients, often as commiseration for the death of a young child – not a situation in which even a militant atheist like Richard Dawkins would come on like, well, Richard Dawkins attacking the consolation of the after-life. Ted, though, presents Emily Dickinson as the unconscious crucible containing the warring spiritual elements of her time: 'At that time, the old Calvinism of the New England States was in open battle against the spirit of the new age – the Higher Criticism that was dissolving the Bible, the broadening, liberalising influence of Transcendentalism, the general scientific scepticism which, in America, was doubly rabid under the backlash of the ruthless, selective pragmatism of the frontier.' So, religion and the forces of scepticism and change. Where does Ted think Emily Dickinson stands, do you think? 'She quarantined herself in Jonathan Edwards's faith that the visible Universe was "an emanation of God for the pure joy of Creation in which creatures find their justification by yielding assent to the beauty of the whole, even though it slay them".' That quotation, by the way, is from Jonathan Edwards. It isn't anywhere in Emily Dickinson herself.

Where does Ted get the idea that Dickinson is interested in the divine? It's via a misreading of a group of her poems – addressed to a Master – which Ted quotes: 'Title divine – is Mine! / The Wife – without the Sign!' For Ted, this represents the transference of human love to something spiritual – from secular to sacred. But we know enough about Emily Dickinson's love life to see how much it flourished, despite her agoraphobia and her single state. She didn't mind being the Wife without the legal title. There are several candidates for her lovers – the already married Otis P. Lord or the Revd Charles Wadsworth. What she didn't want, evidently, was a regular domestic set-up, the grind of marital dailiness. She seems to have felt that great love wasn't for everyday use. She admired her Yorkshire girls, the Brontës, for the purity of their passion.

The paradigm of the double exposure is perfectly illustrated by Eliot and Dickinson. Eliot's writing, Ted argues, is underpinned by a fundamental spiritual crisis, whatever the ostensible subject happens to be in any particular instance. Emily Dickinson embodies, undecided, the spiritual issues of her time: 'she reserved herself in some final suspension of judgment. So her poems record not only her ecstatic devotion [sacred imagery used for secular purpose, I'd say], but the drama of her sharp, sceptical independence, her doubt, and what repeatedly opens under her ecstasy – her despair.' Those last saving sentences are crucial.

They express a reservation about the thesis itself. Suddenly we are confronted with the Emily Dickinson we know from the poetry – the poet of depression who complements the poet of great romantic passion. Without this crucial qualification, Ted's essay would be *parti pris* to the point of obtuseness. As it is, his religious reading of Emily Dickinson is markedly skewed, if still influential – influential, I'd say, because we like the idea that under the particulars of the individual poems there exists a single key. There is an Edward Casaubon in us all, yearning for the key to all mythologies.

As there sometimes is. Ted is absolutely correct about the template unifying Sylvia Plath's poetry and prose, what he calls in a letter to me 'the DNA of her poetic metabolism' – the great drama of death and rebirth that is so clearly played out in *The Bell Jar* as a theme and variations. In 'The Rabbit Catcher', the snares which bring death are paradoxically compared to 'birth pangs' set close together. In 'Ariel' the invocation of Godiva's nudity and self-sacrifice (casting off 'Dead hands, dead stringencies') is followed immediately by the rebirth of 'And now I / Foam to wheat ...'

As for Ted's reading of Shakespeare, there is once more the controlling template. Again Ted uses the metaphor of the 'tragic/dramatic/poetic DNA'. In the same letter (13 November 1989) that he writes about Sylvia, he outlines his scheme for Shakespeare. At the behest of Donya Feuer, a director at the Swedish National Theatre, Ted was to create a single drama from Shakespeare's last thirteen plays – 'crushed into a single drama, or rather ... dismantled and then reassembled as a single complex, like an immense Rubik's cube in a spontaneous slow-motion solving of itself'. Ted's idea is summarised clearly in a letter (20 June 1990) to me and my wife, a Shakespearean scholar: 'a single tragic myth, made out of the plots of the two long poems ['The Rape of Lucrece' and 'Venus and Adonis'] and used as a dramatic template for all the tragedies'. Essentially, Ted identifies a double exposure in Shakespeare: an interchange between the repressive Puritan imperative and the old pagan worship of Nature and sex. Like Eliot, Shakespeare is expressing the zeitgeist – the conflict between repression and licence. The pagan imperative, in Ted's account, survives in Catholicism, which is paganism adapted for everyday use. Behind the Catholic, the pagan – another double exposure. The Virgin Mary is also the pagan Venus in Ted's account. In Shakespeare's later plays the one impulse is constantly and suddenly taken over by the other. The predatory Tarquin is superseded by sexually reluctant Adonis. And vice versa. The clearest example is *Measure for Measure*, though that wasn't part of Ted's account until my wife pointed out to him how perfectly Angelo fitted his Shakespearean schema. Angelo begins as a Puritan but ends by being licentious.

In his letter of 13 November 1989, Ted summarises his general position by proposing a book about Eliot, Plath and Shakespeare as three mythical poets. 'So I had the idea of putting these pieces, the Eliot Piece and the Shakespeare letters together. A book about three mythic poets. I don't think the disproportion in some aspects of stature matters: my point is that all three are exclusively mythical poets, writing only out of their myth (once it has evolved and become active) or rather only within their myth – being unable, actually, to write outside it.' Three double exposures, in fact.

The idea of double exposure also applies to Ted's exposition of metre. When Ted wrote his book of children's verse *What is the Truth?*, the then children's editor at Fabers, Phyllis Hunt, an ex-pupil of Dame Helen Gardner, came to me, deeply troubled. She thought there were several metrical mistakes or awkwardnesses, but she was afraid, too much in awe of Ted, to raise her worries with him. I read the typescript and agreed with her that the metre was sometimes irregular and said I'd write to Ted – citing the lines I thought questionable and saying that children tended to like their metre to be satisfyingly regular. On 16 May 1982, he replied:

> Thank you for the long painstaking letter … All your points gave me pause. You're quite right about several things. That Swallow poem out – for instance. Knock the last verse off the mouse – I quite like it, but the fox came first and the detail there is necessary, as things go.
>
> I'll look at all the metrical pieces over the next couple of weeks. I want to replace the goat piece – 'each rose fails' – alltogether, and one or two of the others. Also, I really ought to have a bee. My difficulty with the lollopy rhythmical lines is that for my first writing years I wrote not ing [*sic*] else (Kipling), and so soon got to the point where my main pleasure in those metres is giving them a twist – and setting some other metre, inside them, against them. So you have the two oscillating along together. [Double exposure.] The problem is – others hear them differently.
>
> Roy Fuller quoted my romantic line 'Hearing the horizons endure' as an example of metrical imbecility, and called it (I think) 'unsayable'. On the other hand, I was specially proud of it. In fact, it still seems to me that if you're going to say it at all, you can only say it as I want it said. It's just that Roy Fuller refuses to surrender his officer's moustache, even provisionally.

I love this correspondence. Neither of us is embarrassed. We're both poets riveted by particularities, technical details that would bore many a reader. Ted ends with a mock exam paper: 'Meanwhile: Eng. Lit. paper 108. Question 1: 'Even the loose stones that cover the highway' a) Identify author and context. b) Scan.

Question 2: 'Young couples nimbly began dancing' a) Identify author and context. b) Scan. Question 3: 'Evening and morning, the steep street of Urbino' a) scan "the steep street" Question 4: Are the above quotations forgettable? If not, give reasons.'

The interesting thing about this little test is that Ted should have had his examples so readily to hand of metrical disruption in the middle of the line. Like all poets, he had thought about metrical technicalities. The irritating thing about Roy Fuller is his assumption that Ted hadn't bothered to think about sound and metre.

My answers all drew the necessary, preordained conclusion – that in each case the poet deliberately disrupted the regularity of his metre for a very specific purpose. 'Even the loose stones that cover the highway' is from *The Prelude*, Book III, line 125. 'Evening and morning, the steep street of Urbino' is from Yeats's 'The People'. 'Young couples nimbly began dancing' is from Keats's *Endymion*, though I couldn't guess where it came from at the time. I conclude: 'Anyway, I take the point. It's just that the poems in *What is the Truth?* which play with metre in this sophisticated way are aimed at the youngest potential readers in terms of subject matter. My guess would be that they'd prefer something regular. Will they appreciate metrical velleities?'

One last example of double exposure just to show how deep it goes in Ted's thinking. One of the great joys of Paul Keegan's *Collected Poems* is the previously uncollected items. One of my favourites is 'Fly Inspects' – in which Ted inverts our prejudice, our association of the fly with dirt and unhealthiness. He offers us instead the counter-intuitive, paradoxical perception of the fly as a sanitary inspector. The wit of this, the sustained invention of the conceit, works only if we remain aware that the fly spreads germs in reality. It begins: 'Fly / Is the Sanitary Inspector. He detects every speck / With his Geiger counter. / Detects it, then inspects it / Through his multiple spectacles. You see him everywhere / Bent over his microscope.' What I love here are the lavish verbal effects that reproduce the fly's meticulous examination of the minutiae: the sounds move on only fractionally. De*tects* every *speck*. Mul*tiple* spec*tacles*. Heaven.

Of course, all metaphor involves double exposure. As readers, we are aware of the thing being described *and* the thing it is compared to. No wonder the idea of double exposure is central to Ted's criticism and poetry. He is a great metaphorical writer. No wonder I was so drawn to him 40 years ago.

Ted Hughes's Letters
(2007)

In 1911, Egon Schiele painted a self-portrait of himself as Eros – in his left hand a terrific, salmon-pink erection, somewhat (I imagine) larger than life. Height 56 cm, width 32 cm, the gouache used to belong to Victor Lownes, who ran the London Playboy Club. I don't think Schiele is painting what Ted Hughes, in a letter to his painter brother, Gerald, disparagingly calls 'transfers': 'any fool can become a mirror if he practise hard.' Schiele's gouache isn't mimesis. It is frank subjectivity. That is how erections feel – larger than life. That is why men like them. They enlarge us.

Let me begin with Ted Hughes's erections – with a commendably indiscreet moment in this commendably discreet selection of his letters, tactfully chosen and scrupulously, unostentatiously annotated by Christopher Reid, Hughes's former editor at Fabers, as I was. (I have only two improvements to offer for the paperback: on page 153, Hughes writes, 'Sylvia detests Lyde'; she must mean Joe Lyde, whose jazz is played in 'St Botolph's' from *Birthday Letters*. On page 658, Hughes is speculating about the euphoria felt by the surprised prey of wild animals: maybe a cross-reference to 'Trophies', also from *Birthday Letters*, would be in order?) On 23 October 1956, Hughes was in Yorkshire at his parents' house. Sylvia Plath, his new wife, was in Cambridge. Their marriage was a secret because the couple feared (needlessly, as it proved) that Plath's Fulbright Scholarship would be withdrawn. They met at the weekends. 'Above all, save every whisper until Saturday, save every little bit of you. I can hardly remember you without feeling sick and getting aching erections. I shall pour all this into you on Saturday and fill you and fill myself with you and kill myself on you.' Let's be clear about what Hughes is saying. He is telling her not to masturbate, to restrain herself as he is evidently restraining himself.

There may also be a suggestion that their pillow talk should be saved till Saturday and not committed to the page. Not that much *is* committed to the page. Compared to, say, Joyce's erotic letters to Nora, this sequence of intimate letters is strangely continent, strangely literary. (Perhaps strangely only to non-writers. There is an apocryphal story told about Brian Friel that illustrates the central, defining importance of writing to writers. Friel is said to have asked his wife of many years whether she would have loved him had he not been a

---

Letters of Ted Hughes, selected and edited by Christopher Reid (Faber and Faber, 2007).

writer at all. Of course, she reassuringly replied. It is mischievously said that the dramatist was so offended he didn't speak to her for a month.) This sequence is full of schemes, poetic regimens, technical tips, pinpoint criticisms of poetic weaknesses, and a stockpile of 'saleable', somewhat tedious plots – with only odd moments of passion. 'I shall kiss you into blisters.' 'I could crush you into my pores.' 'That night was nothing but getting to know how smooth your body is. The memory of it goes through me like brandy.'

We read writers' letters for two reasons – high-mindedly, for the light they shed on the finished writing; and, less laudably perhaps, but undeniably, for what Hughes, in a letter to his mother-in-law Aurelia Plath, accurately calls 'the inside-dope'. Christopher Reid, constrained by considerations of length – these 700-odd pages represent the tiniest sliver of the total correspondence – has properly opted for a narrative of Hughes's writing: 'the story is above all that of Hughes the writer.' He specifically tells us that this is not 'a biography in disguise'. He tells us that he hasn't been constrained by conditions of propriety. I believe him when he says he has had 'unimpaired editorial freedom'. But, however correct his preference for art over gossip, the effect overall is slightly deadening, even a bit dull. Of course we are grateful for indispensable glosses and authorial commentary on the work. Yet the effect is to turn Hughes into a slight monomaniac – banging on, justifying, explaining, bent on leaving a paper trail for posterity. Here there are several pages of commentary, for instance, on *The House of Aries*, a play produced by the BBC in 1960. They end 'so much for the House of Aries. I'm afraid I've been very obscure. And tedious.' Too true. What Hughes says to Aurelia Plath about her selection of Sylvia's letters applies equally here: 'all these letters exist within a single relationship, and this entails, eventually, beyond a certain critical mass of text, a feeling of monotony and narrowness.' In that case, the claustrophobia of Sylvia talking and talking to her mother. Here, Ted Hughes filibusters on the subject of poetry.

Nevertheless, inevitably, the suicides of Sylvia Plath and Assia Wevill are touched on, often movingly, but with this proviso, formulated shrewdly by Christopher Reid: these terrible episodes, he says, are 'retailed as fully as the partial – in a double sense – nature of the telling will allow.' Hughes found these events completely intractable. As who wouldn't. It is one thing to accept blanket blame, as he does, unflinchingly, in a letter to Aurelia Plath – 'I don't want ever to be forgiven. I don't mean that I shall become a public shrine of mourning and remorse, I would sooner become the opposite. But if there is an eternity, I am damned in it.' It is another to confront the less cosmic, actual circumstances, the whys and the hows, and the how exactlys. In his play *Old Times*, Harold Pinter (whose *The Caretaker* Hughes disliked, mysteriously, as a trite outing for Jung's Ego–Id polarity) ends with a trio of characters unable to reconstruct more than the charred remnants of their actual, shared, damaged sexual experience. Much the same thing happens with Ted Hughes. When Sylvia Plath kills herself, Hughes's adultery is assigned a minor role – the spear carrier – in his letter to Aurelia Plath (13 May 1963): 'my love for her *simply* underwent temporary imprisonment by something which can only be described as madness, as much an attempt to free myself from the strangling quality of our closeness as *by any outer cause*' (my italics). Assia Wevill gets the same short shrift in *Birthday Letters*, where she is 'Slightly filthy with erotic mystery', but absolved of blame, as everyone is absolved of blame in *Birthday Letters*, because she is the agent of Fate – Fate that she, Ted and Sylvia are, dreamers all, sleepwalking towards. It is hard not to be impatient with the facile *broad* brush of *Birthday Letters*, hard not to invoke Edmund in *Lear* I.ii: 'This is the excellent foppery of the world, that, when we are sick in fortune, – often the surfeit of our own behaviour, – we make guilty of our disasters the sun, the moon, and the stars; as if we were villains by necessity, fools by heavenly compulsion, knaves, thieves, and treachers by spherical predominance, drunkards, liars, and *adulterers* by an enforced obedience of planetary influence … ' (my italics).

There is a biography in embryo in this volume – or trace elements of one, which are easy to miss. To Terry Gifford on 16 January 1994, Hughes writes about putting 'the human being back in contact with the human animal' and adumbrates the possible situations that help this procedure. They include having a child (reasonably enough to anyone who's seen a child being born) and the 'hectic bout of adultery'. On page 296, a footnote tells us that a letter to Richard Murphy, dated 10 October 1969, was written 'from Lumb Bank [a remote house Hughes bought in Yorkshire] where TH had moved with his children, and with Brenda Hedden, with whom he had been conducting an affair, and her children'. Assia Wevill killed herself on 25 March 1969. In a letter to Assia Wevill's sister, Celia Chakin, dated 14 April 1969, Hughes writes: 'Assia was my true wife and the best friend I ever had … ' – just as he had written to Aurelia Plath, on 13 May 1963, 'My love for her [Sylvia] simply continues, I look on her as my wife and the only one I shall ever marry …' I don't mean to be censorious or moralising. It is easy to find contradictions and complications in a lifetime's correspondence. (For example, Autumn 1986, to Anne Stevenson, Sylvia's biographer-in-waiting, Hughes denies ever having been bothered by fame at the beginning of his marriage. On the contrary: 'I would have liked a bit of fame in those days, but it seemed far off.' We can check. Early December 1960, Hughes is complaining to Aurelia and Warren Plath that his induction into London literary life, 'becoming something of a public figure', has left him drained of energy. Again, in 22 April 1961, he notes ruefully: 'I've been in the news a bit too much lately, I'm beginning to feel news-burned.' QED) The fact of his sexuality – that erection at the top of this piece – is something neither he nor the majority of his readers ever quite face. He uses his lifelong belief in astrology as an alibi: to his sister, Olwyn, in the late summer of 1962, he makes plans for a private bank account, an exit strategy, the marriage being over for practical purposes: 'I'm aghast when I see how incredibly I've confined & stunted my existence ... However, by progression I now have Leo in the Ascendant instead of Cancer, which just about expresses the change I feel.' He glances at it now and again in this correspondence. To his son Nicholas (who has just ended a relationship) he hints at Sylvia's unreasonable restrictions (undated 1986): 'It meant, Nicholas, that meeting any female between 17 and 39 was out. Your mother banished all her old friends, girl friends, in case one of them set eyes on me – presumably. And if she saw me talking with a girl student, I was in court. Foolish of her, and foolish of me to encourage her to think her laws were reasonable ... one person cannot live within another's magic circle, as an enchanted prisoner.' The poet as Proust's Albertine, *La Prisonnière*. On the one hand, Sylvia is unreasonably jealous – and, therefore, we assume, has nothing to fear. On the other hand, implicitly, a man needs more than one sexual partner. Isn't there a covert appeal to male camaraderie here? Nothing is quite spelled out.

In *Birthday Letters*, 'Fidelity' touches, rather bafflingly, even crassly, on this subject. The poem is constructed around a chivalric ideal in which Hughes, the knight, undergoes a kind of test – sleeping with two naked women every night without sleeping with either. Because he is so 'focused', so 'locked onto' Sylvia. The two naked women exist invisibly in a blind spot created by Sylvia's brilliance. One woman respects his celibacy. The other 'Did all she could to get me inside her'. The sexual stupidity here is striking. Were you wishing to demonstrate fidelity, you couldn't choose a more unpromising, un-reassuring scenario than sharing your bed with two other naked women.

The fox-cub poem 'Epiphany' in *Birthday Letters* is an allegory of wildness, which is also about his untamed sexuality. Hughes meets a man with a fox-cub inside his jacket. The price is a pound. He decides against buying the cub – weighing the cramped domestic conditions, a new baby, against the potential 'mannerless energy' of 'an unpredictable, / Powerful, bounding fox'. By refusing the cub, Hughes 'walked on / As if out of my own life'. And he concludes, enigmatically, 'Our marriage had failed.' Enigmatically, that is, if it is only a fox-cub. If it symbolises something untamed, undomesticated, unruly and *animal* – something that a good marriage could accommodate – it becomes relatively straightforward. But the young Hughes is censoring his own behaviour – and therefore denying, as he sees it, his true inner self.

According to Elaine Feinstein's biography, in 'real life', Hughes was more candid about his requirements – and her conclusions are based on interviews with Brenda Hedden and on correspondence in the Hughes archive in Emory. He was frank about his need for more than one sexual partner: Brenda Hedden told Elaine Feinstein that 'Ted was a man who needed several women ... other men do, don't they? He isn't unique.' Carol Hughes married Hughes in August 1970 and therefore overlapped with Brenda Hedden, whose involvement began in 1968 and seems to have petered out in September 1970, ending finally in 1971. Carol accompanied Ted on literary trips to Israel and Persia. Just as well. In Australia, at the Adelaide Literary Festival, in 1976, Hughes began an affair with Jill Barber, the press co-ordinator, who actually lived in London. At the same time, Hughes was having an affair with the novelist Emma Tennant. Jill Barber knew about this and was unworried by it. Emma Tennant discovered the rival relationship by seeing the obviously intimate pair at a party. Meanwhile Carol Hughes was at Court Green mourning her father, Jack Orchard, who died in February 1976. Hughes visited at the weekends. The affair with Jill Barber continued until she went to live in New York in 1980.

It is too easy to be censorious. We simply don't know enough. The affair with Jill Barber probably began as a counter-weight to the hatred of militant feminists who hounded him at Adelaide, accusing him of murdering Sylvia Plath. Public vilification is hard to bear on your own. Thereafter there was loyalty, gratitude, sexual attraction, sexual imprinting, fear of fatal consequences should he attempt to leave. Philanderer, a word sometimes applied to Hughes, even by friends, seems inadequate. His letters to Assia Wevill, for example, are tender and loving in the face of her sometimes exasperating behaviour. We forgive serial marriages, one love replacing another. But why is this more commendable than continuing to love one person while loving another? It is more normal, of course, but is it more commendable? Serial adultery we understand, are familiar with. Multiple adultery seems beyond our comprehension for no necessary reason. Kindness, gratitude, habit must play their part – doubling in ways that are not unthinkable. Habit, for instance, will hold you and slacken the hold on you.

Nevertheless, it is impossible to write sheer, pure, impure sexual energy out of the picture. In *Passion Play* (1981), one of the great plays of the last century, Peter Nichols has the courage to voice the male sexual imperative: 'I'm an unemotional man who's inspired a passion in my partner. [A picture restorer, James, is addressing a painting of Christ.] And I needn't tell *you* what passion means. Suffering, self-inflicted torture, masochism, all that's holy. Like that exquisite depiction of a bleeding corpse that's waiting for me in Zurich. By day I'll patch it up, repair the blood and wounds where they've been knocked around over the years, but every night I'll fuck as though life depended on it. Which of course it does.' He doesn't just mean reproduction. He means being alive, feeling alive. As for the analogy with Christ's Passion – his wife Eleanor sings in Bach's *Matthew Passion* – we can compare Tom Stoppard's *The Invention of Love*, where the middle-aged Housman, *smitten* still by Moses Jackson, parses the middle-aged Horace faced with Venus waging war. Or think of Kipling's ' " *The joy of an old wound waking*" ' (in 'The Oldest Song'). It is no accident that we favour the word 'smitten' to describe sexual passion.

Of course, we would like not to succumb. We would like to behave impeccably. Nineteenth-century literature is founded on the conflict between passion and duty, from *Jane Eyre* to *The Mill on the Floss*. Sense and susceptibility. In all of us, there is a real struggle between the Puritan and the Hedonist – a struggle realer for Hughes than most, so much so that it informs his reading of Shakespeare in *Shakespeare and the Goddess of Complete Being* – where he is on the side of completeness, of licence, of pagan candour, a Nietzschean immoralist. As he is in *Gaudete*, where, *mutatitis mutandis*, the Revd Lumb gets to go with nearly every female in sight. Rejoice.

In a letter to Daniel Weissbort (undated 1976) he writes: 'the real subject of poetry might be what we really feel about what really happens to us, and the real language might be a very plain & direct business.' To Anne Sexton (9 August 1967) he writes: 'Anyway, you've no need to worry. When you've got it you've got it – you don't have to bother about poetry, you just have to be truthful (which is where the brain and all its hideous lies leap in, I know).' It seems so simple. Tell it how it is. As an imperative, it *is* simple. But what really happens to us isn't. We tell the story of ourselves to our own advantage, from our own confusion. In Hughes's case, his openness was as illusory as our own. In *Winter Pollen*, the essay 'Superstitions' mounts a concessive defence of astrology: 'To an outsider, astrology is a procession of puerile absurdities. A Babel of gibberish.' It has no way of shedding its mistakes as science does. Yet, reviewing Louis MacNeice's *Astrology*, Hughes offers up Evangeline Adams as testable data, showing that astrology works, whether as magic or as a science. In this volume of letters, astrology is a persistent *point de repère*, a significant example of what Bridget Jones calls 'mentionitis'. Page 14, 'astrological maps'; page 19, 'I've worked it out by parental temperaments, zodiacal, and such'; page 22, 'my host – a monstrously built Gemini'; page 30, Sylvia is 'Scorpio Oct 27th, moon in Libra, last degrees of Aries rising and has her Mars smack on my sun'; page 47, 'with two Leos you will have to look out' (of his brother Gerald's children); page 49, 'I had to stay at Leeds for an hour, so I bought a glass of milk and a HOROSCOPE and read our different fortunes for the month – all very non-committal & unconvincing as usual'; page 62, 'I can put it down to the conjunction of the moon and saturn'; page 78 shows us Sylvia's astrological chart; page 94, Hughes is trying, unsuccessfully, to place a newspaper advertisement as a professional astrologer.

I could go on, believe me. But there is a comic thread through these letters that conveniently epitomises Hughes's astrological obsession and the rational world's refusal to accede to his belief. The rational world in this case is Faber and Faber. When *Wodwo* is accepted, Hughes asks his editor, Charles Monteith, if the book can be published on 9 May, 'the day of days', as he knows from 'thousands of hours studying Astrology'. Christopher Reid notes drily that '*Wodwo* was in fact published on 18 May 1967.' Frank Pike at Fabers was asked if *Crow* could be published on 1 October, because 'Newton and Kepler are in agreement, that is a great day in heaven.' Reid notes: '*Crow*'s eventual publication date was 12 October.' It wasn't until the publication of *Season Songs* on 13 May 1976 that Faber obliged Hughes.

There is a key quote on page 104: 'There is no explanation for it, though astrology, of course, explains it all.' Hughes believed that rationality was limiting. It is obvious from these letters that astrology shut down far too much. In a key letter to Lucas Myers (19 June 1959) Hughes advances the theory that 'most poetry, particularly modern poetry, is quite without this wholeness – men make their whole style out of one filament of the thick rope of human nature.' This is one with the title of his Shakespearean opus, *Shakespeare and the Goddess of Complete Being*. Joyce leaves behind him a record of his complete being in his work. Hughes's record is short-circuited by astrology – by the autocomplete of astrology as the explanation for everything. Which is why, despite Hughes's moving last letters about the final, painful disclosure of the Sylvia Plath saga – complete disclosure that he hoped would cure his cancer – *Birthday Letters* are a failure as a full record and therefore as poetry. Every poem virtually is a memory arranged to reflect a tragic telos. It makes for falsity and formal monotony. Fixed stars govern a life – as Plath wrote in 'Words'. The danger for Hughes is that they're fixed like the World's Series is fixed in *The Great Gatsby* by Meyer Wolfsheim.

Of course, there are great things in these letters – a marvellous account of receiving the Queen's Gold Medal for poetry, written for Frieda, and completely different from the account he gave me. He is genuinely modest about his work: 'the poems in my book [*Hawk in the Rain*] seem crude in pitch for the most part'; of *Lupercal*, 'much better than my earlier ones, but gravely crippled by the awful emotional dryness I've felt over here [USA]'. Regularly, if not as frequently as you might expect, you encounter delightful touches: on Fortnum and Mason's 'deep carpets, sturgeon's tongues, bowing uniformed attendants, cassowary brains in melon syrup'. This is Frieda learning to speak: 'issueing a stream of Japanese, with the beginnings of translation – app-uh, for apple, ooo-en, for open …' The famous are brought before us: 'Neruda – he read torrentially for about 25 minutes off a piece of paper about 3" by 4". Then he turned it over, & read on.' T. S. Eliot: 'His smile is like that of a person recovering from some serious operation ... Eliot isn't at all unguarded in his remarks. He has huge thick hands – unexpected.'

You might think letters were Hughes's forte, his natural mode, since the Shakespeare book emerged from letters written to the Swedish director Donya Feuer, and given the epistolary template of *Birthday Letters*. However, letters are only letters finally. However many miraculous touches, finished writing is better for second thoughts, and we should curb our expectations. Sometime in the summer of 1959, Hughes wrote to his parents an account of the bears in Yellowstone National Park, Wyoming. 'Tuesday we went round the park look-ing at the geysers, whole valleys full of these things – most are just holes in the caked white ground – steaming, & bubbling water, a really hellish land-scape, sulphur smells.' Compare Kipling in Japan in *From Sea to Sea*: 'In the end we found an impoverished and second-hand Hell ... Water, in which bad eggs had been boiled, stood in blister-lipped pools ... ' Of course, Kipling's *Letters of Travel* were composed for publication. In this case, it is possible to compare the roughed-out original letter with the finished version, thirty-odd years later in *Birthday Letters*, 'The 59th Bear'. The writing is better but the incident is worked up – the bear allegorised to stand in for the death pursuing Sylvia Plath. In the letter, Ted and Sylvia count sixty-seven bears. In the poem, the lethal bear that suddenly displaces the amiable bears fed by the tourists is the fifty-ninth. The original has details 'missing' from the final poetic narrative: 'we heard it sucking our oranges'; a car comes and 'the bear ran to hide behind our tent – hitting a guy rope & shaking the whole place.' On the other hand, generally the detail is improved: 'He'd left matted hairs. I glued them in my Shakespeare'; the hiding bear's 'breathing / Heavy after the night's gourmandizing, / Rasped close to the canvas – only inches / From your face that, big-eyed, stared at me / Staring at you.' (A reprise of the close of 'Full Moon and Little Frieda' – 'The moon has stepped back like an artist gazing amazed at a work / That points at him amazed' – yet tremendous, all the same.) Tremendous, but about to be pressed into a thesis. Just a little reminiscent of a politician, gifted with oratory, but burdened with a party agenda.

A. E. Housman's Letters
(2007)

Arnold Schoenberg thought everything about a great man should interest us – and he concluded by saying he would have liked to see Mahler tying his tie. In fact, the more personal, the better. In an interview once, the aristocratic wizard Nabokov, describing his working day, alluded to his daily 'enthronement' – almost like one of those kings whose toilet arrangements were semi-public, and whose courtiers vied for the position of Gentleman of the Chamber. We like knowing that the lavatories in Morris's Kelmscott Manor were double. Brian Boyd, Nabokov's biographer, tells us that when he taught at Cornell University, the novelist – poor and indifferent to horticulture – would recline in a deckchair surrounded by yard-high grass, drinking cocktails from a jam jar. Housman, after Edmund Gosse died, hoped that his diary would be made use of – 'full and not excessively discreet use'. When I shook hands with Auden, I looked down to see if he was wearing leather gloves. Nothing is too trivial. We read the letters of great men praying for the keys to their art, but alert to moments of unguarded intimacy. There's the big issue and there's the private clue secreted in the text. We pry and we prey. We would like to discover, but we are happy to uncover – or perhaps the verb should be 'to undercover'.

Beerbohm thought Housman a dull dog: 'he was like an absconding cashier. We certainly wished he would abscond – sitting silent and then saying only "there is a bit of a nip in the air, don't you think?"'

So it was with wry amusement that I found myself trying to decide – as I read my way through this beautiful two volume, 1,228-page edition of Housman's letters – which letter was the dullest. There are many contenders, many one-line missives that are the opposite of one-liners: 'Dear Rothenstein [Housman gets a sole mention in Rothenstein's memoirs – about Housman's dislike of Rothenstein's representations of him], I shall be very pleased to dine with you on Friday at 7.15. [26 February 1906]' The runaway winner is, however, a telegram to Housman's publisher, Grant Richards, 27 October 1933: 'Yes Housman.' The dullness is of no importance. Most of life is dull – which is why human beings prize excitement so highly. In *The Curtain*, Milan Kundera notes that tedium is now a major subject for the novel. Jane Austen in *Emma* gives us

The Letters of A. E. Housman, edited by Archie Burnett (Clarendon Press, 2007).

a chapter on gruel, the constituents of gruel, the preparation of gruel, the efficacy of gruel in warding off medical complaints – in a way that pre-empts the non-events of *Waiting for Godot* and makes Beckett look belated. Mr Wodehouse is only ostensibly boring because Jane Austen is the great poet of boredom – her detail is almost epic in its disclosure, her small talk splits the atom of ennui and her aesthetic courage in sustaining these epics of emptiness is what makes them hilarious.

Nor is it important that these meticulously edited letters are not completely free from mistakes. As early as page 5, the numbers in the text do not correspond to their footnotes. But it is easy to see which should be married to which. And on page 458 of Vol. I, the footnote is unable to decide whether Grant Richards's 'pet bruiser' is Frank Moran or Frank Morgan. The otherwise excellent editor, Archie Burnett, might be consoled to learn that, after a day of proofreading that went on till 3 a.m., I told Ted Hughes that we could probably read through his anthology *The Rattle Bag* once more before his early train back to Exeter. His left hand lifted his hair back into place and he said levelly, 'Every book should have a leavening of misprints.' We went to bed.

What do these letters tell us? He could be facetious: he signs himself 'Alfred Edouard Maisonhomme' and tells Edith Wharton that the correct French pronunciation is 'Oozman'. They tell us that Housman was vain and punished himself by refusing all public honours. They recount Housman's generous dealings with his publisher Grant Richards – first refusing any royalties on *A Shropshire Lad* (he preferred a lower price and a large audience); then lending his publisher large sums (Richards went bankrupt twice). Richards, Housman complained to his brother, 'has not paid me a penny of royalties on *Last Poems*, and has intercepted the first year's royalties from the American publishers. He also owes me £750 which I lent him four or five years ago.' Housman was firm with Richards and yet managed to maintain cordial relations. We learn, obliquely, about Housman's foreign rent boys – to Richards in Paris: 'I cannot offer you anything of an invitation, for I shall have a friend with me who would not mix with you nor you with him.' Aged seventy and seriously unwell, Housman writes to his sister about his 'companion', 'who regards me as a benefactor'.

We learn about Housman's educated interest in illicit literature: he read the banned *Ulysses* (without much pleasure) and the banned *Lady Chatterley*, not to mention the letters of Corvo ('I have been more amused with things written in urinals') and *Fanny Hill*. He also read Proust (without being carried away) and the poetry of Anna Akhmatova. He corresponded expertly with T. S. Eliot about Wilkie Collins. It is well known that the poet of pastoral ploughmen also flew in an aeroplane – but perhaps less well known that this was a frequent occurrence, undeterred by crashes. (Housman reckoned that any crash made it statistically unlikely *he* would crash.) But he seems to have been fearless: 'the machine was not particularly unsteady, *except in taking off and landing*' (my italics). One similar surprise is when the pastoral meets *Trainspotting* – in his last illness, Housman takes heroin: 'I am fed on toast, chicken-broth, orange juice, champagne, breast of turkey, Brand's essence of chicken. I am very weak. The other night they gave me an injection of heroin instead of my usual soporific, and I learned what it is to be totally deprived of intellect.'

The unbending scholar of legend could be quite frisky: 'Your attentive housemaids however seem to have retained two pair of boots as a souvenir, and perhaps you will notice them wearing them for ear-rings.' But you have to read all the letters to find the truth in all its contrariety. Punitively modest as a rule, Housman, in the only surviving letter to the great (unrequited) love of his life, is reduced to boasting about sales: 'there are no means of driving the knowledge into your thick head, what a bloody good poet I am.'

Marianne Moore
(2004)

There are obvious, major editorial flaws in *The Poems of Marianne Moore*. Grace Schulman's worthy aim – to give us the first, belated, chronological edition of Moore's work, so that readers can assess her development – has been sabotaged by financial considerations. We are given the work in chronological order, but the texts are chosen without any editorial method. What was needed was a variorum edition, giving all the versions of each poem, arranged chronologically. Obviously, the decision not to do so was dictated by commercial considerations – pricing, in a word. There are too many variant texts of each poem to permit total inclusiveness. Moore was an assiduous reviser and restless recaster, rivalled only by Robert Lowell.

Stanzaic versions, sometimes rhyming, were replaced by free-verse versions. She split up several sequences or suppressed elements in the sequences. Both sequences and suppressed elements are restored here – three times in the main text (pruned of their umbrella titles), sometimes only in the notes. Moore's work was never finished. She was like Degas, whose friends came to dread the painter's frowning appraisal of his own work in their possession – the prelude to removing the picture in question to the artist's studio, sometimes never to be seen again.

Forbidden every variant, allowed a selection in her notes, the crucial editorial choice becomes therefore the main text of any poem. Which of several variants should be chosen? And on what grounds? Grace Schulman has opted for what she describes in her introduction as 'conscientious inconsistency'. In other words, complete absence of editorial method. She pleases herself. It is as if R. B. McKerrow's theory of copy text had never been formulated. The copy text has to be the author's last redaction – in other words, in this case, Marianne Moore's 1967 *Complete Poems*, whether we agree with her decisions or not.

Mrs Schulman's problems are further complicated (she thinks) by hitherto unpublished work and variant versions that exist in the Marianne Moore archive, to which the editor has access. A variorum edition might include any interesting variants from this source. In an edition like the one under review – *not* a variorum – these unpublished versions have no editorial validity, however interesting

---

The Poems of Marianne Moore, edited by Grace Schulman (Faber and Faber, 2003).

they might be. For no good editorial reason, Mrs Schulman also reprints several poems that Marianne Moore decided to suppress. More than twice as many poems appear here than the 102 that made up *Complete Poems*.

Edward Mendelson faced a similar problem with W. H. Auden, many of whose revisions and excisions seemed mistaken to his readership. Mendelson solved the problem by issuing a *Collected Poems* which respected the poet's judgements and decisions. Then he issued *The English Auden* – a volume that reprinted the poems in their familiar, first-published form. Grace Schulman's problems are more acute. There are more published variants – starting with the original magazine publication and metamorphosing through various subsequent collections. 'Poetry' is the most notorious example. By the time *Complete Poems* appeared in 1967, Moore had whittled its original twenty-nine lines down to three. She included a longer version in her notes. It is this version that Mrs Schulman prints as her main text. In her notes, Mrs Schulman reprints the latest, three-line version; the thirteen-line version in *Observations* (1925); and, utterly mysteriously, the otiose (because identical) *Complete Poems* notes text that she prints in the main text.

This isn't an editorial dilemma, but straightforward scholarly slovenliness. Another example is the misprint in line 6 of 'A Grave', where 'The first stand in a procession, each with an emerald turkey-foot at the top' should be 'The firs stand in a procession, each with an emerald turkey-foot at the top'. In Marianne Moore's own notes to 'Picking and Choosing' – as reprinted here on page 138 – we are offered sources for quotations from Erté and Isaac Walton's *The Compleat Angler*. Neither Walton nor Erté is quoted in 'Picking and Choosing'. The notes belong to the next poem, 'England' – which apparently has no authorial notes at all in this edition. On page 413 surely there should have been an editorial note pointing out that the last lines of 'Garter Snake' and 'Eloquence' (two poems salvaged from the Rosenbach Museum archive and printed in the notes) are repeated in another poem, 'The Monkey Puzzle'. Not that this problem would have arisen had Mrs Schulman respected Marianne Moore's decision not to publish 'Garter Snake' and 'Eloquence'. On page 387 Marianne Moore's own note refers to *Animals for Show and Pleasure in Ancient Rome* – a book also referred to on page 385, where the title is unitalicised. There is no cross-reference. On the same page 385 a word in Greek in *Complete Poems* here appears transliterated because the printing software has failed. 'England' is printed here in a different layout from the version in *Complete Poems*, but nothing in the editorial note (page 410) alerts us. These examples are indicative, not exhaustive. Individually, they are less important than the decision to print only a selection of Marianne Moore's translations of La Fontaine, or the decision not to print all Marianne Moore's own, varying notes but instead 'a partial view of the author's notes as they are found in all of her editions'. Cumulatively, however, these slips are unsettling.

Admirers of Marianne Moore's poetry can always produce a vivid anthology of moments, of bravura descriptive touches. The 'kiwi's rain-shawl / of haired feathers' ('The Mind is an Enchanting Thing'); 'the lion's ferocious chrysanthemum head' ('The Monkey Puzzle'); 'snakes' hypodermic teeth' and the witty 'semi-precious cat's eyes of the owl' ('The Hero'); the reindeer as a 'candelabrum-headed ornament / for a place where ornaments are scarce' ('Rigorists'); the 'coral feet' of a dead seagull, 'parting its beak to greet / men long dead' ('A Talisman'); the pangolin's 'scale / lapping scale with spruce-cone regularity', 'This near-artichoke' ('The Pangolin'); 'The / soot-brown tail-tuft on / a kind of lion- / tail', 'when a tiger / *coughs*' (my italics) ('The Buffalo'); the 'fern-seed footprints' of 'The Jerboa', its 'three-cornered smooth-working Chippendale claw'. In the same poem, we find Moore's wonderful periphrasis for a mirage: 'the 'translucent mistake / of the desert'. 'No Swan So Fine' notices the swan's 'gondoliering legs'. Then there is the mussel, 'opening and shutting itself like / / an / injured fan', in 'The Fish'. Or the swans' 'flamingo-coloured, maple- / leaf like feet' in 'Critics and Connoisseurs'. Consider, too, these elephant trunks: 'Uplifted and waved till immobilized / wisteria-like'; 'rests his hunting-horn-curled trunk on shadowed stone'. Or 'the elephant's *stiff* / ear' (my italics) ('Elephants'). Or the horse's 'nose rigid and suede nostrils spread' ('Tom Fool at Jamaica').

These accurate, meditated, 'spontaneous' descriptive flourishes align Marianne Moore with the occasional *sprezzatura* of Wallace Stevens and the habitual bravura of Kipling. This is the story of three bears: Kipling's bear ('cinnamon-bear cub' in *From Sea to Sea*), Stevens's bear ('the ponderous cinnamon' in 'Notes Toward a Supreme Fiction') and Moore's bear ('A bear with fur that appeared to have been licked backward' from her translation of La Fontaine's 'The Bear and the Garden-Lover'). You have to know (wet) bear fur really well to recognise the accuracy of Moore's line.

Compare, too, Moore's 'the waterfall that never seems to fall – / an endless skein swayed by the wind' ('An Octopus') with Kipling's 'a blown thread of white vapour' (*From Sea to Sea*). And observe Moore's influence as Elizabeth Bishop surpasses her in 'Song for the Rainy Season': 'the lint / of the waterfalls cling'.

A hyper-real clarity distinguishes these *aperçus*. Yet they exist in poems whose arguments are often crepuscular. In his essay on Moore's ostrich poem, 'He Digesteth Harde Yron', in *The Necessary Angel*, Wallace Stevens touches on the problem of meaning, both particularly and in general. In general, he says, poetry's meaning is not a profound thought to be abstracted – 'the extraction of a meaning from the poem and appraisement of it by rational standards of truth

[is] due to enthusiasm for moral or religious truth.' In other words, Stevens differs from Arnold: poetry does not tell us how to live. For Stevens, poetry's importance, its profound value, is to make reality itself a revelation, to make the merely given an unlooked-for gift. 'The reality so imposed need not be a great reality.' In other words, 'fire in the dove-neck's / iridescence' or the hyper-real clarity I praised after collating that anthology of vivid examples.

When Stevens comes to the particular poem, however, he mistakes Marianne Moore's emphasis, I think: 'the gist of the poem is that the camel-sparrow [the hump-backed ostrich] has escaped the greed that has led to the extinction of other birds linked to it in size.' The 'mistake' is hardly surprising, hardly unique. In her memoir, an accurate, aleatoric, eclectic poem of accumulation, patient detail, fearless triviality, Elizabeth Bishop recalls that Marianne Moore had a chainless bicycle – in its way, the perfect image for poems whose construction contains nearly always an inexplicable element, some opacity that sets you down at your destination, little the wiser about the means of transportation. Eliot, shrewd editor that he was, knew this, I believe, and therefore suggested Moore place first at the opening of *Selected Poems* the completely lucid, the uniquely lucid 'The Steeple-Jack' – thereby ensuring a readership that would patiently immerse itself in the less immediately rewarding poems with their pockets of fog. (And, of course, creating thereby the editorial problems of chronology that this volume is designed to resolve.)

Moore knew she had a problem with clarity. She knew she had a problem with clarity in 'He "Digesteth Harde Yron"'. She wrote to her brother (21 January 1941): 'We, – Bear [Moore's mother's nickname] & me – accept your overture concerning ye Estrich – "He digesteth hard yron". That's what he's gonna do. / / I rekkonize my trouble, as being too oblique & obscure, as a result of hating Crudeness (& Alvin E. Magary condescension and insulting didacticism). Always What I learn to regret, I try to avoid in the next try, it is very hard to REarrange a thing that has fallen in to the mold already. And *I shall endeavour* to be CLEARER.'

Stevens thought 'He "Digesteth Harde Yron"' was about surviving extinction by 'solicitude for its own welfare and that of its chicks'. He is avoiding the clear pointer at the end of the first stanza: 'the large sparrow / Xenophon saw walking by a stream – was and is / a symbol of justice.' Moore's poem is a meditation on justice – a knotty attempt to discern the real constituents of an abstract noun apparently so obvious it merits no further analysis. It is also embarrassed by the bald magnitude of its theme – something Stevens instinctively realises when he discounts the truth value of meaning – and the theme is therefore 'dressed' with interesting information, digressive frills and furbelows. The accumulation of bizarre facts is likely to bury the line of argument.

One thing Moore wishes to say about justice is bound up in her choice of the ostrich as symbol: justice is intuitive and innate. It requires no theoretical justification:

> The power of the visible
> is the invisible; as even where
> no tree of freedom grows,
> so-called brute courage knows.

'*Brute* courage' – the ostrich defending its young is a perfect example – is 'so-called' because it comes from a spiritual impulse. The 'tree of freedom' is at once the liberty tree and the idea of an evolving *system* of justice. Even without the concept of justice, we have an innate sense of fairness and unfairness.

There are problems of argumentation here, however. 'The power of the visible' assumes that this power is moral. But suppose 'the power of the visible' were a tyranny … 'Brute courage' refers here to animal courage, but the phrase is commonly used of unthinking human courage.

Marianne Moore also wishes to oppose principle to unthinking exercise of power. We are helped to her meaning here by a letter to Lloyd Frankenberg (26 December 1943): 'I believe that the invisible and sword of the spirit could and *shall* make the bayonet and the machine-gun impossible':

> Heroism is exhausting, yet
> it contradicts a greed that did not wisely spare
> the harmless solitaire …

Again, there is a problem of argumentation: 'greed' is less clear than 'power' would have been. *Greed.* Were the auk and the solitaire and the roc killed simply for food in excess of what was needed for subsistence?

Marianne Moore also wishes to praise the panoply of justice:

> Six hundred ostrich-brains served
> at one banquet, the ostrich-plumed-tipped tent
> and desert spear, jewel-
> gorgeous ugly egg-shell
> goblets, eight pairs of ostriches
> in harness, dramatise a meaning
> always missed by the externalist.

The outward sign of inner splendour, material mirroring the moral, is the intended drift here – but, unfortunately for the argument advanced by Moore, the outward symbolic grandeur involves the slaughter of the very bird that is emblematic of justice. There is a real mismatch, a thoroughly awkward fit of subject and anecdotal information.

To summarise: Wallace Stevens is wrong on two counts. He misreads the particular 'gist' of this particular poem. Moreover, though I agree with the general principles he promulgates about meaning – the unimportance of obvious profundity – I think he is obtuse in deriving them from this Marianne Moore poem, or any Marianne Moore poem. She is consistently the figure envisaged in Stevens's 'A High-Toned Old Christian Woman'. Think how many of her poems have moments of candid moralising in praise of freedom, justice and hope: 'love / is the only fortress / strong enough to trust to' ('The Paper Nautilus'); 'What is there // like fortitude?' ('Nevertheless'); 'the wisest is he who's not sure that he knows' ('Elephants'); 'the power of relinquishing / what one would keep; that is freedom' ('His Shield'); 'Hate-hardened heart, heart of iron, / iron is iron till it is rust', 'Beauty is everlasting / and dust is for a time' ('In Distrust of Merits').

Of course, like Stevens, she was embarrassed by what she called, in that already cited letter to her brother, 'Alvin E. Magary condescension and insulting didacticism' – so these moralising precepts were dressed up. In Moore, the oblique modernist was also the Victorian belletrist sewing on sequins of shiny fact. She never stopped rummaging in the dressing-up box. Her poems were cosmetic creations designed to make-over some plain, flat-chested, uninflected moralising.

The strategy extended to her own social personality. Her hats were a strenuous attempt at a personal distinctive style. Her letters reveal someone deeply aware of dress. 'My blue dress with the crystal-and-gold buttons and zigzag gold belt is self-sustaining,' she observed to Hildegarde Watson (11 May 1956). She admired the sartorial eccentricity of Edith Sitwell in a letter to Mary Shoemaker (9 April 1954): 'Edith was wearing an emerald satin Chinese brocade coat and large pale broach (jade perhaps) and very large square cut aquamarines (rings); she has just returned from Hollywood.' Moore was like a young writer bent on manufacturing a style – a set of 'characteristics' whose purpose is to differentiate him or her from other writers, whereas true style is an extension of the writer's natural personality. Think of e e cummings's worked-up 'originality' – the lower case, eccentricities of punctuation, his hectic faux-naïf tone and his febrile faux-naïf sentiments – then remember Wallace Stevens's hapless, neutral comment on Marianne Moore's style: 'Miss Moore's finical phraseology is an element in her procedure.' *Finical*. There was always something *voulu*, something concocted, about even her opinions. Grace Schulman's introduction mentions a 1951 essay in which Moore lists Edward Kauffer as 'one of the few real artists alive today'. According to Grace Schulman, Moore places him in the company of 'Pablo Casals, Soledad, Hans Mardersteig, Alec Guinness, and the Lippizan horsemen'. It is the last item here that ignites one's irritation at the palpable affectation of the list. No Picasso, no Stravinsky, not even Charlie Chaplin. Nothing vulgar, nothing with obvious value, only a few precious items calculated to distinguish their owner from *hoi polloi*. Opinions as fashionably unfashionable accessories.

Her need to decorate the Isaac Watts element of pulpitry in her poetry is manifested in her 1937 review of *Harmonium* and *Ideas of Order*, where she 'analyses' Stevens's 'Bantams in Pinewoods': 'upon the general marine volume of statement is set a parachute-spinnaker of verbiage which looms out like half a cantaloupe and gives the body of the theme the air of a fabled argosy advancing.' Deep profundities, then, buoying up *verbiage* like a tea-clipper cramming on canvas.

This 'verbiage' has the side-effect of obfuscating her argument's direction, of course, but Marianne Moore was argumentatively incompetent in any case. Her reviews are quaint, mannered, unclear pastiches of preciseness. Now and then, there is a defiant flourish of theoretical credo. In that same piece about Wallace Stevens (*Poetry*, February 1937) she writes: 'we are able here to see the salutary effect of insisting that a piece of writing please the writer himself before it pleases anyone else; *and how a poet may be a wall of incorruptibleness against violating the essential order of contributing vagueness*' (my italics). In a letter to Lloyd Frankenberg (26 December 1943), she presents this 'vagueness', this blurred 'poetic' suggestiveness, not as a counter-balance to her didacticism, but as a courtesy to the reader: 'a poem is not a poem, surely, unless there is a margin of undidactic implication, – an area which the reader can make his own.' As she became older, she became more fretful, less inclined to justify her slightly addled poetic procedures. One of the reasons 'Poetry' was slashed to three lines was to present the essence of her argument unencumbered. Another poem, 'Picking and Choosing', seems to be about the simplicity of good literary criticism. In its final version, 'Poetry' argues that, despite its artifice, poetry can be genuine. The excised remainder of the poem, she explained to Grace Schulman, 'seemed to be padding' – or *verbiage*.

On top of that, as her letters make clear, she eventually became aware of her intrinsic ratiocinative disability. In the same letter to Frankenberg, she notes: 'one's reasoning is a strange thing; is really *not* reason, is a mingling of resistances, unperceptiveness, un-coordination and helplessness.' In its way, this is a brilliant account of how we actually think, the process of thought, which could not be more different from Mr Ramsay's logical progress through the alphabet in *To the Lighthouse*. But it bodes badly for the cogent expression of that thought once it has mysteriously arrived. To Ezra Pound (30 July 1950) she writes, re her La Fontaine translations: 'a mixed metaphor is better to me than a right one. A sentence does not have to have a verb as far as I am concerned. But la Fontaine is, as you suggested, better "formal" and unimpaired by the bizarre.'

Consider this letter to Hildegarde Watson (8 September 1954) in which Marianne Moore evokes the house she is vacationing in that used to belong to the scholar F. O. Mathiessen. The tone is finical but the description bleeds from Ingres to bookcases. Thinking as a kind of haemorrhage: 'the hair fine precision of the Ingres 1818 group by the bureau, – of parents, children, & spinet the slightly smiling daughter turning from the keyboard on which one hand is resting, the detail of the father's stock, vest & overcoat buttons; and the University – not to say Harvard – flavour of the bookcases upstairs and down'. The babble of consciousness. Compare her remark to Elizabeth Bishop (9 June 1956): 'I am intolerable, the way I jam things together.'

Sometimes, it works. As it does sometimes in Kerouac. Though it is too long to quote here, no one should miss her account of being taken by George Plimpton to the fight between Floyd Patterson and George Chuvalo – the penultimate, pell-mell, all-inclusive, observant letter in *The Selected Letters of Marianne Moore* (edited by Bonnie Costello, Celeste Goodridge and Cristanne Miller). It is dated 5 February 1965.

Surprisingly frequently, it doesn't work. Reviewing *The Complete Prose* in the *Times Literary Supplement* (6 February 1987), Thom Gunn observed evenly: 'Her poetry fascinates, but its plain sense is often harder to arrive at than those traditional-looking summings-up would seem to indicate, and we continue wondering about it, annotating, considering, memorising, searching out its obscure corners, because it still fascinates even when it bewilders us.' Even the loyal Elizabeth Bishop noted that 'her poems showed a mind not much like anyone else's' and reported that 'when she wrote an acrostic on the name of one of her oldest and closest friends, it too was semi-concealed, by being written upside down.' Moore's biographer, Charles Molesworth, quotes from Malvina Hoffman's memoir, *Yesterday is Tomorrow*, which was polished and edited by Moore: 'I confess I found her poetry hard to understand, so I would ask her to read one of her poems aloud to me. Then I would say, "I really don't know what that's all about, because of my own ignorance, I'm sure, but just possibly you might explain it to me". She would start explaining it, and then she'd say, "You know, I don't really understand much of it myself", and she'd laugh and say, "Of course, I was convinced I understood it when I wrote it. I'll have to work some more on it", and then there would be jottings in the margin, and revisions.'

Elizabeth Bishop's memoir volunteers: 'She said her poem "Spencer's

Ireland" was not about *loving* Ireland, as people seemed to think, but about *disapproving* of it.' If anything, 'people' seem to be in the right – but it is hard to tell. Moore's 'Voracities and Verities / Sometimes Are Interacting' is a more compact illustration of her difficulty with argument. Here is the whole poem:

> I don't like diamonds;
> the emerald's 'grass-lamp glow' is better;
>   and unobtrusiveness is dazzling,
>   upon occasion.
>   Some kinds of gratitude are trying.
>
>   Poets, don't make a fuss;
> the elephant's 'crooked trumpet' 'doth write';
>   and to a tiger-book I am reading –
>   I think you know the one –
>   I am under obligation.
>
>   One may be pardoned, yes I know
>   one may, for love undying.

There is an advocacy of modesty here reminiscent of George Herbert, a repudiation of showiness and braggadocio, that is relatively easy to follow. The moral gist is undisguised. Compare Moore on reticence, citing T. S. Eliot on Lancelot Andrewes: 'he is wholly in his subject, unaware of anything else.' Perhaps there is a local problem with 'Some kinds of gratitude are trying' – a line that I think means gratitude where there is no choice; for example, gratitude enforced by brilliance. I don't think the line means, as it possibly could, that some expressions of gratitude are 'trying' because they are overdone. The second stanza instructs poets that they are nothing special.

The real interpretative difficulty is the relationship of the last two lines to the rest of the poem. 'One may be pardoned, yes I know / one may, for love undying.' Molesworth refers us to St Paul's Letter to the Ephesians for clarification. Not in my Bible. If we say that this is a poem about hyperbole versus unadorned truth, about voracity versus verity, then, taking our hint from the subtitle, the last two lines must be a rare example of their coincidence. One may exaggerate where love is concerned. The poem is much illuminated by Moore's essay 'Feeling and Precision' (1944): in it, she deplores hyperbole because it is imprecise; then she says, 'Sir Francis Bacon was probably right when he said, "Hyperbole is comely only in love".' Without this (involuntary, explanatory) note, those last two lines would plunge the reader into sudden, possibly perpetual darkness.

'The Jerboa' touches on the same central theme of modesty versus excess.

Oddly, again like Herbert, the procedure of the poem seems to contradict its moral. (Think of the intricate artifice of Herbert's 'The Wreath', whose form is just as much a *carmen figuratum* as the more ostentatious 'Easter Wings'.) Part I of 'The Jerboa' is a plethora of information that lives up to its subtitle, 'Too Much' – slightly disingenuously lives up, since Moore expects us to take pleasure in her trawl through rare particularities. Part II is subtitled 'Abundance' – and set in the desert. The subtitle is ironic in two ways. On the one hand, 'Abundance' looks like an obvious misnomer. On the other hand, the ascetic is offered as real abundance.

The six-line stanzaic form of 'The Jerboa' rhymes four lines out of the six, roughly speaking. And it moves for the most part with hypnotic conviction, though the line-breaks are mostly counter-intuitive. (Moore wrote to her niece Marianne Craig Moore on 5 May 1942: 'Nor do I object to having the line begin "weak", or to having what would naturally be the end of the line, come in the middle of the line, because I think of the stanza, rather than the line, as the unit … I do not try to make this kind of [syllabic] pattern, it is instinctive, and usually I would prefer not to divide words at the end of lines but am willing to, for the sake of the larger and more inclusive symmetry.') As quotation shows, in 'The Jerboa' the stanza is not an inviolable unit, any more than the line:

> … this cone
> of the Pompeys, which is known
>
> now as the Popes', passed
> for art. A huge cast
>   bronze, dwarfing the peacock
>   statue in the garden of the Vatican,
>   it looks like a work of art made to give
>   to a Pompey, or native
>
> of Thebes.

The rhymes are 'passed', 'cast', 'give' and 'native'. The momentum ignores the end of the stanza. On the whole, this is plausible rather than factitious. You don't feel the contrivance of a cummings, his manufactured originality. Or you don't until some clumsiness alerts you to the ugliness of an individual line like 'necks rearing in back in the': the Egyptians looked on all animals as theirs, including

> the wild ostrich herd
> with hard feet and bird
>   necks rearing *in back in the*

> *dust like a serpent preparing to strike*, cranes,
>   mongooses, storks, anoas, Nile geese …

The italicised section, with its duff, inert simile, suddenly leaks all conviction – leaving the reader with a line resembling the worst of Brodsky: 'necks rearing in back in the'. Just to preserve decorum, the same thing happens in 'He "Digesteth Harde Yron"':

> … And what could have been more fit
> for the Chinese lawn it
>
>   gazed on as a gift to an
>   emperor who admired strange birds, than this
> one, who builds his mud-made
> nest in dust yet will wade
>   in lake or sea till only the head shows.

The rhymes are 'made' and 'wade', but you suddenly feel they come at too high a price – the eccentricity of the 'line' 'nest in dust yet will wade'. Not to mention 'gazed on as a gift to an'. What was delightfully different strikes one in seconds as hideously mannered. And what this inchoate digression – melding the ornithological hobby of a Chinese emperor to the nesting habits of the ostrich – has to do with the theme of justice escapes me.

Not a negligible poet, far from it, but an overrated one, Marianne Moore is a perfect example of the cult of personality. Her popularity is partially accounted for by the endorsement of T. S. Eliot and by his cunning editorial ploy, which ensured readers encountered 'The Steeple-Jack' before the other less amenable poetry. For the rest, Moore is the perfect American poet – reassuringly weirdo, confirming the populist stereotype, yet combining highbrow and baseball, recognisable as Jackson Pollock, and no one you needed actually to read.

V. S. Naipaul

(2001)

V. S. Naipaul's 'Michael X and the Black Power Killings in Trinidad' (1973) begins, not with the murder weapon but its innocent accomplice: 'A corner file is a three-sided file, triangular in section, and it is used in Trinidad for sharpening cutlasses.'

This first sentence could be Browning in *his* murder mystery, *The Ring and the Book*, evoking that Genoese dagger 'Triangular i' the blade'. It was Browning who asked, rhetorically, 'Is fiction which makes fact alive, fact too?' Of course, there is nothing fictional about that 'corner file'. But, in conjunction with Naipaul's title, its presence in that opening sentence constricts our breathing. And the 'dull' factual record which follows is therefore radioactive, a mundane transaction whose very ordinariness seethes with irony:

> On December 31st, 1971, in the country town of Arima, some eighteen miles from Port of Spain, Steve Yeates bought such a file, six inches long. Yeates, a thirty-three-year-old Negro, ex-RAF, was the bodyguard and companion of Michael de Freitas – also known as Michael X and Michael Abdul Malik. The file, bought from Coobal's Hardware, cost a Trinidad dollar, 20p. It was charged to the account of 'Mr Abdull Mallic, Arima', and Yeates signed the charge bill 'Muhammed Akbar'. This was Yeates's 'Muslim' name. In the Malik setup in Arima – the 'commune', the 'organisation' – Yeates was Supreme Captain of the Fruit of Islam, as well as Lieutenant Colonel (and perhaps the only member) of Malik's Black Liberation Army.

Meticulous, evidential prose, forensic in tone, transcribing errors of orthography, judicious in its deployment of inverted commas, *dry*. Yet as distant as possible from a legal deposition and fraught with fear and foreboding – thanks to the art of that first sentence, its perfectly placed pellet of poison. '*Used in Trinidad for sharpening cutlasses.*'

Might it be the case that V. S. Naipaul's essays in reportage – undertaken, *faute de mieux*, to bridge 'a creative gap' when no novel 'offered itself' to Naipaul – actually constitute his central achievement? More controversially, might

---

V. S. Naipaul: Half a Life (Picador, 2001).

it not also be the case that these factual excursuses are his greater achievement because they disclose fictional properties, fictional inflections, fictional arrangement? Greater, then, because, much more than orderly exposition and objective analysis, they evidence selection and a solipsistic certainty verging on omniscience – qualities we more readily associate with novelistic art.

'Michael X and the Black Power Killings in Trinidad' is Naipaul's account of Michael Abdul Malik's life and death by hanging. It is primarily a factual report based on the court proceedings, the legal record. (Even here, Naipaul's ruthless cropping of the picture is clear if you compare his account with that of his wife Patricia Hale, as it appeared in the *New Review*, Vol. 2, No. 14, May 1975. Sonny Parmassar's role as witness for the prosecution is edited out. Sam Brown, a defendant against whom all charges were dropped, fails to feature in Naipaul's narrative.) But 'The Killings in Trinidad' is also an analysis of motive and causation – an *argument* advanced which is only quasi-factual, necessarily speculative and perhaps solipsistic, whose conviction rests as much on the novelistic presentation as on the objective, abstract merit of the arguments. In short, because we believe in the corner file's undeniability, because it tells, we take on trust what Naipaul's other file tells us about Malik's motivation. Perhaps wrongly.

At the end of his essay on Michael X, Naipaul returns to the murder of Gail Benson, with which he began. His opening pages end on a horrific post-mortem fact about the burial: 'She was not yet completely dead: dirt from her burial hole would work its way into her intestines.' The final account is fuller, too full to quote – full of the murderers' panic and incompetence, until Yeates, who had bought the corner file, takes 'lucid' action. That one adjective, 'lucid', with its connotations of rationality, in conjunction with irrational, sordid action, is the measure of Naipaul's ironic, unsentimental talent. 'The broad blade went in six inches, and Benson made a gurgling noise.' But Benson's feet were 'still beating about' as they filled in her grave. We are given the complete police inventory of her buried belongings: 'one tube Avon Rose-mint cream', 'one Liberation of Jerusalem medallion with 7.6.1967 stamped thereon', 'one brown small tablespoon', 'one blue ballpoint pen'.

It is these insignificant, irrefutable details that underwrite Naipaul's analysis of Malik and the Black Power phenomenon. Naipaul's exact ear for Caribbean patois makes its contribution, too. Naipaul is expert at the elision of verisimilitude into analytic truth. This is Rawle Maximin, a minor character on the very edge of the Malik drama: 'Michael impress me a lot when he come back. He always move in a big way. If they are selling orange juice in that bar there for a dollar a glass and they are selling that same orange juice in that other bar for two dollars, he want the two-dollars one. If you go to the supermarket with him he fulling up two trolleys, one with meat only ... I liked him very much.

He never made me feel less than a man. And he always give. I still have a pair of black socks of his.'

A blue ballpoint pen. A pair of black socks. And, on the same continuum, Malik as the creation of gullible, guilty white radicals – who fashioned this pimp, petty criminal and extortionist into a racial victim, an icon of liberal guilt. If, temporarily, Malik was famous, internationally fêted and financed, it was only because he plagiarised the rhetoric of American Black Power – just as English pop stars made 'cover' versions of US hits. Malcolm X. Michael X. He had no original talent. And, as Naipaul rightly points out, Black Power was more or less meaningless in a Trinidadian context – where there was no white power to oppose. (If anything, it came to mean black racism directed against the creole.) Thus far, Naipaul's analysis is unarguable – even if it means that he has little sympathy to spare for Malik's victim, Gail Benson, who, in this analysis, is partly responsible for her fate. (He takes his horror and revulsion as read. But this isn't the same thing as sympathy.)

The real point of dissent should come with the most seductively elegant of Naipaul's analytic propositions – that Malik was a novelist. Which, of course, in a sense, he was. Narrated by a thirty-year-old Englishwoman, Lena Boyd-Richardson, Malik's 'novel' about himself was written 'in a cheap lined quarto writing pad' – 'solid unparagraphed pages in pencil or ballpoint, the writing small, very little crossed out, the number of words noted at the top of each page'. There were at least fifty pages of inadvertently hilarious self-aggrandise-ment. A dust-free copy of 'Salammbo that masterpiece of Flaubert's' convinces the upper-crust Lena Boyd-Richardson that 'he not only have books but actu-ally reads and understands them' – two qualifications which carefully eliminate competing eventualities, the possession of unread books, and the non-compre-hension of 'read' books. But Mike is a man of culture: he plays 'Thihikosky 1812' on his gramophone.

From this hint, from the talentless tyro, vulnerable to ridicule, Naipaul extrapolates in every direction – past and future. 'Malik was made by words, his and other people's.' So much for the past. The future is more problematic. We are offered the murders of Gail Benson and Joseph Skerritt as 'literary murder'. An afternoon bathing party is 'like an episode in a dense novel' – with 'many purposes' and 'many meanings'. Of course, Naipaul knows that Malik 'had no skills as a novelist, not even an elementary gift of language'. So he makes Malik a novelist in a different medium – life. 'When he transferred his fantasy to real life, he went to work like the kind of novelist he would have liked to be. Such plotting, such symbolism! The blood of the calf at Christmas time, the blood of Gail Benson in the new year. And then, at the end of the sacrificial day, the cleansing in the river, with Benson's surrogate pyre on the bank.' The bathers had lit a fire. Here Naipaul's fanciful over-interpretation is credited to the lesser novelist, Malik. But it is actually Naipaul's idea, not Malik's. 'So many other details: so many things that had to be worked out' – a makeover, then, in which Malik the murderer becomes Malik the writer. The conceit is daring and grants Malik a transposed talent, a creativity in life – which is a stupid idea even in its own terms. The murders are horribly bungled, not perfectly plotted. The whole thing is a hash.

We need to ask why Naipaul should require Malik to be a novelist of any kind. The idea imposes a kind of unity, it is true, even at the cost of some plausibility. But there is a deeper reason. It lies in Naipaul's need for a doppelgänger, a secret-sharer, a failed version of himself.

Finding the Centre (1984) is Naipaul's touching autobiographical account of the failed literary ambitions of his father, Seepersad – the rationalist *Guardian* correspondent who was compelled to sacrifice to Kali, to bend before a superstition he did not believe in, to capitulate to provincial conformity. Seepersad went mad and his madness took the form of being unable to see himself in the mirror. On the one hand, this is pathology based on wordplay – Seepersad has lost face when he climbs down and makes the sacrifice. On the other hand, the form his madness took represents for Naipaul the crucial loss of individuality, the idea of the unique self he seeks in his fiction and non-fiction alike. His father, Seepersad, the failed novelist, is the primal trauma – and therefore father of many secret-sharers, a numerous progeny in Naipaul's œuvre. Abreaction seems not to have worked for Naipaul, despite his several fictional and non-fictional revisitings of the original site.

Typically, paradigmatically, there is a sense of smallness, limitation amounting to suffocation, in the colonial outpost, wherever it is. However, the journey to the centre from outer utter obscurity – to London, say – is a failure and the stifled provincial self simply thins into non-existence. Writing as a form of escape and self-assertion fails to overcome the thin, papery feeling. Travel and change of place similarly fail. So do sexuality and indulgence. Finally, mediocrity is embraced and, with it, a kind of null peace.

Naturally, there are variants, but the template asserts itself in essentials. Malik is a Trinidadian half-caste, whose mother comes to London as a brothel madam. She represents humiliation. 'He is without a personality' until he remakes himself as a Negro leader and achieves a measure of fame – which is critically unstable because founded on nothing true. Malik returns to Trinidad, where the murders are a desperate assertion of black power – as opposed to hollow black rhetoric. They are an intuitive, mad attempt to lend truth-value to theatrical posturing. Naipaul, always sensitive to fame and the failure of fame, understands Malik's half-success in this deranged self-assertion. If not fame, then infamy. The interesting figure here is Stanley Abbott, Malik's accessory in both murders: 'His was the true agony,' Naipaul concludes; 'he rotted for nearly six years in a death cell, and was hanged only in April 1979. *He never became known outside Trinidad*' (my italics). Naipaul presents this as a simple irony. In fact, it is a statement which issues from the secret recesses of Naipaul's own psychic paranoia, his own area of darkness.

The Mimic Men (1967) reprises features of the paradigm as Ralph Singh experiences near-invisibility in immediately post-war London: 'I had tried to give myself a personality. It was something I had tried more than once before, and waited for the response in the eyes of others. But now I no longer knew what I was; ambition became confused, then faded; and I found myself longing for the certainties of my life on the island of Isabella, certainties which I had once dismissed as shipwreck.' Singh returns to Isabella, fluke entrepreneurial success in real estate, then brief political success – before failure, exile and inevitable obscurity, obscurity and fall typified by a chance encounter in a West End department store, where Singh confronts a sales assistant. 'Her face was familiar, and a quick glance at the name pinned to her blouse left no room for doubt. We had last met at a conference of non-aligned nations; her husband had been one of the firebrands. We had seen one another in a glittering blur of parties and dinners.' Now she has to work in the basement of a store. Singh remembers a man, 'the third secretary of her embassy', at the airport, presenting her with flowers, breaking with protocol because he is 'desperate to keep his job in the diplomatic service, *fearful of being recalled to the drabness of his own background*' (my italics).

In *Among the Believers* (1981) Islam itself is Naipaul's secret-sharer – made to exemplify his neurosis, as we can readily see from the examples he gives of Westernised Iranians returning to Teheran and fundamentalism. On American television, he sees a self-assertive woman in the *chador* defending Islam: 'an American or non-Islamic education had given the woman with the *chador* her competence and authority. Now she appeared to be questioning the value of the kind of person she had become; she was denying some of her own gifts.' In Naipaul's terms, she was accepting conformity and the loss of self. He turns then to a novel, *Foreigner*, by a young Iranian woman, Nahid Rachlin. The novel's heroine has failed to find a proper self in the United States: 'she has always been a stranger, solitary in spite of husband and friends, always at a loss sexually and socially; she cannot say why she has done anything, why she has lived the American life.' Eventually, she chooses quiescence, 'turning away from the life of intellect and endeavour'. What is peace and renunciation for her is defeat in Naipaul's system. Naipaul is sometimes criticised for criticising Islam without declaring his Hindu roots, his undisclosed religious rivalry. I think this inaccurate and unjust. By succumbing to Islam, they are, as it were, worshipping Kali.

It is the act of conformity that appals Naipaul as much as the orthodoxy itself.

Near the end of *Among the Believers*, Naipaul relates the story of Nusrat, a journalist who inadvertently provokes an extremist Islamic furore that almost closes his paper down. He survives but he is fundamentally defeated: 'he still had plans to go abroad and study mass media. But he spoke about it differently now. He was a penitent, and he wished now to serve his country and its ideology.' For Edward Said, anecdote is inadmissible evidence against Islam. But intuitions are not always or only prejudices. Sometimes they represent coherent conclusions for which the working has not been shown. One should respect Naipaul's heightened sensitivity to the renunciation of individuality. A believer, though, might see renunciation as the salutary sacrifice of egotism. The question is this: is Naipaul's criticism just because it is based on recognition of a syndrome? Or is it unjust because it imposes a private neurosis and passes it off as objective analysis? Is it insight or overlay?

In 'The Return of Eva Perón' (1972), Argentina and Uruguay are made to fit Naipaul's personal paradigm. Repetitions across books alert the reader. In Iran, 'I felt I was in a city where a calamity had occurred.' In Montevideo, 'even without the slogans on the walls, the visitor would know he is in a city where, as in a fairy story, a hidden calamity has occurred.' In post-revolutionary Iran, 'for seven months no one in this country has done a stroke of work.' In Argentina, a society has been destroyed by idleness, originally sustained by land and by the export of wheat and beef to England – the equivalent of Iranian oil wealth. One analysis – fits all!

Too many of Naipaul's personal obsessions appear in his anatomy of Argentina for it to be convincing. The sense of mediocrity: 'when the real world is felt to be outside, everyone at home is inadequate and fraudulent.' The desire to escape: 'for intellectuals and artists as well, the better ones, who are not afraid of the outside world, there is this great anxiety of being imprisoned in Argentina.' There are two representatives of fame in 'The Return of Eva Perón'. One is Eva herself, fascinating to Naipaul because she comes from nothing, from a backwater in a backwater – perhaps the town of Los Toldos, or Junín, forty kilometres away. Yet she achieves celebrity, then posthumous celebrity – like a writer. Her embalmed body is lost, then rediscovered – like a body of writing. The other celebrity is Borges, who is introduced thus: 'Borges, speaking of the fame of writers, said: "The important thing is the image you create of yourself in other people's minds."' Naipaul slyly shows Borges creating his image, carefully repeating himself, playing his *discos*, while preserving his private self. For Naipaul, fame is an index of the unique self and its successful imposition on the world.

There are other Naipaulian predispositions. Sexual perversity – the macho preference for sodomy to degrade women – signals inner emptiness. National hollowness issues in the temptation to magic – whether it be the plagiarised jargon of guerillas or the atavistic mumbo-jumbo of *espiritismo*. Seepersad Naipaul and Kali again.

The Enigma of Arrival (1987) has an interesting variant: Naipaul's attempt to embrace a positive quiescence in the form of eventless English rural obscurity – as well as the more usual scenario of the anonymous, alien, engulfing, obliterating city. Naipaul's 'novel' is thinly disguised autobiography and intended as a tribute to rural subtlety. Kipling's 'A Habitation Enforced' – an account of the assimilation of two Americans into an English community – deals less tediously with the same theme of micro-sensitivities. Naipaul's 'novel' aims at an austere fidelity to the infinitesimal uneventfulness of country life, a slowness barely distinguishable from stasis – but the result is not far removed from a meticulous description of an abstract monochrome canvas, a concussive non-event.

Half a Life, Naipaul's new novel, reprises many of these psychic topoi, as its title suggests. It is a curiously spectral performance, reminiscent of the whitewashed walls of Buenos Aires in 'The Return of Eva Perón' – where old graffiti survive like 'the ghost of a ghost'. *Half a Life* begins with the inescapable, accidental fame conferred on Willie Chandran's father by a paragraph in Somerset Maugham: 'I recognised that breaking out had become impossible, and I settled down to live the strange life that fate had bestowed on me.' The father has already been coerced by a combination of events, a half-comic tendency to self-sacrifice and a fatalistic compliancy – an ironic unfolding of events almost Kunderan in its calm, intricate comedy. The intervention of Maugham, crucially contingent, sets in train Naipaul's theme – the individual as victim of circumstance.

As a result of the Maugham connection, the son sails to England, enrols in a college, is sexually initiated, writes radio scripts and publishes an unsuccessful book of short stories. His plots and incidents are plagiarised from films and Maxim Gorky and transposed to an Indian context. Meanwhile London's usual identity-erasing power is making itself felt: 'Willie could only go back to India, and he didn't want that. All that he had now was an idea – and it was like a belief in magic – that one day something would happen, an illumination would come to him, and he would be taken by a set of events to the place he should go.' That place is Mozambique. Willie goes there with Ana, whom he marries after she has written a fan-letter, praising his stories for their expression of an individuality otherwise ignored in fiction: 'I feel I had to write to you because in your stories for the first time I find moments that are like moments in my own [Portuguese-African] life.' He is content enough at first. Then he is unfaithful – 'it was like being given a new idea of myself.' After eighteen years, he leaves to join his sister in Berlin. Always he has felt 'another self inside him', that he and Ana have presented 'characters' to a social world inhabited by other 'characters', other constructs. The (unrealised) intention is to elevate what was formerly an analysis of the colonial mentality to a universal, metaphysical conundrum – along the high-minded, low-spirited lines of Arnold's 'The Buried Life'.

The best moment comes early when a barman writes Willie's name on a membership card – 'making little circles with his pen before he began to write, like a weight-lifter making feints at a mighty weight on the floor before he actually lifted'. It is good. But it isn't new. In *A House for Mr Biswas*, Tara signed her name 'with great deliberation and much dancing of the pen above the paper'. The earlier version is laconic, perfect. The later is a little over-emphatic. It is difficult not to feel the same about the hiding places of Naipaul's art. Themes that have served him in the past now look over-exposed, a bit blunt. What they need is a file.

J. M. Coetzee
(2007)

Italo Svevo (aka Aron Ettore Schmitz), Paul Celan (aka Paul Antschel), Sándor Márai (aka Grosschmidt), Robert Walser, Robert Musil, Bruno Schulz ... The roll call of names in J. M. Coetzee's new collection of essays, *Inner Workings*, is enough to evoke the endless, unanswerable examination paper of nightmare. Plus the additional, draughty, scrotumtightening angst brought on by wearing no trousers. In a word, *Weltliteraturangst*.

Relax. Just as London clubs have house-ties for the tie-less, J. M. Coetzee has the trousers to hand. *Wilkommen. Bienvenue.* The essays here, reviews and introductions mainly, taken from the years 2000 to 2005, are welcoming, informative, readable, lucid, plain, purged of exclusive, forbiddingly professionalised jargon. They remind one that Coetzee was once a university professor in Cape Town and then in Chicago – someone, in other words, used to explaining, unafraid of explaining, prepared to risk clarity. Not quite of the pre-Theory generation, Coetzee has certainly internalised post-colonialism and knows his Derrida, but many of these pieces were written for the *New York Review of Books* – and are unapologetic, high-class literary journalism written for the intelligent general reader. Trousers for the *sans-culottes* outside academe. And Coetzee has the writer's instinctive scepticism about Theory: 'despite all the cleverness that has been exercised in film theory since the 1950s to bring film into line as just another system of signs, there remains something irreducibly different about the photographic image, namely that it bears in or with itself the trace of a real historical past.' (One should note, inconveniently, that this idea of the photographic image was first formulated by the theorist Roland Barthes in *Camera Lucida*.)

Like Coetzee's fiction, his literary criticism is super-competent, rather than dazzling. You won't come away whistling the tunes. There are no memorable phrases in the criticism, just as there is no *writing* in the fiction. They do the job. It is no surprise – but a rare misjudgement – that Coetzee should prefer the drab of Bellow's early prose to the throbbing, seething carnival of *Augie March*. He professes to admire the 'verve' of *Augie* but he swiftly lodges a reservation ('portentous rumination and gaseous language') – whereas the early glum existentialist writing is designated 'Bellow's most masterly understated prose'. I

J. M. Coetzee: *Inner Workings: Literary Essays 2000–2005* (Harvill Secker, 2007).

prefer the straight-cut velvet strides with the crimson stripe to grey polyester keks from Topman.

Typically, these essays describe some quasi-epiphanic particular – a childhood memory, a passage of fiction, a telling poem – then, beginning with the date of birth, divulge useful biographical background, before the œuvre is outlined, analysed in detail and reliably evaluated. Coetzee is Swiss in his calm neutrality. His steady regard for Nadine Gordimer is apparent, but his negatives are unflinchingly recorded where they are deserved: 'if the writing tends to be somewhat bodiless, somewhat sketchy by comparison with her major period, if the devotion to the texture of the real that characterises her best work is now only intermittent, if she is sometimes content to gesture toward what she means rather than pinning it down exactly in words …' There is, you will have realised from the syntax, a modification, a qualification in the offing. But the damage has already been done. Coetzee is a polite critic but one of unbiddable integrity.

He is also quietly learned, well read in his subject. Gordimer again: 'In its inspiration *The Pick-Up* is clearly indebted to Albert Camus's story "The Adulterous Woman".' '*The Victim* is Bellow's most Dostoevskian book. The plot is adapted from Dostoevsky's *The Eternal Husband*.' The portrayal of Joseph in Bellow's *Dangling Man* is haunted by 'the lonely, humiliated clerks of Dostoevsky, brooding their revenge; the Roquentin of Sartre's *Nausea* … the lonely young poet of Rilke's *Notebooks of Malte Laurids Brigge*'. Not just trousers, then, but haunted second-leg trousers. Coetzee is a conscientious, fearless flagger-up of indebtedness – in Márquez to Sophocles and Faulkner.

Analysing the paedophilia in Gabriel García Márquez's *Memories of My Melancholy Whores*, Coetzee also expertly demonstrates its debt to Yasunari Kawabata – first via Márquez's early story 'Sleeping Beauty and the Airplane' and *its* debt to Kawabata's 'House of the Sleeping Beauties'. This citation isn't simply expertise. It reflects an abiding preoccupation. In *Giving Offense* (1996), Coetzee observed, calmly, irrefutably, that the idea of children's sexual innocence is a construct imposed by society: 'we have all been children and know – unless we prefer to forget – how little innocent we were.'

So Coetzee is strikingly alert to the subject of sex between younger girls and older men. He chooses to print the Márquez piece (2005) next to a V. S. Naipaul piece (2001). There is an acknowledged shared theme, an interest in common which invites our interest. When he discusses Naipaul's *Half a Life*, he sedulously notes Willie Chandran's recourse to 'African prostitutes, many of them, by Western standards, children'. One of the charges levelled against the fornicating academic in Coetzee's *Disgrace* is the discrepancy in age between him and his student. I was struck by this sentence in the Naipaul essay: 'The African women he [Chandran] sleeps with test *the truth of his desire* in an equally naked way' (my italics). What does that italicised passage mean? It can mean two things. Either it is the statement of an ageing man whose desire is fearful of failing. Or it is a comment on the strange sexual desires that some ageing men discover within them – to their surprise, their excitement and perhaps to their queasy horror.

J. M. Coetzee's *Disgrace*
(2010)

In the François Pinault collection at Punta della Dogana in Venice, there is a series of ten paintings by Cy Twombly called *The Coronation of Sesostris* (2000). They were formerly hung in the Palazzo Grassi. They are characteristically Twombly exercises in sophisticated infantilism of depiction, coupled with a kind of Alzheimer's calligraphy, which is uncertain – taking a line for a few hesitant childish steps, trembly, wobbly, twombly steps. (A very different thing from Klee's famous definition of drawing: taking a line for a walk.) The series depicts a child's red asymmetric sun like a sprocket, which becomes a barge that departs from Paphos to oblivion and the next world. Life's journey. Number 2 is inscribed 'solar barge'. Number 3 has the following pencilled writing:

> Eros weaver of myth
> Eros sweet and bitter
> Eros bringer of pain
> Eros.

Number 5 is a *very* beautiful barge like a Venetian *traghetto* with figures standing in it like long-stemmed flowers, fragrant dripping colours. At its far right there are blossoms of blood. Number 6 has more blotches of blood, more pencil writing:

> when they leave
> do you think they hesitate
> turn and make a farewell sign
> some gesture of regret
> when they leave
> the music is loudest
> the sun high
>
> and you dizzy with wine
> befuddled with being
> sink into your body

J. M. Coetzee: *Disgrace* (Secker & Warburg, 1999).

> as though it were real
> as if yours to keep
>
> you neither see their [illegible]
>
> nor hear their silence

The difficulty of the writing, its illegibility, is a crucial part of the effect. Rather like a lecturer who whispers and so ensures silence and attention. Or a lover whose pillow talk can hardly be heard. And the tottering, faltering script is also crucial because it personalises these perennial sentiments, renders the archetypes innocent.

Number 7 displays a yellow smear of barge and below it two reflections, shadow smudges in grey. It is as beautiful as anything in Turner and bettered only by some of Whistler's Venetian pastels.

The series depicts the myth of love – its intoxicating power, those *ravishing* reds and yellows, those luscious lavenders, and its end in darkness, the blacks in the final canvas. Everything depends on the pigment. It does not fail us.

J. M. Coetzee's *Disgrace* is quite a good novel. It has narrative compulsion; interesting things happen; the formal organisation is intricate and intellectually absorbing to clarify. And it raises controversial issues with an air of commendably cool impartiality. Actually, the issues it raises are not controversial at first sight. Is it wrong for a university professor to sleep with a student half his age? Obviously. We have sexual harassment committees to deal with these infringements of propriety. Now that the white man's hegemony has been overturned in Africa, how far forward does shared colonial guilt stretch? What punishment, what retaliation, is inevitable here after centuries of transgression? Is the idea of truth and reconciliation between the races sentimental, wishful thinking, a pragmatic impossibility? Now the roles have been reversed, should the whites accept what has been the lot of blacks for centuries?

Nearly twenty years ago, in *Giving Offense*, Coetzee flatly stated that the idea of childhood innocence was a social construct – useful, essential even, but a misdescription. We have only to remember our own childhoods, our interest in sexual matters, to realise 'how little innocent we were'. He is not afraid of being unpopular. Something similarly courageous happens in *Disgrace*. Coetzee takes our accepted, unquestioned moral simplicities and redescribes them, restoring their precious difficulty – without ever quite overthrowing the valuable guidelines to which we subscribe. *Disgrace* is not an obviously iconoclastic novel. It doesn't 'take issue' with issues. So it might be possible to describe it, negatively, as morally equivocal, ethically equivocating. I wouldn't do so myself. I think it is morally subtle, calmly intelligent.

It restores to the debate the blood heat of experience.

When Professor David Lurie sleeps with his student Melanie Isaacs and is discovered, he accepts his guilt and the loss of his university post. He refuses the compromise proffered by the university disciplinary committee – a statement of apology and regret, a public display of breast-beating repentance. The academic community is affronted by the meagreness of his admission. And the meagreness of Lurie's guilty plea reflects his mixed feelings. After the hearing, he is asked by students of WAR (Women Against Rape) what he feels about the illicit relationship now. He says he found it 'enriching'.

Then why apologise at all? Because objectively he can see how disgusting society finds the idea of an old man bedding a young girl. He himself has a highly developed sense of self-disgust. The trouble is that his examples of decay are stock, a recital by rote, an identity parade of clichés: he feels his proximity to 'the tramps and drifters with their stained raincoats and cracked false teeth and hairy earholes'. Compare E. M. Forster's bleaker notation: 'hairs clotted round the anus'. *Disgrace* is fundamentally a novel about growing old – old and physically unacceptable. Yeats's 'Sailing to Byzantium' is a *point de repère* throughout the second half of the novel: 'That is no country for old men.' Coetzee is telling us, implicitly, that the moral objection is also an aesthetic objection.

While he accepts his misconduct sincerely, he wishes to inflect the brute fact with saving subjectivity. He is visited by Eros. 'I became a servant of Eros.' That is how he puts it to himself, to the committee and, later, to the girl's father. As a formula, you can see immediately that it won't be very persuasive – either to a disciplinary committee, or to the average reader – in its subjectivity, in its frail evocation of Greek myth. It doesn't look like argument or evidence; it looks like a convenience, an excuse.

By the end of the novel Lurie is a vegetarian, with a sympathy for animals you wouldn't have predicted at the novel's onset. He goes out of his way to incinerate personally dogs that have been put down at the clinic where he works. He cannot bear the way the regular workers beat out the inconvenient rigor mortis in the limbs, using shovels, as the corpses pass along the conveyor belt. He wants dignity for these animals.

Why? Because he knows he is an animal himself. This is a very literary novel, a novel by a teacher of literature about a teacher of literature. Wordsworth features. Byron in Italy is a frequent reference point. At the end of Chapter 10, Coetzee writes 'In adultery, all the tedium of marriage rediscovered.' He is referring to Byron but quoting *Madame Bovary*, apparently unaware – even though elsewhere in *Disgrace* Flaubert's heroine is explicitly alluded to, an ironic reference to the excitements of adultery.

In 'Sailing to Byzantium', Yeats writes: 'fastened to a dying animal / It [the heart] knows not what it is.' These lines, although unquoted by Coetzee, are crucial to an accurate reading of the novel and its complicated moral compass.

At the novel's end, Lurie has become fond of a dog with a withered hindquarter. Although he knows the animal is effectively finished, he preserves it from lethal injection week after week. Finally, the injection is administered and the novel ends. Lurie is that dog – an injured animal with which he identifies. What is the point of limping on?

His daughter, Lucy, a lesbian, and most of the women in the novel, express a distaste for male libido, its coerciveness, its imperative, even when it isn't rape. Lucy is raped by three Africans and appeals to her father in these terms: 'Maybe, for men, hating the woman makes sex more exciting. You are a man, you ought to know.' He doesn't flinch but he introduces a critical modification: 'Perhaps. Sometimes. For some men.' He is resisting not a caricature but a coarse blanket characterisation. All men are not the same. (Later, Lurie *wills* an imaginative identification with the rapists.)

The nearest Lurie (and Coetzee) come to endorsing Lucy's version of male sexuality is in Chapter 20, where it is seen as a kind of poison: 'That is what Soraya and the others were for: to suck the complex proteins out of his blood like snake-venom.' But equally this applies to women, who also need someone to suck out their venom. Byron's cat on a hot tin roof, his mistress Teresa Guiccioli, is Lurie's example. From this position, sexual desire is a burden, not a blessing – something Lurie has intermittently felt.

The problem of libido – a necessary animal instinct, an essential, impersonal instinct, without which the human race would die out – is ventilated by Lurie when he discusses a dog that has internalised its shame, its disgrace. Beaten for sexual arousal, it grows ashamed of its essential nature. The selfish gene needs to propagate. It is natural for men to desire women sexually. Coetzee's implication is that men are being made to feel ashamed of this natural impulse. And that it would be a tragedy if men internalised this disapproval. Lurie proclaims himself 'enriched'.

Objectively, man must propagate his species in the only way possible. The subjectivity of sex, however, is something else. There is, for Lurie – and by implication for all of us – a difference in different sexual relations. The novel begins with Lurie's visits to a prostitute, working under the assumed name of Soraya. This is an arrangement, a convenience, something essentially pragmatic, though more than tinged with affection. For him, it is also personal; for her, not. For her, it is financial and she withdraws when the relationship looks like overflowing the hired room and the physical transaction. Lurie regrets the termination of the relationship but is scarcely heartbroken.

With his student, Melanie Isaacs, it is different, even exalted. And it is at this very early point that the novel fails, that Coetzee fails as a writer. He cannot convince us with the power of his prose. And he knows it. Analysing the relationship between himself and Melanie, Lurie says to her father (Chapter 19): 'I lack the lyrical. I manage love too well. Even when I burn I don't sing, if you understand me.' Coetzee tries to tell us how it feels in the flames that can consume our scruples, dissolve the dross and purify us into desire. The prose lacks the lyrical: 'when he takes her in his arms, her limbs crumple *like a marionette's*. Words *heavy as clubs thud into the delicate whorl of her ear*' (my italics). And when it tries for the lyrical, it's karaoke: 'Strange love! Yet from the quiver of Aphrodite, goddess of the foaming waves, no doubt about that.' The novelist mouthing to the old music like John Redwood famously faking the Welsh anthem. This initial reference to Eros inaugurates a repeated motif, which also encompasses allusions to *Antony and Cleopatra*: 'immortal longing'; 'she has immortal longings.'

It makes it no better that Coetzee knows his shortcomings – that they are dramatised here in the opera about Byron and his mistress Teresa Guiccioli which Lurie is trying to write. In the course of which, he discovers that the *plink-plunk* of a toy banjo, the comic register, most accurately reflects his inspiration. Martin Amis, in a recent interview (*Prospect*, 1 February 2010), dismissed Coetzee as a serious writer, quoting two consecutive clichés: watching someone like a hawk; a voice loud enough to wake the dead. Stilted prose and clichés are everywhere in Coetzee – those thudding, those hammering hearts, those days that are numbered, those fates worse than death, those limbs turning to water, those Aunt Sallies, the hum of that distant traffic – but not in sufficient numbers to poison the prose permanently. There are moments of brief paralysis but they pass.

More important than the dips are the failures to attempt the top notes. Coetzee writes the way Fred Astaire sings – carefully competent in a narrow vocal range.

(And Coetzee can't dance.)

But he is intelligent and, in his way, fearless. It takes gall to insist on animality – the reprehensible, irrefutable facts of life. And it takes intellectual toughness to insist on sexual transcendence without resorting to 'love' as an explanation. What Coetzee offers is not the gestalt of sexual transcendence, however, but academic exposition.

Early on, at a lecture by Lurie, we learn about the 'perfective' form of a verb – the difference between 'usurp upon' and 'usurp', the latter being a completed action. 'Two weeks ago he was in a classroom explaining to the bored youth of the country the distinction between *drink* and *drink up*, *burned* and *burnt*. The perfective, signifying an action carried through to its conclusion. How far away it all seems! I live, I have lived, I lived.'

This last example gives us the primary application of the perfective tense in *Disgrace*. Lurie imagines himself to be somewhere between 'I have lived' and 'I lived', close to a state of completion. It is a way of summoning the ageing process. And when, on the last page, Lurie consigns the defective dog to the flames, the perfective is summoned again: 'the next day wheel the bag into the flames and see that it is burnt, burnt up.'

It is also a way of epitomising his character – which is complete beyond change. Hence his refusal to endure counselling or proclaim the possibility of moral improvement as a way of reducing his punishment. He is, like Byron's Lara, a Lucifer figure who accepts himself as he is: 'a being who chooses his own path, who lives dangerously, even creating danger for himself'.

Lastly (it is doing quite a bit), the perfective applies to the sexual impulse itself – to desire as a desire for completion. 'The seed of generation, driven to perfect itself, driving deep into the woman's body, driving to bring the future into being. Drive, driven.'

We are a long way by now from the moral simpletons sitting on university committees.

And the committee for truth and reconciliation? The crux here is Lucy's rape by three African intruders, her refusal to press charges against the rapists, her subsequent resulting pregnancy. Her position is quietist. She would like peace. She decides on the politics of appeasement while denying that her position has anything at all to do with white guilt and the colonial history of repression. At the end of Chapter 13, Lurie and Lucy consider the rapes as revenge. For Lurie, this cannot justify them: 'Do you hope you can expiate the crimes of the past by suffering in the present?' She insists this is a misreading of her position: 'Guilt and salvation are abstractions. I don't act in terms of abstractions.' But for a long time she refuses to clarify her position.

When she finally does, it is because she cannot conquer her fear. Lurie encourages her to see an impersonal historical motive behind the rapes, but she can see only how personal the rapes were: 'it was done with such personal hatred.' Of the men, she says: 'I think they *do* rape.' At the same time, she begins to accept that the rapists may be telling themselves that rape is the price she must pay for staying on.

The arguments begin to separate and clarify. On the one hand, Lurie and Lucy can see an historical impetus behind this incident. (Or perhaps it is only an historical pretext.) On the other hand, both are actually outraged. There is a parallel here between Lurie's acceptance of his expulsion from the university and the reservation he makes for the role of Eros. He is wrong, but he is right. In terms of the rape, her experience is one of humiliation, of personal disgrace.

Lurie's attitude is double – partially a rationalisation but primarily a cry of outrage. He attacks one of the rapists. He wants Petrus to be less detached, less phlegmatic: '*Violation*: that is the word he would like to force out of Petrus. *Yes, it was a violation*, he would like to hear Petrus say; *yes, it was an outrage.*' Petrus is related in some loose way to one of the rapists, he is Lucy's neighbour and former employee. He did not warn Lucy. He seems to be protecting his relative, certainly denying all guilt – and, finally, offering to marry Lucy as a form of protection. She seems prepared to accept the offer of protection, with her actual status – wife, concubine – left to Petrus's discretion. Her final position is identical to her father's final position at the close of *Disgrace*: 'no property, no rights, no dignity … like a dog'. They are both dogs – the image of ignominy chosen by K at the end of Kafka's *The Trial*. Petrus, however, does not renew the offer. We are not told what finally transpires.

It seems relatively clear. There is an explanation which is historical but it is an overview that does not begin to address the realities of the rape. The 'explanation' is *bien pensant* but bogus while the rape is a concrete truth.

There is an additional complication: Lurie's desire for a demonstration of regret by Petrus is exactly what he himself resisted giving the university committee. Petrus says the rapes were wrong. Lurie says his relations with Melanie were wrong. But beyond this, both men are reserving their position. They are not disclosing everything. What Petrus is keeping back we never discover – because his English is imperfect, and, anyway, according to Coetzee, English is a broken, hollow medium for talking about Africa. (At which point, for the first time, I'd want to press a charge of convenient equivocation.)

There is a further logical difficulty, caused by the link between the rape plot with the misconduct plot: Lurie is compelled to acknowledge a logical connection between himself and the three rapists. 'They were not raping, they were mating. It was not the pleasure principle that ran the show but the testicles, sacs bulging with seed aching to perfect itself. And now, lo and behold, *the child*!' The pregnancy. Not Eros, because done in hatred, but obedient to a process more compelling than both – the principle of reproduction. The rape and its motives are subsumed by biology. It doesn't matter to nature what anyone thought while the egg was fertilised by the spermatozoa. The pregnancy changes the terms of the argument. The pregnancy can't change the terms of the argument. We feel the pain, the awkwardness, the impossibility – because the argument is doing the splits. Morally, we are stretched, if aesthetically we are a little starved.

Geoffrey Hill, Christopher Logue, Seamus Heaney

(2005)

Three or four years ago, the music critic Hugh Canning was interviewing Pierre Boulez for the *Sunday Times*. Mostly it was the self-deprecating elder statesman, the affable publicist for musical modernism, who was smoothly on message. Then, out of nowhere, we suddenly saw the Darmstadt firebrand – who had once booed Stravinsky, aligning himself with Schoenberg's withering characterisation of Stravinsky as *der kleine Modernsky*.

Asked by Canning about Shostakovich's music, Boulez launched an analogy with olive oil and its pressings – *extra virgine*, *virgine* and so on – concluding that Shostakovich's music was a third pressing of Mahler. A music of aesthetic exhaustion. A dilute, flavourless derivative. Mahler features here as a symbolic figure, not as a specific source. He stands for the burden of the past. When you listen to Shostakovich's music, with its fundamentally familiar and reassuring nineteenth-century sound-world, you can hear the aesthetic problem of twentieth-century Russian modernists. Significantly, there was no full Russian translation of *Ulysses* until relatively recently. Effectively excluded from the European avant-garde, writers and composers made decisions that were political as well as aesthetic. They were in delicate, dangerous negotiations with communist doctrine. If their work was to be politically correct, it had to address the lowest common denominator. The avant-garde wasn't allowed to get ahead of itself – or the proletariat. By 1928, RAPP (the Russian Association of Proletarian Writers) was a powerful force for socialist purity and artistic conservatism. Not only that. Stalin might be on the phone at any minute.

When *Doctor Zhivago* was acclaimed by Edmund Wilson, both Nabokov and Stravinsky thought it eerily, unironically nineteenth-century, an old-fashioned novel encumbered with hoop skirts and a bustle. 'I have read *Dr Zhivago* in Russian and am saddened and disappointed by the book. It is awfully old and reminds me of Peredvishniky [a group of traditional narrative painters in the 1870s]. How strange,' Stravinsky concluded in a letter to Suvchinsky (27 January 1961) 'to have written such a book after the event of James Joyce.'

Geoffrey Hill, *Scenes from Comus* (Penguin, 2005); Christopher Logue, *Cold Calls: War Music Continued* (Faber and Faber, 2005); Robert Henryson, *The Testament of Cresseid*, translated by Seamus Heaney (Enitharmon, 2005).

Here is a sample of Geoffrey Hill's lexis taken from *Scenes from Comus*: 'pillage', 'portal', 'assail', 'benefaction', 'far-illuminant', 'clamour', 'sans', 'succubine', 'whereas', 'wherewith', 'bowered', 'spirituous', 'gristing-chamber', 'excoriate', 'disembarrassing', 'vesture', 'swart', 'declivitous', 'laggard', 'circadian', 'haemony', 'murrain'd', 'uncomely swags', 'equipollence', *'superbia'*, *'pondus'*, 'inurement', 'gloam', 'troth-plight', 'numen', 'wit-bibber', 'couvade', 'sunder', 'soughing', 'besprent', 'apologetical', 'greaves'. Whereas 'whereas' is still in use, 'wherewith' is these days less often sighted in poetry than in legal documents. Individually, none of these words is impossible in 2005. Some are inevitable in a poem at least partially 'about' Milton's *Comus*. And Hill might justifiably lament the lack of learning in his readership and its restricted vocabulary. He probably aligns himself with the Eliot of 'The Social Function of Poetry', who theorised that our ability to feel 'the emotion of civilised beings' depended on 'those few men who combine an exceptional sensibility with an exceptional power over words'.

Nevertheless, en masse, this musty vocabulary is a throwback, putting 'diction' back in the 'dictionary'. As Hill himself acknowledges in his epigraph to Part II: *'nello stile antico'*. This epigraph is aware, unapologetic, a pointed antithesis to Dante's *'dolce stil nuovo'*. It is also tactically shrewd – a dummy concession that concedes nothing to potential detractors. It merely states that the poet *knows* his poetry is old-fashioned. Square brackets: [Now fuck off.] Academics in particular like Geoffrey Hill's poetry because it sounds old-fashioned. They confuse greatness with reminiscence. They hear 'a grand and crabby music', as instructed by the poet. And there is always a general readership for 'traditional' poetry. The Archbishop of Canterbury* is an unsurprising admirer. But is it the third pressing of Milton?

There is, however, a dutiful vein of the 'contemporary' here also. It is deployed with the stiffness of Larkin's maladroit version of *being on the pill* – 'And she's taking pills.' A list: 'chill-out', 'titagrams', 'balls-ache', 'twaddle', 'Heavy Metal', 'clones', 'He was his own man', 'blue / movie', 'pinched for cash', 'flight paths', 'off sick', 'weirdo', 'win some, lose some'. In their attenuated, antiquated environment, these innocuous idiomatic turns jump out like Sid Vicious on *Songs of Praise*. I think 'titagram' is Hill's mishearing of a 'stripagram'. And 'chill-out' doubles as a reference to the 'winter-sun' in Reykjavik. Laid back it isn't. But it means well – without really meaning anything. It constitutes a gestural answer to those who think they're reading a third pressing of Milton.

The poet and priest Alice Goodman, Geoffrey Hill's wife, may be responsible for this leavening. She is 30 years Hill's junior and American. Her small

---

* Rowan Williams

talk must therefore differ from her husband's avowedly non-existent small talk. Her everyday vernacular must represent an alternative, a de facto contradiction to his staid word-hoard – and perhaps an implicit reproach or even a source of friction and possible influence. At the time of *Nixon in China*, the John Adams opera whose libretto she wrote in 1987, Goodman was reported in a newspaper interview as saying that the people involved in the project were 30 years old and serious. The collaboration wasn't, she feistily complained, a bunch of kids sitting around in sneakers 'popping gum'. I wonder whose criticism she was answering? I can't imagine Geoffrey Hill writing, as Goodman did, an aria for Nixon with the first line, 'It's prime time in the USA.'

From the internal evidence here, I can't imagine either that Hill much likes the music of John Adams with its minimalist 'simplicity'. Actually, Adams's 'simplicity' manages a Wagnerian scale in *Nixon* for the landing of Air Force One, a texture in *Big Sur* comparable to Debussy's *La Mer*, and is capable of hearing, and playfully reproducing, Schoenberg's sound-world in Looney Tunes. The individual talent recognisably develops a tradition. Here, the music Hill admires is that of Hugh Wood, whose Opus 6 in 1965 was *Scenes from Comus* and whose 70th birthday is 'celebrated' by Hill's *Scenes from Comus*. They are two artists who share a disdain for the popular: 'the self servers now in full career'. Wood's music, as characterised by Hill, is 'caustic attrition and noble rest- / oration of music's power to console'.

It's surprising to learn that Hill chose Jimi Hendrix's version of 'The Star-Spangled Banner' when he appeared on Michael Berkeley's *Private Passions*. But it's meant to be surprising. It is chosen for effect. Like the judicious sprinkling of colloquialisms in the poetry, this preference is intended as a counter-intuitive act of seasoning – pepper on strawberries, mint on mango. Intriguingly perverse. And patently fraudulent. It is of a piece with J. H. Prynne's enthusiasm for techno. The advertised unworldliness of both poets is that of Gilbert Osmond. They never take their eyes off the world – even as they turn their back on it.

This element of calculation operates perfectly properly, if a mite mechanically, whenever Hill sets down a line – or even a line-break. Take that 'rest- / oration' and the way it insists on the presence of 'oration' in 'restoration' – and thus equates their two musics in counterpoint, the poet's, the composer's. Note, too, the balance between 'attrition' on the one hand, and 'restoration' on the other. This tic of contradiction and equilibrium, of paradox, is continuous, not to say relentless. (My italics except where specified.) For example: 'clamours of | diminution'. For example: 'a dark glow'. For example: 'a gross *finery*'. For example: 'I have made – *singularly* – a *double* life.' For example: 'implausible, credible muse.' For example: 'The self-flensing ocean / making haphazard signals, *idle, urgent*'. For example: in Stanza 56, 'Can't tell you' and 'I cán tell you'.

For example: 'alight with *dull* rain'. For example: 'penury poised upon excess'. For example: 'And that *reason* is articulate in the will // *if you don't think about it.*' This is partly a strident insistence on Hill's careful, not to say automatically, agonised choice of words. Which reminds me (Part III, Stanza 3): '(strange form of words, // that, *not to mention* – it has a name)' (Hill's italics). It has two. It is the rhetorical figure *occupatio*, or *occultatio*. And it is part of Hill's pattern of contradiction. You say you don't mention something, but you do. For example, finally: 'That there are immoderate measures in plenty' balances the idea of measure as limitation against excess. Then: 'that plenty is a term of moderation' in which the word 'plenty' can mean 'That's enough, stop.' Lastly: 'that moderation is used by some to excess', there can be excessive moderation.

These contradictions serve one overall theme of *Scenes from Comus*, which is that Geoffrey Hill isn't the entirely austere soul of popular reputation. Taking his hint perhaps from Hugh Wood's setting of *Comus*, Hill feels for the son of Bacchus and Circe. His epigraph from Milton's *Comus* is an admission that no one is immune from lust: 'Who knows not *Circe* / The daughter of the Sun?' In Milton's original, the question refers to Circe's notoriety. Here it is a rhetorical question, an admission of shared guilt. Richard Morrison in the *Financial Times* (23 March 2002) reported that 'Hugh Wood's "Scenes from Comus" cheekily turns Milton's allegory upside-down, so that the virginal heroine – rather than primly defending her honour against the beastly Comus – rather seems to revel in whatever it is that happens in the "wilde woode". Certainly the best bit of the work … is the terrific orgiastic dance that explodes at its heart.'

Hill's *Scenes from Comus* shows us the depredations of age. Hill is 70, too, candidly self-disgusted, a taker of sleeping pills, a snoring old man, who is 'tired now the whole time': 'I snorkel into contrived sleep, I wake, / I address the mirror: *spare me my own* / *rancour and ugliness.* It too is naked.' The poem also shows us Hill's contradictions: 'Chastity makes its bed / with sensuality, could not otherwise / use such authoritative vehemence / devoid of knowingness. / It's an attractive doctrine to me now.' What does this mean? The need to ward off sensuality is vehement because chastity knows intimately what the attraction of sensuality is. It feels the force of sexual arousal. Were sexual temptation weak, it could be dismissed readily, casually. There would be no need for vehemence. Why is this doctrine attractive to the 70-year-old Geoffrey Hill? Because his reluctant old man's chastity may contain the promise of its opposite.

Hill is often portrayed as an austere moralist. In Part II, Stanza 79, he shows us, admirably, that moral display is easy when there is no temptation: 'Moral vanity / is his [Comus's] parole, in the off season, / *at any time mere sensuality* / *seems to lie dormant.* I know well / the bristling strut, demonic rectitude, / the rod and glass, the masks of his fixation' (my italics). In other words, it is easy to moralise when arousal isn't in contention. No erection, no problem.

Contradiction is there, too, in Part III, 'A Description of the Antimasque': 'I think I shall disguise myself | as an óld mán / and get among the women one last time / in a wolf's pelt of harmlessness, holiness even.'

Scenes from Comus is set in Reykjavik, the capital of Iceland. Hill is staying in the Radisson Saga hotel on the sixth floor, where he reads Icelandic Christian poetry, particularly the Passion-Psalms of Iceland's most famous poet, the seventeenth-century Hallgrimur Petursson. From his hotel window, Hill can see the commemorative church, the Hallgrimskirkja. There he imagines the progress of Milton's masque across the border into Wales, giving a big thank you in Welsh, *diolch yn fawr*, to the 'Lord / President of Cymru'. Then he imagines its staging: he imagines torches 'tossing swart-blooded fire' and then rescinds the idea. 'Can't have been torches in thát space; try / candelabra'.

There are difficulties, however – difficulties of Geoffrey Hill's own making. Even though he claims 'I'm wresting myself into simplicity', his other observation is truer: 'That I mean what I say | saying it obscurely.' Admirers of Hill are aware that there is a difficulty about his difficulty. And the usual arguments have been trundled out to excuse Hill's hectic, unsleeping obscurity. It is sometimes said of Hill, as of Henry James, that the expression is difficult because the thought being expressed cannot be simplified. Peter McDonald in the *Times Literary Supplement* has evolved a new tactic – extensive quotation of Hill's clear, merely competent nature description, as if its genius were indisputable, then a bold rejection of the idea that Hill *is* difficult. 'Ever since *Canaan* (1996), it has been easy to deplore Hill's "difficulty", without seeing any difficulty in the term itself; but the poetry has been substantial, rather than "difficult", *with the directness and candour of profound originality*' (my incredulous italics).

One thing is certain about *Scenes from Comus*. It is very difficult to work out precisely what is going on. Specifically in Part II, Stanza 73. For a second, we think we know where we are: 'Four days on floor six of the Radisson / Saga | and thís had to happen'. What exactly is 'thís'? Is it the failure of room service, the arrival of a hooker, or the unplanned onset of inspiration? I exaggerate, obviously, provoked by Hill's niggardly reticence. 'Four days on floor six of the Radisson / Saga | and thís had to happen: high density, / high intensity spaces / of imagination.' Inspiration looks the most likely explanation. But it could also be the onset of love: 'To be reborn into love is to live / a posthumous life' (Stanza 58). In Stanza 50, there is a reference to Lawrence's *The Rainbow* which seems to postulate a suspended betrothal: 'now there's no going back – / like *Wedding at the Marsh*, the true fiction / set in the one frame; or the book set down / marked at that page, not closed, and not returned to.' The narrative is halted just before the wedding. The business remains unfinished, an erotic aporia. This may link with the reference in Stanza 21 to Milton's first wife, Mary Powell. They were married in June 1643 but with Milton's consent she left in July – and Milton wasn't to see her again for two years, and therefore, as Dr Johnson said, he was 'determined to repudiate her for disobedience'.

It isn't clear.

Might Hill's crisis be the realisation that he had squandered an early love? (This is, of course, the starting point of Basil Bunting's great poem *Briggflats*.) Here (Part III, Stanza 7): 'Memory of her body is what carries me.' Part III has Hill contemplating 'Reversed film' (Stanza 7), while acknowledging the fault in himself (Stanza 8): 'The clue's in the projector, out of focus / for fifty years.' Not simply blurred but blind. The regret for the crass mistake, the missed opportunity, is seen as blindness: Gloucester's 'numskull friend / with his tarred whited sockets', Milton's *gutta serena*, where the pupil is unclouded by morbid humour. In Part III, Stanza 8, the result of this blindness is a single ticket symbolic of solitariness: '*Admit One* // to the theatre, the observatory, to the small / cinema showing new foreign films, / the museum of glances, the Ecclesia // Sancti Pauli in Walton Street.' These are Hill's 50-year-old undergraduate memories of Oxford. Ecclesia Sancti Pauli is now Freud's, a wine bar. The cinema, then the Scala, is now the Phoenix.

If the regret is still potent and the love still alive, after all these years, perhaps this would account for Hill's oblique treatment. One is reminded of Wendy Cope's brilliantly shrewd analysis of obscurity in contemporary poetry: 'the reason modern poetry is difficult is so that the poet's wife can't understand it.'

There is also an analogy implied between the sinking of HMS *Hood* in 1941 – after only two minutes of battle with the *Bismarck*. This sudden catastrophe is invoked several times: Part I, stanzas 10, 14; Part II, stanzas 31, 62, 71. Is the visitation in the Radisson Saga comparable? Or is the *Hood* just a reminder of death's closeness?

It isn't clear.

What is clear is that Hill is interested in 'alchemy', by which he means anything that will transform the dross of experience: 'Any fire to transmute these fraudulent base years!' It can be sex: 'Sexual love – instinctively alchemical: / early sexual love'.

When Hill's poetry *is* clear – and therefore easy to judge – you understand why it often isn't. We are continually being told that Hill is a great poet – by George Steiner, A. N. Wilson, Peter McDonald, Harold Bloom, the Archbishop of Canterbury.

But is this great poetry? 'Stations of the cross are not standard school / crossings, unless for non-standard children.' This ponderous jokiness wouldn't pass muster in a Michael Rosen poem for children, even a sub-standard one. 'The voice of prophecy clings to its logged spar': how irritating, how facetious is that pun on 'logged'?

> There is a dogged beauty in the world,
> unembarrassing goodness, honesty unfazed.
> There's also the corrupter, the abuser,
> the abused corrupted in accepted ways,
> the ways of death, the deadliness of life.

Is this great poetry, this bonging, platitude, that good and evil coexist? Are its admirers mistaking prophecy for poetry? And are they mistaking preachiness for prophecy? It might be Les Murray in pulpit mode, wagging his finger: 'There is justice, there is death, / humanist: you can't have both.' Or, worse, Rowan Williams. Or, worse still, Rabbi Lionel Blue.

And what about Part II, Stanza 47?

> The small oaks crest the ridge, the sun appears
> cresting this instant. Their topmost ranks
> take fire and vaporise
> or find some other form wherewith to be
> *not of this world* ... [my italics]

Line-breaks have never been Hill's strong point, but the 'line' 'or find some other form wherewith to be' takes the poisoned Winalot. The description of dawn – a kind of naturalised version of the burning bush – is perfectly passable, but easily surpassable. In fact, Part II, Stanza 39, is an accurate self-diagnosis of Hill's weakness as a poet: there he accuses his writing of academicism ('rewriting his own deepest reading') and expresses a yearning for a more direct contact with the earth's sensuous qualia. It is Arnold's problem repeated a century later – the moral poet so concerned to tell us how to live that abstract precept supplants specific detail. Empedocles's lamentation for his lost contact with the natural world drowns out Callicles as he hymns that world into being. There is a telling moment when Hill sees from his hotel window 'the consular flag / of a Scandinavian kingdom'. *Which* kingdom? It is typical, too, that Hill's yearning for direct contact with the earth, lost since childhood, should be expressed via the figure of Comus. 'Give me a break / in concentration, só I can concentrate, / as I once did – a Comus child – on pignuts.' Like Milton in Dr Johnson's version, Hill sees nature 'through the spectacles of books' – as he is doubtless well aware.

This is what happens when Hill tries to ground his abstractions: his subject in Part II, Stanza 53, is 'love's grief', which he finds a common condition, a condition he wryly designates 'popular': 'always popular, / like ghosted memoirs or the old / fashioned chara-tours, / like the Welsh hills covered in rhododen-drons'. Three similes, each ironically indecorous, and every one a facetious dud.

Throughout *Scenes from Comus* there are little disclaimers, little assertions of spontaneity, as if Hill in the Radisson Saga were making it up like Ezra Pound in his cage at Pisa, without access to books. 'These short ones are the sock-fillers.' 'Need to think about this.' 'Save these for the antimasque.' 'I was not at my best when I wrote that.' 'Somewhere I have lost *Milton on Music* / and *The English Masque*. Sometime in the last days.' We are being told, in certain terms, that the sequence is provisional.

This does not excuse the prevalent lack of clarity.

This is Hill feeling suicidal. I think. In Part II, Stanza 41, the falling autumn leaves are described on All Souls Day. Playing with the idea that rats leave the sinking ship – perhaps an allusion to the *Hood* – Hill explains that prayer has 'ratted' on him just as the leaves have 'ratted' on their branches. Not the most uncontrived refurbishment of a cliché. The connection is made, however, between Hill and the leaves. (The leaves have 'high / spirituous colours, or wan, or putrid brown'. Which helps the reader to visualise the leaves, I find.) The stanza ends with a surrogate suicide: 'And I say: wátch – watch this phe-nomenon, / this other selving; it is yours to keep, / whose shadow reaches out, grows, is *unhinged*, / flung on the shattered pavement, breaks apart' (my pun-seeking italics).

In Part II, Stanza 40, Hill adopts a police witness-statement mode to inter-rogate his experience or perhaps another's experience of Hill in genius mode. I'm not sure.

> Go through it all again: Is this
> the genius that approached you? Does it
> have a name? Said | wísh I could draw you,
> draw you so that you seem
> not to be hiding, wísh I could draw you in? Concede some kind of epic
> statement.
> Sleep alone | fertile and barren friend.
> Insulted witness of proven chastity.
> Name of hotel?

Behind this baffling terseness seems to be the re-enacted encounter between the lady and Comus. But my guess – and it is only a guess – is that in the Radis-son Saga the genders have been reversed. Here Hill is the lady clinging to his chastity.

Stanza 54 returns to the criminal topos, in a way that maybe explains it as a metaphor. Here the crime before the jury is 'overnight seduction by a minor art' – poetry, presumably – which 'carries [a] life' sentence. Who knows? In this third pressing of Milton, the only thing that remotely resembles modernism is Hill's obscurity, *passim*.

With Seamus Heaney's lovely translation of Henryson's great poem 'The Testament of Cresseid', and Christopher Logue's latest imitation of Homer, *Cold Calls*, the relationship of past to present is less problematic. Logue's versions of the *Iliad* are often erroneously called translations. They are in fact nothing of the kind. The miraculous massed fragments of *War Music* make an original poem based on Homer's story – cut, selected, revamped, re-created, emphases altered. It is Homer brilliantly vandalised, crammed with anachronisms, yet able to retain an 'authentic' flavour – no, the actual *taste* – of Homer. This is achieved by virtue of Logue's rhythmic template, which is the blank-verse line, deployed with great intuitive freedom and final fidelity. The faint antiquarian whiff is finely judged and matched by Logue's striking contemporary touches. The enterprise itself is one of the great glories of twentieth-century poetry. Spectacularly lucid, uniquely exciting, it stands with *The Waste Land*, *The Pisan Cantos* and *The Sea and the Mirror*. A completely gripping classic in its own right, it is a hymn to war and is both ancient and modern.

Heaney's retelling of Henryson's retelling resembles Logue. It, too, is ancient and modern, but more comfortably so. We register contemporary or dialect touches without the shock of Logue's radicalism: 'the weather went / From close to frosty' is a lovely addition to Henryson's plainer account of 'the wedder richt feruent'. Heaney's 'I could see away on every side of me' nicely Irishes the original's Scottish Chaucerian: 'That I micht se on euuerie syde me by.' *Close. Away.* These are optional extras that we would not be without. They are immediately as essential as this marginal alteration to Henryson's 'quhen Titan had his bemis bricht / Withdrawn doun and sylit vnder cure [cover]': 'And draped and sealed the brightness of the day'.

Heaney's ground measure is also the iambic pentameter, but he allows himself educated licence. In these four lines, only the first is strictly iambic:

> The northern wind had purified the air
> And hunted the cloud-cover off the sky.
> The frost froze hard, the blast came bitterly
> From the pole-star, whistling loud and shrill.

Apart from Henryson's great dénouement – when Cresseid, the disfigured leper, fails to recognise Troilus or be recognised by him – the most telling moment occurs early in the poem. It is when Henryson tells us about the decline of Diomede's erotic interest in Cresseid. Henryson's lines are laconic, ruthlessly matter of fact: 'Quhen Diomeid had all his appetyte, / *And mair*, fulfillit of this fair ladie …' (my italics). The apparently careless addition, 'and mair', with its emphatic caesura, is incomparable. Heaney cannot match this. Instead of the flat, authentic, spoken note, Heaney, just this once, gets literary: 'When Diomede had sated his desire / And over-sated it on this fair lady.' But could anyone match Henryson here? Elsewhere, Heaney is perfectly contained. Henryson's 'out of his nois the meldrop fast can rin' becomes 'And from his nose there streamed a steady nose-run.' You feel like Polonius acclaiming the moblèd Queen. *Steady* is good. One last niggle, though. When Cresseid realises that the giver of alms was in fact Troilus, Heaney writes: 'When Cresseid understood that it was he / A stun of pain, a stroke sharper than steel, / Went through her heart and to the ground she fell.' *Stun* is good. More than good. But we have seen it before, in *Station Island*: 'And then a stun of pain seemed to go through him // and he trembled like a heatwave and faded.'

Still, it's a marvellous thing to have a translation which does away with the difficulty of Henryson's Scots and perfectly preserves so many things that are already perfect in the original. My copy is covered with pencilled ticks and the words 'in the original'. The translator as a window cleaner – of genius.

Kundera's *Italics*
(2006)

When we speak of style, we often, wrongly, confine our attention to prose style – its lexis, its taxis, its habitual quirks, its peculiarities, its allegedly distinguishing features.

But how distinguishing are they?

For instance, we can see how Martin Amis's characteristic repetitions – those pithy, prodding repetitions, those accretions, those comic, muscular prose push-ups, the pumping of irony – develop out of Kurt Vonnegut and out of Heller's Möbius-strip logical oubliettes in *Catch-22* – a baffled trope which, in its turn, owes a great deal to Beckett's more torpid, depleted dialogue in *Godot*. 'So the only time you did any actual bouncing was when you had failed: as a bouncer. Bouncing was a mop-up operation made necessary by faulty bouncing. Only bad bouncers bounced. It might have sounded complicated, but it wasn't' (Martin Amis's short story 'State of England').

This is a passage of comic repetition from *Slowness* in which Kundera expends himself on a subject near to the young Amis's heart: the vulva. 'The vulva portal is important, of course (of course, who would deny that?), but too officially important, a registered site classified, documented, explicated, examined, experimented on, watched, sung, celebrated. Vulva: noisy crossroads where all of chattering humankind meets, a tunnel generations file through. Only the gullible believe in the intimacy of that site, the most public site of all.' It isn't Amis, but stylistically it almost might be – its unstoppable riff riding on the comic impulse to exaggerate, to argue, to let rip with its rhetoric, with its repetition. We are being tickled, mercilessly, in the same place, by a comic genius.

We can see that Nabokov's prose style carries itself magisterially like the thing of distinction and precision it is. Conveniently forgetting the purged, plainer prose of the early novels – the less *written* prose of *Invitation to a Beheading*, say – we see it as undaunted by the dictionary, confidently recherché in its diction, aristocratic in its imagery. 'I gave her to hold in her awkward fist *the sceptre of my passion*' (my italics) – *Lolita*. But is this enough? Is the prose distinctive enough, so singularly Nabokovian, that it is unfailingly recognisable – unmistakable? Coleridge, in 1798, writing to Wordsworth in Goslar, said of lines in 'There Was a Boy' that he would have recognised them anywhere: 'had I met these lines running wild in the deserts of Arabia, I should have instantly screamed out, "Wordsworth!"'

Is that regal randiness, that sceptre, hallmarked as Nabokov's and his alone?

This is Milan Kundera in *The Book of Laughter and Forgetting* when he describes the frustration of the student's night with Kristyna in 'The Angels Hover Over the Student's Couch': 'Instantly she seized *the sceptre of his love*, upright in her honour, and squeezed it with all her splendid honesty: strongly, sincerely, fervently, like a mother, like a sister, like a friend' (my italics). But she doesn't move it like a lover – up and down.

You see? Which is the genuine article, which is the pretender to the throne? In fact, they are both brilliant – and both genuine. So what do we conclude? We need not go so far as Borges, who, renouncing the elaborate poetic style of his youth, dense with images and metaphor, felt that these superficialities, though chosen to give him a contrived distinctiveness, were not fundamentally distinctive. Sometimes this is true. Every writer has experienced, now and again, the shock of reproduction – the unlooked for encounter with one of his images, or rather its lost identical twin, in another writer's work. Not often, but even once or twice is often enough to unsettle the idea of implacable originality.

For Borges, however, the young stylistically baroque poet and the older prose writer with the purged style are fundamentally the same person. They share a style, despite their differences in written style – the shared attitudes, ways of thinking, which are visible under the earlier 'striving for strident novelty'.

And I want to say, too, that larger, less local stylistic tropes can be both shared and personalised. Look at Amis's debt to the dance-steps of repetition in Vonnegut, Heller and (ultimately) Beckett. Beckett? Beckett is a writer Amis actively dislikes, a writer who provoked both aesthetic disagreement and near-fracas between Amis and Salman Rushdie, as Amis memorably recounts in *Experience*. Amis epitomised Beckett's style as 'maximum ugliness and a lot of negatives'. When Rushdie failed to quote any Beckett, Amis improvised: 'Nor it the nothing never is'; 'neither nowhere nothing is not.' 'By this stage Salman looked like a falcon staring through a venetian blind.'

All the same, however convinced Amis is that his admiration is exclusive – to the nifty Vonnegut and Heller, the nattiness of Nabokov, the reach of Bellow – he is also kitted out in the deliberately dud chic of Samuel Beckett. Surprisingly, somewhere along the line, the thread goes back to the threadbare Beckett – just as the comic prose style of Amis *père* owes a great deal to Richmal Crompton and *Just William*. Amis *fils*'s prose style is indebted *and* independent. It begins, like many styles, by aping others and ends by imitating itself. Repetition as consolidation.

We need to see that style is more than prose style.

And, anyway, in the Kundera passage about the student's sceptre, what is the relationship of those accumulating adverbs ('strongly, sincerely ...') and that accretion of similes ('like a mother, like a sister ...') to Martin Amis? Merely contingent, I would say. The relationship is that of two comic writers who know the value of insistence – of stoking the joke by repeating it, with variations, immediately the audience laughs.

Instructed by a thousand blurbs, we think we know that Hemingway's style is 'simple, terse', a patented amalgam of short sentences, of dialogue that is adverbially uninflected. 'Hills Like White Elephants' is almost wholly dialogue without qualification, without overt authorial guidance. We are accustomed to Hemingway's insistent polysyndeton, his near biblical reliance on the simple copula 'and'. Austerely simple, almost artless. But look at this subtle sentence from 'Cat in the Rain' and the way the end returns us, trapped, claustrophobic, to its beginning: 'Across the square in the doorway of the café a waiter stood looking out at the empty square.' Hemingway can afford to be subtle, because he is repeating the trope: 'The sea broke in a long line in the rain and slipped back down the beach to come up and break again in a long line in the rain.' Each sentence is trapped in repetition – and the two sentences repeat the trope. Hemingway has long sentences, too, that reproduce the digressions and reprises of vernacular speech:

> That night in the mess after the spaghetti course, which every one ate very quickly and seriously, lifting the spaghetti on the fork until the loose ends hung clear then lowering it into the mouth, or else using a continuous lift and sucking into the mouth, helping ourselves to wine from the grass-covered gallon flask; it swung in a metal cradle and you pulled the neck of the flask down with the forefinger and the wine, clear, red, tannic and lovely, poured into the glass held with the same hand; after this course, the captain commenced picking on the priest.

There are other long sentences that reproduce Hemingway's debt to Joyce's stream of consciousness.

Even prose style is more complicated, more 'contradictory', than we at first imagine. And then there is style itself, the thing that engrosses prose style.

We recognise Milan Kundera's style – even though we do not speak Czech. We read him in translation. And there are the inevitable mistakes in translation as Kundera's Czech or French is filtered to us imperfectly. There was, of course, the travesty of translations of *The Joke* – which Kundera has ruefully recorded in *Testaments Betrayed* and *The Art of the Novel*. Translators world-wide worked from the French version – a version that rearranged the order of Kundera's chapters and rewrote the prose. But there are less melodramatic inadvertencies. For example, in *Slowness*, we read: 'being naked like this in this huge glassed-in space is *so unaccustomed for him* that all he can think of is the weirdness of the situation.' Like so many errors of translation, it seems plausible if indefinably awkward. It should be 'so unfamiliar to him'. Kundera's own composition directly into French is itself an act of quasi-translation – because his French is the pure, simple, transparent French of the foreigner. It is a style without visibility. It is like Zeiss glass.

The point is that, despite these many obstacles, we can identify something we call Kunderan – a style that cannot be the prose style, which we have no way of knowing unless we are Czech, but which is a way of seeing, a way of thinking, unique to Milan Kundera.

In his essay on Baudelaire in *French Poets and Novelists*, Henry James jeers – in his elaborate Jamesian way – at the idea of art for art's sake. He marvels that anyone should imagine art could ever be free of a moral viewpoint. Obviously, advocates of art for art's sake envisage an art freed from moralism – a different thing, by which they mean conventional morality, the moral of the story, moral instruction, prescriptive moralism. By moral, however, James doesn't mean moralistic – *the Hippocratic option*, something like a dose of medicine, which can be administered or withheld from the text. James argues, rather, that a writer's morality will inform every aspect of composition. It cannot be withheld. It is everywhere in the choice and treatment of the subject. The moral, as James formulates it, is the way a writer thinks – what we would now call the writer's 'take' on his subject matter.

Here is a check list and a trailer. Helplessly declarative, Kundera's style reveals itself, frankly, forthrightly – in plot, his treatment of sex, his concentration on internals rather than externals, his theorems, his fusion of fiction and essay, dream and reality, his distrust of moral exhibitionism, his hatred of sentimentality, his irony, and his use of theme and variations.

Plot

In *The Art of the Novel*, Kundera observes that, since Flaubert, plot has been routinely disparaged by subsequent writers. And it is true that Joyce in 'Calypso', for example, inverts the traditional economy of the novel so that background supersedes foreground. We learn a great deal about frying kidneys, their pliant flesh, the noise a cat makes, 'warmbubbled milk', a chipped eggcup, a hair-pin used as a reading aid. The plot element in the chapter – Molly's letter from Blazes Boylan – is registered, only to be quickly concealed under her pillow. It is Joyce's way of saying that life is plotless. It is part of his realism, which is part of his radical modernism. George Eliot makes much the same point in *The Mill on the Floss*, when Mr Riley recommends Mr Stelling as a tutor for Tom when Tulliver seeks his advice. Riley knows nothing about Stelling, or tutors, but is reluctant to disclose his ignorance when Tulliver's request flatters his 'expertise'. George Eliot concludes that plotting and malice are not necessary to ruin the lives of our neighbours – that indolence will do. 'Plotting covetousness and deliberate contrivance, in order to compass a selfish end, are nowhere abundant but in the world of the dramatist.'

So what *is* plot? Plot is contrived narrative excitement. You might expect Kundera to forgo plot. You might think that a writer famous for his essays within the novel, his excursuses, his meditations, would neglect plot – but, ever the contrarian, he *embraces* it. He *sexualises* plot. I don't mean that he writes about sex, though of course he does write about sex. I mean that he brings sexuality's interest in excitement, in deliberate arousal, to plot. Just as sexual fantasies exist in their moment – to be swiftly forgotten, irretrievable even, until inevitably rediscovered – so Kundera's plots exist in the heightened world of fiction.

In *The Joke*, a suicide pill turns out to be a laxative. In *The Farewell Party*, Jakub's suicide pill, after much narrative tantalising, turns out to be a suicide pill that kills Ruzena. In *Ignorance*, we are invited to entertain the idea that Irena is the young girl Josef once treated badly – so badly she tried to kill herself and lost an ear to gangrene. In fact, this person is Milada. *Finally*, Kundera refuses the massive contrivance, but for a time it is *entertained* by the narrative, as a kind of fantasy.

In *The Farewell Party*, the police inspector investigating Ruzena's death analyses everyone's possible motives like a detective in an Agatha Christie novel – before pointing out that suicide isn't a criminal offence. It is parodic and significant as an indication of Kundera's attitude to plot – which is self-conscious, playful, teasingly undecided. This attitude is evident throughout: we wonder if Skreta's impregnations will be discovered, whether Ruzena and Klima's wife will have a confrontation – and both possibilities are raised, then rendered benign by Kundera. This is a kind of *flirtation with plot*. It is true, too, that only convention explains why – for someone so anxious to avoid paternity and find another candidate for fatherhood – Klima doesn't realise very early on that Ruzena has another lover, the 'maniac on the motorcycle'.

Sex

We could have started with sex. In a sense, we *did* start with sex. Kundera is unusually frank about sex – as above, when the erotic downgrading of the vulva is the prelude to the upgrading of the anus as an erotic site of excitement. A comic, provisional judgement, this, playful rather than absolute, that tells us something about perversity and sexual boredom – and something about sexual excitement. Kundera has many, many interesting and expert things to say about sexual behaviour. In *Immortality*, he touches definitively on the volatility of desire: 'this disappearance of feeling (sudden, quick, easy!) seemed breathtaking, unbelievable! *It fascinated him much more than his sudden infatuation had two years earlier*' (my italics).

But I think a central insight is his understanding of the role excitement plays in sexuality. And he is the Linnaeus of what sexually excites human beings – his tone pitched somewhere between the analytic, the comically detached and the cheerfully aroused. Kundera is not a writer to pretend to the coldness of a speculum. Nothing is more evanescent than the mental cues of erotic excitement, but Kundera has an almost unique and exemplary erotic memory.

In 'Edward and God', Edward is excited – in the nick of time – by the (nameless) directress's nakedness in combination with her praying. This isn't the sexualised nun topos – filth where we might expect purity. It is its inversion, or at least a variant, the idea that desire can be so acute it will override ideology, principle, even personality. The directress is an atheist – but she is an atheist who is prepared to degrade herself for sex. And Kundera knows that degradation is sexually exciting.

He also knows that obscenity is exciting. In *Ignorance*, Irena's sexual encounter with Josef is (ironically) ignited by 'dirty Czech words' – 'a total accord in an explosion of obscenities'. This is ironical because neither Irena nor Josef have any other desire to resume their Czech roots. Their sexual desire, though, is rooted in the Czech language. Kundera understands the sexual power of speech, that it is more than a synonym for explicitness, for utter nakedness. He knows, too, that it is much more difficult to overcome this particular taboo than it is merely to take off one's clothes. Why is that? Obscene speech returns us to our original, infantile encounters with the idea of sexuality – the incredulous disgust and swooning excitement at the dirtiness involved.

First sex, early-twenties sex, has all the physicality, all the strenuous overacting, of *silent film*. Then couples find themselves *in the talkies*.

Kundera knows this and has plotted its stages, in different terminology, in *Immortality* – where Rubens catalogues *the period of athletic muteness, the period of metaphors, the period of obscene truth, the mystical period*. This last period is when the participants realise that their sexual fantasies are not generated by themselves, but are authored by a sexuality shared with all other human beings – an impersonal stream of filth that we experience as personal.

It is to Kundera's great credit that, describing Irena and Josef's superb sex, he sidesteps all obvious comedy, all coarse irony. (There is quiet irony in the inter-cut sex scenes between Irena's husband and Irena's mother.) He resists *the writer's* automatic irony, *Flaubertian irony*, at the idea of anonymous sex. (Josef has forgotten their previous fleeting encounter. He doesn't know Irena's name.) He ends the chapter with this simile, comparing her 'lewdnesses' to poetry: 'as if a poet were writing his greatest poem with ink that instantly disappears.' As the ink does – for Josef, too, as he contemplates Irena's sleeping body. 'He was still looking at her crotch, that tiny little area that, with admirable economy of space, provides for four sovereign functions: arousal; copulation; procreation; urination. [We can hear the detached scientific cadences of Joyce's 'Ithaca' at this point. But it is soon to be displaced.] He gazed a long while at that sad space with its spell broken, and was gripped by an immense, immense sadness.'

Degradation. Obscenity. And their crucial relationship to love. 'The old moralizing truth that sex has no meaning without love was suddenly vindicated and gained new significance,' thinks Rubens – as he imagines the terror and excitement of sharing his beloved with another man. Not, then, the expected, anodyne truism – that sex is an expression of love. Instead, the idea that love is a route to arousal – that the *violation* of love's exclusivity is sexually exciting. These are dangerous things to admit in the present sexually censorious climate. As a matter of fact, it is dangerous to think about sexual excitement itself at a time when pornography, for instance, is uniformly categorised as 'boring'. Other people's pornography, perhaps. One's own pornography, one's own sexual imagination, is one of the things, like cooking, that distinguishes us from animals. Animals are without self-consciousness. They simply *are* what they are. Human beings can *choose.* We can decide to be animals, for instance. We can induce sexual excitement – and we do. If we don't, something dies in us.

Kundera writes better than most writers about sexuality because he is fearless in an area drenched with fear, hypocrisy and the legislative impulse that comes from fear and hypocrisy. Kundera's 'laws' of sexuality are descriptive, not prescriptive. Whereas D. H. Lawrence, say, was a hybrid – part analyst, part ideologue. Lawrence's sexual writings can be acute and accurate – think of the erotic bond of infantilism between Mrs Bolton and Clifford Chatterley, or the lesbian encounter in the swimming pool between Ursula Brangwen and Winifred Inger. In both, Lawrence is true to the erotic excitement of the perverse – and communicates the 'awful daring of a moment's surrender' to his readers. We feel the frisson. But Lawrence can also be tainted with idealistic prescriptiveness, with erotic bossiness and disapproval. Lawrence was so committed to the body and so mistrustful of the mind that the imagination is outlawed from the bedroom. In Kundera it definitely isn't. Sex is in the head. Whether it takes place in the boudoir or out of doors.

Hatred of Moral Exhibitionism and Sentimentality

But sex is only one thing that defines Kundera's moral imagination – his style. For example, Kundera coined the term *moral exhibitionism* – in a disagreement with Václav Havel – to describe behaviour designed to advertise and broadcast moral superiority rather than accomplish any practical purpose. Kundera's morality is against moral exhibitionism – of the vaunting kind practised by another political exile, Joseph Brodsky. I am thinking of Brodsky's 1984 Commencement Address to the students of Williams College – in which Brodsky's moral boasts are perfunctorily disguised as the account of a man in a Russian camp, a man who can be no one else but Brodsky. The disguise is an admission of shamelessness – a perfect example of the rhetorical figure *occultatio*, in which omission and denial effectively include and admit. The standard example is Mark Antony's refusal to attribute indefensible motives to the assassins of Julius Caesar. They are raised – and 'dismissed'. Of course, the attraction of a writer like Brodsky to moral simpletons is the kitsch morality he underwrites.

Moral exhibitionism in *Slowness* is largely embodied in the egregious figure of the morally competitive Berck. In *Immortality*, we find it in Bettina von Arnim, the advocate of passion, and Deputy Bertrand Bertrand: 'in a recent programme against euthanasia Bertrand Bertrand had himself filmed at the bedside of a patient who couldn't move, whose tongue had been amputated, who was blind and suffered constant pain.' Like Berck at the bedside of an AIDS patient in the later book, Bertrand Bertrand is publicly discomfited on television. The patient screams – a 'horrible, animal sound' that silences the deputy's platitudes and reduces him to petrified smiling. Berck is also embarrassed by his public failure to equal his rival Duberque, who kisses the AIDS victim. Berck, like Bertrand Bertrand, is left 'smiling inanely'. In *The Unbearable Lightness of Being*, Franz observes the moral competitiveness of the French against the Americans. There is a German poet and pop singer 'who had already written nine hundred and thirty songs for peace and against war'. There is an American film actress, whose personal pique, at being rebuked for pushiness, is turned into a photo opportunity: 'the actress gave a long look into his lens, the tears flowing down her cheeks.'

These are all examples of egotism masquerading as altruism, of self-advancement disguised as self-effacement. The self-publicist sells his self-serving actions as self-sacrifice for a larger cause. The moral life is lived out in the telephoto lens, *for* the telephoto lens.

Kundera's larger target is sentimentality. What he calls, in *Testaments Betrayed*, the heart's 'Reign of Terror', 'this imbecile sentimental Inquisition'.

(A trope Kundera perhaps owes to Sterne's 'the *Magna Charta* of stupidity' from *Tristram Shandy*.) And he is unsparing, fearless. Investors in their own images – Brodsky, Bertrand Bertrand, Berck – are all easy targets as they preen and posture in mirrors of the media. Starving African children are not. But Kundera observes, mordantly enough, that famine is edited on television. The dying old are edited out. Kundera's target is only partly the presentation of disaster. That would be easy, free of danger. (Compare Paul in *Immortality*: 'We have long become used to the idea that in such reports children tend to be singled out as a special, exceptionally valuable type of humanity.')

More dangerously, however, it is also an attack on the sentimental pretence that we care: Kundera trails his coat by listing the good things he has eaten – 'a magnificent Bordeaux, duck, dessert' – before talking about famine in an African country 'whose name is already forgotten (all this happened a good two or three years ago, how could anyone remember all those names!)'. He makes a point, though, of recalling that the dessert is 'a house secret'. This admission – of near indifference – is dangerous because it is true. And I would compare it to the bracing, tonic truthfulness of Jane Austen, who dryly and unanswerably remarked after a battle, 'How horrible it is to have so many people killed! And what a blessing that one cares for none of them!' None of us says so, but none of us eats less, or enjoys food less, because there is a famine in Africa. To do so would be absurd.

It is axiomatic, too, in Kundera that the Czech political experience has been sentimentalised by the West. In *Ignorance*, he is prepared to cast a cold eye on love: 'the notion of love (of great love, of one-and-only love) itself also derives, probably, from the narrow bounds of time we are granted. If that time were boundless, would Josef be so attached to his deceased wife? We who must die so soon – we just don't know.'

Dangerous, provocative, comic truths that Kundera's mother warned against: 'Milanku, stop making jokes. No one will understand you. You will offend everyone and everyone will end up hating you.' Of course Kundera will not win the Nobel Prize. Brodsky will win the Nobel Prize – again and again.

The Empty Physical Outline

We know what Karenin looks like in *The Unbearable Lightness of Being*. He has the head of an Alsatian and the body of a St Bernard. On the other hand, we have no idea what Tomas looks like or what Tereza looks like – beyond the stated fact of her beauty. Even the courtyard Tomas stares at – the courtyard whose dirty walls are mentioned twice – is visualised in more detail. When we think of Sabina, we think of her bra, her panties and her bowler hat. She is as she is represented on the dust jacket of the Twentieth Anniversary Edition – a Magritte with props to imply the absent flesh. She has no physical substance. There isn't a face under the hat. She is an example of the unbearable lightness of being.

No, she isn't.

She is there for us – though we could not pick her out in an identity parade.

(And her pattern of behaviour is presented as a recurring *series* of betrayals – the opposite of lightness, which depends on the idea that *einmal ist keinmal*.)

In *The Art of the Novel*, Kundera explains his new economy for the novel. It will be like Janáček's music – sudden, direct, shorn of transitions. The reader will supply all this physical information for himself. Kundera wishes to advance beyond the verbose. He wants to restrict himself to the strictly necessary.

Yet is physical description otiose? George Eliot in *Adam Bede* comments wryly on this business of description and how little it advances us: 'I will not be so much of a tailor as to trouble your imagination with the difference of costume.' For her, as for Kundera, physical description is a chore – a bit of novelistic housework suddenly rendered superfluous by the invention of the dishwasher, as it were. But for a genius like Dickens? Mr Bagstock with the complexion of a Stilton cheese and eyes like a prawn? Whose eyes, when he laughs, produce *gravy* at the corners? Or the description in *Our Mutual Friend* of Mrs Podsnap, who has nostrils *like a rocking horse*? Or think of Grandma Lausch in *The Adventures of Augie March* – who has half a Murad cigarette (cut by scissors from her sewing kit) in a holder held between her thin hard gums. Or think of Augie's African-American girlfriend with 'her cute little saddle nose'.

This kind of physical description is beyond George Eliot's reach. On the whole, her mugshots are workmanlike, neither perfunctory nor piercingly accurate. Only Grandcourt – 'neutral as an alligator' in *Daniel Deronda* – comes close to the full Dickensian portrait and then only because he is without any interior life.

We will never know if Kundera is the equal of Dickens – because there is no evidence. There are no workaday descriptions to dismiss. Where the two writers are comparable – in the area of what I call *the metonymic detail* – they are comparable.

Mr Murdstone, you will recall, has 'the dotted indication of the strong black beard he shaved close every day'. Readers require no more than David's shorthand to bring Murdstone physically before them. No one wants to read a facial inventory. Nor is it necessary. This is Kundera evoking an aroused woman – one of Tomas's window-cleaning conquests in *The Unbearable Lightness* – in one detail. Blotches. 'As her towering frame fell on its back, he caught among the red blotches on her face the frightened expression of equilibrium lost.' We are familiar with those blotches, the faint generic mottling of desire. Like Mr Murdstone's strong shaven beard, the blotches are singular and shared, distinguishing and familiar.

These *metonymic details* do the descriptive work of several unmentioned features. Another example is Tereza's hands, their nervous movements, to which Kundera and Tomas return: her hands shake with weakness just as Dubcek's breathing loses its coordination. Eventually, Tereza makes 'those abrupt, angular movements that so annoyed and displeased him'. We hardly need to know what they are. Everyone knows what it is to be irritated by someone's habitual neurotic gestures.

When Kundera extends his descriptive notation, it is usually because the plot turns on some physical aspect of the character. He tells us only what we need to know.

In *Life is Elsewhere*, we need to know what Jaromil looks like – 'he had a beautiful, fine, tiny nose and a small, mildly receding chin' – because he is a narcissist, whose facial defects have to be neutralised by an alleged resemblance to the chinless Rilke. Jaromil is vain and insecure: 'he examined and adjusted his appearance at every opportunity.'

We need to know that the editor in *The Unbearable Lightness* is tall, stooped, with black hair and a big chin, because Tomas chooses physical characteristics the opposite of another editor he wants to protect – and manages to describe a real person inadvertently. In *The Farewell Party*, we need to know that Olga's breasts are unattractive. Dr Skreta describes them to Jakub as 'tiny and [they] hang from her chest like a pair of prunes'. The breasts will be part of the problematic, automatic, suddenly unstable love-making between Olga and Jakub. In 'Let the Old Dead Make Room for the Young Dead', one of Kundera's most brilliant stories, the two protagonists are nameless, but we know that the man is developing a bald spot and that the woman is older, with missing back teeth and a long scar on her stomach from an operation. The narrative turns on the reluctance of both to settle into erotic silence – to age, to age definitively, to age without reprieve.

What we know about Tereza in *The Unbearable Lightness* is physically slight, but telling. We are told that her areolae are large – 'big crimson targets painted by a primitivist of pornography'. This is essential information because it is an emblem of Tereza's problematic relationship to her body. (Though you might wonder why we know *nothing* about Agnes's body in *Immortality*, since she too has a difficult relationship with her body.)

Let me return to the customer with blotches. She is nameless, but memorable when aroused, blotchy when aroused. Kundera provides additional detail. She is physically unusual, indeed bizarre: 'she was very tall, quite a bit taller than he was, and she had a delicate and very long nose in a face so unusual that it was impossible to call it attractive (everyone would have protested!), yet (in Tomas's eyes at least) it could not be called unattractive. She was wearing slacks and a white blouse, and looked like an odd combination of giraffe, stork, and sensitive young boy.' There is an unaccustomed amount of physical information here. But it is strangely inert detail – insistent without being completely plausible. A giraffe, a stork. The problem is, I think, that Kundera cannot quite bring himself to be completely explicit. (Maybe because the passage is written from Tomas's viewpoint – and he is unaware of exactly why he finds her attractive.) The woman's attraction is that she is androgynous, an inflection underlined by her sexual behaviour – which copies every erotic move by Tomas, including touching his anus.

Interestingly, Tomas refers to sexual memory – of reducing her to a 'chemical formula capable of defining her uniqueness (her millionth part dissimilarity)'. But she is clearly *very* dissimilar from most women. Tomas uses the word 'bizarre'. What makes her attractive – her mannishness – is left out of Tomas's analysis. Her 'uniqueness' is said to consist of clumsy ardour, surprised fear and surrender. The woman is there to illustrate a theorem, an article of belief, but is not an apt example. Fundamentally, Kundera believes that only a 'millionth part' differentiates us from others. Description, therefore, is futile since most people are mostly the same – with only the scintilla of difference, the *crucial*, the *defining* scintilla, requiring the novelist's attention.

Kundera's Theorems

These crucial *physical* differences require the novelist's *descriptive* attention. But, as a novelist, Kundera is more interested in *psychological* differences – in *theorems of behaviour*, requiring the novelist's *analytic* attention. In the afterword to *Life is Elsewhere*, he calls them 'basic categories of human existence' – and invokes the idea of the '*anthropologic laboratory*'.

These theorems are expressed in italics.

They charm us by their elegance, their laconic clarity, as much as by their truth. All one's analogies naturally incline to geometry – I'd call them *occult axioms* because they reveal hidden principles of human behaviour; in *Immortality* and in *Slowness*, Kundera coins the phrase *existential mathematics*. But their apparent irrefutability isn't mathematical at all. They have the feel of logic. Which depends crucially on the swiftness of formulation – an expressive inflection that derives from the fairy tale, at the opposite pole to logic.

Kundera may invoke Janáček's modernism, but I can hear something folkloric in the prose. Just as there is minimal description in the fairy tale – the ugly stepmother, the handsome prince, the beautiful princess, the wise king – so Kundera's characters are equally unburdened. And his narrative is unburdened, too, moving speedily, unhesitatingly, in a couple of sentences through material that might provide Henry James with two or three novels. 'The most downcast of men died after a short spell behind bars, and Tereza and her mother went to live in a small town near the mountains with her mother's swindler. The swindler worked in an office, her mother in a shop. Her mother gave birth to three more children. Then she looked in the mirror again and discovered that she was old and ugly.' This is *the abbreviation of the folkloric*. It comes from the end of Chapter 4 of *The Unbearable Lightness of Being*.

This is from the beginning of Chapter 6: 'She was willing to do anything to gain her mother's love. She ran the household, took care of her siblings, and spent all day Sunday cleaning house and doing the family wash. It was a pity, because she was the brightest in her class. She yearned for something higher, but in the small town there was nothing higher for her. Whenever she did the clothes, she kept a book next to the tub. As she turned the pages, the washing water dripped all over them.' We can glean the ghost of Cinderella from the prose – its simplicity refuses all argument, refuses to admit question.

In *The Art of the Novel*, Kundera says flatly that he is not a psychological novelist. By which he means, I think, the novelist who is interested in extremities of behaviour – the Raskolnikovs, the Stavrogins, who come with case histories and moral conundrums. Description in Dostoevsky is also argument – an argument to see the character *his* way. In the fairy tale, the prose is an imposition – a series of indubitable *données*. This is from Chapter 22 of *The Unbearable Lightness*: 'Hearing the word now made her desire to obey even stronger, *because doing a stranger's bidding is a special madness ...*' (my italics). Is it? Of course it isn't. But we don't question it in these pages because they are inflected – subtly, even homoeopathically – with the arbitrariness of the fairy tale. And that arbitrariness, that unquestionability, is bound up with Kundera's characteristic swiftness of narration. It may come via Kafka – another genius of the arbitrary – but its ultimate source is the folkloric.

We respond to these theorems as women respond to Josef's command to 'strip'. They are categorical statements, as 'strip' is a categorical imperative. You will remember that Josef's command occasionally fails. The woman who is androgynous, a cross between a stork, a giraffe and a young boy, counter-commands: 'No, you first!' This is the essence of these *occult theorems* that command our assent. Sometimes they don't. And that is perfect for Kundera – who has no desire to lay down the law.

In Kundera's ongoing moral accountancy these italicised axioms are subtotals only. He uses italics for any identified trope of human behaviour – the 'timidity of the dead' in *Ignorance*. Hence, too, his interest in definition, in 'Sixty-Three Words' in *The Art of the Novel*.

These theorems *have* to emerge from specifics, from detail. They are at once universal and provisional. They express general truths but truths that emerge from specific matrices. He is after all a novelist.

Kundera's Exfoliating Irony

What kind of ironic writer is Kundera?

In *The Farewell Party*, the famous trumpeter Klima has made a nurse pregnant. The guitarist in his band quotes Nietzsche: '"When dealing with women, bring your whip," he cited Nietzsche, a philosopher whose other utterances were totally unknown to him.' The citation demonstrates knowledge, but the opposite is true. Then the drummer offers to run the nurse over with his car. 'The guitarist was the youngest member of the band; he loved Klima and Klima was moved by his words: "you're very nice," Klima told him.' The irony is the opposition of niceness and the offer to murder.

Equally, classically Kunderan is Jaromil's flinching from sex with a cinematography student and his pretence that the decision is a high-minded fidelity. Kundera tells us that the reason is the terrible communist underpants he is ashamed to be seen in. The opposition is between the high-minded pretence and the rude actuality – moral grandeur versus the grotesque gusset. Kunderan irony has a large weighting of the ridiculous, the raspberry, the deflationary, the coarse, the corporeal. One chapter of *Life is Elsewhere* is entitled 'The Poet Masturbates'.

Irony itself is essentially a simple mechanism. A statement means the opposite of what it says. Sarcasm is, therefore, the most common form of irony. In Swift's *A Modest Proposal*, the speaker advocates the breeding of Irish children as a supply of food for the English tables. He does not mean it. Or, rather, Swift does not mean it. He means the opposite. This is the essential ironic mechanism.

(Of course, it does not explain why *A Modest Proposal* is effective – which is because it is hilariously fertile, heartlessly inventive, in the way it embroiders the initial proposition. The speaker envisages a culture of competition, for example, in which mothers will compete to bring the plumpest child to table. And there is the additional irony that the writer claims impartiality, disinterestedness, on the grounds that he has no children – and therefore cannot profit from the scheme. Or *suffer* from it, is the unspoken, implicit irony.)

Henry James, in his preface to *What Maisie Knew*, writes about 'the full ironic truth'. By this, he means the maximum inversion, a diametric opposition. So that Maisie's acute and finally unflinching moral sense should emerge from a situation saturated in immorality and sexual irregularity. In *The Ambassadors*, Lambert Strether goes to Paris with the mission to rescue Chad Newsome from the immoral embrace of Marie de Vionnet – and concludes by begging him to stay with her. These are examples of the full ironic truth.

Sometimes, though, the ironic truth is less 'full' or its ironic mechanisms more difficult to identify. In *The Rape of the Lock*, Pope describes the clutter on Belinda's dressing table: 'Puffs, powder, patches, Bibles, billet-doux'. We can see that the bibles are anomalous. We are aware of the ironic intention, but it seems different from Swift's *Modest Proposal*. It isn't. 'Bibles' are the opposite of 'billet-doux'.

The first sentence of Jane Austen's *Pride and Prejudice* is famously ironic. 'It is a truth universally acknowledged, that a man in possession of a good fortune must be in want of a wife.' Asked to explain the irony, commentators usually say that *no* truth is 'universally acknowledged'. Or that there is an ironic gap between the idea of a *universal* truth and the paltriness of a man seeking a partner. This is closer. Actually, the irony in the sentence is triggered by the verbal tension, the *opposition*, between 'possession' and 'want'. How can a glut create a shortage?

Even though the mechanism of irony is always the same in essence, writers inflect irony according to their temperament. Swift's irony is mordant, savage, acid with sarcasm. Jane Austen's irony is milder, amused by human foible. James's irony is radical, but occluded – because it is gradualist, conducted over the course of a long narrative.

And Kundera's irony?

In *Slowness*, there is a Czech scientist whose career as an entomologist has been destroyed by the communist regime. He has been forced to eke out a living by manual labour, like many other persecuted Czech intellectuals. One compensation he clings to is his labourer's physique. He goes to the hotel pool: 'with joyous and conscious vanity, he means to show off his body to the feeble intellectuals of this sophisticated, overcultivated, and ultimately perfidious country.' This is from Chapter 27.

He re-enters the narrative, at its outermost periphery, in Chapter 36.

By now, the pool is the locus for two other narratives. In the first, the nude Vincent is simulating intercourse with the nude Julie at the edge of the pool. In the second, because she has been sexually rejected by a French intellectual, a TV presenter in a white dress is about to simulate a kind of suicide by jumping into the pool. She is followed to the pool by her cameraman boyfriend in his pyjamas – whom she has sexually rejected in her turn.

The scientist does not wish to look like a voyeur, but he wants to know if the body of the man apparently having pool-side intercourse is 'in good shape'. He performs handstands – seven – a demonstration of physical prowess that is also metonymic of moral superiority. When the TV presenter throws herself into the water, he realises he will have to save her from herself. The camera-man boyfriend is sobbing at the pool's edge, on his knees. And as the scientist plunges to the rescue, we see him through the cameraman's eyes: 'an unknown man – tall, strong, *strangely misshapen*' (my italics). His body isn't handsome. It is deformed by labour.

This is Kunderan irony. It is patient and it is lethal. It spares nothing. Nothing is exempt.

Above all, it is thorough. Nothing is missed. It is quietly, meticulously merciless.

For this isn't the end of the irony playing on the scientist. He still has a precious crowned tooth to lose. The irony here is that this 'trivial' loss will wring from him a cry of pain more genuinely tragic than his earlier sentimental political self-regard. It is the opposite of what we might expect.

Nor is it the beginning. The long train of ironies begins benignly enough much earlier, in Chapter 16. These ironies *exfoliate* with extraordinary rapidity *like time-lapse photography* – yet the rapidity never once betrays Kundera into implausibility. The scientist is first mistaken for an important post-communist person. The opposite is true. Despite his alleged importance, he is ignored and left alone. The opposite of what you might expect. At the conference entrance, a secretary fails to understand his name twice. She pretends she had heard it – the opposite is true – and leafs through her typed list. He points out his name – which is misspelt – and pretends that the secretary knows about Jan Hus and the invention of a diacritical mark. The opposite is true. She is ignorant. She confuses Hus with Luther. The scientist acts 'as if he had not heard the French girl's gaffe'. He pretends that Czechs are prepared to die patriotically for these diacritical marks. The opposite is true.

His air of melancholic pride, a piece of moral conceit, comes from his dissident status – the loss of his job for political reasons. But Kundera is swift to point out that it isn't courage, but cowardice, its opposite, that has cost him his post. Two dissidents have morally blackmailed him by asking to use his office for a semi-clandestine meeting. He hadn't the courage to face down their blackmail. In time, however, he has persuaded himself that his courage, 'his personal revolt against the hated regime', was responsible for his decision – the opposite of the truth. Now the scientist is the beneficiary of political sentimentality – the kind Joyce coldly ridicules in 'Ivy Day in the Committee Room'. Unprepossessing in himself, he is glamorised in the eyes of others by the political *Sturm und Drang* of the Prague Spring. The spurious glamour is the opposite of the truth.

Waiting to deliver his paper – whose value, he knows, is nugatory because his scientific work has been irrecoverably damaged – he fingers it nervously in his pocket. A touch of novelistic genius. Before he delivers it, he comments on the political background to his attendance at the conference – and is moved by his own predicament. At the same time, he is queasy – the opposite – because he reminds himself of his father, 'who as an old man was continually in an emotional state and wept at every turn'. Everyone is touched, there is a round of applause, a standing ovation. Relishing his moment of glory, the scientist bows and returns to his place.

There the glory evaporates. He feels ridiculous. He has forgotten to read his paper. What is more, muffled laughter indicates that the audience has noticed, too. The mood has swung to its opposite. And so on, and on. In a continuous wave of irony fed by micro-irony after micro-irony – *an exfoliation like time-lapse photography.*

In *The Unbearable Lightness of Being*, Tomas is asked to sign a protest letter by his son (whom he hasn't seen for years) and an editor. Eventually, he decides not to sign. Several days later, 'he could no longer quite remember what had prompted his decision.' But Kundera can. In this respect, he is Jamesian. James records not only the insights of his characters, but also their mistaken ideas, and the motivation for both. Kundera, too, follows the intricacies of Tomas's vacillation to their conclusion.

Theme and Variations as Method: The Essayistic Novelist

Kundera is the novelist of theme and variations, a novelist who pursues his variations through *non-fiction* as well as fiction. One of the most moving passages in the whole of his fiction is the death of his own father in Chapter 13 of *The Book of Laughter and Forgetting* – a passage that juxtaposes grief with embarrassment, intimacy with a coarse communal world. Ironic opposites. A grave, melancholy zeugma.

But Kundera's deaths are exemplary.

When Jaromil dies in *Life is Elsewhere*, the last thing he sees is a look of fear pass over his own features. This is because his mother's shared features are bent anxiously over his at the moment of death. The death, then, is touched with narcissistic absurdity – 'it seemed he was bending over a still pond watching his own likeness' – and it is immensely sad. When Agnes is dying in *Immortality*, the nurse tells her that her husband Paul is on his way. She is so absorbed in dying that at first she doesn't understand. Then she smiles: 'Paul! Yes, Paul. Paul. Paul.

It was the smile of a sudden encounter with a lost world. *It was like being shown a teddy-bear you haven't seen for fifty years, and recognising him'* (my italics). When Agnes's father dies, like her, he would prefer not to be seen dying, and he recites a Goethe poem which makes it clear that death is welcome, as it will be to her – because it is a rest from existence.

Before he dies, Agnes's father destroys as much of his life as he can – photographs, for instance. This is because he dreads what we might call the *immortality of impertinence.* Kundera has a powerful passage about the destruction of privacy that follows death. '[Laura, his other daughter] fought for the rights of the living against the unjustified demands of the dead. The face that will disappear tomorrow under the earth or into the fire does not belong to the future dead but purely and entirely to the living, who are hungry and need to eat the dead, their letters, their money, their photographs, their old loves, their secrets.' This kind of immortality is a violation and an impertinence.

In *Immortality*, Kundera's theme is advertised in his title. His central strategy is a counterpoint, between the true story of Goethe and his dealings with Bettina von Arnim, and the fictional story of Agnes.

With the facts, he adopts a fictional tone. And he reflects essayistically on his fictional creations as if they were factual. He is *an essayistic novelist.* I don't mean that his novels simply mix essay and fiction. I mean that Kundera's unique tone makes the two categories, separate in most people's minds, blend and bleed into each other.

(This permeable membrane between fictional and factual is further extended as Kundera's fiction develops. Reality and dream – interchangeably Kafkaesque – begin to bleed into each other in the same way, in *The Unbearable Lightness*, in *Immortality*, in *The Book of Laughter and Forgetting*, in *Identity*.)

In *Immortality*, we encounter the idea that gestures outlast their moment of inception. They are 'more individual than the individual'. We learn, too, that faces are not individual, despite our prejudice to the contrary. They are a dismal form of immortality we share with our parents.

Immortality, in fact, in this account seems undesirable.

Artists try to manage their immortality, but rarely succeed. The 127th biography of Hemingway tells us he was a congenital liar and impotent from July 1959. Kundera is aware that immortality is often ridiculous – arbitrarily contrived by the circumstances of dying. Tycho Brahe's bladder burst; Robert Musil died lifting weights. The demeaning is more memorable: Kundera cites Jimmy Carter stumbling weakly as he jogged. Goethe's wife, Christianne, is remembered only by Bettina von Arnim's quip – as the 'fat sausage'. Goethe fears for his immortality – fears that he may survive only in her version. Whereas he has been grooming his immortality – collaborating with Eckermann, writing his autobiography, *Dichtung und Wahrheit*. He is looking after his immortality – as Kundera hilariously, brilliantly observes – having a smoking jacket made for it, a new tie.

We learn also that immortality isn't a condition of stasis for immortals but a perpetual process – continuous assessment. For the more ordinary members of the human race, immortality has to be worked for. After all, the human being is a shared, anonymous schema that belongs to everyone. Immortality involves self-assertion, therefore.

The photographic lens now means that chance moments can achieve a kind of dreadful unwanted immortality.

On the whole, Kundera believes that immortality is a curse – an infringement of privacy. Some of his characters disagree. Laura, the hysteric sister of the placid Agnes, thinks in Berkeleyan terms that *esse* is *percipi* – to be is to be perceived. 'I have been really happy,' she says, 'because I knew that Bernard was thinking of me, that I was present in his head, that I was alive in him.' She leaves him, of course – attempting suicide along the way. Suicide being another form of immortality. 'She is thinking of suicide because she sees it as a way to *stay*. To stay with him. To stay with us. To engrave herself forever on all our memories. To force her body into our lives.'

Then there is the immortality of shared sexual fantasies – the precious sewer that runs through all of us. Which we have already looked into.

The enduring charm of Kundera's fiction isn't this reductive *catalogue raisonné*, but the sense that, as we read, there is a melody, fugitive, varied, disappearing, reappearing. Like the paternity motif in *The Farewell Party*. It is the sound of thought singing, being as *musically* intelligent as only Kundera can be.

Kundera's *The Curtain*
(2007)

In *A Passage to India*, E. M. Forster writes: 'Most of life is so dull that there is nothing to be said about it, and the books and talk that would describe it as interesting are obliged to exaggerate, in the hope of justifying their own existence.' Milan Kundera disagrees. The novels he admires lend significance to life without betraying its essential banality. When the sensational happens – as it sometimes does – it is purged of exaggeration, dressed in plausibility.

Kundera's reading of Anna Karenina's suicide – a refined version of his previous accounts in *The Art of the Novel* and *Testaments Betrayed* – is a miracle of renarration, divested of superficial melodrama. He contrasts her suicide with Oedipus blinding himself when he sees Jocasta, his wife and mother, hanged. Rather than tragedy, Kundera persuasively argues, Tolstoy gives us *'the prose of a suicide'*. Her death isn't a fated conclusion or a grand gesture in Kundera's account. It is rather an accumulation of infinitesimally tiny details until they reach a critical mass. Kundera reads Tolstoy's text like a safe-cracker, alert to virtually inaudible shifts in the aural atmosphere – until the safe door swings open, unlocked and lucid, and her suicide gives up its secret.

This 'Essay in Seven Parts', *The Curtain*, is a brilliant and beautifully intricate continuous argument. Its main thesis is the absolutely *true* idea that the novel shows us the prose of life, the unedited version, with its absence of grand events, the sense of life's inevitable undramatic *defeat*. Kundera's image for this is the curtain that the novel draws back so we can see what is actually there. There are no screens around the hospital bed. In the novel, Achilles has broken teeth, as it were. In Homer, orthodontics aren't an issue. There, Life is on a larger scale, an epic scale. The surgical truss hasn't even a supporting role.

The Curtain is crammed with memorable phrases, exciting provocations, and breathtaking insights. Kundera's gift for coining phrases is easily the equal of Musil's, whose epitome of kitsch Kundera quotes: 'bread drenched in perfume'. For example: 'forgetting, which never stops enlarging its enormous cemetery'. He tells us that the novel isn't an inferior form of history: 'The novelist is not a valet to historians.' And he is ironically scathing about the idea that novelists would be bereft of ideas without assistance from the professional thinkers. We learn, too, that the poetics of the novel are constantly shifting; that literary

Milan Kundera: *The Curtain* (Faber and Faber, 2007).

judgements are subjective, yet aspire to objectivity. Yes, we say, yes.

And sometimes when we say 'no', we want to say 'yes'. Consider this ravishing, poetic account of description, for example: 'compassion for the ephemeral'. Kundera 'argues' that the increase of description in the nineteenth-century novel – what a brilliant observation of something obvious and easy to overlook – is caused by accelerating historical change, the obliteration of daily dross. (He must be thinking of the famous communist underpants in *Life is Elsewhere*, forgotten underpants so ugly they were an obstacle to coitus.) I think rather that the increase is a result of the changing economy of narration: the anecdotal narrator of eighteenth-century fiction, like anyone else *telling* a story, concentrates on the story, not on embellishment. There is a Hemingway story in which a pilot describes parachutes opening like 'great big beautiful morning glories' before catching fire. He is mocked by the other pilots – as a *writer*. They are discomfited by his conflation of two different types of narration: telling/talking and describing/writing. Omniscience is impersonal and dispenses with the spoken voice. The altered narrative convention permits and requires greater descriptive detail. But you don't have to agree to be charmed by the panache of Kundera's critical prose.

Sometimes Kundera misrepresents rival art forms in order to award the novel all three places on the winners' podium. He over-emphasises drama's tendency to the dramatic: 'In the theater', he writes, 'a great action could only be born of some other great action.' In other words, the drama is short on the novel's defining prose ingredient. There, the curtains are drawn to reveal *theatrical* action. This isn't true of Chekhov. Who else would subtitle *The Seagull*, in which a woman goes mad and a young man shoots himself, 'A Comedy in Four Acts'? Kundera identifies 'the soft gleam of the comical', irony, as central to the novel. It is there in Chekhov. And so is the prose element so crucial to Kundera's account of the novel. Mad Nina may say, 'I am a seagull. No, that's not it' – but she also remembers the room used to be 'a drawing room' and she gives an objective, accurate account of her bad acting. *She asks for a drink of water.*

As for Kostya's suicide, the fatal shot is passed off by Dr Dorn as a burst bottle of ether. In fact, ultimately, Kostya and Anna Karenina kill themselves for the same reason. He isn't the successful writer he wants to be, though he is published. He is still in love with Nina and learns that she still loves Trigorin, who has deserted her and her child. None of this is new, or reason for suicide. Anna Karenina, Kundera argues, has a troubled relationship with Vronsky, but the efficient cause of her suicide is aesthetic. Surrounded by ugliness of every sort, she is reminded of the first time she met Vronsky – when a railway worker fell to his death under the train wheels. She can 'give her love story a finished, beautiful shape' by ending her life in the same way. She succumbs to symmetry.

So does Chekhov's Kostya. Just before she leaves, Nina recites lines from Kostya's absurd symbolist play performed at the beginning of *The Seagull*. Including this incitement to symmetry: 'All living things have completed their cycle of sorrow …' The implicit imperative is impossible for Kostya to resist – even though he is anxious, moments before he pulls the trigger, that his mother should not be upset by encountering Nina.

The Curtain is great criticism. It is an account of the novel, its shifting poetics, and a record of Kundera's own meticulous reading – what *he* reads, *how* he reads, and therefore how we now have to read also. My account of *The Seagull* is a disagreement, but a disagreement indebted to Kundera – *unthinkable* without Kundera.

Christopher Logue
(2007)

We begin *in medias res*. This is the death of Pyrop in *GBH*. Pyrop, 'the richest and the fattest Greek', whose wealth is founded on 'a chariot factory plus numerous farms'. He crouches down 'as timid and fearful as a dog / About to shit'. He begs: 'My mother is alone, and old, and sick.' (Logue is good at begging for one's life: in *All Day Permanent Red*, Pathenos begs his life from Hector: 'Pathenos kisses Hector's wrist. / His eyes are full of words.') Anyway, back to Pyrop. He flees, pursued by arrows – arrows that 'go so fast their shanks ignite!' And the canine simile comes true: 'he cannot hold his mud.' He shits himself. In its way, this passage is a compendium of Logue's routine narrative talent: the swiftness of the laconic characterisation, the brevity and conviction of the backstory – that chariot *factory*, whose inflection of modernism renders the spoiled rich boy stereotype ironic – the traditional, conventional image of cowardice, the *cur*, remade so we read the dog's costive, curved trembling as fear – the cartoon exaggeration of the arrows bursting into flames, the scatological comedy of the coward's loss of bowel control. But the genius here is in Logue's account of his scream: 'his voice, / So high, so piteous and profound'. *Profound*. It is a witty, ironic and truly imagined counter-intuitive adjective. And it is an adjective that places Logue in the august company of Conrad and Tolstoy. This is Conrad in *Lord Jim*, another novel in which a coward and a dog, a cur, are conflated outside the court as the disgraced Jim leaves and someone aims a kick and an insult ('cur') at a stray dog – an insult Jim appropriates. Later in the novel, Tuan Jim is fighting it out with Gentleman Brown. There is a casualty in an early skirmish: 'He was a strong man and died hard, with moans now loud, now sinking to a strange confidential note of pain.' *Confidential*. *Profound*. And this is Tolstoy in *The Sebastopol Sketches*: he is describing the surgeons at work, amputating limbs: 'you will see the apothecary assistant fling the severed arm into a corner [*fling!*]; you will see another wounded man who is lying on a stretcher in the same room and watching the operation on his companion, writhing and groaning *less with physical pain than with the psychological agony of apprehension*' (my italics). This is Tolstoy in *War and Peace* anatomising the moan: at the battle of Austerlitz (Chapter 18) Nicolai Rostov sees heaped-up bodies of the dead and wounded,

Lecture given at the University of Bristol, 7 November 2007.

'like ridges of dung on well-kept ploughland': the wounded are moaning 'and their shrieks and groans had a painful and sometimes affected sound, it seemed to Rostov.' Not just Rostov. Tolstoy, too, in an earlier chapter (16): this time it's an observation of Prince Andrei as he passes a soldier being flogged for petty theft: 'and still he heard the dull thuds and the desperate but affected scream.' *Confidential. Profound. Affected.*

In *Kings* Logue has Hephaestus, the crippled armourer, tell a joke to his fellow-gods about human beings. In *The Iliad*, the gods laugh *at* Hephaestus – for being a cripple. Not the same thing as Hephaestus cracking a joke. Again, it is a characteristic passage which, at the same time, puts Logue in the best literary company: 'Then, turning on his silver crutch / Towards his cousin gods, Hephaestus / Made his nose red, put on Lord Nestor's voice, / And asked: "How can a mortal make God smile?" // (Two ... three ...) // "Tell Him his plans."' There is a general point here, an ironic cosmological–metaphysical point: that human beings constantly appeal to the gods but that intervention is complicated, complicated by divided patronage – Hera, wife of Zeus, hates the Trojans but Zeus favours Priam. Intervention is also complicated by perfunctory attention. All this provisionality, this contingency, is there in Homer. What Logue brings to Homer is contemporary *sprezzatura* – the reference to the timing of the joke itself, the pause ('Two ... three ...') before the punch line. There aren't many representations of mimicry in poetry, either: 'Made his nose red, put on Lord Nestor's voice'. In literature, mimicry is rare enough. In real life, though, mimicry is rife. Joyce – the great includer – has mimicry in *Portrait of the Artist as a Young Man*. This is Mr Dedalus imitating the Bishop of Armargh, 'the tub of guts up in Armargh': 'he twisted his features into a grimace of heavy bestiality and made a lapping noise with his lips.' And this is Mr Dedalus again, taking off a hotel keeper: 'He inclined his head, closed his eyes, and, licking his lips profusely, began to speak with the voice of the hotel keeper.' In *Ulysses*, it is Buck Mulligan who is the mimic: 'Buck Mulligan, hewing thick slices from the loaf, said in an old woman's wheedling voice: – When I makes tea I makes tea, as old mother Grogan said. And when I makes water I makes water.' Moments later Mulligan's voice has changed to the 'finical sweet voice' of scholarship: 'He turned to Stephen and asked in a fine puzzled voice, lifting his brows: – Can you recall, brother, is mother Grogan's tea and waterpot spoken of in the Mabinogion or is it in the Upanishads?' Although Shakespeare refers to mimicry – Ulysses reporting Achilles's and Patroclus's piss-takes of the Greek court – the first person in literature actually to *enact* this is Jane Austen, when Emma mimics Miss Bates to the uncomfortable delight of Mrs Weston: 'For shame, Emma! Do not mimic her. You divert me against my conscience.' Emma's mimicry is provoked by the possibility of Jane Fairfax marrying Mr Knightley. Miss

Bates is Jane Fairfax's aunt:

'How could he bear to have Miss Bates belonging to him? – To have her haunting the Abbey, and thanking him all day long for his great kindness in marrying Jane? – "So very kind and obliging! – But he always had been such a very kind neighbour!" And then fly off, half through a sentence, to her mother's old petticoat, "Not that it was such a very old petticoat either – for still it would last a great while – and, indeed, she must thankfully say that their petticoats were all very strong."' Once more Logue is in the best literary company. Only the greatest writers consider these previously unconsidered trifles. Writing is partly about extending the franchise – about inclusivity, about the overlooked detail which is overlooked because it is familiar. And that touch of mimicry demonstrates Logue's alertness to micro-events at the periphery of classical actions – and the epic is, almost by definition, alien to miniaturised touches – a stroke by which Hephaestus escapes the dour cliché of his given, traditional characterisation.

Another example of an extra, a side-dish. Logue's title, *All Day Permanent Red*, takes as its subject the first battle scenes in *The Iliad*. Logue's title perfectly describes the continuous spilling of blood – its finality, battle's permanent result. But a great deal of Logue's wit is lost if his title isn't sourced – and with the wit, the metaphorical vividness of the implied comparison and thrilling discrepancy in the comparison between battle and a brand of lipstick seen by Logue at a Boots cosmetics counter. The same powerful discrepancy is at work when Lord Panda kills Quist with an arrow: 'To the sigh of the string, see Panda's shot float off; / To the slap of the string on the stave, float on / Over the strip for a beat, a beat; and then / Carry a tunnel the width of a lipstick through Quist's neck.' The effectiveness of all metaphor depends on, not the justice of the comparison, but also the distance between the tenor and the vehicle, between the things compared – in this case, a hideous, neat wound and an agent of beautification. Likewise the wound inflicted and boasted about: 'Laid his trunk open from shoulder to hip – / Like a beauty-queen's sash.' Compare, too, this ironically inflected image of battle: 'They stood close. / Closer; thigh in thigh; mask twisted over iron mask, / Like kissing ...'

Another example of an extra, the additional touch. Zeus praises Priam's sexual prowess: 'A stallion man – once taken for Myself – / Who serviced 50 strapping wives from 50 towns, / Without complaint – to unify my Ilium.' Four pages later, in Section II, Logue's intelligent imagination gives us the consequence of this virility: Priam gives audience to a young man: 'Who's there?' / 'Manto, sir.' / 'Manto?' / 'Yes, sir. Your youngest son.' Again there is a parallel with another great writer – Evelyn Waugh. In *Vile Bodies*, Fanny Throbbing has difficulty remembering her son, Miles. She is on a Channel crossing, talking to Kitty Blackwater, who says: 'Why, look, there's Miles.' 'Miles?' 'Your son, darling. My nephew, you know.' '*Miles*. Do you know, Kitty, I believe it is. He never comes to see me now, the naughty boy.' The coincidence of genius, but Logue is the greater genius here because he has thought himself into antiquity and aristocracy. Waugh, brilliantly, funnily, has only thought himself into aristocracy. Logue, too, is here purged of exaggeration. It is funny without striving to be hilarious. In the Waugh, it is a joke about promiscuity – about Fanny Throbbing's throbbing fanny – in Logue it is an act of historical imagination as well as a joke, a plausible joke added to Homer – Homer who isn't without humour – famously, there is laughter in heaven – but Homer is hardly Les Dawson.

These touches, additional to Homer, are never allowed to clutter the narrative line. A couple of years ago, I met Philip Pullman, whose *Dark Materials*, after their successful dramatisation at the National Theatre, were about to be turned into a film by Tom Stoppard. Except that Stoppard had been sacked – regretfully sacked, but sacked. Why? Because his script 'didn't tell the story'. Pullman is a writer for whom narrative is central. The other day he gave an interview to Claudia FitzHerbert for the *Literary Review*. In it is he praised David Lindsay, a forgotten writer, in these (for me, paradoxical) terms: 'The first book I think really did what fantasy can do, besides *Paradise Lost*, was a book published in 1920 called *A Voyage to Arcturus* by David Lindsay. [And this is where it gets paradoxical for me.] It's a very poorly written, clumsily constructed book which nevertheless has the force, the power, the intensity of genius.' In other words, in Pullman's hierarchy of talents, narrative is king – description, form, imagery, the sentence, are subject gifts, utterly subordinate. Logue, I can report, feels something similar – the primacy of narrative. Whenever he and I have edited a text together – *Kings*, *All Day Permanent Red*, *Cold Calls* (I had no editorial input for *The Husbands*, which was brilliantly transformed from a rather humdrum initial text by Liane Aukin) – on these occasions Christopher's central aim, constant worry, is that the narrative should *read* – and read quickly. He has been very kind about my epic poem *History: The Home Movie* – but all the same I remember his first comment, his initial reaction, which was how difficult my poem was to read. 'It takes forever.' I would have been crestfallen if I'd thought I'd been aiming to tell a story in quite the same speedy way as Christopher. My method was the opposite. I wanted to slow the action down. To tell my episodes in nearly continuous close-up. In 1996, the Glasgow Citizens' Theatre wanted me to write a dramatisation of *History: The Home Movie*. I mentioned this to Ian McEwan, who advised against, telling me that my poem was already a film in essence. When I offered it to Paweł Pawlikowski, the film director, he turned it down – because it was 'already a film', 'with nothing for me to do.' So Ian was right – in a way. Actually, I knew that my version of film was scanted: the classic syntax of film, to which Logue is much truer, is 'long-shot, middle-shot, close-up', 'middle-shot, close-up, long-shot', etc. – a variety. I consciously embraced the close-up.

Logue's Homer is crammed with film directions, as everyone knows. Knows incorrectly, misleadingly, I want to argue – though *War Music is* unambiguously visual. However, overall, it's cinemascope, wide-screen, favouring the long-shot. While the first obviously filmic instruction is 'Reverse the shot. / / Go close' the shot isn't in close-up. It's more a middle-shot following a long-shot: 'Hear Agamemnon, Lord of Lords, Autarch of Argos, / Whose eminent domain includes all southern Greece ...' Actually, as *Logue's Homer* has gone on, the number of film references has steadily diminished. 'Back-lit by long-necked flames' is from *Kings*. But *most* occur in *War Music*, *Patrocleia* and *GBH*: 'Cut to the fleet'; 'Sea-bird's eye view'; 'Close-up on Bombax'; 'Quick cuts like these may give / Some definition to the mind's wild eye / That follow-spots Achilles' sacred pair – [of horses] .' Even in *War Music* there are not that many film directions. And it is noticeable here, in this last example, the medium switches to the theatre: the spotlight that follows a principal as he or she moves on stage: 'the mind's wild eye / That follow-spots Achilles' sacred pair'. Nevertheless, the film script is implied throughout the poem by Logue's scene setting, which is in note form – the beautifully written 'unwritten' notation of the film script. Ian McEwan says somewhere – the introduction to his script of Timothy Mo's novel *Sour Sweet*, I think – that scripts are a holiday from writing proper because you don't need to describe a rainy night with its glinting tarmac. Instead you type one word: *rain*. And you've just spent thousands of pounds by specifying a rain machine – because the elements can't be trusted.

Logue adapts this economy to his own ends. What in McEwan's analysis is non-writing becomes a kind of laconic brilliance in Logue. And this takes us back to Philip Pullman and the narrative imperative. Description is never allowed to slow down the narrative. Dawn: 'Bright apricot rifts the far black.' It is vital but it is always brief and filmic – an image, another image. 'Swifts flit from spear to spear.' For flames: 'Gold holly in the hearth.' Over and out. 'Moist wind. Black wind. Rainbearing wind. / The tents like lanterns; green beneath dark hulls.' (There are tents like glow-worms in Tennyson's *Princess*.) Here Nestor is going to visit Achilles, with his son Antilochus. The dialogue between Nestor and Achilles is broken by an image: 'Their shadows on the textile'.

This break is interesting, a sign of narrative tact. When Patrick Marber was directing my play '1953', a version of Racine's *Andromaque*, he explained to me early on that Racine was essentially radio drama – so we would need a billiard table to provide physical diversion, to disguise the speeches, to break them up with action. It came up through the floor. I can't remember what it cost. It was over-budget but Patrick gave his director's fee to the Almeida to make up the set-budget shortfall. Patrick also made me cut the introduction to a bit of retrospective narration. My character began *in medias res*, then broke off, with the words, 'But let me tell you exactly what happened ...' That guide line went because it was a *warning* that a speech was about to break on the audience.

There are many speeches in *Logue's Homer*, because there are many speeches in Homer. But Logue is careful to spike the speech with radiant detail. Before Achilles addresses his Myrmidons: 'First light. / Men stand before the level feathers of their breath. / A messenger runs from the pearl-fringed tent.'

Logue's Homer is often praised by classical scholars as a translation. It isn't. Occasionally, classical scholars complain that it isn't. The praise comes from a perfectly reasonable pride that wants to see an academic speciality brought home to a popular audience. (The poetry audience is small. The classical audience is even smaller – and anxious to overpraise Tony Harrison's versions and to inflate Derek Walcott's *Omeros*.) Logue is clear about the status of his poem. It is not a translation. He has no Greek. It is crammed with contemporary references. It is an original poem based on Homer's *Iliad*. And yet the scholars are, if not right, not entirely wrong either. *War Music*, or *Logue's Homer*, isn't an entirely modern poem either – despite its references to Rommel ('grim under his tan' at Alamein), scattered warriors 'like shoppers trapped by a calamity', Palt's 'Porsche-fine chariot', Diomed's arrow-stuck shield like 'microphones on politicians' stands', *Miss Herber's Diary*, 1908, describing the Limpopo, '300,000 plunging tons of aircraft carrier', seat belts, an Uzi automatic, that beauty queen's sash, a Tiger tank, 'blood like car-wash', a dead warrior called 'Bubblegum', a cyclorama, Stalingrad West, a photographer whose colour 'picture went around the world', 'Dark glasses in parked cars', eyelets in mesh 'like runway lights', 'psychotherapists'. Then there is 'Quinamid / The son of a Dardanian astrologer / Who disregarded what his father said / And came to Troy in a taxi.'

I wanted Christopher to call it *World War One* – suggesting therefore that this was the first war, the template for all subsequent wars, and to suggest that it was twentieth-century as well as an example of antiquity. Like Christopher's poem itself. How is this brilliant hybridity achieved?

Partly by his epic similes. Passages of meditation, convalescent from the action, lead to epic similes – peculiar to the classical epic, yet, in this poem, more often than not, extending the comparison beyond its normal limits, into the twentieth century. Matthew Arnold in 'Sohrab and Rustum' takes the reader from the battlefield in Persia by the River Oxus to Pekin and a Chinese porcelain-maker – without distorting decorum. The figure allows for distance between the subject and the comparison. It is defined by the distance. Logue stretches it even further. Frequently, a Logue epic simile will take us into the twentieth-century world of car parks or an earthquake at Skopje (in *Kings*, Part II: originally, 'As in the spring of 1961, / Elly, Hugo Claus and I'; in the revise 'as tourists, my friends and I'. In his *Areté* interview, Logue confesses to temporary funk and embarrassment about these updates.)

Primarily, though, the hybridity is achieved by the dynamic of free verse and blank verse, by the choicely candid anachronisms, by the alternation between filmic shorthand and sinuous Miltonic syntax. On the one hand, there is terseness and telegraphese: 'Taking their elbows. Raising them.' On the other hand, there is the majestic unhurried Miltonic paragraph: 'Now, / Almost by touch, the Council's tumult died, as / Gowned, down the flight of steps that join / The Temple's precinct to the court, / Surrounded by Troy's dukes, Prince Hector comes.' The last line is a perfect iambic pentameter. About ten years ago, the *New Yorker* (then under Tina Brown's editorship) commissioned a profile (in the end, unpublished) of Christopher by Fernanda Eberstadt, a young novelist Christopher assured me had once been a girlfriend of Mick Jagger. She phoned me. I answered questions and forgot my answers – until I had to recall them when the *New Yorker* fact-checkers were going through the text. (It obviously came quite close to being published.) One statement I was asked to verify made no sense to me. The fact-checkers don't read your supposedly actual sentences back to you: they ask you to verify a paraphrase, or sometimes a hint. Anyway, I denied saying the thing I was supposed to have said – mainly because it made no sense to me. Later I remembered. You will see why the metaphor made no sense in paraphrase. I had compared Christopher's use of the iambic pentameter to the Edward Sorel *New Yorker* cover that marked the beginning of Tina Brown's reign as editor. You will recall that several luminaries left the magazine – among them Garrison Keillor – when this English editorial 'vandal' took over from Bob Gottlieb, who had taken over from the legendary, abstemious, Kellogg's-cornflake-eating Mr Shawn. Tina's way of dealing with this flak was to make a joke via Ed Sorel. Sorel's cartoon showed one of those Central Park horse-drawn barouche-landaus – with a Punk Mohican, complete with piercings, sprawled across the seat of the landau. This is what Christopher Logue does with the staid old iambic pentameter. There is plenty of free verse in *Logue's Homer*. But the iambic pentameter is the engine, the rhythmic *point de repère*. (I treasure a memory of sitting in the Pizzaria Amalfi on Southampton Row. Christopher is affronted because I say a line doesn't scan. Counting the beats on his fingertips, he recites the line, adamant – and then concedes.) The iambic pentameter is the dominant vehicle – but Logue makes it carry all kinds of hip, contemporary stuff: 'Nasty, Thersites' little dog, / Now licking this, now tasting that.' In fact, two tetrameters, but you get the idea. (And I want to quote this because it was one of my contributions, if I remember rightly. I should say that Logue's easy

consent to the editing process, his unembarrassed willingness to accept suggestions, is an index of his complete artistic confidence.)

Sorel's cartoon reminds me of the important role that film cartoon plays
in *War Music*. Logue is interested in violence and the difficulties of portraying
action in poetry. Action film is what film is made for. Poetry is handicapped by
comparison. Christopher told me that he read sports journalism – particularly
boxing reports, though wrestling (the forearm smash, the headlock, the body-
slam) makes a more prominent contribution to Logue's warrior lexis. Sports
journalism's tendency to hyperbole – that ball that goes screaming into the top-
left-hand corner of the net – becomes in Logue a readiness to *big* it. Anaxapart,
'(Who once had 50 stitches in his face)', is given a little extra: '(And you could
strike a match upon that scar).' There is an element of comic super-size-me,
Christopher:

> Cut to the Fleet.
> Then to the strip between the rampart and the ditch.
>
> The air near Ajax was so thick with arrows, that,
> As they came, their shanks tickered against each other;
> [remember those arrows so fast they ignited as they fizzed after Pyrop]
> And under them the Trojans swarmed so thick
> Ajax outspread his arms, turned his spear flat,
> And simply pushed. Yet they came clamouring back until
> So many Trojans had a go at him
> The iron chaps of Ajax' helmet slapped his cheeks
> [a verbal nudge: slapstick is what we're watching]
> To soft red pulp, and his head reached back and forth
> Like a clapper inside a bell made out of sword blades ...

They're having a bit of a ding-dong: the verbal triggers, the vulgar animating
clichés, are only just out of sight. The cartoon comedy intensifies until Logue
treats us to the classic vaudeville double-take:

> Maybe, even with no breath left,
> Big Ajax might have stood it yet; yet
> Big and all as he was, Prince Hector meant to burn that ship:
> And God was pleased to let him.
>
> Pulling the Trojans back a yard or two
> He baited Ajax with his throat; and Ajax took.
> As the spear lifted, Hector skipped in range;

> As Ajax readied, Hector bared his throat again;
> And, as Ajax lunged, Hector jived on his right heel
> And snicked the haft clean through its neck
> Pruning the bronze nose off – Aie! – it was good to watch
> Big Ajax and his spear blundering about for, O,
> Two seconds went before he noticed it had gone.

We have seen this, or something similar, a hundred times on Looney Toons: it is the candles on the birthday cake that, wait a minute, are actually sticks of dynamite. The violence here is boldly inflected with comedy – the self-conscious hyper-violence of *Itchy & Scratchy* parodying the unselfconscious comic violence of *Tom and Jerry*. Compare: 'As Akafact fell back, back arched, / God blew the javelin straight; and thus / Mid-air, the cold bronze apex sank / Between his teeth and tongue, parted his brain, / Pressed on, [so far, so brutal: until the saving grotesque verb] and *stapled* him against the upturned hull. / [Logue immediately serious once more] His dead jaw gaped. His soul / Crawled off his tongue and vanished into sunlight.'

Of course, death in battle is often grotesque, often edged with comedy anyway. And Logue can write this, too. I am going to read you the deaths of Lycon and Panotis in *Patrocleia*, but first I want to read Robert Wynkfielde's account of Mary Queen of Scots being beheaded on 8 February 1586:

> she kneeling down upon the cushion most resolutely, and without any token or fear of death, she spake aloud this Psalm in Latin, *In Te Domine confido, non confundar in eternam*, etc. Then, groping for the block [she has a caule pinned over her head], she laid down her head, putting her chin over the block with both her hands, which, holding there still, had been cut off had they not been espied. Then lying upon the block most quietly, and stretching out her arms, she cried, *In manus tuas, Domine*, etc., three or four times. Then she, lying very still upon the block, one of the executioners holding her slightly with one of his hands, she endured two strokes of the other executioner with an axe, she making very small noise or none at all, and not stirring any part of her from the place where she lay; and so the executioner cut off her head, saving one little gristle; which being cut asunder, he lift up her head to the view of all the assembly and bade *God save the Queen.*

Bear that gristle in mind. It is more plausible than the loyal, blood-soaked dog that takes refuge in the dead Queen's petticoats – found, however, when the executioner is taking the Queen's garters ...

Of several incidents, consider two:
Panotis' chariot yawed and tipped him
Back off the plate by Little Ajax' feet.
Neither had room to strike; and so the Greek
Knocked his head back with a forearm smash
And in the space his swaying made, close lopped.
Blood dulled both sides of the leafy blade.
Fate caught Panotis' body; death his head.
Nearer the ditch Arcadeum met Lycon:
Catching each other's eye both cast, both missed,
Both ran together, and both struck; but
Only Lycon missed both times.
His neck was cut clean through
Except for a skein of flesh off which
His head hung down like a melon.

The iambic metre deliquesces in the last line quoted. It is lumpish, rhythmically awkward – grotesque.

Logue is good at these particulars.

He is equally good at battle in general. A small anthology: 'The noise they make while fighting is so loud / That what you see is like a silent film'; 'Impacted battle. Dust above a herd. / Hands wielding broken spearpoles rise through ice-hot twilight flecked with points. / And where you end and where the dust begins / Or if it is the dust or men that move / And whether they are Greek or Trojan, well / Only this much is certain: when a lull comes – they do – / You hear the whole ridge coughing'; 'Sunlight like lamplight'; 'Sparks from the bronze'; 'And when the armies met, they paused, / And then they swayed, and then they moved / Much like a forest making its way through a forest.' And this, one of my favourite passages, describes the facing armies, while their chiefs confer about a single combat:

Fierce chrome. Weapon-grade chrome
Trembling above the slopes.
And standing on it, leaning on their spears, among their wheels,
The enemies. And over all,
The city's altars. Smoking.

A messenger runs between the lines.

Then nothing

Then a boy selling water.

Then nothing.

Then nothing.

'Come on! Come *on!*'

Then 50 kings walk through

And greet –

Every marooned moment in one's life is there in that 'Then nothing' – followed by 'Then nothing'. A repetition worthy of John Cage or a sulking luggage carousel.

Logue has another great repetition in *Patrocleia*, one of the boldest repetitions in literature, calm and incomparable. It is after the death of Sarpedon.

And God turned to Apollo, saying: 'Mousegod, take my Sarpedon
                         out of range
And clarify his wounds with mountain water.
Moisten his body with tinctures of white myrrh
And violet iodine; and when these chrisms dry
Fold him in miniver that never wears
And lints that never fade
And call My two blind footmen, Sleep and Death,
To carry him to Lycia by Taurus,
Where, playing stone chimes and tambourines,
His group will consecrate his death,
Before whose memory the stones shall fade.'
And Apollo took Sarpedon out of range
And clarified his wounds with mountain water;
Moistened his body with tinctures of white myrrh
And violet iodine; and when these chrisms dried
He folded him in miniver and lints
That never wear, that never fade;
And called God's two blind footmen, Sleep and Death,
Who carried him
Before whose memory the stones shall fade
To Lycia by Taurus.

Has the essence of ritual ever been bettered?

And how final that final alteration, that final reordering of clauses, is: not ending on 'Before whose memory the stones shall fade' but ending instead on 'To Lycia by Taurus.' Not: '"And call My two blind footmen, Sleep and Death, / To carry him to Lycia by Taurus, / Where, playing stone chimes and tambourines, / His group will consecrate his death, / Before whose memory the stones shall fade."' Not that, but this, with chimes and tambourines edited out: 'And called God's two blind footmen, Sleep and Death, / Who carried him / Before whose memory the stones shall fade / To Lycia by Taurus.' Not the continuous memory, but the final, fixed place of death – the site of the grave.

In *Kings*, the villain is Agamemnon, who has appropriated Briseis, greedily, over-weaningly. Achilles is given his disgusted denunciation – 'Cuntstruck', 'Cheesey Lung'. Both my suggestions – the latter taken from Mann's *The Magic Mountain*. But the real triumph here is to give Agamemnon good lines, too: he is addressing the angry Achilles: 'God made you fast. Some say the fastest. And some say / More beautiful than any other man. / Indubitably He made you strong and brave. / So tell me this: who made you sour? / For you are sour, boy Achilleus, sour.' Agamemnon's conclusion is telling, damaging: 'Thank you, Greece. / As is so often true, / Silence has won the argument. / Achilles speaks as if I found you on a vase, / So leave his stone-age values to the sky.' This Agamemnon is a politician, a modern politician, deploying all those euphemistic Westminster–Whitehall formulae – as when he tells Achilles, 'Go home. Go now. / The time has come for you to see / More of your family.'

The greatest triumph in characterisation is Logue's rebranding of Helen of Troy. He negotiates her beauty perfectly: 'as she walked across / The level leading to the lower flight / One of our earth's great leaders gasped, and stood, / And then another stood, and then the rest / Casting their gasps before her feet / As would the world its hats before a god.' Her maids dust her with gold. She is also human. She is Elly. Her maid calls her 'Sweetie'. And with a perfect stroke of completely unexpected characterisation, Logue makes her *regret* the whole elopement with Paris to Troy. Sometimes she dreams she is back in Greece again, a girl, 'at home, / And as they did, my brothers come, and pull my covers off.' She would like Paris killed: 'And on the Wall: "God kill him," (Helen to herself).' Her confidences to Priam are a convincing account of amorous confusion, of antipathetic sexual power, of self-loathing:

> I need forgiveness, too.
> Not that I am the kind of she who calls the priest
> Each time she has a cold.
> I always wanted my marriage to be perfect.
> To be his. Just his. As his land is his.

> And that is what my father wanted, too.
> As did the world. And they are right. Quite right.
> But then this thing. Your son.
> I did not want to give that man a single thought.
> He will not apologise. He says
> A higher power gave me to him.

This is the voice of the divorcee, pitying her first abandoned husband, but in the grip of a categorical imperative, irresistible but deeply resented: 'Poor Menelaos. He hid his grief.' *Poor Menelaos*. This is great art.

In Book III of Homer, Helen regrets the grace and grandeur of Agamemnon's court. She regrets not seeing her favourite child, now grown up (the Greek word for 'grown-up' is uncertain: it could mean 'last born'). She wishes she had died. She be-whores herself (we assume – the Greek word's connotation is uncertain: it means 'dog-faced'). Logue takes this general disposition – general apart from the missed child – and rethinks its nostalgia. The pity for Menelaos, this nostalgia for ordinariness and simplicity – for peace, for domestic peace – isn't Homer. It's Logue – out there on his own.

In April 1999, I was asked by the *Guardian* to recommend a book for the decade. This is what I wrote: '*The Husbands* – Christopher Logue's version of Books III and IV of Homer's *Iliad*. It is partly syntactic magic – the dynamic of long, clear sentences, effortlessly extending like clean-cut marble staircases, set beside single words which are radioactive in their isolation. And it is partly the conflation of the iambic pentameter and the candidly contemporary, which, together with Logue's narrative and pictorial gifts, make this one of the great works of our time, not just the decade.'

Counter-Intuitive Larkin
(2008)

When I was Poetry Editor at Fabers in 1986, I published Barbara Everett's *Poets in Their Time: From Donne to Larkin*. Charles Monteith, the ex-chairman of Fabers – loveable, lazy and anecdotal, lord of the late arrival and the long lunch hour – happened to read the chapter on Larkin's 'Sympathy in White Major'. Barbara Everett's argument turned on how much Larkin owed to Gautier's 'Symphonie en blanc majeur'. Charles was incredulous and dismissive. The very idea of 'Philip' being influenced by a foreign poet, he said, with a gentle smile that gradually broadened to show his well-spaced, tawny teeth, was 'ludicrous'. He had fallen for the propaganda – Larkin's bluff, insular, faux-xenophobic self-caricature. Several years before, John Fuller's Sycamore Press had published Larkin's imitation of Baudelaire's 'Femmes damnées'. That rather gave the lie to Larkin's affectation of insularity, an insularity honed and practised and best illustrated by his answer to Ian Hamilton's question about foreign poetry. Larkin chose the simple ironical expedient of repetition in italics: *Foreign poetry?*

Let me start with an easily understood example of the counter-intuitive in Larkin – 'Dublinesque'. We know Larkin abominated the three *P*s, Picasso, Pound and Charlie Parker, yet 'Dublinesque' is a poem written in free verse. Rare for Larkin. I have been wondering about the significance of Larkin's title 'Dublinesque'. What is the significance of the affix 'esque' here? Normally, it implies something characteristic, something typical, something expected, something formulaic. *Shandyesque*, for instance, something like *Tristram Shandy* – say, a whimsical digressiveness, or in Jane Austen's *Northanger Abbey* the ostentatious buttonholing of a fictive participant reader, not the abstract, token, frequently apostrophised reader of 'Gentle Reader' but someone to argue with, dissent from. At the end of Chapter 5 of *Northanger Abbey*, Jane Austen launches an ironic defence of the novel – necessarily ironic because *Northanger Abbey* is an attack on the Gothic novel. Austen laments 'a general wish of decrying the capacity and undervaluing the labour of the novelist, and of slighting the performances which have only genius, wit, and taste to recommend them'. She then follows Sterne's example in literalising the implied reader of any novel. What Sterne does as a novelist is to underline, spell out, the conventions of the novel. Here is Austen aping his example. ' " I am no novel reader – I seldom look

Lecture given to the Larkin Conference, University of Hull, June 2007.

into novels – Do not imagine that *I* often read novels – It is really very well for a novel." – Such is the common cant. – "And what are you reading Miss —?" "Oh, it is only a novel!" replies the young lady; while she lays down the novel with affected indifference, or momentary shame.' This is Shandyesque. And it is no accident that Sterne is mentioned, name-checked, on the same page. My point, though, is this. You would never apply 'Shandyesque' to *Tristram Shandy*. That would be otiose, redundant, circular. The 'esque' form is adjectivally reserved for the imitation, whether conscious or unconscious. It is rather like the term 'realistic', which is reserved for imitations of reality, not reality itself. My late colleague Tony Nuttall had a good example: false teeth are realistic. Real teeth are not.

Larkin's 'Dublinesque', then, is faintly fictive, not Dublin exactly, but Dublin as a literary topos – as we can see from the opening props – those 'stucco *side-streets*' that make me sceptically alert to the grandeur of stucco in sidestreets. Pebble-dash is more like it. I associate stucco with Eaton Square, those dazzling Antarcticas of expensive whitewash. I quote from Wikipedia: 'its "aristocratic" Baroque-looking stucco decoration was used frequently in upper-class apartments of the 19th and early 20th century.' Those 'race-guides and rosaries' are laconic alliterative shorthand, too. They do the job perfectly – too perfectly, perhaps, because they come with a tinge of cliché. A deliberate tinge of cliché, I want to argue. Not quite the accordion for Paris, of course. All together subtler. But the two props work like autocomplete on a laptop. We have been here before. This is a short cut. The two Rs, rosaries and race-guides, summon up the ould sod as surely as R & R would summon up 'Rest and Recuperation' in an American context. And that stucco takes us into the past. This is historical Dublin, perhaps ambiguously prolonged into the present. The scene is anachronistic, or touched with anachronism, and somehow typical. Dublinesque, in fact.

I think we can deduce this from the clothes the mourning prostitutes are wearing: these are period, though they could just conceivably be sixties and hippy. 'A troop of streetwalkers / In wide flowered hats, / Leg-of-mutton sleeves, / And ankle-length dresses'. The emphasis on clothes you might expect to find in Lawrence, but it is uncharacteristic of Larkin, this itemised wardrobe, and it is another indication that we are looking at the past – even as the poem also persuades us we are looking at the present. Partly because Larkin uses the present tense throughout: 'A funeral passes.'

Repetitions are always interesting in Larkin. Here, there are two (my italics). 'There is an air of great friendliness, / *As if* they were honouring / One they were fond of.' Again: 'A voice is heard singing / Of Kitty or Katy, / *As if* the name meant once / All love, all beauty.' Those 'as if's, two of them, tell us, inaudibly, at the frontiers of consciousness, that we are watching a simulation, a figment of the past. The first 'as if' is important, too, because it establishes that the dead person is also a streetwalker. It is explanatory. The 'as if' has the sense of 'because'. 'There is an air of great friendliness, / As if [because] they were honouring / One they were fond of.' The usual penumbra of doubt that accompanies 'as if' is muted here. Think about the expression 'as if' on its own. There it means completely unlikely. The second 'as if' – 'As if the name meant once / All love, all beauty' – is properly provisional. It isn't the case that the name meant 'All love, all beauty'. The person mourned is a tart. The all-important name is actually indefinite, is either Kitty or Katy. The poem doesn't know which. So 'Dublinesque' becomes a poem in the present and in the past, a poem with implicit strictures and reservations, a poem about sentimentality, actually, whose afflatus – 'All love, all beauty' – is phoney, *has* to be phoney – and yet demonstrates how powerful, how unstoppable sentimentality can be – and how close to sentiment it is. The last line of the poem overrides – and is intended to override – the reservations seeded everywhere before its sudden, undeniably moving advent.

I hope it is clear that, in my non-Derridean way, I have just deconstructed 'Dublinesque'. Larkin is undeceived and deceived in equal measure. He connives at the deception. Connive: 3. To feign ignorance of or fail to take measures against a wrong, thus implying tacit encouragement or consent: 'The guards were suspected of conniving at the prisoner's escape.' (Latin *connivere*, 'to close the eyes'.)

We think Larkin is the unromantic, *l'homme moyen sensuel*, undeceived. But he is romantic. His yearning always gets under the wire, under the wary radar. The poetry is a form of smuggling, an exercise in hidden contraband.

Take 'Reference Back', the poem about Larkin playing jazz records and his mother listening. This poem shares with 'Dublinesque' a nympholepsy – specifically, the convenient idea that the past is a place far enough away for us to indulge the pretence that it is the location of something irrecoverable, something valuable, central even, but lost to us now. Nympholepsy: a frenzy for something unattainable.

'Reference Back' refers in its title to the past. The poem again has some interesting repetitions: '*That was a pretty one*, I heard you call / from the *unsatisfactory* hall / To the *unsatisfactory* room where I / Played record after record, idly, / Wasting my time at home, that you / Looked so much forward to.' Let me make the set-up absolutely clear. Larkin is upstairs in his room. His mother is calling up from the hallway. The room and the hallway are 'unsatisfactory' because the young Larkin is defeating the purpose of his visit, his 'time at home' that his mother had looked forward to. He isn't just wasting time, he's wasting his 'time-at-home', by being remote. The micro-epiphany he records is 'the sudden bridge' between him and his mother created by their shared pleasure in King Oliver's *Riverside Blues*. The distant past of 'antique negroes', 30 years before, has impinged on the present. What is bridged is the gap between his mother's *'unsatisfactory* age' and Larkin's *'unsatisfactory* prime'. There are, then, four *unsatisfactorys* in 'Reference Back'. I think we can assume that Larkin thinks this near remembered past – when Larkin was in his prime, a condition immediately discounted here – was unsatisfactory.

It is the last stanza which puzzles me and which requires a certain amount of unpacking. 'Truly, though our element is time, / We are not suited to the long perspectives / Open at each instant of our lives.' That seems straightforward. At every moment, we can take the long view. But it doesn't suit us to do so. For two reasons. First, we are confronted by things completely lost: 'long perspectives' 'link us to our losses'. Second, and 'worse', is the consciousness of something, not lost, but depleted, *unsatisfactory*, when compared to its previous state: 'worse, / They show us what we have *as it once was*, / Blindingly undiminished'(my italics). Let's look at Larkin's title again: 'Reference Back'. Larkin, past his prime, is looking back on a younger Larkin in his unsatisfactory prime, remembering something he cannot remember and something he can remember. What he can remember is the spark that passed between him and his mother. What he cannot remember is King Oliver and his band recording *Riverside Blues*. Yet the syntax allows cunningly for both. 'And now / I shall, I suppose, always remember how / The flock of notes those antique negroes blew / Out of Chicago air into / A huge remembering pre-electric horn ...' Repetitions again, this time of 'remember': 'I shall, I suppose, always remember' – what? – 'a huge remembering horn'. A not-quite infinite regressus of memory, in which what is remembered is something remembering. And actually, Larkin cannot remember this because the recording took place only the year after he was born.

I know. Of course, what Larkin will 'always remember' is, in fact, 'the sudden bridge' the jazz made between him and his mother.

> And now
>> I shall, I suppose, always remember how
>> The flock of notes those antique negroes blew
>> Out of Chicago air into
>> A huge remembering pre-electric horn
>> The year after I was born
>> Three decades later made this sudden bridge
>> From your unsatisfactory age
>> To my unsatisfactory prime.

The object of the verb 'remember' is 'this sudden bridge'. But for a long syntactic moment, Larkin invites us quite deliberately to think he can remember the impossibly distant past. Why? Because in an imaginary past, sufficiently distant, beyond our ken, is the idea, the ideal. King Oliver isn't playing jazz simply. He is taking part in a miracle where a *flock* of notes is created out of thin air. For a second or two, Larkin seems to have witnessed this miracle. We have an idea of perfection even if we have never experienced it – and if we have to locate it somewhere, the past is the only place, since the present is 'unsatisfactory'. For Larkin the romantic can't quite see this perfection, which is presented to us oxymoronically: 'Blindingly undiminished.' How can he see it is 'undiminished' if its brightness blinds him? Again, though, the paradox is curiously weightless. What we are offered is something stupendous – something stupendous, something beautiful, erected on the slight remark *That was a pretty one.*

The poem insists on two contradictory positions. One, that the past is a convenient fiction where we can house our yearnings. Two, these yearnings were once actually fulfilled, in reality, in the past: 'as it once was'; 'we could have kept it so.' The syntax is affirmative even if the poem ends on a note of inevitable emotional entropy: 'just as though / By acting differently we could have kept it so.'

Sometimes in Larkin, the weighting of a poem can be deceptive, deliberately so. In 'Wild Oats', there are two girls, but only one of them, the 'friend in specs', is described intensively. The poem appears to be about Larkin's sclerotic emotions: 'an agreement / That I was too selfish, withdrawn, / And easily bored to love. / Well, useful to get that learnt.' There Larkin stands, heartless in the dock, as meagre as Camus's Meursault. 'Wild Oats' is an ironic title: there is nothing wild in this notation of emotional failure with its drolly observed ragged endgame: 'Parting, after about five / Rehearsals.'

Initially, the poem seems to be an account of duffers like that given to Jenny Bunn by Graham McClintoch in Kingsley Amis's *Take a Girl Like You.* You'll remember that Graham kisses Jenny and she responds politely. Graham immediately picks up on the lack of ardour, the subtle rebuff, and unburdens himself of a credo (Chapter 14) that divides the world into the attractive and the unattractive. Jenny is attractive, Graham is unattractive. 'You can't imagine,' he tells her, 'what's it's like not to know what it is to meet an attractive person who's also attracted to you, can you? [A fine obstacle course: the Amis prose style already in its hobbled stride.] Because unattractive men don't want unattractive girls, you see. They want attractive girls. They merely *get* unattractive girls. I think a lot of people feel vaguely when they see two duffers marrying that the duffers must prefer it that way. Which is rather like saying that slum-dwellers would rather live in slums than anywhere else.'

All of Larkin's focus and attention seems concentrated on the failure of two duffers to marry. We are given the inventory of emotional failure, item by item: 'Wrote over four hundred letters, / Gave a ten-guinea ring / I got back in the end [In the end! The phrase adumbrates an elided struggle of competing mulishness], and met / At numerous cathedral cities / Unknown to the clergy'. In so far as the other girl appears, her demeanour is tinged with amused contempt: 'I believe / I met beautiful twice. She was trying / Both times (so I thought) not to laugh.' Then Larkin reveals that he has kept two snapshots of beautiful in his wallet – snapshots he describes as 'unlucky charms'. Unlucky charms: a wry throwaway, a bathetic inversion of 'lucky charms'. The tone is undramatic, downbeat, *ironic*, but the import is otherwise. The import is romantic. Why has Larkin kept the two snaps? They are introduced as an after-thought – by way of being by the way. But they are freighted with mute significance. The true significance of the snaps is to be found in the first stanza, where Larkin's unromantic, comic delivery – 'the whole shooting match' – deliberately masks his deep romantic involvement. It is easy to miss its significance. 'Faces in those days sparked / The whole shooting match off, and I doubt / If ever one had like hers.' *And I doubt / If ever one had like hers.* He is smitten. 'But it was the friend I took out.' Despite this, he goes on being smitten – hence the snapshots in the wallet and hence the failure of the relationship with the friend. They may have an 'agreement / That I was too selfish, withdrawn, / And easily bored to love', but Larkin, the poem whispers – barely audibly but unmistakably – is already deeply, helplessly, inextricably in love with the other girl, the 'bosomy rose with fur gloves on'. Andrew Motion's biography supplies probable prototypes, but I don't think particular identifiable individuals will unlock the poem, which is written out of a central emotional conviction – a belief in romantic love itself.

In Tom Stoppard's play *The Real Thing*, the hero Henry explains to his wife Annie how he knows that she is having an affair with Billy: 'I know it's him. Billy, Billy, Billy, the name keeps dropping, each time without significance, but it can't help itself. Hapless as a secret in a computer. Blip, blip, Billy, Billy.' Something like this happens in *Required Writing*.

There Larkin periodically gestures towards his core belief in romantic love. At the end of his essay on Housman, for example: 'For as Housman himself said, anyone who thinks he has loved more than one person has simply never really loved at all.' (Where did Housman say this? Archie Burnett, the Housman scholar, tells me that on page 449 of Grant Richards's *Housman 1897–1936* (Second Impression, 1942) there is a biographical reminiscence of Joan Thomson, daughter of Sir J. J. Thomson, Master of Trinity from 1918 to 1940: 'Housman would not tolerate the idea that it was possible for a man truly to love more than one woman in his life; anyone who considered that he had done so had simply never really loved at all.')

In 'Big Victims', he quotes the opening to Emily Dickinson's 'My Life had stood – a Loaded Gun – / In Corners – till a Day / The Owner passed – identified – / And carried Me away' and comments: 'This is romantic love in a nutshell.' At the end of his piece on Hardy's poetry, he praises Hardy's directness. In fact, he is also praising Hardy's romantic temperament: 'He can often be extremely direct. "Not a line of her writing have I, not a thread of her hair." Donne couldn't be more direct than that.'

In 'Wild Oats' Larkin isn't direct at all. He is deceptive, deliberately devious. There is a secret narrative, an implied romantic narrative, overlaid by the cover story about an unsatisfactory relationship that dwindled to a pedestrian conclusion – a cover story told with rueful ironic humour. The title is typical – at once an ironic joke about prudence and tameness, and at the same time a signal inviting us to look at the edges of the too neat story, where wild oats grow.

'An Arundel Tomb' famously ends with this endorsement of romantic love: 'What will survive of us is love.' Donne couldn't be more direct than that. But this famous last line is famously qualified with reservations: 'Our almost-instinct almost true.' We are invited to look in two directions at once. Like 'Dublinesque', 'An Arundel Tomb' is a liminal poem existing at the precise border where sentimentality and sentiment meet. Conventional wisdom has it that, after *The North Ship*, Larkin shed the influence of Yeats, the old spell-binding tenor. Away went the elaborate bow ties and on came the bicycle clips. What actually occurred was that Yeats went undercover. He was wearing a wire and Larkin was still tuned to his master's voice. One of those double hearing aids was in fact an ear-piece. It isn't that Larkin is belting out lines like 'Life scarce can cast a fragrance on the wind' (from 'Meditations in Time of Civil War') or 'Was there another Troy for her to burn?' ('No Second Troy'). But the *sense*, the romantic heft, is often plangent, as it is in 'Wild Oats'. Andrew Motion identifies Jane Exall as the 'bosomy rose' but I think the real prototype is Maud Gonne, the fugitive love of Yeats's life.

'An Arundel Tomb' is a much loved Larkin poem that describes a characteristic arc, one shared with 'High Windows' and 'Sad Steps', of prose to passion – an idea I shall return to. But I think 'An Arundel Tomb' rather over-valued. It is basically iambic with slippage. There are some finely judged metrical effects. For instance, the last two lines of the first stanza: 'Side by side, their faces blurred, / The earl and countess lie in stone, / Their proper habits vaguely shown / As jointed armour, stiffened pleat, / [And here the metre relents, marking a shift in the tone, a hint of potential irony] And that faint hint of the absurd – / The little dogs under their feet.' Nothing would have been easier for Larkin than to re-establish his metre by writing 'beneath' for 'under'. The ceremonial tone and formal sentiment find their objective correlative in the armour

and the *stiffened* pleat. There is a starchiness hereabouts that would accommodate 'beneath' for the more workaday word, 'under'. Additionally, the couple's
faces are 'blurred' and their clothing 'vaguely shown': what we feel here is distance rather than intimacy. With the dogs, though, our ears should warn us that
instability is in the offing.

There are similar delicate metrical effects in the second stanza, which supplies the detail around which the poem gathers its meaning. The earl is holding
the countess's hand. Again, it is the last two lines of the stanza that subtly vary
the metre. At the same time, though, the rhymes are banal and contrived for no
obvious reason other than incompetence. 'Pre-baroque' and 'shock' is good, but
'until', 'still' and 'and' are posted like lookouts at the end of the line. Every one a
kind of cliff-hanger clinging by its fingernails. They are not integral to their lines
and they are obtrusive and feeble. 'Such plainness of the pre-baroque / Hardly
involves the eye, until / It meets his left-hand gauntlet, still / Clasped empty in
the other; and /[here the metre shifts with beautiful appropriateness] One sees,
with a sharp tender shock / His hand withdrawn, holding her hand.' The shock
lodges itself in the ear also.

I think Larkin, as happens quite often – and this, too, is Yeatsian – finds it
difficult to thread his thought through the rhyme scheme. There can be two
results. Murky exposition or enfeebled rhymes. Larkin knew this and says (in his
interview with John Haffenden) that 'technically it's a bit muddy in the middle
– the fourth and fifth stanzas seem trudging somehow, with awful rhymes like
voyage/damage.' The third stanza begins to test Larkin's skill. 'They would not
think to lie so long.' He begins with this lightly archaic construction, meaning the
monument was never meant to last this long. 'Such faithfulness in effigy / Was
just a detail friends would see: / [that is, a detail only friends would see in their
living memories] A sculptor's sweet commissioned grace / Thrown off in helping to prolong / The Latin names around the base.' As readers, we have to keep
at bay unhelpful readings like the idea that the hand-holding is merely a piece of
sculptural eking out. The real sense is that friends who remembered the couple
would relish this tribute to their love. The sculptor is responsible, it is part of
his metier, an inspired touch, but pure professionalism, 'sweet commissioned
grace', part of a project to memorialise the dead couple, to ensure their names
[in Latin around the base] live on a little longer. So Larkin cunningly vacillates.
We are touched. We are touched by a touch of the artist. It isn't innocent.

The next three stanzas are social history. In its way, 'An Arundel Tomb' is a
political poem. Larkin records his implicit verdict on the present – in an aurally
clumsy phrase – 'An unarmorial age'. The difficulty of these stanzas is their difficulty – the inept conduct of Larkin's argument. 'They would not guess how
early in / Their supine stationary voyage / The air would change to sound-

less damage.' I am unsure what this third line means: 'The air would change to soundless damage.' What follows helps a little, since it describes particular social change: the break between aristocracy and their tenants. We can work out, too, that the inability to read Latin is intended by the lines 'How soon succeeding eyes begin / To look, not read.' So 'soundless damage' must be damage to the social fabric. Why is it 'soundless', though? The 'air' must mean, slightly baf-flingly, the general social 'atmosphere', what's in the air. 'Soundless' presumably carries the implication that the changes – damage from the earl and countess's point of view – were effected without violent revolution. But I freely confess that the line is gnomic as far as I am concerned.

Motion tells us that the sculpture was damaged in the Reformation and Civil War and that the hand-holding is a later addition by Edward Richardson in the nineteenth century – to disguise the damage. However, Larkin did not know this when he wrote the poem, but knew, as Motion puts it, 'subsequently'. In any case, none of this gets into the poem, though you might deduce a reference to the Reformation in the perhaps contrasted 'soundless damage'.

The succeeding stanza is clearer, and has some nice touches (that 'bright / Litter of birdcalls'), but the rhymes are again fabricated. Look what they do to the integrity of Larkin's lines. 'Of time. Snow fell, undated. Light.' The next line is: 'Each summer thronged the glass. A bright.' 'Breadths' and 'paths' is a satisfying rhyme, but it comes at a cost. The 'lengths and breadths / Of time' is a strikingly empty phrase. The *breadth* of time it took to write this lecture. See what I mean?

The penultimate stanza is smoke and mirrors more than it is cogent syntax. 'Now, helpless in the hollow of / An unarmorial age, a trough / Of smoke in slow suspended skeins / Above their scrap of history, / Only an attitude remains.' I have no idea what this means. The earl and countess are lying in a hollow. Is the hollow the same thing as the trough of smoke? That seems more unlikely than likely, because the trough is said to be above their scrap of history. But I really don't know how to interpret 'the hollow of an unarmorial age'. Nor can I make much of the 'smoke in slow suspended skeins'. It is an evocation of the unarmorial age, but more evocative than precise. Is it Larkin's idea of the Industrial Revolution? You almost wonder, desperately, if the couple haven't been made into a gift ashtray. I admit defeat, but the responsibility, the blame is Larkin's.

Andrew Motion's biography tells us that Larkin wrote on the end of the manuscript draft: 'Love isn't stronger than death just because statues hold hands for 600 years.' Larkin is consciously refuting the Song of Songs 8:6: 'for love is strong as death.' And logically that – 'Love isn't stronger than death' – is the enforced conclusion of the poem. 'Time has transfigured them into / Untruth.'

There is, apparently, no way around this. It fills the doorway like a bouncer saying 'I'm afraid *not*, sir. If I could just stop you there, sir.' It is reinforced by another denial: the earl and countess didn't mean it. I take it this isn't a reference to the Victorian repairs, but the primacy of the sculptor's role. 'The stone fidelity / They hardly meant ...' Thereafter, though, the qualifications are themselves qualified. *Prove* is a very strong verb and almost cancels the *almosts* in 'Our almost-instinct almost true'. It again becomes a question of weighting. The last line has all the force of a last line. It simply overrides the prior qualifications so that we, and Larkin, enjoy the afflatus unqualified. It is an indulged poetic fiction. When we speak about poetic justice we mean something perfectly balanced, where the offence and its punishment are exactly matched. This poetic fiction is perfectly balanced between complete endorsement and careful reservations. It is a curious form of co-existence, a two-state solution, where each exists independently of the other. Like the duck-rabbit in gestalt psychology, you can't hold the two interpretations simultaneously. They alternate.

Sometime in the early eighties, the drama editor at Fabers, Frank Pike, went to visit Larkin on Faber business. This involved staying the night in Hull – as it still does – so Larkin had the task of entertaining Frank. After a Chinese meal, Larkin took Frank to an amateur boxing match. As the boxers bobbed and weaved, feinted, dodged, ducked, pawed distantly at each other, Larkin turned to Frank and said lugubriously: 'Only connect.' Referring, of course, to E. M. Forster's hallowed liberal-humanist nostrum from *Howards End*: only connect the prose and the passion. In Forster's novel, the passion is represented by the Schlegels, while the prose is represented by the Wilcoxes. It isn't quite this simple, however, because Forster takes some pains to complicate what might seem a trite polarity. Helen and Meg Schlegel are passionate enough, but their pedantic brother, Tibby, displays a donnish slightly inhuman frigidity. And Meg Schlegel can see that people like Henry Wilcox, business people, the sons of Martha, have a saving *usefulness*: 'If the Wilcoxes hadn't worked and died in England for thousands of years, you and I [Meg says to her censorious sister] couldn't sit here without having our throats cut. There would be no trains, no ships to carry us literary people about in.' Remember, it is Henry who has saved Howards End from destruction.

Forster's polarity between prose and passion and their conflation are clearer in *The Longest Journey*. Forster fuses them in the famous scene where Rickie goes back into the arbour to retrieve his sandwiches and finds the bully Gerald (with the body of a Greek athlete and the face of an English one) locked in an embrace with Agnes. Forster conflates prose (those mislaid sandwiches) and passionate love. 'But they [Agnes and Gerald] had got into heaven, and nothing could get them out of it. Others might think them surly or prosaic. He [Rickie] knew … and so in time to come when the gates of heaven had shut, some faint radiance, some echo of wisdom might remain with him outside.' The same conflation, the same instinct, shows itself in Virginia Woolf, who inherits it from Forster. This is a famous hybrid sentence from *To the Lighthouse*, concerning not sandwiches but Mrs Ramsay's *bœuf en daube*: 'It partook, she felt, helping Mr Bankes to a specially tender piece, of eternity.'

This tradition, this fusion of the banal and the brilliant, is picked up by Larkin. Only connect the down-to-earth with the dazzling; the hedging, the hesitation, with the high romantic. We've seen this fusion at work in 'Wild Oats' and 'Reference Back'. I'd like now, if I can carry your scepticism with me, to look at Larkin the secular mystic – what you might call the Marriage of Heaven and Hull. 'It partook, she felt, helping Mr Bankes to a specially tender piece, of eternity.' Bear that sentence in mind.

The last stanza of 'Solar' can serve as a starting point. Andrew Motion quotes the stanza on its own – an unconscious act of criticism and improvement. Shorn of its inferior preceding stanzas, its power is enhanced. 'Coined there among / Lonely horizontals / You exist openly. / Our needs hourly / Climb and return like angels. / Unclosing like a hand, / You give for ever.' The sun as an image of self-sufficiency, of singleness married to inexhaustible generosity, to perpetual open-handedness. What is given is the coin of itself. We don't need the reference to Jacob's Ladder to sense the religious dimension. The anthropomorphism of the sun is crucial to this, too. There is something here that is fearless and generous that we might be tempted to worship. I am interested in the word 'unclosing'. Larkin partly chooses this word, rather than the more obvious 'opening', because he has already used 'openly' only eight words earlier. The other reason for choosing 'unclosing' is that it strongly suggests its opposite, 'closing' – more than 'open' suggests 'shut' – and the contrast enhances the generosity. There is a moment in Scott Fitzgerald's *Tender is the Night*, when the novelist describes the Divers' beach in the South of France: 'The hotel and its bright tan prayer rug of a beach were one.' Fitzgerald and Larkin are playing with a cliché, a figure of speech, literalising and transfiguring it. Sun worshippers both. The stale hyperbole is invigorated and brought to blazing life. From the prose of Ambre Solaire to solar energy.

'High Windows' starts with prose and ends with passion. The poem is a radical tonal journey from the coarse to the exalted. 'When I see a couple of kids / And guess he's fucking her' to 'and is nowhere, and is endless'. So many of Larkin's poems are about the gap between the ideal and the real – 'Essential Beauty' being the *locus classicus*.

'High Windows' seems a relatively simple poem about solipsism, the prison of the self. In Michael Frayn's early philosophical book, *Constructions*, his image for the mind is a suitcase – a suitcase capable of containing everything except itself. In 'High Windows', each generation sees its own limitations and *idealises* the subsequent generation – because it can't escape itself. Larkin's generation is unhappy, but previous generations could see the release from fear of God and guilt about sin. Larkin, in his turn, idealises the present younger generation for their sexual liberation. The idealism is actually ignorance turned inside out and Larkin's image for this is high windows – of the kind that let in light but which are too high to see through and discover what is on the other side.

The last stanza nevertheless isn't purely ironic – though it is 'nowhere', a species of fiction, a non-existent alternative. It is also a vision of heaven – hinted at in the fourth line: 'I know this is paradise.' By the end this means more than sensual 'bliss'. That bliss is desecularised and given 'real' spiritual content.

I want to make an analogy with Le Corbusier's chapel at Ronchamp, Notre-Dame-du-Haut. There is a side altar there of solid concrete, a giant inverted ingot, with a simple white linen runner on top of it. Behind the altar is a kind of chimney, a whitewashed tunnel reaching up to the sky. But all you can see from the inside is the downward flood of light. And though the source is unseen, you can see the light's intensity grows higher up. It is the perfect metaphor for spirituality.

Larkin's poem has a tightening rhyme scheme (with only one duff rhyme) that mirrors the poem's growth in intensity. The last lines are both negative and promissory. 'The sun-comprehending glass' offers both understanding of the sun and physical containment of the sun. The glass shows – after a line-break freighted with suspense – nothing, and is nowhere, and is ironic, even bathetic, while at the same time it promises an infinity that is 'endless'. And the final word casts its spell on the other words, 'nothing' and 'nowhere', so they become not empty but cleansed of physical reality. A nirvana for the non-believer.

I want to turn now to 'The Explosion', which, like 'Solar' turns partially on a bit of subtle, semiconscious wordplay – this time, blow-up and blown up, explosion and enlargement, as in the Antonioni film *Blow-Up*, with David Hemmings and Vanessa Redgrave. 'The Explosion' is written in trochees, rather uncertainly for the first two undecided lines: 'On the day of the explosion / Shadows pointed towards the pithead.' The first conversational line isn't obviously trochaic, but becomes so in retrospect. The second would be more pronouncedly trochaic if Larkin had written: 'Shadows pointed to the pithead.' Obviously, then, he begins by wanting to finesse the Hiawatha metre. It soon establishes itself and forces on Larkin some contrived, awkwardly maladroit locutions: 'Coughing oath-edged talk and pipe-smoke.' Oath-edged, like the beards and moleskins, locates the poem in the elastic past, where reality is more permissible and permeable, as in 'Dublinesque'. And I believe that 'The Explosion' toys, quite seriously, with the mystical, leaving a trail of Christian trace elements. Those 'tall gates standing open' are at once the colliery gates and also perhaps those heavenly gates evoked by Forster in *The Longest Journey*. On its own, this detail would count for nothing, of course, but the touches accumulate. 'At noon, there came a tremor ... sun, / Scarfed as in a heat-haze, dimmed.' In the conventional narrative, this is barely plausible. Why should an underground explosion, that 'tremor', cause the sun to dim? We are surely looking at a quasi-Calvary: Luke, Matthew and Mark all record an eclipse of the sun from the sixth to the ninth hour. What Koestler called *Darkness at Noon*. In Luke 23:45 we read: 'And the sun was darkened, and the veil of the temple was rent in the midst.' Doesn't Larkin conflate the veil and the eclipse? 'Sun, / *Scarfed* as in a heat haze, dimmed.' And consider the second line. Even on a strictly secular reading, it is ominous: 'Shadows pointed towards the pithead.' Why would those shadows be 'pointing'? It reads like an omen. And to me 'pithead' suggests a near-miss – 'godhead' – but only retrospectively, when all the other evidence is in. The evidence, though, is inconclusive. It is meant to be inconclusive, to exist at the periphery of our vision, at the far borders of our disbelief. We are addressing an aura, an inexplicable suggestion.

And then Larkin's poem risks unclosing its hand to show us what might be there. The italicised sixth stanza alludes to two different passages in the Bible. '*The dead go on before us, they / Are sitting in God's house in comfort, / We shall see them face to face –*' The third Epistle of St John 1:14 is actually an excuse for not writing more: 'But I trust I shall shortly see thee, and we shall speak face to face.' The other biblical passage is that standby at weddings, I Corinthians 13:12, the passage about the importance of charity/love and the imperfection of human knowledge: 'when I was a child, I understood as a child, I thought as a child: but when I became a man, I put away childish things. // For now we see through a glass, darkly; but then face to face: now I know in part; but then shall I know even as I am known.' Neither passage is an exact match for the words in the poem. The best match is Richard Francis Weymouth's New Testament of 1903, an idiomatic translation into everyday English from the text of 'The Resultant Greek Testament' by R. F. Weymouth. This reads: 'For the present we see things as if in a mirror, and are puzzled; but then we shall see them face to face. For the present the knowledge I gain is imperfect; but then I shall know fully, even as I am fully known.' Of course, Larkin is covered. He's quoting from the chapel walls.

The point is, though, that Larkin should now be so direct in his religious citation. Before, we were given elusive allusion, evocation. To conclude, Larkin protects himself with hearsay – 'It was said' – but (*mot juste*) wishes on his readers a miracle, a poetic miracle perhaps, but one containing the idea of the resurrection of the body. 'Wives saw the men of the explosion // Larger than in life they managed – / Gold as on a coin, or walking / Somehow from the sun towards them.' This miracle, of invulnerability to bodily injury, is epitomised in the unbroken eggs – which are an index of its impossibility, its imaginative fragility; which are also perfect because they particularise one person, one individual, so we see him face to face, as it were. It isn't true. It is an idealisation: 'Larger than in life they managed'. The traditional halo is assimilated to a face on a gold coin. But the unbroken eggs are the telling, the clinching, the circumstantial detail on which the poem ends.

Finally, I'm going to stretch your tolerance a bit by poking behind the opening poem in *High Windows*: 'To the Sea.' This is obviously a kind of companion piece to 'Show Saturday' – the celebration of an English rite, something specifically and eternally English going on: 'Still going on, all of it, still going on.' Compare 'Show Saturday': 'Regenerate union. Let it always be there.' In addition, though, 'To the Sea' is also like 'The Explosion' – the opening poem, like the closing poem, is ghosted by eternity. The interpretative key is the line 'The miniature gaiety of seasides'. Why 'miniature'? Partly because the seaside is 'Under the sky', 'crowded under the low horizon', as if it were squashed and miniature by contrast. But it is 'miniature' mainly because Larkin is returning to his childhood, where everything seems smaller than it did at the time. Not just going to the seaside after a long time. In reality, there is nothing miniature about the seaside itself. You go to your old classroom and squeeze into your old desk. He is going back in time a bit like Alice entering Wonderland. He is an adult actually revisiting his childhood. It's a little like the skewed mysticism of 'Burnt Norton' – at once impossible and obvious.

The first line – 'To step over the low wall that divides' – tells us a great deal. It is a low wall but it also *seems* low now that Larkin has grown up. He once described childhood as a 'forgotten boredom' but here it is vivid and welcome. A species of time-travel has been accomplished. An ordinary miracle.

'It partook, she felt, helping Mr Bankes to a specially tender piece, of eternity.' Or consider A. E. Housman writing to Arthur Pollard on 17 January 1923 about the death of Moses Jackson. This is high romanticism, this is unblunted passion at its most direct: 'Now I can die myself: I could not have borne to leave him behind me in a world where anything might happen to him.' The next day, 18 January 1923, Housman writes to Grant Richards, his publisher: 'I am told that the Brighter London Society are printing Lovat Fraser's illustrations to *A Shropshire Lad* on calendar covers.' The prose and the passion coarsely connected – as they are in life, always.

Rebecca Gilman: Dramatist
(2004)

Rebecca Gilman is thiry-eight and she is already an important writer.

In January 1999, the Royal Court Theatre put on *The Glory of Living* in the Theatre Upstairs to considerable acclaim. In February of this year, *Spinning into Butter*, her play about racism, had a six-week run, also at the Royal Court. Although the brilliant Emma Fielding took the lead and gave a performance characteristically rich in detail and inflection, the English critics were unimpressed. John Peter in the *Sunday Times* was the exception. Michael Billington's *Guardian* review conceded the importance of Gilman's subject. By and large, however, the critical response was an affected yawn – in the States, *Spinning into Butter* had occasioned controversy but *we* were less hysterical about race. Gilman's new play, *Boy Gets Girl*, is about stalking and has just opened to mixed press in New York. It seems likely that this play too will be staged by the Royal Court. Yet another play, *Blue Surge*, about prostitution is also likely to find its way to Sloane Square.

Her early plays are as yet unseen in England. They are *Smaller and Clearer as the Years Go By*, *The Land of Little Horses*, *The Adventures of Bobbi and Vaughan*, *Little Eva Takes a Trip*, *Speech Therapy* and *The American in Me*. In interview, she has described them as 'plays about IVF, crime and capitalism'. Even this laconic summary of a summary has its idiosyncratic note.

IVF?

It is, of course, a topical issue – ripe for television debate between the moral majority and medical advance. In the hands of Rebecca Gilman, the debate is guaranteed greater subtlety. More importantly, she guarantees drama, the powerful complicated emotions generated between couples in this situation – desperation, hope, exhaustion, *conflict*. Though she admires Shaw – 'I ended up reading all George Bernard Shaw's plays back to back' – her plays anatomise issues without staging debate. There is no sense that her characters are ideologies rather than individuals. (*Viscount Viewpoint looks through his lorgnette at Mr Opinion.*)

In fact, the issue at stake in *The Glory of Living* isn't easily identified. Gilman's own epitome isn't an epitome at all. It is actually a sociological overview: '[it's] about a society that doesn't care for poor people or for its children and about how that impacts on individuals.' Reading this worthy, frowning, reductive summation, I am reminded of John Ray, Jnr, Ph.D. – who ends Nabokov's cod-foreword to *Lolita* with this resonant platitude: '"Lolita" should make all of us – parents, social workers, educators – apply ourselves with still greater vigilance and vision to the task of bringing up a better generation in a safer world.' How authentically inauthentic those cadences are.

'Society' isn't a character – supercilious, careless, bored, brusque – in the ironically titled *The Glory of Living*. Nor is it an obligatory background presence as, say, South African apartheid is in Fugard's *Boesman and Lena*. Gilman's inert overt political analysis is at several removes from the dense, violent, puzzling texture of her play – which opens with the fifteen-year-old Lisa talking over the TV while her mother balls a customer behind a shaking sheet in the same room, in the only room. Pretty soon Lisa is married to a psychopath, Clint, for whom she procures partners who are subsequently disposed of. Her twin kids are cared for by Clint's mother.

The term dirty realism might have been invented for *The Glory of Living*. Clint, emphatically tautological, accuses Lisa of infidelity while he was in jail: 'I ain't sittin' in no goddamn jail again while you go out getting it with some goddamn nigger gettin' it on day and night with some goddamn nigger.' Lisa's denial grounds itself in physical impossibility: she was pregnant, 'big as a fuckin' house'. And afterwards: 'my cooter was all ripped up to hell and sore. Hell it was sore. And they shaved off all my hair down there and man did it itch. Shit.' The *noir*-ish events are without glamour but exude authenticity. We feel the voyeuristic pull of Diane Arbus or Weegee's photojournalism.

The plot almost certainly owes something to real life. Or it may derive from Terence Malick's *Badlands* – itself the true story of nineteen-year-old Charlie Starkweather and his fourteen-year-old girlfriend Caril Ann Fugate. Starkweather died in the arms of Old Sparky but Fugate was paroled in 1976. Their murderous spree through Wyoming and Nebraska was re-enacted in Robert Markowitz's two-part film for TV, *Murder in the Heartland*, starring Tim Roth and Fairuza Balk. Not one film, then, but two – which reflects the fascination exercised by gratuitous violence. It might be Coleridge's 'motiveless malignity', except that the Starkweather killings were genuinely baseless, bled of affect. 'Malignity' suggests a moral sense quite at odds with the untroubled, smiling arrest photographs of Starkweather and Fugate. Fugate escaped the electric chair because of her affecting testimony – which some thought was the pretence of remorse.

This ambiguity is central to the Starkweather story and *The Glory of Living*. On the one hand, glazed detachment and the *acte gratuite*, on the other, a costive, rudimentary remorse open to the charge of insincerity. Lisa not only procures women for her husband; she also shoots them afterwards. For the first half of the play, we infer Clint is the murderer. It's his gun. Lisa is covered with bruises. She phones the police anonymously with details of the bodies' where-abouts – clearly at some risk to herself. What engages us throughout – but more forcibly when Lisa is known to be the murderer – is the need to decide, and the *impossibility* of deciding, whether Lisa feels anything at all. Our bias as an audi-ence is to exculpate the woman while inculpating the man. Lisa is clearly acting under duress – the bruises, Clint's candid, visible violence. Yet, asked why she tipped off the police, her answer doesn't refer us directly to any obvious spring of feeling: 'I hated ta think a' her down there. Maybe gettin' eaten up by birds or somethin'.' And she has to *think* to discover this reason – a queasiness that comes close to feeling sorry for flesh, but not remorse itself at all.

Finally, her lawyer puts to her the crucial question: 'Are you sorry you killed those girls?' Lisa's answer is 'Yes' – a flicker of sensibility that is extinguished in the immediately subsequent dialogue. 'CARL: Really? LISA: I guess. CARL: Lisa! LISA: They was gonna die anyway.' This is the authentic voice of redneck exis-tentialism. Her victims do not matter: 'That girl I killed, and them two other people, if I hadn't called the police, if that guy hadn't of lived, wouldn't any-body even know they was gone.' Lisa's own death doesn't matter: 'you tell me one way that it matters.' These particular lives are manifestly expendable. They make no significant difference. *The Glory of Living*.

The play ends with Lisa's lawyer teaching her the value of the notes on her toy piano – the sole gift from her long-disappeared father – and we read this as poignant and subtly symbolic of moral values, of order.

Gilman wants to keep us in a state of moral suspense. This girl's body lan-guage articulates her discomfiture when her mother is servicing a trick. Clint notices: 'So see honey, I can see as how you're not comfortable with what your mama puts on.' Three years later, the same girl laughs straightforwardly ('Yeah, so?') when Clint dismisses her mother as a 'drunk whore'. Apparently, she has become more callous.

Given any audience's powerful instinct – to mitigate, to excuse, to salvage – the difficulty for Gilman is to establish Lisa's lack of affect, her moral blank-ness. This audience prejudice short-circuits the moral suspense and unbalances the play – though it could be countered in performance by an expressive facial blankness and coarse bodily movement, clear conventional signals of dimin-ished normality.

Without this crucial conflict, this complication, other subtle touches go for nothing. For instance, there is a moment of immense dramatic power when the police transcriber, after hearing Lisa's testimony, asks, 'Is pin-the-tail-on-the-donkey hyphenated?' Only moments before we have heard Lisa's account of how she injected Draino into the neck of one of her victims – matter-of-fact, orderly, unmoved. The discrepancy between the murder details and orthography heightens the terrible nature of those details. At which point, the intervention of the transcriber – a necessary professional question, otiose in human terms – is seen to be poised. How is one to decide its status? Does it illustrate inadvertency? Does it illustrate absence of affect – or the *appearance* of absence of affect? Or does it show the way that the ordinary and the ironic persist in the most appalling circumstances. Think of *Lolita*, of Humbert's car, tightly wedged between two newcomers, after he has murdered Quilty. *Parking!*

Were Lisa's lack of affect sturdily established – as a plausible alternative to her other role as the fundamentally innocent agent of Clint's violence – this incident with the transcriber would significantly complicate our reading of Lisa. We'd see how easy it is to create the *appearance* of the failure of feeling. As evidence, it would count in Lisa's favour. It would mitigate her apparent emotional neutrality, her moral inertness.

Other touches in the play are equally subtle. When Lisa tells detective Burrows that she was missing her babies 'somethin' awful', we believe her. She satisfies our need to discover the human in her. But this has to be qualified by the emptiness of Clint's automatic expressions of affection: particularly the repeated 'I can't believe I wasn't there for you' and 'You are all there is, Lisa girl.' These conventional endearments, culled as they are from TV and the movies, carry no evidential weight in Clint's favour. At the same time, they cast doubt on Lisa's equally clichéd expressions of affection for two children she scarcely ever sees.

The Glory of Living engages us by setting up contradictory signals, preferring moral suspense to moral certainty, the problematic to the prejudged. The play is neither low-life documentary nor slum tourism. Gilman asks her audience to discriminate, to weigh the dramatic conflict, in a way that makes passive voyeurism impossible. Take Steve Culverhouse. His slightly subnormal girlfriend, Carol, has been killed by Lisa. His testimony is vivid. He knows he has an unanswerable argument: 'Her skin was cracked open. Her skin was cracked open and she was leakin' water through her skin.' He is certain that Lisa enjoyed killing: 'she was wearin' a big smile.' The poverty, the thinness of his life, is put before us: 'we liked to walk on the road and look for nuts and bolts.'

And then the complications kick in. He denies Carol was retarded and is immediately confronted with evidence that shows he is lying. He himself had suggested Carol was mentally simple – perhaps to convey to Lisa that sexual latitude wasn't out of the question. We know from a prior scene that Carol is sexually compliant but Steve denies the lawyer's suggestion that she was sexually interested in Clint. His prevarication, however, doesn't diminish his (beautifully transcribed) declaration of love: 'Look, mister? I just want you to know, the thing was, I never even asked her to sleep with me. I never asked her 'cause I loved her.' He is fatally compromised.

The official version and the actuality cannot be reconciled or resolved – as they are also opposed in the case of Lisa, whose character is insoluble. It is this discrepancy between what is *supposed* to be the case and what is *actually* the case that provides the dramatic energy of Gilman's plays and links them despite their very different settings – a college in Vermont, New York and, in *The Glory of Living*, the back of beyond.

The issue addressed in *Spinning into Butter* is race and the conflict between public pronouncement and private attitude. The plot is simple. At Belmont College in Vermont, a black student, Simon Brick, receives racist hate mail. The teaching staff and the (largely white) student body are much exercised about the proper response to this unexpected occurrence. The staff and students organise public forums designed to demonstrate their impeccable liberal credentials – in a comedy of political correctness. Simon, the black student in question, never appears on stage – a sly stroke of irony. He is an issue rather than an individual. It transpires finally that he has written the offensive notes to himself. When this is discovered, he is promptly expelled by the very staff who were earlier so keen to 'defend' him. In the play's last lines, the Dean – almost the only sympathetic character – is heard talking to Simon on the phone, trying to elicit his side of the story.

The dean of Belmont College is Sarah Matthews. The molten core of the play is a speech in which she confesses to Ross (her ex-boyfriend and a member of the faculty) that she is afraid of black people – in spite of taking 'every class on African-American literature and theory' at graduate school. 'Now, I'm fully aware that black people have agency and are responsible and can help themselves, but I think they don't do it because they're lazy and stupid.' She has left her previous job, in Lancaster, a predominately black college, to get away from black people: 'they're too damn scary.'

In interview, Rebecca Gilman has said 'my conclusion is that everyone is racist' and that racism isn't restricted to the obvious candidates – economically disadvantaged, white supremacists. The English press accepted this as an adequate summary of *Spinning into Butter* – and dismissed it as obvious. In *Time Out*, Jane Edwardes concluded: 'that none of us is free of racism is hardly a revelation.' Nicholas de Jongh was equally dismissive: 'a ponderous demonstration of the fairly obvious'.

Actually, the play itself is much more subtle than Gilman's press encapsulation – an encapsulation which would align her with two of the play's shallower characters, the teachers Ross and Strauss: 'Dean Strauss got up and said to, you know, look inside ourselves [reports the self-serving student Greg] and see were we culpable at all.' Ross agrees: 'that's what we need to reveal. That racism isn't someone else's problem. It's our problem.'

In fact, Sarah's speech isn't the confession of wholesale, across-the-board racism that it was widely perceived to be. It does contain some shocking gener-alisations. For example: 'They weren't going to do anything with their lives. Not because they couldn't, but because they didn't want to. Because they were lazy and stupid.' But equally the speech secretes its own crucial modifications, its own important *discriminations*: 'some of them were great, and some of them were okay and some of them were pains in the ass, and some of them were awful.' Actually, Sarah's fundamental benevolence is never in question. Her nega-tive feelings are not the entire picture. She can see that there are exceptions: 'There were plenty of nice kids, but they weren't the ones you noticed. You noticed the awful ones because they dominated the landscape.'

Her problem is that the evil of racial discrimination – judgement on the sole basis of skin colour – does not allow her to exercise proper discrimination. Local judgements of individuals are perceived as judgements of the entire race. Grada-tions of judgement are impossible – illegitimate – as the problem is framed. For example, Sarah, shockingly, thinks Toni Morrison's novels 'suck' – and, judging by the reasons Sarah impatiently adduces, I would guess that Rebecca Gilman shares her literary judgement. The difficulty is that this perfectly proper literary judgement is likely to be seen as racist in North America. In other words, racial discrimination renders all discriminations suspect – because they are perceived as representative, not as particular.

The speech itself doesn't make this point explicitly. We are rather in the pres-ence of Sarah's pained confusion. She herself *accepts* the way the problem has been framed. Her negative judgements, her reservations, her fears, amalgamate – and convict her of racism in her own mind. Her positive feelings, her essential good faith, are discounted. Gilman's own position is less cloudy. But as a true dramatist, she chooses to stage Sarah's confused turmoil rather than a limpid analysis of the issues. The authorial position (and Gilman is far too intelligent not to have one) is given to two discredited characters.

Virginia Woolf's *Between the Acts* plants the authorial message on the Revd Streatfield – a man undersold to the reader as the human equivalent of a corner-cupboard or the top-beam of a gate. He actually asks, 'What message was our pageant meant to convey?' And then answers, 'Each is part of the whole.' Which is indeed Woolf's message. In *Spinning into Butter*, Gilman uses this useful device herself.

There are two student characters, both unsympathetic. One, Patrick Chibas, is a Nuyorican student whom Sarah is trying to help financially. He is graceless, prickly about his precise racial identity – and sympathetically exasperated to be perceived not as an individual but as a *cause*. In the end, he makes one of Gil-man's two most important points. It is this. He feels, correctly, that Sarah has idealised him. She has: 'I just wanted you to get the scholarship. I thought you'd, you know, take it and go on to solve the red tide or something.' Finally, Patrick explodes: 'I'm not some genius or something. I'm just whatever I am ...' In other words, the wholesale *idealisation* of a race is subtly demeaning. This is clear from the Chibas interchange. It is underlined, however, by a crude parallel. In New York, the academic Ross has seen for the second time a down-and-out on the subway – reading a laminated card with a biblical text on it. Ross is impressed: 'I felt both times that he was a man about to disintegrate. A man who kept himself in one piece by a dedicated devotion to God. But a devotion that was so fragile that he literally had to keep it here, before his face, like a beacon.' It is, of course, pure fantasy, based on ignorance. And later in the play Sarah excoriates it: 'You were idealising him.' And she *twice* makes the point: 'To idealise is to fundamentally mark as different; it is not to respect.' She then explicitly makes the connection with Patrick Chibas – pointing up her realisation that she has patronised by idealising him, by failing to see him as he actually is.

The other source of authorial analysis is Greg, the President of the newly formed Students for Tolerance. Greg's interest in the Simon Brick affair is at first largely confined to bulking out his curriculum vitae: 'Well, I mean, to be perfectly honest, I'm applying to law school and the resumé is a little thin, if you know what I mean. I mean, something like this would definitely add a line.' He proves a crucial (if inadvertent) contributor to the play's analysis of racism. The students gradually free themselves of faculty participation and meet in secret. 'Students for Tolerance', however, needs the attendance of 'students of colour', otherwise it is white and without credibility. In the very last stages of the play – as the sacked Sarah is packing up – the self-seeking careerist delivers this telling speech: 'In fact, we kept asking all the black people there, you know, why did he do it? [Send himself racist hate mail] And finally, this guy Jason said, "I don't know why he did it. It's not like we all think alike, just because we're black." You know? His whole point was that he wasn't the spokesperson for his race. He said, "That's just one of those things you white people assume about blacks, That we all think alike." But then, this girl Lisa said, "But, now you're saying that all *white* people think alike. How is that any different? (*Laughs*) We went around and around with that for an hour practically.'

It is immensely cunning of Rebecca Gilman to give this important truth – that in the end there are only individuals and not representatives – to an equivocal character and immensely skilful to articulate it using the inarticulate patterns of his speech.

In essence, then, *Spinning into Butter* argues, first, that it is an act of disrespect, an assertion of inequality, to idealise a race – as Sarah does Patrick Chibas, as Ross does the poor crank on the subway. Second, shared racial characteristics are far outweighed by individual differences. We are not defined by racial identity any more than we are defined by our gender or sexual orientation. It is fundamental and trivial. It follows from this that Sarah is entitled to denominate lazy and stupid blacks as lazy and stupid. She is allowed to discriminate – to distinguish between 'loud and belligerent and abusive' blacks and the 'plenty of nice kids'. Once allow the distinction and the self-accusation of racism vanishes. Neither the nice blacks nor the 'fucking rude and loud and stupid' blacks are representative.

Given the current climate of opinion in America, you can see why Gilman wouldn't want to spell this out in interview. Additionally, it would destroy the carefully concealed drift of her play – which isn't a tract but a subtly presented and subtly argued exposition. The one other sympathetic character is Meyers, the fifty-year-old security guard. And he finally does not endorse Sarah. Rather, he confesses his disappointment in her. 'I thought you were different. But I guess you were just hiding out, huh?' In other words, he sees her as a covert racist – with a problem still to solve. Which is Sarah's own view of herself. This is dramatically shrewd, an act of profound calculation, for Rebecca Gilman to preface Greg's clinching (if occluded) contribution to the debate with Meyers's considered appraisal of Sarah's racism. Greg is made to look like a digression into the merely lightweight examination of the problem.

Conscious of the issues, critics tend to simplify Gilman's work. Several complained about the sketchiness of the characters around Sarah Matthews and tended to treat *Spinning into Butter* as a round-table discussion on race. It's true that the main focus *is* on Sarah, but race isn't the only subject. She has a mother who is a lush. She has been having an affair with Ross while his regular girlfriend, Petra, is on sabbatical in Europe. These additional narratives lend Sarah substance. They also contribute to the overall shape because they are only superficially digressive – in each case there is a discrepancy between the official, public position and the private reality. Sarah is a model of efficiency whose chaotic mother is a potential liability. Petra and Ross have made an agreement – to allow each other erotic adventures during their year-long separation. Ross is stupidly surprised to discover that, despite their rational agreement, Petra is angry and humiliated by Ross's affair with Sarah. Under the rational, then, are powerful and chaotic currents, atavistic, subrational categorical imperatives. Likewise, Sarah knows what the publicly acceptable position on race is – she is simply unable in private to subscribe to it.

Spinning into Butter is an elegantly constructed theme and variations: even the debate about Belmont's architecture bodies forth the fissure between the publicly acceptable and the actual. For Strauss, 'They were master craftsmen'. For Dean Kenney, 'Put a marble on that floor and it will roll straight to the corner.' In the past, these two have had an affair – a back-story, again with bearing on the central issue, since Kenney still lays claim to deep feelings for Strauss, a man of manifestly coarse egotism. 'I think I may be the only person in the world who fully understands him. He's very vulnerable.' A semi-public avowal of private sensitivity which the play allows us to see as a laughable fiction. Academic rivalry, too, is presented as a variation on the holier-than-thou, competitive responses to the Simon Brick affair. Ross, hearing of a classmate's success, wonders 'if David's still fat' – and we glimpse the personal envy informing the apparently objective assessment of academic achievement.

Boy Gets Girl is Rebecca Gilman's examination of human sexual behaviour. Theresa Bedell is a journalist who is stalked and terrified by a man she has met only twice. The first occasion is a brief blind date – involving conversation and a beer. On the second occasion, Theresa has already identified something sufficiently odd in the man's behaviour – he bombards her with flowers – and she terminates the 'relationship'. Things rapidly accelerate until Theresa's apartment is wrecked, she receives obscene and violent letters and phone messages, and fears for her life to the extent that she changes her name and moves to Denver. The play is characteristically well researched and expert – even though the blind date is psychologically improbable, given Theresa's tough intelligence and independence, the actual presentation of this stilted encounter is a tour de force. The other difficulty with the play is that, although it is extraordinarily exciting, there is no dramatic conflict – obviously the dramatic sympathy for the stalker is nil, so we aren't given his point of view. Instead Gilman gives us debate. This makes the ending problematic in terms of the action – as opposed to the issues, which have by then been fully ventilated. Gilman is very professional, however. So at the climax, she introduces two narrative possibilities: that Tony, the stalker, will be caught by the police and that therefore Theresa's identity and life need not be changed. The second, alarming possibility is that the stalker and stalkee will confront each other in a violent episode. In the event, we are spared these turns of fate. Instead Gilman ends her play emblematically. In her new identity – as Claire Howells – Theresa introduces herself and shakes hands with her boss, Howard, and her colleague, Mercer. The emblem is this: in our culture, women change their natural behaviour to accommodate male behaviour. Changing your name and identity is only an extreme version of the normal.

And this seems to be Gilman's axis of interest throughout *Boy Gets Girl* – the continuum she perceives between extreme behaviour and 'normal' behaviour. At first the idea is mounted that stalkers are only following a version of Hollywood male behaviour – persistence gets the girl. Hence the title. The stalker is following cultural instructions. Indeed, everyone, male and female, is following a culturally created and culturally endorsed paradigm. Men are instructed to regard women as sexual objects and women are implicitly taught by the culture to enjoy being looked at – in other words, to accede to their role as sexual object.

Of course, Gilman doesn't leave the debate there. Theresa, for example, is a baseball expert and a Yankees fan – even though there is evidence of her bookishness in her citations of Edith Wharton, Hawthorne and William Dean Howells (who eventually supplies Theresa's protective alias). Her male colleague, Mercer, and the stalker himself know very little about baseball. So that, if there *are* cultural male and female stereotypes, Gilman wants to show us that they are eroded. One of the faintly creepy things about the stalker is that he overvalues his mother's cooking. On the other hand, *he* cooks, since he knows that many women no longer cook. And in fact, Theresa's kitchen consists of a pot and a pan. Neither of them conforms to the cultural stereotype.

These are small touches. The main proponent of the culturally determined reading of the stalker is Mercer. Mercer is planning an article about stalking which will take Theresa's experience as a starting point for a larger meditation on male/female sexual relations. He admits he has considered fucking Theresa – briefly, reflexively, as a passing thought. He explains this mental-event as the product of culture. He is shrewd enough to realise, however, that he cannot *say* many women enjoy being looked at sexually in this way – given the present climate of intelligent opinion. Gilman, though, supplies us with a secretary, the pea-brained Harriet, who buys into the coarsest version of women the culture has to offer. Harriet is culturally conformist to her last cell – which makes her a rather token figure in the drama. She needs to be less of a caricature.

Theresa opposes Mercer's plan to use her experience as a pretext for his meditation on sexual relations. He proposes to go ahead anyway. That is, like the stalker, Mercer is prepared simply to ignore a woman's emphatically expressed wishes when they conflict with his own. Which brings us to the crux of *Boy Gets Girl*. The stalker, his violence and his impersonal libido, isn't so anomalous. He exists on a continuum with 'normal' male behaviour – which is Mercer's thesis, even as he illustrates it inadvertently, without seeing the parallel.

Nothing is so simple. The main spokesman for an alternative analysis is the seventy-year-old pornographer, Les Kennat, whom Theresa is sent to interview for her magazine. Gilman reuses the device of placing authorial truth within a tainted source. On the face of it, Kennat is as much a caricature of acculturated maleness as the secretary Harriet is a caricature of acculturated femaleness. Theresa's article makes mock of him by attaching an ironic epithet whenever she uses his name – 'breast-loving' or 'fan of mammary glands'. Les gets off on big tits. When Theresa accuses him of exploiting women, he returns his standard answer – that his films celebrate women. Where is the trickle of pure truth in this mantled pool? It is the idea that sexual behaviour is biological, atavistic, given, distorted and influenced by the culture, but finally hard-wired into us.

Take breasts, for instance. Mercer, advancing the culturally conditioned line, is significantly inconsistent in a discussion with his boss, Howard. He argues that 'we're taught to like breasts, but the size we like, even, goes up and down. Literally. You can get breast implants now that you can inflate or deflate according to the fashion.' Howard, though, realises that Mercer prefers small breasts to large breasts and gets him to admit his preference – without Mercer realising how much it damages his thesis. Kennat likes large breasts, the bigger the better. Both men have an *unalterable* sexual preference which isn't subject to stock-market fluctuation or any other societal influence. Kennat wants Theresa to admit that she, too, has sexual preferences that are entirely physical and that precede the assessment of personality. His example is 'tight buns'. Theresa will not admit to Kennat that she also routinely treats male bodies as sexual objects – checking out either a wish-list or a hate-list. We are not convinced by her denial. We think she may be *in denial*.

Finally, *Boy Gets Girl* brings us the reconciler in the form of Detective Beck – who is thematically over-useful, a bit of an authorial convenience. Her own swiftly divulged background is that of someone who has both accepted and rebelled against conventional expectations of her as a woman. Unlike her brothers, she has had to pay for her own education, at Hunter College, because she was expected to marry the man selected by her parents. She felt unable to insist that her parents paid for her education also. Theresa provides a convenient parallel of automatic female accession to male expectations: an old drunk in a bar asked her to kiss him on the mouth and, loathing it, she complied. Why? So as not to hurt his feelings. 'I was supposed to be nice.' Similarly, the 'mistake' she makes with her stalker is a failure of frankness. Her excuses for not wishing to see him again all centre on her own inadequacy, pressure of work, rather than on his own mildly repugnant personality. Theresa is letting him off lightly. Detective Beck articulates for us the play's final, unfinalised position: 'we can't always tell how much is us and how much is the world around us.' The private, then, and the public yet again – not discrepant, but interfused. This summation is followed by the direction 'beat' and preceded by Theresa's question 'I don't understand the connection.' In every way the sentence is dramatically highlighted, just as in *Spinning into Butter* we encounter the theatrically cordoned off '(beat) to idealise is not to respect (beat)'.

As I said, Gilman once confessed to reading the whole of Shaw 'back to back'. We tend to think of the drama of ideas as an intrinsically lesser form – which is prone to the tendentious and which gravitates inexorably towards the consensus. But in the hands of a dramatist as accomplished as Gilman the ideas are subtle, subversive, original, compelling – and, therefore, dramatic. Tom Stoppard said: 'Shaw raises conversation to the power of drama. And he does it for three acts.' But Shaw was opinionated. As a genre, the play of ideas is playful but also finally a game with a result – a winner and a loser. It would be an act of extraordinary dramatic continence for an intelligent author to repress his or her own opinion. Not all arguments are equal. Even Stoppard, theatre's most gifted imaginative barrister, capable of defending the indefensible, eventually wants to decide on the truth – despite the impulse instinct in his comment, 'I write plays because dialogue is the most respectable way of contradicting myself.' An extraordinary number of Stoppard's plays contain a lecture or are constructed around a lecture which in effect resolves the issues being discussed. Think of Housman in *The Invention of Love*, George in *Jumpers* toiling away at his lecture, Bernard's lecture in *Arcadia*, Henry's mini-lecture on writing in *The Real Thing*, Cecily's lecture in *Travesties*, or Anderson's philosophical lecture on natural justice in *Professional Foul*. Stoppard has said that, although ideas are his initial motivation, they are nothing without a narrative. He has also said that 'if I were to write an essay instead of a play about any of these subjects it wouldn't be a profound essay.' Substitute 'lecture' for 'essay' and you realise Stoppard has done precisely that. But he is a lecturer of genius.

By which I do not mean that his ideas are 'profound'. The lecture is not the place for complicated ideas. It is the place for clear ideas, for precise distinctions and discriminations – memorably, wittily expressed. No one will ever forget Henry's cricket-bat metaphor, which distinguishes between good and bad writing: 'this thing here, which looks like a wooden club, is actually several pieces of particular wood cunningly put together in a certain way so that the whole thing is sprung, like a dance floor. It's for hitting cricket balls with. If you get it right, the cricket ball will travel two hundred yards in four seconds, and all you'll have done is give it a knock like knocking the top of a bottle of stout, and it makes a noise like a trout taking a fly ... (*He clucks his tongue to make the noise.*) What we're trying to do is write cricket bats, so that when we throw up an idea and give it a little knock, it might *travel* ...'

Rebecca Gilman deals with issues and ideas, but she has neither Stoppard's epigrammatic force nor his comic gifts. Her strengths are mainstream. Her dialogue and her narratives, unlike Stoppard's, are naturalistic. She can be very funny. But essentially her kind of play isn't fundamentally comedic and so she can't allow herself the full-frontal candour of Stoppard offloading his views. Gilman's naturalism means that she must avoid even the appearance of ventriloquism. On the whole, she is successful, but her opinions are there to be found – well concealed but identifiably authorial.

In *Blue Surge* the Stoppard principle obtains within Gilman's naturalism. Her central idea is neither intricate nor profound nor subtle. But the play memorably and dramatically embodies its concerns. We are shown the obverse of the American Dream – in which the poor are inescapably fucked. The play begins, brilliantly, with two scenes in a massage parlour in which the cops fluff an undercover bust of the sex racket. Where Stoppard makes phrases, Gilman offers us pitch-perfect drunk dialogue and everywhere demonstrates her aural Velcro: the police detective Curt, from a dirt-poor background, is discussing the unbridgeable gulf between him and his girlfriend. His father was a grave-robber, his mother a loser. She is an artist from a rich background. Curt's definition of rich – 'they have rooms in their house they don't even use'- gives us a vivid idea of how psychically poor he sees himself to be. He touches on her art:

> CURT: … Collages of female body parts and cuts of meat. What's that word you use?
> BETH: I don't know.
> CURT: Not subliminal.
> BETH: I don't know.
> CURT: Subversive. Your art wasn't really subversive.

The title refers to the Duke Ellington song 'Blue Serge', about a cheap suit. The rich girlfriend has introduced him to it. He thinks that the title refers to the blues, a surge of sadness. The lesson is that the sadness is connected with the poverty implicit in the cheap material. In this world, women are bartenders or prostitutes, the men cops or security guards. The poor can really talk only to the poor because their memories are too 'gross' for polite company. If the poor have ambitions – and they do – life makes them impossible to realise. In *Blue Surge* the regular guy is poor but honest and ends up as a security guard who is himself under TV surveillance – to make sure he doesn't read or study on his night-shift job. The other route is that of Sandy, the hooker who still isn't twenty. She would like to break free – at times – but actually accepts that the only way her life can really improve is by working as a ho. The poor in this play are like the spider in the bath – defeated by the smooth porcelain of circumstance. There are long speeches of self-analysis here but they are saved from preachiness by the self-excoriation, the self-loathing and the self-pity. The central fault of the rich is not their greed or their selfishness – but that they have no idea what it is to be poor. The end of *Blue Surge* will be accused of sentimentality: the whore and the security guard agree to hold hands, to comfort each other for their different failures. But they and their author know that nothing is going to change. She is comforting him for his absurd attachment to the idea of improvement – the world of role models and self-improvement. She is, in a sense, giving him a hand-job – synthetic comfort of a kind. And so the play ends as it began. She cares for him. But it's still a hand-job.

Joyce's *Exiles*
(2006)

Jealousy is central to Joyce's *Exiles* – now playing at the National Theatre's Cottesloe in a brilliantly calm, quietly acted, subtly paced production, directed by James Macdonald. Without raising its voice, it does thorough justice to Joyce's bold, patient play that, for the most part, is written in a level, clear whisper – and is all the more shocking for that. (Before it opened, Philip Hensher, the columnist, announced in the *Guardian* that *Exiles* is a notorious clunker. Not so notoriously reliable a clunker, you might think, as Philip Hensher, who consistently confuses being opinionated with being thoughtful.) The understated acting is flawless, the opposite of histrionic, and matches Joyce's muted tones – though at the play's centre is a potentially melodramatic situation. Richard Rowan, a Joycean–Nietzschean writer, at once morally courageous and morally narcissistic, wishes to overstep conventions, to propose moral liberty for himself, his wife and his old friend Robert Hand. Perhaps his wife would like to have an affair with Hand. If so, Rowan is prepared to face the truth of this path of action – its pain, the jealousy. Except, of course, that he isn't prepared – being human and therefore jealous. As a thought-experiment, it blows up in his face.

In *De l'amour*, Stendhal famously compared love to the Milky Way – 'a shining mass made of millions of little stars, many of them nebulae'. He proposed an astronomy of the heart, stating that, out of these millions, only 'four or five hundred of the small successive feelings' that 'go to make up love' had been identified – and those the obvious ones. He was against the idea of love as something single and simplified. You could therefore argue that he anticipates the modernist inquiry into feelings. Jealousy is an equally interesting subject for the modernists and their readers. Though it has left its indelible mark on all of us – like the mark left by the dead centipede on the dining-room wall in Alain Robbe-Grillet's *La Jalousie* – we know very little about it. Everyone has experienced it, no one properly understands it. Jealousy is something we suffer.

In Jonson's *Every Man in His Humour* and *Volpone*, we have Kitely and Corvino – pathologies seen from the outside, though even here Jonson engineers a shift from ridicule to prurient morbidity. We pay attention when Corvino threatens to slit Celia's nostrils 'Like a raw rochet [a fish]'. And Jonson is acute about the eternal reciprocity of jealousy: MOSCA: 'they that use themselves most licence / Are still most jealous.' With Othello, the internals of jealousy are swiftly, accurately set down: the noble Moor embodies the central paradox of jealousy – the oxymoronic spasm caused by the fusion of love and hatred, by the mind in contradiction, the nauseous mix of thwarted grandeur and gut reaction.

But there is more, much more to be said about jealousy and its cerebral operations. Jealousy is the emotion of magnification, of scholarly paranoia, of obsessive sifting of 'evidence' – the footnotes of the sick soul. When Thomas Rymer mocked the role of the handkerchief in *Othello*, its weightless triviality as evidence, he failed to see that this was exactly Shakespeare's point – that 'trifles light as air / Are to the jealous, confirmations strong / As proofs of holy writ.'

There is more authentic disgust perhaps, more *actualité*, in Leontes's retching cry that he has 'drunk, and seen the spider'. Robbe-Grillet's novel teaches us that jealousy is a yearning for certainty, conclusiveness, for mathematical proof – hence those Euclidean sentences 'describing' the architecture of the house and courtyard and veranda – sentences that leave us none the wiser for all their pained precision. Jealousy involves the policing of detail, unblinking alertness, a forensic search for clues, a sense that the very configuration of the furniture can provide clues to the secret thoughts of their sometime occupants. Consider how the unhappy but unsuspecting Isabel Archer suddenly *sees* the significance – the implied intimacy – of Gilbert Osmond sitting in an armchair while Madame Merle is standing.

Jealousy is the *illusion* of clairvoyance. Robbe-Grillet's novel shares with Pinter's drama the sense that there is a weasel under the cocktail cabinet. Jealousy is a vigil and a rapt boredom – hence the repetition of detail in *La Jalousie*. Think of the jealous Sylvia Plath and her poem 'The Courage of Shutting-Up', which offers the figure of a gramophone needle 'tattooing over and over the same blue grievances'. Here is the 'after' – justified jealousy, not merely suspicion. Patrick Marber's *Closer* showed us the terrible need to know the details that pain us: who can forget Julia Roberts's reply in the Mike Nichols film to her husband's question about her lover's semen? 'IT TASTES LIKE YOU BUT SWEETER.' As Nina Raine's play *Rabbit* tells us, sexual jealousy is pornographic: it is about who put what into which hole.

Tom Stoppard's great play *The Real Thing* intelligently, shrewdly, offers a more familiar, temperate jealousy – less 'dramatic' than Marber's upper case, but just as unhappy and plausibly reticent. The playwright hero, Henry, ransacks Annie's belongings off-stage. His guilty wife movingly comments: 'Don't be like this, Hen. You're not like this.' Nor is he – and for the rest of the play he controls himself – like Maggie Verver in *The Golden Bowl*, like almost every betrayed person we know. We learn to live with pain. We wean ourselves off wailing and whining – and, finally, wincing. We get over ourselves – and it.

Joyce's contributions to this topos in *Exiles* are several. He importantly shows us that jealousy is sometimes about as manageable as acute diarrhoea. Richard Rowan is morally rational, he thinks, but unable to deny the pain he has theoretically accepted. His final words are: 'I have a deep, deep wound of doubt in my soul … My wound tires me' (*tires* is a verb of genius – persuasive, modest, depleted, plausible). Joyce also demonstrates, brilliantly, that jealousy is inflected by the whole envelope of circumstances. Jealousy uses all our insecurities, feeds off them. *Exiles* is a deceptive play. It feels simple only because its exposition, its build-up, is so steady, so gradual. This is a dramatic sleight. In fact, it is thick with absorbing complication.

It begins low-key with Brigid, the Rowans' maid, exchanging banal information – pitch-perfect Irish lower-class vernacular, realised by Áine Ní Mhuirí with marvellous quiet accuracy – about this and that with Beatrice Justice. 'The mistress and Master Archie is at the bath … Practise [the piano], how are you! Is it Master Archie? He is mad after the milkman's horse now.' It is as precise as Gretta Conroy's dialect at the end of 'The Dead'. And, like the entire cast, she *never* sounds like an actor. This production is all naturalism of gesture and delivery. The actors do hardly anything and yet they achieve transparency. When Beatrice (stunningly played by Marcella Plunkett) opens her spectacle case and slides on her spectacles, it is an event in this epic of physical containment.

Soon, however, the unmarried Beatrice Justice and Richard Rowan are having an allusive conversation freighted with unresolved implication. At first, we think there is an amorous understanding between them. There is certainly intimacy of a kind. Rowan refers to a previous conversation: 'Have you thought over what I told you when you were here last?' As in a Neil LaBute play, the obvious narrative hook catches our attention. He has told her, we guess, that he loves her. 'Very much,' she replies. Rowan continues: 'You must have known it before. Did you? (*She does not answer*) Do you blame me?' In point of fact, though, this means something else, it transpires: he has told her that he has been writing about her. He asks if she would like to see what he has written, even though some of it is cruel. At this point, when the intimacy between them seems largely aesthetic, Rowan suddenly becomes explicit if interrogatory: 'Then it is my mind that attracts you? … Perhaps you feel that some new thing is gathering in my brain; perhaps you feel that you should know it. Is that the reason [you come to the house]?' You feel he is repressing the reason he would like to hear her give. A great deal is 'understood' in this Ibsenite exchange. And this wary young woman replies with candour that she comes to the house, not to give Archie his piano lesson, but because 'Otherwise I could not see you.' It is an unambiguous, unexpected declaration which takes us back to the beginning of their conversation. With this difference – she, not he, has spoken in effect of love.

Almost immediately, Rowan's wife, Bertha, is seen succumbing to the advances of Beatrice Justice's cousin and ex-fiancé, Robert Hand – who also happens to be Rowan's oldest friend. Hand is temperamentally different from Rowan. He is a romantic by temperament and Joyce mildly ironises him – partly through Bertha's contained, prosaic responses. While gifting him endearments Joyce himself used to his wife, Nora – 'Your face is a flower too – but more beautiful. A wild flower blooming in a hedge' – Hand is also undermined by overstatement. As he kisses Bertha, Hand invokes a Wagnerian *Liebestod*: 'To end it all – death. To fall from a great high cliff, down, right down into the sea ... Listening to music and in the arms of the woman I love – the sea, music and death.'

We have heard Rowan, on the other hand, be cool, measured and unsentimental about his dying father: 'I was a boy of fourteen. He called me to his bedside. He knew I wanted to go to the theatre to hear *Carmen*. He told my mother to give me a shilling. I kissed him and went. When I came home he was dead. Those were his last thoughts as far as I know.' He is also unsentimentally unforgiving about his dead mother: 'How can my words hurt her poor body that rots in the grave? Do you think I do not pity her cold blighted love for me?'

So: a conventional romantic makes conventional adulterous advances to a wife, while the intellectually tougher, more original husband, Rowan, seems to have a parallel understanding with Beatrice Justice. The plot, it appears, has some of the fearful symmetry we associate with Henry James's *What Maisie Knew*. (There, you recall, Maisie brings together the estranged partners of her estranged parents.) At this juncture, however, Joyce springs his surprise, a twist worthy of LaBute. The wife, Bertha, is debriefed by Rowan, reporting to her husband every move in the little minuet of lust.

Richard Rowan's reaction is to feel betrayed. Despite his tacit encouragement, he wants to denounce his old friend. In Act II, however, the friends discuss the situation – and Rowan is far from the aggrieved, deceived husband he initially seemed. His motives are clamorous and contradictory. He has been unfaithful to Bertha on many occasions and confessed because he believes they should live in truth. (Hand, the conventional romantic, is more cynical and pragmatic. Just as later, he proposes to Bertha a revenge fuck for Beatrice Justice.) This is an argument for sexual equality. He feels his initial erotic certitude – or illusion of certitude – is no longer there. If Hand feels more certain, then it is he who deserves Bertha and Rowan would be prepared to cede her to him, to relinquish her. He wishes to grant his wife liberty – on principle. He also, less high-mindedly, wants to be betrayed by his wife and best friend – craftily, secretly, for shameful erotic reasons. He wants to approach intimacy with his best friend via that friend's physical relationship with his wife. Additionally,

Bertha suspects that Rowan is encouraging her so that he can feel free to betray her with Beatrice Justice.

Joyce does not insist on a hierarchy of motivation. All these motives play their part. It is also suggested by Joyce, I think, that Rowan's refusal to flinch from pursuing the 'principles' he has worked out, is part of his own self-romanticising – as the father of a bastard, the controversial writer who once eloped with his 'wife', as a figure of moral fearlessness, as a flouter of convention, as a kind of Nietzschean *Übermensch*, who will think the unthinkable – and act on it. Rowan has his own romanticism, which is more dangerous than that of Hand. And it leaves him, by the end of the play, denying love like Birkin in *Women in Love*: 'It is not in the darkness of belief that I desire you. But in restless living wounding doubt. To hold you by no bonds, even of love, to be united with you in body and soul in utter nakedness.' It sounds like Lawrence. It sounds like a writer – theorising under torture, finding a form of words with which to contain and elevate the demeaning pain. We, the audience, like Rowan, cannot be certain that Bertha has not succumbed. She and Hand appear to agree a story – but it may be a true one. Rowan's chafing, unresolved ignorance is also ours. That is Joyce's final coup in *Exiles*.

Harold Pinter Remembered
(2009)

I think everyone was a little nervous of Harold. Including Harold, sometimes. He was affable, warm, generous, impulsive – and unpredictable. Like his plays, where the hyper-banal surfaces – the synthetic memories and false nostalgia of *Old Times*, the aural drivel of Rose in *The Room*, the bogus familial warmth of *The Homecoming* – are fragile and about to be displaced by something ugly and authentic, something obscure and violent. Plays where on countless occasions – think of Lenny in *The Homecoming* or the alcoholic Hirst in *No Man's Land* – a speech will take off into dramatic Tourette's, unstoppable and at the edge of sense. The plays are edgy, alert to something sinister at the periphery. Harold once described his plays as being about the weasel under the cocktail cabinet. Later, he repudiated this description. In fact, it is the perfect encapsulation, but no one likes to be fixed in a formulated phrase – particularly a phrase of one's own coinage. The plays are unstable, never more dangerous than when the surface of the dialogue is at its emptiest: think of *One for the Road*, with its grotesque affability – signalled by the title's pub-speak – and its pragmatic, morally drained, unexcitable sadism.

Style, wrote Buffon, *c'est l'homme*. With Harold, it was as well to be aware that the weasel wasn't confined to the drama. It might draw blood on the domestic stage. He was all about surprise and social suspense.

I first met him in Claire Tomalin's basement kitchen in Gloucester Crescent at an impromptu party. Claire was the literary editor of the *New Statesman*. I was her summer stand-in theatre critic (while Benedict Nightingale was having his annual fortnight's holiday) and I had reviewed *No Man's Land*, with Gielgud as Spooner and Ralph Richardson as Hirst. Harold thanked me for the review. I was emboldened and explained that I'd had two putative interpretations – both wrong, I now think – but not enough space (800 words) to adequately ventilate the two takes on his play. He looked at me quizzically, almost boyishly, his eyes smiling. 'How can I help you?' he said. 'Well,' I said, 'I was wondering if I was right.' He stopped smiling, reached into the inside pocket of his jacket and took out a spectacle case. Opening it, he put on a pair of dark glasses and looked at me, enigmatically, eyelessly. After a pause: 'Search me, squire.'

My theory was that the non-sequiturs and anacoluthon in the dialogue of the two principals was there to conceal some deeper malaise – a flimsy alibi, nonsense overlaying madness, perhaps, grammatical confusion masking mental disintegration, ageing, say, or a deeper derangement. The supporting cast had the feel of high-class minders. There was a sense of supervision. But nothing specific, something present and incorrect. Think Tennessee Williams. It is easy enough to see the influence of Hemingway's 'The Killers' on Pinter the dramatist: the banalities of the menu rendered radioactive with menace by Hemingway's title. But Tennessee Williams is there, too: in *Cat on a Hot Tin Roof*, Big Daddy's cancer, Brick's sexual revulsion, his relationship to Skipper, are all hidden but looming large. In *A Street Car Named Desire*, Blanche Dubois has a front, a façade to match the façade of the Pollitts in *Cat*. We wait for the revelation, for the weasel under Brick's cocktail cabinet, for Blanche's bright, mannered chit-chat to morph into misery. The difference between Pinter and Williams is the degree of explicitness. In Williams, the plot is stripped bare so you can see the dramatic ticking. In Pinter, the sheets are dirty but difficult to interpret. Especially when the dramatist is ostentatiously sporting dark glasses. You don't get to the bottom of anything – or not immediately, or obviously.

In fact, there are answers: *No Man's Land* is a play about alcoholism, about 'the great malt that wounds' and the title follows from that – a metaphor for the stranded mind with its damaged short-term memory. Hirst drinks, collapses, is carried off, and immediately re-enters to a situation that now seems entirely new. His consciousness is severely curtailed by drink. He exists only in the moment, the lucid nanosecond shrouded in darkness. He is as impaired as Martin Amis's John Self in *Money*, who drinks so much that four minutes' sleep is indistinguishable from twenty-four hours' sleep. Being dissolute to this extent is the dissolution of all certainties. Hirst *improvises* for the length of Pinter's play. Which ends, conclusively, I'd say, with Hirst's words: 'I'll drink to that.'

The next time I met Harold – perhaps a year later – I was Reviews Editor at Ian Hamilton's the *New Review* and I had written a *New Statesman* assessment of Harold's *Poems and Prose 1949–1977* that was scathingly amused in tone. (I admired the more recent dramatic poetry.) I'd forgotten the review. It was a bleak party, a scratch affair, with eye-watering salt and vinegar crisps and inferior wine in Ian's mean office. Everyone smoked.

Harold was wedded to the world of little magazines – including *Areté*. What was that about? It was partly superstitious appeasement, I think. Harold remembered his beginnings, his first poems in Tambimutu's *Poetry London*. (He was often pissed off, but he was never grand or pompous. His favoured formula for praise was 'bloody good', either in block capitals or booming actor's baritone.) And it was partly sentimental nostalgia for the camaraderie of failure, and partly a specific piety about poetry, which for him was the heart of the little magazine. Xandra Gowrie saw me standing on my own and introduced me to Harold. 'Actually,' I said, 'Harold and I have already met.'

Without taking his eyes off me, he took a drink. 'Only once.' He took another drink.

It wasn't quite 'fuck off' but it was a near thing. And beautifully delivered.

At another party – there will be a lot of parties in this piece – for Michael Horovitz's magazine *New Departures*, an intermittent, highly intermittent, but tenacious publication, Harold was at his most expansive. He was recommending a hotel to me – 'perfect for writing. You should go there.' I was bemused by his imperfect sense of my finances – and my working methods – but Harold wasn't lording it. He was lauding the hotel and genuinely trying to be helpful. He found it hard to write and valued anything that might help the process. 'What's it called?' I asked. He blinked. 'Bugger.' And he turned to find Antonia: 'What's the name of that hotel? The one that's good for writing? Christ.'

At the launch party for Ian McEwan's *Black Dogs* at a Chinese restaurant in Chelsea Harbour, Harold asked me what I was doing. I said I was teaching at Oxford, at New College. 'How do you like it? You know, I never went to the varsity.' I found it endearing that he used the term 'varsity' – as if to demonstrate his lack of a university education. 'I like it very much. Last week I gave a class on *The Homecoming*.' 'Did they like it, the kids?' 'Yes, very much.' 'Good.'

'But they were puzzled by Ruth.' 'Were they?' 'Yes.' And then I risked it, he was so pleased and friendly: 'But she's a tart, isn't she, Harold?' He wasn't angry. He was full of delighted mischief: 'You can't ask me a thing like that!' And he laughed.

But he didn't deny it. *The Homecoming* has an important stage direction describing the set. The wall between the sitting room and the staircase isn't there. So your assumption is that this is an exploded view, a stage-design convention, so the audience can see what would otherwise be hidden. Later on, Lenny tells us that the wall has been knocked through. In other words, the apparently imaginary is actually real. The play turns on the play between the imaginary and the real, between fantasy and actuality. They are in constant negotiation. Until, finally, the lines of demarcation are drawn – and Ruth reveals herself to be tough and knowledgeable when it comes to the terms of her role as a prostitute. She is more convincing in this role, much more convincing, than she was as the alleged wife of an academic, a philosopher in a thinly realised USA. *The Homecoming* is about a communal male sexual fantasy – and it is outlined very near the beginning of the play when the father, Max, rips the piss out of his homosexual brother, Sam: 'When you find the right girl, Sam, let your family know, don't forget, we'll give you a number one send-off, I promise you. You can bring her to live here, she can keep us all happy. We'd take it in turns to give her a walk round the park.' This prolepsis prefigures the advent of Teddy and Ruth just sufficiently for the audience to discount it, if they remember it at all. But the main plot is there in three sentences.

Pinter is groundbreaking in his treatment of sexual fantasy – in *The Lover* and *Ashes to Ashes* particularly. The earlier play turns on the crucial moment when the shared, transgressive fantasy – transgressive as all effective sexual fantasies are – moves from the ring-fenced imagination into the ordinary arena and ceases to be fantasy. The later play, *Ashes to Ashes*, is one of Pinter's masterpieces – because it shows us that sexual fantasy, though never innocent, can segue into something unspeakable, the darkness of the holocaust. As the lamps (practicals, as they are called) become brighter, the stage itself darkens – the perfect image for what the play has felt and faltered its way towards. The sinister autonomy of the imagination. As the fantasy clarifies, it reveals its bilious blacks.

Another party, this time at Ruthie and Richard Rogers's house, for a private performance of *Ashes to Ashes*, directed by my daughter Nina. Afterwards, Harold makes a warm speech, praising the actors, Kathy Tozer and Elliot Levey, and the director. I'm standing next to my old boss at Fabers, Matthew Evans. 'Good night for the Raine family,' he says with his irresistible grin. 'I'm just going to say hello to Harold.'

He is back in thirty seconds, grin gone. 'What a fucker.'

'What happened?'

'I said "Hello, Harold. How are you?" And he said, "Fuck off. I sent you my new play [*Celebration*] a week ago and you haven't said what you think, whether you liked it. You're supposed to be my publisher. Fuck off."'

You didn't want to get on the wrong side of Harold. When I still worked at Fabers, sometime in the late eighties, a confrère of Harold's rang to ask if I would publish their joint translations of the Nicaraguan poet and politician Ernesto Cardenal. The intermediary on the phone would do the translations, Harold would 'add the poetry'. I said that I'd be pleased to consider the translations when they had been done. (Actually, I had heard Cardenal read in India and I had not been impressed.) But that wasn't the question: the question was, would I agree in advance to publish the poems? I said I couldn't do that, but I would be very pleased to … etc. My interlocutor lost his temper, appealed to Harold's reputation, but I was firm. He was equally firm. They wouldn't undertake the work without a guarantee of publication. Which I wouldn't give.

I then read the New Directions two-volume *Poems of Ernesto Cardenal*, translated by Alastair Reid. I thought they were no good, but I read on very carefully – knowing that one day I might find myself in an argument with Harold. I wanted to acquit myself as well as possible in what might be a noisy, public viva voce. For about a year, whenever the firm threw a party, I scanned the guest list – and if Harold had accepted, I strategically absented myself.

Perhaps unnecessarily. Perhaps not. It depended on whether Harold had had a drink, and how much. When the fatwa against Salman Rushdie was in its second or third year, there was a meeting of Rushdie's supporters at Westminster Hall. Tom Stoppard was the main speaker and delivered a cogent speech arguing that Rushdie couldn't be defended on the basis of freedom of speech – because our own society accepts all kinds of limitations on freedom of speech. Such a defence would be illogical, therefore. And Stoppard proposed a defence based on common humanity – that what was threatened by the Ayatollah Khomeini fell short of human standards of behaviour.

Afterwards, Harold, a glass of white wine in hand, asked me if Tom was against freedom of speech. I put my hand on his shoulder and assured him that Stoppard was in favour of freedom of speech. He was convinced. Immediately. Abruptly.

Touching Harold ... At the first night of *Celebration* at the Almeida, just before the performance, without thinking, I kissed him on both cheeks. A mistake. Unmistakably, though he was affable still. There wasn't a trace of the luvvy in him. When the performance was over, he was standing in the court of the Almeida, receiving congratulations, holding court. I said that he must be tired. What the fuck do you mean? Weeks of rehearsal, I began, the strain of a first night. He cut me off. 'Astonishing what stupid things people say. Of course I'm not tired. I'm going off now to have dinner with Antonia.' At which point, I was rescued by an old friend of Harold, who asked him to go into the bar to meet his new wife. 'Bring her out here.'

At the first night of *Moonlight*, I asked him, before the performance, how he was feeling. 'Bloody nervous, I don't mind telling you.' The nervous side coexisted with the brusque, dismissive side and it was very endearing. I saw it once on television, when he did a *Face to Face* with Jeremy Isaacs. I think he was spooked by the singular conditions of the programme – no prior sight of the questions, no prior discussion, in fact no meeting with the interviewer before the interview. Isaacs's second question was really a statement: of course, he said, you've read Wittgenstein. It was enough to panic Harold, the possibility of a public viva on Wittgenstein. In fact, it would panic most people, but it had a special terror for Harold. ('I didn't go to the varsity ... ') He reached uncertainly for his glass of water. It shook in his hands. I felt like a son watching his father.

In 1994, Nigel Williams approached me about a possible *Arena* programme about my long poem *History: The Home Movie*. In the end, Nigel's condition, after a night of drinking and discussion, was that my father should be filmed. I refused. Nigel: 'You and bloody Harold Pinter. He wouldn't let me film his father either.' I think we were both right to feel protective and wary. And nervous.

Harold was very generous to *Areté* – giving the magazine a little play, poems, prose-poems, a letter written about *Waiting for Godot* when he was still a jobbing actor, a sizeable chunk of his screenplay for *Lolita*. More than that, he was enthusiastic about the work of other writers which appeared in the magazine. In Issue 1, there was a little sketch by Patrick Marber. Harold left a number on my answer machine. I rang him back. 'Bloody funny play by Patrick Marber [*Casting*]. I read it to Antonia. Did all the parts. Bloody funny. Well done.'

When *Areté* decided to give a 10th Anniversary party for contributors, Frances Stonor Saunders telephoned Harold to see if he could come. Phew. She then rang me, in a state of shock. THIS IS A PRIVATE NUMBER. HOW DID YOU GET THIS NUMBER? A tirade. It's nothing, I said. It's Harold. I'll email him. Don't worry. This is my letter.

Dear Harold,

I hear you turned your *Flammenwerfer* on my editorial assistant, the delightful Frances Stonor Saunders – whom you've met, and liked, in other circumstances. It really wasn't her fault that she rang your private number. It was in my address book – because you gave it to me, twice, without saying it was Top Secret. You were anxious to discuss the first issue of *Areté* and Patrick's little sketch *Casting*. The second time, you wanted to hear my reactions to your *Lolita* script.

Anyway, I think being scorched by you is one of life's central experiences – from which Fran will benefit in due course.

She is contacting you in a good cause. I know you are a great supporter of *Areté*. You've been very generous with your contributions in the past. It was a particular pleasure to scandalise the literary world with 'Modern Love' in the last number.

We need to broaden our subscription base. To do this, we need a bit of publicity. (You may think that 'Modern Love' is an ample enough contribution.) We are giving a party for contributors on 17 January, a Saturday, in Oxford, to say thank you to them and also to attract some press coverage. Obviously, we would like you to be there. Tom (Stoppard) has promised to be there. Francis (Wyndham) will be there. Antonia can cast a nostalgic glance at the Dragon (just round the corner from where we live).

I know this is an enormous favour to ask, but might you be able to come? The food will be good (River Café chefs).

Much Love,
Craig

PS Do you remember telling Ian Hamilton off in about 1978 for giving

your phone number to a photographer called Dmitri Somebody or Other?
You said: Don't give my number to any Tom, Dick or fucking Dimitri ... Legendary.

A couple of nervous days passed (during which I remembered the photographer's surname: Kasterine). Then Harold emailed an explanation and an apology and an acceptance.

In T. S. Eliot's essay on *Hamlet*, we find the following crucial passage. It explains a lot about Harold and the connection between the writer and the man, why they were of a piece. 'The intense feeling, ecstatic or terrible, without an object or *exceeding its object*, is something which every person of sensibility has known; it is doubtless a subject of study for pathologists. It often occurs in adolescence: the ordinary person puts these feelings to sleep, or trims down his feelings to fit the business world; the artist keeps them alive by his ability to intensify the world to his emotions' (my italics). We all know what it is like to lose our temper – sometimes about very small things; *especially* things – but mostly we control it. Harold was incapable of tailoring his feelings to fit the social world. He wasn't a trimmer. That was the price we sometimes paid for the art – willingly.

He *was* one of life's central experiences – *Flammenwerfer* and all.

Short Bit about Beckett
(2006)

Beckett is a very uneven writer, blighted from the beginning by the prior prodigality of Joyce. Beckett chooses to portray his personal dilemma – how to match *Ulysses* using his own drastically limited literary gifts – as merely another instance of a general condition of entropy. His writing comes out of an aesthetic of exhaustion. This is his existential alibi for his meagre native abilities. Interestingly, though, his contempt for literature, for theatre, his determination to write aesthetically punitive, self-mocking works of art, eventually produces some of the greatest theatrical effects, the most striking stage imagery. Not the jejune anti-theatre of *Godot*, nor the torpid yet risibly melodramatic pessimism of *Endgame* ('You know what she died of, Mother Pegg? Of darkness'!) – rather that restless, disembodied mouth in space, throbbing on the retina, in *Not I*. Or the three Dantesque heads in *Play*, up to their necks in urns as they eternally rehearse their erotic triangle – looking like Ser Brunetto in Canto XV of the *Inferno*, with '*cotto aspetto*' (a cooked face), their features 'so lost to age and aspect as to seem almost part of urns' – *terra cotta*, in other words.

Don Paterson
(2007)

Even in bed I pose.
– Thom Gunn, 'Carnal Knowledge'

Don Paterson's first book, *Nil Nil*, won the Forward Poetry Prize for the best first collection. 'A Private Bottling', from *God's Gift to Women*, his second collection, won first prize in the 1994 Arvon Poetry Competition. The book, published in 1997, won both the Geoffrey Faber Memorial Prize and the T. S. Eliot Prize. His fourth collection, *Landing Light* (2003), won the Whitbread Prize for Poetry and the T. S. Eliot Prize for a second time.

The two great, natural enemies of poetry are exaggeration and euphemism. Good poetry is accurate, precise poetry.

I want to begin with Don Paterson and sex.

A quotation from Don Paterson's book of aphorisms, *The Book of Shadows* (2004). 'In some Neanderthal part of me, every husband poses an affront.' More a boast than an aphorism, this hybrid indulges and rejoices in its primitivism just as surely as it deplores it. It is a revel and a boast – and a serio-jocose warning to lock up our wives. (Compare another aphorism sixty pages later: 'Only having children makes any sense of our *biological* contact. Finally, some reward for the torment of those drip-fed poisons [hormones, testosterone], reptilian tics and *Neanderthal lunges* whose derangement shapes half the day' (my italics). You would be naive not to hear the sexual braggadocio of the alpha male here, too. These days, we reserve the expression 'breast-beating' for ostentation of a self-righteous kind. But it could easily engross the engorged, tormented, tumescent, red-blooded self-portrait offered here – the semi-explicit Polaroid pretending to be an 'aphorism', but thumping its chest.

It isn't just me. In his enthusiastic review (*London Review of Books*, 21 August 1997) of Paterson's second book, *God's Gift to Women*, even Robert Crawford noted that 'the title of the volume is qualified by irony, but it remains a vaunt.' However, we were invited, a touch quixotically, to think the book was *about* young Scottish males examining what it is like to be men – where 'the boozed-up Scots male emerges as a damaged damager'.

Another quotation from *The Book of Shadows*: 'anal sex has one serious advantage: there are few cinematic precedents that instruct either party how they should *look*.'

Again, this is a hybrid 'aphorism'. It says that, in these intimate moments, the participants should be spontaneous, should abandon themselves, should be sensually sincere rather than sexually correct. It also says that, however deplorably, Don Paterson is self-conscious about how he *looks* in sexual situations.

He isn't simply a participant; he is a performer, an actor, or something lesser: Paterson in his posing pouch. A symbolic figure, I'm afraid.

If you asked most people to report on anal sex, the lack of *style* guidelines – on positioning, posture and facial expression – would be the last thing on their minds. Particularly facial expression. Should orgasm in the anus and the vagina produce different facial expressions? Is there a subtle shift in features when we shift from hand to mouth? You feel like summoning Beckett's jaded Molloy, whose first sexual act might have been with a man or a woman. He can't decide. 'Is it love in the rectum?' he ruminates. Of course, this is exaggerated indifference – necessary for Beckett's bleak comedy, agnostic in the face of love itself, let alone sex. But it is a tonic antidote to Paterson's humourless, faux-comic, joshing exaggerations.

For Paterson, normal sex is evidently, if reluctantly, influenced by filmic precedent. This follows logically from the noted absence of examples in the anal field. He may also be implying that we are all moulded by the movies ... And it is true that the trench-coated, smoking Albert Camus modelled himself on Humphrey Bogart – gratified by certain facial coincidences. Further down the scale, Ian Hamilton was an accurate pastiche of Bogart smoking gestures. And, more parochially still, Peter Porter's side-parting and horn-rims clearly aped those of Michael Caine in *The Ipcress File*.

But bedroom behaviour? Surely the days have gone forever when the man, obedient to Hollywood, lit two post-coital cigarettes and passed one wordlessly to his partner? (This, of course, was a synecdoche for sexual intercourse.) Even the most intimate movie is less explicit than pornography – though both are mendacious as a matter of course. Failure isn't box office. *Slowness* isn't box office. Commercial celluloid coitus is a curtailed explosion of mutual gratification – usually standing up, if we are to believe Paul Verhoeven and Joe Eszterhas's *Basic Instinct* or *Fatal Attraction*. No one really believes it – not even Don Paterson.

But he does believe in passion. In his heart of hearts. It is an abiding theme of his poetry.

Not real passion, however. Exaggerated passion. The kind of passion punters think it is the business of poetry to promote. 'Obeah' (in *Nil Nil*, 1993) is typical. Sexual obsession portrayed as magic, as voodoo – where the woman's power over men is depicted as a host of parked cars outside her house, each with a 'gibbeted mascot' in the windscreen – the voodoo doll assimilated to car accessories. It is about as plausible as Mickey Sabbath (in Roth's *Sabbath's Theater*), 'overcome by a stupendous deforming emotion', joined by four other lovers who also masturbate over the grave of the sexual genius Drenka Balich. Roth, of course, can cover himself with the curtain of comedy. Paterson is serious – if not literal – about his melodramatic, metaphorical scenario. Alas. There is no ironic gap between the actuality and the image. 'Obeah' is all over-statement.

The last allegedly significant poet to truckle to this appetite for sexual kitsch was Robert Graves. This is 'The Watch':

> Since the night in which you *stole*
> *Like a phantom* to my bed,
> *Seized my throat* and from it wrung
> Vows that could not be unsaid:
>
> Here beneath my arching ribs
> Red-hot embers, primed to be
> Blown upon by winds of love,
> *Scorch away mortality.*
>
> Like sledgehammers my two fists,
> My broad forehead grim with pride,
> Muscles corded on my calves
> And my frame gigantified … [my italics]

Ho, yus, as William Brown would say: *stole / Like a phantom, Seized my throat.* There is a classical tradition here of amorous hyperbole that both Graves and Paterson draw on – selectively. Paterson's 'The Lover' (in *God's Gift to Women*) is 'after Propertius' (in fact, Book II, 27, of *Elegies*): in it, Paterson, putting his mouth where the money is, wooing the paying public, argues that immortality is conferred on the lover. Who is knocked down by a car – but whose fatal accident is erased in a kind of Nicholson Baker fermata. Time is stopped and the accident is cancelled. Compare Graves's *Scorch away mortality.* Actually, (the frequently humorous, savingly wry) Propertius is as general as Graves: he merely says his mistress's voice could recall him from the banks of the Styx. The kerb, the car, the ambulance, are all Paterson's invention. What was allowably rhetorical in the original has been made bathetically literal. Pure tosh – he *and* Graves – as distilled as a single malt.

Which brings us to the 1994 Arvon prize-winning 'A Private Bottling'. The narrative here is that the male, in the wee small hours, drinks his way through 'a chain of nips', samples of 'the extinct malts / of Ardlussa, Ladyburn and Dalintober'. Each malt recalls 'a micro-episode' of the man's love affair with a woman. Not that any episodes are specified. All the detail is lavished on the drink.

Paterson has touched on this scenario in *The Book of Shadows*: 'When I'm drunk the ghosts of all my old lovers file through me one by one; I realise I had never stopped loving them, only buried them alive in me.' You get the picture: morbid, brooding, boozer's gloom, but portrayed in 'A Private Bottling' as ineradicable passion, realised in the imagination with 'something like an infinite sensitivity'. The man regrets their unborn sons and daughters – and *their* unborn children.

At the very end, there nearly is a new note when the speaker appears to realise the sentimentality of his ritual. It is almost an emotionally intelligent moment. 'So finally, let me propose a toast: / not to love, or life, or real feeling, / but to their sentimental residue; / to your sweet memory, but not to you.' Of course, the distinction is hollow – and is intended by Paterson to be hollow. The speaker, try as he may, is still (sentimentally) hopelessly in love.

But the poem has already been poisoned – by the melodrama of the ritual, a sort of Scottish *Ashes and Diamonds*; by the coarse way the wife is marginalised; by the inept metaphor used to describe the man's entry to the marital bed. Viz.: 'then slip back to the bed where she lies curled, / *replace the live egg of her burning ass / gently, in the cold nest of my lap,* / as dead to her as she is to the world' (my italics). I'm reminded of Hopkins's hilariously extrapolated metaphor in a letter to Robert Bridges: 'No, Philip Rathbone never wrote. The teapot of inclination has been tilted several times till the spout of intention very nearly teemed out the liquor of execution (I am speaking of myself now, not of Mr Rathbone, and must point out the extraordinary merit of the figure I am employing: I shall work it up), but till now it has not filled the cup and saucer of communication.'

Worse than any of these specific flaws, though, is a general disposition to annex mystical territory, a grandiose pretence, a self-aggrandising weakness for talking things up. In a word, exaggeration, a kind of immodesty that relies on no one calling your bluff: '*This is no romantic fantasy*: my father / used to know a man who'd taste the sea, / then leave his nets strung out along the bay / because there were no fish in it that day' (my italics). Why would anyone credit this baloney, unless you were Jeanette Winterson? A few lines later, our speaker is claiming to have found God on the radio: 'as once, through the hiss and backwash, / I steered the dial into the voice of God / slightly to the left of Hilversum, / half-drowned by some big, blurry waltz / the way some stars obscure their dwarf companions / for centuries, till someone thinks to look.' Isolated like this, the claim looks so fatuous, it must be ironic – but it is clear from the rest of Paterson's work that he is an amateur astronomer. (Not that that saves him from maladroitness here: according to the analogy, God is a dwarf companion of the waltz tune.)

These assertions are of a piece with the claim, in the same poem, to be able to detect 'the light charge and the trace of zinc / tap-water picks up at the moon's eclipse'. The absurd paper currency of runaway poetic inflation.

Paterson alludes to Rimbaud's 'Le Bateau ivre' in 'The Wreck', a poem that describes a drunken fuck: 'We slung the drunk boat out of port // and watched our unreal sober life / unmoor.' The poem ends on a realistic, chastened, wary note: the lovers separate and make 'our way alone / up the mined beach of the dawn'. What precedes this commendably realistic metaphor, however, is rhetorical overreach: 'But what lovers we were, what lovers, / even when it was all over.' Just a minute, when it was all over, you were picking your way warily up the beach – well away from amorous plenitude, crippled with caution. Actually, I think the second line is pure filler for the rhyme – and is made a nonsense of by the trammelled close of the poem. But the romantic overstatement is there in the conflation of wine, bells and hearts: 'the deadweight, bull-black wines we swung / towards each other rang and rang // like bells of blood, our own great hearts.' You get, aurally, from the chime of glasses to the shudder of bells and the beating of hearts by abusing your poetic licence. And what are those '*bull-black* wines' the poet is quaffing? You can't buy those at Oddbins.

The major improbability comes with the sex itself – which is metaphorical and observes, pedantically, painfully, dutifully, the sea-going decorum: we 'stripped off in the timbered dark, // gently hooked each other on / like aqualungs, and thundered down // to mine our lovely secret wreck'.

The sex in the prose poem 'Colophon' is less strained and as good as it gets in Paterson's work. Which isn't brilliant. 'I took three Nurofen and hit the sack. – Praying, as usual, that you'd follow me through; that beautiful pause; and you always would, and did, letting me stiffen under your cool hand till, before we knew it, it became a hitch, a copla, a hyphen between us, something as much yours as mine, or neither, no part of us, till we were both lost on the bridge of it.' Recognisable sex at last (though the reliance on prayer seems perverse, when you can *ask*). And a genuine attempt to describe the trance-like quality sex sometimes achieves. A pity, therefore, that the word 'hitch' suggests 'obstacle' more than it suggests 'connection' or 'tie'. By 'copla' Paterson presumably intends not the Spanish dance but 'copula' – as in 'copulate'. (This verbal incompetence is something I will return to.)

Euphemism, metaphor, analogy, are all dangers for Paterson when he turns to sex. Reviewing *Landing Light*, Patrick Crotty (*Times Literary Supplement*, 12 December 2003) praised 'Letter to the Twins': 'if erotic writing of such force and subtlety is rare, its framing in the context of advice to children is indicative of the capacity to carry off bold imaginative risks that makes Paterson unique among poets of his generation.' The first thing to say is that the poem is addressed primarily to Romulus and Remus – and only secondarily to Paterson's own twin children. This is essential because Paterson's concluding comparison of the cervix to a 'wet snout' wouldn't make sense without the suckling wolf of legend: 'and as you lie there by her [your lover's] side, and feel / the wet snout of her womb nuzzle and lather / your fingertips – then you might recall / your mother; or her who said she was your mother.' That last line is a minor miracle of ugliness. You want to take it to Lourdes.

The *disadvantage* of addressing this paean to erotic gentleness to Romulus and Remus is that Romulus slew Remus and organised the rape of the Sabine women.

The centre of 'Letter to the Twins' is a major site of pious euphemism that almost persuades you the frankly fornicating boyo and boastful buck is preferable. It begins well, though: 'First, she will address you in a tongue / so secret she must close her mouth on yours.' The brief hopefulness vanishes immediately: 'In the curves and corners of this silent song / will lie the whole code of your intercourse.' *And corners* is an empty alliterative reflex, without meaning.

Then Paterson comes to the breasts and the pudenda. 'The roses of her breast will draw in tight.' *The roses.* Poetry that makes you long for prose – for the precise, vivid prose of Ian McEwan, say, watching a woman's nipple wrinkle and gather like a peach stone (*The Cement Garden*, page 135: 'I touched a nipple with the end of my finger. It was hard and wrinkled like a peach stone'). The pubes in Paterson are 'parched scrubland', suddenly wet, 'as though you'd found the stream / running through it like a seam of milk'. The second line here is padding for the rhyme and 'seam' suggests a 'join' as much as it suggests a 'vein'. The (nameless) clitoris is 'where the pearl sits knuckled in its silk'. I have been looking at my knuckles for any resemblance to the clitoris. I conclude that Paterson must mean that the tumescent clitoris bulges like an unwrinkled knuckle. If so, there is a size problem, a serious discrepancy. This, however, is no more physiologically improbable than the cervix nuzzling the fingers – a thing not seen in nature.

The vagina (also unnamed) is 'that ochre-pink anemone' – which 'relaxes' and 'unknots' when your hand applies 'white spit'. The spit is good. But *unknots*? Isn't that anatomically unthinkable, too? Even with poetic licence, even with relaxed semantic rigour?

Paterson goes on. The next step is to insert fingers into the vagina: 'to make **that** shape **that** boys, alas, / will know already as the sign for *gun* / et slide it with a woman's gentleness / till you meet **that** other muzzle coming down'

(Paterson's italics, my bold: there are nine 'that's in twelve lines). It could be Rowan Williams deploring the gun lobby. The 'other muzzle' is of course the cervix. The first muzzle is the gun's. I read this and long for Donne, who touches his mistress like a surgeon tenting (exploring) a wound – a tender simile of genuine originality, both shocking and apt.

The penultimate stanza, before the wet wolf nose, is an instruction to the twins to realise that *this* is where they came from, their route into the world. It is stiff with solemnity and concludes in euphemism and bathos: 'Now, in all humility, retrace / your steps, **that** you might understand in full / the privilege **that** brought you to this place, / **that let you know the break below the wool**.' The 'parched scrubland' has now become 'wool'. Which rhymes with 'full'. Has being born ever been so difficult to understand?

There are two poems in *Landing Light* that you might think show a glimmer of self-awareness, of self-criticism, a vestigial wariness of exaggeration and romantic rhetoric. They are 'My Love' and 'The Shut-In'. The argument of both is that the lover is in love with love – rather than the loved one. In 'The Shut-In', the poet, waiting for his lover, is happy to be locked in, for illicit drinking after closing time, because this preserves the perfection of anticipation. He has a glass of beer, Stevenson's allegory of love's selflessness, 'The Bottle Imp', to read, and the *prospect* of meeting the lover – who is now locked out by the lock-in, thus saving both parties from 'the vast / infinitesimal letdown of each other'. Even here, though, the romantic Paterson salvages his sentimentality from the situation. The 'vast' letdown is *not* 'infinite' but 'infinitesimal'. So high are his expectations, that even the tiniest short-fall is 'vast'.

(No wonder, then, that in *The Book of Shadows*, he records 'the poems and songs I laid at her feet'. Ultimately, Paterson's love poetry is seldom disobliging or so much as tinged with discrimination.)

In 'My Love', momentarily, there is something wryly truthful about the romantic temperament in these lines: 'When our lover mercifully departs / and lets us get back to the business of love again'. As there is also something ironically self-aware in the distinction Paterson makes between those who reverently secrete their love away, like taking the sacrament, and those who make a song and dance 'that the whole world / might know'. (Not '*so* that the whole world *would* know': the linguistic patina is that slightly archaic mode of love poetry favoured by Geoffrey Grigson, which was already dated all those years ago.) The second option – shouting the odds – 'was always more my style', Paterson informs us. He beats the drum (the moon as bodhrán, to be imprecise and over the top) for love. A bodhrán is an Irish frame drum.

Crucially, though, his drumming is a pain in the arse: 'but truth told, I was terrible: / the idiot at the session spoiling it.' Just when you think Paterson has renounced romantic excess, sent it packing, it re-enters through the back door, bragging and exaggerating. 'The last time [he drummed for love], I peeled off my shirt / and found a coffee bruise that ran from hip to wrist.' No half-measures for him, then. The bruise was so bad, we are told, that '*Two years* passed before a soul could touch me' (my italics). Only two years, eh?

With Don Paterson, all that phoney stuff is for real.

And 'My Love' ends with grotesque melodrama: the astronomer Camille Flammarion gives a signed copy of his study of the planets to a girl he compliments on her skin. Coincidentally enough, 'Two years later', she returns the volume, this time signed '*with my love*' – and bound with her own skin, her 'lunar vellum' (there is a lunar decorum to sustain).

So you see: *even people who don't drum very well are capable of extreme sacrifices when they are in love, a force which should never be underestimated.*

The tendency to exaggeration is endemic in Paterson's poetry and not restricted to the subjects of love and sex. This is partly cultural. Paterson comes from a culture that prizes the anecdote and the exaggeration that goes with it. In *Huckleberry Finn*, Twain meticulously distinguishes between his true narrative crammed with exceptional events and the bogus yarn, the tall story that emerges 'naturally' from the vernacular. 'I've always reckoned that looking at the new moon over your left shoulder is one of the carelessest and foolishest things a body can do,' says Huck. 'Old Hank Bunker done it once, and bragged about it; and in less than two years [*two years!*] he got drunk and fell off of the shot-tower and spread himself out so that he was just a kind of layer, as you might say; and they slid him edgeways between two barn doors for a coffin, and buried him so, *so they say, but I didn't see it. Pap told me*' (my italics).

Paterson is in the grip of the vernacular culture because its currency is overstatement, good *craic*, memorability at all costs. In the title poem of *Nil Nil*, football scores are 'so obscene / no respectable journal will print them'. (Aye, I ken he disna really mean it.) 'Amnesia', in the same volume, tells us that 'Blind Annie Spall' had her eyes 'put out before the war / just in time to never see the daughter / with the hare-lip'. In 'Homesick Paterson' (*God's Gift to Women*), we read: 'His Ma had pit his shed in wi an aix.' (His mother had parted his hair with an axe.) Authentic pub phrase-making. Compare Mr Dedalus in *Ulysses*, saying the sky is as 'uncertain as a child's bottom' or that a bishop has 'a belly on him like a poisoned pup'. Phrases that impress Leopold Bloom. One Paterson poem finishes with a variant on the old joke question: Do you know [the plays of Shakespeare / the Scottish moors]? Answer: No, but if you hum it, I'll pick it out on the piano. 'Homesick Paterson' ends with a woman acquaintance attempting to renew relations with the poet-musician: 'wee man, dye ken, you were the best?' Paterson brushes her off: '*Nae requests.*'

In the same volume, 'Postmodern' tricks out a tall story with literary garnish. Told in the Scots vernacular, it relates how a man records a hardcore Swedish porn film with his camcorder – masturbating the while. He then distributes the camcorder version to the clientele of his pub and it does the rounds – finally returned to him with strange looks he doesn't understand. It transpires that he has also recorded his masturbating reflection. As he discovers when masturbating to the recording yet again. He stops, but the reflection continues. There is one moment of truth in this farrago – the real sex of 'the big box o' Scotties, the wife's cocoa-butter'. The title, 'Postmodern', is Paterson's aesthetic alibi for the evident Neanderthal relish in the hypocritical anecdote. Were the clientele, then, borrowing the video for purposes other than masturbation themselves? 'Postmodern' means that the reader is part of the text, the viewer part of the film – and that the poet is intellectually superior to his narrator. But the 'sophisticated' writer definitely joins in the belly laugh. The distancing is nothing but *mauvaise foi* – when caught enjoying a dirty joke.

The exaggeration is habitual and damaging. It harms a poem about class, 'An Elliptical Stylus' in *Nil Nil*. An uncle has an 'elliptical stylus' on his record player. It brings out the tiniest musical detail. Paterson and his father go in search of one – and are pooh-poohed and put in their place by the serving assistant, who will not sell them an elliptical stylus because their equipment is too primitive and needs to be upgraded. Fair enough, you might think. But Paterson is enraged by the shop assistant's visible pleasure in their discomfiture – and it is precisely here that the poem goes wrong. It exaggerates. It lies. 'Still smirking, he sent us from the shop / with a box of needles, thick as carpet tacks, / the only sort they made to fit our model.' In other words, needles for a wind-up gramophone. Don Paterson was born in 1963. No record shop would have stocked those ancient needles for twenty years before he was born. What actually happened in the shop might have been interesting, but Paterson doesn't tell us. We get the worked-up version, raising its voice.

(Unless, of course, the whole thing is an allegory about writing – and the 'elliptical stylus' is purely symbolic, not a hi-fi accessory at all.)

Working-class writers (of whom I'm one) have to guard against chippy parables of insult and oppression. In the *Independent Magazine* (24 March 1990), Tony Harrison was interviewed by Mark Lawson. Harrison ended with an anecdote about his father at the National Theatre. This is Lawson's version: 'Perhaps it should be, then, a story not about the baker's son [Tony Harrison] but the baker himself which stands as a final illustration of England and her divisions. All Northern men had a suit which they kept for best. Mr Harrison senior wore his to the opening of *The Misanthrope* [in Harrison's translation]. Going to check in coats, his son left him at the door of the stalls. When the poet returned, his dad looked distressed: "Tony, Tony," he said, "everyone's been giving me their tickets." '

Harrison's implication is that his father was handed tickets *because he was working class*. I don't believe it. At the door of the stalls, there would have been National Theatre employees to intervene. The other implication is that *no one would tender a ticket to a middle-class person*. Otherwise there would be no slight to Mr Harrison senior. But to make that hypothesis plausible, you'd have to believe that ushers at the National Theatre, despite their suits, are instantly identifiable as working class.

I think I know what really happened. Harrison has transformed his (guilty) embarrassment – at his father's wincing inferiority – into anger at the upper class. My own father, a more ebullient specimen, would have been embarrassing in a different way. At the New Theatre touring performance of the Glyndebourne production of *The Electrification of the Soviet Union* (for which I wrote the libretto), my father embarrassed me and my mother by a breathtaking display of egotism, as he told anyone who would listen about his role as Blinky Bill in *The Belle of New York* performed by the Shildon Amateur Operatic Society sometime in the thirties. He even sang at the top of his voice. Phew. I don't mind telling you.

I much prefer Paterson's allegory of deracination '11:00: Baldovan' in *God's Gift to Women*. It is about the young Paterson and another boy, Ross Mudie, going on the bus to Hilltown from wherever they live. There is a mountaineering metaphor because they are scaling the social heights: 'Base camp. Horizontal sleet. Two small boys / have raised the steel flag of the 20 terminus: // me and Ross Mudie are going up the Hilltown / for the first time ever on our own.' The poem is gravid with the small change of anxiety: 'where we should sit, when to pull the bell, even // if we have enough money for the fare'. Thereafter, things take a surreal turn, an acceptably skewed version of alienation, of lost bearings: 'streets that suddenly forget / their names'. And the return to home, where everything will be utterly changed: 'our sisters and mothers are fifty years dead.' Anyone who has ever been lost, anyone who as a child was anxious about being lost, will respond to the queasy morph of nightmare.

There *are* good things in Paterson's five books: skimming stones 'the fit and weight of a sleek fobwatch'; the enchanting and accurate depiction of a baby's first smile ('and his four-day-old smile dawned on him again'); dead seagulls ('Where their eyes had been were inkwells'); a friendly snatch of intimate male dialogue in the tropics ('Silence. *Turned out nice again.* Slow breath. / *Away and fuck off.* Silence'); the perfect match of allegory to actuality in 'The Ferryman's Arms', where the coin for Charon is 'slotting / a coin in the tongue' of the pool table, whose balls 'were deposited with an abrupt intestinal rumble'. There is real wit in 'The Alexandrian Library' (*Nil Nil*): 'you trip on a pile of misprinted erratum slips.' Paterson's version of Rimbaud's 'Oraison du soir' improves the last line of the original. This is Rimbaud taking a piss: 'Je pisse vers les cieux bruns, très haut et très loin, / Avec l'assentiment des grands heliotropes.' This is Paterson taking a piss ('Morning Prayer'): 'I pish gloriously into the dawn skies / while below me the spattered ferns nod their assent.'

The next poem in *Nil Nil*, 'Filter', is also about pissing but illustrates a persistent fault in Paterson's poetry – misleading exposition, lack of clarity:

> Thrown out in a glittering arc
>   as clear as the winterbourne,
> the jug of Murphy's I threw back
>   goes hissing off the stone.
>
> Whatever I do with all the black
>   is my business alone.

The disentangled sense is that the poet drinks black stout but pisses clear piss, filtering off the 'black' – the black which takes on further connotations of pessimism, depression, melancholy, privacy. The problem is the play on 'thrown out' and 'threw back'. Obviously Paterson intends a linguistic playfulness like that in 'Orchitis': he is phoning a cousin to find out about an inflammation of the testicles: 'Terrified, *I held the line* while he *fished* through / his lecture notes.' In 'Filter', though, the play brings semantic opacity. 'Thrown out' isn't obviously applicable to pissing. It more obviously summons the sense of 'disposing' or 'getting rid of'. Likewise, 'threw back' doesn't immediately suggest 'swigging' but 'throwing something back' or 'returning something'. Of the two, 'thrown out' is the most seriously misleading. Without the preceding Rimbaud poem, the reader would be in trouble. If anything, 'thrown out' suggests renunciation of drink.

Compare 'My Love' and these two enigmatic lines: 'Even in its lowest coin, it kills us to keep love, / kills us to give it away.' I think they mean this: he believes that it is painful to keep love secret and equally painful to broadcast the secret. This (purely notional) polarity would be clearer were Paterson's lines less misleading – clearer. *Keeping* something and *giving something away* suggests possession and divestment – not discretion and disclosure. Another example of syntactic ineptitude.

In his aphorisms and public pronouncements, Paterson likes to embrace simplicity: 'only the rarest artists move towards simplicity. The rest *progress*, which invariably means complication, as if you measured your advance by the number of readers you leave behind' (*The Book of Shadows*). His poetic practice contradicts this. (What do you think a 'quilted coat with one long arm' might be? Answer at the end of this essay.) Following the example of Paul Muldoon, Paterson has favoured the kind of poem that is its own narrative oubliette. I'm thinking of a poem like 'Next to Nothing' in *Nil Nil*, which concludes, tellingly, with this gnomic line: 'The recorded voice addresses its own echo.' The poem describes a moment out of time at a country railway station – 'frozen sun', 'fixed stars', 'the ghost of the lame porter' who vanishes as time resumes, but reality is now ghosted by the metaphysical – that echo on the public address system. The next poem, 'The Trans-Siberian Express', leaves us contemplating facing mirrors: 'stretched to vanishing point'. His work has affinities with the drawings of Escher. The Goddess Aporia presides over many poems and he himself summons Orpheus, if a 'scrawny Orpheus': 'as soon as he knew we were all drawn into his magic, crushed it in his hand, as if out of pure scorn for us.' This idea of incompletion, of tantalus, explains Paterson's fondness for evoking Scheherazade: '*But Scheherazade saw the approach of the dawn / and discreetly fell silent.*' Significantly, in *Landing Light*, this poem, 'The Long Story', has no full stop after that last word *silent*.

There are some simple poems in these collections, but they expose Paterson's weakness. 'Waking with Russell', for instance, has one good line – about the baby's first smiles – which I have already quoted. But it begins with an echo of Paul Muldoon: 'Whatever the difference is, it all began.' Compare Muldoon's 'October 1950': 'whatever it is, it all comes down to this'; 'whatever it is, it goes back to this night'; 'whatever it is, it leaves me in the dark.' The end is sentimental and clumsy: 'How fine, I thought, this waking amongst men! / I kissed your mouth and pledged myself forever.' There is a technical reason, too, for the poem's failure: it is a sonnet that uses only two rhymes: began / again / grin / *cammin* / ran / on / men; lovers / waver / rediscovered / ever / giver / river / forever. The rhetorical afflatus of that last line is at least partially caused by the strain of the rhyme scheme. With half-rhymes, of course, the scheme isn't *very* demanding, but it creates some fatal padding early in the poem: 'and his four-day-old smile dawned on him again, / possessed him, *till it would not fall or waver*'(my italics). How does a smile fall? We know how faces fall, but not how smiles fall. And shouldn't the sequence of events be 'waver' then 'fall'?

You might argue that the opaque syntax prevalent in Paterson's poetry is part of the Escher aesthetic. After all, the last poem in *God's Gift to Women*, '02:50: Newtyle' is 'completed' on the ISBN page of *Landing Light*. Paterson is not above teasing his readers. But his incompetence is shared with Yeats. I choose from a hundred possible examples in Yeats this stanza from 'In Memory of Major Robert Gregory':

And that enquiring man John Synge comes next,
That dying chose the living world for text
And never could have rested in the tomb
But that, long travelling, he had come
Towards nightfall upon certain set apart
In a most desolate stony place,
Towards nightfall upon a race
Passionate and simple like his heart. [my italics]

Padding, confusion, reprise. Usually in Yeats, the flaw is the separation of subject and predicate by unwieldy parenthesis. I will spare you. To be in such exalted company might cheer Paterson. It shouldn't. A fault is a fault.

And this is Paterson toiling away in 'Letter to the Twins':

But were I to commend just one reserve
of study [what is a reserve of study?] – one I promise that will teach
you nothing of use, and so not merely serve

to deepen your attachment or your debt,
where each small talent added to the horde
is doubled in its spending, and somehow yet
no more or less than its own clean reward –

it would be this: the honouring of your lover ...

You wouldn't like to be compelled, on pain of death, to produce an accurate paraphrase.

My 'favourite' example is from 'The White Lie' in *Landing Light*, but it is only one of many:

Everything we know to be the case
draws its signal colour off the sight
till what falls into that intellectual night

we tunnel into this view or another
falls as we have fallen.

Don't worry. It's him, not you. (Apart from 'intellectual night' – which is Pope.)

With these gifts of clarity, Rilke seems the last poet Paterson should try to translate. The versions in *Orpheus*, however, have been well received, by, among others, Jeremy Noel-Tod, the former assistant editor of *Areté*. In the *Daily Telegraph* (5 November 2006), he praised Paterson's 'near-Tennysonian ear', singling out this undistinguished, hyper-ordinary line from 'The Venturers': 'and their pitchers filled with well-water and oil'. Those of you who think that 'Tennysonian' means assonantal glissandos like 'The moan of doves in immemorial elms / And murmuring of innumerable bees' will be puzzled by the comparison invoked. There is, however, a line from *The Princess* that I often point out to my undergraduates. Jeremy Noel-Tod may have it in mind: 'Laborious orient ivory sphere in sphere'. Tennyson is describing one of those ivory ornaments – like an astrolabe, wheels within wheels – carved out of a single piece. Appropriately, a unified sound is enclosed in nearly every word: 'Lab*ori*ous *ori*ent iv*ory* sph*ere* in sph*ere*'. I guess Noel-Tod detected a similar effect in 'filled', 'well' and 'oil' – a replenishment of sound. But 'near-Tennysonian' isn't close enough. What I hear is an ugly rhythm.

There are two versions of Rilke in *Landing Light*, 'Palm' and 'Archaic Torso'. They illustrate, perfectly clearly, Paterson's lack of clarity. In the first, Rilke's conceit is that the palm of the hand was once a sole. (Not the fish.) Rilke's poem begins: '*Innres der Hand. Sohle, die nicht mehr geht ...*' Or: 'Interior of the hand. Sole, which no longer walks ...' The Rilke is as clear as Rilke ever is. This is Paterson: 'Nowadays, this footsole treads on nothing ...' Only his title – an addition to Rilke; the Orpheus sequence is without titles – is a help. The poem's equation of the hand and the foot is eliminated.

In 'Archaic Torso of Apollo' (I quote Stephen Mitchell's translation), Rilke writes that, although only the torso survives, it glows with power like a lamp: 'Otherwise the curved breast could not dazzle you so, nor could / a smile run through the placid hips and thighs / to that dark centre where procreation flared.' Pretty clear. In fact, clearer than the original. This is Paterson smudging the original smudge: 'Or the double axe / of the breast couldn't blind you, nor that grin / flash along the crease of the loins / down to the low centre of his sex.' The muffed imported metaphor ('double axe' for Rilke's 'prow'), the euphemism ('his sex') I haven't seen since David Harsent's *A Violent Country* 40 years ago – are both the maimed offspring of the rhyme scheme.

'Unicorn' in *Orpheus* is a bit better. What in Mitchell's Rilke is 'graceful movements, the way it stood' is made gratifyingly specific in Paterson: 'its bearing, its stride, its high, clear whinny'. Paterson's 'the stable of its nothingness' is a brilliant amplification of Rilke's plainer 'in dem Raume'. The problems come in the last two lines. Rilke: '*Zu einer Jungfrau kam es weiss herbei – / und war im Silber-Spiegel und in ihr.*' (Mitchell: 'It drew nearer to a virgin, white, gleaming – / and was, inside the mirror and in her.') That is, the unicorn was in the mirror *and* in her. Paterson's version is a travesty: 'It grew inside a young girl's looking glass, / then one day walked out and passed into her.'

That weakness for exaggeration again.

And 'the quilted coat with one long arm' ('God's Gift to Women')? A rather strange straitjacket. Strange because they usually have two long arms – in my constrained experience. Quilting optional, as a rule. Perversely misleading, then – and typical.

Kafka: *The Trial*

(2001)

Breakfast is central to Kafka's *The Trial*. Joseph K's bad day begins with the failure of his breakfast to show up: 'Someone must have been telling lies about Joseph K, for without having done anything wrong, he was arrested one fine morning. His landlady's cook, who always brought him his breakfast at eight o'clock, failed to appear on this occasion.' A bathetic zeugma – two disruptions of differing magnitude – whose differential appears not to strike the narrator or Joseph K (who are effectively identical). In two sentences, Kafka establishes immediately the oneiric consciousness – its gaping credulity, its tendency to naturalise the extraordinary.

But *The Trial* is a dream that never once steps outside itself to tip off the reader. Kafka is careful to maintain the appearance of extended chronology – the narrative lasts from K's thirtieth birthday to the eve of his thirty-first. Dream chronology is non-existent or disorderly. At the same time, *The Trial* details, with the pedantry common to sexual fantasy and to dreaming, passivity and pointless action – pointlessness for which flimsy explanation is patiently improvised by Joseph K. He has an appointment with the Court – no time of day specified. He runs across the entire town in case he is late. En route, it occurs to him he could have taken the tram. Why didn't he? His 'explanation' is absurd: 'a sort of defiance had kept K from taking a vehicle to his destination, he loathed the thought of chartering anyone, even the most casual stranger, to help him along in this case of his'. *A tram?* A better reason – it would be subtly demeaning to be excessively punctual. In that case, why is he hurrying to an appointment he may already have missed?

Breakfast for K means breakfast in bed, or at least in the bedroom: 'K waited a little longer, watching *from his pillow* the old lady opposite' (my italics). This old lady 'seemed to be peering at him with a curiosity unusual even for her' – unsurprisingly. Thanks to a syntactical ambiguity, for a moment the old lady seems to be in Joseph K's bed, rather than at the window across the street.

Dubiety and conviction are the twin poles of dreaming. What could be more dubious or plausible than the warder's 'close-fitting black suit'? – 'furnished with all sorts of pleats, pockets, buckles, and buttons, as well as a belt, like a tourist's outfit, and in consequence *looked eminently practical, though one could not quite tell what actual purpose it served*' (my italics).

K returns to his bedroom to search for identification papers, though neither of his warders require them. On his return, the warders, Franz and Willem, are 'devouring his [K's] breakfast' – bread and honey, coffee – in his landlady's living room. (Subsequently, they are whipped for this, in the lumber room of K's bank – where else?) They offer to bring K 'a little breakfast from the coffee-house across the street'. Wordlessly, K returns to his room. There, as if he had completely forgotten the assertion seven pages earlier – that the cook always brings him breakfast – K takes 'from the washstand a fine apple which he had laid out the night before *for his breakfast*' (my italics). K then drinks two glasses of brandy – one to compensate for the lost breakfast, another for courage. That apple is a little oneiric, arbitrary narrative wrinkle – the *other* breakfast – quickly smoothed away: 'now it was all the breakfast he would have.'

As K returns to the fray, his landlady's living room, crammed with 'furniture, rugs, china and photographs' minutes before, is 'now empty'. Noted but not remarkable. He crosses it to get to another lodger's room, Fräulein Bürstner's, now being used as a temporary office and also rearranged. Three young men are looking at her photographs. K doesn't recognise them. He is told by the Inspector they are bank colleagues. Now K knows their names – Rabensteiner, Kullich, Kaminer. The contradiction, the oneiric slippage, is quickly resolved. They are 'not colleagues' but 'subordinate employees'. Resolved, however, only to be further plunged into contradiction. K can recognise their specifics: the one who swings his arms, the one with deep-set eyes, the third with 'his insupportable smile, caused by a chronic muscular twitch'. That smile cannot be suddenly 'insupportable'.

With all this prior knowledge, *'How could he have failed to notice?'*

Because K is in a dream. True, the dream disguises itself as reality with the usual plethora of plausible detail – the way his landlady's apron string makes such 'an unreasonably deep cut in her massive body', the white blouse hanging from the latch of Fräulein Bürster's window. Each makes its contribution to undeniable mimesis – as do, later, the shirt covering the painting on Titorelli's painting, the washerwoman's damp hand pointing directions, K squeezing Leni's wrist so hard she has to leave off interfering with his access to the Advocate. These irrefutabilities cannot be dismissed as figments even when so much else is frustratingly fluid, nonsensically opaque.

Like the business with breakfast. In the evening, K discusses his arrest with his landlady, Frau Grubach. Had he been prepared, he could have acted 'sensibly'. Here Kafka's unsmiling comedy is at its best: 'If immediately on waking I had got up without troubling my head about Anna's absence and had come to you without regarding anyone who tried to bar my way, I could have breakfasted in the kitchen for a change and could have got you to bring me my clothes from my room; in short, if I had behaved sensibly, nothing further would have happened, all this would have been nipped in the bud.' Breakfast again. *If I had behaved sensibly* – that is, 'got you to bring me my clothes from my room'.

And so Kafka's comic epic of aporia and makeshift begins its long ache for closure.

Religious interpretations of *The Trial* depend on K's encounter with the priest in the Cathedral and his account of the parable of the Law – the suppliant is refused admission without explanation until the moment of his death, when he realises that *no one* has entered that door. The doorkeeper then explains that the door is especially for the particular suppliant – and he is now closing it. The Law, then, is whatever would give meaning to an otherwise meaningless existence. Pass through the door and justice would be administered. There is access to meaning, to resolution – which, however, is refused. And then Kafka brilliantly decides to intensify his grand narrative of deferral. The priest interprets the parable and empties it of meaning by flooding it with uncertainty and multiple choice – 'the simple story had lost its clear outline, he wanted to put it out of his mind.' As we do, faced with a possible allegorical solution which then metamorphoses into an infinite hermeneutic regressus.

Kafka's grimmest, blackest jokes are reserved for Joseph K's judicial murder – the locus of all tragic interpretations. Although K is compliant with his executioners, his reasoning is hilariously wonky: 'Are people to say of me after I am gone that at the beginning of my case I wanted it to finish, and at the end wanted it to begin again?' He is prepared to die rather than appear logically inconsistent. And just as the knife is about to go home, he still looks out for a reprieve of some kind. 'Were there some arguments in his favour that had been overlooked?' This is rational enough, but its corollary is a combination of fatuity and pathos: 'logic is doubtless unshakeable, *but it cannot withstand a man who wants to go on living.*' K is about to be proved wrong. In its last paragraph, the comic dream of *The Trial*, with its characteristic arbitrary erotic interludes, achieves the status of nightmare. And even here, the final sentence is a comically futile assertion that attempts to outflank his fate. K's comment on his death – 'Like a dog!' – is a cry with a codicil: 'it was as if he meant the shame of it to outlive him.' An ignominious after-existence is preferable to extinction. K would like to be special K.

Laughter in the Dark: Nabokov
(1998)

Emptying his scorn over the idea that characters sometimes take a novel in directions unenvisaged by their author, Nabokov remarks in *Strong Opinions* that *his* characters are 'galley slaves'. A more characteristically Nabokovian figure for the writer, however, than that of taskmaster, complete with tumescent torso, is that of a woman weak with exertion in a maternity ward. 'I repose like a brand-new mother bathed in lace, with slightly damp skin, so tender and pale that all the freckles show,' he writes on the completion of *Bend Sinister*, 'with a baby in a cradle beside me, his face the colour of an inner tube.' Variations on this trope are relatively frequent in a life crowded with productivity. For *Laughter in the Dark*, though, the image is that of the father with his face averted from an unforgiving index finger. The novel – originally entitled 'Camera Obscura' and written in Russian under the pseudonym of Sirin – was more or less disowned by Nabokov a decade after its first publication. Writing to the American publisher James Laughlin in 1941, he described it as one of his 'worst novels'.

It is certainly true that Nabokov improved. *Bend Sinister* was published in 1947. Compare that baby whose face is 'the colour of an inner tube' with the little girl born to Elisabeth and Albinus in Chapter 2 of *Laughter in the Dark*. Irma's face is, by comparison, a nondescript dab of pigment: 'the baby was at first red and wrinkled like a toy balloon on its decline.' The prose is curiously undistinguished for Nabokov. And throughout the novel one is likely to encounter oddly inert moments – a 'sun-drenched village', the 'diamond-bright world' of the film star, a face 'distorted with fury' or 'a queer sinking in the pit of his stomach'. All the same, if we only consider Nabokov's parentheses in *Laughter in the Dark* (dense, debonair, briskly brilliant) we can see the young novelist already accelerating towards maturity. Take Frau Levandovsky's dachshund, for example, with the soft silky ears: '(inside they resembled dark pink blotting paper, much used).' What could be more appropriate, too, than a parenthesis, to cup and conceal Albinus's secretive action: '(holding the while one hand in his pocket and endeavouring to push off his wedding ring with his thumb)'? The function of the Nabokovian parenthesis is to contain an explosion of observation, a detonation of descriptive assets, an extra intense transaction of linguistic energy, a concentrate – like two boxers at close quarters, neither giving quarter in the blether of boxing gloves. Of course, the classic knockout occurs in *Lolita*, when Humbert laconically adumbrates his mother's death in a freak accident:

'(picnic, lightning)'. Nevertheless, *Laughter in the Dark* brims with these brim-ming asides: 'Irma playing with glass marbles (a rainbow in every one)'; 'the time from his blithely taking that bend until now (a couple of weeks), the place where he was (a clinic at Grasse), the operation he had undergone (trepanning), and the reason for his long period of unconsciousness (effusion of blood into the brain)'.

In each case, the brackets bring focus, qualification, precision, proof – the proof of circumstantial detail. Nabokov is intensely interested in making his fictional world not simply persuasive but undeniable. When he describes Paul Hochenwart's 'vast overcoat' hanging on its coat-hanger, the novelist adds, clinchingly in a clinch of parenthesis: '(a special hanger covered in red silk)'. Here, too, are a couple of refinements which add to the verisimilitude by subtraction: when Rex first appears, he is without the gold cigarette-holder promised by the procuress: 'picking off a bit of the cigarette paper which had stuck to his full, very red lip (where was the golden holder?)'. The other example of subtraction is an admission of intermittent alertness, an unaccountable blank: Albinus, dis-traught with jealousy, 'gazed at her pink wrinkled heel with a bit of black plaster on it – when had she managed to stick it on?'

Few of these quotations have the bravura of later examples, but it would be a mistake to exaggerate the gap between sophisticated Sirin and magisterial late Nabokov. Is, for instance, the blindness of President Poore in that great master-piece *Pnin* any better than the blindness of Albert Albinus? President Poore 'came, a figure of antique dignity, moving in his private darkness to an invisible luncheon'; 'Albinus nodded his head now and then and slowly consumed invis-ible cherries, spitting the invisible stones into his fist.' The linguistic power of both quotations is located in the sleight which offers a particular, specific afflic-tion, poker-faced, as a general condition. Nabokov's parentheses in *Laughter in the Dark* already achieve the status of a stylistic mannerism – at once calculated and involuntary – which will prove to be continuous and as much of a piece as those two identical treatments of blindness. Parentheses, too, are crucial to any discussion of Nabokov's alleged cruelty – an accusation often supported by the citation of *Laughter in the Dark* and Rex's undisguised pleasure in tormenting the helpless Albinus.

The Nabokovian parenthesis is an outburst of manic particularity, at once unstoppable and contained. All writers learn to control and succumb to their instinctive tendencies – which is why Nabokov's parentheses are, as it were, 'strait-brackets'. He is like any performer – a singer, say – who learns to *use* his adrenalin. It is his business, of course, to exude control – clicking the cuffs on his helplessly detailed acts of imagination – but we should never forget the invol-untary, erotic aspect of writing. Particularly so in the case of Nabokov, because it is this quality which is responsible for those charges of coldness shading into cruelty.

Any reader of *Pnin* – a novel which, without abating one jot of ridicule, presents a truly sublime human being – will find it difficult to credit the commonly held notion of Nabokov as the connoisseur of pain. *Pnin* – with its cast of ghosts, its tugs of nostalgia, its gift of dignity to a lonely, ridiculed, exploited, toothless, ideally bald Russian expatriate – is often perceived as the exception in Nabokov's œuvre. It is, rather, a lodestone, directing us to the true north in Nabokov's work.

Part V of Chapter 5 of *Pnin* largely consists of an elegy for Mira Belochkin, an early inamorata of Pnin who has perished in an extermination camp. It traces her history from the precise recollection of their last meeting on the Neva embankment ('the warm rose-red silk lining of her karakul muff') to the obscured fate awaiting her. The three pages or so are beautifully judged – artistically, morally – so that, for example, the girl is not presented sentimentally as the lost love of Pnin's life. Another parenthesis: '(alas, recollections of his marriage to Liza were imperious enough to crowd out any former romance).' Their youthful love affair is described as 'banal and brief'. For all that, the passage is eloquent with considered sentiment. Reading it, one can scarcely believe that a critic as good as Christopher Ricks has identified Nabokov as 'morally attenuated'. One is reminded of Kipling, another writer capable of almost unbearable tenderness, who is nevertheless accused of moral coarseness. Auden, in *New Year Letter*, pronounces him 'horrible'; Orwell finds him 'morally insensitive and aesthetically disgusting'. In both cases, I think the fault lies with the readers – from an understandable desire for uncomplicated morality, for right and its opposite, wrong, for spiritual correctness – but it is a venial, understandable fault connected with the writerly imagination – its iron necessity, its imperium.

This is *Pnin*: 'one had to forget – because one could not live with the thought that this graceful, fragile, tender young woman with those eyes, that smile, those gardens and snows in the background, had been brought in a cattle car to an extermination camp and killed by an injection of phenol into the heart, into the gentle heart one had heard beating under one's lips in the dusk of the past.' This would be enough for most readers. But it is not enough for the writer, whose duty, talent and affliction it is to imagine in circumstantial detail – without which the novel is a desert, since detail is the subsoil, the topsoil and the luminous plant stem rooted in it. 'And since the exact form of her death had not been recorded,' Pnin–Nabokov pressingly continues, 'Mira kept dying a great number of deaths in one's mind, and undergoing a great number of resurrections, only to die again and again, led away by a trained nurse, inoculated with filth, tetanus bacilli, broken glass, gassed in a sham shower-bath with prussic acid, burned alive in a pit on a gasoline-soaked pile of beechwood.'

Mira's many deaths are, of course, representative. She is an emblematic figure – the Holocaust victim. But she is primarily an individual. One word in Nabokov's catalogue tells us as much, though it has apparently nothing to do with her. *Beechwood*. Even the fire is specified, given its singular identity by a novelist helplessly alert to the suggestion of Buchenwald. There is unquestionably something morbid here in the vivid detail – but Nabokov is right to be true to his and our morbidity. As readers we are nostalgic for certainties – the certainty of outrage, for example – but a great writer like Nabokov has an instinct for complication. Even his outrage is complicated. A George Steiner might easily have written, as Nabokov does, that Buchenwald is 'an hour's stroll from Weimar, where walked Goethe, Herder, Schiller, Wieland, the inimitable Kotzebue and others'. It is commonplace now to shake one's rueful head over the spectacle of Germany's uniquely fascinating conjunction of barbarity and the highest civilisation – a paradox of history. It takes a Nabokov to describe his *own* country, 'the country of Tolstoy, Stanislavski, Raskolnikov, and other great and good men', as another 'torture house'. As Eliot remarked justly in *After Strange Gods*, the trouble with Ezra Pound's Hell was that it was for *other* people – not one's friends, or oneself.

And who else but Nabokov would have the intellectual nerve to tinge his moral vision with a sly joke by attributing it to the President of Waindell College – whose afflatus has so far misled him that he believes a fictional character, Raskolnikov, a murderer, to be a 'great and good' man. The moral lesson remains. But the last lesson Nabokov teaches us is that we should be wary of the comfortable complacency to be found in moral pronouncements. Beware the feel-good factor.

Nevertheless, there is some justification for assuming agreement between Pnin and his creator when we learn that Pnin 'did not believe in an autocratic God'. In *Laughter in the Dark*, Rex steps into the vacuum left by the absconded God. He is king. And, pre-Holocaust, he foreshadows with extraordinary prescience the paradox we have already discussed – he is a gifted artist and a gifted sadist. But, in a way, the prescience of Nabokov isn't so remarkable since his vision isn't restricted to the twentieth century in the usual chronologically provincial way. Like his creation, Pnin, he knows that 'the history of man is the history of pain.' There is something sentimental and self-aggrandising in the idea that *this* century is uniquely cruel. Nor is Nabokov interested in supernatural evil: 'the stage manager of this performance was neither God nor the devil. The former was far too grey, and venerable, and old-fashioned; and the latter, surfeited with other people's sins, was a bore to himself and to others as dull as rain ...' Typically, Nabokov's aposiopesis is the occasion for yet another imaginative flourish or two: 'in fact, rain at dawn in the prison-court, where some poor imbecile, *yawning nervously*, is being quietly put to death for the murder of his *grandmother*' (my uncontrollable italics). Anyone who has seen Clouzot's *Le Mystère Picasso* will recognise this restless, unstoppable invention – for which a blank piece of paper, or a blank space in a piece of paper, is the only necessary condition. That dull rain is Nabokov's blank space into which he rapidly sets down a scene full of indisputable particulars.

In Descartes's 'Meditations on First Philosophy', he postulates the following hypothesis in order to make doubt an absolute condition of existence: 'I shall then suppose, not that God who is supremely good and the fountain of truth, but some evil genius not less powerful than deceitful, has employed his whole energies in deceiving me.' There are obvious parallels between Rex and Descartes's deceiver even if they are unintended by Nabokov. A benevolent God and a torpid devil are replaced by 'some evil genius' whose speciality is the inversion of the truth: 'Margot described all the colours to him – the blue wallpaper, the yellow blinds – but, egged on by Rex, she changed all the colours.' In both Descartes and Nabokov, God is expelled from his creation. Which is why Nabokov twice refers, at longish intervals, to Udo Conrad's novel *The Vanishing Trick*. We learn the title at the end of Chapter 16, but the content on the first page of the novel in another parenthesis: '(not the famous Pole, but Udo Conrad who wrote the *Memoirs of a Forgetful Man* and that other thing about the old conjuror who spirited himself away at the farewell performance)'. In *Laughter in the Dark*, God has spirited himself away, or has been spirited away by the novelist. The only trace that remains of the novelist or of God is a deliberately mysterious use of the first person in what is otherwise an impersonal third-person narrative: 'Two hours later Paul appeared. I see he has shaved himself clumsily. Crisscross on his plump cheek was some black sticking plaster.' This occurs in Chapter 9. In Chapter 30, the reader will re-encounter, mysteriously, 'the bit of black sticking plaster' on Margot's heel. One thinks (uneasily) of Joan Clements in *Pnin*: 'But don't you think – haw – that what he is trying to do – haw – practically in all his novels – haw – is – haw – to express the fantastic recurrence of certain situations?'

In *Laughter in the Dark*, Nabokov isn't merely interested in recurrence. He is also interested in inversion. That 'I' may make only one brief Hitchcockian personal appearance, but Nabokov's presence is implied throughout by the patterns of organising intelligence. Rex fills the moral void but Nabokov opposes him on the aesthetic level. Consider, for instance, that sticking plaster coincidence. Rex's attitude to coincidence is hostile and ironic, rather than welcoming: '"A certain man," said Rex, as he turned round the corner with Margot, "once lost a diamond cuff-link in the wide blue sea, and twenty years later, on the exact day, he was eating a large fish – but there was no diamond inside. That's what I like about coincidence."' Rex is against pattern and against moral order. Nevertheless, Nabokov implies both by imposing on Rex and Margot the mythos of Eden – inverted, of course. 'Those friends of yours talked as freely of their love as though they were alone in Paradise – a rather gross Paradise, I'm afraid.' Margot is twice compared to a snake ('there *is* something snakelike about her') and the Rex–Margot ethos is summed up by Albinus in Chapter 39: 'Real life, which was cruel, supple and strong like some anaconda'. And when Rex is discovered by Paul, he is 'like Adam after the Fall' covering 'his nakedness with his hand'.

The principle of inversion adhered to by Nabokov was implicit in his original title, 'Camera Obscura'. This was a 'dark chamber', sometimes large enough for a viewer to stand inside, with a small hole at one side. An inverted image of a scene was formed on an interior screen, which could be traced by an artist. No wonder that Albinus, on beginning to suspect Rex with Margot, should undergo 'the *obscure* sensation of everything's being suddenly turned the other way round' (my italics).

Obviously, the camera obscura has affinities with the modern cinema – hence the original title. The idea of darkness is central to Nabokov's vision, here expressed by a sententious postman. '"Love is blind," remarked the postman thoughtfully.' Thoughtfully and proleptically – for Albinus is about to lose his sight. Literally, this time. There is no need to explain his infatuation. The reasons are superseded by film precedent. Dorianna Karenina is intended to conjure up Marlene Dietrich: 'famous for her exquisite shoulders, her Mona Lisa smile, and her husky grenadier voice'. With Dietrich comes the plot of the *Blue Angel* – and the idea of the obsessed oldster in thrall to silk stockings is validated by a thousand screenings. In any case, the fairy-tale opening of *Laughter in the Dark* ('Once upon a time …') refers us immediately to versions of the old tale in which January falls in love with May – the most famous being Chaucer's 'The Merchant's Tale'.

There is some need, however, to explain Margot's attraction for Rex. Nabokov tries to solve the problem by confronting it: 'their mutual passion was based on a profound affinity of souls, though Margot was a vulgar little Berlin girl and he – a cosmopolitan artist.' Elective affinity is being asked to do rather too much here. In fact, there is another reason, which looks as far ahead as *Lolita*. Though Nabokov is severely restricted in the candour of his analysis – it is after all the thirties – there is a strong implication that Margot's appeal is to the paedophile. At the beach, spectators think Albinus is playing with his daughter. His brother-in-law, outraged, suggests that Margot should be in a reformatory – as if she were under age. She is only just sixteen.

When she first visits Albinus's flat, 'he heard the childish stamping of her footsteps coming up the stairs.' Within, reflected in the mirror, he sees 'a pale grave gentleman walking beside a schoolgirl in her Sunday dress'. As Paul, the brother-in-law, says, so suggestively and incompletely: 'This is not mere vice, it's …' Whatever it *is*, Rex has done it, indulged it some time before Albinus. When Margot was fifteen? She is *said* to be sixteen throughout. She is 16 for a very long time … At twelve 'she became less boisterous.' 'A year later she had grown remarkably pretty, wore a short red frock.' This red frock, in her possession at thirteen, is what Frau Levandovsky advises her to wear to meet Axel Rex – at least three years later. In the interests of minimal plausibility, Nabokov describes it as 'her *old* red frock'. I think we can take the hint, however.

Sex is manifestly an important aspect of the novel but Nabokov is confined by the conventions of his time. The umbrella at the end of Chapter 3 is asked to do a great deal in the way of innuendo – 'this moist ecstasy drumming, drumming against the taut silk overhead.' And the hockey match, where the advances of Rex and the caution of Margot are mirrored in the play on the ice, is bold but successful: 'the goal-keeper pressed his legs together so that his two pads combined to form one single shield.' The hockey match is a very filmic scene of cross-cuts and intermittent dialogue: 'their lips continued to move, but the clamour around them drowned out their swift quarrel.' One thinks of Brando and Eva Marie Saint in *On the Waterfront*, their words wiped out by sirens.

It is Margot's ambition to be a film star. Albinus wants to animate a picture. The irony is that they are *in* a film – a *film noir* with a familiar plot of sugar-daddy, trollop and trollop's pimp. To this tawdry triteness Nabokov adds film behaviour – Albinus pays for a taxi 'as men do in films – blindly thrusting out a coin'; Margot falls in love with 'a life full of the glamour of a first-class film with rocking palm trees and shuddering roses'.

Finally, though, Nabokov abandons his pastiche at the moment he gives the impression of most thoroughly embracing it. The last moments of the novel *feel* filmic, intensely so, but we *see* absolutely nothing – we are trapped inside Albinus's consciousness, his blindness. And, lastly, we are left with a tableau which, though it feels filmic once more, is actually a still. Nor has there been any dialogue. So it isn't a movie; it isn't a talkie. It's a thinkie.

Why did Nabokov change the names of his characters so that the central trio have, as it were, two Christian names? Axel Rex. Margot Peters. Albert Albinus. Does it not hark back to earlier times, biblical times, when human beings were without surnames – but, already, not without sin? When Rex describes Berlin to Albinus 'as if it were a distant picturesque city', we experience a similar pull between time-frames. And we remember yet again the tipsy voice of Joan Clements: 'to express the fantastic recurrence of certain situations'.

Paul Valéry's Notebooks
(2000)

One of Valéry's finest digressions touches on children and their destructiveness. What possesses them? What instinct do they obey? A 'kind of "vertigo" that prompts the child to activate what is there to be activated, – opening the drawer, breaking what is fragile, putting out its tongue (since it is put-outable –)'. He summarises: 'an instinct to try what has not been tried and presents itself as possible.' The whole of Valéry is implicit here – the *enfant terrible*, the intellectual adventurer, the fierce sceptic. The poet understands the solemn absorption of childhood games – that, by analogy, poetry is an exercise in pointless perfection. Valéry has no time for poetry as the shrine of significant ideas. T. S. Eliot dismissed the role of meaning in poetry as a requirement 'to satisfy one habit of the reader's mind, while the poem gets on with its real work – much as the burglar is always provided with a nice piece of meat for the house-dog'. Valéry likewise demotes the paraphrasable content of poetry: 'People say (of Mallarmé or – of me) – So much research and obscurity – all to envelope – what? A smidgeon of thought. The kernel is hard, its content a bit watery. The chest is almost inviolable – a steel, triple lock, and inside – a trouser button.' Mentally, Valéry was always a child – given to secrecy, intellectual brutality, obsessiveness, fierce denunciation, indestructible loyalties, unconquerable aversions, toughness, freedom from sentimentality.

Which is odd, since the life seems almost spectacularly grown up, social, sophisticated.

Paul-Ambroise Valéry was born in 1871. In 1889, his law studies were interrupted for a year by compulsory military service and he began to write poetry as a riposte to the *bêtise* and the boredom. Influential friends included Gide, and Pierre Louÿs, who took him to meet Mallarmé – whence he was to meet and marry Jeannie Gobillard in May 1900. Jeannie's aunt was the painter Berthe Morisot – Manet's sister-in-law, friend of Mallarmé, Degas, Monet. From April 1900 to 1922, Valéry was the secretary to Edouard Lebey, director of the Agence Havas. In England, he met Gosse, Aubrey Beardsley, Meredith, W. E. Henley, T. S. Eliot. He was a central member of the Académie française. This establishment figure turns the odd elegant public eulogy – for Proust, for Bergson – but is at bottom a feral thinker, instinctively vigilant, sceptical and iconoclastic.

Gide's *Journals* recall and celebrate, a little ruefully, the daunting ferocity of Valéry's dismissiveness. In 1907, he complains that 'Valéry will never know how much friendship it costs me to listen to his conversation without an outburst. I go away black and blue all over ... I never argue with him; he merely strangles me and I struggle back.' Valéry had been dismissing 'the Greeks', specifically Homer. In 1938, Valéry hadn't finished finishing off Homer. At a meeting of the radio council, he whispered to Gide: 'Do you know anything more boring than the *Iliad*?' Quick-witted enough to counter, 'Yes, the *Chanson de Roland*', Gide avoided collusion with Valéry's eccentric judgement. Sacred-cowherd versus bloody-minded shambles operative, wielding his cleaver. No contest. Gide concedes Valéry's 'extraordinary intelligence' and 'crushing superiority'. Valéry's approach to literature is Cartesian – a stance of habitual doubt. He never felt the need to believe. In anything. On Proust (in the privacy, the confessional, of the *Cahiers*): 'Montesquiou–Proust–Lucien – three tarts, and what falsettos! Spoiled on fine literature, acute nonsense. Deadly bores, not a whit of intellectual force.' On Flaubert: 'Reading Flaubert is unbearable to anyone who can think – he's incompatible with thought.' It makes one recall T. S. Eliot's just comment: that most critics simply parrot the opinions of the last great master of criticism, until a new master appears and redraws the literary map, banishing cities, populating villages, demoting Milton, promoting Donne.

Valéry was an aphorist, not a systematic thinker – even though he had areas of stubborn interest, of energetic repetition, which might be mistaken for systematic thinking. (Think of his repeated assertions that the language of poetry is non-utilitarian, whereas prose is primarily a semantic carrier.) Again, the accomplished aphorist is, of course, one whose aphorisms have been polished, perfected and repeated in some prior, private space – the *Cahiers*, where else? But, qua aphorist, he is typically provisional, without system. Because the aim is provocation rather than truth. In this sense, the aphorist is pornographer – whose art is an incitement to excitement. 'There is a part of man that feels alive only when creating,' Valéry writes, 'I invent, therefore I am.' For him, thought itself is invention. No wonder Auden admired Valéry and introduced 'Analects' for Vol. XIV of the Jackson Mathews edition of the *Collected Works*. Auden was himself a famous categoriser and deviser of after-dinner intellectual party games. Which writers understood money and would have made investment bankers? Which twentieth-century writers would Wordsworth/Jane Austen/Dickens have admired? And so forth. The impulse is essentially diverting, but cognate with the exam rubric DISCUSS. Sometimes, Valéry's provocations are baldly gnomic, challengingly cryptic. For example: 'The "smile of the Mona Lisa" is empty of thought. Her smile signifies: "I'm not thinking of anything – Leonardo is thinking for me."' What does this mean? It means that it is sentimental to suppose that art is in any sense equivalent to life. Its reality is an illusion. The Mona Lisa is an aesthetic construct. As readers, we are asked to unpack Valéry's elegant, intriguing miniaturisations. We enjoy being made to think.

When Sir Isaiah Berlin appeared on *Desert Island Discs*, Sue Lawley, the presenter, was immediately halted by her guest when she proposed her idea of him as an intellectual. She imagined him as slavishly ratiocinative, perpetually in the toils of great thoughts. Sir Isaiah disabused her. He thought, he said, only when engaged in discussion or reading a book or writing. There were extended periods of vacancy, of near torpor. Compare Valéry's assertion that 'there are also cases when you notice, after the event, that the brilliance of your state of mind has been fired by another person.' Or his observation (familiar to us all) that 'nobody has noticed that there are as many inanities as there are fine things which come to us from ourselves.' Inner resources are all very well, but they require external stimulus.

Gerard Manley Hopkins described the experience of Browning's poetry as comparable to listening to a man with his mouth full of bread and cheese, banging the table and saying he'd stand no more of this d—d nonsense. Valéry is a smoother customer, spreading his foie gras carefully over his dry toast, and enunciating elegant apothegms – pure provocations to thought, to dissent, such as: 'What has been believed by all, always and everywhere, has every likelihood of being untrue.' Or: 'Most people have so vague an idea of poetry that the very vagueness of their idea is, for them, its definition.' Or: 'Every treatise on the arts which falls short of the clarity of a cookery book must be written off as a failure.' Or: 'Those big words, the Infinite, the Absolute, Nature, are the papier-mâché weights that the literary Hercules lifts, waves in the air, puts down again.'

It is possible to agree with the drift of these assertions, without acceding to them in their calculatedly exaggerated forms. The consensus is unreliable – but $2 + 2 = 4$ is widely believed and happens to be true. People with a vague idea of poetry can't be bothered to define it. Clarity is valuable, but maybe the recipe is an inadequate intellectual model. And so on. Pedantry is possible but impossibly pedestrian. Valéry is a polemicist. He is not a literary critic. The texture of the text may be theoretically all-important to him but it attracts very little of his real attention. And it is dangerous, I think, to value his coinages because they foreshadow systematic critics like Barthes or Derrida – as if the literary past were validated by its anticipation and endorsement of current intellectual fashions. We disclaim the idea of literary progress – and yet implicitly claim it for our own era. The diversity of the written word shouldn't be reduced to a word from our sponsor. In any case, Valéry's phrases are the products of a phrase-maker, a man who entertains ideas. The parallel must be with Oscar Wilde's 'The Critic as Artist', in which Gilbert launches a raft of critical positions that appear to anticipate late-twentieth-century radical theories. But Wilde's final, considered view is voiced by Gilbert's interlocutor, whose dry epitome of the arguments is reductively comic. When gathered together, the individual improbabilities are collectively fatuous:

You have told me many strange things tonight, Gilbert. You have told me that it is more difficult to talk about a thing than to do it, and that to do nothing at all is the most difficult thing in the world; you have told me that all Art is immoral, and all thought dangerous; that criticism is more creative than creation, and that the highest criticism is that which reveals in a work of Art what the artist had not put there; that it is exactly because a man cannot do a thing that he is the proper judge of it; and that the true critic is unfair, insincere, and not rational.

With that, Ernest visits on Gilbert's intellectual improvisations the *coup de grâce* – 'My friend, you are a dreamer.' Valéry's aphorisms, too, are provisional, cerebral reveries, intellectual entertainments.

An obvious feature of Valéry's thought is his contradictions. They scarcely amount to the systematic, sustained, worked incoherence of classic deconstruction, where each statement is the cradle or the prophet of its immediate opposite. In classic deconstruction, the 'progress' of the argument serves only to illustrate the central tenet that language is incapable of semantic stability. At any moment, a statement is required to surrender its semantic certainty to an alternative identity, to its opposite – like an Alzheimer's sufferer.

Or consider the debate in the *Cahiers* which revolves around interpretation and seems to foreshadow debate about the Death of the Author. Undoubtedly, Valéry wanted to redress the balance of power as between author and reader. He began by interrogating the input of the author: 'a work is executed by a multitude of minds and circumstances (ancestors, climates of opinion, chance events, previous writers, etc.) under the Author's supervision.' The creative mind, then, cannot exist in isolation. It is continuous with its cultural context at a million points. Unlike the body containing it. There is no spiritual epidermis. Eliot puts it thus: 'at the moment of composition, no poet can repair the damage of a lifetime.' Nevertheless, the author isn't dead. The author has simply taken the job of supervisor.

'Once a work is published its author's interpretation of it has no more validity than anyone else's.' This isn't, I think, the incitement to unbridled multiplicity of interpretation it initially seems. The statement is true only because the author may not have successfully realised his intention, as the full quotation shows: 'if I make Pierre's portrait and someone finds it more like Jacques, there's nothing to be said against this; his opinion is as good as mine. My intention was merely my intention and the work is – what it is.' The insistence here is on the finished work alone. Elsewhere, Valéry notes ruefully, drolly, that 'a bad book might very well be a masterpiece – inside the writer.' A statement like the following rather reinforces the idea of the author: 'a literary work represents primarily the last instant of its composition: the instant when the author has re-read and accepted it as his own, definitively.'

On the other hand, what about this repudiation of the author? 'When a work of art is very beautiful, it loses its author. It no longer belongs to him. It belongs to everyone. It devours its father – He was only the means. It sloughs him off.' Here, Valéry means only that the very beautiful literary work – as a condition of its beauty – necessarily conceals the means of its production, its authorship. Beauty is finish, perfection – rather than the laborious creation of the effect. Additionally, Valéry may also mean that the creation of the beautiful means the suppression of the original authorial intention. Aesthetic opportunism, the embrace of chance, is a favoured methodology for which Valéry finds analogies outside the arts proper. 'A hunter with lightning reflexes. It's the same in war, and on the stock-exchange.' The author serves the art work rather than himself. The self is sacrificed to the poem. Nevertheless, this is manifestly an act of authorship and not abdication.

In 1942, however, Valéry wrote, 'what is produced and affirmed in this way is no longer the product of somebody, but a sort of manifestation of intrinsic, impersonal qualities of the complex function which is Language – a rare manifestation, in conditions that come together as rarely as those that create a diamond from carbon.' Again, though, the argument here arises out of the idea of perfection and therefore the elimination of all trace of the contriving, failing, fixing *bricoleur* who is the author of the sublime artefact. On the one hand, there is the restaurant, the temple of pure consumption; on the other, there is the kitchen, with its overflowing bins, court bouillon and bad temper.

In 1942, Valéry defined the 'deepest problem in art' 'to produce a work formed in such a way that, with variations in taste and needs (impossible to predict) that will occur in the future, it can be interpreted differently from how it was in its own time, and take on a meaning unforeseen by its author, and answer to some thirst of the new era, or create that thirst within it.' This may seem radical. But it scarcely differs from Valéry's earlier affirmation that the purpose of a poem was not necessarily to express a message but rather to receive meaning from its readers: 'few people imagine one can produce a work specially written – not with a view to giving the reader something, but with a view to receiving. To offer the reader the chance of a pleasure – active work – instead of proposing a passive enjoyment. A text fabricated expressly to receive a meaning – and that not only one meaning, but as many meanings as the operation of a mind upon the text can elicit from it.' Valéry continues: 'but do not believe this is a novelty. It's no more than doing consciously what is necessarily done unconsciously every time language is used.' While this empowers the reader, it is also an aesthetic that derives from *symbolisme* – and therefore confers a job on the reader, the necessary work entailed by *'une série de déchiffrements'* specified by Mallarmé's account of the reader's duty. The poet is the employer and the reader his employee – however much responsibility is devolved on the reader. Regardless of whether the reader finds his way into the sandtrap or onto the fairway, the golf course is constructed by the poet.

Valéry was not a theoretician. He was an aphorist and provocateur. Ultimately, he could see that theory has one crucial limitation: generalisation. On the one hand, there is connoisseurship, taste, specificity, discrimination; on the other hand, there is the blanket flatness of theory. Generalisation – the essence of theory – is always vulnerable to detail, to the exception.

True, aphorism and theory have the impulse to generalisation in common – but only theory is constrained to be strictly true. The aphoristic form allows for exaggeration, distortion in the interests of memorability, suggestiveness – in short, poetic licence. Current theory's predetermined indeterminacy seeks to emulate the aphorism's generic intellectual irresponsibility – but the element of predestination crucially countermands the pretence to free play.

'An artist's theories', Valéry wrote, 'always lure him into liking what he doesn't like and not liking what he likes.' Was T. S. Eliot so impressed by the truth of this that he copied it? Or did the same truth strike him independently? In *After Strange Gods*, warily, wearily, Eliot blurs the distinction between the terms 'romantic' and 'classical' – 'whichever you like *in theory*, it is suspicious if you prefer works altogether of one class in practice: probably you have either made the terms merely names for what you admire and for what you dislike, or you have forced and falsified your tastes' (my italics). And in *The Use of Poetry and the Use of Criticism* he asserts that 'we should begin to learn to distinguish the appreciation of poetry from theorizing about poetry.'

Valéry was of course temperamentally a classicist – like Eliot. He believed in impersonality, in attentiveness to the poem's voice. Rather than a vehicle for self-expression, the poem should seek the status of object. Emotion was a matter for scepticism, particularly with regard to composition: 'the idea that by suspending the intellect, and by plunging into emotion, into the apparently unconditional – into some febrile liberty – one comes closer to ever more precious things – is an error and an absurdity. To be drunk without alcohol, to be drunk on the self yields no more than the other state; it isn't rich in revelations.' The greatness of Valéry is his restlessness and his unsentimental honesty – which are the same thing. Victor Hugo was a constant source of irritation to Valéry. Mallarmé was the mentor and exemplar whom he frankly loved. Yet in these *Cahiers* we find Valéry helplessly impartial – praising Hugo for an incomparable line and lamenting Mallarmé's inevitable historical limitations.

Auden's Early Poetry
(2005)

Right from the beginning, Auden seemed distinctive and original. Cyril Connolly, in *W. H. Auden: A Tribute* (edited by Stephen Spender), illustrated Auden's extraordinary charisma by recounting a dream he'd had early in his acquaintance with the poet. In the dream, Auden showed Connolly his breasts: 'Let me show you my lemons.' It seems to me, however, that the problem is defining what it was that made Auden seem so individual, so singular.

He ended up a more conventional poet than he began. And this wasn't just the usual switch from obscurity to lucidity, from self-conscious *art* to a greater reliance on the power of subject matter. We're familiar enough with that arc – almost as familiar as we are with the creeping conservatism in politics that comes with old age, a process that attracted dry comedy from Robert Frost in 'Precaution': 'I never dared be radical when young / For fear it would make me conservative when old.'

In the beginning, several features at once made Auden's poetry as distinctive as his quasi-albino face. I'm going to discuss five characteristics of Auden's style – style in the broad sense as well as the stylistic texture of the writing. Style is also a frame of mind, a frame of reference, the writer's whole moral being. Here are the five things.

1. Language. Auden's early poetry has its own idiolect. It is almost as distinctive as the speech tic of Ma Jingle in *Pickwick Papers* ('it was tiresome, very') – most obviously in the omission of definite articles. 'In month of August to a cottage coming.' But also in his fearless embrace of inversions ('to a cottage coming') and unusual word order ('In month of August to a cottage coming'). That's from his poem '1929'. The lack of definite articles, the unidiomatic word order, is usually attributed to the influence of Anglo-Saxon alliterative poetry, but that doesn't quite cover it. I think that Auden, like any intelligent new boy, decided to forge a distinctive style, a radical style, *artificially*. It's not a question of influence. It's a question of *willing a new style into existence*. It's a determination to be *different*. Sometimes when you read Auden you might easily be reading someone *parsing* a translation from Latin. Or perhaps giving a literal translation from German. 'In month of August to a cottage coming.'

Talk given as part of the *New Yorker* Festival, 2005.

Or: 'All this time was anxiety at night.' And how does Auden say that he is on a hilltop saying something to himself? 'And I above standing, saying in thinking.' It almost sounds like Clough's hexameters, themselves a Latin metre and excessively dependent on the present participle in English ('Waiting, and watching, and looking! Let love be its own inspiration!'). Compare Hemingway in *For Whom the Bell Tolls*, where he creates an idiosyncratic English to represent the dynamitist Robert Jordan thinking in Spanish: 'In this you have to have very much head and be very cold in the head.' So my first point is that Auden sounds like himself more than he sounds like anybody else – or, as is generally the case with poetry, like everybody else.

2. His way with paraphrase and refurbished commonplace. Of course, this is a feature of all poetry, which differs from prose in being more self-conscious. A novelist might write: the curtains were striped orange and lemon. A poet would write: 'Oranges and lemons sang the jolly striped curtains.' That's not Auden but a poet called Henry Marsh – in a poem called 'Ninewells', from a collection called *A Turbulent Wake*. Auden does the same kind of thing. Only more so. Like any really clever young poet, the young Auden is a tweaker, an improver, an aesthetic malcontent – a man to add a moustache to the Mona Lisa. Not the weeping willow, say, with a weeping lover under it, but instead an *abject* willow and a *sulking* lover. 'Underneath the abject willow, / Lover, sulk no more.' In 'A Free One', Auden gives us a poem about someone free from fear, existentially confident, because undeceived. This person exploits his poise, his looks, his manner – exploits not his arresting profile, but his '*accosting* profile'. In the same poem, not an inner peace but an 'intrinsic peace'. In '1929' Auden doesn't order a meal and consult his watch; instead the ordinary is encrypted: 'Order to stewards and the study of time'. He doesn't mark his pupils' exercise books: 'Correct in books' is his laconic three-word paraphrase. From a train, Auden sees the telephone wires dip from pole to pole. He infuses this with an ethical, moral dimension and a piece of word-play about slackers: 'I watched from train, / Slackening of wire and posts' sharp reprimand.'

3. A sophisticated refusal to accept the current currency of poetic ideas. He is the young poet as iconoclast. Love isn't a token for Auden. He interrogates it. Even when he is prepared to concede a little inner euphoria, a willingness 'To love my life' (in '1929'), he first insists on 'Those ducks' indifference, that friend's hysteria'. Then, what he has to say about love isn't riding on a cushion of afflatus: 'So, insecure, he loves and love / is insecure.' When Auden writes about the subjectivity of what we understand by Law ('Law Like

Love'), he concludes by saying that, for him, Law is like love. *And then what he understands by love*: 'Like love we don't know where or why, / Like love we can't compel or fly, / Like love we often weep, / Like love we seldom keep.' It isn't the sentimental equation of law and love that we might expect in a lesser poet. Love here is irrational and inexplicable ('Like love we don't know where or why'). Love isn't quite under our control: you will recall that St Augustine thought that, before the Fall, man could decide whether or not to have an erection. In Auden, and in life, it isn't a question of choice: 'Like love we can't compel or fly.' Love is also sad ('Like love we often weep'), and often broken/unfaithful ('Like love we seldom keep'). When we read Auden on the 'bright / [but] *tiny* world of lovers' arms' (III of 'Ten Songs': 'Warm are the still and lucky miles'), we feel the invigorating scepticism of modernism. Modernism is thought to be many things, but centrally it is an inquiry into the nature of feeling, a scepticism about romantic exaggeration that we might typify by Prokofiev's 1919 piano suite, 'Sarcasms'. Or else by Joyce's attacks on sentimentality in *Dubliners*. When trouble arrives in Auden – as it does in 'O What Is That Sound?' – lovers' vows are weak: 'No, I promised to love you, dear, / But I must be leaving.' Or think about the famous apostrophe to the lover once thought to be Benjamin Britten, now thought to be Michael Yates by Auden scholars: 'Lay your sleeping head, my love, / Human on my faithless arm.' (Note Auden's invisible rhyme scheme, by the way – he rhymes 'love' with 'grave', 'from' and 'harm', appropriately in a poem where falling in love is paraphrased as love's 'ordinary swoon', where the illusion of nobility is embraced as an illusion.) Auden the iconoclast turns aside from the tragic: in 'Who's Who' we learn that the subject of a shilling life was susceptible emotionally, but unexceptional: 'Love made him weep his pints like you and me.' There's a robust reductiveness here that refuses to give love the red carpet treatment.

4. Nor is art the high calling it is in 'Lycidas', where 'Fame is the spur' and 'That last infirmity of Noble mind'. In Auden, art is a compensation for failure elsewhere, failure in the difficult love he proposes: 'again some writer / runs howling to his art' ('Journey to Iceland'). There is an unmistakable edge of contempt in that '*some* writer'.

5. Auden's early poetry specialises in incandescent specifics shorn of explanation – detailed detail that glows in the obscurity surrounding it: 'the fuming alkali-tip / Or by the flooded football ground'; 'The hard bitch and the riding master, / Stiff underground; deep in the clear lake / The lolling bridegroom, beautiful, there.' These telling details gain their power because they

don't tell. In the prose, it's different. There, the details tell quite clearly. This is from a BBC Midland Home Service broadcast in 1939: *China*. First, Auden tells you what war *isn't* like. It isn't tidy. It isn't like those 'lucid tidy maps of battle', 'the pincer movements working with mathematical precision'. Then he tells us what war *is*: 'War is lying in a stable with a gangrenous leg. War is drinking hot water in a barn and worrying about one's wife.'

I want to illustrate these points by using Auden's poem 'Journey to Iceland'. For instance, my point about Auden's language, and his instinct to tweak and to metaphrase: when he describes a 'scolding flag' we recognise and register the brilliance before we understand the mechanism of the image. A *scolding* is a 'tongue-wagging'.

What's 'Journey to Iceland' about? What's the theme of the poem? It's this. In going to a remote place like Iceland, we imagine we are leaving behind our neuroses and our troubled former selves – selves tormented by sex and egotism ('pale / from too much passion of kissing', 'those whose dreams accuse them of being / spitefully alive'). But of course, desert purity is impossible, the ascetic life is impossible, even though the Icelandic landscape seems to promise a volcanic featurelessness.

In a way, 'Journey to Iceland' is a travel poem, but it ruptures the genre. On our travels, we hope to be in good health, not to be ill. Auden's way of saying this is a counter-intuitive periphrasis. *Let me be far from any physician.* With this way of saying this comes the notion that doctors are responsible for illness. Also there is a suggestion of death-wish. Of wishing to be far from help. Hence the first stanza's conclusion: 'and North means to all *Reject*.' Auden is saying that he wants to turn his back on the whole idea of illness and cure.

The poem has its Guide Book element, but it is reduced, a concentrate. It is a Guide Book's *index*. It isn't a *guide* at all.

This is a slightly edited chunk from the middle:

> Here let …
> the student of prose and conduct [find] places to visit,
> the site of a church where a bishop was put in a bag,
>> the bath of a great historian, the fort where
>> an outlaw dreaded the dark,
>
> remember the doomed man thrown by his horse and crying
> *Beautiful is the hillside. I will not go.*
>> the old woman confessing *He that I loved the*
>> *best, to him I was worst.*

Europe is absent: this is an island and should be
a refuge ...

But is it ...?
    A narrow bridge over a torrent,
        a small farm under a crag

are natural settings for the jealousies of a province:
a weak vow of fidelity is made at a cairn,
    within the indigenous figure on horseback
        on the bridle-path down by the lake

his blood moves also by furtive and crooked inches,
asks all our questions: *Where is the homage? When*
    shall justice be done? Who is against me?
        Why am I always alone? ...

Tears fall in all the rivers: again some driver
pulls on his gloves and in a blinding snowstorm starts
    upon a fatal journey, again some writer
        runs howling to his art.

We are thoroughly lost in Auden's gnomic citations: 'the site of a church where a bishop was put in a bag, / the bath of a great historian, the fort where / an outlaw dreaded the dark'. Gnomic, then, but gripping. And this technique works like the romantic genre of the fragment, or Pound's four-word poem 'Papyrus': 'Spring ... Too long ... Gongula ...' John Fuller's *Commentary* will tell you all the background that, in one sense, you don't need, background that will undermine Auden's special laconic effects.

These discrete, gnomic details exercise their dark power – and then lead into the theme of the poem. Which is, as we said, the idea that in going to a remote place like Iceland, we imagine we are leaving behind our neuroses and our troubled former selves. However, a Wilfred Thesiger desert purity is impossible, the ascetic life is a chimera, an illusion.

The catalogue of sights to be seen gradually morphs into a catalogue permeated with the *difficulty* the traveller hoped had been left behind. We encounter it first in the outlaw who dreaded the dark. This might be because of some frightful misdeed committed like Macbeth's. Or because revenge is more likely to take place under cover of nightfall.

But it actually sounds as if the tough outlaw is like a child who is afraid of the dark.

Then we encounter 'the doomed man thrown by his horse' – and Auden gives us *in two lines* man's futile defiance of death and death's implacable cancel-lation of life's beauty: '*Beautiful is the hillside. I will not go.*' The inversion lends plangency to what would otherwise be a bald statement. There is a massive dif-ference between 'Beautiful is the hillside' and 'The hillside is beautiful.' And '*I will not go*' for 'I refuse to die' is at once a superstitious euphemism and a child's cry of defiance: I won't go.

Then there is the old woman confessing '*He that I loved the / best, to him I was worst.*' In Iceland, *in Arcadia, ego* – ego and perversity. All the things the speaker hoped to have left behind. Likewise, the 'indigenous figure', the local, the native Icelander, knows nothing of passion and purity – or even of straightforwardness and honesty: 'his blood moves also by furtive and crooked inches.' This is a vari-ant on standard 'creeping blood' as we find it, say, in *In Memoriam*. 'Be near me when my light is low, / When the blood creeps ...' (Stanza 50). It is the oppo-site of T. S. Eliot's 'blood shaking the heart'. This indigenous figure, the local type, proves to be universal ('his blood moves *also*') – the voice of the insistent, unsleeping ego: he asks '*Where is the homage? When / shall justice be done? Who is against me? / Why am I always alone?*'

A journey to Iceland simply proves that 'the fabulous / country [is] impar-tially far.'

One point here is crucial. It is implied rather than directly stated, but it is cen-tral to Auden's idiosyncratic insight. It is that adults remain children – children who hide their true emotions, but experience their force undiminished. 'Again some writer / runs howling to his art.' Behind this shocking, ironic, reductive image is the psychic topos of childhood – where we run to our comforter, our unwashed quilt, the better to suck our thumbs.

This is Ted Hughes writing to his son Nicholas:

> Nicholas, don't you know about people this first and most crucial fact: every single one is, and is painfully every moment aware of it, still a child ... Everybody tries to protect this vulnerable two three four five six seven eight year old inside ... [by] a whole armour of secondary self, the artificially constructed being that deals with the outer world, and the crush of circumstances ... But when you develop a strong defining self for the child behind that armour, and you make your dealings and negotia-tions only with that child, you find that everyone becomes, in a way, like your own child ... And in fact, that child is the only real thing in them.

There's a difference between Auden's sense of the inner child and Ted Hughes's sense. Auden is less sentimental. Hughes is dangerously near to counselling (*le mot juste*) us to get in touch with our inner child as if that were merely vulnerability. Auden, I think more intelligently, remembers childhood as it actually is: cruel, sentimental, egotistical, self-serving – and willing to hurt because easily hurt. *'Where is the homage? When / shall justice be done? Who is against me?'* Surely, everyone's childhood is here, if only in part.

Auden, an exceptionally intelligent poet, really got back to childhood. This is the end of his poem 'Schoolchildren':

> But watch them, set against our size and timing
> their almost neuter, their slightly awkward perfection;
> for the sex is there, the broken bootlace is broken:
>> the professor's dream is not true.
>
> Yet the tyranny is so easy. An improper word
> scribbled upon a fountain, is that all the rebellion?
> A storm of tears wept in a corner, are these
>> the seeds of a new life?'

The myth of childhood happiness. Schooldays are the happiest days of your life. In this poem, Auden's argument, his thesis, is that children are a kind of prisoner, torpid, submissive, conformist, but prisoners of convention. Their innocence is wished on them: 'the condemned see only the fallacious angels of a vision.' And the poem ends as these things will always end – in tears. 'A storm of tears wept in a corner.' Auden knows that tears, unhappiness, constitute a good part of childhood. He's good on tears. 'The boiling tears amid the hot-house plants' ('A Bride in the 30's').

If you become a legend in your lifetime, you acquire anecdotes.

When David Hockney drew Auden in Christ Church, he was accompanied by R. B. Kitaj. As they went out under Tom Tower, Kitaj turned to Hockney: 'If that's what his face looks like, what do you think his scrotum looks like?'

That's a finished anecdote, with a punch line, but I want to leave you with something less complete, more like the early Auden, a little fragment of the quieter, stranger truth. When I met Auden, we shook hands and I glanced down involuntarily, to see if he was wearing leather gloves.

Auden's Prose
(2008)

1972. A face disguised as a dried riverbed. I met Auden at dinner shortly after he moved to Christ Church from St Mark's Place in New York. Photographs of that iconic, seamed face didn't prepare me for the distressed reality. It was past plastic surgery. Palmistry seemed a more appropriate skill. It looked a hard face to keep clean. There was detritus in the tear ducts, dottle at the corners of the mouth, fluff in the fissures. It was like the dirty photograph of a face found in the depths of a schoolboy's pocket. The conversation was, if anything, stranger still. By that time, Auden specialised in end-stopped conversational gambits – like Mr F's Aunt in *Little Dorrit*, who gnomically remarks 'There's mile-stones on the Dover road.' He wasn't senile, but there was something sclerotic about the non-sequiturs and conversational lacunae. The abrupt dogma arrived *in medias res*. I remember him saying that all Victorian novelists treated money like fairy gold. William Dorrit, I agreed, is restored to riches inexplicably by 'a flourish of his pen'. But I offered Mr Micawber not as a contradiction, rather as a refinement: annual income, annual expenditure … Auden cut me short: 'Fairy gold.'

Two nights later, he was on television, being interviewed by Richard Crossman, who had been his Oxford contemporary. (They may even have slept together as undergraduates.) The repertoire of bon mots was repeated – eerily, pitiably at cross-purposes to Crossman's questions. The impression given was of eccentricity. In fact, the end was in sight.

The portents were there much earlier. A 1953 piece on *Huckleberry Finn* and *Oliver Twist* (a comparison thriftily recycled) argues that the European and American attitudes to money are significantly different. You can see where the idea of money as fairy gold originated. It isn't simply that we have no idea of what actually takes place, say, in Dickens's Circumlocution Office – how its employees actually earn their money. (Dickens's point being, of course, that they do nothing to earn their salaries. They are busily idle.) In Europe, apparently, money is regarded simply as a means to freedom, to please yourself, to independence. In America, money is a sign of manhood. It shows that the wage-earner has conquered an inimical outside nature. This is, of course, confident *ex cathedra* claptrap. Run it past yourself a couple of times – and watch the nifty

W. H. Auden: Prose. Volume III: 1949–1955, edited by Edward Mendelson (Faber and Faber, 2008).

formulation run out of conviction and start to look shifty.

Compare this assessment of Freud. (Auden is reviewing the first volume of Ernest Jones's biography.) 'A very great man still if every one of his theories should turn out to be false.' Apply this to Gordon Brown and you quickly realise how frail the proposition is. Even if you fail at everything, you can still be a success. Tell that to the back-benchers. It is true that I have quoted the proposition out of context – but the context hardly makes sense without an additional explanatory context (a piece on Saint-John Perse) and is in any case so much protective polystyrene. Of the same order of magnitude (or should that be minitude?) is the assertion that only sadism and lack of love can explain the treatment of mental disorders by physical intervention – hypnosis, medication, electro-shock therapy. For Auden, these procedures are 'morally revolting'. The alternative is Freud's talking cure – psychoanalysis. Yet, if as he maintains, neurosis is not part of 'the natural order' (that is, cyclical, changeable) but part of 'the historical order' (linear, one-off and therefore unchangeable), then the psychoanalytical 'cure' has no hope of success. It is, by definition, ineffectual – not on the face it a strong argument for Freud's greatness.

Reading his review of James L. Clifford's biography of Samuel Johnson makes it clear that Auden was aware of his weakness for pontification. Johnson wasn't tempted by drink or by whores. He was drawn, Auden tells us, to a different form of debauchery, something subtler but finally just as destructive: 'as soon as I enter the door of a tavern,' Johnson said, 'I experience an oblivion of care, and a freedom from solicitude: when I am seated, I find the master courteous, and the servants obsequious to my call; anxious to know and ready to supply my wants: wine there exhilarates my spirits, and prompts me to free conversation and an interchange of discourse with those whom I most love: I dogmatise and am contradicted, and in this conflict of opinions and sentiments I find delight.' The idea of contradiction is an ideal, the merest pious aspiration. Johnson liked holding forth – and so did Auden. That is partly why he is so quick to identify the trait in others. They are rivals, competing for air-time.

His publisher T. S. Eliot, for instance, despite his mild curate's prose manner, is keen to supplant Matthew Arnold and 'every bit as violently polemical a writer as, say, D. H. Lawrence'. It's like the assembly in Lord of the Flies. In all Auden's pieces on Eliot, you sense the struggle for the conch. The younger poet is keen to twist it out of the hands of his illustrious mentor. Sometimes with justice: Auden is quick to spot the mismatch between Eliot's account of his prosody and his actual practice in the verse plays. Sometimes with scant justice and flagrant inaccuracy: 'what struck me most on rereading his poems straight through is how little, stylistically, Mr Eliot has changed.' Eliot? The Picasso of poetry? Think about the virtuosic display of multiple styles in The Waste Land.

Philip Larkin, diagnosing the relative failure of Auden's poetry after leaving England for America, singled out literature. For him, Auden had lost his real subject – Europe and its ominous politics – and found only literature to replace it. He became 'a walking readers' digest'. Larkin's damning verdict – the verdict of a former fan – is borne out by much in this volume. Everything in it is written for money, like everything Dr Johnson wrote. Sometimes it seems designed to attract dollars – to sound impressive rather than to be convincing. This is the aphorist's weakness. It is also the needy writer toadying to academic professionalism. Auden was too shrewd not to realise the danger. To Chester Kallman about a 1950 Mount Holyoke lecture: 'The first lecture was last night and the most severe I have ever given – a cross between Whitehead and Heidegger.' Enough to bring tears to your eyes, detritus to the tear ducts.

Zbigniew Herbert
(2008)

In 1988, I was in Bophal as part of a poetry festival. There was a poster promising Ashbery, Ginsberg, and other big-hitters of world poetry. None of whom turned up – mostly for medical reasons. The mischievous seventy-four-year-old Chilean poet Nicanor Parra asked me who I was there 'instead of'. I didn't understand the question. Nicanor explained: 'I am ere instead of Neruda.' 'But Neruda has been dead for twenty years,' I said. Nicanor smiled ruefully: 'No difference. I am ere instead of Neruda.' At the same festival, the Swedish poet Tomas Tranströmer explained the mechanism of international poetic celebrity to me: that every country has several good poets at any given time, but only one is chosen for export. Arbitrarily, not necessarily the best. Foreigners can remember only one foreign name from each foreign country. In Czechoslovakia, it is easy to check out the principle: in prose, Kundera, but not Škvorecký; in poetry, Holub, not Hanzlik.

In Poland, however, things are different. There are *three* poets: two Nobel Laureates, Czesław Miłosz, Wisława Szymborska – and the un-garlanded Zbigniew Herbert. Miłosz writes the kind of poetry we half expect of poets. It is high-minded, morally unflinching. It is Nobel. Herbert's *Collected Poems* comes with a paean from Seamus Heaney, lauding Herbert as if he were a Laureate, too: 'he shoulders the whole sky and the scope of human dignity and responsibility.' The empty alliteration – 'sky' and 'scope' – should make us wary. Herbert's poetry has what T. S. Eliot called 'the unpleasantness of great poetry'. Or the cussedness. Existentially, temperamentally, poetically, he is a contrarian – someone unsuited to the Swedish Academy in Stockholm. The poetry, its attitudes, are designed to disconcert us. When he strikes an anti-attitude, its tonic purpose is to pain us and himself.

Miłosz was a communist apostate who thrived in Californian exile, safely and honourably returning to his native country, to Krakow, only when socialism had atrophied. Herbert travelled to the West, too – but found himself returning several times to a system he had never served. Why? He wrote about this decision twice: in 'The Return of the Proconsul' and 'Mr Cogito – The Return'. Mr Cogito is a figure for Herbert's refusal of poetic afflatus: I think therefore I am.

The Collected Poems of Zbigniew Herbert, translated and edited by Alissa Valles, with additional translations by Peter Dale Scott and Czesław Miłosz (Atlantic, 2008).

And that includes the unthinkable and the borderline-rational. In 'Mr Cogito – The Return', Herbert goes back to Poland knowing 'he will regret it greatly.' He wants his own language, not phrase-book foreign expressions. The West's conspicuous consumption bores him. He is like Vissarion Belinsky, preferring persecution to peace on the periphery of neglect. 'He cares about his own wound': this is how Herbert identifies with his country. He wants to return to 'the treasure house / of all misfortune'. And he recognises, too, in his horribly mixed motives the desire for 'impossible happiness'.

And why did Herbert not succumb to communism's high-minded ideal of equality like so many twentieth-century intellectuals, like Miłosz, like Aragon, like Picasso, like Sartre? Was it because – Brodsky's empty brag – he saw through the system at the age of nine? No, it was because communism offended his taste. It was vulgar. And his taste was snobbish and 'rightly' so, as he records in 'The Power of Taste': none of the Nobel characteristics were needed: 'It did not take any great character / our refusal dissent and persistence / we had a scrap of necessary courage / but essentially it was a matter of taste / Yes taste / which has fibres of soul and the gristle of conscience.'

When Miłosz, in *The Captive Mind*, relates his own revolt from communism, it is also in terms of taste – finally, he couldn't stomach it. Miłosz describes a cumulative moral revulsion, at which he finally gags, unable to swallow another toad sandwich. Herbert, if I can put it like this, would rather starve than eat a single toad sandwich. But before you applaud Herbert's untempted, intransigent virtue, consider 'Mr Cogito on Virtue': 'that whimpering old maid / in her hideous Salvation Army hat' whose breath smells of mothballs. No temptress. And in 'The Return of the Proconsul', Herbert imagines a scenario of calculated compromise: 'I must come to terms with my face again / with my lower lip so it knows how to curb its scorn / with my eyes so they remain ideally empty / and with that miserable chin the hare of my face / which trembles when the chief of guards walks in.'

Herbert's political poems frequently take the form of contrarian parables, parables refitted to address Herbert's particular circumstances. As a form, the parable derives from Constantine Cavafy. Poems like 'Ithaca' and 'Waiting for the Barbarians' are Herbert's fortifying, fructifying exemplars. Famously, 'Waiting for the Barbarians' ends on a paradoxical, but psychologically plausible, note of contrariety. After a day spent dreading the arrival of the destructive barbarians, the speaker is made aware of how his mindset is structured around the threat – when, worryingly, by evening, the threat of the barbarians has not materialised.

Herbert warmed to this kind of cerebral perversity. Intellectually, the obvious is mildly insulting. Thus, we know the myth of Procrustes, who tortured unwary travellers on his bed. Herbert makes this a parable of purges, of the political lopping and crushing and unjointing and stretching required by the ideal of equality.

My favourite Herbert poem, 'Photograph', strategically deploys the biblical myth of Abraham and Isaac to illuminate the communist idea that the end justifies the means, that the immediate sacrifice is justified by the eventual millennial outcome: 'my little boy my Isaac bend your head / just a moment of pain and then you will be / anything you like – a swallow a lily of the valley.' Abraham thinks he is preserving Isaac's innocence and rewarding him with freedom. Herbert, perversely, beautifully, is true to the allure of political ideas. Abraham doesn't know he is lying – to Isaac and to himself. People aren't evil, aren't cynical. They act from the best motives, so they think. The lies are beautiful or we wouldn't believe them: Isaac dead will be 'pretty as a fern's cathedral preserved in coal'. What a ravishing image that is. How difficult it is to resist. In fact, Abraham is acting on orders from on high, obedient to a fault – to history or heaven. Somewhere in the poem is a reproach to Herbert's father – for not fleeing to safety while it was still possible. But this, too, is seen in a long historical perspective: the titular photograph, of the child Herbert, is taken 'before the second Persian war'. The error is as ingrained, as ancient as ancient history itself.

Even love is given the contrarian treatment. For Herbert, it isn't simple: in 'Maturity', Herbert looks at the sexual basis of love: 'In a nest pleated from the flesh / there lived a bird /its wings beat about the heart / we mostly called it: unrest / and sometimes love.' In the prose poem 'Shell', Herbert articulates a truth not often found in love poems: 'In front of the mirror in my parents' bedroom there lay a pink shell. I stole up to it on tiptoe and in a swift motion, raised it to my ear. I wanted to catch it when it wasn't pining with its monotonous sound. Though I was little, I knew that even if you love someone very much, it sometimes happens that you forget all about it.'

You will have noticed that Herbert's poems are sparing with punctuation. This is not because there was a shortage of semicolons under communism. Let me explain indirectly. A beautiful line from 'Arion': 'the sea gently rocks the land.' Actually, the opposite is true. This sea rocking the land like a cradle is a poetic transfer of instability and movement to the land – a subtle quiet barely visible metaphor. Henry James, Saul Bellow and John Updike have all experimented with unpunctuated adjectives. Why does this work so powerfully? What is the difference between 'a subtle, quiet, barely visible metaphor' and 'a subtle quiet barely visible metaphor'? Poetry refuses the automatic. It is considered. It wears its art on its sleeve – even when, especially when, it is 'artlessly' unpunctuated.

And, oh, I was there instead of Ted Hughes.

Not about Heroes
(2008)

Not about Heroes is the title of Stephen MacDonald's 1983 play, now being revived at the Trafalgar Studios. It is taken from the first sentence of the preface to Wilfred Owen's poems: 'This book is not about heroes.' The First World War has a unique status among conflicts. By common consent it was the war that revealed war as a dirty, unheroic business – an outraged discovery, you feel, that may have surprised the gobsmacked poets but could scarcely have been much of a surprise to the common soldier. Tennyson's 'Charge of the Light Brigade' will serve as a marker for military myopia in previous poetry: 'When can their glory fade?' Before that, Horace's 'Dulce et decorum est pro patria mori' (It is sweet and honourable to die for one's country') held the line valiantly against realists and sceptics.

Or so it seems. In fact, Thersites in Shakespeare's brilliantly cynical *Troilus and Cressida* rips the piss out of those classical values *farci* with noble fatuities. And Thersites isn't the only ironic voice in the play. Events speak for themselves: when Achilles kills Hector, it isn't single combat but a cowardly attack by Achilles's Myrmidons. Not that Hector is heroic: like a mercenary, he kills someone for his golden armour.

And in Arthur Hugh Clough's great poem *Amours de Voyage* (1858) its queasy hero, Claude, is caught up in the siege of Rome by the French in 1849. He reminds me of Dylan Thomas when war was declared in 1939. Thomas was reluctant to donate his 'one and only body' to the nation. This is Claude's take (in cod-classical hexameters) on the Horace, a brilliantly wheedling alibi, an elaborate conscientious objection:

> Dulce it is, and decorum, no doubt, for the country to fall, – to
> Offer one's blood an oblation to Freedom, and die for the Cause; yet
> Still, individual culture is also something, and no man
> Finds quite distinct the assurance that he of all others is called on,
> Or would be justified even, in taking away from the world that
> Precious creature, himself.

So Owen and Sassoon weren't the first to appreciate the force of fear and cowardly self-interest. Not that they talk much about either. In fact, their astonished revulsion has its own stricken nobility – its own zeroism, its own strenuous posturing. Which is partly why it goes down so well with sentimental readers – who, deprived of heroism, are equally willing to embrace its unidentical twin – unmitigated horror.

It is the replacement of overstatement by another form of overstatement.

When John Humphrys was talking to surgeons in Iraq on the *Today* programme last week, he relayed something of the real thing – surgeons operating in helmets and *laughing* as the mortars went overhead. Oddly enough, this kind of real war gets into Sassoon's prose, the great *Memoirs of an Infantry Officer* and also (intermittently) into Owen's journal entries and letters: 'I don't take the cigarette out of my mouth when I write Deceased over their letters'; 'we carried on [advancing] like a crowd moving off a cricket field'; 'the seeng-seeng-seeng of the bullets reminded me of Mary's canary.' Mostly, though, it's *angoisse*: 'No Man's Land under snow is like the face of the moon, chaotic, crater-ridden, uninhabitable, awful, the abode of madness.' Look at those adjectives and the way they weaken as they strive for effect: *the abode of madness.*

It's a pity that, for Owen, the poetry is in the pity. Discomfiting detail, awkward accuracy, doesn't get into his poetry – which consistently succumbs to poetry's greatest weakness – easy, posturing eloquence. At least Sassoon, with his debt to Kipling's *Barrack-Room Ballads*, has an effective line in the sardonic.

Neither, though, can compete with Orwell, whose first-hand account of the Spanish Civil War, *Homage to Catalonia*, is a distinctive mixture of understated old Etonian vernacular ('hurt like the devil', 'hurting damnably', 'the mud was unspeakable') and utterly authentic reportage. Shot in the neck, Orwell is transported in a field ambulance: 'Bang, bump, wallop! It took me back to my early childhood and a dreadful thing called the Wiggle-Woggle at the White City Exhibition.' Preparing for action, Orwell 'oiled my ten Mexican cartridges, dirtied my bayonet (the things give your position away if they flash too much), and packed up a hunk of bread.' You could comb through the whole of Owen's poetry and find nothing so vivid. With four exceptions – 'Anthem for Doomed Youth', 'Spring Offensive', 'Futility' and 'Send-Off' – Owen's poems are written, oddly enough, by Outraged, Tunbridge Wells.

Opera as a Flawed Form
(2004)

Princess Margaret described opera as fat people shouting at each other. A memorable epitome, but one which, if true, would hardly explain why we persist. *When* opera works, it works as one, the whole works work – the singing, the music, the words, the acting, the design and the lighting. We experience these several things as a single bolt of pleasure – a piercing spear of sound, something so powerful, so prolonged, so *held*, it is almost painful.

(Yes, it's *supposed* to remind you of sex.)

It's 1987. I'm in the singers' kitchen at Glyndebourne watching Mirella Freni sing *Butterfly* on the TV. The sound is OK, the picture passable. Six or seven of the singers are taking in *Butterfly*'s fantasy of Pinkerton's return, the thread of smoke on the skyline, etc. (I will return to that etcetera.) They are the kind of hard-boiled professionals who will say their last job was singing Purcell's *Dildo in Anus*. And you can see the play of colour from the TV reflected in the tears washing down every face. I reflect that these are some of the same people who, only a few hours ago, were dismissing Stephen Sondheim's *Pacific Overtures* as 'fucking *Puccini*'.

Now it's 1991. I'm in Cheltenham to hear the first performance of Michael Berkeley's opera about Kipling, *Baa Baa Black Sheep*. On the drive from Oxford, I've read aloud to my wife David Malouf's wonderfully direct, uncluttered libretto. Well, nine tenths of it. The journey time hasn't been quite long enough. At the interval, my wife and I are *amazed* to hear people complaining they can't hear the words. We can, perfectly. In the second half, we continue to hear the words perfectly – until the last ten minutes, when words fail me and words fail my wife – as they have been failing quite a lot of the audience for most of the evening. We've reached the bit I didn't manage to finish in the car.

If you can't hear the words, the music can't do its work. The music is written with the words in mind. When we listen to *lieder* or, say, a performance of *Four Last Songs*, the importance of the words is taken for granted. *They are printed in the programme.* That's how important, how *indispensable*, they are. Without the words, imagine trying to make sense of Jessye Norman singing Ravel's *Shéhérazade* in her continent-encompassing but consonant-free delivery.

And yet, with opera, how dispensable they seem. In fact, we commonly sit through opera without even being clear about the plot, let alone knowing what the individual words are on about. How often have we looked in the programme at the plot summary of an unfamiliar opera – 'In the ducal court at Mantua, Domitila, the Contessa Pedroni d'Almovadro, is plotting with Madriagra, the one-legged dwarf ...' – and decided to pick it up as the piece goes along? Not even Tom Stoppard could produce a readable summary. It's an oxymoron. Whereas an *unreadable* summary is a tautology. It will never work until it is available in pill form.

Which brings me to that etcetera. The libretto of *Madame Butterfly* was written by Luigi Illica and Giuseppe Giacosa. 'Etcetera' is the opaque word that epitomises the epitome. It tells us nothing. It is summary. These are the words of Butterfly's 'Un bel dì' aria. Even without the music, they are brilliant and heartbreaking. Pinkerton, the naval love-rat, has returned to America during the first interval – itself one of the great operatic narrative coups. The last time we saw Butterfly, she and Pinkerton were in ecstatic duet on their way to bed for the first time. The contrast, therefore, is acute and bleak. Butterfly refuses to see Pinkerton's desertion as a desertion. Instead, she imagines his return. She tells herself the *story* of his return – using the most basic narrative technique possible, the suspense of '*e poi*', 'and then'. It feels improvised and spontaneous, but it is so detailed, so vivid, that we know she must have rehearsed it, *elaborated* it, many, many, many times.

> One fine day I will see a thread of smoke out to sea, right on the horizon's edge. And then, the ship appears. Then the white ship enters the port. Thunders its salute. Can you see? It's come. I do not go down to meet it. Not I. I place myself there on the crest of the hill and wait. And wait. For a long time. And the long wait doesn't feel a long time. And out of the crowd of people comes a man. A little dot approaches up the hill. Who knows? Who knows? And how he will be met – who can say? Who can say? He will call Butterfly from a long way away. I won't answer. I'll stay hidden. A little bit as a joke. And so as not to die at the first meeting. And he, a little bit anxious, will call, Little wife and Scent of verbena – the names he gave me when he was here. All this will come to pass. I promise you ...

It is one of the great poems, a conflict of improvised fantasy and undeniable detail: 'Who can say?' set against that thread of smoke and the wholly plausible, yet counter-intuitive, assertion that 'the long wait doesn't seem a long time.' The words are irresistible. We step on the trap of Butterfly hiding for a 'joke' and fall endlessly into the deep pit of emotion – 'so as not to die at the first meeting'.

But you have to hear the words. The reason all those singers at Glyndebourne were so completely wiped out by 'Un bel dì' was because there were subtitles on the TV.

Years ago, I took part in a discussion about surtitles in the Covent Garden foyer with David Pountney (then still at the ENO) and the composer Nigel Osborne. It was a contest between common sense and a kind of aesthetic vested interest. As a director, David Pountney didn't want his audience distracted from his staging even for a nanosecond. Nigel the composer clearly felt that inaudible words were caused by poor diction, poor acoustics – and reflected very badly on the composer's technical competence. Set properly and sung properly, the words should be seventy per cent audible in a decent acoustic. Seventy per cent, he alleged, was the 'scientific' measurement of audibility when our opera, *The Electrification of the Soviet Union*, played in Wuppertal. (You can't measure audibility. Think how subjective all hearing is.) The first night at Glyndebourne, I was under the strong illusion that the words were at least ninety per cent audible. However, I suggested a more modest figure to my wife – seventy per cent. She smiled politely over my shoulder and answered discreetly, 'Seven per cent. Sorry.' You see, when rehearsals have been going on for eight weeks, everyone in the opera house knows all the words by heart. Naturally, they can hear them. They've had eight weeks' preparation.

But opera is a flawed form. It was noticeable at the Covent Garden 'Words and Music' session that Nigel, even as he was making his claim for seventy per cent audibility, had to raise his voice. Why? Because a rehearsal of *Carmen* was taking place on the main stage behind him – a hundred yards away, separated from the foyer by two sets of double doors and a dense velvet curtain. Although he was only a yard or two away from his audience, he had a slight difficulty in making himself heard because of a band a hundred yards *behind* him. Imagine that orchestra in front of him, between himself and his audience, and you have the flawed operatic form.

Of course, nowadays, the use of surtitles is common. Covent Garden uses them – because it is no longer socially plausible to pretend that audiences are fluent in Italian, German and Czech, let alone *sung* Italian, German and Czech. They never were. So surtitles have arrived, but only for opera in foreign languages. Everything performed in English is slightly inaudible.

It's 1993. The composer Alejandro Viñao is trying to persuade me to collaborate on an opera. He is darkly handsome. His eyes glitter. His hair is vinyl. I fear the worst. 'What do you think of opera?' he asks. 'It doesn't work,' I reply. His dark brown eyes narrow. 'You're absolutely right,' he says. 'But why?'

'You can't hear the words,' I say.

'Because of the music, yes,' he nods and pauses. 'Well, don't expect me to tone down my music for your words.'

'That was quick,' I say. 'Goodbye.'

He smiles. He grins. 'The answer is to build surtitles into the project right from the beginning. No surtitles, no opera.'

Together we write *Rashomon* and I really enjoy working with him. The music is wonderful, but when it is loud, the singer isn't a goldfish mouthing a mute aria. The words can be heard because they can be seen. We experience surtitles for opera in English as unnecessary. But they aren't. That's the trick.

Influences

(2004)

A general truth about writers and the importance of writing to writers. It defines them – they think.

I have always thought Yeats's poem 'The Choice' ridiculous because it proposes perfection of the life *or* art. As if the two were necessarily incompatible. Whereas, in actuality, few of us are asked to choose. Why not both?

Yet, without thinking a choice of that kind at all necessary, a writer might mentally refer everything in his life to the idea of writing. I remember losing my virginity and thinking on the bus ride home that now I could write a novel. And then thinking that I hadn't seen a bull-fight, so the novelist's career was still closed to me. You see, all writers think all the time about writing and its role in their lives. (One thinks of the fatuous poet in Bruce Chatwin's *In Patagonia*: 'She is a hard mistress. She casts her spell.' He is speaking of Patagonia, but it could be art.)

At the same time, when I was growing up 40 years ago, it was life, it was experience, that decided whether you were going to be a writer. Or not. Writing had more to do with the *corrida* than it had to do with the conduct of words in a sentence. The model was Hemingway – a writer with street cred, prairie cred, matador cred, marlin-fishing cred, pampas cred. It took me a long time to believe in Pampers cred – that poetry could be written about changing nappies. 'We have squeezed / a fluent ideogram / of cleansing cream / across the baby's bottom.' This was a real discovery, I felt, like Picasso saying Van Gogh invented boots as a subject for art. I'd invented Boots the Chemist for poetry. (Not that it was long before critics – suffering withdrawal symptoms – were denouncing this stuff as 'domestic' and demanding 'bulletins from the front-line'.)

What got me back to Dad's Army and the home front? A tea-break in the storm of stupidity raging in my head. And this passage from Joyce's *Ulysses*: 'His hand accepted the moist tender gland and slid it into a side pocket. Then it fetched up three coins from his trousers' pocket and laid them on the rubber prickles. They lay, were read quickly and quickly slid, disc by disc, into the till.' The adjectival precision of 'moist tender', the little dance, the quick step around 'quickly'. If buying a kidney could be so interesting, then all that *other* stuff was, well, baloney.

Poetry and Language
(2004)

Consider the word *Houyhnhnms* for a moment.

It is a word that is never typed or written other than anxiously. Its orthography resists complacency. It opposes the virtual invisibility that overtakes the familiar.

Which is just as well, because this one word, on its own, demonstrates the power of language to equal the actual world.

For literary theoreticians, it is axiomatic that language is unequal to the task of encompassing reality. Its failure is inevitable, a given.

Then we consider Swift's brilliant one word encapsulation of the shuddering breath in a horse's nostrils. Or *mkgnao* – Joyce's more accurate word for the approximate and conventional *miaow*. Both words are triumphs of mimesis. Of course, you might object that neither of these words is a word. *Mkgnao* is not a proper word, runs the objection. To which there is an answer: it is now. And so are Joyce's two sharply observed and minutely differentiated alternatives: *mrkgnao* and *mrkrgnao*. Each of which is frriendlier. Language is not limited to the hobbled, hideous, trammelled practice of the average theoretician. Or even the average writer.

Another objection might be that *Houyhnhnms* isn't exact. It is a bold equivalent. It is essentially metaphoric. The answer is the same: a natural resource of language, metaphor doesn't preclude accuracy and exactness. We know the difference between a good accurate metaphor and a bad inexact metaphor: the good metaphor's equivalence is incontestable. Joyce's *Sllt* convinces us: this is the noise the machine makes.

Let me make a parallel with dialect in literature. In an early chapter of *The Bostonians*, Henry James considers Ransom's Southern dialect and announces that it is not in his power by any combination of words to render Ransom's 'speech. In a sense, this represents a defeat for language – except that really it is only a local defeat for Henry James's language. Kipling, though less intelligent than James, is a greater *writer* – at any rate, a writer more interested in capturing externals by means of words.

This is Kipling in *Something of Myself*: 'it was necessary that every word should tell, carry, weigh, taste and, if need were, smell.' Once raised to this standard – a high standard – language is likely to succeed in precise ways. Conrad is often cited by literary theoreticians as a writer who mistrusts language. As proof, they invariably cite this passage from *Under Western Eyes*: 'The epigrammatic saying that speech has been given us for the purpose of concealing our thoughts came into his mind.' In fact, this statement is a tribute to language's subtlety, not its limitations. And one should bear in mind Conrad's fervent credo in the preface to *The Nigger of the 'Narcissus'*: 'My task which I am trying to achieve is, *by the power of the written word* to make you hear, to make you feel – it is, before all, to make you *see*.'

In 'The First Letter' in Kipling's *Just So Stories*, Tegumai says to his daughter (who has written the first letter, in pictures): 'It *is* a great invention, and some day men will call it writing. At present it is only pictures, and, as we have seen to-day, pictures are not always properly understood. But a time will come, O Babe of Tegumai, when we shall make letters – all twenty-six of 'em, – and when we shall be able to read as well as to write, and then *we shall always say exactly what we mean without mistakes*' (my italics).

Kipling's way with words is exact and economical. James's reality is internal, rather, the accurate accountancy of mental events. (James's expansive, wordy prose is mildly ironised in 'The Elephant's Child'. James appears there as the Bi-Coloured-Python-Rock-Snake, telling the elephant's child that the crocodile 'will permanently vitiate your future career'.) Unsurprisingly, Kipling assesses the problem of dialect more shrewdly than James. In a letter of 1893, to a tyro writer, Kipling advises: 'The dialect is unnecessarily misspelled. All you have to do is to give the reader a notion of the dialect. If he knows it he will read in the rest. If he does not no amount of commas and elisions will help him.' He is, of course, right. Think of trying to pronounce a foreign word from its phonetic rendition in a phrase book. Exact, but unintelligible unless you *already* know what it sounds like.

Debra Gillett, an actress friend, was in Gorky's *Vassa*, translated by Tanya Alexander and Tim Suter. Even though, as our friend explained, the actors had a pronunciation chart which they sedulously consulted, nearly all the Russian names were mispronounced by the cast. After the dress rehearsal, Mrs Alexander tried to correct the errors, but by then it was too late. The mispronunciation was unbudgeably there – in the vocal chords, the lips, the teeth and the tongues of the cast. In what actors call the muscle memory.

Dickens's renditions of Yorkshire in *Nicholas Nickleby* are brilliant, subtle even – to those who know the dialect. For others they are unreadable. 'Hoold 'em toight, while ar coot treaces. Hang on tiv 'em sumhoo. Well deane, my lod.' Or: hold them tight while I cut the traces. Hang on to them somehow. Well done, my lad. As it happens, I was educated in Yorkshire, so I can understand that 'By, me lugs uz card terday' means 'Well, my ears are cold today.' Or that 'Give us yer gowk' means 'Will you give me your apple core?'

Kipling's Yorkshire, the Yorkshire of Learoyd in *On Greenhow Hill*, is a cunning, tactful, accurate, unpedantic combination of dialect words and dialect constructions, with minimal orthographical change. 'Six candles we had, and we crawled and climbed all that day while they lasted, and I said to mysen, "'Liza Roantree hasn't six months to live." And when we came into th'daylight again we were like dead men to look at, an' Blast come behind us without so much as waggin' his tail. When I saw 'Liza again she looked at me a minute and says, "Who's telled tha? For I see tha knows." And she tried to smile as she kissed me and I fair broke down.'

The isle is full of noises, says Caliban, by way of challenge. It is also full of sights. The writer's job is to use words so skilfully that what is out there – actual, but actually unseen – should be seen, fixed and preserved. Great literature allows us to quote reality. This is Seamus Heaney on the noise and feel of a spade hitting an obstacle: 'The plate *scrabs* field-stones / and a tremor blunts in the shaft / at small come-uppances meeting / the driven edge' (my italics). This is Kipling on the noise of the bell at Kyoto in Japan: 'A knuckle rapped lightly on the lip of the bell – it was not more than five feet from the ground – made the great monster breathe heavily.'

The real ringing is the result of a battering ram. But Kipling's evocation exposes the thinness of the given, automatic, reflexive word 'ringing'. His prose demonstrates vividly the power of considered alternatives: 'The boom of the smitten bronze was swallowed up by the earth below and the hillside behind, so that its volume was not proportionate to the size of the bell, exactly as the men had said. An English ringer would have made thrice as much of it. But then he would have lost the crawling jar that ran through the rock-stone and pine for twenty yards round, that beat through the body of the listener and died away under his feet like the shock of a distant blasting.' *Crawling jar.* Great literature makes reality portable. Words are a handle.

In Kipling's collected travel writings, the two volumes of *From Sea to Sea* (Macmillan, 1914, from which the above quotations are taken), there are many modest disclaimers. On page 401: 'the defilement of the pen'; 'it's all beautiful and it can't be described.' On page 373: 'these be only feeble words.' On page 328: 'alas for the incompleteness of the written word.' On page 106: 'You will understand that these foolish tales are introduced in order to cover the fact that this pen cannot describe the glories of the Upper Geyser basin.' On page 111: 'neither pen nor brush could ever portray its splendours adequately.' On page 317: 'but all the telling you in print will never make you understand the exquisite finish.' Faced with this anthology of reservations, any literary theoretician would claim support for the idea that language is *intrinsically* and inevitably inadequate to reality.

However, this last disclaimer, one of many, is succeeded by this passage describing a Japanese shop, a structure so delicate 'you could kick [it] in with your foot and pound [it] to matchwood with your fists.' What can one say to the simplicity of Kipling's essentialism? The language isn't at all bravura, but everything is *there*. And that includes emptiness.

As you will discover when you read the passage, the essential thing for Kipling to describe is invisible – positive emptiness, artistic emptiness, aesthetically chosen emptiness.

It also includes the *absence* of imperfections:

Behold a *bunnia*'s shop. He sells rice and chillies and dried fish and wooden scoops made of bamboo. The front of his shop is very solid. It is made of half-inch battens nailed side by side. Not one of the battens is broken; and each one is foursquare perfectly. Feeling ashamed of himself for this surly barring up of his house, he fills one-half the frontage with oiled paper stretched upon quarter-inch framing. Not a single square of oil paper has a hole in it, and not one of the squares, which in more uncivilised countries would hold a pane of glass if strong enough, is out of line.

The shopkeeper himself is an arrangement of clean colours: 'And the *bunnia*, clothed in a blue dressing-gown, with thick white stockings on his feet, sits behind, not among his wares, on a pale gold-coloured mat of soft rice straw bound with black list at the edges. This mat is two inches thick, three feet wide and six long ... By the *bunnia*'s side is a pouch of green leather tied with a red silk cord, holding tobacco fine cut as cotton. He fills a long black and red lacquered pipe, lights it at the charcoal of the brazier, takes two whiffs, and the pipe is empty. Still there is no speck on the mat.'

This inherent artistry, extending even to smoking, is shown by Kipling to be a conscious exercise of taste: 'a room floored with pale gold and roofed with panels of grained cedar. There is nothing in the room save a blood-red blanket laid out smoothly as a sheet of paper. Beyond the room is a passage of polished wood, so polished that it gives back the reflections of the white paper wall. At the end of the passage and clearly visible to this unique *bunnia* is a dwarfed pine two feet high in a green glazed pot, and by its side is a branch of azalea, blood-red as the blanket, set in a pale grey crackle-pot. The *bunnia* has put it there for his own pleasure, for the delight of his eyes, because he loves it.'

The *bunnia* understands the poetry of arrangement. Or should that be, the arrangement of poetry? Kipling's description can also be used to account for the way space works in poetry – to isolate and highlight the individual word or the single cadence. There are, of course, larger formal satisfactions – the shape of a whole poem – which readers for content, consumers of ideas, will inevitably miss. But poetry should always provide these local intensities as well. A musical analogy: Anton Webern's 'Five Pieces for Orchestra', Opus 10, which takes about four minutes to play. The fourth piece is six bars long and lasts less than 25 seconds. Webern apparently told his teacher Schoenberg that he was composing 'a kind of symphony. I mean a series of pieces belonging to each other.' Actually, to my ear, the music is neither symphonic nor related. The sound episodes are too short for 'episode' to be the right word, with its connotation of continuity. The music is more like fireworks.

Or one sip of a great wine.

Then a sip of another.

Space is a simple way of isolating each phrase.

All good poetry is Japanese in the speed at which it must be read. Poetry is slow and separate and significant. A creative director at Davidson Pearce, an advertising agency, once solemnly informed me that poetry was diametrically opposed to advertising. I contradicted him. Poetry and advertising share a method – the minimum words for the maximum impact. Less is more.

You may think that Robert Frost's colloquial pentameter subverts this notion. It does. This is how his 'New Hampshire' garrulously begins: 'I met a lady from the South who said / (You won't believe she said it, but she said it)'. But it is precisely this subversion that provides the axiomatic intensity. Nothing is more gripping than sabotage. And Frost's relaxed speech patterns are densely focused speech acts: in that 'New Hampshire' quotation, the three apparently carelessly repeated 'said's are also an act of lingering, of insisting on the presence of the speaking voice.

Like Frost, Browning is another speech-based poet, but his method is dense rather than airy with 'redundancies'. His crowded text is impossible to read with any rapidity. Think of parenthetical, unstoppable, unstoppably medical Karshish: 'Sends greeting (health and knowledge, fame with peace) / Three samples of true snakestone – rarer still, / One of the other sort, the melon-shaped, / (But fitter, pounded fine, for charms than drugs) / And writeth now the twenty-second time.' All poetry readers are slow readers – even the fast readers.

The line is central to poetry – a basic act of isolation, of focus, of pause, of the part asserting its equality to the whole. A painting analogy: we weigh the density of the pigment on the loaded brush. A drawing analogy: the line records the subject and the adventure of the graphite negotiating the texture of the drawing paper. In poetry there is overall effect, but there are local decisions of equal importance – without which there is no overall effect. Aesthetic decisions – word arrangements, beauties, calculated uglinesses – are imperatives which have to be attended to.

Kipling's *From Sea to Sea* tells the legend of a Japanese emperor at the Nikko River, trying to compose the scene, feeling it lacked 'a dash of colour'. First, he tries 'a little child in a blue and white dressing gown under the awful trees'. Interrupted in his aesthetic pursuits by a beggar, the king absent-mindedly sweeps off the beggar's head with his sword. The blood spilt solves the problem and the king orders a vermilion lacquer bridge to be built. It is a purely aesthetic decision – emphasised by the king's instruction that no one is to step on this red bridge and that another utilitarian grey bridge should be built for his subjects. The imperious amoral aesthetic instinct here – displayed so candidly by Kipling – reminds me of the Jewish painter in the Łódź ghetto who could not help relishing the restricted palette of his bleak landscape and surroundings.

The aesthetic instinct is autonomous and imperious. It is also curious and tasteless. Let me explain that last adjective 'tasteless': in the interests of aesthetic taste (that vermilion bridge), conventional taste, that is to say, 'good' taste, with its moral dimension, has to be set aside. At least initially.

As a small child Kipling was brought up by his Indian *ayah*. The family house in Bombay was near the burning ghats where the dead bodies were incinerated. Vultures flapped and lolloped on the lookout for tidbits. So, one day, a child's hand was found in the family garden. The young Rudyard was forbidden by his mother to mention it. 'I wanted to see that hand,' he writes in his autobiography, *Something of Myself.*

The impulse here is cognate with Kipling's strange injunction in *From Sea to Sea* (Vol. I, page 449): 'When you come to Japan, look at Farsari's *hara-kiri* pictures and his photos of the last crucifixion (twenty years ago) in Japan.' The aesthetic cannot really afford to be squeamish. Of course, the moral will always make itself felt. Here Kipling concedes that there is 'a strain of bloodthirstiness in their [Japanese] compositions.' And he knows their 'grim fidelity' will 'make you uncomfortable'.

But the same element exists in his own writing and in the writing of any good writer. Graham Greene vulgarised the idea, typically, with his insistence that every writer has a chip of ice in his heart. Which carries the suggestion of coldness. Whereas the truth is not coldness, but accuracy and inclusiveness. The moral is always tempted to censor, occlude, to prefer what *ought* to be the case to what actually *is* the case. All good writers are Nietzschean in that sense. This is Kipling again, in *Something of Myself*: '(Also, by pure luck, I had sight of the first sickening uprush and vomit of iridescent coal-dusted water into the hold of a ship, a crippled iron hulk, sinking at her moorings.)' Not a thought for the owners, the loss, the insurance. '*By pure luck ...*' The true morality of art is its accuracy.

Short Introduction to T. S. Eliot
(2008)

Round the corner from Faber and Faber, the publishing house where T. S. Eliot worked from 1925 until his death, there is a joke shop in Southampton Row. Eliot could be a bit of a joker. As a publisher, he liked pranks – book committee meetings disrupted by fireworks in the coal-scuttle. He and his poetry are full of surprises. For instance, he once wrote that the artist aspires to the condition of a music-hall comedian. He was talking about popularity and audiences, but his remark is a joke – a humorous refashioning of Walter Pater's famous aesthetic axiom that all art aspires to the condition of music.

Eliot was one of the great high modernists, who were notorious for their unbending intellectualism and their artistic difficulty. His reputation is forbidding. The labyrinthine complexities of the great modernists require a guide and a guide book, a Baedeker for readers liable to lose themselves: Eliot has his B. C. Southam, Ezra Pound has Edwards and Vasse, James Joyce has Don Gifford and Weldon Thornton – a posse of scouts scrutinising the spoor, in scholarly pursuit of their fugitive quarry and the fleeting evanescence of meaning.

This view of modernism has been so influential it has spawned a post-modern poetic school led by J. H. Prynne, whose purpose is to be difficult – emulatively difficult. (Not difficult to be difficult, actually.) And this take on modernism has created the critical idea of a 'new poetic' – essentially the notion that the reader shouldn't expect anything in the way of conventional 'meaning', since the poetry was anyway fetched up from the dark womb of the poet's unconscious.

All contemporary poetry, when it *is* contemporary, is initially baffling to its readers. Browning's poetry was once thought to be so difficult that a Browning Society was formed to annotate and explain it. Wordsworth's simplicity in *Lyrical Ballads* had its own contemporary opacity. Why was *this* poetry at all? And when Eliot began, there were plenty of critics who thought his work too intellectual, insufficiently emotional, to be poetry. Where was the afflatus, the uplift and the separation from ordinary prosaic life?

It looks very different now, almost a century since Eliot's early poems were published. We can see, for example, what a brilliant, if surprising, nature poet Eliot was, despite his justified reputation as a poet of the metropolis. Nightingales 'let their liquid siftings fall / To stain the stiff dishonoured shroud'. His eye is meticulous and unflinching: 'Along the garden-wall the bees / With hairy bellies pass between / The staminate and pistillate, / Blest office of the epicene.' Or Eliot lets us see the sea in all its variety: 'Faced by the snarled and yelping seas'; 'Out at sea the dawn wind / Wrinkles and slides'; 'What seas what shores what grey rocks and what islands / What water lapping the bow / And scent of pine and the woodthrush singing through fog'; 'Phlebas the Phoenician, a fort-night dead, / Forgot the cry of gulls, and the deep sea swell / And the profit and loss'; 'Dropping from fingers of surf'; of mermaids, 'I have seen them riding sea-ward on the waves / Combing the white hair of the waves blown back / When the wind blows the water white and black. '

These descriptions are easy to appreciate. So is their converse, drab daili-ness, the dramatically pedestrian, the pointedly unlovely: 'You curled the papers from your hair, / Or clasped the yellow soles of feet / In the palms of both soiled hands'; 'But Doris, towelled from the bath, / Enters padding on broad feet'; or 'Sweeney shifts from ham to ham / Stirring the water in his bath'. In 'Aunt Helen', Eliot is funny about death: 'the undertaker wiped his feet.'

Sometimes the plangent and the prosaic are conjoined, as they are in 'A Game of Chess' from *The Waste Land*, where sinuous Shakespearean pastiche meets the Vic from *EastEnders*. The verse demonstrates a fundamental hybrid-ity: not a centaur, exactly – more like a stallion's head joined to the backside of a pantomime horse. On the one hand, 'In vials of ivory and coloured glass / Unstoppered, lurked her strange synthetic perfumes, / Unguent, pow-dered, or liquid' (*Lurked!*). On the other leg: 'Well, that Sunday Albert was home, they had a hot gammon, / And they asked me in to dinner, to get the beauty of it hot –'

Poetry is written out of the true self, in all its complexity, in all its saving incoherence, its authentic internal contradictions, its existential candour, a self utterly remote from the self deduced by the world, the glib caricature we rec-ognise reflected in the eyes of others, 'eyes that fix you in a formulated phrase.' About this, too, Eliot could be seriously comic: 'How unpleasant to meet Mr Eliot! / With his features of clerical cut, / And his brow so grim / And his mouth so prim.'

The Laureate

(2005)

It must have been some time in 1984. I was Poetry Editor at Faber and Faber. Ted Hughes, one of 'my' authors, was discussing the appointment of the next Poet Laureate. At that stage, Philip Larkin was the popular favourite and seemed the foregone conclusion. 'Of course,' I said, 'no one in their right mind would really want it.' Ted's eyes studied the carpet and then looked straight into mine. You could see what women saw in him. There was a pause. What followed had the quiet force of a proposal. It was a proposition of sorts. 'You'd get some terrific fishing.' He said it quietly, without the hint of a smile. He was absolutely serious.

When he was subsequently appointed, his patriotism, his feel for England and his sense of its heritage, its psychic geography, became palpable. As did his Yorkshire financial acumen. Hughes's Laureate poems fetched top rates from the broadsheets, rates negotiated by Desmond Clarke, the then Sales Manager at Fabers – who screwed £1,000 out of Donald Trelford, as the then editor of the *Observer* was on his way to meet Gorbachev. There was a lucrative reading tour, again organised by Clarke and gingerly agreed to by Hughes, who hedged any public appearance with conditions – no introductions, no signings, no journalists, note-takers, tape-recordings. He took every aspect of the job seriously.

In no time, of course, *Private Eye* was turning out parodies – parodies that were very funny and bore hardly any resemblance to Hughes's Laureate poems. They were travesties, actually. His first poem, 'Rain-Charm for the Duchy', gave the *Eye* the hint it needed. It was subtitled 'A Blessed, Devout Drench for the Christening of His Royal Highness Prince Harry', but it was an authentic Hughes masterpiece, describing a rain storm in Cornwall after a long drought. Its connection with Prince Harry was minimal and all in the subtitle. But what a poem! 'The pavements danced, like cinders in a riddle.' And it wasn't all nature: 'A girl in high heels, her handbag above her head, / / Risked it across the square's lit metals.' It ends with a roll-call of rising rivers: the Barle, the Lyn, the Mole, the Taw, the Torridge, the Okement, the Tamar, the Lyd, the Lew, the Wolf, the Thrushel, the Tavy, the Erme, the Dart, the Teign, the Exe ... Well, he was a fisherman as well as a poet. One of his best books was *River*.

The *Eye* parodies seized on two things – the lack of connection with the ostensible royal starting point and a cliché about Hughes's poetry, that it is violent. As it happens, there is no violence in any of Hughes's Laureate poems.

The mockery began – undeterred by this minor infringement of the facts. In the *Eye* of February 1992, almost ten years later, the joke was still going strong: 'The Lion and the Unicorn', 'Lines Written by the Poet Laureate to Celebrate 40 Years of the Reign of Her Majesty Queen Elizabeth II' goes like this. 'Unicorn. Gentle / Erect, vulnerable./ Grazing./ Silver horn glistens/ In sun./ Corkscrew-like.// Lion in bushes./ Golden mane, mangy/ Roar./ Spring. Rip. Tear./ Teeth sink into soft belly.// Unicorn squeals./ Too late. Blood, guts./ Gush, Grisly./ Lion chews./ Only horn left.// Happy anniversary,/ Ma'am. (*Is this bad enough? TH*) .'

The appointment of the Poet Laureate is a national event like the Oxford and Cambridge Boat Race or the Grand National. People who are normally uninterested in racing shells, and who wouldn't know a cox from a Golden Delicious, tune in to *Grandstand* on BBC One. People who wouldn't know what Wincanton or *Timeform* are suddenly have a little each-way bet at their local Ladbrokes. When the Laureate stakes open, you would be forgiven for thinking that Britain is a nation of poetry lovers, passionately interested in the outcome. If you are a poet, journalists whose shelves are crammed with slim volumes of contemporary poetry ring you up – and invite you to apply for the job, outline your credentials and disparage possible rivals. (Or, in the case of Tony Harrison, ostentatiously decline the post in advance, in verse wi' clogs on – cloggerel – the better to advertise your republican credentials.) The main point, though, is that you should kneecap any poet who presumes to be visible.

And this goes on after the appointment is made. Immediately after Andrew Motion was appointed in 1999, informed opinion canvassed by the *Guardian* included this anonymous verdict: 'bag o' shite'. The abbreviated 'of' hinted at a Scottish author and no one in the poetry world would have much difficulty identifying the bald, ugly, graceless, unaccountably overrated, technically clunky, Muldoon-derivative who was the source of that remark. Interviewed down the line in Australia, Motion was understandably nonplussed when Francine Stock put this verdict to him on Radio 4's *Front Row*. You could hear the gulp all the way from Sydney where the programme caught up with him – bringing news of the flak caused by his appointment. It was his first taste of the animosity that goes with the post and the tasting took place in public. If he was expecting congratulations, he was wrong.

When the Laureate poems appeared, the daily broadsheets and the Sundays were equally eager to solicit instant (negative) opinion. There was an assumption that Laureate-baiting was a wholesome, red-blooded national sport. If you refused to participate, you were definitely meant to feel like a spoilsport. Motion's first poem, 'Epithalamium', was occasioned by the marriage of Prince Edward to Sophie Rhys-Jones and it was a trim bit of trimming – a poem that described a wedding and the meaning of the marriage vows. St George's Chapel, Windsor, was in the subtitle, but Edward and Sophie were subsumed into anonymous symbolic figures, 'two human voices'. It was a plausible solution to the problem of occasional verse: the birth poem, the christening poem, the archetypal-situation poem.

However, though Motion hasn't really continued this strategy, he has written some perfectly creditable Laureate poems. Nothing approaching Hughes's 'Rain-Charm for the Duchy', of course, but mostly competent efforts all the same.

One failure (uncollected) was 'Cost of Life: Paddington Rail Crash'. The reasons for its failure are instructive. The rhetorical organisation of the poem centres around the imperative 'imagine' and 'then imagine', seven times in the course of the poem. (I hesitate to point out that this tactic is an inadvertent, unconscious lift from a poem of mine called 'The Man Who Invented Pain', which includes the lines 'Imagine held hats' as well as 'And then imagine / the rest of the day.') The poem fails because it hasn't the courage to really imagine the details. It doesn't want to pry and so manages to be prurient. And its ending, which gives us ghost commuters returning to their homes, derives too blatantly from the close of Wilfred Owen's 'The Send-Off'.

The worst line is this overwritten, sentimental evocation of the mobile phone: 'still weeping in the ash-mess hiding human bone'. Contrast Ian McEwan's brilliant and instant *Guardian* response to the events of 9/11, both a meditation on the mobile phone and the nature of imagination: 'This is the nature of empathy, to think oneself into the minds of others. These are the mechanics of compassion: you are under the bedclothes, unable to sleep, and you are crouching in the brushed-steel lavatory at the rear of the plane, whispering a final message to your loved one.' *Imagine*, Motion's poem instructs us, but it is McEwan's prose that succeeds in placing his readers in seat 23C: 'Here is your seat belt. There is the magazine you were reading before it all began.'

But we should get Motion's failure into perspective. Few writers write as well as McEwan. Several other good writers, better writers than Motion, were humiliated by the events of 9/11. Moreover, the Laureate has an extra imperative, one special to his role: he must avoid offence, lapses in taste, the mention of a 'brushed-steel lavatory' in the context of a tragedy. And good taste is the enemy of literature. 'Picture This', Motion's goodish poem on the Queen Mother's birthday, bravely attempts to allude to the problems experienced by the Royal family in 1997. Motion's poem is organised around the idea of photographs on public occasions – 'the hats, the hats, the hats' – and then 'the photos no one took of you': 'the grandmother-confessor-friend, the mourner / at divorces and the rest'. He would claim, I think, to have faced up to royal realities *in so far as it is possible* in a poem of this kind. But that phrase 'and the rest' is an inevitable cop-out, covering a multitude of peccadilloes, from Sarah Ferguson having her toes sucked to Major Ferguson on his way to a massage parlour.

It isn't that I'd like Laureate poems entitled 'On the Occasion of James Hewitt Visiting Princess Diana for the Purpose of Consolation' or 'Imagine Being a Tampax: Intimate Thoughts on the Mobile Phone'. Well, maybe I would. But this kind of public poetry can't go there. When it tries to, even modestly, it comes unstuck. 'Remember This' deals with the death of the Queen Mother and has some accomplished touches, 'the flower-lit coffin', and a graceful close: 'you helped give a shape / to slipstreaming time / with a wave of your hand.' But it also has the temerity to take us into the royal bedroom and into the grave itself, without really describing either. 'Held in a trance of fading light' is gestural, a million miles away from the dirty business of dying, with its tubes and snoring, snagged breath. Illness 'and the rest' is where we are. This isn't real poetry. It's like eye drops: they sting a bit and you can't see properly, so the poet kids himself he's moved us.

I prefer the Queen Mother as she appears in Adam Thirlwell's novel *Politics*, a portrait that is true, funny and manifestly affectionate, but which might easily get a Poet Laureate the sack: 'Moshe looked at Elizabeth Windsor, fondly. Indulgently, he observed the ragged points of her scuffed and skyblue shoes. *Time was running out*, he thought. He guessed at the enticements beneath her artfully draped chiffon. Her legs, he admitted, were odd. Her shins were thick with ulcers. They looked like plastic. She had the legs of an unusual Barbie doll. And her arms were cracked and bruised.' Ah yes, we think, a real old person. Like the moment when all the Royals were gathered for a communal photograph and Diana's dress was dark with baby drool from Prince William.

When Andrew Motion wants to be tough, he is tough in cipher. His poem about the death of Princess Diana, 'Mythology', is widely regarded as sentimental. It is actually very cool and even-handed about Diana's collusive relationship with the press. In the myth, Diana's hounds savage Actaeon. Here, she is 'breathless, hunted by [her] own quick hounds'.

Motion isn't stupid. His worst poem, on the English Rugby World Cup victory, knows full well that it is a bad poem – knows that badness is inevitable and therefore chooses, tongue in cheek, the limerick form.

I think we should reappoint him. He's done a good job in nearly impossible circumstances. When I said earlier that the press wants poets to kneecap each other, I forgot that, in the case of Andrew Motion, this is impossible. In his early teens, both kneecaps were surgically removed. He keeps them in a jar of formaldehyde. I think they should be purchased for the nation, as a national treasure.

Consider the Hipster: How Good is David Foster Wallace?

(2011)

I blame Zadie Smith. Here she is in the *Guardian* Books of the Year 2000:

> In the end it was young American writing that rocked my world, and, more than anything else, David Foster Wallace's *Brief Interviews with Hideous Men*. Foster Wallace is proving to be the kind of writer I was sort of hoping didn't exist – a visionary, a craftsman, a comedian and as serious as it is possible to be without accidentally writing a religious text. He can do anything with a piece of prose, and it is a humbling experience to see him go to work on what has passed up till now as 'modern fiction'. He's so modern he's in a different time-space continuum from the rest of us. Goddamn him.

But she isn't entirely to blame. Foster Wallace's publisher has something to answer for. As reproduced on various paperbacks, this quotation has been doctored. So: 'a visionary, a craftsman, a comedian and as serious as it is possible to be without writing a religious text. He's so modern he's in a different time-space continuum from the rest of us. Goddamn him.' No elision marks. The quotation begins, without preliminaries, at 'a visionary'. The word 'accidentally' has been edited out. So Foster Wallace is now an established secular seer, the acceptable face of mysticism. The whole idea of works in progress – 'is proving to be' – has been erased. And that is why the sentence has been dropped describing Foster Wallace going 'to work on what has passed up till now as "modern fiction"'. The publisher prefers the completed arc to the ongoing effort.

Her 2008 essay *Brief Interviews with Hideous Men: The Difficult Gifts of David Foster Wallace*, was completed after his suicide. It is a more defensive, discriminating display of stubborn defiance. But the damage was already done.

When you stand in front of a big Rothko, one of the big red ones shown at Tate Modern in 2008, it is impossible to see the entire canvas – to see it steadily and see it whole, in the words of Matthew Arnold. You can't get far enough back, so your eye is compelled to ponder the pigment in close up. The long view

---

Infinite Jest (Abacus, 1997); *The Pale King* (Hamish Hamilton, 2011).

is impossible. You might as well have a painting an inch from your eyeball. It is curious how powerfully disorienting it is to be visually stifled, to be deprived of conventional space, to be unable to see every border. Reading David Foster Wallace – *Infinite Jest*, *The Pale King* – is a little like that (though *The Pale King* is more pleasingly organised and shapely, perhaps thanks to the editorial intervention of Michael Pietsch). Size matters. Especially when the size doesn't permit you to judge the actual size. Jonathan Franzen, in a *New Yorker* piece (18 April 2011), reminisced that Foster Wallace had signed one of his books for Franzen: 'on the title page ... was an outline of an erection so huge that it ran off the page, annotated with a little arrow and the remark "scale 100%".' You see? Well, no, you don't quite.

What you sense, though, is ambition. Which is universally praised. Almost as though it were achievement. This is Updike on ambition. He is talking to Ian McEwan (*Areté*, Issue 15, Autumn 2004): 'There's a number of young American writers but they don't have much of a platform, I think. They either write a magnum opus or nothing.' McEwan: 'The wish to write the great American novel seems strong.' Updike: 'I know. And it seems to me such a bogus ambition, such a crippling ambition to *begin* with. Better to begin modestly and it becomes great under your hands. You discover its greatness. *Ulysses* began as a short story, one more Dubliner. But to begin with the notion of bigness is daunting to the author and I would think somewhat paralysing.'

David Foster Wallace certainly found it so and we have *The Pale King* only because his editor tidied the loose ends and made 'the story and characters as comprehensible as possible' – which obviously meant binning what Foster Wallace called 'Zero drafts' and 'freewriting'. 'Binning' in this case means the University of Texas's Harry Ransom Center – where 'the complete original drafts of these chapters, and the entire mass of material from which [*The Pale King*] was *culled*' (my italics) will eventually be deposited.

Famously, Foster Wallace was a tennis player – a gifted junior. Nabokov on Joyce: 'my prose is patball compared to Joyce's champion game.' In his introduction to *Lolita*, Martin Amis demurred, placing Nabokov higher than Joyce when he considered Nabokov's solid series of Grand Slam titles. This is Foster Wallace on Hal Incadenza's style of tennis in *Infinite Jest*: 'Hal's game involves attrition. He'll probe, pecking, until some angle opens up. Until then he'll probe. He'd rather run his man ragged, wear him down. Three different opponents this past summer had to go to oxygen during breaks.' Often the breathless reader of Foster Wallace feels like an opponent being worn down in an 'endless butterfly-shaped rally' – by the prose of attrition, accumulation, accretion. If this is Joyce, it is Joyce restricted to 'Ithaca', the catechistic pedantic section of *Ulysses* described by Joyce as the novel's ugly duckling. It is prose of the long game by a talented writer with limitations. There are very few aces.

In his essay about Tracy Austin, he produces an ace. The basketball player Michael Jordan 'hanging in midair like a Chagall bride'. Here are some more examples of touch-play. Listen to the clever dull clinks in this sentence: 'the station's flagpole's flag's rope's pulleys and joists clinked dully in the wind' (*The Pale King*, page 512). Or 'dogs lay throbbing in the smoke tree's shade' (*The Pale King*, page 56). 'A nameless cat oozes by on the broad windowsill' (*Infinite Jest*, page 278). Or 'the room's carbonated silence' (*Infinite Jest*, page 8). There aren't many of these outright winners.

In his *New York Times* piece (20 August 2006) about Federer and Nadal at Wimbledon, Foster Wallace revisits the idea that 'there is about world-class athletes carving out exemptions from physical laws a transcendent beauty that makes manifest God in man' ('How Tracy Austin Broke My Heart'). In the *New York Times*, he modestly credits a driver with this perception: in 'the literally withering heat and then wind and rain of the '06 fortnight, then you are apt to have what one of the tournament's press bus drivers describes as a "bloody near-religious experience". It may be tempting, at first, to hear a phrase like this as just one more of the over-heated tropes that people resort to to describe the feeling of the Federer Moment. But the driver's phrase turns out to be true – literally, for an instant ecstatically – though it takes some time and serious watching to see this truth emerge.' And he tells us how Federer's view of the ball is bigger. The word 'literally' is repeated twice in that passage. This is artless, even clumsy, but it is also artful. It insists. Foster Wallace wants to persuade us that a metaphor, a hyperbole, is literally true. That a metaphor isn't a metaphor at all.

Are we convinced? As we *are* convinced by Michael Jordan 'like a Chagall bride'. Prepare yourself for 'today's power-baseline game' and the arduous prose that Foster Wallace deploys to capture it.

Nadal is serving a lot faster than he did in Paris, and this one's down the center. Federer floats a soft forehand high over the net, which he can get away with because Nadal never comes in behind his serve. The Spaniard now hits a characteristically heavy topspin forehand deep to Federer's backhand; Federer comes back with an even heavier topspin backhand, almost a clay-court shot. It's unexpected and backs Nadal up, slightly, and his response is a low hard short ball that lands just past the service line's T on Federer's forehand side. Against most other opponents, Federer could simply end the point on a ball like this, but one reason Nadal gives him trouble is that he's faster than the others, can get to stuff they can't; and so Federer here just hits a flat, medium-hard cross-court forehand, going not for a winner but for a low, shallowly angled ball that forces Nadal up and out to the deuce side [right-hand side], his backhand. Nadal, on the run, backhands it hard down the line to Federer's backhand; Federer slices it right back down the same line, slow and floaty with backspin, making Nadal come back to the same spot. Nadal slices the ball right back – three shots now all down the same line – and Federer slices the ball back to the same spot yet again, this one even slower and floatier, and Nadal gets planted and hits a big two-hander back down the same line – it's like Nadal's camped out now on his deuce side; he's no longer moving all the way back to the baseline's center between shots; Federer's hypnotised him a little. Federer now hits a very hard, deep topspin backhand, the kind that hisses, to a point just slightly on the ad [advantage] side of Nadal's baseline, which Nadal gets to and forehands cross-court; and Federer responds with an even harder, heavier cross-court backhand, baseline-deep and moving so fast that Nadal has to hit the forehand off his back foot and then scramble to get back to center as the shot lands maybe two feet short on Federer's backhand side again. Federer steps to this ball and now hits a totally different cross-court backhand, this one much shorter and sharper-angled, an angle no one would anticipate, and so heavy and blurred with topspin that it lands shallow and just inside the sideline and takes off hard after the bounce, and Nadal can't move in to cut it off and can't get to it laterally along the baseline, because of all the angle and topspin – end of point. It's a spectacular winner, a Federer Moment; but watching it live, you can see that it's also a winner that Federer started setting up four or even five shots earlier. Everything after that first down-the-line slice was designed by the Swiss to manoeuvre Nadal and lull him and then disrupt his rhythm and balance and open up that last, unimaginable angle – an angle that would have been impossible without extreme topspin.

Zadie Smith: 'He can do anything with a piece of prose.' Well, it's OK. It's serviceable prose, if oddly academic, apart from a couple of touches: 'the kind that hisses'; 'blurred with topspin'. It's top-class *radio*: you can almost hear Raymond Glendenning quickening his naturally excitable pace as he holds the mike to his handlebar moustache. But it isn't better than television. And it's nothing like being at Wimbledon. And God is nowhere to be seen. Of course, action is very difficult to capture on the page. A picture is worth a thousand words. Timothy Mo once told me that the narrative secret of the fight sequences in his novel *Sour Sweet* was to *analyse* the action rather than to describe it straight. Which is what Foster Wallace does, too. We know beyond doubt that Federer doesn't go for the outright winner straight away. Neither does Foster Wallace.

And sometimes, it pays off. On page 157 of *Infinite Jest*, 'Winter BS 1960 – Tucson AZ', he gives us the extended drunken monologue of James Incandenza's father to the ten-year-old Jim. It is a twelve-page tour de force of fluidity, untouched by the usual comedy that drunkenness mostly attracts in fiction: 'C'mere c'mere c'mere c'mere'; 'What say I put the last of this out of its amber misery.' The slurs are all in the syntax. It is, surprisingly, eloquent – eloquent with the soaked misery of a son (now a father) telling *his* son how his father had no emotional investment in him as a son. It comes out of nowhere, holds you, disappears. James Incandenza says nothing – and that, too, is eloquent in its different, telling way.

In *The Pale King*, the sustained monologue of Meredith Rand – the pretty girl whose 'burdensome beauty' takes her into the loony bin – succeeds in holding the reader's attention for sixty pages of unflinching, repetitive disclosure to Shane Drinion, a worker ant at the IRS with the gift of attention. (He is also gifted, helplessly, with the ability to levitate when he is paying absolute attention. He stands for the reader. He is, though, an old-fashioned, implausible confidant, lent improbable individuality by his silent levitation.) Equally gripping, equally flawed, is Fogle's powerful – because affectless – account of his father's death on the Chicago subway. He is caught in the doors. Fogle can't help parenthetically reporting that the train 'was stainless steel and tan plastic, with both full and partially pulled-off holly decals around some of the car's windows'.

Chapter 39 has a compelling account of an irritable carpentry teacher losing his thumb while demonstrating how dangerous the machine can be. It has none of the economy of Robert Frost's 'Out, Out –'. Sample: 'For reasons now lost in the administrative mists [*sic*], Industrial Arts was then required of male tenth-graders across the upper Midwest, giving the Vocational Ed pupils a last chance to savage and torment the College Prep boys from whom they'd been (in Michigan) split off the previous year. And Leonard Stecyk had an especially hard time of it in Mr Ingle's third-hour Industrial Arts class at Charles E. Potter High School in the autumn of 1969. It was not just that at almost sixteen Stecyk was 5'1" and a 105 pounds soaking wet ...' Etc. Amazingly the moment of thumb-loss survives the pedantry of its setting forth.

Sometimes it doesn't pay off. For example, *Infinite Jest*, page 273, contains this list of inmates in rehab: 'it was one reason he'd even been able to stick out his nine residential months here with twenty-one other newly detoxed housebreakers, hoods, whores, fired execs, Avon ladies, subway musicians, beer-bloated construction workers, vagrants, indignant car salesmen, bulimic trauma-mamas, hunky artists, mincing pillow-biters, North End hard guys, pimply kids with electric nose-rings, denial-ridden housewives and etc.' Whitman could do lists. Randall Jarrell memorably said of a passage in Whitman's *Song of Myself* that 'anyone who could call this a list would boil his babies up for soap.'

Foster Wallace loves lists, he has a crush on lists, but he can't do them: 'also available are lobster rolls, lobster turnovers, lobster sauté, Down East lobster salad, lobster bisque, lobster ravioli, and deep-fried lobster dumplings. Lobster thermidor is available at a sit-down restaurant.' Of course, the excess is meant to mirror the excess. But it is the chute school of prose – pour it on, wholesale – taken from the New Journalism's prodigal use of space – and done to death.

In 'Consider the Lobster', there is an ominous, a terrible sentence: 'all this is right there in the encyclopedia.' Foster Wallace's default narrative mode is to aspire to the encyclopedia. With it comes bureaucratic locution, mannered and stilted: 'Be apprised, though'; 'see, for example, the aforementioned Main Eating Tent'; 'a good percentage of the total noise was masticatory'; 'the smells, which latter are strong and only partly food-related'; 'the above-mentioned paradox'; 'as a purely observational sick-note, be apprised'; 'is it all right to boil a sentient creature alive just for our gustatory pleasure?'; 'Be further advised'; 'suffice it to say' (all from 'Consider the Lobster', but I could throw in 'in videos heretofore' from 'Big Red Son', his essay on pornography. Or this government leafletese from *Infinite Jest*, about a kid who has eaten mould: his mother, 'countenancing evidence of oral contact with same', is upset. *Countenancing. With same.*

Did I mention coaxials? In 'Big Red Son', Foster Wallace describes the klieg-glitter of Caesar's Forum and mentions that 'mysterious bundles of co-ax emerge from under the Forum doors.' A flourish of technical expertise. No explanation. On page 183 of *Infinite Jest*, we read 'pumps the music up the coaxial medulla'; on page 241, 'high-voltage grids and coaxial chokers strung with beads of ceramic insulators'; on page 268, 'all this year's conspicuous tech-wonks mounting the heaters and stringing the lights and running coaxial shunts'; on page 369 of *The Pale King*, 'I've seen two IBM RPGs in a closet with an unbelievable tangle of co-ax.' Co-axial cable is plural – cables with a flexible, tubular, insulating layer. Sleeved electrical sphagetti. Now you know.

There is a place for the technical in literature. Think of the numbles passage in *Gawain and the Green Knight*, with its detailed description / instructions for preparing game – detailed and nine tenths unintelligible. Think of Shakespeare flaunting nautical terms at the beginning of *The Tempest* – 'Bring her to try wi'th' maincourse' – as an economical shorthand to summon up a ship. In Foster Wallace, though, there is a wonk who is unable to resist the lure of insider dealing. Acronyms abound. Self-congratulatory. Exclusive. Inner circle.

Detail is the essence of fiction. But in Foster Wallace there is no essence, no concentration, no selection. As he increasingly realised. In *The Pale King*, he makes a bogus appearance as 'David Wallace' in Chapter 24 and decries his favoured fictional method:

> I am about art here, not simple reproduction. What logorrheic colleagues like Fogle [elsewhere designated as 'Irrelevant Fogle'] failed to understand is that there are vastly different kinds of truth, some of which are incompatible with one another. Example: A 100 percent accurate, comprehensive list of the exact size and shape of every blade of grass in my front lawn is 'true', but it is not a truth that anyone will have any interest in. What renders a truth meaningful, worthwhile, & c. is its relevance, which in turn requires extraordinary discernment and sensitivity to context, questions of value, and overall point – otherwise *we might as well just be computers downloading raw data to one another.* [my italics].

This is a motif of *The Pale King*. Fogle constantly worries if his deposition and life story is 'relevant'. On page 340, there is an induction lecture on the need for selectivity. One IRS agent gets tetchy about the irrelevant detail supplied by another, Sylvanshine: Sylvanshine (paradoxically) adds into his reports touches we readers recognise as novelistic colour – not strictly utilitarian but supplying felt life, concreteness, description. Sylvanshine, it turns out, is a 'fact psychic': his brain bombards him with random facts, like who invented luggage wheels, who sprayed the candy-frosting coat on a cup-cake, a Hostess cup-cake, and what that person's bowling average is.

The *cri de cœur* of 'David Wallace' in Chapter 24 is followed by *pages* on 'logistical absurdities' – like the irrational layout of the access road to the IRS HQ in Peroria. *Like traffic cones.* The narrative problem is formulated but left unsolved. Perhaps it is a ponderous joke. Perhaps Foster Wallace couldn't stop himself. That's just the way his mind worked. I think he couldn't stop himself bingeing. It isn't a joke.

'Irrelevant Fogle' casts some light here. He is a 'wastoid', a drug-taker, who finds salvation in the IRS, in the heroism of accountancy. One of the drugs he previously favoured was Obetrol, 'chemically related to Dexedrine'. He describes its effect as increasing awareness:

> I'm still not entirely sure what I meant by this, nor why it seemed so profound and cool not only to be in a room but be totally aware that I was in the room, seated in a certain position listening to a specific track of an album whose cover was a certain specific combination of colors and designs – being in a state of heightened enough awareness to be able to

say to myself, '*I am in this room right now. The shadow of the foot* [a neon street sign] *is rotating on the east wall. The shadow is not recognisable as a foot because of the deformation of the angle of the light of the sun's position behind the sign. I am seated upright in a dark-green easy chair with a cigarette burn on the right armrest. The cigarette burn is black and imperfectly round. The track I am listening to is "The Big Ship" off of Brian Eno's* Another Green World, *whose cover has colorful cutout figures inside a white frame.*'

He concludes: 'Stated so openly, this amount of detail might seem tedious, but it wasn't.' It was 'paying attention' – the very thing needed to sift and sort tax returns at IRS. The analysis of Obertrol and its effects is expert, probably first-hand, and would account for the overkill in the prose, its willingness to include, its tolerance of superfluous detail.

We know that Foster Wallace took drugs in large quantities. If you want to know how to cook up crack cocaine and smoke the rocks, see pages 237–8 of *Infinite Jest*. Drugs figure prominently in *Infinite Jest* and less large but meaning-fully in *The Pale King*. Jonathan Franzen in his *New Yorker* piece proposes that a significant proportion of Foster Wallace's readership was made up of drug users or former drug users – familiar with disabling paranoia, and the mental impedi-menta of drug use. *Infinite Jest* has quite a funny early chapter about giving up drugs, disposing of bongs, while at the same time ordering a huge assignment of Bob Hope from a female contact. (Dope to you and me.) I imagine that recid-ivist drug users find this hilarious – whereas I was only aware of how much its comedy owed to Heller's *Catch-22*. 'He had never been so anxious for the arrival of a woman he did not want to see.' *Catch-22* is parent to any number of comic paradoxes and double-binds in Foster Wallace's fiction.

And Foster Wallace's humorous riffs are drug-dependent, too. As chillis are categorised in terms of hotness by multiples of chilli pods, so some of these jokes should be designated by one joint, two joints, three joints and four joints. On page 218 of *Infinite Jest*, we are told of a demon tennis doubles pair who are unbeatable because they are Siamese twins joined at the head so they share a brain – and are therefore perfectly coordinated. Except, the spoilsport interjects, that their movement, their court coverage, would be significantly impaired, handicapped even. A four joint (!) riff. On the same page is another giggle-weed joke about a woman, met via email, who in person turned out to have 'like just one enormous tit in the exact middle of her chest or something like that'.

Foster Wallace's weakness for comic exaggeration is also, I believe, drug-related. In 'Big Red Son', the essay on the porn Oscars, there are people who get too close to the mike 'and produce a jolt of feedback that sends people and cocktails flying out of chairs in the first rows of tables'. I don't think so. The drugs are talking. The drugs are writing – as they are in Chapter 29 of *The Pale King*, the chapter about various forms of shit in various places, which ends with this anecdote of coarse farce. A bunch of students think it's funny to sit a naked arse on the sleeping faces of fellow-students and disappear before they're fully awake. However, Diabolo the Left-Handed Surrealist (don't ask)

> waited until Fat Marcus the Moneylender's ass was right down next to him, touching his face but not with the full weight of the ass on him yet, and jerked up and bit into Fat Marcus's ass. And I'm not talking a lover-nip here, I'm talking a full front Doberman-type sinking of his whole frontal set of teeth into the buttock arc of Marcus's ass, so that even down by his ankle I could see blood going down the Surrealist's chin and see Fat Marcus the Moneylender's ass flexing as he reared back and let out a scream that made the windows shiver and knocked the two guys holding Diabolo the Left-Handed Surrealist's shoulders back against a row of no-eye masks the spic's got on his wall that all fell and made a racket and could see the horrible thing of this unbelievably obese guy rearing back and up and trying with all his weight to get his ass out of the teeth of Diabolo the Left-Handed Surrealist, who gentlemen just let me say was letting go, the kid was a Gila monster, even as fat Marcus had both hands hooked in the kid's nose trying to peel him off his ass and Fat Marcus's main stooge Marvin 'the Stooge' Flotkoetter actually bent in and was biting Diabolo the Left-Handed Surrealist's ear and cheek, trying to make him let go, and both him and Diabolo were growling and Diabolo was shaking his head trying to tear the mouthful of ass clear out of Fat Marcus's ass and his nose and ear were bleeding and blood was just shooting I mean arterially shooting in all directions out of Marcus's ass and into the mattress and his pants and Fat Marcus took a shit in fear and pain ...

There is one significant word here – 'unbelievably' ...

You can find something similar in 'Big Red Son', page 21, a foot-noted brawl involving several participants and culminating in the 'dislodging [of] H H's special autotint trifocals and sending them out into an arc across the room and into the forbidding décolletage of Ms Christy Canyon, never to be recovered (the glasses) or even ever seen again.' I can't make my fingers type out the whole thing. You'll just have to take my word for it. I spliffed my sides laughing.

I know: these are anecdotes; exaggeration is the staple of anecdote; but neither of these gross-out sequences works as successfully as the cartoon violence they emulate. Nor are they offered in the spirit of irony. This is Jackass – the

Prose Version. And it doesn't work. Not without a hit of Bob from a bong.

Much has been made of Foster Wallace's determination to surpass *Infinite Jest*, to break new ground with *The Pale King*. We have already noted his unease about downloading life in his fiction, file after file of raw data. Central to this determination is his choice of subject: the IRS, tax collectors in America. What could be further from a doped tennis academy, the drug-addled experiences of low-lifer Don Gately and a film so funny that it killed people who couldn't stop watching it. (They died laughing. Ho, ho.) Strangely, the theme of *The Pale King* is predicted in *Infinite Jest*: 'That boring activities become, perversely, much less boring if you concentrate on them' (page 203). Compare Shane Drinion in *The Pale King* (page 456): 'Well, I would say almost anything you pay close, direct attention to becomes interesting.' To write about boredom – that would be new, testing, difficult.

There is a key chapter which records unflinchingly IRS operatives turning pages. 'Matt Redgate turns a page. R. Jarvis Brown turns a page.' And so on, for four pages. The joke is that these pages are laid out in double column – like book-keeping entries. Reviewers have singled out these pages as radical, if rebarbative, mimesis of crushing monotony. They all omit to say that there are three anomalous sentences interpolated into the mindless catalogue of repetition. Viz.: 'Devils are actually angels'; 'Two clocks, two ghosts, one square acre of hidden mirror'; 'Every love story is a ghost story.' From the remnant of *The Pale King* that has reached publication, it is possible to say more about the ghosts. They are different from the phantoms who bother IRS operatives at the edge of terminal boredom. The two ghosts are Frederick Blumquist, fifty-three, who died at his desk, unnoticed for four days, and Garrity, 'a line inspector for Mid West Mirror Works', also the victim of monotony in the workplace.

The ghosts are interesting because they demonstrate Foster Wallace's failure of nerve about his project. He isn't convinced he can make the boring interesting. The small change of experience – those tax inspectors – isn't enough, so he throws ersatz money at the project. We're looking at narrative inflation, fiduciary paper, quantitative easing – a fact psychic, ghosts and (spectacularly unpersuasive) a blow-job given ('woodpeckerishly') to the author (in a footnote) by a complete IRS stranger nicknamed 'the Iranian Crisis'. She has mistaken 'David Wallace' for another David Wallace, higher up the tax hierarchy who therefore requires 'every courtesy' – a phrase she takes to mean fellation. We are in the presence of screwball comedy, I fear.

(It takes a very good writer like Adam Mars-Jones to make small change go a long way, as he does in *Cedilla* for nigh on 1,000 pages. That novel is like the miracle of the loaves and the fishes. Two sardines and one tin of tuna, as it were, are somehow deliciously extended without any sense of strain. Not a lot happens. Mars-Jones's gay hero is confined to a wheelchair, so not a lot *can* happen. The *blurb* to *Cedilla* is a masterpiece of comedy, funnier than anything Foster Wallace wrote. But Mars-Jones is an acerbic critic, so Foster Wallace acclaim isn't on offer, only continent praise. No one is marvelling at the scale of *Cedilla* or its predecessor, *Pilcrow*, because they are so ostentatiously miniature despite their manifest length. Nicholson Baker is another novelist who can take out Foster Wallace – in straight sets – as he captures minutiae, like his baby daughter's genitalia. 'Her captivating coffee bean' couldn't be improved on.)

Actually, Foster Wallace's new project isn't *that* different from the old one. Of course, *Infinite Jest* is superficially more zany than *The Pale King*, but it occurred to me unbidden that the minutiae of tennis – those 'sticks', those heads, that stringing, ranking, training, instructional film, the wood Wilsons in their 'trapezoid presses', armfuls of 'sticks' like an 'obscene bouquet' and so forth – are just as unpromising, just as boring, as the IRS. *Infinite Jest* is encyclopedic about tennis – everything you need to know and more. On page 110, you can learn how to hit a forehand. Sample: 'the fluid transfer of weight to the front foot as the ball ...' Check it out. It's roughly equivalent to 'Jay Landauer turns a page. Ryne Hobratschk turns a page and then folds over the page of a computer printout that's lined up next to the original file he just turned a page of.' Foster Wallace isn't a genius. He is a top contestant on Mastermind and his special subject is tennis – followed by taxation as an encore. An analogy prompted by the quizzing of Hal Incandenza on page 95 of *Infinite Jest* – he memorises everything he reads: 'He can scan the page, rotate it, fold the corner down and clean under his nails with it, all mentally.' Asked to define *acutance*, he answers: 'a measure of resolution directly proportional to the resolved ratio of a given pulse's digital code.' Anyone wanting to be baffled – seeing difficulty as a condition of great modern literature – will see this as a way to separate the dilettante from the true disciple.

In 'Reflections of a Kept Ape', Ian McEwan addresses the problem of the second novel. The story is narrated by an ape who is the (neglected) lover of the novelist Sally Klee. He rifles her locked desk drawer (from the rear, removing the back panel) when she is out and discovers that her days of 'writing' are actually days of typing – she has been typing out her first novel again, word for word identical. It is a piquant version of the problem – what next? – heightened for comic purpose.

The Pale King owes a surprising amount to its predecessor *Infinite Jest*. For example, on page 43 of *Infinite Jest*, Orin Incandenza sees 'the sun like a sneaky keyhole view of hell'. Anyone who hates this kind of rhetorical prose will be irritated by its recycling on page 156 of *The Pale King*: 'the sun overhead like a peephole into hell's own self-consuming heart'. (Why do novelists think this kind of stuff is poetic when it is only overwritten?) On page 9 of *The Pale King*: 'Look down your shirt and spell *attic.*' On page 973 of *Infinite Jest*: 'He remembered being young on the playground and telling Maureen Duffy to look down her shirt and spell *attic.*' (The feeblest of jokes recycled. Spell it aloud.) In *The Pale King* (page 392): 'an adult who has recently inhaled helium out of a decorative balloon'. *Infinite Jest* (page 318): 'some helium-voiced girl'.

The Pale King begins with a page and a half of uncharacteristic prose – definitely *written*, less vernacular, less discursive. Pietsch, the editor, has chosen well. It looks like new territory. It isn't. And it isn't very good. There is a morning breeze 'like a mother's soft hand on your cheek'. There is 'ale-colored sunshine and pale sky' – just as on page 213 of *Infinite Jest* there was 'a bubble of ale-colored autumn sunlight'. Beyond the field, 'the shush of the interstate off past the windbreak', whereas *Infinite Jest* (page 16) had 'the street's passing traffic is constant and seems to go "Hush, hush, hush".' This is better than the even more gussied 'long-haul trucks on 54 for Santa Fe whose tires' plaint had the quality of distant surf's lalation'. *Plaint. Lalation.* This is what a *writer* can do to that old familiar, the surf of traffic. On this opening page, we have the 'tobacco-brown river', so striking that it's given a second outing on page 270 as 'the tobacco-colored Illinois River', just before a telling paragraph on traffic cones ... Then there are 'horses in the distance standing rigid and still as toys' – so rigid and still, in fact, that in the next sentence they are 'all nodding'.

I daresay repetitions can be excused by the unfinished state of *The Pale King* So what if the insects are repetitively 'electric'? If Jonathan Franzen affirms that 'David wrote about weather *as well as anyone who ever put words on paper*' (my emphasis: has he been talking to Zadie Smith?), what does it matter that this brilliance comes around like a suitcase on a luggage carousel? Is it the same suitcase? It looks slightly different. My examples are taken not from *The Pale King* but *Infinite Jest*. Page 43: 'heat shimmers off the deck like fumes from fuel. There's that mirage thing where the extreme heat makes the dry deck look wet with fuel.' Page 109: 'air that swam and shimmered like the area behind jet engines'. Page 136: 'the air has that spilled-fuel shimmer to it.' Page 17: 'dazzling sunlight and cracked earth with heat-shimmers over it'.

And what about the clichés? The borrowings? Not just the huge debt to Heller's *Catch-22*. Nor the comparable debt to Salinger, whose brilliant but disturbed Glass family have been cloned by Foster Wallace as the 'genius' Incandenzas. Particular felonies. Page 1's 'weeping trees and coins of sunlight', courtesy of Joyce's 'Nestor': 'On his wise shoulders through the checkerwork of leaves the sun flung spangles, dancing coins.' Meredith Rand 'exhales two brief tusks of smoke' on page 465. In *Lolita*, Chapter 11, 'the smoke she exhaled from her nostrils was like a pair of tusks.' *Infinite Jest* gives us, courtesy of *Pnin*, this image (page 5): 'my chest bumps like a drier with shoes in it.' Pnin, you'll recall, gives his landlord's washing machine a pair of gym shoes to 'play with' and hears 'a dreadful arhythmical tramp'.

As for gussied clichés: 'the gathering storms' and 'lost in the administrative mists' (*PK*, page 416); 'nail-tough' for hard as nails (*IJ*, page 137); for gooseflesh, 'his bare arms had the plucked-chicken look of chilled and bare skin in its grotesque sleeveless dress' (*IJ*, page 127); 'vanished in some bureaucratic puff of violet smoke' (*PK*, page 11); 'his trademark fedora' ('Big Red Son', page 13); 'his trademark glower' ('Big Red Son', page 15); 'a thorny question' ('Big Red Son', page 18); 'either the iceberg's tip or the camel's straw' ('Big Red Son', page 21: 2 for 1); 'flinty-eyed casino guys' ('Big Red Son', page 46); 'a flinty-eyed entourage of bureaucrats and implementers' (*PK*, page 147); 'that whole Pandora's box of worms' (*IJ*, page 49); 'lets his psychological hair down' (*IJ*, page 79); 'but the real coffin-nail for videophony' (*IJ*, page 147); 'makes a freebase hangover look like a day at the emotional beach' (*IJ*, page 271). I could multiply examples. Flinty-eyed is a bit of a favourite ('flinty-eyed tire-executive's daughters', *IJ*, page 218), but let's stop with tight as a drum: needlepoint's 'sterile white cotton stretched drum-tight in its round frame' (*IJ*, page 275); 'Ewell's drum-tight bunk' (*IJ*, page 209); 'the drum-tight bed' (*IJ*, page 214).

Obviously a style so dependent on the vernacular is bound to contain an admixture of clichés. So let me conclude with Foster Wallace's central weakness: his lack of economy, that fatal prolixity. Here is an insincere smile from the beginning of *Infinite Jest*: the Dean of ETA's 'fixed smile nevertheless has the impermanent quality of something stamped into uncooperative material.' Not bad. Passable. Another insincere smile, also from *Infinite Jest* (page 75): 'And she gave him back a frightening smile, a smile empty of all affect, as if someone had contracted her circumorals with a thigmotactic electrode. The teeth of the smile evidenced a clinical depressive's classical inattention to oral hygiene.'

Insincere smiles. Now think of Henry James in *The Bostonians* summoning up Oliver Chancellor's smile, 'like a ray of moonlight on a prison wall'. Or Byron on Castlereagh's smile, 'like the silver plate on a coffin lid'. Both better because swifter. (The cliché is 'rapier wit'. With David Foster Wallace, it is Swiss army knife wit. Specifically, the SwissChamp XLT, which looks like a cheese mite under a microscope.) Neither the James nor the Byron is as brilliant as Twain describing the mirthless laugh of Sherburn in Chapter 22 of *Huckleberry Finn*: 'the kind that makes you feel like when you are eating bread that's got sand in it.'

Mostly Foster Wallace doesn't try as hard as he does in these examples. This is a description of a Mrs Sloper in *The Pale King*: 'the DDP's horrific secretary /

receptionist, Mrs Sloper, who on this first day gave me the exact same look of incurious distaste I would receive from her for the next thirteen months, and wore (this I sure remember) a lavenderish pants suit against which the abundant rouge and kohl were even more ghastly. She was maybe fifty, and very thin and tendony, and had the same asymmetrical beehive coiffure as two different older females in my own family, and was made up like an embalmed clown, the stuff of nightmares.' *The stuff of nightmares.*

This is Saul Bellow on Grandma Lausch: 'with the holder in her dark little gums between which all her guile, malice, and command issued, she had her best inspirations of strategy. She was wrinkled as an old paper bag, an autocrat, hard-shelled and jesuitical, a pouncy old hawk of a Bolshevik, her small ribboned gray feet immobile on the shoe-kit and stool Simon had made in manual-training class.' Bellow's *Augie March* is a vernacular masterpiece, relaxed but precise. He could really write. I think that Foster Wallace thought he was doing something similar. He wasn't.

Eliot's Inferno: The Letters
(2009)

Letters give us the life as lived – day to day, shapeless, haphazard, contingent, imperfect, authentic. That is their value. Life-writing, biography, is plotted, shaped by an argument and is summary, selective and often tendentious. There is a lovely moment in these letters when the shivering Eliot, trapped on the top of a French mountain, a long mule ride from civilisation, is writing to Richard Aldington on a defective typewriter. It sticks and repeats. 'I'm writing there fore the r therefore more briefly than I intended and shall do when I get to Nice again and hie h ire hire a typewriter *merde*.' Half of each letter is missing. 'This type looks just like Hebrew.' For a brief existential moment, the amused irritation of a complicated, deeply troubled man, at the end of his tether, whose dangerously loopy wife is in a nursing home, 'recovering' but actually on the edge. The typewriter is part of unedited, impure, actual life. It wouldn't make it into the Life.

We read the letters of writers for high reasons – to illuminate their art. And for low reasons – to discover, as it were, what they were like in bed. We would like to catch them unbuttoned, if possible with their trousers down. Curiosity is a powerful, ineradicable human instinct. In T. S. Eliot's case, hostile critics are eager for shameful revelations of anti-Semitism and misogyny.

Vol. II covers the inception of the *Criterion*, usefully outlines the magazine's Tory, classicist, reactionary stance and reproduces much repetitive editorial boiler-plate. The drab commendably elided by biography. Eliot's editorial persona is in place, except to Ezra Pound: 'It doan matter a toad's fart,' writes Eliot, emulating Ezra's forthright, backwoods manner. There isn't much here to compel the ordinary reader, except for unsurprising moments of venial hypocrisy. To Middleton Murry, on the death of Katherine Mansfield, Eliot condoles and promises an assessment of her work in the *Criterion*. It never appeared. Eliot's verdict (to Pound) on Katherine Mansfield in Vol. I: 'simply one of the most persistent and thickskinned toadies and one of the vulgarest women Lady R [Rothermere] has ever met and is also a sentimental crank.'

On 11 May 1923, Eliot writes to Ford Madox Ford: 'I like your essay "From this Grey Rock" very much.' On 4 October, Eliot is complaining to Pound that Ford is 'rhetorical, verbose and damned vulgar'. To Gertrude Stein, Eliot pro-

The Letters of T. S. Eliot. Volume I: 1898–1922. Volume II: 1923–1925. Edited by Valerie Eliot and Hugh Haughton (Faber and Faber, 2009).

fesses to be 'immensely interested in everything you write'. A little earlier, he states she 'is quite meaningless to me'. She is published in the *Criterion*, 1 January 1926. He flatters Saintsbury as the 'most eminent critic of our time', publishes him, benefits from his status, and to Lady Rothermere damns as dull his article on 'Dullness'. He needed names, even while he predicted disaster for the *Dial* because of 'its mania for popular names'.

These discrepancies, these social compromises – tactful, hypocritical, tactical, strategic – aren't uncommon currency. None of us is totally honest. If we were, there would be devastation all around us – as there is around Gregers Werle, the truth-teller in Ibsen's *The Wild Duck*.

Actually, Eliot's integrity, probity and impartiality are more or less permanently present and correct. Sometimes irritatingly so for a friend like Virginia Woolf: 'drop by drop of his agonized perplexities fall ever so finely through pure cambric.' This volume begins with a letter to his elder brother Henry Ware Eliot, expressing a scruple about money and whether Eliot should cash Henry's fraternal cheque. It ends with Eliot attempting to persuade F. L. Lucas to let Fabers and Gwyer see his purported novel. Lucas had rinsed *The Waste Land*. But Eliot displays an unruffled, urbane impartiality. As he does to John Crowe Ransom: 'I have probably a higher opinion of your verse than you have of mine.' Ransom had also been rude about *The Waste Land*. He publishes Clive Bell in the *Criterion* despite Bell's attack on him in the *Nation*. He seems not to have harboured disabling grudges.

His doctor Hubert Higgins proffers his 'most respectful admiration' for what he identifies as Eliot's 'new England conscience'. In his dealings with Lloyds Bank, Eliot is concerned to behave well, to avoid 'ingratitude': 'If I left the bank now I should simply be hanging another millstone round my conscience.' He is principled to people and (a rare quality) to institutions. He takes no payment for his editorial work for the *Criterion*. He thanks Edmund Wilson, but enters the reservation that praise is less pleasing if he, Eliot, is used as a stick to beat Pound. He wants justice, poetic justice, for Pound, too. He touches this sore patch again when he writes to Gilbert Seldes at the *Dial*. It isn't a pose, it is a preoccupation. Eliot is sometimes seen as a cold careerist. Here we watch him sedulously supporting two often exasperating comrades-in-arms, raucous Pound and the swiftly nettled Wyndham Lewis. About Lewis, Eliot mildly remarks that he is so insolent it is difficult to patch up quarrels. He explains truthfully to Lewis: 'You surely know by this time that I have had a continuous and disinterested desire to push your work as far as in my power.'

Faber have reissued Vol. I with approximately 200 new letters. Many of these new letters, perhaps half, are not by Eliot, but by his wife Vivien, his mother, his father ('I hope that a cure for syphilis will never be discovered. It is God's punishment for nastiness'), his brother and his patron John Quinn. Eliot's own new letters are mostly brief, businesslike and boring. But there is one fragment of a letter to his brother, consoling Henry over a disappointed love affair and adding that he (Eliot) lives 'among a set of people some of whom would probably shock your friends (all of them) terribly by varieties of "immorality" with no pretense' (Clive Bell's relationship with Mary Hutchinson, Bertrand Russell's relationship with Ottoline Morrell, and Bloomsbury homosexuality *passim*).

In Earl Griggs's magisterial six-volume edition of Coleridge's letters, there is, in the final volume, an appendix containing newly discovered letters from 1795 to 1831. These late finds are inevitable. There will be further Eliot letters – little caches like those to Edgar Jepson incorporated here. Normally, the Griggs method is the only sensible one. But Eliot's letters are a special case. When Vol. I originally appeared, there were accusations of suppression when ill-disposed critics failed to find evidence of careerism and rabid anti-Semitism. The record has to be as complete as it can be – now. The distortion of editorial method, the extra expense to the reader, is inevitable in the mistrustful critical climate created by Anthony Julius's study of Eliot's alleged anti-Semitism and Julius's more aggressive supporters.

Actually, in two volumes of about 1,700 pages, there are perhaps two (maybe three) questionable moments, none of them conclusive. Length less than a page in all. There *is* open anti-Semitism in these letters, expressed by John Quinn (flagrantly) and Eliot's mother (regretfully). In the past, Eliot has been found guilty by association, by the company he keeps. Eliot's mother is uneasy with her prejudice: 'Have I previously answered your letter? It seems as if I had previously referred to the Jew, Bodenheim. It is very bad in me, but I have an instinctive antipathy to Jews, just as I have to certain animals. Of course there are Jews and Jews, and I must not be so much narrow-minded, as narrow in my sympathies. There must be something in them which to me is antipathetic. Father never liked to have business dealings with them, and they took advantage of Henry in the Publisher's Press.' In castigating herself, Mrs Eliot seems to be referring to a previous letter of Eliot's – perhaps complaining about the reference to Bodenheim? She is certainly responding to something already raised, something more likely to be a demurral from her favourite son than an endorsement. She is explaining, backing down.

Quinn is an unapologetic anti-Semite. But we should mark the continence of Eliot, when compared to Quinn: 'the streets and sidewalks are infested ... with swarms of horrible looking Jews, low, squat, animal-like.' Eliot is more concerned that Horace Liveright, his Jewish publisher, should pay up monies owed. He upbraids Liveright directly in the end. To Quinn, who is his proxy in dealing with Eliot's New York business affairs, Eliot writes: 'I am very annoyed about this, *although it is the sort of behaviour which I have been led to expect from Liveright* [my italics]. I am sick of doing business with Jew publishers who will not carry out their part of the contract unless they are forced to; I have not the time nor can I at this distance keep my eye on him incessantly and I hate to bother you with these affairs. I wish I could find a decent Christian publisher in New York who could be trusted.' The prejudice is initially against Liveright. It then engrosses the Jewish sector of American publishing – but isn't hopeful that a decent Christian publisher can be found either. Eliot endorses a prejudice about Jewish publishers and their methods but includes Christian publishers in his disillusionment. (The *OED* records, by the way, 'Jew' as a formerly acceptable adjective, interchangeable with 'Jewish', but no longer allowable or neutral.)

Later (16 February 1925) Eliot writes to Herbert Read: 'I have the same racial prejudice myself; and I am always inclined to suspect the racial envy and jealousy which makes that people [the Jews] inclined to Bolshevism in some form (not always political) though I suspect something of this destructive instinct in Disraeli; in spite of the conventional Tory exaltation of him.' Read's letter is missing. The racial prejudice so openly admitted isn't, read carefully, an admission of anti-Semitism, but an admission of a prejudice that Jews are inclined to 'Bolshevism', in this case, a generalised iconoclasm. Not such a damaging charge, you might think. And, as in the case of his mother, Eliot is prepared to set this down as prejudice. Contrast Quinn, contrast any anti-Semite. They don't describe themselves as *prejudiced*.

Some readers, including the composer Thomas Adès, have related the accusation of 'Bolshevism' to Nazi anti-Semitism and Nazism's idea that the Jews were responsible for the communist revolution. But Eliot was not a Nazi: *The Rock* ironises the Blackshirts and their anti-Semitism. More, Bolshevism here is a tendency to iconoclasm, not something purely political. Eliot cites Disraeli – not an obvious Bolshevik.

Anthony Julius's review of these letters (the *Sunday Telegraph*, 13 December 2009) addresses neither of these incidences, concentrating instead on the 'anti-Semitism' of the postscript of a letter to Mark Van Doren (24 February 1925). Eliot was reviewing *Spring Thunder and Other Poems* by Van Doren for *The Nation* – praising the ruralism of Van Doren and Frost, as a contrast to the 'sham originality' of city-based poetry. The postscript reads: 'If the allusions to Jews are undesirable you may omit them.' To me, this indicates Eliot's sensitivity to Jewish sensitivities. It is not therefore an admission of anti-Semitism – which is what Julius perversely takes it to be: 'he was well aware of the offence that his anti-Semitism was capable of causing and was even willing on occasion to submit to censorship in that respect.' A strange anti-Semite, then, this T. S. Eliot – willing to pander and self-censor, alert to putative offence. (In his *T. S. Eliot:*

Anti-Semitism and Literary Form, Julius portrays Eliot as blind to Jewish offence.) And the 'offensive' sentence itself in Eliot's review? 'Here too the metic plays a large part; for the metic, like the Jew, can only thoroughly naturalise himself in cities.' You might think that the belief that Jewish migrants are more likely to settle in cities than in the countryside isn't the most rabid form of anti-Semitism, but Julius is an adept at evidential massage. He defines 'metic' as 'roughly speaking' meaning 'unwelcome foreigner'. How roughly, how inaccurately speaking, is that exactly? 'Metic' means 'resident alien'.

Had Julius read the volumes under review more carefully, he would have remembered that in the first volume in a letter written by Eliot to Mary Hutchinson (11 July 1919), Eliot describes himself thus: 'remember I am a *metic* – a foreigner, and that I *want* to understand you, and all the background and tradition of you.' This quotation makes Anthony Julius's antagonistic gloss untenable.

Julius concludes by noting that 'the deniers' of Eliot's anti-Semitism have not addressed this postscript. He means me. And I have now. I note, finally, the spin on the term 'deniers' – Holocaust deniers is Julius's contemptible innuendo. And I reject it.

This augmented Vol. I includes one new, dangerously flirtatious letter from Vivien to Scofield Thayer, the super-rich American who owned the *Dial*. You get a pretty good idea of how Vivien vamped. She boasts about Bertrand Russell: 'He is all over me, is Bertie, and I simply love him.' Tom is in America: 'Rather unwise perhaps to leave so attractive a wife alone and to her own devices.' She vaunts her initiated marital status: 'grass widows do seem, I find, to be so very *very* attractive, *much more* than spinsters! Now WHY is that?' Dangerous, yet harmless – play-acting, with the Post Office as pimp and the Atlantic as chaperone. The editors think that Vivien may have had an affair with Russell in the summer of 1915, shortly after her marriage to Eliot. In Vol. II, they quote a letter of Russell's to Ottoline Morrell (September 1915): Vivien, wrote Russell, had 'a great deal of mental passion & *no* physical passion, a universal vanity, that makes her desire every man's devotion, & a fastidiousness that makes any expression of their devotion disgusting to her.' This is taken as evidence of an affair: 'it is possible he was briefly her lover in the course of that summer.' It seems obvious that Russell is a disgruntled and disappointed lover in a state of sexual frustration. Vivien wasn't putting out, she was putting him on. (Vivien wasn't having it off, she was having him on.)

In *Pride and Prejudice*, Charlotte Lucas marries the repugnant Mr Collins in the spirit of unillusioned pragmatism. She needs a husband and an establishment. Her observation tells her the majority of marriages are romantically unsuccessful, whatever their inception, and she embraces this empirical fact.

Her letters to Lizzie Bennet concentrate exclusively on the positive aspects of her new situation. She has entered the opacity of marriage – what Henry Ware Eliot calls 'a bourne of which no traveler ever tells'. 'It is the most secret of all secret cults.' The Eliot marriage, spectacularly pored over, is no exception. We know less than we think. How could it be otherwise?

His parents, his family disapproved. Eliot's father 'wish[ed] I liked his wife, but I don't'. His mother (25 March 1923) writes to his brother: 'Mrs Haigh-Wood is very pleasant, but she is not congenial to me, and I can not forget. She is not a person of high principle and I should not want to be much with her. I do not think Tom entirely trusts her. He makes the best of his marriage which was a great misfortune, and becomes more and more so.' We know the marriage failed. We know that the vivacious, breathy, babbling, careless, flighty, flirtatious, faintly vulgar Vivien went mad. We don't know precisely how the marriage felt, day in, day out. There are no diaries and not that many letters detailing the friction or the happiness. For the most part, what remain to us are the lacunae of married life seen from the outside. This is normal. Quarrels between partners are seldom set down on Basildon Bond. Happiness, too, has to be inferred from tender nicknames: Wee, Wonkypenky.

One thing is clear. Eliot championed Vivien's literary talent, publishing her in the *Criterion* and constantly telling his friends how talented she was: 'she has already a very exceptional and individual style.' He defends her *against her own criticisms* to Sydney Schiff (21 October 1924). Writing to Aldington, he affirms 'she has an original mind, and I consider not at all a feminine one.' Ottoline Morrell is told (1 May 1925): 'And I think that she is a *very* clever and original writer.' He tells Bertrand Russell (7 May 1925): 'she writes *extremely* well (stories etc) and [with] great originality.' This genuine regard for her talent contributes to an aberrant moment when Eliot succumbs to Vivien's contagious hysteria. In June 1925, he writes a deranged letter to Marianne Moore, in reply to a perfectly polite rejection of a story by Vivien sent to the *Dial*. Moore's letter is anodyne, an editorial bromide, but Eliot is toweringly insulted and reminds Marianne Moore how obligated as a writer she is for Eliot's support. The episode is a *folie à deux*.

But she was always a handful – risky, rash, indiscreet. To Mary Hutchinson, when the marriage is not obviously in trouble, Vivien writes (25 August 1920): 'As to Tom – a lot seemed to happen in that time between my leaving Bosham [their place in the country] and his going to France. I had rather an affair with him, for one thing. It began when we were staying with the Schiffs for the Peace weekend. Don't you yourself find that staying in people's houses together is very conducive to reviving passion?' Eliot, by contrast, was guarded with everyone, except Ezra Pound and (later) Geoffrey Faber. (And, unaccountably, once, to John Middleton Murry.) Hugh Walpole's diary can be trusted: 'he is a very quiet man and of course I am a little afraid of him.'

After endless *Criterion* palaver, Vol. II suddenly ignites. In 'What Dante Means to Me', Eliot said his early poetry aimed to 'establish a relationship between the medieval inferno and modern life'. Geoffrey Faber reassures Eliot that a letter detailing his personal travails is 'combusted'. No matter. At the end of the second volume we are given terrible glimpses of Eliot's personal inferno.

Another thing we can be sure of – that Vivien's mental deterioration was largely caused by physical debility aggravated by incompetent physicians. She has 'catarrh of the intestines, with occasional enteritis'. Her ailments are prescribed 'the electric treatment, the Plombières treatment, which is most disagreeable of all' – a form of colonic irrigation. The 'root and core of Vivien's illness' is 'malnutrition'. She has bronchitis, 'completely numb, terrible palpitations', 'septic influenza', 'entero-colitis', 'enteric influenza', an 'extraordinary excess of streptococcus fecalis', 'chronic anaemia and defective circulation', 'trigerminal neuralgia', 'terrific rheumatism all over her body', 'general neuritis', 'serious liver trouble', shingles, 'liver and intestine ... nearly paralysed'. She is given 'bioplastina injections' to relieve her anaemia.

What a bill of health. For which Eliot paid in every sense. He is blamed by posterity, and indeed blames himself constantly: in mid-April 1925, he writes to Middleton Murry, 'But the dilemma – to kill another person by being dead, or to kill them by being alive? Is it best to make oneself a machine, and kill them by not giving nourishment, or to be alive, and kill them by wanting something that one *cannot* get from that person?' He thinks his decision to be a machine – in order to endure – has '*killed V*'. He elaborates: 'Can I exorcise this desire for what I cannot have, for someone I cannot see, and give to her [Vivien], life, and save my soul?' Valerie Eliot thinks the 'someone I cannot see' is a reference to Emily Hale. It is difficult to be sure. It might be an abstract ideal, a standard Vivien did not meet in her person and personality – 'by wanting something that one *cannot* get from that person'.

Murry's advice is *sauve qui peut*, risibly sub-Lawrentian, chilling in its irresponsibility: 'Do whatever your being says you must, and trample down what your mind says you ought. Put resolutely away from yourself all sense of guilt for the past: *put that responsibility on to the universe* [my incredulous italics].' Murry hadn't the measure of Eliot's agonised, unrelenting, New England conscience.

Writing to Leonard Woolf (29 April 1925), Eliot continues his self-excoriation but perhaps explains what being a 'machine' means, once stripped of self-dramatising rhetoric, a tendency he analysed in literature: 'I think that the years of loneliness since marriage ... may be enough to account for her fear of being left.' Virginia Woolf records Eliot accusing himself humbly 'of being the American husband'. *The American husband.* In other words, the absentee, workaholic husband who sends his family away to the country while he remains, a slave in the city. The *Criterion*. Lloyds Bank. Reviewing. Lecturing.

Meanwhile, Vivien is going steadily mad: a letter to Pound has some words underlined seven times. On 2 November 1925, Vivien writes to Eliot from her nursing home: 'Please write to this doctor instantly and tell him the truth, that we have had sexual relations. // Do these things for me. Especially about our married life and make him see it *had* been good. All here believe not. Also explain about the scars on my back.'

Those scars stand for all we will never know about the Eliot marriage. They remain unexplained. We have her word for it, however, that things '*had* been good'. Once. And the lost happiness is what Vivien clings to as her mind disintegrates. To Ellen Kelmond, the Eliots' maid, she writes (20 December 1925): 'But Ellen dear tell him his wife does love him and still loves him and always has loved him (he does not believe I do) ... If Mr Eliot does not arrive till night, what shall I do? I shall go mad Ellen.'

She threatens suicide – to Ellen, to Dr Hubert Higgins. Eliot expresses his (groundless) guilt: 'And the fact that living with me has done her so much damage does not help me come to any decision.' Vivien, though, blames herself: 'When I think of all that my husband has done for me, and of all the life I smashed up (as I do think of it, all night and much of the day) I do not know why I don't go out and hang myself.'

Eliot behaves impeccably, incapable of taking Murry's advice. He copes with the *Criterion* and continues to care for Vivien, who is being harrowed in her own unreachable hell – the hapless contrivance of a multitude of incompetent general practitioners and cranky specialists. It is heartbreaking.

Bryan Forbes
(2010)

About five years ago, Christopher Hampton received a package from Bryan Forbes. It contained the yellowing pages of a film script, Hampton's adaptation from his first play *When Did You Last See Your Mother?*, written so long ago Hampton had forgotten it. Forbes thought he was unlikely to make the film now – he is eighty-four and in poor health.

Tony Battita owns the smallest house in New York, one up, one down, propped against the back wall of a courtyard off Jones Street in Greenwich Village. As a young man, he worked in a bookshop patronised by Scott Fitzgerald. They became friends over one summer and subsequently Battita wrote a memoir of his encounter with Fitzgerald. When Adam Mars-Jones met Battita a few years ago, Battita's sole income in his old age was (he said) from Bryan Forbes, who renewed the film option on his memoir every year.

Forbes has been an actor, a producer, a director and a screenwriter. Nearly all his work as writer and/or director is based on prior fiction. He is responsible for two masterpieces, *Whistle Down the Wind* (1961) and *King Rat* (1965). *Whistle Down the Wind* takes its narrative from a novel by Mary Hayley Bell, the wife of John Mills and the mother of Hayley Mills, who took the lead role of Kathy. The script was by Willis Hall and Keith Waterhouse. *King Rat*, written and directed by Bryan Forbes, is based on *Shogun* by James Clavell.

This does not make him derivative. There is a kind of genius in knowing what to adapt. Shakespeare was touched with this genius, too. His sources run to eight volumes, edited by Geoffrey Bullough. Who else could see the point of Lodge's *Rosalynde?* Great fiction resists digestion, break-down, simplification. It is itself an anaconda capable of swallowing the largesse of life. Opera and film are vegetarian, vegan, elvers and adders by comparison. Complication and ramification stretch their capacity, rack their remit, dislocate their jaws. Avoid *War and Peace*. Pass on Proust.

Pushkin's *Evgeny Onegin* is perfect for opera or film: a rake goes into the country, is bored, and fights a duel, killing his opponent; a provincial girl falls in love with him and tells him in a note; he turns her down, perfunctorily; ten years later, he sees her at a ball in St Petersburg and falls in love with her. It is too late. She loves him still but she is married and immovable in her fidelity.

Not difficult to follow. From this near anecdote, a successful opera by Tchaikovsky and a good film by Martha Fiennes with wonderful performances by

Liv Tyler (the most vulnerable mouth in movies) and Ralph Fiennes (the most versatile mouth, capable of shy beauty and thin contempt, just as his eyes can be tender or empty as a seagull's).

In *Whistle Down the Wind*, three Lancashire kids, Kathy, Nan and Charlie, find a murderer in their barn and mistake him for Jesus. The synopsis doesn't short-change you. The plot essentials are all there. In *King Rat* an American corporal is a black-market racketeer in a Japanese concentration camp. His illegal activities are opposed by the camp's military policeman, the Provost-Marshal Robin Grey. It is rather the reverse of good versus corruption. Corporal King has charm, chutzpah and gleeful entrepreneurial genius plus a human warmth denied his sourly meticulous opponent. It could almost be the artist versus the critic, Hans Sachs versus Beckmesser. Or talent versus hierarchy, Mozart versus Salieri – Pushkin again; a short play this time, seized on by a dramatist, Peter Shaffer. At any rate, both the expected conflict and the inversion of our sympathies – we prefer corrupt Corporal King to Grey, the envious policeman – are clearly, limpidly plotted. There is a brilliant plot *elision* when Grey gets wind that King is doing a deal with a diamond and pursues him. We never know how Grey knows so much. We aren't told. It isn't explained. Forbes knows enough not to explain, to move with the momentum, to look away from the balance sheet and trust to the total.

The advantage in filmic terms is clear. In *Séance on a Wet Afternoon*, for example, we watch the husband Billy (Richard Attenborough) and the wife Myra (Kim Stanley) quarrel about the wording of a ransom note, composed of letters cut out of magazines and newspapers. This in itself is a superb way of summarising the plot for us, without the two principals telling each other things they must already know for the benefit of the cinema audience. Instead of a press release, we watch the two characters arguing at the periphery of the plot. Is 'lock' the right word for the kidnap victim's hair, which is straight? Doesn't 'lock' suggest 'curl'? What about 'some'? Wouldn't 'piece' be more accurate? It is vivid and bizarre and unforgettable. There is, too, a moment I would designate as Forbesian: when Myra asks about 'whom'. ' "Whom" doesn't have an "e", does it?' The clarity of the plot means that we (and the characters) can almost forget it and live in the shadows it casts.

There is a moment of calculated inadvertency when the kidnapped little girl asks why she is in hospital. (The couple have dressed a room in their house to look like a private room in a hospital.) When she is told she has German measles, she confounds her captors: 'Had it.' Their momentary stay is double German measles. Then the girl says the 'doctor' doesn't smell like a doctor – he should smell 'all pepperminty'. Typically in a Forbes film, you turn away from melodrama towards the ineradicably humdrum. And you can afford to because the narrative has been purged of complication to make way for detail. For instance, Billy parks his motorbike and sidecar at a disused, defunct dog track. We can see the betting guichets, windows saying 'Forecast 2/–' The point of this is thematic: Myra is a spiritualist medium, also in the business of forecasting.

Her idea is to kidnap the daughter of a rich couple, keep her in isolation in a mock hospital, tended by masked doctor and nurse, then tell the anguished parents where their child can be found, this establishing her gifts as a medium beyond doubt. It is to be a lie that will serve the truth.

The irony is that Myra holds a séance for a police inspector (Patrick Magee) who says he is president of a psychical research association and that he is seeking her assistance to solve the case. (His immediate underling is married to someone who attends Myra's séances regularly. He himself is agnostic.) At this final séance, Myra goes into control, quite genuinely, and gives everything away – that the girl saw Billy and that therefore he should take her and kill her. Ergo, though we have thought of her as fraudulent, she does have a genuine, irresistible mediumistic gift. And it does for her. The form is the anecdotal twist, the candid, radical inversion.

Unfortunately, it is flawed as a mechanism because the séance, though *genuine*, isn't mediumistic. She isn't in touch with the dead. She is not a medium. She is merely recounting and enacting what has happened quite recently. There is no predictive element, nothing supernatural, though the film tries to pass it off as spiritualist. It is an involuntary confession.

More interesting than the given kidnap plot, with its familiar formulaic elements, as well as its bizarre inflections, is the back-story of the couple, which is eked out and withheld in an almost Pinterian way. (I shall have more to say about Pinter and Forbes.) We learn they have lost a child, Arthur. The kidnap victim can go in 'Arthur's bed'. Later we learn that Arthur was born dead and that Myra 'never knew him'. This correction to Myra's indulgently inaccurate narrative configuration of her history is the culmination of various smothered irritations on Billy's part: for example, when Myra says that temperatures are not unusual in children, he objects 'How would you know?' We hear her version of marital events first: that Billy depends on her. 'Why did I ever marry, Billy? Because you're weak, because you need me.' We also learn that Billy 'tried living without me – I took you back.' And certainly, Billy seems weak. He accedes to her plan. And yet, at one point, he mentions the 'time you were ill' after Arthur died. Truth is so pliable in her mouth, we come to realise, that her words are not to be trusted. Early in the film, she says to him that he wants 'that car' and he cuts her off: 'I'm not doing it for a car.' She is deeply unreliable as a witness. We deduce this against the tide of the dialogue whose sweep is controlled by her. Eventually we conclude that the 'time you were ill' is Billy's euphemism for 'mad'.

The balance of power between them isn't wholly clarified, but by the end it begins to look as if he is acting out of love rather than weakness. He cares for her. He fears not her but her madness.

Against the clarity of the film noir plot – kidnap, the sexual hold of the wife over the husband, leading to a criminal act – we have a less familiar scenario in which the weak, psychologically damaged person exercises power. Forbes gives us a lethal version of the art of tears, of tears as a weapon, a form of psychological warfare, the threat of the suicide bomb. Billy tries not to upset her in case he triggers the destruct mechanism.

In *King Rat* there is a subtext of homosexuality, as well as overt reference. A doctor in Changi camp is tartly disapproving of Stevens, a male nurse: 'Stop trying to pretend you're Florence Nightingale' (the gender is important as well as the self-importance implied by the comparison) and 'you shave your legs and you're a liar, Stevens.' The hostility here is realistic, but isn't shared by Forbes, who is invariably empathetic to homosexuality across his œuvre. Cicely Courtneidge is a sympathetic lesbian thesp, an ancient principal boy, in *The L-Shaped Room*; another Stevens in *The League of Gentlemen* is a blackmailed homosexual portrayed compassionately, while routinely ribbed by Lexy, who has queasily to share a room with him. In *King Rat*, Corporal King develops a friendship with an upper-class British officer called Marlowe (James Fox). Marlowe injures his arm, which becomes gangrenous. King arranges for antibiotics, superficially in return for a favour connected to a scam. There is a telling moment when King takes Marlowe's face in his hands and brings his own face close – to persuade him forcefully – but easily read also as a gesture that might lead to a kiss. And his words are a variant on classic, exclusive romantic love, a version of 'Let Rome in Tiber melt.' They are: 'either way, it's just you and me.' When the antibiotics are administered (by Stevens), we see Corporal King for the first time without a shirt. (Usually, he is impeccably dressed in newly pressed shirts. Everyone else is in rags.) His naked torso is conflated with the ejaculation of the hypodermic while it is being tested. The equation couldn't be clearer. Or more subtle. It is a great moment which explains the powerful, unacknowledged same-sex love between the two men.

The other great moment in *King Rat* is the death of Hawkins's dog, put down on Grey's orders after it has savaged some hens. The custodian of the hens wants revenge. He *loves* his hens. Hawkins *loves* his dog. We are made to realise how bent, how intense, emotions can become in this claustrophobic world. The effect on Hawkins of losing the dog is shown in a brief aside. Hawkins is talking to himself in a tone of sweet reasonableness: 'Wife took it very badly. We did the right thing having him put down. He didn't feel a thing, just went to sleep.' Three ordinary sentences, deceptively low key and conversational, which show us that, far from being reconciled to the dog's death, Hawkins has gone mad.

The symbolic significance of the dog is beautifully disguised by this human drama and – when it is then cooked by Corporal King and eaten to up-beat martial music – further obscured by the importunate realia of human greed. 'Do you think it needs more salt?' 'I wouldn't know. I'm drooling so much, I've lost my sense of taste.' 'The greatest thing since Bisto.' Ethical, sentimental objections to eating the dog are briskly swept aside by King: 'lobster, geese – so don't tell me about Hawkins' dog.' They inhabit a world where dog eats dog – here literalised, a predatory world in which it is every man for himself. Except for the most ostensibly selfish, pragmatic person of all – Corporal King, who finds the necessary drugs to save Marlowe's arm. *King Rat* is a love story, a surprising, subtle love story, almost invisible, then suddenly clear, like the mercury in a thermometer.

Forbes has a gift for implication, a natural feel for structure. In *Only Two Can Play*, his adaptation of Kingsley Amis's novel *That Uncertain Feeling*, the denouement may seem an unlikely twist. John Lewis, the randy librarian (played by Peter Sellers, looking oddly like Milo O'Shea), turns down Elizabeth Gruffydd-Williams (the *appetitlich* Mai Zetterling). Now why would he do that when everything was at last going well? The twist is prepared for. The conclusion, though a shock, is logical. Forbes sets up a motif of domestic service – not so very different, actually, from the domesticity that Lewis is in flight from, what is designated as 'soap lodged behind the old wedding ring'. Elizabeth Gruffydd-Williams's initial lover, Bill, is employed to carry her poodle (Scampi) and to baby-sit Lewis's kids so he can be freed to attend her party. There are many obstacles to their congress. For example, Elizabeth takes Lewis back to her empty house because it is the staff night off. 'Curiously enough, the staff are off tonight.' Lewis inquires after her husband: 'Vernon out too?' 'Yes, strangely enough.' Lewis then says sotto voce: 'Well, he's staff too.' As she disrobes, leaving a trail of clothes, she also leaves a set of instructions. Lewis is ordered (charmingly) to make screwdrivers and find cigarettes. The lovers are then interrupted by her husband returning with an impromptu party of friends. When he tries to escape, Lewis finds himself trapped and taking their coats – as if he were staff. At the library, she is procuring promotion for Lewis, fixing a job for him, and at the erotic level she regards herself, unacceptably, as the boss. When she asks Lewis to buy a new suit, he tells her to buy Bill a new dog collar instead. It is the culmination of an intricately deployed motif.

Forbes's dialogue is a curious blend of Noel Coward and Harold Pinter. There are a great many elegantly turned, dry, well-aimed sentences. The doctor in *King Rat* specialises in cool irony: 'Don't eat too much rich food and you should play the violin again.' In *The League of Gentlemen*, the wit is Bond before the Bond films: Rupert steals a car and, asked from where, replies 'Harrods – put it on your account.' The Jack Hawkins character begins the film by emerging, Bond-like, in black tie, from a manhole in the street, before driving off in a Rolls-Royce. (Compare Sean Connery in *Dr No* stripping off his wet suit to reveal a dinner jacket complete with buttonhole.) His name (significantly enough) is Mr Hyde. When Hyde tells them the project is to rob a bank, Rupert quips, 'I do hope he doesn't have the National Provincial in mind. They're being rather decent to me at the moment.' *The League of Gentlemen* is an early, probably seminal, example of the team-heist movie. Steven Soderbergh's Oceans 11 series is the latest spin-off. Every man has a specialism essential to the success of the heist. This involves Forbes in a series of mini-back-stories – a skill he had already practised in *The L-Shaped Room*, where the inhabitants of the house are so vividly sketched they swamp the main story-line. The basement prostitute (Pat Phoenix) is unsentimentally well written: during the war, she had an affair with a Yank who was killed. Then there were one or two others – before he was dead. Her working partner is called Jean – 'not her real name, but I couldn't pronounce her name.' (She's Hungarian.)

The League of Gentlemen has been influential, but it is also influenced. Pinter makes his influence felt in the back-story of Weaver, the bomb-disposal expert. We first encounter him sitting in silence while his gaga father-in-law watches the TV, which is talked down by his jabbering wife: 'That girl still in the iron lung, is she, Daddy?' Forbes has made contact with *The Room* and elsewhere you can see him fighting off filmic working-class dialogue but sometimes succumbing. 'Humphries, what's this bleeding ladder doing here.' Comedy sometimes carries off the proletarian dialogue – Anthony Newley as the shyster Clarke in *The Cockleshell Heroes*, for example, of whom Sergeant Craig says, 'You're coming back to me like a song, you are.' The working-class dialogue is more problematic in *The Angry Silence*, the Forbes/Attenborough film about trades union malpractice – a cover of Elia Kazan's *On the Waterfront*. The best dialogue is Pinterian, drily comic: someone says he's in favour of mixed marriages between the Scots and the English.

The best moment in *The Angry Silence* has nothing to do with the film's thesis about outside communist agitators and the importance of the individual, of Tom Curtis versus union victimisation. Curtis's little boy gets out of bed. He obviously hasn't been to sleep at all. When his father asks him why he isn't asleep, he replies, 'My heart stopped.' *On the Waterfront* has survived better largely because Marlon Brando's performance and his character transcend the message. Attenborough is a lesser actor playing a character with only one dimension – stubborn victimhood. *The League of Gentlemen* has its limitations, too. The comic interlude in the army camp is funny but an unnecessary, implausibly risky strategy: why not just nick the weapons by night? Since they are kept quite a distance from the camp, it isn't necessary to distract the army's attention by impersonating a brigadier-general pursuing a complaint about the food. And the actual heist, when it comes, is decidedly unthrilling. Most of it consists in driving through sluggish traffic. There is one burst of – harmlessly demonstrative – gunfire. Smoke bombs and gas masks just don't cut it any more, if they ever did. We have left them behind for electronically detonated plasma bags, for swashes of blood, for disembowellings and decapitations in tasteless Technicolor.

Whereas *Whistle Down the Wind* hasn't dated at all, despite a plethora of authentic contemporary references – to Radio Luxembourg's 'Beat the Clock' (with Michael Miles) and TV's 'Wagon Train'. It remains a masterpiece. How? The danger for this film is sentimentality. But it is a danger triumphantly avoided – in large measure because the innocence that lets the children believe that the murderer is Christ is steeped in two opposing impulses, credulousness and scepticism. The 'evidence' for their belief is the physical reality of the man himself, his beard, his presence in 'our barn', the misprision when they take his alarmed expletive 'Jesus Christ!' as an answer to the question 'Who is it?' Their Christianity isn't sophisticated: it comes from carols, particularly 'We Three Kings', which underscores the action in the soundtrack, when they bring him their own gifts – fruit pie, toothpaste and so on. While he is irrefutably 'asleep in the hay' – they don't distinguish between Baby Jesus in the manger and the grown-up Jesus – the children still interrogate the evidence. The film lives in the fissure, the fracture, between belief and scepticism.

Our sceptical representative is the young boy, Charlie ('our Charles'). Even before the discovery in the barn, he shows he has a head on his shoulders: when his sister tells him that the Salvation Army woman lives in Jesus's house, he retorts, 'Don't talk wet. How can she, when he's dead?' And later, when he is taken to see the man in the barn, his shrewdness is ready: 'It's just a fella.' 'It's not a fella, it's Jesus.' To which he counters: 'That isn't Jesus. Jesus wore a long dress.' 'That was in them days.' Then he is converted, having been held back only because his sisters tried to keep it secret from him.

His expression of faith is incomparable, a brilliant piece of writing. 'O gentle Jesus! *Boom!*'

Alongside this reverence, spiked with excitement, we are shown the real world of children, depicted in dialect, *grounded* in dialect. The boredom of childhood: '198: that's the number of eggs [for breakfast] since last Easter.' The transactions between siblings, the snubs, the retaliations: the sisters are conducting an enigmatic conversation at the table, about what they won't say. Our Charles: 'I know what you're talking about?' Nan: 'What?' Charles: 'I'm not telling you. Shan't tell you anything ever again.' When he tries again ('Are we playing with Jackie Greenwood?'), he is rebuffed: 'One of us might be, two of us aren't.' To which he responds: 'You rotten cows.'

Whistle Down the Wind uses the magic realism that is childhood. On the one hand, the impossible, the return of the Messiah, Jesus in the barn – in the same way that Bulgakov has the Devil descend on Moscow in *The Master and Margarita*. On the other hand, folded newspaper sticks, a newspaper to blaze up a fire, the literalism of childhood, the gift to Jesus of *Shirley* with a free gift inside (an Arabian charm bracelet). The pawky independence of Charles, who wants to call his kitten from the rescued litter 'Spider'. Charles responding as his sisters protest and mock: 'When it grows up I'll teach it to hate yours and eat it up.' You see, not in the least sentimental. Blazing with truth. Unextinguishable.

Alan Bennett: The Angst in the Axminster
(2009)

What we write about, what we choose to write about, chooses us. This is what I want to say about writing – that it isn't unlike sexuality. We have strong, inexplicable preferences. Some things excite us, other things don't. Some thoughts excite us, while others leave us unaroused.

And every writer knows what it is like to have an idea which, by being trailed, by being discussed, by having its execution postponed, loses its ability to constrict our breath. Instead, our breath dulls its vividness. It becomes overfamiliar and invisible as a source of excitement. Reviewing Andrew Motion's biography of Philip Larkin in the *London Review of Books*, Alan Bennett addressed the subject of sexual excitement in the context of Larkin's collection of pornography stashed in his attic at Pearson Park. After a time, Bennett reflected, after several years, it must have been about as exciting as *Beowulf.*

This is rather different from the usual hypocritical, predetermined disclaimer that pornography is 'boring'. It is an admission that once, for a time, it was as exciting as *Gawain and the Green Knight.*

Or Simon Armitage's great remaking of *Gawain and the Green Knight* – with its vivid hunting scenes (the boar trapped against a river bank), its parallel sex scenes (the comic gulf between the wife's candid come-on and the cornered, hunted Gawain), its self-conscious awareness of the romance as a genre, and its determination to give us the faint sexual smell concealed by the powerful euphemistic perfumes of *amour courtois*. Armitage's version is the literary equivalent of marrying your deceased wife's sister. The same, yet excitingly new, incitingly different.

But it is the sameness that is fundamental – in sex and in subject matter. Individual examples may lose their power, but the unchanging topoi exert their tyranny. Individuals outlive their charge, their capacity to shock, to stir, but the templates tempt to eternity. Think how often we see a man divorce only to marry the same woman, barely disguised by trivial differences. What interests me is seeing the same type – of situation, of subject, *of something* – exciting the interest of the writer in Alan Bennett.

Ten years ago, maybe less, I picked up and read, on a whim, Alan Bennett's wonderful play for television *Our Winnie* (1982). I wrote him a postcard praising this perfect play about imperfection. I admired the artistic courage necessary to write about Winnie's condition, Down's Syndrome – an area full of sensitivities and constantly at risk from sentimentality. For me, the use of dialect was crucial in warding off the spectre of piety. Bennett deploys it sparingly but so accurately that it establishes the unquestionable reality of the situation and characters. 'It's done well has this coat.' 'We don't want to keep your Aunty Ida stood waiting.' 'Only think on.' 'I reckon nothing to it.' The authority of the dialogue colours and extends to the set-up. Which therefore doesn't feel set up.

There is a motif running through *Our Winnie* of natural behaviour and 'appropriate' behaviour. An art student is photographing the cemetery attendants and attempting to catch them in unguarded moments, when they aren't being dutiful, when they are off duty – smoking, say, while arranging wreaths. This divergence also applies to Down's. We know what we are supposed to feel about Down's Syndrome children, but the embarrassed frisson is persistent and instinctive, if controllable.

The central plot turns on an art student who takes an illicit photograph of Winnie at the cemetery where she, her mother, Cora, and her 'Aunty Ida' are visiting the grave of Winnie's father, Frank. (I think Ida isn't an actual aunt, but a friend given a courtesy title.) In Kipling's autobiographical memoir, *Something of Myself*, he recounts that one day in India, the vultures dropped into the garden a child's hand from a Parsee burial tower. Unflinchingly, Kipling records his emotion: he wanted to see the hand. Fascination. Curiosity. Art is ruthless. And, though Bennett disapproves of the art student, by writing about Winnie himself, he knows that he, too, is implicated in the process of exploitation.

Waiting for Godot, Endgame, Happy Days, are all plays about the terminal condition of art and the world. Early Beckett buttonholes us and torpidly, transparently bangs on about the depletion of drama. It tepidly twins artistic entropy with a doomed, cooling planet, parallels aesthetic exhaustion and the second law of thermodynamics. Alan Bennett, though, isn't, on the face of it, a writer of the same play in different guises. He is notably various, conspicuously versatile. *Our Winnie, Playing Sandwiches, The Madness of George III*: two television screenplays, one full-length stage play. One television monologue delivered by a male child molester, compulsively (and compassionately) confessional, the other television play having at its heart a central but non-speaking role – Winnie, a sub-normal Down's Syndrome girl. The stage play is about the temporary madness of an English monarch. If you then include, say, *A Question of Attribution* (about Anthony Blunt, art historian and spy) and *The Habit of Art* (about W. H. Auden and Benjamin Britten) the overall view looks even more gratifyingly various.

On the face of it.

Actually, these very different plays share a family resemblance, a common trait – the hot blush, an interest in exposure, a fascination with shame. Humiliation is Bennett's figure in the carpet, the Angst in the Axminster. This is Cora, Winnie's mother, talking to Ida about being the parent of a Down's Syndrome child. It occurs right at the end of the play, after, as it were, the implicit dramatic representation: 'Once we knew for certain, I didn't go out. Didn't go anywhere. I wouldn't take her out. Dad had it all to do. Dad and you. The housework. The shopping. Everything. It was long enough before I came round. Still, life has to go on, I suppose. Folks stare. They look at her and they don't realise. Then when they do realise, they look away. You don't want them to stare, and yet you don't want them to look away either. I don't know.' The shame is hinted at earlier when Cora reminisces about the wife of the doctor who delivered Winnie: 'Always used to speak.' It is a throwaway remark, in an agglomeration of random observations, but an important one. Either some people didn't speak, or Cora feared they wouldn't – after the discovery that Winnie had Down's Syndrome.

As well as shame, there is something hidden in Cora's speech. ('Dad and you.') It is the love between Ida and Cora's dead husband, Frank. Ida's response risks piousness but is in fact a double entendre: 'It's a good job there's love.' Meaning love overcomes the shame of Winnie's disability. And meaning – no, not meaning, *gesturing towards* – the compensatory love between Ida and Frank that is the secret, undisclosed by-product of this marital catastrophe. Rather as Maisie brings together her two step-parents, Sir Claude and Mrs Beale, in James's *What Maisie Knew*, Winnie has brought Ida and Frank together. The occluded relationship between Frank and Ida lends meaning also to Ida's earlier remark 'I can see him [Frank] in Winnie so clear sometimes.' Winnie, of course, has her own value, but she has an additional value for Ida as an imperfect, invaluably precious souvenir of Frank. Ironically, Cora, throughout, harps on Ida's failure to marry, her lack of knowledge of married life.

In his introduction to *Rolling Home*, Alan Bennett's 2003 collection of films for television, he writes: 'A writer isn't the best person to analyse his or her work or to detect and detail its preoccupations.' I have never believed that the writer is as poorly placed as the reader, or the inferior of the critic. The writer is privileged. Of course he is. And Bennett goes on to outline his preoccupation with the writer's relationship to his material – the writer's ruthless exploitation of real life for the sake of his art. He says the tenacity of this preoccupation, its recurrence in his work, shows he doesn't know exactly what he thinks about the artist and life. This is disingenuous. He knows that art involves violation, as his citation of his parents demonstrates: 'My parents were both shy people, so it's not simply a case of not presenting them in an unfavourable light, which I've never had reason to do; but presenting them at all would, if they knew of it, seem to them a violation.' The violation of privacy, that is, bringing with it the violation of exposure. In real life, people want at the very least to tell their own story. Bennett, though, isn't only interested in the artist's ethical dilemma. He is drawn to exposure itself – its gestalt, its actual manifestations, the ways in which we adapt and deal with shame.

Think of *Forty Years On*, a mélange of sublimely silly sketches, strung on the frayed thread of English history – a purported review, but actually a revue. *Forty Years On* reaches its surprising, even *arbitrary*, but undeniable climax with Neville Chamberlain shamed and ridiculed at the Court of History: 'You are charged that on the night of September 30th, 1938, you did indecently expose yourself at the windows of your home, No. 10 Downing Street, clad only in a scrap of paper and shouting "Peace with Honour".'

Indecently expose yourself.

Now think of *Kafka's Dick*. The title tells us most of what we need to know. Kafka's shaming secret is the size of his penis: 'H E R M A N N K: The long and short of it is: my son is ashamed of his old man. B R O D: We know that. That's what all the books say, starting with mine. H E R M A N N K: No, not me. He's ashamed of his old man. K A F K A: Don't listen. Please don't listen. H E R M A N N K: Putting it bluntly: his old man doesn't compare with his old man's old man. His, Mine. (*He makes an unequivocal gesture.*)'

In *A Question of Attribution*, Bennett's art historian knows that behind the painting, over-painted, is a hidden figure, and behind that hidden figure, another figure painted out. Bennett *is* interested in the artist's relation to his raw material, but what links these various dramas is the indecent exposure of the decently hidden – the king's piss, the monarch's *merde*, the tangle on the wrong side of the official tapestry, the private view, the view of the privates.

Biographers appear to have less of this pudeur than Alan Bennett. Jeremy Treglown began the authorised biography of Henry Green (Henry Yorke), but found himself obstructed by the son, Sebastian Yorke. There was a love-child, with her real father's idiosyncratic, unique laugh. Treglown identified her – something that would have been impossible without hints and a certain passive connivance from the son. So why the (inconsistent) obstruction? Treglown differs from many modern biographers by doubting that truth and interest legitimises the biographical project. He believes that biography should be a hybrid of sympathy and objectivity. Listening to him lecture (on 8 February 2006), I found myself thinking it might be interesting to write the life of one of our leading biographers – Hermione Lee, say – and discover how intimate revelations were received by the life-writer. Publicity is more usually attendant on the famous: as the king says in a (cut) draft of *The Madness*, 'if you're poorly it's safer to be poor and ordinary' – or a humble biographer. I mention this because Alan Bennett is a shy subject himself and, at his request, his friends are properly protective of his privacy. None of them would contribute to this celebration. And, as a result perhaps, I find myself reluctant to reminisce about a shared trip to Russia. Alan's version – edited for public consumption – has already been published.

We sometimes pretend that privacy is a good in itself. But the desire for privacy is always partly a fear of shame. I don't mean to imply that Bennett, uniquely, has something to be ashamed of. I take it that every one of us has something we are ashamed of, something we wouldn't like others to know about. Biographers not excepted.

There is a problem with *The Madness of George III*. It is this. Bennett is drawn to George III's humiliation as the king is gripped by madness and loses control of his faculties and his sphincter. And we are greatly moved by the Queen's impotent concern, love and loyalty. As we are by the king's recovery, discovered to the audience by his reading of the mad scenes in *King Lear*. And yet, in order to saturate us in the king's madness, without boring us with incoherence, the play needs to diversify and therefore shows us how this affects the body politic, the government, the political rivalry between Pitt and Fox, the monarch and the Prince of Wales. We attend the political manoeuvrings but it is the king being blistered that pains us – and hypnotises Bennett the writer. The play, he writes in his preface, is 'about the madness of George III, the rest amusing, intriguing, but incidental'. Bennett the historian is there, too, lucidly, wittily explaining the parliamentary ins-and-outs, but he is secondary. The flaw in the play is that, presented as contemporary history by Bennett, there is a contrast between several doctors who are quacks and Willis, who apparently succeeds by his methods – methods that involve systematic humiliation, the use of the strait-jacket and the gag, the denial of kingship, the insistence on indignity, and colossal *presumption*. We see the justice when the cured King George tells Willis (in the indirect royal mode): 'You may tell Dr Willis that the ceremony will not be such a burden as the want of ceremony has been. And do not look at me, sir. Presume not I am the thing I was. I am not the patient. Be off, sir. Back to your sheep and pigs. The King is himself again. God save the King.' It is possible, given Bennett's presentation, to see this as the speech of an ingrate. In fact, we know that Willis achieved *nothing* with his brutal methods. We know that George III was suffering from porphyria, a toxic physical condition, and that he was to suffer again without recovery. But we do not know this in Bennett's play: the awkward expository scene in which a modern medical practitioner gives us the lowdown on porphyria was quickly and rightly dropped. Even included, it is unsatisfactory because the information comes too late for us to appreciate the irony of Willis's 'cure'.

There is something similarly problematic in *An Englishman Abroad*, the Guy Burgess half of the double-bill, *Single Spies*. We are in a familiar area. The shamed, disgraced Burgess is beyond the pale, figuratively and literally – in exile in Moscow. Bennett's thesis is given to Coral Browne, the actress, who in real life encountered Burgess in Russia while playing Gertrude in a *Hamlet* for cultural export. The thesis is that Burgess wasn't the unprincipled traitor of the tabloid press, but a man acting on principles that differ from our own. A commendably intelligent reconfiguration of the cliché. Burgess keeps asking Coral Browne about various friends – Auden, Cyril Connolly – because Bennett knows that public shame means the loss of your friends. These days Burgess can only struggle to keep up appearances – hence his request for a suit from his tailor. Now I come to the unsatisfactory part: in order for Coral Browne to vent her speech about differing principles, there has to be a recipient and a pretext. A firm of outfitters refuses to supply Burgess with a pair of pyjamas. So Coral Browne explodes. And we hear our author's message. The problem for the playwright is that Burgess's tailor and his shirt-maker have already readily (and inconveniently) supplied the required goods without a murmur. Bennett wriggles out of the difficulty (just) by making the pyjama refusenik not English (and therefore a representative hypocrite) but Hungarian. The Hungarian firm remembers the Soviet invasion of Hungary and takes a principled stand against Burgess, who would have been partially responsible. Yet another set of principles. Here, the exasperated Forsterian side of Bennett (Forster said he would rather betray his country than betray a friend) is improved, subtilised politically by a need to face the historical facts – namely, the readiness of the retail trade, unimpaired by *any* principle, motivated solely by monetary considerations, to supply the traitor.

Playing Sandwiches deals directly with a subject also present in *The Habit of Art*, where Benjamin Britten worries that his public will recognise a pattern of paedophilia in *Death in Venice*: ' "Here we go again," is what they're saying. *"Peter Grimes, Billy Budd, The Turn of the Screw.* Britten's perennial theme of innocence corrupted." Sometimes I think they'll come for me as they came for Grimes.' Britten is keen to transmute his desire into a seduction by beauty. Auden is blunt: 'Ben, fuck the book. I can't write a furtive libretto. You like boys, Ben. No amount of dressing Tadzio up as a vision of Apollo can alter the fact...' In *Playing Sandwiches*, the love object isn't a boy but a little girl. Wilfred's monologue culminates in prison, where he has been beaten up, violated as George III was violated. Rough treatment, in both cases, administered by the ignorant righteous. And Wilfred's paedophilia isn't madness, though society chooses to see it as madness. He is a man who loves children, who notices them ('I didn't foist them off like grown-ups do. I looked at them. I listened to them'), who is aware of them, alert to every detail ('Apricot satin, little buttons down the front'; 'Bonny little thing, only her mother's put her some earrings in, stud things. And one in her little nose and she can't be more than seven'). He loves children but he also desires them. There is a dark irony in his regret that this seven-year-old is adult before her time. Bennett's sympathy is largely invested in Wilfred, but the dramatist in him is true to the element of self-deception. Wilfred's version of events is one of surprised innocence. He and the little girl play sandwiches, hand over hand, then he pretends to be asleep: 'She kept wanting to hold my hand but I wouldn't. Her little hand kept pecking at my hand, like a little bird trying to get in. Only my hand was a fist, honestly. Tight, she couldn't get in. "There's nothing in there for you," I said, "I don't have anything for little girls. My shop's closed." "No it's not," she says and slips her little finger in between my fingers and wiggles it about and looks at me and laughs. She laughs again. She knew what she was doing. She must have known what she was doing. So I took her in the bushes.' She seduces him. In *his* account. (Compare Britten on Aschenbach's seduction by the beauty of Tadzio. Compare, too, Humbert Humbert, another paedophile, on Lolita: 'Now I am going to tell you something very strange: it was she who seduced me.') But Bennett has already shown Wilfred preparing for the aftermath, his exit-strategy, by giving a false name to the mother, Hargreaves instead of Paterson. So, *he* must have known what he was doing – or about to do.

Seduction is susceptibly slanted to cliché. I mentioned the wife in *Gawain and the Green Knight*. She is close to caricature, veering on the vamp. Her approach is unambiguous. She is putting out, unmistakably. But the titillating topos – phew – is savingly inflected with comedy. It is Gawain's strategic 'incomprehension', his deliberate semiological blindness, his queasy politesse, that brings the scene alive.

All seductions are bespoke. When Bob Doran is seduced by Polly in Joyce's story 'The Boarding House', he afterwards recalls the circumstances, the detail, with 'the curious patient memory of the celibate': 'Then late one night as he was undressing for bed she had tapped at his door, timidly. She wanted to relight her candle at his, for hers had been blown out by a gust. It was her bath night. She wore a loose open combing-jacket of printed flannel. Her white instep shone in the opening of her furry slippers and the blood glowed warmly behind her perfumed skin. From her hands too as she lit and steadied her candle a faint perfume arose.' The eroticism here is grounded in the ordinary particulars – not Polly's breasts, not her inviting eyes, but the naked instep, the printed flannel, and a redolent related adjective and noun: 'loose *open*' and 'in the *opening*'. Seduction for everyday use, purged of the theatrical, the staged. Joyce's exposition is itself patient, attentive, lingering. Exactly like Bennett's very different encounter.

Compare Scott Fitzgerald's account of child abuse in *Tender is the Night*, when Nicole's father, Devereux Warren, confesses to incest: 'we were just like lovers – and then all at once we were lovers – and ten minutes after it happened I could have shot myself – except I guess I'm such a God-damned degenerate I didn't have the nerve to do it.' As summary, as unspecific, as the guilty Devereux Warren could wish – a plausibly vague non-account. It has none of Bennett's or Joyce's brilliantly methodical, dry-mouthed detail.

Playing Sandwiches is, with another monologue, *A Woman of No Importance*, one of Bennett's masterpieces. Wilfred's 'seduction' is utterly persuasive in the way it shows desire distorting objectivity. At the same time, it is undeniably plausible that, to Wilfred, the little girl of seven meant every last detail. His misinterpretation, the entire narrative of the molestation, from game to assault, is unerringly convincing – something a writer couldn't invent. Except that is exactly what great writers do – invent the truth. Invent the truth because, imaginatively, they inhabit the truth.

This is George Eliot, a great novelist and a Victorian woman cohabiting with a married man, writing about the shame visited on the Bulstrodes: 'openminded as she was, she nevertheless shrank from the words which would have expressed their mutual consciousness as she would have shrunk from flakes of fire.' Shame – hiding its face from itself. This is Daniel Deronda shrinking from the shame of his obscure parentage: 'Secrets about which he, Daniel, could never enquire; for to speak or be spoken to about these new thoughts seemed like falling flakes of fire to his imagination.' Same image, same topos. If you don't want to know what you already know, look away now.

A Woman of No Importance is a characteristic masterpiece.

Bennett isn't always characteristic, however. *Kafka's Dick*, for example, is Bennett's lively but misguided attempt to match the surreal dazzle of Stoppard's *Jumpers* and *Travesties* (just as *Enjoy* is an attempt to absorb Orton). In Russia, I heard Bennett claim kinship with the writers of Orel as another 'provincial' writer. Everyone was offended. Alan protested: 'I meant provincial like Chekhov.' And he is Chekhovian by nature, mesmerised by the mediocre. His forte is insight into the ordinary, sympathy for the sidelined – the bus shelter, the biscuit barrel, as it were, rather than Stoppard's radical razzle-dazzle, those impossibly extended rallies at the net. Bennett's 'You prick in a bottle. You turd in a hat' irresistibly recalls Stoppard's more bravura 'You jumped-up phrasemaking smart-alecy arty-intellectual Balkan turd.' Bennett's dialogue draws on the Marx Brothers – pithy exchanges, repeating the previous speaker, as stylised as Stoppard's limericks in *Travesties*. Herman Kafka arrives as a policeman who can't remember Sydney the insurance man's name; Inspector Bones in *Jumpers* randomly apostrophises Sydney, Charlie and Clarence as he fumbles George's name. When characters refer to Kafka as 'the Czech Chekhov', 'the Prague Proust', you can feel the contrivance. In Stoppard, the fizz is naturally sparkling. All these details are mere details, however, when you consider the indebted theatrical topos – Stoppard's patent – of historical figures reincarnated under the aegis of farce.

Kafka's Dick is as absorbing as an algebraic equation and as heartless as a theorem. Our attention is engaged by the debate about the private lives of public figures but we couldn't care less about the characters. The play catches fire intermittently but its light is borrowed from Stoppard.

Whereas *A Woman of No Importance* creates a person – 'Miss Schofield is a bore' – as only Bennett could. The monologue is the opposite of heartless, though Bennett's introduction doesn't flinch from acknowledging its 'relentless nature', its 'unremitting detail', its 'tedium'. Its title is taken from Oscar Wilde but it is resolutely the opposite of witty. Samuel Beckett, writing to Alan Schneider, the director responsible for many first productions of Beckett plays in America, frequently alludes to the punitive quality of his art, the desire to affront his audience. *Waiting for Godot* candidly sets out to bore us. A glance at the programme told the first audiences that Godot would not materialise. Vladimir and Estragon are virtually interchangeable ciphers. Their individuality is rudimentary. So the play is a form of slow strangulation, a tightening of dental floss around our interest – till we drop off. Bennett knows about boredom. And he knows Miss Schofield is a woman of no importance – except to herself.

Whereas Beckett's anti-art is deliberately slovenly, Bennett pays meticulous attention to the asphyxiating detail of Miss Schofield's existence – her racial prejudice, her snobbery, her condescension, her cattiness ('She shouldn't wear trousers') and her hopeless, hidden crush on Mr Skidmore, which is imperfectly concealed from others. In *Emma*, Jane Austen risks giving her readers six pages on gruel, Mr Wodehouse's mantra on his grandchildren, the repetitive small change of local society. She is Chekhov before Chekhov – before the Chekhov who wrote 'A Boring Story'. She can make Beckett's parsimony of narrative event look belated. And this is the tradition that Bennett writes in. Where dullness is risked and rhetoric denied. And where we are greatly moved by the absolutely ordinary. Miss Schofield *is* a bore but Bennett makes us realise, with matchless pathos, how important she is to herself. As we are important to ourselves. When she is dying, she notices a fly: 'I've got a fly: keeps coming down. Must like me.' 'I said to Nurse Gillis, "It's singled me out." She laughed.' There is something indomitable and laughable here that touches us profoundly while conceding nothing to sentimentality. Bennett is bleaker than Beckett because he never exaggerates. Beckett, by comparison, is romantic, all black hyperbole.

Salinger: 'A Perfect Day for Bananafish'
(2010)

The title. In a recent *London Review of Books* (2 February 2010), Alex Abramov-ich told us his professor, Stanley Sultan, thought 'bananafish' was a euphemism for condoms. Ingenious, but wrong. Because out of character. Seymour Glass wouldn't toy with that kind of double entendre with a child – unlike Septimus Hodge in Stoppard's *Arcadia*. Hodge, the tutor, tells Thomasina Coverly, his young but not entirely innocent charge, that 'carnal embrace' is hugging a side of beef. Seymour isn't like that. The explanation is the dish of fried fish with banana, mentioned by Elizabeth Bishop in a letter to her Aunt Grace (23 September 1960): 'The fish was excellent (I ate nothing but fish and bananas for three days).' Nothing surreal, then, about bananafish, except in Seymour's playful, extrapolated fantasy – rather a species of 'soul food'. Think of chicken Maryland and substitute fish for the chicken. There is nothing sinister here, merely a menu.

The ending. There is a two-volume, probably pirated, undated, anony-mously published edition of Salinger's *Complete Uncollected Short Stories*, written for a more commercial market than the *New Yorker*. I bought both volumes for 10p each over twenty years ago. Though the edition includes 'Hapworth 16, 1924', Salinger's last published story (in the *New Yorker*), the twenty-one other stories are apprentice work.

For example, 'Personal Notes on an Infantryman' (1942). It is narrated in the first person by an enlisted infantry officer who is redirecting a stray recruit – an unfit middle-aged man named Lawlor. Lawlor has come to the wrong office. The officer examines Lawlor's application papers and discovers he is 'a techni-cal foreman in a key war industry'. In other words, he needn't join up. He is doing vital war work. His actions are voluntary. And he has found a job replace-ment. The officer (and Salinger) floats a hint that the recruit might be escaping marital problems: 'How does your wife feel about you going to war?' According to Lawlor, she is 'delighted'. It isn't clear whether this is sarcasm. The other information gleaned by the officer from the application papers is that Lawlor is married and has two sons.

After Lawlor has left for the proper recruitment office, the phone rings. It is Lawlor's wife: 'I explained to her that I was not the recruiting officer and there was nothing I could do. If he wanted to join the army and was mentally, physi-cally, and morally fit – then there wasn't anything the recruiting officer could do either, except swear him in. I said there was always the possibility that he wouldn't pass the physical exam.' An unusual conversation, you might think. If this isn't the recruiting office, how does Mrs Lawlor happen to have the number?

It gets odder. The narrator announces that Mrs Lawlor has 'the sweetest voice I know'. *Know?* Why not, say, one of the sweetest voices I've heard? The glitch looks like a slip when the story continues with the officer watching over the new recruit in training: 'he was a darned good soldier.' Lawlor is about to be shipped into war action when his name is suddenly dropped from the list. He comes to complain to the officer-narrator – who denies responsibility. Lawlor then blames Mrs Lawlor and asks if she has phoned again. Or if she has phoned Lawlor's Captain. '"I don't think so,"I said.' Lawlor salutes, about-faces and leaves the orderly room.

Eventually Lawlor becomes a 'buck sergeant' and is shipped to the Front and the officer telephones Mrs Lawlor. At which point I can reveal Salinger's reveal. The twist is that Lawlor is the narrator's father. And Mrs Lawlor is the narrator's mother. To raise his mother's spirits, he first of all tells her what a gallant soldier Lawlor is. Then he tells her that he and his brother Pete saw off their father: 'Dad started to salute us, but we kissed him goodbye.'

This is a very costly reveal, since it so taxes the reader's belief and patience. The explanation, the reason why neither son nor father acknowledges their relationship is implicit in that final goodbye, in which the salute is overtaken by a kiss. Here is a man who is heroically putting service before self. Tell it to the marines.

Here, the twist in the tail – the staple of the anecdotal form – involves a kind of narrative torture, a diet of improbability, for the simplest of narrative satisfactions, that bonne-bouche of surprise at the end.

And there is a final surprise in this sentimental war-time story of hard-boiled soft-centred heroism. The final two sentences read: 'Pete's my brother. He was an ensign in the navy.' *Was.* Dead now, you see. Quite quiet, quite subtle, beside its demonstrative, baying counterpart.

'A Perfect Day for Bananafish' shares narrative DNA with this coarse story. It, too, uses a (counter-intuitive) reveal, an anecdotal twist. Salinger's stories are never avant-garde in their methods and approach. They always seem reader-friendly, well-made *New Yorker* stories – at first sight. 'A Perfect Day for Bananafish' is an orderly dialectic: we infer that Muriel's mother is mistaken in her analysis of Seymour as a danger; then we observe Seymour talking charmingly, whimsically, sanely to Sybil Carpenter, the little girl. Thesis: the hectic, italicised, auto-destructive, psychoanalysis-inflected melodrama of Muriel's mother. Antithesis: Seymour dealing with a small child's imperiousness (and mild, enjoyable fear) with all the aplomb of Peter Brook. Or a silent shrink – the soul of quiet containment at his end of the couch.

Synthesis: not what you have been led to expect. Muriel's mad mother is very nearly right about Seymour's madness. 'He glanced at the girl lying asleep on one of the twin beds. Then he went over to one of the pieces of luggage, opened it, and from under a pile of shorts and undershirts he took out an Ortgies caliber 7.65 automatic. He released the magazine, looked at it, then reinserted it. He cocked the piece. Then he went over and sat down on the unoccupied twin bed, looked at the girl, aimed the pistol, and fired the bullet through his right temple.' Don't be fooled by the methodical prose, its calm, unhurried exposition. This is a violent twist in the tail.

What differentiates it from 'Personal Notes on an Infantryman' is the complete absence of explanation. The expertise – that Ortgies 7.65 – is an important Hemingway effect. For the end to work, we have to feel the detail is authentic and snugly in place. The detail is there, as it often is in Hemingway, instead of an explanation. Like Kipling, Hemingway was a great eliminator – and so is Salinger. Hemingway explained, more than once, the iceberg theory of composition, this time to George Plimpton in the *Paris Review*: 'if it is any use to know it, I always try to write on the principle of the iceberg. There is seven eighths of it under water for every part that shows. Anything you know you can eliminate and that only strengthens your iceberg. It is the part that doesn't show. If a writer omits something because he does not know it then there is a hole in the story.'

Despite its understated tone, the ending of 'A Perfect Day for Bananafish' is candidly sensational. Not 'shock and awe' so much as 'shock and or'. That 'or' stands for the possible explanations we attempt to bring to the narrative – using what we can of the glimpsed, fragmentary back-story. It is 1948: 'He calls me Miss Spiritual tramp of 1948.' According to *Raise High the Roofbeam, Carpenters*, they were married in 1942. Muriel has waited for Seymour '*all* through the war' – unlike 'all those crazy little wives who –' They, Muriel and Seymour, have stayed in the same hotel but 'we couldn't get the room we had before the war.'

Six years of married life, by my calculation.

This isn't, then, a honeymoon horror story. The couple are well acquainted – though manifestly unsuited to each other, at least on the surface. He is interested in German poetry, she in prêt-à-porter. On the other hand, the wife is affectionately unruffled by the bizarre behaviour so alarming to her mother. In so far as we can hazard, 'A Perfect Day for Bananafish' is a post-traumatic-stress story, reasonably closely related to Hemingway's 'Big Two-Hearted River', though you might think 1948 is a long time after the end of the war. Maybe. Maybe not.

Throughout, Salinger's technique is the conflation of exact notation of externals and the severely restricted access to the past and, more particularly, the interior, the theatre of the mind. So: the unimportant in fierce focus; the crucial inner drama invisible, except for examples of enigmatic behaviour. On the one hand: 'She washed her comb and brush. She took the spot out of the skirt of her beige suit. She moved a button on her Saks blouse. She tweezed out two freshly surfaced hairs in her mole.' On the other hand: 'The trees. That business with the window. Those horrible things he said to Granny about her plans for passing away. What he did with all those lovely pictures from Bermuda – everything.' Everything – and, curiously, nothing. At once specific, but tantalisingly shielded – hidden by banal consumerism, 'that awful dinner dress', 'your blue coat'. We never find out what Seymour did with Granny's chair, but we know Muriel has had some of the padding taken out of her blue coat.

In *Raise High the Roofbeam, Carpenters*, the later prequel to 'A Perfect Day for Bananafish', Salinger experiments with a narrator's characterised voice – that of Buddy Glass, Seymour's younger brother. It is accurate but more hospitable to digression and relaxed 'personal' observation. But the anecdotal twist is there – the missing bridegroom elopes with his 'jilted' bride. And the core method – highly focused specifics and a balancing occlusion – continues to be crucial. *Raise High the Roofbeam, Carpenters* ends with the idea of a wedding present: 'Just the cigar, in a small, nice box. Possibly with a blank sheet of paper enclosed, by way of explanation.' The minuscule cigar-toting deaf-mute uncle ('Muriel's father's uncle') who beams, enigmatically, is Salinger's figure for his technique. Nothing could be more particular, more bizarre, than the externals: the feet that don't touch the cab floor; the unlit 'clear Havana cigar'; the silk top hat that is four inches short of the cab roof, so small is the uncle. Yet we have no access to his inner life. He is as inexplicable as a character in a fairy tale.

And of course he also stands for, or stands in for, the absconded bridegroom, Seymour, who is the potent absent presence throughout the narrative. In their apartment, Buddy Glass and Seymour, 'defiantly sentimental', have taped up photographs of fellow-participants of the radio quiz show *It's a Wise Child. Defiantly sentimental.* This is the key-note of *Raise High the Roofbeam, Carpenters.* The young Seymour read a Tao parable to the bawling, preliterate Franny, when his sister was still in her cradle. In essence, the import of the parable is this: ignore the outer trappings and penetrate beyond them to the spiritual essence under the surface. (The great horse expert mistakes the gender and colour of the horse he chooses, but chooses a superb horse nevertheless.) Seymour's diary, rather too conveniently to hand, shows us Seymour's determination to transfigure his wife-to-be and her ghastly mother, Mrs Fedder, who thinks Seymour is a latent homosexual with schizoid tendencies: 'She's an irritating, opinionated woman, a type Buddy can't stand. I don't think he could see her for what she is. A person deprived for life, of any understanding or taste for the main current of poetry that flows through things, all things. She might as well be dead, and yet she goes on living, stopping off at delicatessens, seeing her analyst, consuming a novel every night, putting on her girdle, plotting for Muriel's health and prosperity. I love her. I find her unimaginably brave.' This is 'defiantly sentimental'. But it is sentimental, perversely counter-intuitive, in the Glass family manner. Remember Zooey on the radio embracing standard housing, architectural prefabrication, because you would encounter a new family every night, not knowing which house was yours.

But Salinger isn't buying it. *'A type Buddy can't stand.'* And this is Boo Boo Glass on Muriel, Seymour's intended: 'She's a zero in my opinion but terrific looking.' It is also Boo Boo who writes on the bathroom-cabinet mirror, 'Raise high the roofbeam, carpenters. Like Ares comes the bridegroom, taller far than a tall man. Love, Irving Sappho, formerly under contract to Elysium Studios Ltd. Please be happy happy *happy* with your beautiful Muriel. This is an order. I outrank everybody on this block.'

Boo Boo and Buddy are still in thrall to Seymour's cast of mind, his wishful thinking, his sentimental imagination, his gift for poetic fiction. But they know it is fiction. It is no accident that *Raise High the Roofbeam, Carpenters* informs its readers after three pages that '[Seymour] committed suicide in 1948, while he was on vacation in Florida with his wife.' The deaf mute is also a figure for Seymour's hope that below the impermeable surface there is delight, peace, tranquillity. Salinger – and his creation Seymour – would like to succumb to the sentimental. But the sentimental flies in the face of facts. 'When I was a child, I spake as a child, I understood as a child, I thought as a child: but when I became a man, I put away childish things' (1 Corinthians 13:11.)

This is where all Salinger's fiction is sited – on the fracture-line between childhood and adulthood. Think of 'Down at the Dinghy', where the child senses the anti-Semitic insult but mishears 'kike' as 'kite'. Right on the border of innocence and experience. Think of Holden Caulfield's symbolic patch of prematurely greying hair. (All part of a pattern: see my piece on *The Catcher in the Rye* in my essay collection *In Defence of T. S. Eliot*.)

In her *New Yorker* review of Martin Amis's memoir, *Experience*, Joan Acocella, with her habitual acuteness, fingered an omission in the narrative, the dog that didn't bark in the night. Amis's memoir made no mention of his divorce from Antonia Phillips. Instead, the novelist was simply married to Isabel Fonseca. In 1984, Martin and I were the subjects of a joint profile by a friend, Redmond O'Hanlon, in *Tatler* (then edited by another friend, Mark Boxer). We were cajoled and betrayed. We gave the interview in Martin's work flat. Everything thereafter at dinner was 'off the record'. The profile was amazingly indiscreet, a comprehensive breach of trust. But it was also a true off-the-record record of the subsequent drunk conversation, unbuttoned because – stupidly

– we felt protected by friendship. The article should have been called 'Friendly Fire'. Martin made Redmond take out *every* reference to his wife Antonia, even anodyne references. She was not the subject of the profile. I assume this is why she plays no part in *Experience*. Antonia values her privacy. Everything else we had to live with.

In her review, Joan Acocella located Martin's divorce – its pain, its grief – in his account of the tribulations with his teeth. 'The teeth are the divorce,' she wrote, invoking psychoanalysis with its flair for solving everyday encryption.

'A Perfect Day for Bananafish' contains a similar transposition. If we want to know about the marriage between Seymour Glass and Muriel, all we have to do is observe the relationship between Seymour and Sybil Carpenter. Salinger is routinely praised for his observation of children. We feel their innocence and Salinger's empathic, observant tenderness. This is a slightly sentimental reading. Not wholly sentimental, because it is true that Salinger prizes children and is charmed by them – by their candour and directness. However, Sybil Carpenter is a portrait of a real child – imperious, self-centred, jealous, ruthless, rivalrous. And innocent. Too innocent to disguise her feelings.

> 'Next time, push her off,' Sybil said.
> 'Push who off?'
> 'Sharon Lipschutz.'
> …
> 'Don't let go,' Sybil *ordered*.' [my italics]

Seymour is humouring her confident egotism. As he humours his wife's placid assumptions of centrality and irrefutability, while her once charming innocence hardens into cast-iron stupidity. It's all there if you look.

One word more about the back-story. In the later novella, *Raise High the Roofbeam, Carpenters*, we learn that Seymour had qualms about the marriage. After all, he doesn't show up to his own wedding ceremonials. We aren't told why. Or, rather, we learn from his diary that Seymour was 'too keyed up' to go through with the planned, conventional wedding. Or as the boiler-plated Maid of Honour sceptically puts it, 'indis*posed* by *happ*iness'. We share her scepticism, I think. He and Muriel elope.

Nor, in 'A Perfect Day for Bananafish', are we told why he changed his mind. Instead, the back-story is grainy, incomplete, hypnotic, tantalising. As the aesthetic of the Hemingway short story demands. Might it be that in his famous concrete bunker the Salinger project was to fill in the details, to complete the jigsaw, to construct something completely different – a *War and Peace*, a family saga – with timed information releases? A gradual epic like an IV drip?

Sex: Mrs Whitehouse and Mrs Eagleton
(2010)

Hugo (with halitosis) and Tamina (with reluctance) are having sexual intercourse. She is being taken from behind. In Milan Kundera's *The Book of Laughter and Forgetting* we encounter this truthful sentence: 'At the same moment, Hugo opened his eyes, and seeing the eye of Tamina's backside, he felt a bolt of ecstasy run through him.'

Familiar, dear reader? Or matching nothing in your experience? – perhaps you are a virgin. Or a missionary.

Bear this sentence in mind.

On Saturday, 9 April 1983, with my wife and two children, I returned towards midnight to a rented holiday cottage near Padstow in Cornwall – one of those beautiful, slightly Spartan, thick-walled, window-seated houses, with sand on the lino in the kitchen. In a terrace of ten cottages, we were the third. There was no phone. (And no mobiles in those days.) Our immediate neighbour, a Jehovah's Witness, knocked on our door to tell us that Blake Morrison from the *Observer* had telephoned her number asking to speak to me. There was, apparently, going to be something in next day's paper I should be aware of.

I was definitely worried. I still don't know how Blake, then the *Observer's* literary editor, knew where I was, let alone acquired my neighbour's number. He must have done a lot of phoning.

The next morning, we drove up the steep hill, then wormed and coaxed the car along the cramped lanes to Padstow, where I bought the papers and found myself on the front page. I had attracted the attention of Mary Whitehouse, the scourge of indecency. Mrs Whitehouse had read a poem I'd published in the *New Statesman* and was threatening legal action under the Obscene Publications Act. The poem was called 'Arsehole'.

In 1982, the year before, Mrs Whitehouse had prosecuted Michael Bogdanov, the director of Howard Brenton's play *The Romans in Britain*. The play opened on 13 October 1980 and the writ was delivered at the Stage Door of the National Theatre on 10 December 1980. In May 1982, Bogdanov was sent for trial at the Old Bailey. However, he was acquitted when it was established that Mrs Whitehouse's solicitor had been seated in the rear stalls when he 'saw' a penis exposed on stage. It was, in fact, the thumb of actor Greg Hicks, standing in for the genitalia his hands were actually concealing.

Now cut to 18 October 2010, when I learn from the *Evening Standard* that I have been shortlisted for the Bad Sex Award annually handed down by the *Literary Review*. The other contenders, according to Londoner's Diary, are Ian McEwan, Martin Amis and Tony Blair. Evidently, the judges have read Terry Eagleton's review of *Heartbreak*, my first novel, in the *London Review of Books*: they cite the same passage, describing an arsehole, that Eagleton singled out as offensive.

(The final shortlist was rather different: Alastair Campbell, Jonathan Franzen, Rowan Somerville (the winner), Neel Mukherjee, Christos Tsiolkas, Annabel Lyon, me and Adam Ross.)

Twenty-seven years separate these events. In that time, Mrs Whitehouse, herself the reincarnation of Mrs Grundy, has become Mrs Eagleton, the burly sister of Bertolt Brecht, pantomime dame and scourge of bad taste.

No one, in the present pious climate, would dream of criticising a gay writer for this freedom. Not Alan Hollinghurst: '[I] sniffed through the dry smell of the talc to his own rectal smell – a soft stench like stale flower-water. [Flower-water courtesy of Joyce's 'Calypso'.] His asshole was a clean pale purple, and shone with my saliva.' More recently, Colm Tóibín's 'Barcelona, 1975', in *The Empty Family*, has an extended description of anal intercourse. I'm glad both have the freedom being denied heterosexual writers.

My crisis coincides with a crisis for literature. And it isn't, in retrospect, a sudden crisis. It has been happening for quite a long time. Sometime in the eighties, Ian McEwan attended a conference at which leftist intellectuals tried to codify the correct socialist attitude to sex. He was denounced from the floor. Andrew Motion, in his biography of Philip Larkin, published his shock that Larkin used pornography. His hypocritical eyes have never strayed up to the top shelf, curved with the weight of dirty magazines – which are bought by no one...

In 1992, Nicholson Baker writes *Vox*, a funny, tender book about phone sex, and follows it by *The Fermata*, which proves fatal for his reputation. In interview, he admits to renting porn videos. *The Fermata* starts from the comic premise that its protagonist, Arno Strine, can sometimes stop time and during the *fermata* satisfy his curiosity about women's bodies and underwear. This unachievable, *imaginary* nirvana – the *vain* hope of every heterosexual male in the world – is pronounced 'creepy', denounced as 'voyeuristic' by literalists. As if men weren't interested in how women look naked. As if men wouldn't vote for this power provided the secrecy of the ballot box was protected.

In *Encounter*, Milan Kundera says, 'In the twentieth century the novel discovered sexuality, gradually and in all its dimensions.' This is true, but our culture is now in the process of denial. My old friend Martin Amis recently stated that it is impossible to describe sex other than pornographically. An abdication of the writer's responsibility, in my view. It was not always so – especially in the novels of Martin Amis, which, allowing for comic exaggeration, were essentially truthful, keen to embrace the failures of flesh, the embarrassments of ecstasy. (Glance at Amis's 'Let Me Count the Times' – a parable of inhibition and internalised hypocrisy.) Take a less contentious example: Christopher Hampton on his screenplay *Able's Will*: 'I was interested in breaking a bit of new ground [in 1976]. For example, the scene where two characters are having sex and talking at the same time, which is something you seldom see on screen but often happens in life, seemed quite bold at the time.' This is the writer's job – to describe sex accurately, to resist the censored versions of sex forced on us by prudes (Mrs Eagleton) and the stylised, grandiose versions wished on us by Hollywood (say, Joe Eszterhas). Accuracy doesn't mean pornography, though it will include elements some regard as pornographic.

In Adrian Lyne's *Fatal Attraction* the first encounter between Michael Douglas and Glenn Close is the time-lapse version of sexual intercourse – rapid simultaneous orgasms of both gurning partners after a few moments of frenetic friction, *while both are standing up*. I saw the same simulation recently at the National Theatre's production of *Danton's Death* when Toby Stephens helped himself to a whore. I find this unacceptable – offensive, actually – because it is such a crude approximation to the truth. Women aren't that light and men aren't that strong – and it is a lot easier lying down. Standing sexual intercourse isn't impossible, we know, but rare in real life.

Male writers are afraid of female disapproval. And some female writers aren't about to cede this power – or their special authority. On *Saturday Review* (Radio 4), I heard Louise Doughty and Bidisha disparaging John Updike as a chronicler of sex. Tom Sutcliffe and John Carey thought Updike wrote about sex well. Bidisha was dismissive. She co-opted Louise Doughty to her irrefutable, undisclosed position – which was that women *knew* sex wasn't like that. I wondered about the dogmatism. A moment's thought will tell you women's sexual experience is enormously various – and that Bidisha has no special authority. Her gender gives her no access to the spectrum of women's desires or sexual behaviour. The variety of sexual experience – male and female – is what the writer should be trying to set down, as accurately as possible.

As I looked at that front page in Padstow, the seagulls bickering around me, I suddenly relaxed. I knew something Mrs Whitehouse didn't know. My poem was a translation of a sonnet by Verlaine and Rimbaud. Mrs Whitehouse had had over a hundred years to get litigious about this great work of art – which captures accurately and forever the power of sexual excitement to transcend the primitive plumbing so essential to sexual joy. Yeats, in 'Crazy Jane Talks with the Bishop', famously wrote that Love had pitched his mansion in the place of excrement. Rimbaud's account of the place of excrement brilliantly invokes food and consuming hunger: *'le tube d'où descend la céleste praline.'* Get your dictionaries out. Mrs Eagleton of course will wrinkle her blunt nose every time she rootles in her box of Milk Tray.

PART TWO

Art – Reading the Detail

Seurat's Courage

(1997)

Has Seurat sabotaged perfect beauty in favour of modern life?

At the National Gallery just now you can see Seurat's *Bathers at Asnières* (1884), with preparatory drawings and oil sketches, sources and analogues, and subsequent representations of the Clichy district by the likes of Émile Bernard and Van Gogh.

Two metres by three metres, it fills one wall – a silent, still, difficult, ironic masterpiece. Its hazy colours recall the faded pigments of a Piero della Francesca fresco, as do its vivid yet flat figures. The scene is monumental enough to hint at higher things; it gestures towards the contemplative, it is composed and quasi-meditative – and then it insists on what Matthew Arnold called the 'object as in itself it really is'. *Bathers at Asnières* is the suburban scene in a trance of torpor. Its figures are not spiritually naked but nearer a banal vacancy. Seurat evokes the idea of epiphany, a transfiguration of the ordinary, then settles for a mildly hedonistic vapidity. He was too intelligent a painter to exaggerate or sentimentalise his subject matter. He was a painter of modern life, but one who ignored Baudelaire's stipulation to heroise the stove-pipe hat and the pipe-clayed spats. Seurat's preferred note was tougher, ugly, accurate, secular, ironic.

In Fellini's film *La Strada* (1954), the Clown is killed by Zampanò, when the Strongman meets his teasing rival by chance on a deserted road. The Clown, in mufti, is repairing a flat tyre. The two men exchange a few blows in a ragged, realistic fight. The Clown dies only because he bangs his head against the metal corner of this car: the two men separate, the Clown looks at his wrist and complains that the Strongman has broken his watch, then he lies down and dies. *That watch.* Bizarre, less symbolic than comically incongruous, a pedestrian interpolation at the moment of pathos, it is also a perfect example of modernism. Modernism refuses to edit in the interests of afflatus. The process begins with Flaubert, its first uncompromising practitioner.

When Emma Bovary's arsenic poisoning enters its final phase, her daughter, Berthe, is brought to the bedroom. The burning candles remind the little girl of New Year's day, of being woken early, of gifts. Her eyes cast about, looking for her stocking, cubist with presents, depending from the mantelpiece. Her innocent, infantile egotism takes its place with the other infantile egotisms gathered around the deathbed. Pathos is stayed, impurities are unflinchingly reported, the grotesque is given its due. Ironies are treasured.

Philip Larkin thought that photography epitomised this tendency to embrace the awkward and inconvenient: 'But o, photography! as no art is, / Faithful and disappointing! that records / Dull days as dull, and hold-it smiles as frauds, / And will not censor blemishes / Like washing-lines, and Hall's-Distemper boards.' *And will not censor blemishes*. My argument is that, to the heartbreaking beauty of the preparatory drawings, Seurat, in the finished picture, brought blemishes. Deliberately.

The magic of the drawings is cognate with photography, though far from photography's vaunted accuracy of finish. The curators have assembled a dozen or so early drawings so we can see Seurat's technique mature rapidly. When it arrives it is incomparable. Let me try to describe it. Using the texture of the paper as a central part of the process, Seurat's Conté crayon develops its image as if the paper were light-sensitive. The results look like a photographic detail enlarged to a grainy shimmer. More than usually, the process of drawing seems to be preserved in the finished drawing. And the process is also akin to brass-rubbing: it is sculptural in its emphasis on shape, on outline rather than line. And its textures summon up the surface of polished granite – not a high, machined polish, but a worn patina, still preserving its precious irregularities.

A good chalk drawing of Seurat by his art-school contemporary Ernest-Joseph Laurent shows us, by contrast, how little store Seurat set by the line. Seurat's *Woman Reading* has already moved beyond convention, where what is captured is aura, as though drawing were a species of spiritualism. The woman is there in outline, granite, granular, her one distinguishing feature a downcast eyelid – a detail which is indistinct, almost an accident of the paper, yet utterly authoritative and precise. That eye is reading, not resting. The drawing is a record of discovery. Seurat finds what is there within the paper. He doesn't seem to draw *on* the paper. This sense of finding images is reinforced by the presence of the MICHALLET watermark in several drawings. In the portrait of Aman-Jean it is picked out vertically in the top left of the drawing.

This exhibition shows Seurat working towards the brilliant unfinished finish, which privileges texture over line. Not all the early drawings are uniformly successful. *Locomotive*, for example, tries to make Conté crayon work like charcoal. The enlargement effect is in abeyance and, in spite of the conveniently obnubilated subject, the texture is curiously perfunctory and the stylised smoke a particular failure. In *Two Men Walking in a Field*, Seurat addresses the problem of total texture – background, middle-ground, foreground. He favours overlaid wispy lines, a little like fibreglass, which can stand for cracked earth, scrubby vegetation, brambles, in a non-representational way. As texture it fails, because it is so clearly a device – clever, relatively versatile, but without the inevitability of the granites conjured out of the paper by his Conté crayon.

These granites are at once monumental, particularly where the human figure is in question, and capable of the subtlest inflections – as when, for instance, Seurat manages to specify a heavy twill material for the cloak of *The Nanny*. As a technique, it is perfect for textures, and eventually it marginalised other interesting stylistic experiments – like the pencilled ur-cubist, Gris-like rendition of *Woman Seated on a Bench*, or the worn dry-point quality of the charcoal sketch *The Seamstress: A Painting on the Wall*. These explorations are broken off in favour of the sculpted Conté crayon, where the image seems to seep out of the paper like the legendary veronica.

The technique has its limitations. It can make for some difficulty with a thing as intricate as the ear. Aman-Jean's portrait has wonderful spikes of hair in his back crown and a linen cravat whose white weave is almost palpable – and yet his earlobe is the size of a small mastoid. Seurat has given his fellow-artist a thick ear. Apart from that, it is a marvellous drawing, whose effect is at first academic – though a glance at Seurat's early charcoal study *Standing Man, Hands Outstretched* merely emphasises the extraordinary distance between the earlier, meticulous work (with its graphic, ragged prepuce and its cock and balls the dark shade of furniture stain) and the essentially suggestive later piece. The *Portrait of Aman-Jean* is deliciously granular and shimmers in a way that anticipates Seurat's pointillisme – though pointillisme is, of course, a theory of colour. Here the dots are created by the surface of the paper. They are brought out rather than brought there by the crayon. Later the dots are put there by the point of the brush: Seurat's *Bridge at Courbevoie* is fully fledged pointillisme, whereas *Bathers at Asnières* has a single pocket of touches to the hat of Echo. Pointillisme, for all its laborious application, can create a permanent spontaneity of effect because, as viewer, you are as aware of the representation as of the scene represented. In *Bridge at Courbevoie*, smoke emerges from a background chimney like a gyre of midges. In fact, the whole picture is so minutely speckled, you half feel that the marks may just take off like a host of insects.

The wall of nine drawings for *Bathers at Asnières* is a miracle of obvious, unsurpassed, immediate beauty, classical and perfect. It is unforgettable and flawless. In particular, there is a previously unknown drawing, *Study for 'Bathers at Asnières'*, which materialised (the *mot juste* for Seurat's technique) during research for this exhibition. The drawing is crucial for a proper understanding of Seurat's final grand oil, though it is possible to deduce the same argument from *Seated Nude Boy*, which is part of the holdings of the National Gallery of Scotland. One thinks of Michelangelo's idealised heads. Very little else can begin to compare with Seurat's frank pursuit of balance and beauty, poise and perfection. In the drawings, both figures are naked, more boyish, slighter, vulnerable – and edited for effect, idealised. The genitalia of the standing boy are invisible.

Instead, the emphasis is on his tilted, boyishly sturdy waist and one prominent buttock, muscular and pleasingly scalloped. Adolescence on the cusp of manhood. The seated nude, on the other hand, is more fragile – curved shoulders, narrow neck, a long slim thigh. Knee, calf and complicated hands have been silently censored to keep the simplicity and balance. Not that you notice until you look at the final oil.

In the big picture, the catalogue argues, Seurat effects an elision of this classicism with the realities of contemporary Asnières. I think this idea is wrong. What takes place is not an accommodation, but rather a repudiation of the idea of classical perfection – in favour of the task of painting modern life. In the final picture, both these figures are clothed. The swimming costumes make an enormous difference. The seated figure is deliberately and systematically deprived of beauty – the profile coarsened, the nose enlarged, the upper lip an ungainly flap. The hands reappear. The knee turns down into an amputated calf, a stump. Beauty, texture, intricacy, have gone. In their place is a pair of cotton swimming trunks and a hair-style like a ginger wig. Echo's buttocks are out of sight underwater and clad in a costume, too. The figure from Ovid has been metamorphosed into an ordinary urchin. These decisions show exemplary artistic courage.

To forgo obvious beauty, irresistible beauty, is never easy. Matthew Arnold wrote that poetry should be a criticism of life. Oscar Wilde misinterpreted this to mean that art was a series of cosmetic improvements on life in the interests of beauty. What Arnold really meant by 'criticism', whether of an artwork or life, was that it should not remake the object under scrutiny, but describe it accurately – as it really is. The greatest artists take their stand with Arnold, even if this involves uglinesses of every kind. It isn't the business of art to flatter reality. Seurat's Conté crayon confers a twilit charisma on *Hats, Shoes and Undergarments*, not to mention a pair of elasticated boots. But he could also see these items as in fact they really were – banal, obvious, devoid of poetry, but redeemed by their irrefutable reality, the truth of their ordinary ugliness. In the final oil, the boots have their loops restored and they move, with that one touch, from the abstract world of shape into the welter of seams, stitching, shoe-horns, polish and welts ...

When Claudio Abbado had been with the Berlin Philharmonic for a year, the BBC screened a documentary in which the conductor rehearsed a young violinist protégée. At one point, he interrupted her playing to tell her she was making a particular passage too beautiful. 'It should be an ugly sound,' he advised. Seurat's great picture is a similar discovery – that great art is not necessarily synonymous with beauty. There is love and there is sex.

There are other, less obvious satisfactions. Think how powerful the idea of obscenity is. *Bathers at Asnières* offers immense formal satisfactions, all of them orchestrated by the figure of Echo, who is a self-conscious synecdoche in a picture where so many things are echoes of other things. Those loops on the boots, for example, mimic the flick of red hair at the base of their owner's neck. His half-visible straw boater parallels the submerged figure with his back to us. Then there is the reclining, bowler-hatted figure in the foreground, whose little spaniel mirrors its master: both are looking over their shoulders and presenting a profile. The dog's long tail picks up on its master's long brown trousers.

This figure is also the lynch-pin of one of the picture's two compositional templates. He is the apex of a triangle which runs (echoically) from the background triangle of sail on the left to the other triangle of sail to the right. The left-hand side of the triangle runs from the sail to the bowler-hatted figure, through a series of echoing intermediate figures – a stretched-out figure in a pink shirt, then two figures both with raised knees, the stretched figure of the bowler-hatted dog-owner. The right-hand side of the triangle runs from the bowler-hat to the right-hand triangular sail, via the bather on the bank, the submerged figure whose back is turned, and the wherry with its two passengers. The river itself forms a further, overlapping triangle, whose apex is the bottom-right-hand corner of the painting. The base of both triangles is the background of Clichy, which is a shared horizontal. These two triangles echo each other as they overlap like an old-fashioned W, which was a double V: W.

In addition there is a second compositional shape which counters the picture's tendency to tilt to the right. The figure of Echo has raised hands and his bent elbows bring us back into the picture. The controlling shape here is the ellipse, like a ring of Saturn. We see this shape in the wherry, in the skiff, in the elongated green (of rushes? of grass?) in the river, as well as in the sandy shape of the river-bank. The figures make a flattened ellipse, too. From Echo the eye moves to the figure with his back to us, to the figure in the straw hat with raised knees, to the man in the 'wig', and back to Echo. The man in the bowler-hat is partly co-opted to this template and partly an echo of it – an entire ellipse in himself. The rim of his bowler is a further, echoic, mini-ellipse. Echo, then, is internalised, formal, silent and central to the composition.

Room 4 of this exhibition, 'Tradition and the Ideal', assembles classical sources for Seurat's masterpiece – sources which, in my view, are so many rogue echoes. Poussin's *Finding of Moses* and Flandrin's *Priam's Son* are two examples of paintings adduced to over-argue the case for the classical source as a justification of the painting of modern life. Everything here is irrelevant and misleading. The room epitomises the art-historian's fatal tendency to treat art as a relay in which the dull torch of tradition is passed, ever guttering anew, from artist to artist.

The key to Seurat's attitude lies in *Les Poseuses: Small Version*. Here the models are clearly intended to invoke the Three Graces, but the models (equally clearly) exist also in relation to *La Grande Jatte*, which apparently forms a whole wall in this painting. *La Grande Jatte* looks, in fact, like a window – a picture window – through which we can see the fully clothed, parasol-bearing Parisian public. Alongside there are these nude women who are surrounded by the clothes they have taken off, their shoes and their parasols. These models, then are not the Three Graces, Seurat insists; they are ordinary women like those at the edge of the Seine, ordinary women who just happen to have taken their clothes off. The classical is present in *Les Poseuses* but it is present only to be ironised by a great painter of modern life. Seurat was capable of classicism's easy, familiar 'poetry', but he preferred the more arduous truth of depicting the truth, the whole truth and nothing but the truth.

Old Friends in Venice
(1995)

Early evening. The lagoon like sandpaper, sparking with lights. Competing bands in Piazza San Marco. Two swallows like the hands of Edward Scissorhands. Mooring posts putting their heads together. A sparrow pursuing a hard crumb of *grissini* like a hockey puck across the restaurant floor. The Palazzo Ducale's faded pinks. Backpackers recognisable by their mosquito bites. The centipede in sole and in the hotel bath. Early morning. Hosing the chairs outside Florian's. The lagoon its usual drab olive, the colour of military fatigues. Local colour ...

I am here to see old friends I haven't seen for twenty years – Vittore Carpaccio's *L'uomo dal berretto rosso* and Antonello da Messina's *La Pietà* in the Museo Correr and Brancusi's *Bird in Space* at the Palazzo Guggenheim, among others. Unlike friends, art, of course, does not change. On the other hand, the postcard, like the photograph it really is, will tell us less and less as it gradually supplants the original to which it was initially a crude aide-mémoire. One's reluctance to buy postcards has everything to do with the fresh sensation of the original still vibrant in the optic nerve: the postcard colours are dramatically inaccurate and, as with all photographs, the detail is diminished and the volume of information reduced to a whisper. Over twenty years, however, it is the postcard which constitutes the work of art for all practical purposes – and a visit to Venice is the only way to supplant the copy by the original. The postcard, the reproduction, may be better than nothing, but it isn't everything: it *can't* be everything. In the Accademia, I check out the postcards against the originals I've just been looking at: Giorgione's *La Vecchia* and *La Tempesta* are both cropped, and, in fact, *La Tempesta* has lost the male figure on the left of the canvas, while *La Vecchia* has lost the final flourish of the moralising banner '*Col tempo*'. You shrug. Well, you can't have everything.

But why can't you have everything? Because, apparently, it is a law of life. At the Museo Correr, I arrive, prepared for the Carpaccio portrait head by several hours of looking at the narrative-epic Carpaccios in the Accademia. There is an aesthetic mystery here. A Carpaccio like *L'apparizione dei crocifissi del Monte Ararat nella chiesa di Sant'Antonio di Castello* doesn't lead you to expect the in-your-face face of *L'uomo dal berretto rosso* with its dispassionate accuracy. Instead there are twenty-nine figures in a dim church – a kind of sediment at the bottom of the painting. And, while there *are* portraits in *Arrivo degli ambasciatori inglesi*, they are too strenuously differentiated and the background figures are studiously composed, rather like a still from Resnais's *L'Année dernière à Marienbad*. 'Wooden' is the word that comes to mind, though there is quite a good cross-eyed burgher just below the feet of a middle-ground dwarf.

In *Il martrito dei pellegrini e i funerali di Orsola*, all motion and actions are portrayed by Carpaccio with a curious abruptness – particularly the two central 'running' figures, who are leaning forward in a way that makes you long for Muybridge. The posture is theoretical and the eye rumbles it immediately. The two figures are not running. They are having their first lessons in running. In other words, the Carpaccios in the Accademia demonstrate skill and the limitations of that skill, whereas the Correr's portrait is a masterpiece. The contradiction is resolved, perhaps in the only way possible. Sometime in the last twenty years, this particular friend has changed his name to *Gentiluomo dal berretto rosso*. But gentrification isn't the only bit of tampering with the birth certificate. This famous Carpaccio is no longer by Carpaccio, but by a *'Pittore ferrarese / bolognese'* – a painter, one might add, with skills well beyond Carpaccio. Twenty years ago at the Correr competing attributions were often pencilled and biroed on the walls under the official labelling. But it is unusual to see an 'unauthored' painting, as this one now is, retain its prominence and importance in the collection as a whole. The picture itself, rather than the name attached to it, is what grants it special status. We have come a long way from Berenson's specious attributions, once thought an indispensable guarantee of authenticity.

What makes a great portrait? Karl Kraus defined the portrait as a picture in which the mouth is wrong. So perhaps a great portrait is merely a picture in which the mouth is right – and certainly, in this case, the mouth is crucial to the painting, those thin lips at once pragmatic and pinched, tough and a touch apprehensive. The more you look at the mouth, the more enigmatic it becomes. Like the *Mona Lisa*. And, at once, a critical pitfall reveals itself. No one wants to sound like Pater on the *Mona Lisa*, where the picture is a pretext for free association: 'She is older than the rocks among which she sits; like the vampire, she has been dead many times, and learned the secrets of the grave.' On the other hand, there is the less risky but totally uninformative procedure recommended by Degas: 'Among people who understand, words are not necessary. You say humph, he, ha, and everything has been said.' Would it were true. Humph. He, ha.

In the case of Giorgione's *La Vecchia*, it is possible to speak of the painter's intention – so clearly signposted in the words *'Col tempo'*. The portrait itself is beautifully carried out, in addition to the primary moral purpose. The palette is strictly circumscribed – white, dirty pink, brown. The three-quarter face isn't dramatically old, but the nose's wings are big with age, the mouth is open to breathe and one lower canine stands up and out – an irregularity which is paralleled in the fold of her under-blouse. The fringe of her shawl picks up the haze of hair hanging from her left brow. The picture, then, is composed. And if you compare it to Giuseppe Nogari's *Vecchia con ciotala* (also in the Accademia), the difference is at once apparent. Here, everything centres on the easy pathos of the old woman's eyes, brimming like oysters in their ichor.

The Giorgione reminds us of T. S. Eliot's disquisition on meaning in poetry (*The Use of Poetry and the Use of Criticism*, 1933): 'the chief use of the "meaning" of a poem, in the ordinary sense, may be ... to satisfy one habit of the reader, to keep his mind diverted and quiet, while the poem does its work upon him: much as the imaginary burglar is always provided with a bit of nice meat for the house dog.' Giorgione's meaning is a *tempus fugit* – contemporaries would have rested comfortably enough on this solid and stable truth while the composition did its proper work.

However, it is not always true that the ultimate painterly values are exclusively aesthetic in portraiture: Whistler – need it be said? – intends to shock us when he entitles his portrait of his mother *Composition in Grey and Black*. In many portraits, though not all, there is a psychological dimension. In the Giorgione, this dimension is muted: the old woman is herself unreflective; she glances at the painter; she inhabits her old age unselfconsciously, like an animal. The psychological possibilities are therefore as restricted as Giorgione's palette.

But in many portraits the aim is to admit the viewer to the psyche of the sitter – to tell us what kind of person we are looking at. And this aim coincides with an almost ineradicable human instinct. In Gentile Bellini's *Ritratto del Doge Giovanni Mocenigo*, in the Museo Correr, the artist has chosen for us the moment of coincidence between familiar power and the ebbing of testosterone – the flat, inexpressive eyes, the razor-blade mouth, on the one hand; on the other, the pinkly feminine, palpy skin, almost beardless and belying the obvious habit of authority.

Part of the brilliance of *Gentiluomo dal berretto rosso* is the utterly contemporary immediacy of the face. He looks like the brother of Philip Roth. But, while we *recognise* this face, its level, quizzical gaze, the face itself guards its interpretation. The expression isn't open but closed – suffused with wary neutrality. I used to think this a tough face, but, since restoration, a small fleck of paint has gone missing from the left of the mouth – and this introduces a quality of undecidedness that I hadn't previously seen; perhaps because this quality wasn't here when the fleck of paint was.

Restoration is always controversial, of course. But the restoration of Antonello da Messina's *La Pietà* isn't controversial. It is a complete catastrophe which has destroyed a masterpiece. It, too, has been retitled: *Pietà con tre angeli*. I now have three different postcards of this picture, one of which represents its present condition in which the head of Christ is virtually wiped clean of features, let alone *expression*. The angels are outlines – facially empty, their arms and legs now pigment-free. There is no modelling. Instead there is a notice: 'although this painting has been defaced and also damaged by previous restoration it still conserves the charm of Antonello's strong figurative expression.' The wings of the angels survive and so does the body of Christ. In so far as one can guess at the face, the lips are closed – unlike Antonello's *Pietà* in the Prado (again 'Sostenido por un ángel'), where Christ is exhausted and open-mouthed like someone who has run a long way, watched by a weeping angel. The facial expression of the Christ at the Correr has to be conjectural, so little remains. You could say it is serene with fatigue, but the weariness is entirely in the body – the parted thighs, the total limpness, especially of the left wrist, which, because it isn't a *gesture*, is devoid of camp and replete with death. Two delicate, asymmetric creases are eloquent at his slim waist. The chin is on the chest – formerly with a little under-scrub of beard. The whole is a kind of pictorial transferred epithet (or, rather, *was* a transferred epithet) in which the young angels lend their childishness to the figure of Christ. It amounts to a curious reversal of a familiar situation – the sleepy adult being half helped by children back to his own bed. Thank goodness for my old, curled postcard from 1975 with its pragmatic overpainting – its restoration as repair.

Which brings me to the Guggenheim and Brancusi's *Bird in Space*. Like Giacometti's great masterpiece *Statue of a Headless Woman Walking* (1932), this sculpture has been damaged. On the wall of the Guggenheim–Ray and Patsy Nasher Giacometti Gallery, we read the maestro Giacometti on the qualities of plaster: '*Il gesso e una material senza peso, la più spirituale.*' There is a bronze replica of *Woman Walking* of the same date and it is, by comparison, coarse. It is, as it were, the postcard – of bronze. The plaster statue has certainly been broken once through the top of the thighs and perhaps also through the buttocks. The cracks are clearly visible from the back, where the left buttock is a sweet fraction lower than the right because the left leg is inched forward. Nevertheless, this is really a sculpture whose effect is purely frontal and, from the front, by a miracle, the repair(s) are invisible. A purist would, of course, have left the statue in two or three pieces. As it is, the statue stands there in its purity and pallor like a holy ghost. Indefinite article.

One notices the repair to Brancusi's bird because the repair isn't successful. It was, according to the deputy director, the patient and shrewd Philip Rylands, broken in the sixties. Everything depends on the singleness of Brancusi's vision and, for my money, the best version is the 1929 plaster version. The Guggenheim's version is polished brass and has been repaired at its slimmest, most crucial point, and its materially weakest point, too. The bird's mass must be weightless, *in space*, and Brancusi achieves this effect by poising the long body on what seems an impossibly fine waist above the tail. If, however, this really *is* impossibly thin, the aesthetic finesse is nullified. Now what you see at the Guggenheim is the mistake, the fatal miscalculation, and not the idea of weightlessness.

The Guggenheim Collection has changed considerably in the last twenty years. It is open the year round (except Tuesdays and Christmas Day), whereas when Peggy Guggenheim was alive, it was open Monday, Wednesday and Friday from 3 to 5 p.m. What you see has changed, too. The whole lower floor of the palazzo is now administrative, so there is no longer room to show the artistic mistakes, the duff purchases made by Peggy Guggenheim as her collection neared the contemporary. According to Philip Rylands, there is an unwritten ethic that institutions 'don't de-accession the work of living artists'. All the same, the bureaucratic expansion means you no longer see, say, Günther Uecker's *Nail Construction*, which, as I remember it, was six-inch nails in a colander. Nor do you see any Alan Davie. Nor Leslie Thornton. Nor Reg Butler. Nor Kenneth Armitage. Nor Lynn Chadwick. Nor Fritz Hundertwasser. Not, perhaps, that it matters very much. But it does demonstrate, I think, how uncertain Peggy Guggenheim's taste actually was.

When I put it to Philip Rylands that the collection tailed off, he agreed, but he was careful to put the Guggenheim Collection in perspective. Undoubtedly, the collection is unique in Italy – far and away the best of its kind, since it is international, whereas modern Italian collections tend to be about modern Italian painting. Nevertheless, the Guggenheim has gaps in its completeness: there is no German expressionism, no Matisse and no later abstract expressionism. Pursuing what he called 'the mirage of completeness', it would be 'tremendously amusing' if, as deputy director, he had an executive, purchasing function. In fact, there have been additions as the Guggenheim has accepted (very selectively) five or six works *as gifts*. For example, such a pragmatic acquisition would be the Fontana donated by the Fontana Foundation.

What of Peggy Guggenheim's taste and flair? Rylands is loyal and affectionate but unable to suppress his intelligence completely. Thus, buying a 1911 Picasso in 1941 in New York represents expenditure rather than artistic risk. On the other hand, Peggy Guggenheim was instrumental in creating American abstract expressionism, in stealing the idea of the avant-garde from Paris, in setting up Pollock, Motherwell and Rothko.

Pollock, it seems to me, is the crucial figure in the question of Peggy Guggenheim's taste. Two things that Philip Rylands told me about Peggy Guggenheim strike me as relevant here, though at the time they seemed merely anecdotal. On reflection, they seem symbolic and symptomatic. Her mode of conversation, he said, was to ask questions and not listen to the answers. This peremptory care-lessness is reflected in the old Guggenheim catalogue, printed in June 1973, long before Philip Rylands was in a position of responsibility: in it, Klee's *Portrait of Mme P in the South* is printed back to front. Perhaps she stopped looking at her pictures? Even then, you would think she would notice the signature was back-wards. The other anecdote was that she read Henry James – 'all the time', 'of course, she didn't understand a word, but, then, who does?' James's *What Maisie Knew* was a particular favourite, apparently – and Mr Rylands explains the attrac-tion for Peggy Guggenheim as residing in the punning title, the maze.

At the time, I begin by agreeing and cite the notorious sentence from the book: 'but if he had an idea at the back of his head she had also one in a recess as deep, and for a time, while they sat together, there was an extraordinary mute passage between her vision of this vision of his, his vision of her vision, and her vision of his vision of her vision.'

But if this seems like a maze, it isn't difficult to penetrate the centre. Don-nishly, I began a tutorial on *What Maisie Knew*, explaining that Mrs Wix is the moral centre of the novel, despite her ignominious squint and her perspiring bulk ('as I'm perspiring now'). 'But,' objects Rylands, 'Maisie is so cruel to Mrs Wix.' Me: 'Yes, but Mrs Wix keeps Maisie on the moral straight and narrow –' And I break off – conscious then, as now, that close analysis can appear boring. But at 4 a.m. I realise that 'boring' is not the right word, that 'taxing' or 'tiring' or 'exhausting' or 'hard work' are more just words. And at 4 a.m. I am awoken by the thought that this is an allegory of Peggy Guggenheim's attitude to art in general: it is *comfortable* to consign art to the unfathomable. 'She didn't understand a word, but, then, who does?' And the paintings of Jackson Pollock are perfectly suited to this attitude because they are *simply* incomprehensible. Therefore there is no need to think.

When I asked Philip Rylands about the value of Pollock's work, he answered that he would never be dislodged from the text books and that he was a con-troversial painter only to the man in the street. Of course, there would be 'little rituals of revisionism' – suggestions, for example, that Pollock's wife, Lee Kras-ner, was the better painter, or that someone had 'dripped' before Pollock – but his place in art history was assured. His importance, according to Rylands, was that he had freed the artist from the responsibility to paint *anything* – figurative or abstracted. Pollock withdraws from direct contact with the canvas and so puts us in direct touch with his psyche. Some artist-students from NYU, Rylands remembers, responded to Pollock 'without fear of incomprehension'.

In the current Guggenheim catalogue, the entry on Rothko's *Sacrifice* (April 1946) is a perfect example of this eagerness to arrive at the intellectu-ally undemanding area of complete abstraction, where there can be no fear of 'incomprehension'. 'Figurative and literary allusions, albeit disguised, persist here.' 'The title may be inspired by Rothko's interest in Greek tragedy and Friedrich Nietzsche's examination of its origins.' *But* 'despite the persistence of these references, overtly representative images have disappeared, signaling a move towards the complete abstraction of Rothko's mature style.' All this is completely wrong. The title's connotations are Hebraic, not Hellenistic. The Jewish Rothko is alluding to the idea of the scapegoat – a subject also treated by Holman Hunt. 'Overtly representative images' have *not* disappeared: the goat is at the bottom left of the canvas, reduced to a blue shadow below a *stain* of blood with spray at the edges. The desert sun is a black circle containing a pale yellow circle and there are mirage effects in grey. But Rothko's brilliant talent is all there in the laconic rendition of the goat – its horns, the forelegs drifting to the left like threads of a prayer shawl, the pot-bellied gravity of the body. It is a wonderful and essentially figurative painting. But you have to think.

Pollock saves us, Peggy Guggenheim, NYU art-students and the world at large from the need to think. We are put in direct touch with the artist's psyche. As a theory, it has all the appeal of fast-food, all the ease of McDonald's. But consider how difficult it is to be in touch with the psyche of a sitter when you're looking at a portrait, even though its very purpose is to do just that, at least in part. We can't really be sure we're receiving the artist's idea of the sitter, or that the artist's idea was right in any case.

In other words, we're back with Henry James – we're contemplating our vision of the artist's vision of the sitter's vision.

And here at least, with the portrait, viewer and artist are pulling in the same direction. The danger – we have already pointed out – is that we fantasise like Pater. Portraiture is only theoretically an act of divulgence.

How much less likely, then, that Jackson Pollock, by virtue of withdrawing from direct contact with the canvas, can put us in direct contact with his psyche – whatever *that* is.

I don't mean to imply that the argument against Pollock is an argument against the use of chance in art. Obviously, this is not a possible argumentative move, because capitalising on chance is an element in all artistic creation. But what becomes important with Pollock and with a creative environment where chance is maximised to the fullest extent is this – the crucial need for the artist to exercise *critical* judgement, to destroy everything that doesn't succeed in aesthetic terms, *not* in terms of how he happens to feel his psyche has found itself expressed. In these terms, Pollock had virtually no aesthetic judgement. His pictures aren't either good or bad. As we view them in the Guggenheim, they are uniformly mediocre. To see this, you only have to compare Pollock's aptly named *Alchemy* (turning dross into gold) with Klee's exquisite *Magic Garden*

(1926), whose basic material is plaster on mesh, slightly sunken, covered with texturally rich (not to say edible) colours. On this ravishing surface are scratched various figurative elements – a house with a fire escape, a little mad face, a glass containing a woman's face and neck which are also a wine glass. The charm of the whole comes from the way in which Klee harmonises his colour chaos. The effect is of looking at an infinitely untidy dressing table – covered in spilled cosmetics, absorbing explosions of eyeshadow, smeared lipsticks – and finding in it a thrilling peace and unity. To be a great abstract painter, like Klee, or Kandinsky, you have to have an optic nerve of exquisite sensibility. Or Rothko. Or Howard Hodgkin. Or Vuillard. Pollock plainly possessed no such thing. His appeal is different. He is recognisable. And you don't have to *think* about his pictures. Exactly like Henry James. No one understands him either.

Claes Oldenburg and Coosje van Bruggen
(1999)

In a way, the most exciting and convincing thing I saw in Venice was a piece of performance art by Bryan Robertson at breakfast. At the mention of Oldenburg, Bryan announced, 'Old grey dusty things. Every museum in America has an obligatory soft drum kit floppily collecting dust in a corner.' Whereupon, he sank like a soufflé into himself. The legendary Boneless Wonder. A puff ball suddenly short of puff.

The first sight of the Claes Oldenburg–Coosje van Bruggen exhibition in the Museo Correr is in Piazza San Marco as you approach from the Campanile end. From an upstairs window a yellow plastic rubbish-chute protrudes, one of those chains of sturdy builders' buckets. From it hangs a dark brown torrent of arrested dirt. Minutes before, I had been admiring the Pollock in a pizza. Thus prepared, I admired this radical, in-your-face mission statement – to refurbish the Museo Correr and rid it of its Renaissance rubbish. Or, if not a mission statement, a pre-emptive joke aimed at sceptics – that the exhibition itself was rubbish. (An equally plausible construction.)

But, as I neared the installation, I realised that the apparent chain of buckets was not in fact telescopic. Their configuration was much more a segmented length of flexible pipe – a sewage outlet. So I stood underneath, pondering the feathered suspension of liquid shit. It swayed in the breeze like a layer-cut wig, or black and brown strips of seaweed, with its coiffure faintly suggestive of Olivier as Henry V. Prompted maybe by the intimate connection between sewage and sea, I reflected that it could perhaps be intended to represent kelp or tangle – (*laminaria digitata*) that leonine seaweed. It was only the cover of the catalogue which alerted me to my misprision. Oldenburg and Van Bruggen actually intended to represent a lion's tail – appropriately enough, given the winged lion's symbolic Venetian role. T. S. Eliot's famous Venice poem asks 'Who clipped the lion's wings, / And flea'd his rump and pared his claws?' Now we know. Guilt at my misinterpretation was mitigated by the catalogue's reproduction of Oldenburg's preparatory sketch (not in the exhibition), entitled *Broom*, in which the lion's tail is assimilated to a painter's brush, mopping up little dumps and droppings of pigment. So – back to shit again, by a Joycean 'commodius vicus of recirculation'.

Exhibition at the Museo Correr, Venice Biennale, 1999.

My hermeneutical 'failure' prompts several arguable propositions relevant to the Oldenburg–Van Bruggen project.

How much of their work is any good? How much is shit? (Bryan Robertson at breakfast again: 'some beautiful things and some over-inflated jokes'.) How much do the (comparatively rare) successes depend on the transfiguration of rubbish? Specifically, the detritus of American life, typically magnified by Oldenburg's signature suburban surrealism. How important is it that the iconic banality should be recognisable? How much delay in recognition is permissible? How much delay is desirable? Is multiplicity of interpretation an index of profundity? Or merely a sentimental and redundant tenet left over from New Criticism – namely, the idea, fostered by William Empson's confused, overrated and idolised *Seven Types of Ambiguity*, that the essence of poetry is ambiguity, that singleness and richness are incompatible, contradictory features? Clearly, Oldenburg's wife, the literary half of this partnership, Coosje van Bruggen, instinctively favours such a position.

In the irritating (because simultaneously transmitted) videos which accompany the exhibition, she presents herself as the writer and conceptual enricher in the relationship. She contributes to the 'thinking process' – adding complexity and commentary, believing that 'not one way but two ways [of interpretation] will make it [the art-work] last'. Thus, in *Spoonbridge and Cherry* (1988, Minneapolis, Minnesota) the spoon was Claes's but the cherry was added by Coosje. (A straightforward enough female sexual reference and one insistent on equality, on balance. The cherry has a stalk, just like the masculine spoon.) And in the catalogue interview, Van Bruggen is relaxed, not to say encouraging, about multiplicity of interpretation: 'while the work functions as the sign we intended it to be, at the same time members of the community bring their own interpretations to it.'

Which, of course, consoled me for my gaffe. On the other hand, given the only tenuous resemblance of their sculpture to a lion's (non-segmented) tail, perhaps I needed no reassuring: I could be confidently cock-eyed, since the mote on my retina was induced by the beam in theirs. In the exhibition itself, *Bottle of Notes* (1993) reinforced the idea of complication – is, indeed, a piece which is about the very meaning of meaning. It equates complexity with profundity. Such an equation is frequently true (especially in literature) but not *necessarily* true: it must take into consideration Eliot's opposing, higher valuation of 'A condition of complete simplicity / (Costing not less than everything)'. Profundity, of course, ensures that those vulnerable 'over-inflated jokes' are protected. Coosje van Bruggen is there to mitigate the flip side of Oldenburg. *Bottle of Notes* is a metal bottle consisting of words, of joined-up writing, coloured white – a continuum which contains further, *blue,* joined-up writing. The proverbial message in the bottle, therefore, is itself contained within a message. Form and content, that old circus act of inseparable Siamese twins, are with us once more. Wow. 'Tell me now what is *claritas* and you win the cigar,' Lynch says to Dedalus in Joyce's *Portrait of the Artist as a Young Man.*

This take on interpretation, however, so favoured by Van Bruggen, actually runs contrary to the spirit of the very best Oldenburg. She favours *kinesis*, the idea of 'the unsettling beauty of the imperfect condition', things exploding, imploding, whereas Oldenburg seeks 'classical equilibrium' – 'I tend to think art has a kind of stasis to it.' And *he*, after all, is the artist, not she. What she *helps* him to is change – relief from the monstrous monotony of his basic methodology. Mere defamiliarisation is in itself no guarantee of artistic success. Think of successful defamiliarisation and think of, for example, Colette's inspirational transformations in her libretto for Ravel's *L'Enfant et les sortilèges* – those shepherds and shepherdesses from the torn nursery wallpaper who lament their lost 'green sheep upon the mauve grass'. A witty and beautifully judged ironic pathos. Without Colette's taste and imagination, defamiliarisation isn't much more than a methodological cliché. It all depends on the how and the who. Oldenburg is overconfidently democratic when he says that 'essentially the use of an object, a simple object that people know from their own experience, is a radical act in itself. Almost any situation for such an object in a large scale is going to be a radical statement. You're not expected to monumentalise simple, ordinary things.'

Not unless you're Claes Oldenburg.

Coosje van Bruggen has saved him somewhat from this artistic predictability. Without her, no *Dropped Bowl with Scattered Slices and Peels* (1990), no *Toppling Ladder with Spilling Paint* (1986). So her influence isn't entirely detrimental. But... the merit of Oldenburg is inseparable from the monotony. The artefacts which *work* work in an orthodox Oldenburgian way. The fundamental key is given the spectator as he mounts the flight of stairs to the Museo Correr proper – given with a straightforward clarity that is avoided in the many obfuscations in the catalogue, on video and elsewhere. At the foot of the stairs, suspended above the viewer, are a pink arch, an off-white accordion of stairs, a green obelisk, a faded apricot pediment with two pillars (the right one a touch withered) – classical quotations, in other words, presented as soft furnishings, upholstered so that the steels zips are on view. Dunlopillars. This is partly an in-joke directed at Christo that just about wraps things up. More meaningfully, of course, it is a summoning of classicism – mildly tinged with irony and weightlessness only to avoid solemnity and ponderousness. An evocation and an invocation of classicism.

The best Oldenburgs do not merely indulge the automatic and reflex radicalism of incongruous scale, matching the monumental to the everyday – which would scarcely be an advance on the tedious predictability of René Magritte's outsize matches and combs. The best Oldenburgs discover a classical, Brancusi-like purity of line in the most mundane objects. Which is why, at the top of the Correr stairs, Oldenburg confronts us with two slices of all-American blueberry pie wodged onto the balustrade balls. Europe and the New World – separated only by a flight of stairs.

The essential aesthetic journey to be undertaken is there from the bottom to the top – from Palladio to home-baked pie. And it has to be instant. This stereoscopy, bringing together the old and the new, is a question of identification, though. It isn't a simple matter of juxtaposition – as it often strives to be in the Oldenburg canon. What makes art more than merely conceptual – always – is the account that needs to be taken of the means. Brancusi's various *Birds in Space* are not uniformly good. Obviously, the broken and mended example in the Palazzo Guggenheim is significantly spoilt. Only one or two of the many versions actually work by creating the correct, impossible, but mastered, viable slenderness. Brancusi's several versions of *The Kiss* are by no means equal. Some are downright clumsy. One or two only are perfection. Oldenburg's output is even more uneven – though with notable successes which I will come to, as well as notable failures.

The root impulse in this deliberate conflation of contemporary and classical is political and patriotic, if not downright chauvinistic. To understand it, you need to consider the immediate post-war American imperium – a culture of surpassing vulgarity – of power and perceived aesthetic poverty, of Coca-Cola, of consumerism, of baked-bean baroque. Not even redeemed by a glorious barbarism, America was ketchup and kitsch. Pop Art's response was to brazen it out, to revel in it – to call it Art. Oldenburg's sophisticated, if belated, response is much more subtle – a cultural cringe. He collates the classical and the all-American cliché by discovering beautiful design in the drearily everyday where, very occasionally, it is indubitably to be found. Consider the baseball bat – its shape as intrinsically elegant as the Indian exercise clubs that provided the model for Perrier bottles. The catalogue shows us photographs of bats fresh from the sporting-goods store, mounted on plinths, and conceding nothing to the inevitabilities of the best Arps, and little to the best Brancusis, like *Fish* or *Little Bird II*. The found object meets the connoisseur of the concrete jungle, as Stanley met David Livingstone. A chance in a million. Why?

Because most everyday objects are ugly – and, if they are, nothing will transform them, let alone the pathetically simple magic of enlargement. Enlarge a hideous dust pan and brush – and you get an even uglier dust pan and brush – *Big Sweep* (1999). Or take Oldenburg's monumental *Saw, Sawing* (1996), which contrives to maximise the dime-store horror of the red plastic handle, while losing the extraordinary beauty conferred on the saw model by Oldenburg's instinctive taste. *Study for a Sculpture in the Form of a Saw, Cutting* (1973) is exquisite, constructed from cardboard with inner corrugation, a Batman cut-out of burnt ochre, sprayed silver for the top of the saw-blade. Oldenburg has sensed the beauty in the saw-shape, a beauty all but hidden by the utilitarian materials – the bulbous bright-red plastic, the raw metal screws, which have been fatally restored in the magnified monument.

The baseball bat is a different case. Here the object requires no improvement, nothing but unprejudiced recognition of a beautiful shape. A shape that Oldenburg violates as he scales up the project, since he appears not to realise that the solidity of the baseball bat is nine tenths of its charm. Instead of this matchless hardwood, perfectly turned, we are offered a woven *wicker-work* baseball bat, the size of a small skyscraper. Though constructed from steel, the thing is literally and aesthetically hollow. It is, in theory at least, hard to imagine how anyone could impair the classical beauty of the safety pin – what Russians call an English pin – but Oldenburg contrives just that. How? By the simple expedient of having a metal pin whose width and grey colour look like pumped-up plastic – so that *Corridor Pin* (1999) embodies as much conviction as an inflatable woman with puckered plastic seams. On the other hand, *Dream Pin, Clasp*, a safety pin without the pin, affects one with the force of macabre Lewis Carroll, assisted, if anything, by the nastiness of the materials. The drawing study, curiously, has none of the menace that exudes from the finished sculpture.

This variation in quality control within a single subject is conspicuous in *Monument to the Last Horse* (1990), where a rusty horseshoe with nails laconically evokes the radical, idealised curve of a horse's neck. One nail *is* an ear. The feel of the thing is rather like those bronzes of Picasso done in the thirties from crude plaster or clay maquettes (for example, *Le Guerrier*, 1933). It isn't at all replication or representation – it is pure evocation, classical only in the straitened means employed. What is odd, however, is the failure of the preparatory drawings to capture any horsiness at all – a fatal weakness common to nearly every 'realisation' of Oldenburg's idea, except the one named, *Monument to the Last Horse* (1990).

The great, typical successes are *Flashlight, Final Model* (1980) and *Clothespin – 45 Foot Version, Model* (1976–8). Here Oldenburg finds the indisputably classical in the everyday. The pieces are obvious and eternally surprising. Only an eye of genius could have seen them. But that eye's talent is intermittent. Or is it that art requires not only recognition but contrivance? The flashlight is a profound black and finely finned along its length – the switch suggested by only the faintest variant. Van Bruggen calls this 'an organic cactus-like form', a description that scarcely does justice to the finesse of the fins. The piece is exactly assimilated to the corduroy classical column and rests on its own circle of light. The equation is error-free and ungainsayable and gratifyingly impossible. One plus one is one. Orwell's doublethink redeemed in the aesthetic sphere. But *Flashlight* (1979) fails completely because it is small and (frankly) dumpy. Nor does *Flashlight, Study for Final Version* (1979) work either because, although it, too, is ribbed, it is over-bulky at the bottom and has none of the ravishing balance of *Flashlight, Final Model*. The idea, then, depends crucially on enhancement of the found object. Were those fins actually based on the muffled symmetries of a cactus, *Flashlight, Final Model* (1980) wouldn't work. That clothespin resembles the everyday object as Raquel Welch resembles the readers' wives in 'Your Bit'. Its legs are longer. More curvacious. They go right up to its armpits. Execution is everything.

And execution depends on the artist. Isn't something nearly always lost when the assistants and the factories are employed to realise large-scale projects? Is it heretical to suggest that Oldenburg's strength is more clearly visible in the draw-ings and models than in the factory-finished monuments? In the Correr show, there are some lovely, delicate drawings. *Umbrella, Inscribed 'R. Crusoe'* (1977) is a shamelessly pretty drawing of a red parasol on green grass, Japanese in its simplicity – a work that underlines the crudity of the large sculptural models of Crusoe's umbrella. Van Bruggen may multiply her spells as she wishes – insisting on 'the many associative images connected to this piece [*The Architect's Handkerchief*]' or insisting on the literary *lions* who have worked in Venice. But, in the end, it is Oldenburg's eye which, for better, for worse, for richer and for simplification, is going to decide how this marriage of contemporary and clas-sical will work out.

And those soft, floppy affairs from earlier? That was the first marriage. It didn't work out.

Masterpieces: Things in Particular
(1997)

Interviewed in 1969 by James Mossman for BBC 2, Nabokov said, 'I go by books, not by authors.' And he proceeded to lavish praise on *Anna Karenina* while categorising *War and Peace* as a work 'for that amorphic and limp creature known as "the general reader"'. I feel the same way. I go by pictures, not by painters.

For instance, in a recent *New Yorker*, Adam Gopnik attacked Picasso, exempting only his cubist period. Writing in the *New York Review of Books*, James Fenton was quick to defend Picasso in a prolegomena to his review of John Richardson's second biographical volume. He chose Gopnik's most fatuous attempt at character assassination. Why hadn't Picasso fought in either world war? Fenton neatly retorted that since Spain wasn't a participant in the First World War, there was no obligation on Picasso to enlist. As for the second, it was, and still is, unusual, Fenton noted, for men of fifty-nine to fight. *Touché*.

However, Fenton did not even address Gopnik's more interesting and less easily answerable criticism directed at the coarse poster rhetoric, the indignant voluble gothic of *Guernica*, masquerading as tragedy. Nor those sentimental political props, the doves, the fauns, the pan-pipes, that populate post-war Picasso – every one of them off the peg, drawn from general stores instead of the individual imagination. Glib, prêt-à-porter, apparat chic.

And then I remembered Picasso's bull at MoMA in New York – to the left of the men's toilet as you come out. I saw it in September. It is worth flying the Atlantic for. My notebook says: 'plywood cut-out sculpture'. This seems culpably laconic. But then the sculpture itself is laconic – a white wood simplified outline of a bull in profile, tail down to the left, head to the right and turned to face the viewer. The horns are not pointed but finished with pom-poms, as it were. The lower body of the bull is masked with a second outline, not of white wood, but of a coarser, darker wood, the texture of packing cases. One effect is to multiply the bull's legs, or to supply the usual four with shadow or motion. To this smooth/coarse, white/raw mahogany template, Picasso adds four things: the sinews of the bull, the veins of the bull, the flies on the bull and the sweat on the bull. The sinews and veins are stripped reddish brown twigs which are roughly nailed to the other two textures. The nails are sturdy and have been hammered in, then bent across the twigs. The nail heads bite into the white plywood finish and the packing-case material. Flies and sweat are clusters of gunmetal tin-tacks – darkly glittering, strategically placed where you would expect to find them. The eyes are unforgettable – nuts and bolts right through the head, full of menace. Unforgivably, there is no postcard of this masterpiece – this possibly misremembered masterpiece.

Its relevance to the Gopnik–Fenton dispute is this: you can smell this bull; you can see the sinews; the hair is there before you in the rough hirsuteness of the wood. To the idea of the bull, to its billboard outline, to its almost cartoon conception, Picasso has roughly added its actual roughness, its animal force, its beastliness. It hardly makes sense to speak of this sculpture – so particular, so perfect in its conscious shift from stylisation to realisation – in terms of anything other than itself. The Gopnik–Fenton debate, the prosecution and defence of 'Picasso', is conceived in such broad terms that the verdict, either way, is meaningless. Artists are uneven. We persist, nevertheless, in our pursuit, of Either/Or. Genius or charlatan? It is the idea of genius we should forget. It is a figment. It is a concept fuelled by mankind's unconquerable sentimentality, by our nostalgia for the absolute. Let us stop pretending we can either arraign or acquit, enthrone or depose. Let us look at what is there – the particular in its particularity – and leave the cosmic accountancy to the likes of George Steiner with his silo of crude superlatives.

Writing about Giacometti, Andrew Graham-Dixon was dismissive when he reviewed the retrospective at the Royal Academy. Unpersuaded by Giacometti's genius, Graham-Dixon argued that the large claims made for Giacometti rested on the work of the last twenty years – work which was 'repetitive', showed 'an almost complete lack of imagination', was derivative from Etruscan art and slavishly illustrated the ideas of Jean-Paul Sartre, specifically 'the hell of existential alienation'. Andrew Graham-Dixon isn't unlearned but he is tempted by his silo of crude thunderbolts. When I read his piece, I could not help remembering Giacometti's Afghan hound (or was it a borzoi?) in MoMA. My notebook says 'witty, droll, beautiful'. No subject could be better suited to Giacometti's characteristic etiolation. The artist knows it. His style has met its match, literally. So the sculpture is self-ironical, ruefully humorous. Roquentin, the anti-hero of Sartre's *La Nausée*, with his troubled conflation of the human and the inanimate, could not be more irrelevant to this ironic, affectionate, accurate and exaggerated portrait of an absurd animal – whose absurdity has nothing at all to do with the Absurd of Sartrean existentialism, and everything to do with looking like canine spaghetti.

(A digression: just after Christmas, I saw David Lean's film of *Dr Zhivago*, thirty years after falling in love with Julie Christie. Less susceptible these days, my vision less hampered by romantic haze, I noticed the sexual symbolism for the first time, perhaps alerted by Dirk Bogarde's reminiscence of working with Joe Losey on *The Servant* – Losey wanted the Bogarde character to return from shopping with a string bag containing a marrow, two melons and a jar of salad cream, presumably to underscore the movie's portrayal of repressed homosexual desire, just post-Wolfenden but pre-implementation. Bogarde refused. In the roughly contemporary *Dr Zhivago*, Lean shows us the loss of Lara's virginity, and its implicit brutality, by the zeugma of intercut footage of Cossacks attacking a street demonstration. We see the older man, Komarovsky, lean to Lara and kiss her in the carriage. Cut to close-up of the Cossacks mounting, their haunches hitting the saddles, pumping forcefully down. Cut to the peaceful march and its destruction by the sabre-wielding Cossacks. Back to Komarovsky saying goodbye to Lara. Rod Steiger hands Julie Christie into her carriage, carnally known and conceivably a teeny bit sore – or worse, given the cut back to the march and a huge patch of blood on the snow. I was reminded of the Balthus portrait of André Derain in MoMA. Derain fills the foreground, wearing a dressing gown. The right background depicts a nymphet, raising and clasping one knee, flashing her lingerie like Gerty MacDowell in the 'Nausicaa' episode of *Ulysses* so that Bloom can take himself satisfactorily in hand. Derain, of course, can't see her, posed as he is. His mind could be on quite other things – except that *one* of his fingers is exploring the folds of his fly-fronted shirt, a garment which is here cunningly androgynous, at once flies and hairless fanny. Soon, I thought, some moral terrorist, unable to distinguish between art and reality, is going to demand that this picture be relegated to the stacks.)

Ah yes, art and reality. Looking at Monet's *Water Lilies*, I recalled Clement Greenberg's appropriation of this epic work to the cause of abstract expressionism. First, the picture is an optic experience. The eye is overwhelmed by the gorgeously textured colour, its loud long chord, in which the intimate – a water garden – achieves apotheosis. Greenberg is right: we are being asked to encounter colour itself, for itself, and on a more vehement scale than usual. But he is only partially right because what he says is true of any good picture. The pleasures of pigment are a *sine qua non*. Also, the Monet preserves the crucial link with represented reality – the link significantly severed by, say, Jackson Pollock, or the really good abstract expressionist, Rothko. In the Monet lilies, the representational element, however vestigial, is crucially maintained, and it engages the spectator's necessary (because human) need for art to 'mean' something. In the real world, all colour is abstract. When we look at real lilies, a real water garden, it never occurs to us to ask what they represent or mean. They are. We then enjoy pure colour, pure colour in the abstract, untempered, untampered, natural. Even in Rothko, pure colour isn't pure – it is arranged, prepared for the optic nerve as food is cooked by a master-chef.

At the Frick, I fell in love with the Chinese, downcast eyes of Beatrice of Aragon, a portrait bust by Francesco Laurana (*c.* 1430–1502). She has a faintly aquiline nose (invisible in the postcard's frontal representation) and the marble has been left, not rough exactly, but unpolished, so to speak, at the back – to capture exactly, thrillingly, the muslin texture of her cap. Art constantly moves us with its perfect similes while never once allowing us to confuse the exactitude of comparison with *das Ding an sich*, the thing itself. Equivalence is not the identical. Laurana's portrait head provides another example. There is a blemish in the marble under her left eye. It is an accident. It is a mole. Our pleasure lives in the scarcely discernible, the almost theoretical niche between the two. And in the slightest of angles given to her head, a touch to her left, and in the again barely identifiable niche between her young girl's gravity and her young girl's sadness.

Is Francesco Laurana a genius? Faced with this one perfect work, you see how crude the category is. A catalogue raisonné of a thousand other imperfect pieces by the same artist wouldn't touch this perfect piece in all its singleness.

Earlier in the year I went to Ronchamp to see Le Corbusier's Notre-Dame-du-Haut. There one has to contend with the egotism of Abbé René Bolle-Reddat, the pilgrimage priest, who is much given to scolding imagined infractions and to toneless demonstrations of the chapel's acoustic. Then there are Le Corbusier's sub-Cocteau decorations on the main door and the stained glass. There is a chip missing from the footrest of the hollow cross. A couple of glass tiles are cracked. A window pane at the ceiling line is broken. And yet...

And yet, note the impress of two scallop shells like fossils in the concrete door – an artistic act of commentary on the survival of an ancient tradition into a self-consciously modern era. Sir Walter Ralegh's pilgrim shell of quiet, fragile yet indomitable, linking the alluvial age to the time of reinforced concrete – a simple, symbolic promise of salvation. The architect as saviour, at once secular and numinous. Then there is the side chapel containing a plain one-piece altar of concrete, over which is laid a plain linen strip of altar cloth, on which there rests an open missal. It is the opposite of Catholic baroque. It is Puritan in its insistence on the purity of its means. Above the altar, the interior of the whitewashed tower rising, rising into light – light whose source is invisible but which strengthens from dimness to bright promise as the eye travels up. As an architectural device, it deploys its artifice with extraordinary cunning. It is paradoxical to accuse simplicity of ostentation. Nevertheless, our pleasure in the side altar is poised between the *appeal* of its unadorned mysticism and our awareness of the laconic and calculated means.

The chapel itself is at once high-tech and primitive. On the one hand, there is the reinforced concrete means; on the other hand, the whitewash, the thick walls, the irregular, intuitively placed windows, some profoundly inset, suggest bare, almost chthonic dwellings in some remote Greek village. The roof is said to be based on a crab shell picked up by Le Corbusier in 1946 on Long

Island. Another shell. Not the scallop shell of pilgrimage but a dwelling place. In fact, the whole building is a three-dimensional realisation of those Picassos of the thirties, which, extending cubism, conflate solid geometry and the human figure. Le Corbusier's darkened roof remembers Picasso's cross-hatching, however distantly. At Ronchamp, the constructivist meets the chthonic, the ultra-modernism of Picasso meets the ancient tradition of pilgrimage and prayer. And the chapel itself is both a monument imposing its reality for miles, an emblem of permanence, and a temporary structure whose impermanence is created by the gap between the roof and the supporting structure. The gap is carefully created illusion but it allows us to witness the impossible – a great boat, all curves, carrying the imprint of lengths of wood, being launched into space at the moment of its first movement. Le Corbusier has managed to freeze the second, the nanosecond, when the material becomes immaterial, when matter becomes spirit. Calculation and inspiration – poised between miracle and trick.

For this, one is prepared to put up with any amount of nonsense about 'visual acoustics, a phenomenon brought into the realm of forms', or vaunting claims for architecture as 'the synthesis of the major arts' bringing together 'form, volumes, colour, acoustics, music'. For this, too, one must tolerate the imperfections and unevennesses – largely the result of Le Corbusier's hubris, his sense of himself as Renaissance man. Would he had employed an artist like Matisse on the doors and the windows. Or Miró, since Matisse had already excelled himself at Vence. Le Corbusier's gift for decoration was mediocre compared to his grasp of volume and mass. Nevertheless, Notre-Dame-du-Haut is a great enough work of art to accommodate, if not obliterate, its flaws. The chapel engrosses our undivided, if critical, attention.

In October, there was an exhibition in Vienna at which I saw two great Degas absentees from the Rizzoli *L'opera completa di Degas*. The title of the exhibition was *Meisterwerke aus Schweizer Privatbesitz*, namely the Weinbergs (Rolf and Margit), which explains their absence from the public record. There were six other works by Degas – three drawings (studies for *La famille Bellelli*) and three oils (one copy of a Caroto portrait, another original portrait and an interior). All of them were good – but not as good as the two pictures which would have been outstanding in any company, a pastel of *Madame Ernest May auprès d'un berceau* and an oil entitled *Intérieur (La salle de billard?)*. Until the catalogue arrived, the intervening five months was sufficient for me to misremember each picture slightly. I felt like the hero of Clough's *Amours de Voyage*, who falls in love with Mary Trevellyn, only to discover, after weeks of vain pursuit, that the precise details of her personal appearance have gone missing: 'After all, do I know that I really cared so about her? / Do whatever I will, I cannot call up her image.' I wasn't experiencing the hero's 'pale blank orb', nor 'a sort of featureless outline'. But my recollection wasn't perfect, either. In one picture, there was a little cloud of unknowing I couldn't fill in quite. In the other, I had actually added a detail. Granted these errors of mnemonic transcription, was love at first sight everything I had cracked it up to be?

Yes. Memory is always imperfect – and especially where the greatest art is in question. It seems so unforgettable that one doesn't make the effort to memorise it. The acts of attention associated with falling in love are different in kind from those acts of attention designed to memorise a person's face, or a set of complicated facts, textures, shades.

The easier picture to write about is that of Madame May next to a cradle. The picture was to be of the newborn baby and the proudly pale mother. Degas painted instead a pooped parent, stretched on a chaise, her feet at ten past ten. The centre of the picture, the off-centre (to be strictly accurate), is the veil over the cradle, a blue mist miraculously rendered, a source of painterly difficulty superbly solved. But Degas isn't merely addressing a technical problem – how best to paint a veil – but is, as it were, offering the viewer two matching spectral presences, the faded, exhausted maternal presence, and the more powerful invisibility of the veiled baby. One ghost is potent and the other is flat out. Monsieur Ernest May sent the picture back to the painter.

Finally, we come to *Intérieur (La salle de billard?)*. This is a red oil. But how little that tells us. It is an oil with all the qualities of a pastel. It is matt in texture. Imagine an ochre rust, thick on an iron girder, a dense oxidisation – which is wiped in different degrees, lightly and less lightly, in places firmly, in others finally, to create a room, a red room with two chairs and a table, red also, like the red planes they exist in. And off this red room, another, redder room. The picture tells us, with absolute clarity, without compromising the shades of its own colouristic meaning, that *this* is what absence looks like when we are not there to experience it, to sentimentalise it or to dramatise it. It is a void free of Sartrean *Angst* or Le Corbusier's arranged uplift. No one lives here. Except colour.

Frank Gehry
(1998)

Between two bridges, Frank Gehry's Museo Guggenheim Bilbao erupts, inde-
scribably, on the bank of the Nervión River. The seaport of Bilbao is down the
road a few miles at Santurtzi. Bilbao itself has industrial interests. The maritime
and the industrial significantly inflect Gehry's design. On the one hand, the titanium cladding evokes the surface of the sea – the sea which is often conjured
as a great scaly dragon enfolding the earth in its coils. (See Isaiah, *The Odyssey*,
Gerard Manley Hopkins's 'endragoned seas' and Robert Lowell's 'The Quaker
Graveyard in Nantucket': 'the earth-shaker, green, unwearied, chaste / In his
steel scales'.) On the other hand, should you approach Gehry's creation on a dull
overcast day and glimpse it at the distant end of the Calle de Iparraguirre, what
you will see is a grey cement works, drab with dust – matt, occluded, industrial.
The brilliant exterior isn't always brilliant. It takes its colour – its immediate
colour – from its environs. Place twenty or so red flags next to it, to announce
the exhibition *China: 5,000 Years*, and the titanium tiles are touched with rouge.
Equally, look down the Calle de Iparraguirre on a bright day and the Gehry Guggenheim looks like the beginning of *Smilla's Feeling for Snow*, a spectacle, a frame
from a disaster movie. You see an almost unwatchable bright boil of surf, the
toppling tiers and terraces, a terrifying turbulence and weight of water which
brings home the full meaning of the phrase 'high seas' – a towering, impossible
height, bigger than the nearby buildings, and an impending catastrophic crash.
Gehry's Guggenheim is protean.

It is protean like the famous dog in Joyce's *Ulysses*, a cocklepickers' mongrel
whose subtly shifting identities mirror the ceaseless flux of the ocean alongside:
'he made off like a bounding *hare*, ears flung back, chasing the shadow of a
lowskimming gull. The man's shrieked whistle struck his limp ears. On a field
tenney a *buck* trippant, proper, unattired... The dog yelped running to them,
reared up and pawed them, dropping on all fours, again reared up at them with
mute *bearish* fawning. Unheeded he kept by them as they came towards the
drier sand, a rag of *wolf's* tongue redpanting from his jaws. His speckled body
ambled ahead of them and then loped off at a *calf's* gallop' (my italics).

Seen from the back, the building resembles nothing so much as a futuristic
city, Sylvia Plath's Brasilia, caught in an earthquake – an aesthetic earthquake,
the meltdown and upheaval of Euclidean solid geometry in spectacular spasm.
At night, its floodlit titanium picks up the reflections of the subtly agitated moat-

water and flows like streaming parachute material – a satin shimmer and flux. Its restless versatility as a building is what makes it a significant advance on its precursor, the Philharmonie building of Hans Scharoun in Berlin, whose gold-tinted stucco-aluminium limits itself to the permanent innuendo of transit – by evoking the nomadic tent in its peaks and by evoking metal camera-equipment luggage in its hard, gleaming surface. At any moment, you feel, the Scharoun building might decamp from its position – originally in the shadow of the Berlin Wall. But Gehry's Guggenheim has a longer list of *dramatis personae*, a richer repertoire of roles.

The frontage, seen close to, is no longer the cement works nor the towering high seas, but rather a building of abstract angles, frankly aping the exaggerated stylisation of cubism – like Le Corbusier, Gehry has learned a lot from the Picasso of, say, *Factory at Horta de Ebro* (1909, The Hermitage, Leningrad), where the buildings seek a candid rapprochement with geometry. Thus far, Gehry's Guggenheim fulfils the criteria laid down for art in Wallace Stevens's great masterwork 'Notes Toward a Supreme Fiction'. They are three. In this order: 'It Must Be Abstract'; 'It Must Change'; 'It Must Give Pleasure'.

Oddly enough, by 'abstract', Stevens doesn't mean 'abstract' in the usual sense of 'withdrawn or separated from matter, from material embodiment, from practice, from particular examples'. Rather, he means that the Supreme Fiction should deal in a currency of epitome – in other words, in universals. Figurative reference is allowable provided it is universal. One of the greatest aesthetic thrills delivered by Gehry's Guggenheim is the building's insistence on the frankly figurative, despite its candid cuddling up to conventional cubism – more Juan Gris than Picasso and Braque, perhaps. Seen lengthwise from across the river, the building is ship-shape – ending with two long boats in a state of overlap. Taken with the scales of the titanium tiles – reminiscent of marine life, even though they don't overlap – it is tempting to sum up the figurative allusions in Gehry's design as fish 'n' ships. However, there is a crucial complication to the left of the long boats, or, if you prefer, this great catch of squirming silver.

It is the stone-clad tower, separated from the main building by a pier bridge, bearing a four-lane highway out of Bilbao to the San Sebastián motorway. At the bottom of the tower is a kind of pleat in the stone cladding, through which the cross-hatching of girdered 'machinery' is visible. At the top, the tower is parted asymmetrically like a hand straining open between second and third fingers. The stone tower is open down one complete side, so the viewer can see the apparently hydraulic operating mechanism within the tower. Except that this frank admission of function, this manifestation of machinery, this baring of the device à la Beaubourg, is a joke. It is a joke because the machinery in fact operates nothing. The tower has no function at all. It houses precisely nothing except a fantasy of function. It exists partly to celebrate its own shapeliness – the stone is elegantly curved on each of the planes – in conjunction with the display of ugly machinery. It exists for an additional and vitally important reason which, I believe, focuses the building's flux and yields us its final cause – its aesthetic rationale. While we relish the competing chaos of Gehry's architectural components – the way the building deconstructs itself and insists on its serendipity and its daring resistance to coherence, its openness to suggestion and its embrace of aporia – *nevertheless*, once that tower is seen for what it is the whole building submits to its dominant shaping idea. The tower is the fluke of a whale, partially flensed maybe, which has dived under the bridge – to emerge on the other side, in a chaos of ship-shapes and seething surf, as the Guggenheim in the disguise of that most American of icons, the white whale, a titanium Moby-Dick. In this way, Gehry has balanced his allusions to the industrial and marine life of Bilbao with an American analogy – the whaling industry.

Of course, there is nothing so simple or so vulgar here as the cod-shaped fish restaurant that Gehry made for the town of Kobe in Japan. Gehry is interested, I think, in the drama of the white whale and his building is more like the architectural equivalent of an Eadweard Muybridge sequence – presented out of sequence and in an impacted form, so that it is true to the gestalt of chaos, of drama, of excitement, and intensely wary of the baldly literal. The dive of the stone fluke, for example, is repeated in the titanium slither to the right of the umbrella portico, which itself lifts to reveal windows reminiscent of baleen feeder filters. The umbrella might also be Gehry's gesture towards the flipper – one doesn't want to insist on equation, as if the building were constructed according to the rules of Snap. Gehry's design method is a jumbling together of related imagery – of nautical prows, of skylights and windows that are also fins, of an entrance sign that mimics the fins of the flying fish. The centrality of Melville's albino sperm whale to Gehry's design doesn't rule out reference to industry or the spume and spout of the high seas. Gehry's building goes deep. It has really taken the plunge. It is his Supreme Fiction – and is destined to give lasting pleasure.

One's grumbles are tiny. And they are to do with Spanish workmanship. The stone-tile cladding (exactly the same size as the titanium cladding) is not quite flush when you look at it closely. The fit looks faintly bodged when compared to the general ethos of hi-tech precision, implied by the building as a whole but by the titanium in particular. More, seen from the nose-end, so to speak, there is a distinctly rumpled section of titanium above the administration's stone frontage to the left. The evident forcing of the material here works implacably against the building's overall torrential spontaneity. Finally, the inside of Gehry's Guggenheim is attractive enough and an efficient enough display space – aided, of course, by the relative lack of windows – but it cannot be described as a lucid inner space. The exciting outer chaos necessarily entails an inner uncertainty, an interior unreadability. On my last, fifth day, I discovered a room which had been hiding from me.

The other real problem with Gehry's Guggenheim is nothing to do with Gehry – and everything to do with American cultural imperialism and the relentless export of abstract expressionism, the CIA's chosen aesthetic weapon in the cultural Cold War against Russian socialist realism. (For the fullest possible account of this phenomenon – CIA spooks fostering Rothko, Motherwell, Barnet Newman et al. as a bulwark against communism – see Frances Stonor Saunders's *The Cultural Cold War: The CIA and the World of Arts and Letters* (New Press, 2000).) As one strolls through the twentieth-century paintings showing in *China: 5,000 Years*, it is easy to feel superior to the acreages of socialist realism, to the central smirking figure of Mao, surrounded by ecstatically grinning peasants whose harmony manifests the success of Maoist political doctrine, QED. It's hard, too, not to condescend to paintings where the drama is apparent in *every* facial expression – no one is allowed repose, so the drama isn't a true drama, but the picture of a demonstration. Why ever did the painters forgo the idea of oriental inscrutability? Even sadder in its way is a painting like Guan Zilan's *Retrato de la Srta.L.1929*, in which Matisse has been adapted for Chinese use.

The twentieth-century art here, as opposed to the earlier antiquities, is frankly chauvinist – but it is no worse than the aesthetic chauvinism of the gallery given over to American post-abstract expressionism by Agnes Martin, Brice Marden, Ellsworth Kelly, Robert Mangold, Robert Ryman and Carl Andre. The Chinese are risible because a sluggish but prized tradition is made over to the service of politics – and is afflicted with artistic stasis. The American artists are equally doctrinaire and equally predictable. Given the intentionally nugatory efforts of these painters and sculptors, high on their own theoretical purity, fanatically committed to elimination and evacuation, it is hardly surprising that the room was usually as empty as the vacant canvases. Visitors stayed away in droves – a remarkable achievement when you consider the smoking coils of the queue for admission which didn't slacken till 2 p.m. The trouble with post-abstract expressionism is that it is just as derivative as the Chinese art, just as much the prisoner of its own methodology and its politics.

Its crass certainties, its misrepresentation of derivativeness as a tradition, the doctrinaire misdescription of what is actually painted on the canvas, are all strikingly apparent in the other visiting exhibition at the Bilbao Guggenheim – *After 'Mountains and Sea': Helen Frankenthaler 1956–1959*. Frankenthaler is a moderately talented painter whose technique of 'soak-stain' on unprimed canvas, using oils mixed with turpentine or kerosene, produced some beautiful local effects of 'aura'. Young and beautiful when, at twenty-three, she produced her signature, breakthrough painting, *Mountains and Sea*, Frankenthaler became the companion of the influential critic Clement Greenberg and in 1958 the wife of Robert Motherwell. Her reputation has its erotic dimensions, then. Nevertheless, her work in itself is a million times more interesting than that of her enshrined successors. The Frankenthaler catalogue is remarkable for its peripheral yet prominent awareness of the art historian and his importance as cultural commissar. When the artist comments on her work, she is careful to feed the art historian's appetite for predecessors and successors. It isn't a spontaneous performance but an example of aesthetic correctness: of *Mountains and Sea*, Frankenthaler says to Julia Brown, 'I painted [it] after seeing the cliffs of Nova Scotia. It's a hilly landscape with wild surf rolling against the rocks. Though it was painted in a windowless loft, the memory of the landscape is in the painting, but it also has *equal* [my italics] amounts of Cubism, Pollock, Kandinsky, Gorki.' On the one hand, you can read this as an account of influence. On the other, as a confession of conformity. Frankenthaler is keen to let us know, too, that she has her aesthetic progeny in Morris Louis and Kenneth Noland's use of soak-stain to produce what the catalogue calls 'purely optical paintings' – paintings without 'reference to the natural world or sign of the artist's hand', paintings embodying 'a purely formal approach that took Greenberg's theories to their logical conclusion'.

What we come back to is Clement Greenberg's orthodoxy, the crucial pronouncements of the Berenson of Brooklyn – and the artist's abject impulse to agree, to agree in the face of every awkward fact.

The awkward fact about Frankenthaler's pictures is that they are representational and far from purely formal. How could she not know it? But she issues earnest rebuttals: 'I am affected by nature, and I have made many paintings both "about nature" as well as those that imply the figure, but it's really not a primary concern of mine.' This insistence on the primacy of pigment was once a useful corrective. Texture and tone and brushwork are undeniably central to painting. But it is absurd to airbrush any figurative elements – to say, as Francis Bacon did, that a hypodermic syringe was empty of content and merely a painterly device. The syringe is, of course, pathetically melodramatic. The emphasis on the medium over any content has been taken to fantastic lengths. This is Frankenthaler on subject matter: 'that there is a citron at the foot of a Manet figure has very little to do with the fact of a citron. Manet needed something of that colour and shape there, and that spot of colour refers to every other millimeter of the canvas... For me, a majority of the later Velásquez, Rembrandt and Titian works have as much to do with paint as they do any given subject. The history of painting demonstrates that the application of paint can become the subject.' The history of painting as skewed by Greenberg, perhaps. And should that verb be 'screwed'? Meaning 'deprived of value'.

Frankenthaler's most famous painting has a lot to tell us in this debate about the relative importance of paint and ostensibly representational elements. No one seems to have noticed the obvious about Frankenthaler's *Mountain and Sea*. For all its noisy abstract credentials, the painting depicts a little shadow-coloured crab shape at the bottom centre – unfortunately invisible in the catalogue's reproduction. Not only that: the centre of the picture depicts a great lobster, recognisable by the legs at the back, and the pincers and radio aerials at the front. The charcoal outlines are not spontaneous but indicative. This lobster is accompanied by its own watery reflection. And it is a cooked lobster. Pink, not blue.

I wonder why the artist and the art-world have suppressed this undeniable fact for so long. Actually, I don't wonder at all. An awkward fact, the literal lobster won't take Greenberg's theories to their logical conclusion – paintings without 'reference to the natural world'. All the same, like Gehry's building, the painting is figurative even as it gestures to pure abstraction. And all the better for that. Otherwise, the Museo Guggenheim at Bilbao is crammed with emptiness – a glittering casket without a jewel.

Ron Mueck

(2000)

Four easy pieces: a baby, two men and an old woman, all naked. The primal narrative of Ron Mueck's new show runs from birth to death – from the naked baby to the old woman dying in a hospital bed under a sheet and one cotton cellular blanket. The blanket, 'natural' colour, is the kind one commonly sees in a baby's cot or on a hospital bed. It tells literally like the net layers of Degas's *Little Dancer of Fourteen* at the Boymans-van Beuningen Museum in Rotterdam. However, this simple story – of birth's swift metamorphosis into death – proves not to be so simple, though its complications are always brilliantly clear. Unmistakably profound, the show's profundity is also unmistakably lucid. Its greatness – and it *is* great – is grounded in its absence of ambiguity.

The first piece in Ron Mueck's new sculptural quartet is a baby hung highish on the left-hand wall. It is hermeneutically crucial to the show yet easily, fatally rushed. We see what we already know – rather than what Mueck is actually showing us. Up there on the gallery wall, the baby glances obviously at the crucifixion. The crucifixion is there in the placement of the arms – the body is being lifted under the arms by invisible adult hands, so the elbows are out, away from the body, creating a general cruciform shape. The crucifixion is there, too, in the positioning of the feet: the baby's right big toe is prehensile on the other foot – biologically accurate and an allusion to the traditionally singular nail parsimoniously piercing Christ's overlapping, balletic feet.

So, expert anatomical naturalism conflated with aesthetic allusion – unpretentious accuracy and candid artistic reflexiveness. Rather than the allusion, it is the physical exactitude (so deceptively familiar) which one shouldn't hurry over here at the beginning of the exhibition. We need to balance the blunt allusion with the physical palpability so scrupulously rendered by Mueck, otherwise we are left with a coarse symbolic prolepsis, an interpretative diagram: 'In my beginning is my end,' as T. S. Eliot writes in *East Coker*. Think of *The Shadow of Death*, Holman Hunt's painting of the young Christ in his father's carpentry shop, displaying a wound in the centre of his palm. Curiously, Holman Hunt's solution is also Mueck's – though Mueck is the more subtle and effective. Hunt lavishes attention on the shop – its wood shavings, its ringlets, its sawdust, its gimlets, its planes, augers, braces and bits, chisels, all soliciting the eye as rivals

Anthony d'Offay, 15 September–17 October 2000.

to the stigma spotlit at the centre of the picture. Mueck's baby similarly opposes detail against symbol. For instance, the piece alludes not only to the crucifixion but also by its placement to traditional putti: those arms are almost fledgling wings. But, in a way, slack military puttees are nearer the mark when you look at the baby's creased inner thighs and the sag and slippage of flesh. These legs have never been stood on. In fact, the baby is newborn. Cleverly, it isn't foetal, when every other piece in the show alludes to the foetal curve. It is stretched by its own weight, its own gravity. There is dried blood in the nostrils, a dust of black pudding in the ears, vernix in an armpit. Its umbilical cord has yet to atrophy and fall off.

The painstaking realism we have come to expect from Mueck is also symbolic in two ways: the nipples and the genitalia are enlarged, as they commonly are in newborn babies that still carry the mother's hormones at birth. In other words, at this, the earliest stage of life, the hormonal inheritance is proleptic, too. A glance at the subtly oversized, prematurely adult cock, like an uncircumcised mushroom – with miraculously rendered shadowy veins, so fine they feel like infusoria in the vitreous humour – explains the wary expression in the baby's precocious eyes. The face is grave in its expression, the head slightly turned – full of foresight as it looks towards the next piece, a man naked, curled up in blankets.

On the other hand, the baby has no eyebrows, a missing feature shared by every other figure in the show – as if to assimilate all the figures to a single template. As if to demonstrate the brevity of existence – like Beckett's *Breath*, but with more afflatus. This equation, this collapse of categories, is achieved, too, in the case of the second piece, by the miniaturisation of the man in the foetal position curled inside the blankets, pink inside, grey-blue outside, arranged in a womb-like configuration.

The baby is even smaller than life-size – a scintilla – with a whole wall to itself, its smallness magnified by the surrounding white space. In order to see it properly, therefore, the spectator has to look closely – from a few centimetres away, where the effect of overall smallness is neutralised, where the details fill the eye. It is a visual paradox. In interview, Mueck has several times said that photographs cannot do justice to his work. This is important in three ways. Obviously, a photograph of a piece on its own cannot capture Mueck's alterations to scale. (Which is why newspaper publicity photographs often include a spectator.) Secondly, the camera is fixed and incapable of recording the eye's journey, what Bonnard called the adventures of the optic nerve. Thirdly, compared to a Mueck sculpture, with its extraordinary storm of information, the camera is a niggardly messenger. Photographs tell us so little. Mueck tells us so much.

And has *imagined* so much. The 'computer-generated' special effects – the enlarged penis and nipples – are *true*, accurate 'distortions'. But the baby's face seems well in advance of its body and birth weight. The gaze is adult, the features less carved, less miniaturised, than in real life. The eyelids have those newborn marshmallow puffy folds but the gaze is disconcerting. It puts us out of countenance. It is focused beyond us – unlike the usual initial baby bleariness, all sticky eye and apparently untuned wash of iris. (Retinoscopy shows that new-born babies have anatomically complete visual equipment with a fixed focus initially of eight inches from the bridge of the nose.) Only after four months does a baby arrive at adult visual variation and the depth of field evident here. This isn't Mueck's mistake, though. He knows exactly what he is doing. It is deliberate distortion – of a kind we aren't accustomed to in his work. We are used to radical alterations of scale but fidelity to details. Here, the tampering with detail is considered, measured.

Untitled (Man in Blankets), towards whom the baby looks, demonstrates an aspect of Mueck's eerie skill. The assimilation theme is clear in the womb-like swaddle of blankets, the adult body in the foetal position, the absence of eye-brows. Genitalia – which might have worked against the identification of adult and infant – are out of sight, between the man's legs. At the same time, this is an adult, even if full-bellied, without being fat, like a baby: the upper lip and jawline is rendered with an eight o'clock shadow you could strike a match on. Grey-blue enough to look well used for that purpose. There is dark hair beauti-fully rendered on the forearms. And the adult is sleeping, is *sleeping*. Deeply. Like a baby. Not that Mueck telegraphs this to the viewer with, say, an open mouth or any obvious device. You look and *know* this man isn't dead, but sleeping, like the daughter of Jairus in Luke 8:52: 'She is not dead, she only sleepeth.'

The lack of ambiguity is, I think, crucial to the third figure, *Untitled (Big Man)*, described in the exhibition leaflet as 'a gigantic Buddha-like man crouch-ing contemplatively in a corner'. This description is incorrect in two important respects – the Buddha suggests meditation and calm, as does the equally mis-leading word 'contemplation'. You have to look hard to see what Mueck has captured here. When you have seen it, it is obvious. But Mueck requires the viewer to read this piece as carefully as the baby on the wall. Big Man in the Corner is completely hairless, as if visited by virulent ringworm. His knees are raised and his elbows rest on his knees. Superficially, his position looks relaxed. His elbows are crinkled like peach pits, the skin of his knees worn coarse, leath-ery. The overall flesh is faintly mottled in a way at once aged and babyish – 'bless the mottled little legs ... like Canterbury Brawn,' says Dickens's Mrs Gamp of a young baby. The mottles here are Kinnock-like freckles, large and dim, blotches, so that you suspect the hair was ginger when it existed. Again there are no eyebrows. Or eyelashes. Nor is there any pubic hair. The scrotum is pitted and pimpled like a golf ball, the prominent follicles plucked-looking. The navel is a wad of chewing gum. In other words, naked as a newborn baby – effecting the expected collapse of categories – *and* the body of an old man, hacked in the neck, hairless, two little flat warts whitish over his right eyebrow, a blue vein on the inside of his left thigh, hinting at varicosity. There are tremendous passages in this sculpture – particularly the distressed, crushed, exhausted skin, with another flat wart, where the neck joins the torso, and the prehistoric reptilian feet, each one a dinosaur. Then there is the little toe on the right foot – like a prawn in batter, tail protruding.

It is the eyes that are the key. Like the baby's eyes, they look away from under gathered, frowning 'eyebrows'. And the feet are another key to interpreting this figure. The naked, hairless man is in a corner – but he isn't relaxing against the walls. His back is to the wall. You can see from the whiteness of his toe joints that there is tension – that he is holding himself forcibly into the corner. And you read the gaze: this is a lunatic, a paranoid, catatonic in a corner, and it is Ron Mueck's incomparable genius to have captured this unambiguously and absolutely without theatricality, without melodrama. The inscrutability of the madness rendered lucid and reinforced by the body's particular fatness – not the flab, but the solidity of the mentally ill.

Mueck's *Dead Dad* was unmistakably dead, not sleeping. These figures, too, are miracles of accuracy. Just as the man in blankets is sleeping, not dead; just as the gigantified *Untitled (Big Man)* is clearly mentally disturbed; so the woman in the final piece, which has to be viewed from several metres, is manifestly dying, not sleeping. Her exhausted mouth is open, her knees are raised, she is on her side. Mueck manages these precisions without signposts, without exaggeration – a harder thing than one might think, unless you happened to consult any great artist's notebook sketches, Rembrandt's for instance, where the emotions are frankly caricatured and telegraphed. In theatre, there used to be a kind of actor who traded on facial expression. There still is, as a matter of fact. To those who disliked it, it became known as 'face-acting'. Good actors now try to *feel* the emotion rather than express it. They have what John Travolta called 'transparency'. The audience sees what the actor is feeling without any visible sign. Ron Mueck's extraordinary sculptures work in exactly this way. It is a radical advance on representational sculpture as it has existed for the past few centuries – a fundamental revolution, in fact. T. S. Eliot once quoted a line from Tennyson's 'Mariana' – 'the blue fly sung in the pane' – and noted that 'the line would be ruined if you substituted *sang* for *sung*.' Hearing Tennyson's suddenly freed metre, Eliot announces the arrival of something 'wholly new'. In the same way, Mueck has effected something wholly new. He has emancipated portraiture from elocution without impairing the clarity of what is said. He has brought understatement to the portrayal of emotion in sculpture. The four pieces are at once continuous – the conflation of birth and death, a set of variations on the foetal – and exquisitely individual and defined. This is an exhibition of extraordinary significance that has advanced not only Mueck's standing but the possibilities for sculptural portrait art.

Mueck at Kanazawa

(2008)

The story so far. In 1997, at the Royal Academy, the sensation of *Sensation: Young British Artists from the Saatchi Collection* is neither Damien Hirst's increasingly dowdy, dilapidated, dog-eared shark, nor the homoeopathically talented Tracey Emin, whose empty appliquéd tent is an exact objective correlative of her camp conceptualism. Nor is it yet Marcus Harvey's cool, ironic but cynically hyped portrait of Myra Hindley, whose compositional method is denounced by the tabloids – because the face is an agglomeration of childish handprints. Nor is the sensation of *Sensation* the Jake and Dinos Chapman 1995 fibreglass frieze of girls – naked, prepubescent, wearing only trainers, but sporting several penile noses and open, anal mouths.

Among this clamorous, attention-seeking art there is good work – by Jenny Saville, Rachel Whiteread and the photographer Richard Billingham. And there, on the floor, three feet long, is one indisputable, obvious masterpiece – a single work, the understated *Dead Dad* by Ron Mueck, the Australian son-in-law of Paula Rego – a calmly brilliant sculpture which is the contemporary equivalent of, say, Holbein's subtle portrait of Erasmus, with its engaged intelligence and wryly amused thin mouth.

The greatness of *Dead Dad* is oxymoronic: its very completeness also tells us something is missing. The sculpture dispassionately records every delicate and indelicate bodily detail – detail that is alive with accuracy. Nothing is missing. Tendons, toenails, the direction of dark hair on the calves, the hazy pubes a little stationary mirage, the tidy greying hair, the polished, modest, uncircumcised cosh of the penis at four o'clock, which echoes the thumbs across the open, upturned palms.

And yet this body is unmistakably dead. It is laid out – the opposite of foetal. We are not in the presence of sleep. The eyes have it – significantly pink, fatally, infinitesimally sunken. And the helpless hands have irretrievably lost it.

Everything is there still, but stilled, and something central has gone. The reduction in scale somehow suggests this loss. The body is lesser than life – for some, lighter by twenty-one grams, the weight of the soul: the alleged difference in body weight before and after death.

I talked to Ron Mueck in October 2000, when he was artist in residence

21st Century Museum of Contemporary Art, Kanazawa, 26 April–31 August 2008.

at the National Gallery, and we discussed *Dead Dad*. He was worried about sentimentality: 'I didn't really get on with my father but as I made the piece I found myself thinking about him, caring.' The carefulness of his creation is cognate with care in the broader sense. In fact, sentimentality is nowhere in sight. Though there is sentiment – a completely other thing – it is inextricably fused with another perfectly proper, strong human emotion, curiosity.

Mueck also said that in creating *Dead Dad* he had worked from memory and imagination. *Imagination.* In the Lucian Freud retrospective at Tate Britain in 2002, No. 113, *The Painter's Mother Dead 1989*, was a drawing done from 'life', in the immediate aftermath of death. It records unsparingly the palsied skew death inflicts on the mouth. As I've already said, for Karl Kraus a portrait was a picture in which the mouth was wrong. In death, all the mouths are wrong. The rictus is an oddly painful, unexpected, ugly fact. The undertaker and about twelve hours restore malleability and undo the damage. You have to be at a deathbed to know this. Mueck wasn't – and so couldn't be expected to know and record this expression of fleeting melodrama. *Dead Dad* isn't harmed by this omission.

In fact, on balance, the sculpture perhaps benefits – because Mueck's art is characteristically understated. Not for him the swastikas and hypodermics of, say, Bacon's painterly histrionics. His preferred reference work is Professor R. D. Lockhart's *Living Anatomy* ('A photographic Atlas of Muscles in Action and Surface Contours'). This dislike of emotional Grand Guignol, of grandstanding exhibitionism, is at once typically Australian and classically modernist. Natural taciturnity meets principled artistic restraint. The modernist inquiry into the emotions is predicated on a shared scepticism about the purity and force of what we feel – Eliot, Joyce, Lawrence, Conrad, Camus, all know that we frequently feel less than we are supposed to feel. Or feel it differently. Or adulterated with 'inappropriate' feelings. The modernists know, too, that in literature real but unspectacular emotions – like embarrassment, curiosity – are often ousted by super-sized emotional simplifications.

There is a Mueck piece called *Spooning Couple*: two tiny figures, a man in a T-shirt and a woman in a pair of knickers, cuddle up to each other like spoons, both facing in the same direction. They are bigger than a pair of spoons, more like Brobdingnagian salad servers. One's initial assumption is of cosiness and affection. There isn't any obvious antagonism of the kind recorded in Paul Muldoon's poem 'Asra', where a couple 'wake before dawn; back to back: duellists'.

And yet... all is not well. They are not as comfortable, as relaxed, as they seem at first. Both sets of eyes are open – without eye contact. They are thinking. In silence. About what? We can only guess. Her unclothed torso is turned away from his clothed torso. His naked lower half is against her knickers. The T-shirt is unironed, its white muted. The knickers are somehow indeterminate

– the faded colour purple that results when whites get washed with items which aren't colourfast. Romantic it isn't.

Vladimir Nabokov once asked his protégé, Alfred Appel, how academe was weathering a period of widespread student unrest in the sixties. Appel reported that things at his university were quiet: a nun had complained that couples were 'spooning' at the back of lectures. Nabokov pounced: 'you should have told her to thank God they weren't *forking*.'

Mueck's *Spooning Couple* are definitely not forking. They seem not to be spooning, either, in the erotic sense – they resemble kitchen utensils in close proximity, more than they resemble human beings about to make love. Mueck has given us the habit of affection, the *pose* of cuddling. In *Dead Dad*, he gave us the mystery of death – of to be and not to be. In *Spooning Couple*, he has given us another mystery – the precise moment of sexual evaporation. The emotion here is as miniaturised as the figures – mild worry, 'How did we get here, if this is where we are?'

Mueck has now created by my rough calculation about thirty-five pieces in nine years. There are no failures. (He spoke in 2000 about the pressure of success: 'You have to keep on doing something better. Reviews stop you working for two years.') Only one piece is actual-size – a dog, 'the only life-size thing I've ever done'. I saw the photograph, not the sculpture: the dog was prognathous, either naturally, or as a display of aggression. It had a tiny, volcanic, red, pointed semi-hard-on. The others, whether scaled up or scaled down, are equally painstaking.

And, in every case, the emotion is as accurate as the physical detail. *Ghost*, an early piece, is a wonderful, unexaggerated sculpture depicting an emotion rarely noted by artists – self-consciousness. A gigantified girl in an unflattering swimming costume arranges herself awkwardly – as if she were a tripod rather than a biped – caught between two states, at once pathologically ordinary and a freakish refugee from Diane Arbus's lurid, unforgiving, prying lens. Her size, the scale, is how she feels about her body. Technically, this cognitive dissonance is called anosognosia – which means not being aware of your condition. She *thinks* she is the Incredible Hulk. She is only sick with shyness.

Art historians tend to source Mueck's art in the art of the past – particularly since his residence at the National Gallery – either in dialogue or in debt. The absence of originality is seen in some strange way as a guarantee of worth – and a vindication, therefore, of the art historian's role. Hmm. Mueck's sculptures are meticulously 'copied', meticulously imagined and meticulously *composed* – like all the greatest art of the past. They share these demanding fundamentals. But that is all. Take, for instance, Rogier van der Weyden's *Deposition* in the Mauritshuis in The Hague. Two things immediately strike me. The blood from the wound in Christ's side runs down, *disappears*, under his loincloth, and continues down his leg. *Imagination*. The man holding Christ under his arms has folded back his fur sleeves – so he isn't hampered, or soiled. *Imagination*. The right sleeve nearest to the viewer is painted so that we can see the open fur at the fold – which is like a wound. That visual echo is deliberate artistry.

Now consider a piece from 1998, *Man with Shaved Head*. It frequently provokes in critics a 'comparison' with the Kritian Boy from the Acropolis (*c.* 480 BC). You might equally summon up *The Dying Gaul* (*c.* 230 BC) from the Capitoline Museums in Rome. Neither is properly pertinent. For a start, they both have hair, and it is crucial to Mueck's sculpture that his young man is bald. Why? Because the compositional axis of his sculpture is a parallel – between the circumcised head and shaft of his penis, and the neck and shaved head. Both bulbous paralleled spheres are themselves between two parallels – the cock is between the ankles (he is squatting), the skin-head is between extended arms.

With some justice, Mueck's sculpture could be renamed *Knob Head* without offending *compositional* decorum.

Echoes. Parallels. In *Man with Shaved Head*, the very *idea* itself of parallels is suggested by the man's parallel feet and the parallel arms. Naturally, this is part of Mueck's sculptural stock in trade. He spends, he told me, a lot of time staring at his clay models – trying to *see* them. 'If you've been looking at a piece of clay for hours you can't see it.' He has invented strategies to counter this blasé blindness: he takes photographs; he looks at the piece in a mirror; he glances over his shoulder. In one case, *Big Man* (2000), he lost his rag, bashed it on the head and created a frown from which the sculpture really began. Look for long enough and parallels – natural parallels – will mob the real artist.

For example, the cover of the National Gallery catalogue is a photograph of Mueck's tool board – pliers, pincers, punches, wire-cutters, all suspended from Phillips screws, handles dangling like legs, outlined in crayon on the plywood. There is also an outlined Mueck sculpture of a small baby – its legs an obvious parallel, but an ironic parallel, because its vulnerability also insists on dissimilitude.

Another example, *Pregnant Woman* (2002), demonstrates lucidly how the face and the body can be mirror images of each other. All portrait painters know – if they are any good – that the face is echoic, a rhyming dictionary. The eyes and the nostrils and the eyebrows are examples of almost competitive mimicry. Raise an eyebrow, arch a nostril – snap. In Matisse's 1914 drawing *Elsa Glaser*, the mouth is another eye. In Mueck's *Pregnant Woman*, this network of parallels is extended to an invisible omnipresence.

First things first. You are overwhelmed by the size of the piece. She is larger than life – eight feet tall. But pregnant women at this stage *are* larger than life.

There is, too, something unbelievable, impossible even, about their anatomy. Mueck reminds us of more familiar truths as well. The woman has monumental legs and feet. We think of women as feminine, delicate, *waisted*. And they are. But they are also female, sturdy and monumental. Pregnancy reveals the practicality of the pelvis, like the frame of a rucksack.

Then you are overwhelmed by the detail. Amazingly. The danger of scaling things up, of bigging it, is that there isn't enough detail to go round the acres of extra space, of dead space. Her calves and shins are shaved. There are two very inconspicuous spots on her bum – in exactly the right place. The spot on her left buttock is *just* to the left of her bum crack. The moles are perfect, especially the larger one just above her left armpit.

Then the parallels kick in: the closed rounded eyelids are mini-breasts, the nose a pregnant belly (with a mole placed to echo the bud of the navel). The lips and vagina are an obvious implicit parallel, of course. Her hair parallels her pubic hair – both *wonderfully* accurate, differentiated textures. Her arms mirror her legs, her hands mirror her feet.

Her look is one of exhausted weary concentration. Her eyes are closed. The sculpture is a portrait of fatigue. This is typical of these unsentimental sculptures. *Mother and Child* shows a mother who has just given birth. The baby's colour is deeper, darker, shiny as brawn, say, turned out of a butcher's mould. Its umbilical cord vanishes up the vagina. The vagina is echoed by the baby's buttocks and feet, from which the other end of the umbilical cord protrudes. The woman's facial expression is neutral, bled of melodrama. Just looking, in Updike's phrase. There is no obvious joy, no tears. She is unsmiling. But the real triumph is the woman's hair – uncombed to exactly the right degree.

Sometimes size in Mueck is a metaphor. *A Girl* is newborn and about twelve feet long. The piece's title is typically factual and understated. It is also subtly inflected. There is a faintly sardonic reference to the way – 'it's a girl' – we disclose gender after a birth. 'Female' is correct, the *mot juste*: without connotations, it simply denotes. But the word we actually use in this context is 'girl', or 'boy'. We say 'it's a boy / a girl' not 'it's male / female.' Mueck's title, *A Girl*, is 'sardonic' because, apart from the genitals, his sculpture is devoid of the kind of *femininity* associated with the word 'girl' in English. It is purged of the sentimentality we semi-reflexively bring to birth. When the piece was first shown at Edinburgh in 2006, the catalogue listed its title as the completely neutral *Baby*.

This is the bare fork'd animal. The umbilical cord is a blue twist – yellow at the flat end where it has been cut – set in the navel's holder, the navel's socket. The vagina has a cleft like the cleft in a fountain-pen nib – except that its indelicacy, its robustness, its size, rather reminds one of a set of pliers with a wire-stripping hole. There is blood everywhere – in fact, not *everywhere*, but on the toes, on the vagina, on the umbilical cord, on the arm, on the neck, the upper chest. It has been steeped in blood and lifted from its bloodbath. (When my wife gave birth to our first child in 1975, the first thing I noticed in the delivery suite was the blood, someone else's blood, on the ceiling.)

The newborn's nipples and vagina are enlarged by the presence of the mother's adult hormones. All this demonstrates the accuracy we expect from Mueck – as do the creases in the skin under the left nipple, or the double-creased buttocks with their under-creases, or the deep creases along the back.

Two things make *A Girl* extraordinary. One is the sheer size of the head in relation to the gigantified torso: Mueck captures the element of caricature that is normal in the newborn features and top-heavy head. The other is the metaphor implied by the size: this newborn is already grown up. Look at her ankles, look at *its* ankles – its genderless ankles, its sexless ankles. They are the thick ankles, the creased proleptic ankles, of a very old, sexually undifferentiated person. The speaker of T. S. Eliot's poem 'Journey of the Magi', faced with the Christ-child in Bethlehem, asks: 'were we led all that way for / Birth or Death? There was a Birth, certainly, / We had evidence and no doubt. I had seen birth and death, / But had thought they were different; this Birth was / Hard and bitter agony for us, like Death, our death.' Mueck doesn't ask, querulous, uncertain. He tells us.

I said there were no failures. Perhaps there are – on the studio floor, in the rubbish bins. But I will enter a tiny caveat: some of the larger than life-sized masks run the risk of caricature. There were two in the Edinburgh exhibition: one a self-portrait of Mueck sleeping (*Mask II*, 2001–2), the other a black woman's plump face (*Mask III*, 2005). Of these two, the self-portrait runs the greatest risk, as did the original frowning self-portrait (*Mask*, 1997) – which Mueck explained away by saying it was how he imagined he appeared to his children. Still, we are dealing with greatness here – no question.

Mueck: *Invitation au voyage*
(2009)

There are splashes of white paint, like tiny stars of lichen, on the bows of the boat. Man in a boat, then, or a mollusc in an open, midnight blue, mussel shell? A visual pun: a portrait of vulnerability, of edibility unprotected by a carapace.

The 'man in the boat' is slang for the clitoris. Why? Because the pudenda look like a narrow boat. Mueck's man is naked as a newborn baby in the vagina's open boat. An implication of helplessness.

Perhaps.

An *'Invitation au voyage'*, certainly. But rather different from Baudelaire's imagined, ideal destination of 'luxe, calme et le volupté' in the company of his beloved. Instead, an unanswered question, a taxi-driver's question: *where to?*

Walter Pater's famous prose rhapsody around Leonardo's *Mona Lisa* was included in the *Oxford Book of Modern Verse* by W. B. Yeats, who laid it out typographically as *vers libre*. In 'The Critic as Artist' (1890), Oscar Wilde had already acclaimed its self-standing aesthetic status – quoting it practically verbatim – and disclaimed any requirement for accurate description of the original painting. 'Who…cares whether Mr Pater has put into the portrait of Monna Lisa something that Lionardo never dreamed of?' Wilde thought the Pater a rival work of art, executed by the critic. 'It treats the work of art simply as the starting point for a new creation.'

In brusque, denuded summary, Pater's point is that *La Gioconda*'s physicality, her troubled beauty, expresses every malady of the human soul.

Is that *all?*

Pater exists as a warning and T. S. Eliot was right to stigmatise this kind of 'aesthetic' criticism as illegitimate, as thwarted, ersatz creativity. I will try to avoid it.

In *Ulysses*, Leopold Bloom, on his way to Paddy Dignam's funeral in Glasnevin Cemetery, glimpses a tramp from the cortège: 'On the curbstone before Jimmy Geary the sexton's, an old tramp sat, grumbling, emptying the dirt and stones out of his huge dustbrown yawning boot. After life's journey.' Life's journey: the (appropriately fatigued) cliché is redeemed by the description of the boot.

Exhibition at the National Gallery of Victoria International, Melbourne, 22 January–18 April 2010.

Jorge Luis Borges, in a *Paris Review* interview, asserted that all the great metaphors were unoriginal: 'When I was a young man I was always hunting for new metaphors. Then I found out that really good metaphors are always the same. I mean you compare time to a road, death to sleeping, life to dreaming, and those are the great metaphors in literature because they correspond to something essential. If you invent metaphors, they are apt to be surprising during the fraction of a second, but they strike no deep emotion whatever.'

In fact, it is true that with *Man in a Boat* an allegory irresistibly suggests itself – life as a voyage; life as a journey without a definite destination. There are no oars. The man's arms are folded. He is a naked, middle-aged Moses, afloat in our limitless imaginations and the abstract limbo of the art gallery's 'invisible' walls. He is a man in space.

Pascal famously said, *'Le silence éternel de ces espaces infinis m'effraye.' The silence of interstellar space terrifies me.* And we are comfortably uncomfortable with that bleak immeasurable dread, that blanket angst. But Ron Mueck is offering us something significantly different – a discomfort blanket. Anthony d'Offay, Mueck's dealer, once said to me he thought 'Ron dreams these things.' I'd put it rather differently. *Man in a Boat* is a classic dream image – inexplicable nakedness in a public place, a rowing boat which clearly belongs to someone else. The enigma of total exposure. Nothing hidden. Nothing disclosed.

I first saw *Man in a Boat* at Mueck's National Gallery exhibition in 2003 and again at the Scottish National Gallery of Modern Art in Edinburgh in 2006. My notes record the slight paunch, the hairs above the nipples, the hair on the pale forearms, the pinker hands, the strained tendons on the left side of the neck, the slightly angled head, the faint bristle on the chin, the cock all glans (below it, a crumpled scald of skin). The feet are turned in and tucked away. The upper lip is loose and the hair going grey. Unmistakably, this is not a naked man so much as a man without his clothes.

There are two crucial features: his combed careful hair and the expression in his eyes and face. I should say the expression is guarded, wary. Were he sculpted by Pascal, he would be terrified. Instead, he is sculpted by Mueck – as watchful; as wary of being watched. His right eyebrow is cocked and curious. He is the opposite of a representative figure, a symbolic figure. This isn't Everyman. He's a particular bloke.

In my collected etchings of Rembrandt, there are many self-portraits: *Rembrandt in a Cap, Laughing* (B316, III, Rijksmuseum); *Rembrandt Open-Mouthed, as if Shouting* (B3, I, Rijksmuseum); *Rembrandt Angry* (B10, I, Rijksmuseum); *Rembrandt in a Cap, Open-Mouthed, as if Staring* (B320, Rijksmuseum), and so on. Looking at this range of expressions makes you realise that Frans Hals's *The Laughing Cavalier* is a technical topos as well as a terrific portrait – a technical test, like the spring of lemon peel or mother-of-pearl oyster shell in a still life, or Hockney's rendering of a bigger splash. Hals captures the laugh without confusing it with, say, an angry grimace. Catching an expression unambiguously is a painterly feat. Mueck, capturing an ambiguous expression – the man's determination to disclose nothing, while being exposed in every other possible way – raises the stakes wonderfully. We have an allegory in all its obviousness and the cancellation of that allegory by a pallid, ordinary figure in his contemporary quiddity, his irreducible particularity. The sculpture is all reach and its opposite – just sitting tight. Hardly daring to think.

Modigliani
(2006)

Modigliani is known for his nudes. They are sexy. Art historians find this a problem.

Some of Modigliani's models found this a problem, too. For different reasons. Not for moral reasons like the shiftiness of removing your shift for a shufti – you know, pornography, voyeurism, the male gaze – but for anatomical reasons. As I will explain.

In Tom Stoppard's radio play *In the Native State*, a fictional young poet, Flora Crewe, has been a model for Modi – as she calls Modigliani. She is, shall we say, uninhibited. This is a sample of her racy poetry: 'Sweat collects and holds as a pearl at my throat, / lets go and slides like a tongue-tip / down a Modigliani.' There is a word understood here: 'down a Modigliani [nude]'. Thereafter the poem (and the tongue-tip) head southwards: 'now in the salt-lick', 'a seed pearl returning to the oyster'. Her sister Eleanor offers a gloss on Flora's libidinous temperament: 'Men were not really important to Flora. If they had been, they would have been fewer. She used them like batteries. When things went flat, she'd put in a new one.'

Let Flora Crewe stand for the women in Modigliani's short, serried and, we hope, rank erotic life. Which included a poetic fling (1910–11) with Anna Akhmatova, to whom he gave sixteen portrait drawings – which were lost at Tsarskoye Selo during the first revolution: 'the one that survived is less characteristic of his later nudes than the others,' she confessed in *Poem without a Hero*.

She is seated nude in a wing-backed armchair, her head turned in profile to her left, resting on her shoulder. This tells you nothing. Her eye is closed. Her nose is faintly aquiline. She isn't tall so much as prolonged. And the lines of her slim torso go on endlessly. It inhabits a dark outline. Without the chair – which is five lines only, one broken – the nude would be nothing. The charm is the contrast between her angular curves and the slightly curved angles of the chair. She is more curved. The chair is more angular. But Modigliani hints at marriage – at squaring the circle. The angles have it.

After Akhmatova, there was a subsequent thing with the poet and writer Beatrice Hastings, who had been a circus performer in the Transvaal. Then a final affair with the painter Jeanne Hébuterne, who committed suicide the day

Modigliani and His Models, Royal Academy, 8 July–15 October 2006.

after Modigliani's death, aged thirty-five, from alcohol and tuberculosis in 1920. There were probably others.

Akhmatova, with her fifteen lost drawings, may have been Stoppard's model for the model and poet Flora Crewe – whose nude picture is bought by her jealous fiancé and burned. In any case, Flora Crewe has penetrating things to say about Modigliani's nudes: 'I had to lie with my shoulders flat but my hips twisted towards the canvas; I could hardly move afterwards.'

This is what John Updike means when he says, in *Just Looking*, that Modigliani's *Reclining Nude* (c. 1919) in MoMA is 'anatomically impossible'. To realise this, you turn the picture on its side so you can see *la grande horizontale* in the vertical. As viewers, we are mesmerised by the solid swell of the breasts – which begin at the collarbone, and are so big the woman isn't flat-chested even when lying on her back. (It looks impossible, but it is only rare.) And we are mesmerised by the waist extension – an extra foot, which *is* as impossible as it sounds – so that we don't notice the perfunctory hands.

Modigliani doesn't *want* us to notice the hands. They are finessed away as fatally finicky, a compositional complication. What we are offered is sexy, but a simplification. The pelvis – in a different plane from the upper body – is turned to the viewer to maximise the arc of the hips. The artist has turned his model like a Rubik's cube below the waist. If you are inclined to acquit the artist – from the charge of painting kitsch, of painting sexual fantasy, of beautifying the banal – you call this stylisation. You invoke the Willendorf Venus.

I wonder whether Botticelli's *Venus* isn't a better parallel. All Modigliani's paintings have cubist-lite elements and classical Renaissance traits. (For instance, the visible under-paint, the glimpses of canvas, are meant to evoke the fresco.) Botticelli's nudes are pleasing but anatomically implausible – he can't quite work out how the ankles join the feet. And his *Venus* in the Gemäldegalerie in Berlin has a left arm almost as long as her left leg – she needs it to gather her golden hair over her modesty. But we don't notice, because the eye is conventional and therefore compensates. Human beings interpret, they fudge, they are nostalgic for the normal. At an eclipse of the sun, the temperature drop is radical, dramatic – but our bodies tell us something different, they register a lesser change.

These Renaissance liberties with physiology give Modigliani the necessary licence to undertake his own alterations – to take in, to let out, to tailor his material. For instance, *Reclining Female Nude on a White Cushion* (1917, Staatsgalerie, Stuttgart) has had her (compositionally troublesome) left arm amputated and her pelvis exaggerated – or her waist taken in. The trouble is that Modigliani's nudes tend to the formulaic. Ever seen a Modigliani nude with a dumpy waist? No, of course not. Is this repetition? Or is it perfectionism? Or is it a style?

But just as one inclines to a negative verdict, one remembers Brancusi – an infinitely greater artist than Modigliani, a radical artist whose ideas Modigliani borrowed and popularised. But Brancusi made (at a rough count) twenty-one *Birds in Space*, in a variety of materials – bronze, marble, plaster. I think I saw thirteen on show at the Centre Pompidou, Beaubourg, in 1995, and marvelled at the crucial, infinitesimal differences that meant only two of the thirteen achieved the weightlessness sought by the sculptor. There are also twelve *Fish* by Brancusi and at least sixteen *Sleeping Muses*... No one thinks Brancusi limited or formulaic.

Brancusi was, we tend to forget, a great portraitist – both in his early, conventional sculptures and, on occasion, in his drawings. Think of his great drawing of Joyce – specs, tache – a schoolboy's maladroit simplification of genius. And Modigliani's portraits deserve to be as famous as his nudes. Of course, like the nudes, they over-insist on their stylistic signatures – the blank black asymmetric eyes out of Cézanne and (say) Picasso's 1906 *Portrait of Gertrude Stein*. There is also a debt to Picasso in the empty eye matched with a 'conventional' dark eye – for example, his study for *Les Demoiselles d'Avignon* (1907) in the National Museum for Modern Art in Paris. Don't get me started on his nose-jobs – those wedges out of Africa and Picasso. Not exactly forgeries, but forged originally in someone else's foundry – where they were 'found' by Modigliani.

I'd like to look at Modigliani's portraits of his quondam mistress Beatrice Hastings, the Jewish poet Max Jacob, Cocteau, the sculptor Lipchitz and the painter Diego Rivera. Photographs of all these sitters survive. They show us that Modigliani had a gift for likeness, which he sometimes, rightly, chose to override – in the interest of inspired equivalence. Brancusi's portrait of Joyce is the perfect example of inspired equivalence – a facial kit, a sketch, a gathering together of the *ingredients* for a portrait. In Modigliani, there is nothing so radical, but there *is* a negotiation between likeness and stylistic features. His best portraits are where the two poles are closest – the pictures of children, who are naturally simplified. Children are notoriously difficult to paint convincingly, their features disguised by the anonymity of innocence. Modigliani brings it off triumphantly.

One should add that photographs are, in any case, unreliable guides to a true likeness. The painter Mark Alexander often works from photographs and he once told me that a large part of his task was inventing detail – detail necessary for pictorial conviction that is not supplied by the photographic image. Think, too, about those David Levine caricatures in the *New York Review of Books* – how brilliant they seem until the caricature happens to be of someone you know personally. How, you wonder, did he get Timothy Garton Ash so wrong? The answer is to hand. Consult the author's photograph on his dust jacket – and you will discover not what the author looks like, but how the author would *like* to look. It is from this already tweaked image that poor Levine has to work. First, though, it is the photograph itself which is at fault.

Modigliani's technique of stylisation – its candid asymmetry, its shared cubist elements, its uneven eyes, the jigsaw fit of the nostrils to the outline of the upper lip – is to spike the mannerist touches with plausible and vivid realistic detail. Diego Rivera's eyes are two navels sunk in flesh, the plump fish lips are minimised by the fat moon face. His beard is a seethe of ants. There is an element of brilliant pudgy caricature. Rivera resembles his photograph, but he resembles (we think) Modigliani's painting more. Cocteau complained about his mouth. It is prissy, a rosebud – whereas in photographs it is lean and rather wide. Modigliani's portrait is painted out of homophobic distaste and drawing-room cubism. It is all poise and pose – close to caricature, then, libellous even, but true in the way that Picasso's 1905 portrait of Apollinaire as a pipe-sucking pomegranate is irrefutable.

Lipchitz hardly resembles his photograph at all. The trick, though, is the same. He is given a standard stylised nose out of stores, but his supplementary detail includes asymmetric hair, solid as a wig, an incipient prickle of sparse moustache (like a shaven armpit) and an incipient double chin, whose fold is mirrored in his polo-neck.

There are approximately seven oils and two drawings of Beatrice Hastings – another possible model for Tom Stoppard's Flora Crewe. Her surviving photograph – of a woman in a waisted jacket with mutton-chop sleeves, an elaborate feathered hat and a tough-ish mouth – tells us very little. Modigliani's pencil drawings (c. 1915) tell us more – both about her face and the fleeting influence of Chinoiserie. Two paintings record a Ronald Searle-like upturned nose in oil and pencil (1916), then the same nose repeated in oil, plus hooded cubist eyes, cheekbones she shares with the Max Jacob oil and a boldly rendered check dress taken from Matisse.

In 1916, there is yet another portrait of Beatrice in a high-collared overcoat – at the centre of overlapping planes is the same nose on the same trajectory, one eyebrow only, one blank eye and one black eye. The mouth looks tight – the mouth of a woman at the end of an affair, just ever so slightly pissed off. The picture is full of character. Subsequently, she is more stylised: her widely set eyes closer together, both of them black, the nose straight, seen frontally, the mouth tiny, hardly the width of her nostrils, the columnar neck a beanstalk. The pictures are full of character – of containment, of resignation, of realistic assessment. In approximately two years, Modigliani has exhausted her facial individuality and assimilated her to his style – miraculously without mislaying her likeness.

A last word about Max Jacob. According to Beatrice Hastings, Modigliani 'despised everyone but Picasso and Max Jacob'. She adds that he 'loathed Cocteau'. There are two Modigliani portraits of Jacob – one relatively conventional, one of Jacob in a top hat and a tie whose checks are repeated in the sitter's left eye. It is the mouth that interests me. It is thin, a little pinched, but somehow benignly humorous, as if reflecting on and relishing a joke with a slow burn – the opposite of Cocteau. It bears out Beatrice Hastings's testimony.

Modigliani may not be a great painter – and his early death may have saved him from what Picasso called the 'abject' fate of imitating himself even more than he does now – but what remains is charming, often sexy and unquestionably talented.

Adam Elsheimer
(2006)

You probably haven't heard of Adam Elsheimer, known as Adam of Frankfurt, who died in poverty in Rome in 1610 at the age of thirty-two. Only thirty-four of his works survive. The seven dispersed panels of his *Frankfurt Tabernacle* were finally reconstructed as late as 1981 – when the last was found in Australia. Elsheimer was in any case costively meticulous, working on a miniature scale in oils on small pieces of copper. There is a single surviving canvas – a fine, unostentatiously accurate oil self-portrait, which discloses none of his notorious melancholy, but shows concentration in the eyes and knitted brow, and wittily echoes the sweep of his moustache in the curve of his white starched collar. You would know from this that Elsheimer wasn't a bad painter.

But you wouldn't know from the self-portrait that Elsheimer was a *great* painter. To know that, you need to look at the other paintings – recently on show at Edinburgh and the Dulwich Picture Gallery. Nor is the catalogue much help. You have to have seen the originals. Catalogue reproductions work – as always – only as aides-memoires, useful but depleted. Blown-up details of miniatures are particularly treacherous – overstatements, betrayals, that broadcast painterly whispers. (I will return to this when I write about Elsheimer's *Flight into Egypt*, the version that depicts, for the first time, the Milky Way.)

In fact, because the pictures are the equivalent of painterly small print, you need to read them, carefully, meticulously. Otherwise they are invisible. Or, rather, their greatness is invisible – invisible because it is subtle, miniaturised.

For example, in *The Stoning of St Stephen*, the saint is kneeling, in a rather sumptuous tabard. His mouth is open. So he may be praying. Or he may be in pain, because he is already gashed at the hairline. Behind him a man with rolled-up trousers is holding a small boulder above his head. You suddenly think what stoning actually involves – something more than the three people about to pelt the saint with rocks the size of bread rolls – or rock cakes. And then you notice that the man with the boulder *is standing on tiptoe*, for greater force.

And you know that Elsheimer is a great painter because, allied to a nearly flawless technique, is the ability to imagine his subjects in exemplary detail – in amoral detail, as the imagination does its vital, tasteless work. (The Dickens manuscript of *Martin Chuzzlewit* in the V & A records this late addition: on

The Paintings of Adam Elsheimer, National Gallery of Scotland, 23 June–3 September 2006; Dulwich Picture Gallery, 20 September–3 December 2006.

Montague Tigg's corpse there are meat flies like a scattering of currants. Same thing: the imagination on tiptoe.) The moral context of suffering is suggested by the silk tabard, which depicts Christ carrying the cross. The moral dimension is there, too – in the subtle, understated background detail of two mules baring their teeth at each other. What a dark, laconic glance in the direction of man's inhumanity to man – man's animality to man.

Elsheimer's technique is so secure, so virtuosic, that one almost forgets about it. In *The Flood*, for example, amidst the chaos, there is a breath-taking *portrait* of a bearded man tight-wrapped in a yellow cloak. It isn't a thumbnail sketch *because it isn't even the size of a thumbnail*. Yet you would recognise this person in a crowd on the concourse at Paddington Station – even were you running for a train. Important as these immaculately executed details are, the engine of Elsheimer's greatness is the conception – the intelligence of the idea before brush point touches the copper plate or pecks at the paint. In the *Frankfurt Tabernacle*, one plate depicts *The Testing of the Cross*: a bishop, the sun catching his gilded mitre, watches as a naked figure sits on the angled cross – like someone halfway down a slide. Who would have thought of *testing the true cross for size?* It's a bit like running carbon-dating on the Holy Grail.

In his marvellous memoir *James Joyce and the Making of 'Ulysses'*, Frank Budgen records Joyce looking at a postcard reproduction of a ruminative marble Penelope. He asked Budgen what he thought she was thinking about. His own answer was brilliantly ingenious and profoundly plausible: Joyce said Penelope was trying to remember what Ulysses looked like. 'You see, in those days, they had no photographs.' We like to think our artists are gifted but intellectually wayward, even a bit wonky. They are, of course, extremely intelligent – well, the good ones are. You simply have to realise that real intelligence isn't conventional intelligence, *university* intelligence, but applied *artistic* intelligence.

In his painting of *The Flood*, Elsheimer has given the subject proper thought, brought his artistic intelligence to bear on every detail. Everyone is making for higher ground, but in the left foreground two people are climbing trees. A woman is clinging to a bale, using it for flotation. You can see two babies in wicker panniers on the side of a camel, one with both bare arms hanging out. Two people are sharing a horse, one riding pillion. A little boy is carrying his pet dog under his arm. There is a baby *floating in its crib*.

The obvious danger – that the painting is too busy with detail, too theatrical to be composed – is largely avoided by Elsheimer, whose most crowded compositions are beautifully, simply composed. *The Exaltation of the True Cross* is a good example. On the one hand, there is enough going on – from the ascension of the Virgin Mary to the Tobias character, sitting on a fish with his back to us – for us to be reminded of Robert W. Buss's bustling watercolour of *Dickens Surrounded by His Characters*. There are two compositional devices. One is a centrifuge around the cross itself – as if it were a teaspoon stirring the details. The other is bravura perspective: the miniature foreground fading and diminishing further into the background as the picture recedes into heaven. In *Flight into Egypt*, there is a string motif that ties the details together: Joseph's trousers are tied at the knee with string; his shoes are bound with string; Mary sits side-saddle resting her feet on a rung suspended from ropes; Joseph's hat is suspended from a string; there is a rope bridle; tools and a cloth are roped to the back of the ass.

Sometimes, it has to be said, the subjects do succumb to theatricality. *Three Marys at the Tomb* is a touch over-expressive, *Three Sisters* acted by RADA students. But the stained winding cloth makes its point, and there is a terrific young angel in the foreground, whose profile is so turned away from the viewer to the three women that we see only the suggestion of nose, a rumour of eyelash – and have to make do with one ear seen sideways on like a bracket, and a hairstyle of flowing curls below a tonsure growing out and still straight. The angel's costume is dazzling white and labyrinthine with wrinkles.

Usually, however, Elsheimer brings off the most testing subjects. In his version of *Judith and Holofernes*, the danger is the obvious one of melodrama. Blood issues from the *half*-severed neck and the mouth. But the body language is persuasively, quietly eloquent. Both fists are clenched. The victim's right leg is raised high, as high as Judith's sword is raised for the second blow. One eye of Holofernes is visible – big as the eye of an ox in an abattoir. A dark figure is looking into the tent. On the table are two glass vessels – like an ironic reminder of, hah!, the still life – containing water and oil.

Or consider Elsheimer's *Conversion of Saul*. The conception, yet again, is brilliant – an encounter with the Almighty on the road to Damascus envisaged as a terror of horses. At the absolute pictorial centre, Saul's horse is bucking – *not* rearing in clichéd fashion. Centre *foreground*, we see a sprawled figure, richly gowned enough to be a rival Saul. There is a stallion also on its back, hind legs splayed, the genitalia like a sawn-off blunderbuss. A man is trapped under a horse. A Roman soldier lies, brilliantly foreshortened, in the far foreground: you can see his leather strip skirt, the binding of his sandals, his entire uniform a miracle of suggestion. In the right foreground, a horse *squats* down, flinches away, while someone controls its head. It's better than many of Stubbs's action paintings – I mean, paintings of action – in the Tate.

These spasms of equine panic would test any painter. But Elsheimer is equal to them, as he is equal to depicting drunkenness in his copy of Dürer's *The Witch* – whose foreground is taken up with four dancing, drunken cupids in what looks, appropriately enough, to be a reel. More quietly virtuosic is the small dog in *Jacob's Dream*. How it is that we know the dog has *seen* something is impossible to analyse – but Elsheimer lets us know it for a certainty. Something about the slight angle of the head tells us it isn't looking but that it has *seen*.

Elsheimer painted two versions of *Flight into Egypt*, one of which we have already discussed. The other is the more famous. It is allegedly the first depiction of the Milky Way in Western art. Up to now, I have been mainly concentrating on Elsheimer's imaginative gifts, while noting *en passant* that the technique is secure. In this painting, execution and conception are inextricable, one and the same, and both of them blindingly brilliant. I use the word 'blindingly' deliberately – because it is possible to look at this very great picture and fail to see it. Its greatness is *absolutely invisible* in reproduction. Unless, of course, the details are magnified, a procedure which is fatal for the integrity of this picture and its crucial miniaturism – here applied to a landscape and the night sky, neither of them obviously miniature in themselves. So I need to talk you through it.

The Holy Family are visible in the foreground – a tiny group against an extensive wood, whose trees are like billows of smoke. To the right the moon in the sky is reflected in the river. Its surface looks surprisingly accurate astronomically. Some art historians think he may have used a telescope – perhaps Galileo's. To the left there is a bonfire with a great banner of sparks – watched by a few animals. Just as the moon has its reflection in the river, so this bonfire is a deliberate parallel to the Milky Way above – which is almost obliterated by the fierceness of the fire on the ground. But the fire is also a pointer to the Milky Way – which is barely there, micro-particles, a memory of pollen, whose visibility becomes more palpable *once it is noticed*.

Let me end with the other stars. Auden's poem 'Lullaby', better known by its first line as 'Lay Your Sleeping Head, My Love', has an interesting technical feature. There are a very few scattered full rhymes, but mainly the rhymes are chosen to be invisible: 'from' and 'arm', for example; or 'love' and 'grave'; or 'rocks' and 'wakes'. All of them audible once you have seen them, but intentionally concealed. Or consider the couplets in 'Music is International', Auden's Phi Beta Kappa poem of 1947: 'speaking'/'Greek'; 'thirsty'/'first'; 'important'/'caught'. Same thing. Only different. In Elsheimer's painting at first the stars are invisible, intentionally so: the minuscule points of light are easily read as an accident of light, as pinpricks of light from the outside catching the pigment. The size of these flecks of white and their distribution is impeccably – the *mot juste* – judged. Once seen, the flecks differentiate themselves. Some are larger than others, though all are tiny and initially at the edge of visibility.

Elsheimer even includes a witty joke about visibility. The Holy Family in the foreground have their possessions, as always, tied to the ass. By the light of the flambeau in Joseph's hand, you can see a frying pan, a frying pan with an exceptionally long handle, whose cooking surface gleams like glass – like a *magnifying glass*.

The stars are, in their way, an emblem of Elsheimer himself – a star who is invisible – until you look and see what he has put there.

Klimt

(2008)

Two great portraits by Gustav Klimt, ten years apart, with a shared secret, a *je ne sais quoi* – one of Fritza Riedler (1906), one of Friederike-Maria Beer (1916).

Fritza Riedler's hair is short, no-nonsense, very faintly unkempt with one or two escaping curls. Her teeth display a winning, subtle asymmetry. Her upper-left forearm is so precise in its plumpness that you can guess her age – about forty-six. Her expression is warily intelligent. She might be the (quietly, intelligently sexy) wife of a head of college – were it not that she is richly arrayed like the wealthy person she is. Behind her head, Klimt has placed a secular mosaic-enamel halo, a bit like a stained-glass window, and she is sitting in a backless armchair, which has been transformed by Klimt into a decorative accessory. In the preparatory drawings, the chair is conventional enough – and you can still make out the armrests as well as the (less readable) pleated valances at the base of the chair. However, in the finished portrait, it is a flat honeycomb of blanched-almond statue eyes. Actually, the overall effect created by the chair is the sway of the sea, ripple and wave. Fritza Riedler emerges from the chair, her expensive, pale eau de nil dress pouring down her, like Venus Anadyomene emerging from the ocean – goddess and bluestocking.

Friederike-Maria Beer, with her faint moustache and her pragmatic, assessing eyes, is painted against a background oriental screen of battling warriors – apparently taken from a Korean vase in Klimt's possession. Her standing figure is conterminous with the teeming tapestry 'behind' her. Tapestry and woman exist in the same plane. Her head and her hands are transfigured by the welter of stuff around them, stuff taken, as it were, from the dressing-up box – so they are granted nakedness. They are the only naked things. Which is not the way we usually think of faces and fingers.

The shared secret of these ostensibly different portraits is – accessories, incidentals, decorative 'accidentals', background as foreground, in a single plane. It is the combination of the decorative and the representational, their fusion, that makes him great.

Great artists are like tweed. (Hello, Pseuds' Corner.) For instance, Thrie Estaits' 826 Ettrick Sporting Tweed. From a foot away, it has a clear, defined pattern, a grid of alternating brown and paler brown micro-squares. Something

Exhibition at the Tate Liverpool, 30 May–31 August 2008.

simple, manly, frank. But if you look closely, the material reveals heather threads and green threads, so subtle as to be almost invisible. Hang *on,* you think, these are eye-shadow pastels. Is this tweed by any chance gay? Should it come out of the closet?

These things are an allegory – of the macro and the micro in art – which I will explain, using Picasso as exemplar, and then apply to Gustav Klimt.

Picasso is famously various – the blue period, the pink period, cubism, analytical cubism, the neoclassical period, the surreal thirties, the post-war pro-communist kitsch welter of doves, harlequins, clowns and those lazy cartoon kings. So various, in fact, that it is difficult to see the pattern in the warp and the weft – the pattern, the template, the tweed in his work, the recurrent artistic idea. It's all apparently an inchoate cornucopia, a mass of unexpected threads – Ezra Pound's 'broken bundle of mirrors'.

Coleridge says in *Biographia Literaria* that great artists can be animated for a lifetime by one idea, one discovery. Picasso's dominating idea is sculpture – bringing the values of sculpture to the one-dimensional canvas surface with its familiar illusions of three-dimensionality and perspective. Picasso is interested in every inflection of sculpture, of different kinds of sculpture. For example, *Les Demoiselles d'Avignon*, his brothel picture of 1907, would not be possible without the visual example of African carving. Those bold diagonal strokes representing shade down one side of the nose are a trope taken from the coarsely chiselled profiles of African art. Cubism is, in essence, an equivalent of the radically unstable viewpoint we deploy when we walk round a sculpture. Collage insists on actual three-dimensionality.

A picture like Picasso's *The Two Brothers* (1906, Gósol) reproduces the powdery pinks of terra-cotta garden sculpture in the bollock-naked boys. The little brother being piggybacked has in the corner of his only visible eye a squidged lump of pigment – not a skin tag but a nod, a tribute to the imperfection of swiftly worked clay. In *Dancing Couple* (1921–2, Paris) the man is a stylised self-portrait. (This is another unifying element of Picasso's work in the early twenties: compare *Seated Woman* (1920, Paris) or the two brothers of *Reading the Letter* (1921, Paris), all three of whom are cloned from Picasso's own features.) But the crucial sculptural value is present in the canvas weave itself – whose rough nubbly texture, whose burly Braille, is like unpolished granite. Small wonder, then, that Picasso should also be a brilliantly original, if intermittent, sculptor all his life, as well as a great painter.

Gustav Klimt was a student at the *Kunstgewerbeschule* when the Viennese historical painter Hans Makart was at his most celebrated. Klimt was a fervent admirer. Makart's *The Entry of Charles V into Antwerp* (1878) is representative of this kind of teeming historical painting – bombastic art that Klimt eventually rejected for a different kind of painting which has art historians expressing baffled regret that Klimt somehow failed to register their meticulously researched historical background in his pictures. 'One searches in vain for any sign of these momentous events in Klimt's work,' writes Frank Whitford, looking for signs of the assassination of Archduke Ferdinand at Sarajevo and the collapse of the Hapsburgs and the Austro-Hungarian Empire.

Klimt's flirtation with this kind of epic, overweight, overcrowded picture – somewhere between Wembley Stadium and a mass grave – is pared down, spliced with symbolist aesthetic and allegory, but over-impressed by the idea of size. As if a great picture were a large picture. Klimt's *Beethoven Frieze* (1902) was painted to showcase a monumental sculpture of Beethoven by Max Klinger. It is less pullulating than a Makart but has fatally pompous Wagnerian elements of *Nibelungenlied*. In 'Compassion and Ambition' (what an unassuming subtitle), for example, there is a knight, in golden armour, with a perm like Kevin Keegan of yesteryear, apparently representing the strong *Führer*. He is surrounded by suffering mankind – represented by several supplicating nudes, slightly etiolated but not devoid of comeliness.

Wagner invented the idea of the total artwork, the *Gesamtkunstwerk* – a notion that proved, indirectly, to be Klimt's artistic salvation. (*The Ring* is the ultimate control feat by a control freak.) The Viennese Secession, led by Klimt, among others, was a precursor to the Bauhaus – and the idea that art could be applied to every aspect of life, much as, in nineteenth-century England, Pugin's Roman Catholic aesthetic was (mysteriously, solipsistically) applied to door-knobs, fire irons, floor tiles. Josef Hoffmann, an architect, designed a chair for Klimt, and monogrammed cutlery in a 106-piece set (for Lili and Fritz Waerndorfer, 1904–8), a tea and coffee set for Margaret Wittgenstein-Stonborough, cigarette boxes, vases, buckles – all in *Jugendstil*, the Viennese version of art nouveau. Klimt made book plates, clothing labels (for his mistress Emilie Flöge's dress business). Like Oscar Wilde, like George Bernard Shaw, he believed in dress reform. When he wasn't dressed like a banker in striped morning trousers – with a firm fistful of gloves, and holding the brim of his hat – Klimt was naked under a self-designed burnous.

What Klimt learned from this fusion of art and craft proved to be crucial to his art – saving it from aesthetic inflation. The *Gesamtkunstwerk* gave him his idea, the idea that would lift him above the level of hyper-skilful painter to great artist. Textile was his tweed. His greatest paintings are a conflation of two skills – extraordinary in combination, less extraordinary in isolation. Klimt was a striking portrait painter, swift to achieve a likeness, accurate to the point of genius. He was also, it transpired, a decorative designer of genius. His paintings are very beautiful, *obviously* beautiful – and some, unsurprisingly, have been owned by Estée Lauder and Barbra Streisand. There is a popular appeal here – an appeal it would be snobbish and foolish to resist. Think of Matisse's vibrant charm. Or the way certain Jackson Pollocks have been annexed of late to the decorative camp – unpersuasively in my view. The beauty is all in the flat textile element. The sitters are seen exactly as they are – a different beauty, which can encompass imperfection, the ghost of a moustache, a deformed finger, awkward angularity, prominent teeth, plumpness. The beauty in the portraiture is partly the pleasure of accuracy, but more substantially the pleasure of form – form so delicately done it is almost invisible.

When form is obtrusive it is lesser. In 1981, there was an exhibition of photographs by Helmut Newton (reprinted in *Photographies 1980–1981*) at the Galerie Daniel Templon in rue Beaubourg, Paris. The flyer showed a nude woman, her face in profile, her body three quarters facing the viewer. Her right breast looks us directly in the eye like a target. Her left breast is in profile, more or less. Its under-curve is echoed by the line of her ribcage as it comes to the waist. Her left arm is arranged. It has designs on us. The elbow is posed facing out – to mirror the left breast – and the back of the hand rests against the top of the pelvis. A thing never seen in nature. Utterly artificial. Like a jug handle to echo her jugs.

Now consider Klimt's first portrait of Adele Bloch-Bauer (1907, Neue Galerie, New York, oil and gold on canvas). The chair she sits in burns like a throne… and enfolds her like a floor-length spreading train. She wears two bracelets on her left arm. Her throat is invisible under a choker the size of a small flowerbed. Her dress has jewelled shoulder straps. It is narrow, a kind of textile backgammon board at the bust, the body of the dress an aquarium of golden fish, of eyes like beaten gold, dense with luxury. Painters who have ambitions to paint gold – not an easy thing – should consult this Klimt. He solves the problem directly – by *using* gold.

Madame Bloch-Bauer's face has the slightly retroussé mouth of Tom Stoppard – full lips, handsome without being quite conventionally so. She could be his sister. Her eyes are intelligent and grave. Klimt has painted reserve, distance – flesh and blood, sure enough, but at a lower temperature than the expression usually implies. The hands are remarkable – thin, elegant, perhaps a little cold – and arranged at once elaborately and plausibly. You feel that they are composed by the sitter, not by the artist.

But of course they *are* arranged by Klimt. Madame Bloch-Bauer's hair is equally elaborate, equally composed, cropped at the top by the edge of the canvas. Its extraordinary outline – it might be topiary – is mirrored exactly by the shape of her two hands. Neither the hair nor the hands can be described in words. (The coiffure is as bizarre, in a completely different way, as those Spanish police hats made from melted 78s.) Their shared shape of hair and hands is so utterly out of nature, it resembles nothing except itself – an artificiality the sitter has learned to live with quite easily, quite naturally by now.

Klimt, like his disciple Egon Schiele, is also known for his candid nudes – women masturbating, semi-clothed, innuendoes of lesbianism. Art historians tend to worry away at the moral propriety of these pictures. Are they titillating? They are frankly sexual in the way Donne is in 'On His Mistress Going to Bed', when he instructs his mistress to 'cast all white linen hence' and show herself as to a midwife. It may be thought, in some quarters, to be deplorable but it is natural for men to be interested in women's genitalia. We can take Klimt's nudes as reliable, nay, irrefutable evidence. He himself was unworried, saying that the arse of one of his models was 'more beautiful and intelligent ... than many faces'. Let's not be arse-ist about this. You know what he means.

Everyone knows about these nude pictures – and they are terrific – but Klimt's landscapes are greater and less appreciated. I want to discuss four of these paintings and relate them to Klimt's guiding idea – the conflation of textile with reality. In *Farmhouse with Birches* (1900, private collection) the farmhouse is relegated to the far background. The foreground is taken up with turf, with a few wild flowers in the near foreground. A picture of grass, then, with the trunks of four silver birches. All branches and foliage are out of the picture. On the right, a thin birch trunk runs slightly askew from the top of the canvas to the bottom. The other three trunks to the left come a third of the way down the painting. You have to look at the composition for quite a long time before you identify the textile technique involved. At first, I thought of drawn-thread work – where you pull threads in one direction to create a diaphanous line, like the ladder in a stocking. Then I realised Klimt's birch trunks are mimicking *trapunto* – a sewing technique like infibulation, where raised decorative matter is sewn onto/into the textile, bringing supplementary textures to the flat material.

Beech Forest I (1902, Staatliche Kunstsammlung, Dresden) is the familiar barcode effect, but the horizon five eighths of the way up the painting creates the idea of a loom with warp and weft. *Field of Poppies* (1907, Österreichische Galerie Belvede) is the painterly equivalent of a pretty floral print. When we think about prints, we tend to isolate the pattern and its repeats. Klimt knew, as print designers know, that the pattern is there but is obscured by folds, by the very act of being worn. In *Field of Poppies*, you can hardly stop the feeling in yourself that, could Klimt's landscape only be straightened out, the slightly obscured pattern would be clearly visible – whereas, for the moment, it is merely shy but about to overcome its embarrassment and show us everything.

The Park (1909–10), a great painting, which hangs in MoMA in New York, takes the idea of textile to its most radical expression. Nine tenths of the canvas is foliage, brush-strokes, serried leaves that almost lose their source in nature and become abstract, pure pigment, printed textile close to pattern. Then, right at the very bottom of the painting, Klimt allows us to see tree trunks, dwarfed by the canopy above. The painting is like a swallow dive. I used to think that this name referred to the flight of the bird. In fact, it refers to the action of the gullet. In *The Park*, the eye falls the full length of the picture, headlong through space, from morn to noon, from noon to dewy eve, a summer's day, before Klimt rescues us from vertigo with a gratifying gulp, at the very last moment – returning us to the safety of suddenly recognisable reality.

Richard van den Dool
(2005)

Richard van den Dool was born on 23 October 1949 at Sliedrecht in the Nether-lands, where he now runs the publishing house of Wagner and Van Santen with his first wife, Caroline van Santen. It specialises in poetry, much of it translated, printed in beautifully designed books. He lives in nearby Dordrecht, at the con-fluence of three rivers, with his second wife, Olga, and their daughter Emma.

His education, he says, was 'nothing at all' – three months here, two months there. Aged fifteen, he had 'a year at art school'. Eighty other kids wanted to go and there were only four places. He was 'too young' and stayed only a year. At sixteen, he moved to the Conservatory to study music but left after two weeks. Between the ages of eleven and thirteen, he played the piano 'for hours' and composed every day. He still composes and plays in a group.

His father was a former Tango champion and water-skier – skills picked up in Borneo, where he was a teacher and schools inspector, living the 'gorgeous' life of a bachelor, since his wife and children remained in the Netherlands. On his return, he bought a small printing firm and Richard worked there, designing books and catalogues. It was ten years before Richard, at the age of twenty-six, felt 'OK' with his métier, secure in his craft. He started designing poetry books and literary books. He specialised in graphic design for art books dealing with the seventeenth, eighteenth and nineteenth centuries – and he designed posters and lettering for museum exhibitions. Then, for family reasons, he left the firm. Subsequently, in 1985, he taught at an art school, left that, divorced, fell in love, remarried, set up his own publishing house – and made himself the greatest twentieth-century landscape painter.

The status of landscape painting is problematic. It is the poor relation. This is George Bernard Shaw writing about Dickens's friendship with the painter Clarkson Stanfield: 'Stanfield was a scene painter who appealed to that English love of landscape which is so often confused with a love of art.' In the Nether-lands, of course, landscape painting is more practised and prized.

It begins, probably in the sixteenth century, as background to scenes from the Bible, like the 'Flight into Egypt'. For example, in the Koninklijk Museum voor Schone Kunsten, Antwerp, there is a winter scene painted by Pieter Bruegel the Elder. It depicts cabbages with snow on them and a marvellously humorous snowballing scene, in which one person threatens while the other cringes. The cowering person has hunched shoulders and no neck. People gather round a bonfire. Kids go down a slide, arms out like singers. Pigs are being slaughtered. An idiot is being pulled on a sledge by his mother. You can tell he is an idiot by the hump of his shoulders – a hump that is subtly different from the hunched shoulders of the person about to be snowballed. In the foreground, there is a Madonna figure, sitting side-saddle – with a possible Joseph in front carrying a long, thin, curved saw over his shoulder. On the left-hand side, there appears to be some kind of census taking place – so we infer this is Bethlehem relocated in the Polder.

Here the balance between biblical subject and the matter of real life has shifted towards real life – as it has in Pieter Bruegel the Elder's *Die Anbetung der Könige im Schnee* (1567), in the Museum Oskar Reinhart am Stadtgarten in Winterthur. The kneeling kings in the stable are cropped and the foreground is given over to a village scene, with peasants carrying filled buckets from a hole in the ice. A toddler in a boat-sledge rows on the surface of the ice. You can barely make out the infant Christ at the furthest edge of the painting. The home movie supersedes the main feature film. Which is why I wanted to use this painting on the paperback cover of my epic poem, *History: The Home Movie*.

In the Prado at Madrid, there is another winter landscape by Bruegel. It is called *Winter Landscape with Bird Trap* (1565). The trap is an old door in the woods, propped on a stick. Attached to the stick is a rope leading out of the painting. While there is no religious element, there *are* hordes of people. So we haven't yet reached pure landscape painting.

Dürer is arguably a representative of the transitional phase. His exquisite watercolour landscapes are regarded as purely preparatory by some scholars: a lake scene is later incorporated, as background, in *The Madonna with the Long-Tailed Monkey*. However, Erwin Panovsky argues convincingly – from Dürer's prose writings and his habit of signing studies and drawings – that Dürer anticipated modern taste in sometimes seeing in a sketch artistic value superior to more ambitious painting.

In Poussin, like Bruegel, there is nearly always human reference, however muted. Even in J. M. W. Turner's paintings, there is usually a human pretext, however secondary to the vast surrounding meteorology. In Holland, though, pure landscape painting is a flourishing tradition by the nineteenth century.

And Van den Dool began traditionally enough – painting outside, painting from life, working from preparatory drawings. He also painted nudes and still lifes. 'I've tried everything.' Asked why he specialised in landscape, Van den Dool says, wryly, 'Because it's easier, maybe, than painting women with elegant hands. My nudes were influenced by Gustav Klimt.' The candour and the confidence remind me of Francis Bacon. Asked by Richard Cork why there were no drawings, Bacon replied, 'That's because I can't draw.'

From early on, Van den Dool's paintings show a restricted palette, a disposition to monochrome, but this is misleading: 'I started with lots of colours. Then
at the end, after maybe a year, I painted only with white or blue – on top of the
other colours with transparent paints. It took a very long time.' He exhibited
these works in which the colours were overlaid, but thought them 'not exciting'.
He stopped exhibiting. Then, from 1988 to 1992, he virtually stopped painting,
too – 'the small forests were done then.' In late 1993 and 1994, the breakthrough
came, at the age of forty-five.

Because Van den Dool has so remade landscape painting, his pictures aren't
easy to describe. I have two in front of me. One, unusually, has a title, *Regen*
(*Rain*). Both are painted in oils on identical small wooden boards which measure 19cm x 14cm. These two paintings are part of a series of approximately 200
– begun in 1994 and painted at night, sometimes six or eight in a session. The
series is key.

One reason landscape painting is undervalued is implicit in the Shaw quotation above. It is thought to be pretty. And therefore without profundity.
Complication came in two stages. First, the picturesque – meaning an art that
lent itself readily to pictorial representation – was expanded to include ruins
and nature: as 'Culpability' Noakes remarks, in Tom Stoppard's *Arcadia*, 'Irregularity is one of the chiefest principles of the picturesque style.' It was further
subverted or amplified by the idea of the Sublime. With the Sublime, delicacy,
prettiness, gave way to ruggedness and a touch of terror.

Landscape painting's aesthetic inferiority complex – and its resort to steroids, to the Sublime – is of no concern to us now. It is historical, by which I
mean concluded. It is also a chapter in the history of morality, of Puritanism.
Caspar David Friedrich's landscapes almost always carry a Christian cross. The
cross is like a tiny laundry mark – an index of ownership, of divine authorship.
Pure aesthetic pleasure, what Nabokov called 'aesthetic bliss', tends to bring
with it guilty feelings – and the need for justification. It interests me that Van den
Dool's immensely knowledgeable second wife, Olga, sees her husband's art as
'spiritual' – a word divested of theology but which I take to be a hangover from
this moribund tradition. Actually, I think there is nothing wrong with prettiness.
Nor anything redemptive about ugliness, for that matter. In fact, Van den Dool's
paintings evade both categories by making them irrelevant. The morality of
his paintings is their accuracy, their peculiar mediated accuracy, the considered
accuracy of a painter bent on capturing not spirituality but the spirits of particular places – the precise, fugitive, inexpressible emotions we feel when we look
at landscapes.

Van den Dool's landscapes are not in the least Süß. Neither are they tinged with melodrama. In fact, misleadingly, the first impression is sometimes of dullness. The viewer is expected to read the pigment attentively, to concentrate. It is a little like starting to read Henry James – *The Ambassadors*, say – and discovering that one has 'read' a page and taken in nothing. Initially, Van den Dool's landscapes are difficult, opaque, occluded. The pictures do not try to charm, to glad-hand, to sell themselves. The scenes are sombre, perhaps the result of Van den Dool's depressive temperament – perhaps the medium for that depression. Not that I would account for his skill in terms of his complex psychology or upbringing. His temperament may colour his art, but it cannot account for it. It is noticeable that no one 'explains' Luís Figo's football skills or Roger Federer's art by invoking their unhappy childhoods.

Take *Regen*, dated 1993 and therefore one of the first breakthrough paintings. Long before we see what is being represented, we register the paint crudely, approximately, as six irregular horizontal strata in subdued colours of the same family – dull olive, charcoal-grey, dull olive, thin light lovat, charcoal-olive, khaki with tinges of emerald-green. As it might be, a rectangle of army shirt with a biggish, darker stain of Brasso. Not so much a painting of landscape as the shorthand of rough camouflage.

Of course, the eye is intelligent and quickly interprets and unpacks the picture – but the delay in abstraction, in enigmatic dullness, is crucial. The frank quality of enigma stops this being the kind of picture you might walk past in a museum on your way to the Vermeers and Rembrandts. You can't quite read it. So it differs from all those other traditional landscapes, equally 'rewarding' if read, but too easily 'read' from a distance to detain our impatience. The Van den Dool is poised – briefly, crucially – between abstraction and representation and therefore presents us with a temporary interpretative obstacle.

We can't see it and dismiss it – because we can't quite see it *to* dismiss it.

And when we look properly, we see the work of a recording angel on whom nothing is lost. Unsurprisingly, it is a rainy day, a scene subdued by dirty weather – but that Brasso stain resolves itself into a wood with several birch trees and, in the middle-foreground, perhaps a young fir tree. All this differentiation is the result of almost homoeopathic traces of broken, grubby, snot-coloured verticals – silver-birch trunks – and some phantom overlaid indigo marks. To the right of the wood is a fence. What kind of a fence? Two rows of wooden poles, a fence made from branches or sapling trunks, irregular but straight enough to use as fencing. And this 'detail' is created out of nothing, out of marks made by the point of the brush's shaft roughly scoring the oil paint. The 'roughness' is actually very precise. It tells us the fence isn't regular sawn wood or barbed wire or wire mesh.

In the foreground is a bogland sunken stream. There are reeds, laconically registered by three charcoal-grey patches to the right, each the single stroke of a half-inch starved brush. And there are *disintegrating* bulrushes – four dark minuscule *v-shaped* marks to the left of the picture. Neither let me forget the bluebells beyond the stream, below the fence – just four tiny touches of pale blue. When we look properly, we go from rags – that remnant of army shirt with the Brasso stain – to riches, to a landscape detailed enough to live in.

There are two kinds of painterly realism. The first is the realism of Holbein's portrait in chalk, ink and brush of Sir Thomas Elyot in the Queen's Collection at Windsor. The drawing technique isn't quite invisible, but it is self-effacing, even interred. Consider the hair in this picture. It is inseparable from the marks that represent it. Initially, there are four kinds of hair on view – eyelashes, eyebrows, stubble and fine scalp hair. The weight and texture of each is differentiated by Holbein's perfect, clear graphite gradations. These gradations further, lucidly, differentiate within each type. We distinguish between the mini-splinters and the coarser micro-commas of Elyot's unevenly concentrated facial hair. Holbein establishes the scalp hair's fineness by the two or three long, single, separate threads floating free of the mass. He distinguishes between the spread and separation of the upper eyelashes and the more crushed italics of the lower lashes. And don't get me started on the mole faintly foxing the flesh to the right of the eye. Or the incipient double chin.

The other kind of realism advertises its means, is frank about how it achieves its ends – and our pleasure comes from the chasm between the signified and the signifier. Degas's pastel *Woman Sponging Her Leg in the Bath* shows us the bath-water as flakes of lime-green pastel. We are persuaded by the equivalence and astounded by the licence. We register the medium. In other words, the means are essentially metaphoric. If a poet compares a milk tooth to a segment of sweet corn, the justice of the comparison comes encumbered with micro-objections. So the pleasure of metaphor is not only the likeness invoked, but also the *unlikeness* that is overridden. Teeth are white, sweet corn is yellow – and so forth. In fact, teeth are not white. Nor is sweet corn yellow. And both have a rough edge where they once joined the parent body. In all metaphor, there is an implicit argument to be made for the justice of the comparison – which, in the poetic conceit, is explicit argument because the *contrast*, the *unlikeness*, is what initially strikes the reader. In 'A Valediction Forbidding Mourning', we listen to Donne ingeniously explaining why parting lovers are like stiff twin compasses. We are conscious of an element of imposition, of strenuous persuasion. (Which makes it odd that Donne only implies the real, tender grounds for comparison – the reluctance of the lovers to part that makes 'stiffe' the key word.)

With Richard van den Dool, the paintings are manifestly *painted* and we admire the brilliant economy of means. The mark, the sign, advertises its status as a sign. It says to the viewer, for example, 'I am not a bulrush. I am a dark, divided, minuscule mark no bigger than a crushed gnat. But I can persuade you that my approximation is the perfect equivalence, accurate beyond literal accuracy.' Yet one of Van den Dool's favourite artists is Holbein, a painter who eliminates all space between the brush-stroke and reality. The others are Turner, Klimt, Van Eyck, Tiepolo, Caspar David Friedrich, Matthijs Maris, Mark Rothko and Guardi – the prolific Francesco Guardi, whose *vedute* paintings of Venice were free from the burden of accuracy and included the quite imaginary view (*veduta ideata*).

The second painting in front of me is dated 4/1994. Though it has no title, Van den Dool refers to it as Dartmoor in winter. There is snow on the hilltops, like two lines of converging crumbling surf. Above the hills, low unbroken cloud like dirty snow. Above the cloud, a sky of dull pewter-blue. The middle-ground and foreground are the dead-heather browns of moorland in winter – with added smears of grey-white, which may be a river, or remnants of snow. There are, too, some pollen-coloured threads straggling down from left to bottom right. The yellow threads are created by scraping away the surface brown – perhaps with a fingernail or the shaft of a brush – and they suggest the gradient, steep at first, then levelling out. The lack of any human reference causes inevitable ambiguities of scale. At the centre of the picture is a darker patch – a cave from which the 'river' issues? To the right-hand side of the picture, rubbing has revealed a series of close-packed needles of yellow-green – which follow the grain of the wooden panel and may represent trees in the far distance.

Unlike *Regen*, *Dartmoor* resists resolution and leaves us permanently in the pigment. It refuses to be precisely representational, without in any way diminishing the reality of its mood. It is, too, a picture that changes dramatically, depending on the light – as if light were its own weather.

Browning's notorious Renaissance Duke of Ferrara – autocrat, connoisseur, barbarian, oxymoron – has his wife made away for being too familiar with her social inferiors. He chooses 'never to stoop'. One of Browning's great gifts as a writer is to stoop – to the allegedly 'ignoble', to what is 'beneath' the notice of high-minded, bad poetry. In 'How It Strikes a Contemporary', Browning gives us the poet as harmless intelligencer, considering unconsidered trifles. It is a modest yet exacting role for the writer. In 'Saul', there is a description of darkness and the way that detail develops as the eyes accustom themselves to darkness. Less dramatic, more telling, is Browning's account of what it is like to enter a tent. For this biblical subject – the first encounter between the depressive King Saul and the young David – Browning mimics simple biblical syntax. Like Matthew Arnold in 'Sohrab and Rustum', Browning presses the connective 'and' into such frequent service that what is intended as simplicity almost begins to look mannered. David is speaking:

> Then I, as was meet,
> Knelt down to the God of my fathers, and rose on my feet,
> And ran o'er the sand burnt to powder.
> The tent was unlooped;
> I pulled up the spear that obstructed, and under I stooped;
> *Hands and knees on the slippery grass patch, all withered and gone,*
> That extends to the second enclosure... [my italics]

I have invoked that slippery, dry grass – polished with use – because for everyone who has been a child it is an infallible mnemonic of summer, and because it is the kind of detail that Van den Dool addresses and summons in 147 (3/1994). This painting has a dense, almost uniform, green-blueblack sky above a hill, with a wooded clump at its summit. The hill and the copse are initially undifferentiated. Below the sky, we see a scoured, scarified cinnamon rust – the copse, the stand of trees. The stand is above, but continuous with, dung-coloured beiges scumbled over a near-obliterated green. This green is a faded version of the green sky. It is a green from which all the chlorophyll has fled. The scratches for the trees are all rough verticals. The scratches for the dry, autumnal grass are a mixture. Mostly they are rough horizontals. But there are verticals, and verticals bent left like a left-hand bracket [( ]. All told, they designate a dull tangle, in fact, of the kind you see on lower ski slopes at the end of the season when the snow has melted. Tough grass the texture of baler twine. Dead grass like an etching plate – scratched into being. And, above the grass, a wood like a workman's stiff broom with one or two dead leaves trapped in its twigs.

What are the precedents for this great art? What are Van den Dool's influences?

They go back a long way, well beyond the immediately contemporary, or even the early part of the twentieth century. Were one intent on over-simplification, the early monochrome landscapes might evoke Gerhard Richter – say, the frozen stream between pallid blue-grey banks of *Winterlandschap 1973*, a painting that captures perfectly what skiers know as 'dead light'. In 'dead light', detail is subtly depleted. Asked directly about Richter, Van den Dool simply says, 'I don't think I learned anything from him. These paintings were before or the same time as Richter.'

It is another tempting over-simplification to plot Van den Dool's development as parallel to that of Kandinsky, whose *Landschaft mit dunklem Baum bei Murnau, 1908,* is boldly summary but naturalistically recognisable – and leads to the fauvist quasi-abstract *Landschaft mit roten Flecken, 1913*, which hangs in the Guggenheim in Venice. A nearer parallel might be Mondrian. Mondrian began as a realist painter of landscapes like the watercolour *Geinrust Farm in Watery Landscape 1905–6*. He ended, via the semi-abstract, quasi-fauvist *De Rode Wolk* [*The Red Cloud*] *1907*, as the *outré* abstractionist of *Broadway Boogie-Woogie*. And there *are* Mondrians that might be mistaken for Van den Dools – for example, *Dune Sketch in Bright Stripes* and other seascapes of 1909. In fact, Mondrian and Van den Dool share a common ancestry. Consider an oil painting like *Groot landschap 1907* (in Marty Bax's *Complete Mondrian* as *Riverscape with Row of Trees at Left, Sky with Pink and Yellow-Green Bands 1907*). You could put it next to Van den Dool's striated pinks of 128/1 and claim a family resemblance. When I showed 4/1994, the 'Dartmoor' painting, to the novelist Philip Pullman, he sent me a postcard the next day of Mondrian's *Groot Landschap*. Though the two paintings aren't 'alike' in any obvious way, I could see what he meant. Actually, Van den Dool and Mondrian share a common ancestor. Mondrian's sunset pinks derive from the spectacular Baltic light effects of Caspar David Friedrich.

Rather than Richter or Mondrian, I would cite as truer influences Dutch painters of the nineteenth century. T. S. Eliot, in his essay 'Tradition and the Individual Talent', explained that meaningful originality, as opposed to easy eccentricity, meant developing the tradition, rather than breaking with it. It is easy to be merely different. Richard van den Dool is in the Eliotean tradition. I want to discuss three crucial, representative, influential paintings.

On the landing outside his studio, there is a painting by Henri van Daalhoff (1867–1953) – a landscape with trees, a house in the background. This ostensible subject barely survives the pigment used to render it – a thick *pointillisme*, a *tachisme* that leaves the viewer reading dense, pitted blacks. Through a glass darkly.

Another, favourite artist of Van den Dool's is Matthijs Maris (1839–1917), who lived in London from 1888 till his death, obsessively working over two or three pictures. His *Zelfportret 1860* is an astonishing work, perhaps the greatest self-portrait ever. It is unflattering, even ugly, itself in the tradition of Rembrandt self-portraits – an utterly compelling chiaroscuro, seen from underneath, somewhere between three-quarter face and full face.

Traditionally, sentimentally, we look to portraits for psychological insight, a portrait of the inner man. But it has always seemed to me that only the caricature truly attempts the promised psychic commentary. A David Levine caricature in the *New York Review of Books* primarily seeks, not only resemblance, but brisk, often glib, epitome. For example, Rasputin with staring, white, empty eyes and pinprick pupils, outlined with charcoal like a pince-nez – the Mad Monk of the MGM movie. Nabokov with butterfly net, stalking an open book. Gore Vidal, the author of *Lincoln: A Novel*, visually conflated with his subject. A nude, bisexual Paul Bowles, sucking an erect cigarette holder. The paralysed polio-victim Roosevelt, in a full-length swimming costume, his lower body an uncertain wash of lines in the water. Of these examples, however, only Rasputin and Gore Vidal embody their (arguably, trite) characterisation through the portrayed features. The psychological commentary implicit in the others is achieved not through the face but by the use of props. Accessories are psychological plants – the press release with the author photograph, as it were.

Caricature, then, is commentary. But its insights are opinionated, simplistic and dependent on accessories. The self-portrait goes deeper than caricature, deeper than resemblance, deeper than portraiture. Mainly because the painter knows what is going on under the surface. The Maris self-portrait looks down on the viewer and also casts a cold eye on its subject – the self with the wide Slavic nostrils and the pulled sensuous mouth, as if the upper lip were a repaired hare-lip, its apex slightly off-centre. The mirror here is crucial to this unusual viewpoint. It isn't vertical, in the same plane as the canvas. It is horizontal, flat on a table. Maris looks down at his reflection, looks up – and paints himself looking down.

How does this picture relate to Van den Dool?

We see Maris's features through a dark spatter of granules, of tiny freckles. Compare the tension in the Daalhoff landscape between the tachisme and the traditional subject. How do we read these blemishes? They are, first, an index of candour. The self-portrait is freckled, moled – warts and all. Second, the self-portrait also insists on its pigment. The marks on the skin are also tiny marks made by the painter. Pigment elides with pigmentation. The portrait makes you pay attention to the paint. It is abstract as well as clearly representational. Finally, of course, the freckles refer us to the old speckled mirror Maris looked at to paint his own portrait – and another elision of medium and subject. Through a glass darkly.

(This elision of medium and subject had been done before – differently – by Bruegel. His *Die Anbetung der Könige im Schnee* (1567) is the first (and brilliantly successful) attempt to paint falling snow – the medium through which he 'saw' the three kings at the periphery of village life.)

And compare, too, Willem Witzen (1860–1923), whose late self-portrait is painted in aquarelle with oil on cardboard. *Zelfportret, London, 1889* has a very dark gold background and a face even darker so that the painter looks like one of Velázquez's Negroes. Whistler called the portrait of his mother *Composition in Grey and Black*. Witzen might have called his self-portrait *Composition in Gold and Black*. The figurative reaches after the abstract, like an early Rothko, yet using the monolithic diction of late Rothko. In each case, the impulse to insist on the paint is identical. The medium is the message. As it is in Turner, despite Ruskin's attempts to validate the pictures by translating them back into reality. They are first of all paint. I asked Van den Dool if he took suggestions from the medium itself. 'Not sure about it. No, I don't think so. But it can be very helpful, the paint itself. I don't think so much. I just start it. And wait for what is coming up.'

But none of this is really important. The thing is to describe the quiddity of each picture, its qualia.

Van den Dool's recent work is in close-up – close-ups of leaves, vegetation, undergrowth, grass – with, paradoxically, much larger canvases for the more limited viewpoint. Though I like these pictures a fraction less than the little landscape series, they are immensely charming and engrossing. I have a very beautiful pencil drawing made by Mark Alexander of a Japanese girl, *Yuko Soneoka*, done in 1993. It is as brilliant as the very best of the earliest Augustus John. Perhaps I can use it to explain how Van den Dool's close-ups work. The girl's hair isn't fine. It has the blackness and the coarseness we associate with one type of Japanese hair. Alexander contrasts its vigour with the moulding of her face, small blunt attractive features, which are subtle without being exactly delicate. Alexander has chosen precisely the right weight of pencil, the perfect degree of sharpness in his pencil point, for the hair – so that each strand finds its exact equivalent in the single line.

Similarly, in Van den Dool's paintings of foliage, you experience equity between brush-stroke and the image itself. The coarse grass blade is one brush-stroke, an identical match. Yet overall you see a large-ish canvas filled with white and green-blue marks, feather-shapes or wood-shavings. But it is a painting of undergrowth. As is clear from the photographs on the studio floor – brilliant in their own right as photographs, but without the wonderful brushwork. These are often very bright pictures in pinks, blues, yellows – everything alive with light. The brushwork restores undifferentiated vegetation to its individuality. Each leaf is of course virtually identical. Nature is thrifty. So there is a temptation for painters to 'knit', as Stanley Spencer designated this painterly automatism. Van den Dool refuses this shorthand because he realises that, although the shape may be the same, the angle is always different. No two leaves, therefore, are the same to the accurate eye. As Elizabeth Bishop records in 'Brazil, January 1, 1502': 'Januaries, Nature greets our eyes / exactly as she must have greeted theirs: / every square inch filling in with foliage – / big leaves, little leaves, and giant leaves, / blue, blue-green, and olive...'

Initially you might liken this foliage painting to one of Joan Mitchell's conflations of Monet and abstract expressionism – for example, *L'Arbre de Phyllis 1991*. But *L'Arbre de Phyllis* isn't a detailed picture of nature at all. It is a broad metaphor for nature in the round, for nature seen at a glance, for nature quickly squinted at. It is an approximation. It *reminds* you of nature. It is more coincidence than design. Compare Pollock's *Enchanted Forest 1947* in the Guggenheim in Venice, or his *Autumn Rhythm, Number 30* – disingenuous, opportunistic titles both. Van den Dool's paintings are all specificity.

Photographs on the studio floor corroborate my argument. In one, there are leaves on the ground, each a different colour – a pink leaf next to a yellow leaf, a yellow leaf with copper-green mould at its edges. We rely on our artists to look for us. Without them, we are blind in our approximations. Oscar Wilde said in 'The Decay of Lying' that there were no fogs before Turner. A harmless hyperbole, which only means that it took a Turner to see the beauty and painterly potential of a meteorological condition largely regarded as a nuisance.

In this respect, Van den Dool reminds me of Hopkins, whose 'Inversnaid' celebrates the weeds and the wilderness: 'O let them be left, wildness and wet. / Long live the weeds and the wilderness yet.' The same Hopkins was once seen by a lay-brother at Stonyhurst crouching 'to stare at some wet sand'.

Wet sand.

There is a marvellous Witzen winter landscape in the Rijksmuseum in Amsterdam. In the centre, a line of leafless trees, sheltering a village whose snow-covered houses look like a camp-site. But it is the foreground, taking up perhaps half the canvas, which is extraordinary. It is only snow, with a sparse scattering of uncovered rocks. Yet this familiar, unseen thing strikes you with the force of a great discovery.

As great, if not greater, is Van den Dool's 1994 painting of a small sharp uneven stubble field on a slope – an untidy cul-de-sac of corn, an awkward corner, bordered by clumps of brittle, uncut stalks the reaper couldn't reach. There is a loose tangle of undergrowth in the foreground, a dry dense high hedge or a leafless little wood in the background.

'There is a loose tangle of undergrowth in the foreground.' In Bruegel's *Jäger in Schnee* at the Kunsthistorisches Museum in Vienna, this means the meticulously recorded rusty straggle of brambles in the foreground – whose awkward, untidy, irrepressible loops are unsubdued by snow. We have all 'seen' this a hundred times without seeing it. Unless we are Robert Frost: 'And the ground almost covered smooth in snow, / But a few weeds and stubble showing last' ('Desert Places'). Before Bruegel, no one thought such a thing worth recording. His painting is an *aide-mémoire* actually – but one in which recognition feels like discovery. Our artists exist in order to lend reality to 'reality' – to add the italics of considered attention, to make us read the landscape, for instance, as closely as we must read pictures.

And this is what a great artist like Van den Dool does, too, though slightly differently. In his painting, 'there is a loose tangle of undergrowth in the foreground' means there are a few marks and a few scratches – like bits of wire left on the floor of Alexander Calder's workshop. There are some blue smears. To interpret them, we must bring our reading of nature to our reading of the picture. We have to remember what we read a long time ago – when we were children, when we read our surroundings in unremitting close-up.

In literature, in 1933, T. S. Eliot invented something which was later called reader-response theory by Wolfgang Iser. This means that the reader, under the supervision of the writer, brings his own meaning to the text. A Van den Dool landscape requires reader-response. Under the supervision of the painter, we make those loops, those scratches, into a specific detritus of suckers and angular brambles. The blue seems to be some kind of wild iris. It is too big to be speedwell or forget-me-not. We bring all this to those brilliantly suggestive marks. It is a stereoscopy of precisions – the painter's and the viewer's.

It makes you realise that this kind of modest, dull scene is drenched in its own emotion. It isn't landscape painting. Here, there is nothing generic or generalised. It is a *portrait* of this particular landscape. And no other. We recognise it like an intimate, like a dead loved one returned to us, slightly disguised by paint, so we have to search – like Dante seeking the features of Ser Brunetto under the scorched surface, under the pigment.

Jeff Koons
(2009)

Outside Frank Gehry's quilted, titanium-clad Guggenheim Museum in Bilbao, there is a West Highland terrier puppy, a 'Westie'. You know it's a puppy because its tilted head is larger in proportion to its body than normal: it has that cute caricature quality so endearing in the very young. It is forty-three feet high, made out of 7,000 flowers and is a masterpiece by Jeff Koons. I'm looking now at a photographic reproduction, which differs slightly from my ten-year-old memory of it. The photograph is mostly green with a frosting of flowers – a greenness that assimilates Koons's art to classic topiary and therefore slightly diminishes its shock value and its originality. When I saw it, the 7,000 flowers were largely white and pink and pale blue – emulating the Westie's precious peroxide coat and embodying the irresistible sentimental allure we feel for puppies. Koons was fusing two undeniable emotional categorical imperatives – puppies and fresh flowers in pale pastel shades. There were Japanese tourists at its base having their photographs taken. It sat, winningly, in a permanent pool of 'urine' – actually, the sprinkler system that watered the 7,000 flowers.

In Pasolini's 1968 film *Theorem*, Terence Stamp represented an ideal of beauty – a profile, a face, wrapped in a pale cream cashmere overcoat. Immaculate. Impeccable. The ultimate aspirational love object. Until, that is, a tiny bruise of oil appeared on the overcoat in the latter part of the movie and the perfection evaporated, suddenly volatile, maculate. In his first incarnation, Terence Stamp represents the transfigured flesh that we fall in love with – the heart's hyperbole. Then experience marks the complications of reality, the symbolic soiling of the cashmere overcoat. In the old quad of my college, there is a magnolia tree that suddenly switches on in early May and blazes for a week before depositing a detritus of petals like used toilet paper. Koons is true to the coruscating wattage of flowers and will not, apparently, admit the obverse – those same petals anointed with rust and decay. We are used to the ironies of modernism, its sceptical interrogation of romantic feelings, but Koons is part of a tradition that goes back to the Renaissance, back to Michelangelo's drawings of 'ideal heads', a tradition that admits selection and improvement, a poetic treatment of reality.

To this tradition, however, Koons adds humour. Vladimir Nabokov said in an interview that most people who complained about sentimentality didn't

Exhibition at the Serpentine Gallery, 2 July–13 September 2009.

know what sentiment was. In other words, they are dangerously allied. One man's sentiment is another man's sentimentality. This is Jeff Koons's special territory. His *Puppy* tells us two things – both of them true. First, it is true that human beings are hard-wired to love small animals. It isn't affection we feel for Rottweiler puppies, it is love. They are irresistible. Second, this vivid feeling, this genuine sentiment, is also sentimental because it overrides the ambient facts – the faeces, the ferocity of the mature dog. Koons acknowledges both the improbable emotional purity and the dogged downside by constructing his tribute entirely of flowers. In this way, the floral untruth says it with flowers – and unsays it with flowers. It is at once an expression of sentiment and an acknowledgement of sentimentality.

In August 2006, François Pinault's art collection was shown at the Palazzo Grassi in Venice. Koons's *Balloon Dog* glittered cerise on a pontoon moored outside the palazzo. Inside, there were several examples of Koons's work including a pale violet *Hanging Heart* – a huge stainless-steel sculpture that dominated the ground floor. What kind of a heart? A Valentine heart, a symmetrical heart, a Christmas tree decoration with golden bows, a Walt Disney heart with the promise of amorous, aerobatic bluebirds. It was too good to be true. It was ideal. It was enormous.

It was also genuinely beautiful – as well as unbelievably beautiful.

It wasn't just a Disney animation. It was a fully realised film star in person, so to speak. You could see its aura, touch its tangible charisma, take in and be taken in by its nimbus. It was both intrinsically vulgar and vertiginously numinous. The essence of Jeff Koons, in fact – a heart all hyperbole, all advertising hype, *and* helpless hyper-ventilating surrender to beauty.

The man who doesn't know much about art, but knows what he likes, also 'knows' that nudity in classical art isn't really nudity at all. It is a branch of geometry, a question of form, of abstract shapes, a world from which pubic hair has been banished like the unkempt rough-work of calculation in progress. We can look at classical nudity without the slightest danger of arousal. This is not a pornographic experience. It is an aesthetic experience.

This is a little like saying that classical nudity owes much of its impact to Euclid.

In his pictorial and sculptural series *Made in Heaven*, Jeff Koons engages with this view of art. In 1991, he married the porn-star and Italian politician Ilona Staller and photographed his wife and himself as Adam and Eve in various sexual situations. As in the classical tradition, Mrs Koons is without pubic hair – in this case, though, the aim isn't euphemistic and modest, but explicit and exposed, a full Brazilian. But I'm getting ahead of myself. The series is, above all, a series. The bland refusal to register nudity is there in the marble *Bourgeois*

Bust (1991) of Jeff and Ilona, where her upper arm is amputated like the Venus de Milo. The photographs are transmitted like stills from a movie: *Made in Heaven: Starring Jeff Koons and Cicciolina*. (Cicciolina is Mrs Koons's *nom de guerre*.) On occasion, the pose is far enough away for the sexual act in question to be distanced, if not discreet. On other occasions, though, we can see the artist's penis in the act of penetration (*Ilona's Asshole*, 1991) as well as the working wife's full complement of orifices. Jeff Koons has remarked, counter-intuitively, that what *he* likes about these photographs are the pimples on his wife's backside. Which are visible – if you look for them.

Koons is the Laurence Sterne of the art-world – apparently enamelled with innocence ('I think life is simple'), but actually smart as the smart of a whip, witty, yet as poker-faced as Buster Keaton (whom he has sculpted). In interviews, he has nothing but praise for his fellow-artists; he is assiduously complimentary to anyone who could be described as a mentor. There is, as it were, a perpetual smile on his conventionally handsome face – so unvarying that it is impossible not to detect the imp of intelligence, the innuendo of laughter.

For example. Andy Warhol did a famous series of Elvis silk-screen prints – iconic Elvis, holster tied to his trousers, revolver in his hand. Koons's contribution to this artistic topos is a woman, duplicated: nude but for a vinyl thong; completely nude but for a scrap of black material that conceals nothing of importance. Between these two images is an inflatable lobster. The picture, an oil, is called *Elvis* (2003). There are other versions with a trio of identical women, in different states of nudity, but always with the inflatable lobster. It takes only a moment's thought to work out what the lobster signifies – a real cooked lobster, though red and hard, would serve Koons's purpose less accurately because the real thing isn't inflatable. The actual crustacean is one size fits all, whereas the toy inflatable version mimics the expansiveness and the retractable capacities of the penis in action. In interview, Koons blandly explains the lobster as a reference to the acrobat–artist H. C. Westermann – the claws as an allusion to Westermann's hand-stands. I think we are looking at the original double-entendre that nick-named Presley, Elvis the Pelvis. That, I take it, is the thrust of the Elvis series.

Koons is so various, so inventive, it is no surprise that not everything works as well as the best work. And just occasionally you can detect him playing the art game: in an interview with Peter-Klaus Schuster when there was a Koons installation in the Neue Nationalgalerie in Berlin in 2008, he claimed there was a dark side to his art: 'even though the outside could be joyous, the inside was a little dark. It's like the *Balloon Dog* having this very joyous outside, but at the same time an equestrian, Trojan-horse quality. You could feel the presence of the inside.' Excuse me. *Balloon Dog* is charming because it is as light as the helium inside the fairground original – and if you inhale it, you will emit a tinny giggle. *Balloon Dog* is actually a guard dog – guarding us against taking art too ponderously. It is immensely, monumentally, lightweight. It is self-consciously lightweight. And, like all of Jeff Koons's art, it is aware of previous art. *Aqualung* (1985), to take one little example, is a breathing kit done into bronze – bronze with all its museum connotations – but is in fact a *spoof* sculpture, a 'found' pastiche abstract-futurist sculpture of the kind so prevalent in the forties. The innocence displayed by Koons is really very knowing.

Rodchenko
(2008)

I begin with a spectacular pair of spectacles and I will end with a pair of spectacles. Even if you have never heard the name Alexander Rodchenko, you will know his 1924 image of Osip Brik, the husband of Lili Brik, who was the lover of the poet Mayakovsky. Osip Brik was the co-founder of *LEF* – a magazine whose acronym stands for Levy Front Isskustva, the Leftist Front for the Arts. Rodchenko's iconic image shows these three Cyrillic letters in one lens of Brik's spectacles. Once seen, never forgotten. It is a striking piece of agitprop – propaganda for Brik's magazine and an index of its dedicated leftist vision. It is also subversive – as you would expect from someone whose own sense of artistic self-worth was inseparable from the lens. In effect, Brik, a figure of the avant-garde, is sightless in one eye. The obverse of an heroic historical vision is cultural blindness, narrowness, conformity. Rodchenko's image encompasses both – strikingly, ruefully. Brik was persecuted through the thirties. In 1930 Mayakovsky committed suicide. Rodchenko was expelled in 1931 from the October circle of artists, charged with 'formalism'. I think he could see it coming.

What is the status of photography? It varies. In 1878, photography was a star. In 1878, the murderer and photographer Eadweard Muybridge made his series *Horse in Motion*, which demonstrated that painters – painters as great as Degas – had been getting it wrong. The definitive success of *Horse in Motion* inaugurated further (semi-prurient) series – of naked women and men running and jumping. Just in case we were in any doubt about how these locomotive physical tasks were accomplished by men encumbered only by a cache-sex and sometimes not even that. Photography, it seemed, had definitively replaced painting as the medium for accurately representing reality. If mimesis was your aim, photography was the perfect method. In fact, if David Hockney is right in his book *Secret Knowledge* – and, forget the sentimental art historians, he *is* – for generations, artists had been surreptitiously using the photographic precursor, the *camera obscura*, as an aid to draughtsmanship.

However, these artists discovered that the photographic image is a useful guide to proportion and dimension but niggard of detail. A draughtsman like Ingres was compelled to augment his image with information acquired by 'eyeballing' the sitter directly. The greater depth of focus provided by the

Alexander Rodchenko: Revolution in Photography, Hayward Gallery, 7 February–27 April 2008.

nineteenth-century photographic plate and prolonged exposure provided only a temporary solution. The superiority of the naked eye soon became apparent. It saw more. It saw in cinemascope – a feature the 'panoramic' function on modern cameras is meant to approximate – and it saw quasi-microscopically in intimate close-up. The eye is vari-focal. The camera is not. If the frayed cuff of an extended sleeve is in focus, the face of the sleeve's owner won't be. The photographer chooses between foreground and background. Film chooses, too, and even a focus-puller can't choose both at once, though either is possible successively. No sooner had photography deposed painting than its limitations were revealed. It is a perfect example of 'The Iron Law of Stardom', formulated by Louis Menand in the *New Yorker* (24 March 1997), 'the law of the three-year limit': 'This law dictates that stardom cannot extend for a period greater than three years. There is no penalty for breaking this law, for the simple reason that it is unbreakable.' Yes, I know, and Menand knows, too, the obvious objection: 'Once a star, always a star, of course – and that's the problem. For stardom is not to be confused with being a star... Stardom is the period of inevitability, the time when everything works in a way that makes you think it will work that way forever.' In 1879, the Tay Bridge disaster was commemorated by William McGonagall and recorded photographically. The photographic evidence featured in the inquiry. But the party was almost over. The etymology of the name 'photography' means 'drawing with light' – but the very difference between photography and drawing is that photography is, finally, mechanical. There is no drawing.

By 1880, the jig was up. Even then the writing was on the wall and Larkin's 'Lines on a Young Lady's Photograph Album' were waiting to put the de facto declension of importance into words. Larkin's title, reeking of anachronism and out-of-datedness, is an index that, in the nineteenth century, the verdict was already in and merely waiting for Larkin to clear his throat and find photography guilty – of being prosaic, of being misleadingly literalist: 'But o, photography! as no art is, / Faithful and disappointing! that records / Dull days as dull, and hold-it smiles as frauds, / And will not censor blemishes / Like washing-lines, and Hall's-Distemper boards.' The point – that photography isn't art – has been waiting, patiently, inertly, since 1880, when the Iron Law of Stardom decreed that photography wasn't inevitable.

You can see this clearly in Alexander Rodchenko's question-begging, nervously vaunting credo of 31 October 1934, 'Photography is an Art': 'From being secondary and imitating the etching, painting or carpet [not a mistranslation: carpets were art objects; Gorky showed his collection to Anna Akhmatova], photography has broken free and embarked on its own path...It is growing and establishing its right to the same respect as painting.' What are Rodchenko's arguments for equality? One is to be expected from a communist, that photography is 'essential and accessible' – accessible as an available technique and something easily read by the viewer. This essentially pious, party-line argument from plebiscites can be discounted.

The other arguments advanced – compositions 'that leave Rubens behind', the revelation of the 'unknown' (i.e. undocumented) – can be refuted by example. Like, for instance, 'foreshortening that would be impossible in drawings or paintings'. It is true that some of Rodchenko's most brilliant photographs depend on the radical dislocation of viewpoint – though nothing like as radical as cubism's unfixed viewpoint that brings sculptural in-the-round values to the acknowledged, given two-dimensionality of painting. Three examples: *Pioneer Trumpeter* (1930), *Pioneer* (1928), *On the Telephone* (1928). In the first, we are shown the trumpeter from under his chin. The trumpet is cropped so we see only the mouthpiece and a horseshoe of the trumpet. The picture is turned to the left about ten degrees out of the expected vertical norm. Compositionally, it is quietly, subtly echoic: the trumpeter's nostrils, immediately above the mouthpiece, replicate the mouthpiece almost exactly. The line of his right ear is reproduced, upside down, in the collar of his uniform. The horseshoe of the instrument contains a metal loop – which is mirrored in the dark eyes. The woman on the wall telephone is shot from above, radically foreshortened, holding an awesome black Bakelite exoskeleton and speaking into its periscope. The composition embraces defamiliarisation. Now you don't see it, then you do.

The Russian formalists, including Viktor Shklovsky, who was photographed with Rodchenko, called this technique *ostranenie* – or 'making strange'. One of the best examples in literature is the opening of Nabokov's *King Queen Knave*, which describes perfectly an example of everyday surrealism – the sensation that the station is leaving the train: 'the huge black clock hand is still at rest but is on the point of making its once-a-minute gesture; that resilient jolt will set a whole world in motion. The clock face will slowly turn away, full of despair, contempt, and boredom, as one by one the iron pillars start walking past, bearing away the vault of the station like bland atlantes; the platform will begin to move past, carrying off on an unknown journey cigarette butts, used tickets, flecks of sunlight and spittle.' And so, vividly, irrefutably, on – a tour de force, forcing us to reconsider reality. Rodchenko's telephone is made equally strange.

But of course there is nothing new here. Photography is simply catching up. Consider, for example, Degas's *Stooping Dancer, Seen From Behind* (c. 1877–8), an oil drawing on faded pink paper, dedicated to 'mon ami Mathey'. The right of the drawing is filled with the ballerina's behind – an unruly thatch, an angular mushroom of petticoats, the stiff scratchy tulle brilliantly captured by Degas's starved brush. No arms are visible. No torso, either. It is all arse. The dancer's

head is a darker oblong at the upper right of the skirts. The scumbled shape of
the tutu, the compositional enigma, is quickly deciphered and read. At first, it
might be a mistake, or someone simply trying out a colour to see how it looks.
It looks uncomposed, unbeautiful, unformed, a mass of rough brush-strokes.

In the Musée Rodin (D 556, graphite on paper, 1900) there is a drawing of
a man bending over backwards – seen from the front, all legs and knees – like
a high jumper executing the Fosbury Flop, which, after the 1968 Olympics,
replaced the Straddle technique, which had in turn displaced the Scissors. At the
top of the drawing, you see a phallus, arranged to the viewer's right, limp as a
lock of hair. The upper body is invisible. Mid-left there is a suggestion of head,
etiolated in the same way as the head of Degas's stooping dancer. Our pleasure
is the pleasure of closure like the end of an epic simile – as the initially uncertain
resolves itself.

In other words, photography isn't outpacing art. It is catching up. It is emulative – of Egon Schiele's *Nude with Blue Stockings Bending Forward* (1912, pencil
and gouache on paper, Leopold Museum, Vienna, No. 1441), in which the coccyx
is the summit of the picture. The pose is folded in on itself, a kind of ironic
compositional modesty, showing only one scuffed shoe at the bottom right, and
three brief quotations of blue stocking – a wry pun in this sensual painting
which is all back and vertebrae.

No sooner had painting successfully reasserted its superiority than the
motion picture arrived as another threat. Initially, of course, the movies were
just as sensitive to charges of artlessness. The early auteurs, like Eisenstein and
Dziga Vertov, were careful to compose their shots rather than simply to point
the camera. (You can see why Francis Bacon was later drawn to stills from Eisenstein, like the bleeding, bespectacled nurse on the Odessa steps in *Potemkin*. The
image is viscerally powerful but also carefully composed.) Rodchenko's photography is quick to assimilate the compositional possibilities of Eisenstein and
Vertov. An obvious example is *The Stairs* (1930), where a woman – just off-centre,
plumb in the conventional vertical axis – carries a child up a set of stone steps
sloping steeply, dramatically, from top left to bottom right. Only the narrowing
perspective of the steps tells the viewer that this isn't Viennese *Jugendstil* – a
deliberately flat, decorative surface, intercut, as in a Klimt painting, with the
human form.

Later, of course, as film took hold and enjoyed its own three years of stardom,
photography felt constrained to follow. The photographer Philippe Halsman's
envy of motion pictures is evident in his kitsch skull composed of nude women
– like a Busby Berkeley musical desperately seeking sophistication. Halsman
was fascinated by motion: famously he photographed Marilyn Monroe jumping
barefoot for *Life* and followed it by the Duke and Duchess of Windsor in mid-

air. Other celebrities jumped on to Halsman's band-wagon, which he explained with the theory of 'Jumpology': when asked to jump, celebrities forgot to be celebrities and revealed more of their unguarded selves. Actually, 'Jumpology' is a form of filmic emulation, as are Halsman's exercises in photomontage like *Dalí Atomicus*, where Dalí is in motion, cats are in flight, thrown water is in mid-trajectory, and a chair is levitating. All these are examples of photographs who would like to be motion pictures – when they grow up. Compare Rodchenko's boast in 1934: 'To say nothing of the double exposure (or dissolve to use the cinematic term)...'

In fact, Rodchenko's photographs are as grown up as it gets. If you are looking for obvious composition, his snaps of mass gymnasts exploit natural pattern. Stanley Spencer, painting First World War troops cooking with their skillets for his glorious Resurrection War Memorial at Burghclere, talked about his composition as an *obbligato* of bacon rashers. The proper comparison, however, is not Spencer but Leni Riefenstahl and her dramatic repeats. (At least Rodchenko won't have to face the charges of fascism levelled by Susan Sontag against her photographs celebrating the beauty of the Nuba. The way Rodchenko photographs communist physical culture isn't glorification. It is aestheticising, the obliteration achieved by pattern. Pattern is more important than national prowess.) There is a marvellous photograph, *Scierce: Planks of Wood* (1931), which is arranged around a single formal template set up by the parted legs of the workmen. The wood being carried carries the eye from centre to top left. The stacked planks on the right carry the eye from centre to right. Everything goes its separate way. The photograph is as lovely as a woman opening her legs.

How good is Rodchenko? His most famous photograph is *Mother of the Artist* (1924). All his considerable gifts are here. Pattern *trouvé* is there in the half of the composition given over to his mother's tiny polka-dotted headscarf. The line of her nostrils and her overlapping upper lip are another repeat. And this repeat is itself repeated and inverted in each of her eyebrows. She has a polka-dot of her own, a circular cyst, on the side of her nose – itself circled by the single lens of her spectacles that Rodchenko permits us to see. The art here is hidden. You have to look for it – because, first and last, the photographer is giving you an old woman in her quiddity taking a closer look at something. But there is a message here for us, too. Look. Take a good look. It is a kind of credo.

(In case you were wondering, in 1874 Eadweard Muybridge shot his wife's lover, Major Harry Larkyns (fateful name), and was acquitted on the grounds of 'justifiable homicide'.)

Sickert in Venice
(2009)

In 1995, I talked with Philip Rylands, then deputy director of the Guggenheim Collection in Venice, about Jackson Pollock. It didn't matter that I was unpersuaded by Pollock's painting, Rylands calmly explained, because his place in art history was assured by, among other things, Pollock's anecdotal value. You might call this the Vasari effect. Which is another way of saying we like gossip, recently dignified as life-writing. Do we read Diogenes Laertius's *Lives of the Philosophers* for a measured exposition of these ancient thinkers' philosophical tenets? I think not. We read them, as we read Aubrey's *Brief Lives*, for the scandal, the fresh scurrilities, Robert Lowell's 'ever-lasting dross', dirt with the bloom still unblemished. Think of the fart that inadvertently escaped Edward de Vere, the Earl of Oxford, as he bowed low to Elizabeth I – a fart faithfully, unfaithfully recorded by Aubrey, who also loyally records the monarch's response when de Vere returned to court after seven years of self-imposed exile. 'My Lord, I had forgott the Fart.' Think of Diogenes Laertius's account of Diogenes his namesake, masturbating in public: 'when behaving indecently in the market-place, he wished it were as easy to relieve hunger by rubbing an empty stomach.'

Were Philip Rylands correct, Walter Sickert (or Richard Walter Sickert, as he later preferred to be known) would have an assured place in the history of art. He has anecdotal value. Marjorie Lilly's *Sickert: The Painter and His Circle* is a mine of anecdote: when Sickert's first wife was angry, 'she went very pink... a sort of carnation... charming. I had to fetch my palette and state the tone.' Maddening, perhaps charming. Unruffled or uncaring? Ellen Cobden Sickert had every reason to be cross with Sickert. The couple separated in 1895 because of Sickert's numerous infidelities – with Ada Leverson, friend of Oscar Wilde and grandmother of Francis Wyndham; with, among others, Aggie, the sister of Max Beerbohm. Sickert refused either to apologise or to adapt his behaviour. Ellen Cobden Sickert set down Sickert's misbehaviour in her 1902 novel *Wistons*. Sickert thoroughly approved.

On 3 June 1911, Sickert was jilted at the registry office by his fiancée, a former pupil at the Westminster Technical Institute. He did not repine. On 29 July he married instead Christine Drummond Angus, a woman twelve years his junior, who died in 1920. When asked if he missed her, he said: 'It's not that. My grief is,

Sickert in Venice, Dulwich Picture Gallery, 4 March–7 June 2009.

that she *no longer exists.'* Not then, perhaps, the egotist he often seemed.

Nor simply the immoralist he often seemed. When Arthur Clifton, his dealer, left his wife for Madeline Knox, Sickert terminated his contract with the gallery. On the other hand, Madeline had been a partner at Sickert's etching school. The connotations of 'partner' may be relevant here. Morality? Or jealousy?

Early in his career, Sickert, painting in Venice, living on the Zattere, wrote to Philip Wilson Steer, friend and fellow-painter: 'nearly sat on a scorpion in the w.c. Thought of you at once: of what you would say.' This may account for Sickert's alterations to his Islington house in 1927, where he lived with his third wife, the painter Thérèse Lessore: he had the builders rip out all the conventional lavatory bowls and replace them with French stand-up floor-pans. (It was said, to enjoy the reaction of his discommoded female guests, but perhaps that scorpion played its part.)

Throughout his life, he grew and shaved his beard – beginning lean as Gregory Peck and ending with an ebullient beard like Brian Blessed. Periodically, he shaved off all his hair. He couldn't decide about his Christian name.

And he changed his style all the time. For example, he began by denouncing the use of photographs: 'in proportion as a painter or a draughtsman works from photographs, so he is sapping his powers of observation and expression. It is much as if a swimmer practised in a cork jacket [a life jacket], or a pianist by turning a barrel organ.' By the end of his life, and even earlier, he was using photographs as much as Francis Bacon used them.

And Bacon is an interesting *point de repère* in any discussion of Sickert. There is a direct line that runs from Degas, through Sickert, to Bacon. Degas's *Le Viol* (1874) is a bedroom scene, showing a man, fully dressed with his hands in his pockets, leaning against the door, and a woman with a torn chemise. Obviously, Sickert's Camden Murder series – of naked women and fully clothed men – derives from his beloved (and much quoted) Degas. Sickert's *La Hollandaise* (1906), with its iron bedstead, sunken, perfunctory mattress, and meaty nude, is benefactor to Bacon's *Henrietta Moraes* (1966). Both models' faces are anonymous smudges, the faces of women who have been systematically fucked over. The difference between Bacon and Sickert is that Bacon can be a brilliant and vibrant colourist, whereas Sickert's palette was consistently limited to the dun end of the spectrum. (Which made it difficult when he gave lessons to Winston Churchill, always an energetic colourist, and then Chancellor of the Exchequer.) Nevertheless, there are Bacons that owe everything to Sickert's continent drabs. Compare, for example, the brushwork and the browns of Sickert's *Self-Portrait* (1896) with Bacon's *Study from the Human Body* (1947).

Sickert is important to Bacon, no question. He makes a top-hatted, be-spectacled appearance – perhaps based on the well-known 1923 photograph taken when Sickert lectured in Edinburgh – in Bacon's (1987) *Triptych* (left-hand panel). And the panama-hatted drinkers in the right-hand panel of Bacon's (1965) *Crucifixion* owe everything to Sickert's *Vernet's, Dieppe* (1920): the central male drinker wears an identical hat (and hatband!) and is also in profile.

As well as these (arguable) visual details and parallels, Sickert and Bacon share a temperament. Don't be fooled by the dark, obscure passages in some Sickert paintings, or the smudges and 'accidental' drips and spills in Bacon. Neither painter takes his eye off the object. They are realists, classicists, bent on the unpretty truth. This is why Sickert is so unfair to his first mentor, Whistler, who painted ravishingly beautiful paintings. In Whistler, there is a transaction between truth and beauty, an assimilation which is incomparable. Sickert, like Bacon, was fascinated by crude, uncompromising truth and therefore accused Whistler of too much taste. No surprise, then, that Sickert defended his beloved impressionists against charges of vagueness: for him, impressionism was a 'severe and pure reaction in art', not a 'cult of the vague or a refuge of the negligent'.

Like T. S. Eliot, another classicist in favour of unblinking emotional precision, Sickert was committed to impersonality in art: 'Banish your own person, your life and that means you and your affections and yourself from your theatre.' Little wonder, perhaps, that Sickert, who began as an actor, should have used Mr Nemo (no one) as his stage name. Eliot's range went well beyond the obvious 'poetic' subjects – for example, his prose poem 'Hysteria'. Sickert's brush addressed the subject of *Ennuie* – the dead taste in the mouth, the sticky glass. Both men were profoundly swayed by French cultural life, both men loved the music halls. Both men were realists rather than beauticians.

The always-enterprising Dulwich Gallery is about to show Sickert's Venice paintings. In March 2007, I saw the *Sargent and Venice* exhibition at the Museo Correr in Venice. Sargent is a very good painter but Venice is the graveyard of painters. I have nine pages of notes in my notebook. They end on a note of exasperation. About, note, repetition: 'Too many pictures with cropped prow of gondola in foreground. 10!' Up to then, my comments are appreciative. For example, I admire the way the 'represented ripples bleed into the steps' in *Zattere, Spirito Santo and Scuola, 1902–4*. But the only great painting, among many good pictures, was called *Side Canal, 1880–81* – a watercolour which showed the viewer its *dirty* walls, with the one gondola banished under a bridge and practically invisible. To paint a dirty wall, to think a dirty wall a worthwhile subject – that is genius, that is Vermeer.

Venice is full of fallen plaster, broken brickwork, dirty walls, dowdy poetry – all unpainted, all neglected in favour of the tourist centres of Piazza San Marco, the Palazzo Ducale, San Salute, the Basilica San Marco, the Rialto, the Grand

Canal. Who hasn't been photographed in Piazza San Marco? Everyone who is anyone. Schoenberg. Monet. Leonid Pasternak. Wagner. Stravinsky. And then the nobodies. Piazza San Marco is a site both dulled forever and shiny with constant contact – as meaningless as a politician's handshake. Everyone goes there. Everyone paints it. Imagine it was compulsory to paint the Eiffel Tower and you get the scale of the disaster. It is just this oppression, this tourist tyranny, that Claes Oldenberg addressed in his 1999 exhibition at the Museo Correr, where he sent up the winged Venetian lion and twisted its tail. The tail became a yellow chain of interlocking builder's buckets dangling from the side of the building, its frayed end mimicking a spout of builder's detritus.

Of course, some painters have triumphed in Venice. Whistler, for example – because he sought out the unofficial, the back passages rather than the front entrances. In the *Turner Whistler Monet* exhibition at Tate Britain in 2005, those self-important sites were shrunk to a pretext for the subtlest colours in combination. They were self-evidently secondary to Whistler's rust-gold pastels, restrained blues and greys, on brown or beige paper, that materialised miraculously out of the background like spectral textiles, frail faery fragments from Fortuny's factory: *Red and Gold: Salute Sunset* (1880); *Salute: Sundown* (1880); *Sunset, Venice* (1880) – all of them better than the Turners from which they derive.

By comparison, Sickert hardly survives. You feel the economic imperative. At this time, as Sickert remembered in 1935, his dealers 'bought my canvases in roped up (and unseen) batches of ten at £40 the batch, with one batch thrown in as a make-weight'. It's hardly surprising he painted the subjects that would sell. The three best, genuinely exceptional paintings are oil on panel – one, surprisingly enough, of Piazza San Marco, which normally hangs in the Fitzwilliam Museum in Cambridge. Somehow the official nature of the site is subverted by the way the undisguised grain of the wood is frankly visible through the paint at points. The two masterworks, however, are *The Ghetto, Venice* (1897–8) and *Santa Maria della Salute* (1901). Both are oil on panel. The ghetto pell-mell architectural crowding is a waffle of windows, a dun Mondrian *avant la lettre*, a kind of fretwork that uses the wood on which it is painted. Perhaps it resembles an Andreas Gursky more than a Mondrian: it is at once intensely patterned and idiosyncratic in its detail.

Santa Maria della Salute is oil on panel, tonally red, and still squared up in red, a grid that transforms the familiar church, making of it a mirage, something seen through a veil: 'a rose red city – "half as old as Time"'. Actually, Sickert's red reads as the red of gold – it confers value and splendour as well as unfamiliarity. We see the thing again, thank goodness. It isn't so different now, while Santa Maria della Salute is being restored and is surrounded by scaffolding. My notebook records that in the morning mist the dome of Salute is a fuzzy corduroy cactus. This is what Martin Amis called the war against clichés. Go to the Dulwich Gallery for these three paintings that break the adamantine spell of hypnotic holiday Venice. That will have to suffice until the best living landscape painter, Richard van den Dool, can be persuaded to go to Venice and do it justice.

Vorticists

(2011)

The Vorticists opens at Tate Britain on 14 June and can be seen until 4 September. I saw the show in Venice at the Peggy Guggenheim Foundation.

Who were the Vorticists? Galvanic Ezra Pound was the band's vocalist, belting it out. With his ziggurat hair, he was the impresario, the excitationist, the amplificationist, just as another writer, Marinetti, was the vocal focal point of the Italian Futurists. Every movement needs a writer to whip up the manifesto. The philosopher T. E. Hulme was its theorist. The leading participants were expatriates – the American sculptor Jacob Epstein, the ex-Canadian Wyndham Lewis, the Frenchman Henri Gaudier-Brzeska, the American photographer-in-exile Alvin Langdon Coburn.

The movement was short-lived, barely lasting from 1914 to 1917. Epstein was never an official Vorticist. Nor was David Bomberg. But both could see the commercial point of Vorticism – the biz of the buzz. And they made a more lasting impact than various other English painters who were drawn into the Vortex – Pound's wife Dorothy Shakespear, Jessica Dismorr, Frederick Etchells, Helen Saunders, Christopher Nevinson, the Yorkshireman Edward Wadsworth, William Roberts. Apart from Roberts (barely represented here), none of these slight painters is touched with talent: they are canon fodder. They are the infantry, the grunts, bulking agent, the barium meal which creates the sense of a movement. The flush New York lawyer John Quinn, anti-Semite, lover of Lady Augusta Gregory, patron of W. B. Yeats, T. S. Eliot and the avant-garde magazine *The Dial*, also threw money at and down the Vortex.

And what *was* Vorticism? For all its international recruits, it was a parochial British attempt to emulate and excel Cubism and Futurism. Another ism. No wonder (in 1925) Hans Arp and El Lissitzky co-authored the tri-lingual *Die Kunstismen* (*Isms in Art* in English). Constructivism was set up in Russia. Fernand Léger's Tubism was just round the corner. There was Suprematism, Expressionism, Verismus... Arp and Lissitzky don't mention Vorticism, however. Why not? Because it was effectively invisible, a variant, a hanger-on, a wannabe. Vorticism was keeping up with the Cubists. A great many of the catalogue essays here are intent on translating the art into ideology. Every picture is worth a thousand words. Or more. And we get them. The art historians assiduously mine the art for traces of Bergson, Kant, Newton, Max Stirner, Nietzsche, George Sorel.

Actually, the impulse behind Vorticism, the theory, is simple. The machine is central to Vorticism. Everything is subsumed to the machine. Le Corbusier famously said in 1923 that a house was a machine for living in. By then, the idea was domesticated and cosy. In January 1914, T. E. Hulme wrote that 'the specific differentiating quality of the new art [will be] the idea of machinery.' It is an irony that Langdon Coburn's mechanical Vortographs – disappointing double- and triple-exposures – meant he was swiftly dumped by Pound. (Langdon Coburn's straight photograph portrait of Wyndham Lewis shows an inadvertent apostasy of vision: note the great gathering of Cubist folds in Lewis's ample crotch.)

In *Orlando*, Virginia Woolf definitively mocked the idea that literature, that prose style, was the toy of social conditions: 'Also that the streets were better drained and the houses better lit had its effect upon the style, it cannot be doubted.' Apparently, Wyndham Lewis was of the opposite persuasion. Social conditioning was crucial: he is against prettiness, he favours abstraction, because 'a man who passes his days amid the rigid lines of houses, a plague of cheap ornamentation, noisy street locomotion, the Bedlam of the press, will evidently possess a different habit of vision to a man living amongst the lines of a land-scape.' However, this glib assimilation of seeing to surroundings – falling for a formula – is effectively repudiated by Wyndham Lewis when he subsequently writes: 'In a painting certain forms MUST be SO; in the same meticulous, pro-found manner that your pen or a book must lie on the table at a certain angle, your clothes at night be arranged in a set personal symmetry, certain birds be avoided, a set of railings tapped with your hand as you pass, without missing one.' What does this mean? Lewis is invoking superstition and ritual – and the iron law of instinct.

T. S. Eliot means much the same thing when he writes, in *After Strange Gods*, that theories of Romanticism and Classicism – Eliot was a classicist – count for nothing at the moment of composition, when it is impossible 'to repair the damage of a lifetime'. You can read the sex manual but the warm living woman will come as a complete surprise. In art, the hand and the eye are decisive. The brain guides the eye which guides the hand. Or so we think. But frequently the chain of command is disrupted, reversed, and the mind sees what the hand has already done. We look for inevitability.

And, once or twice, we find it in this exhibition. Jacob Epstein's *Rock Drill* (1913–15) was reconstructed in polyester resin by Ken Cook and Ann Christopher in 1973–4. It is the exemplary Vorticist art work. It shows a man on a tripod who is one with his machine. His drill is also his rigid proboscis, his hard, angled phal-lus. The tripod has weights (embossed Colman Bros Ltd Camborne England) on each leg, just above midpoint – which look like enlarged joints, or a bee's pollen knee-pads (only available in black).

The ribcage of the figure is exactly like the twin cylinders on a motorbike. He is recognisably human, true, but the human body, with its curves and trim little bum, has been made over to the angular machine: it is an armoured exo-skeleton. The arms are like greaves. I thought of Seamus Heaney's description of a motorbike lying in flowers and grass like an unseated knight. And I thought, too, of 'Not My Best Side', U. A. Fanthorpe's marvellous poem about Uccello's St George and the Dragon in the National Gallery. In it, Fanthorpe imagines the young girl being rather taken by the dragon's equipment, when suddenly, irritat-ingly, 'this boy [St George] turned up, wearing machinery'.

Rock Drill is a tour de force, of energy, a vibrant sculptural collage. The head is turned so we can ponder its long, insect profile. It is immensely alien and spooky, even after you realise it is a long welder's mask, untitled and initially unrecogni-sable, tilted but not revealing a face. There is no face. The mask is the face.

The other great work is the Frenchman Henri Gaudier-Brzeska's Hieratic Head of Ezra Pound (1914). No photographic reproduction prepares you for the scale of this piece. Or the satisfying solidity of the marble. In the Palazzo Guggenheim, the authorised copy was beautifully lit so the shadows were incised and the planes visible. The only thing that is Vorticist about the piece is Gaudier-Brzeska's direct carving, without prior clay models or plaster-of-Paris maquettes – an earnest of Vorticist energy, of vitalism. Otherwise, it is more like something found on Easter Island, as its title suggests. Pound's pompadour is subdued by Brzeska so it resembles a Zadie Smith turban – all that hectic hairstyle hidden away. The mouth and the moustache are one – the mouth of a disgusted turbot, as Salman Rushdie once described V. S. Naipaul. What you have here is a genius for simplification. The eyes are dark, triangular, Toblerone slots. The right eye differs from the left by being pointed at the outside corner. The danger for the sculptor in a task like this is not simplification but blandness. You avoid blandness by touches of asymmetry. The nose is a particular success: it may superficially resemble a nose guard on a Norman helmet, but the top-left-hand line of the nose is skewed and angled out, whereas the right-hand line descends a perfect perpendicular. The front of the Pound sculpture is all lines and angles, all non-Euclidean geometry, like a Ben Nicholson drawing, but the back is bulbous and unmistakably represents a scrotum and an impressive glans. To see it is to recall Brancusi's phallic Princesse X, which was removed from the Salon des indépendants on the grounds of obscenity in 1920.

By 1910, Brancusi had made Sleeping Muse I and entered his maturity, leav-ing behind the early (wonderful) realist sculptures. Gaudier-Brzeska was killed at the front in June 1915. The relationship between Brancusi and Gaudier-Brzeska is interesting because both men were aesthetically inclined in the same direction – but Gaudier-Brzeska's telos of simplification isn't achieved. The Hieratic Head is the nearest he comes. There is another Portrait of Ezra Pound (in the catalogue but not displayed in Venice), which is a carved wooden totem with Pound's head at the top. It is undated, so it is difficult to know whether it was influenced by Brancusi's many totemistic sculptures, at least one of which Gaudier-Brzeska might have known. (Brancusi dates a photograph of the piece 1914–17, with the typical chronological imprecision of an artist.) The other Gaudier-Brzeskas exhibited here are well in the rear of the avant-garde, even when they gesture to the future.

For example, you might compare Gaudier-Brzeska's bronze *Fish* (1914) with Brancusi's polished bronze *Fish* (1924–6) in Tate Modern. Gaudier-Brzeska's *Fish* has some of the ugly angularity of modern Israeli jewellery. It is simplified, quasi-representational and fussy. Of course, ten years of Modernism intervene between his and Brancusi's sculpture. But the Brancusi is a miracle, whereas the Gaudier-Brzeska is workmanlike.

Scientists sometimes tell us that the physical universe rests on a few elegantly simple laws, whose truth is borne out by the sheer beauty of the math. Brancusi's *Fish* (1926) is the closest the rest of us will come to knowing what they mean. Every fish's complexity is here – in essence. It is an abstract of the fish. At the same time, strangely, it is a representation of a recognisable fish. It persuades us of its symmetry while being in fact subtly asymmetrical: the nose is sharper than the rounded tail and, to my eye, the left side (viewed from the tail) is infinitesimally more curved than the right. Nothing could be more concrete. Nothing could be more abstract. Brancusi is the Einstein of art.

Nothing in this Vorticist exhibition gets anywhere near Brancusi. Instead we are invited to view a construct, the impedimenta of a movement, rather than a genuine artistic movement. It is employment for the art historians. We get to see exhibition catalogues, the cover and sample pages of *Blast!* including the 'Bless!' pages, which are curiously parsonical in their blessings of our seafarers. 'BLESS the vast planetary abstraction of the OCEAN.' 'BLESS THE ARABS OF THE ATLANTIC.' (Explained, presumably, by camels being traditionally ships of the desert.) And, finally, an evocation of England as 'Industrial Island machine, pyramidal' – striking the key Vorticist note. There are advertisements for lectures, invitations, posters – in fact, more documentation, it sometimes feels, than actual art. And when we get the art, it looks weaker than its Continental counterparts. When you look at Edward Wadsworth's worthy woodcut of a Yorkshire village (1914), it's difficult not to prefer the original, Picasso's *Factory at Horta de Ebro* (1909). When you see Christopher Nevinson's *Marching Men* (1916), it's obviously all about movement. The regiment looks like one man in a Muybridge, a time-lapse sequence squashed together. But then you remember Duchamps's *Nude Descending a Staircase* (1912) and think how radical that is, and how safe the Nevinson is. For all the blasting and bluster, Vorticism is unpersuasive. You can't will an artistic movement into existence – any more than those cynical pop impresarios could persuade the punters that the Monkees were the equal of the Beatles. Not even with Ezra, king of the cadence, singing his heart out for the lads.

Gerhard Richter
(2011)

Artists don't always tell the truth. 'Notes 1964–1965', in Gerhard Richter's *The Daily Practice of Painting: Writings 1962–1993*: 'I don't create blurs. Blurring is not the most important thing; nor is it an identity tag for my pictures.' This section ends: 'The central problem of my painting is light.' In a later 2001 interview with Robert Storr, Richter said, 'But I have a problem with the term *light*. I never in my life knew what to do with that. I know that people have mentioned on some occasions that "Richter is all about light", and that "The paintings have a special light"; and I never knew what they were talking about. I was never interested in light.'

In *Panorama*, the current Richter retrospective at Tate Modern, jointly curated by Nicholas Serota and Mark Godfrey, there is just one example of Richter's candle paintings. *Kerze* (1982) is a very beautiful, accurate painting of a single simple lighted candle. The curators place their emphasis on the traditional connotations of the candle as an emblem of mortality – as we find it in, say, Macbeth's 'brief candle', or Rembrandt's 1641 painting of the Mennonite preacher Anslo and his sickly wife, whose sickness is manifested in a smoking, recently guttered candle. Richter's painting of this candle seems, at first sight, to belong to the candidly classical sector of his art – the works which take Vermeer as their starting point. And *Kerze* does belong in this category. However, it also reveals its kinship with the great body of Richter's work – the light of the candle is a blur. All candle-light is a blur. This is Sylvia Plath's 'By Candlelight': 'this haloey radiance that seems to breathe.' The halo, the nimbus, the blur, the suggestion, the negative capability – by which Keats meant the ability to remain in uncertainty, without any irritable reaching after fact and reason. Keats liked 'the Horizon' to be 'a mystery'.

Speaking of Vermeer, Richter says to Nicholas Serota in the catalogue (2011): 'The fact that his paintings are good, better than most others, has nothing to do with his special way of painting – it's connected with another quality entirely, a mysterious something.' By Vermeer's 'special way of painting' Richter means 'skill', technique, virtuosity. 'It's not about skill, the so-called craft, that's a given, and virtuosity alone has nothing to do with art. I don't know how I can describe the quality that is only found in art (be it music, literature, painting, or whatever), this quality, it's just there, and it endures.'

In the exhibition's penultimate room we find *11 Panes* (2003), a glass-and-wood construction, consisting of eleven superimposed panes of glass, each separated by an inch, that appears to have the clean precision of Bauhaus. It seems austere, almost sterile and limpid, until you stand in front of it – and see your reflection. Or, to be more precise, your reflections. There you stand, pen poised to make notes, and then you notice that there are *three* pens – the main pen and two phantom edding 55s. Your black Levi 501s are triplicated. Your every movement is accompanied by visual echoes of diminishing force. The panes reflect you – and your blur, your shimmer.

Toilet Paper Roll (1965) depicts what it says on the can. The exhibition note links this to Duchamps's ready-mades, the fountain-urinal, etc., but the art history, the constructed back-story, doesn't begin to describe what the viewer sees. There is a temptation – not always resisted here and elsewhere – to see this painting in its art-historical context of Pop banality. But I think we should rather be seeing Richter's toilet roll (one of two) in the context of Chekhov, who once told his wife, Olga Knipper, that a carrot was as mysterious as the universe, just as implacably inexplicable. The toilet roll is a blur, but 'blur' doesn't begin to describe the transfiguration of this ordinary object. It *glows*, more quietly, more subtly, than the LED in your Apple Mac. It is numinous. And it appears to materialise out of the canvas – like ectoplasm – divorced from the banal conditions of its being. The viewer infers a holder, but it isn't shown, so what we see is a kind of levitation – the bog roll still with menace as a hooded cobra. Richter to Robert Storr on his resistance to pictorial rhetoric and thematic grandstanding: 'the demand was, and remains, to address the things that are most important, that concern us all. And so in relation to the history of art, where nobody had ever painted toilet paper, it was time to paint toilet paper, *which is not really banal*' (my italics).

Richter sidesteps the big themes. We are told at Tate Modern that *Uncle Rudi* (2000: a photograph of the 1965 original) 'is one of the first attempts in German art to confront the legacies of the Nazi past and the involvement of family'. Yet the painting is remarkable – and very beautiful – because it is thrillingly devoid of rhetoric. It confronts nothing except this smiling, vague man in the uniform of the Wehrmacht, holding a glove in one hand. The slope of his pocket parallels the slope of his hat. The painting takes the weakness of the snap-shot – which is its lack of visual information – and turns it to pictorial advantage. Richter's painting is wonderfully composed: behind the figure are two horizontals, a fence and a block of buildings, and the figure in the foreground has two rows of six vertical buttons. He is at once the only vertical and at the same time coterminous with his background. The folds of his overcoat join the planks of the fence. The blurred buttons mimic knot-holes. He is there, glimpsed by the camera, but already disappearing, undifferentiated, into his background.

His famous Baader-Meinhof paintings inevitably attract ideological inflation, even though Richter is at pains to repulse it. 'The risk I was running,' Richter told Jan Thorn Prikker in 1989, 'was perfectly clear. There are plenty of examples of people hitching themselves to some big, attractive theme and ending up with mere inanity.' In his pronouncements about the sequence, Richter voices his distrust of ideology: 'They were merely gangsters, of the sort that are around in any period. But those who were full of beliefs, they were dangerous' (interview with Robert Storr). The pictures themselves tell a more complicated story.

The triple portrait of the dead Ulrike Meinhof is based on a photograph in *Stern* that shows the rope burn on her neck. It is a famous image, powerfully iconic. In Richter's versions, it is gradually, successively, eroded. Eyebrow, eyelid, open mouth blur into vagueness. Not all the paintings in this *October 1977* sequence are successful – the double *Aufnahmen* (*Arrest*) is barely readable in either version. Perhaps, however, this is deliberate? There is one anomalous painting, not often commented on. It is *Record Player* (1988), which shows an old-fashioned machine with its vinyl and the needle arm. What is it doing in this violent Stammheim Prison sequence? Apparently, it was used to smuggle a gun. It stands, though, for the artist memorialising and the implication is that repetitive memories are subject to attrition. The whole sequence is not about the sensational image but about the way the sensational fades with repetition. Things get to be blurred... *Man Shot Down*, a version of Andreas Baader dead in his cell, is 'weaker', less detailed, in the second version. But that is Richter's point.

It must be obvious by now that Richter's blur is enormously versatile, put to a plurality of uses. *Hanged* (1988) shows Ulrike Meinhof hanged in her cell. It makes a brilliant distinction between hanging and standing, even as the brushwork disguises the distinction. The figure could be standing, turned, looking away from the viewer. The blurring allows for that interpretation. And yet, the slightest of angles, the passivity of the hands by the side of the body – something mysterious tells us the truth, discovers the truth. The shock is preserved.

If that primitive Dansette-type record player is a wryly transposed self-portrait, what of the candid *Self-Portrait* (1996) in the penultimate room? Richter is looking down, bespectacled, wearing a tie. It isn't a clear image and yet it is full of information. At first, you think the bust is emerging from the canvas, like a brass-rubbing, but soon you realise that it, too, is *disappearing* into the canvas. It is at once a *memento mori* and a statement of reluctance – a figure for art's impersonality. 'It was the opposite of ideology,' he told Storr in the 2001 interview. 'I don't want to be a personality or to have an ideology', he wrote in 1964–5 – in the same notes where he denied the centrality of blurring to his art.

The unblurred paintings exist and are fascinating. Richter has said that *Reader* (1994) reminded him of Vermeer after he had painted it. It is a portrait of his third wife, Sabine Moritz. It invites comparison with Vermeer's *Woman in Blue Reading a Letter*, in which the whole picture is pregnant with implication, with an implicit narrative. The girl –'solid with yearning', as Lowell once wrote – is probably pregnant, separated from her beloved by a great distance (there is a map on the wall behind her) and reading his letter, lips parted in concentration. Richter's painting is slighter because it is less suggestive, more sharply focused, more photographic, tastefully lit. There is something fatally exact in its calculated perfection. *Betty* (1977) shows Richter's daughter lying down, her face on one side with lipsticked lips. It is a painting in which Richter tries to match all the liquid mouths that are so mesmerising in Vermeer. These are ambitious, emulative paintings. Neither equals their source. But in *Betty* (1988), Richter at last equals his classical master. Betty is turned away from the viewer. Art historians invoke Caspar David Friedrich's *Woman at the Window* (1822) but I think it is Vermeer's *Girl with a Pearl Earring*, glancing over her shoulder at us, that Richter has in mind. Betty's left shoulder is in the same position, but her face is turned away. It is Richter's composition which makes this painting a great masterpiece. Betty's blonde hair is gathered like two loosely enfolded wings – the left sweeping to the right, the right going to the left. And this movement is picked up in her arms, the left arm going to the right, the right going to the left. It is a very simple duet, full of felt harmony, but the means disguised to the perfect degree. And the face turned away is another version of the blur, another way of deferring our habituated, instantaneous vision.

In *Frau mit Kind* (1965), a proper reading of the picture shows not a blurred photograph but a series of visual non-sequiturs. A mother on the beach is towelling the small son on her lap. The blurring, created by dragging a dry brush across the canvas, produces an effect like tapestry – of threads and vagueness of outline. One of the important functions of Richter's blur is to detain the viewer, to make him decipher the unfocused information. Attention must be paid. (It was noticeable that, as the curator's guided press tour swept past me, very few people did more than glance at the paintings. To adapt Eliot, they had the meaning but missed the experience.) Her mouth is open, concentrating. The boy's left arm appears to grow out of his face. Her hand and arm grows out of his arm. His right elbow is visible *under* her embracing arm. The boy appears to have three legs – like the Rembrandt etching of a man and woman copulating in bed, where the woman has three arms. The third of these boyish legs may be the beginning of her other leg. The picture isn't what it first appears to be. Similarly, *Nuba* (1964) reverses the Leni Riefenstal photograph it is based on and introduces various minor, crucial changes.

This is a great show, packed with marvellous pictures. There are three cloud pictures, nature's natural blurs, painted from photographs, that are incomparable, the best cloud pictures I have ever seen. There is a stunning picture of Richter's first wife, Ema, walking nude down a staircase. You have to see the original. Richter's paintings are even more unreproducible than most art. Ema is a blur, with high, vague nipples, no navel and a resolute fuzz of pubic hair. Her face is reminiscent of Monica Vitti. The stairs behind her are in violet lines like a measurement chart. Richter's palette is beautifully limited. Down her left side and between her legs is a lovely dark iodine shadow, like a Diane Arbus photograph. The catalogue and wall notes refer us to Duchamps's *Nude Descending a Staircase*, reasonably enough – but what Richter has painted is a ghost, someone not quite there, but with a bra bikini line.

In Richter's (less compelling) abstract paintings, the blur is present in the bold paint dragged horizontally by the squeegee. I would not be surprised to learn that these abstracts are based on photographs dragged out of a laser printer and thus stretched into abstraction. They include one great 'abstract' painting based on the 9/11 attacks – *September* (2005). Essentially, it consists of two verticals and several horizontal broken brush-strokes, discontinuous right across the canvas – the twin towers and the planes as planes. The top of the picture is a dark pall, through which the canvas shows as almost invisible gold filigree. Everything is muted – the purged colours, the subtle imagery. The painting is beautiful, calm and classical. Olympian and contingent. Achieved and undescribable.

Hockney at the Royal Academy
(2012)

The cover for the January/February 1977 issue of the *New Review* was a black-and-white, nude photograph of David Hockney and his friend, the painter R. B. Kitaj. Hockney's studio can be glimpsed beyond the edges of an improvised white cardboard background. Hockney's pelvis has a female breadth. Ron Kitaj is stockier. Hockney is wearing his owlish spectacles, Kitaj a coloured wife-beater, dark socks and gym shoes. Hockney's uncircumcised penis is a slump of tallow. Kitaj's penis is circumcised, a chunky chip-shop vinegar dispenser.

It was a provocation. The witty strap line across the bottom-right-hand corner was 'A Double Issue'. It did not improve the magazine's minuscule circulation. Many newsagents were reluctant to stock it.

The two painters were protesting the displacement of the human figure by conceptual art and abstract expressionism. A dialogue inside asserted the importance of tradition – of a Seurat responding across 300 years to Piero della Francesca. Hockney: 'I can't understand why anybody would think it was a ridiculous thing to do, but there are people who'd say, "You can't do that now."' Both painters favour skill in drawing and the centrality of representation in art. There is a reactionary tincture that might then have excluded Picasso, one of Hockney's heroes: 'it's harder to paint people like they are than to do them like Quasimodo.' Francis Bacon, another man-handler of the human figure, felt the same way. This is Hockney in conversation with Martin Gayford: 'Francis Bacon was the first intelligent painter I met who dismissed a lot of abstract art. He quoted Giacometti, who used to say a lot of abstraction was "the art of the handkerchief" – "*C'est l'art du mouchoir*" – covered in stains and dribbles … I was rather impressed that Francis had the confidence to say that kind of thing at that time. Loads of people would have howled him down.'

It was ever thus – new-fangled fashion and old-fashioned tradition. And now? There are no human figures in Hockney's new landscapes at the Royal Academy, though there is a Range Rover, captured with great freedom and exactitude on an iPad. But the concern with current fashion remains. This is Hockney talking to Marco Livingstone in Enitharmon's excellent *David Hockney: My Yorkshire*: 'Even if you say, "Painting landscape is an old-fashioned thing to do, I didn't think that. I knew, "Oh no, it's not." I would argue with anybody.'

David Hockney RA: A Bigger Picture, Royal Academy, 21 January–9 April 2012.

He would, too. Hockney is a brainy painter, widely read, thoughtful, restless, whose exceptional intelligence is secured by his insider expertise. His mind is intimately aware of what an artist's hand is likely to decide. *Secret Knowledge*, his narrative of the artistic use of mechanical aids (lenses, mirrors, camera obscura, camera lucida) long before the official 'invention' of the camera, is completely persuasive, despite the reservations of art historians. For example, he takes an Ingres drawing and notices a discrepancy – the head is marginally too large for the body: 'if Ingres had moved his camera lucida to get in the clothes, a slight change in the magnification would have occurred, explaining the difference in scale.' He then observes a technical parallel between Ingres and Warhol – who certainly used a projector.

This show of landscapes is fuelled by a similar innovative thesis – Hockney's sense that the camera isn't the end of painting, that photography's hegemony is finished. Figure, landscape – Hockney's abiding concern is with the nature of representation. In literature, this was the argument about realism. Art is never reality. Art is merely realistic – an imitation, a simulacrum. All representations of reality are constructs, conventions, which undergo ongoing adjustment, major and minor.

For Hockney, the camera is only a *near* equivalent to the way we experience reality. And now we are bored: 'visual magic tends to wear out when it is based on the photographic conception of space which immobilises the viewer, distancing him from the view.' Painting can achieve a more accurate degree of involvement. Picasso gives us the visual experience of the breasts and the bum in the same plane: 'because you could see back and front at the same time, you would not ask yourself, where am I? You were *inside* the picture.'

Hockney's aim is to place the viewer *inside* the painting. His means to this end is the bigger picture, which gives the show its title. There is, however, a problem with increasing the scale of the painting – *joins*. *Winter Timber*, 2009 is made up of fifteen sections, five by three. *The Arrival of Spring in Woldgate, East Yorkshire, in 2011* is made up of thirty-two canvases. In other paintings, the frames of the individual sections are clearly visible. In the old days, according to Hockney, large-scale paintings were wound up and down in 'special studios': 'that's how they paint theatrical scenery.' Hockney didn't have the advantage afforded to a painter like David – hence the joins, which he returns to, uneasily easy, in conversation with Marco Livingstone: 'Long ago I realised that the join doesn't disturb at all. Your eye fills it in'; 'you don't really notice the joins after a while.' In fact, you do – with the odd exception.

When Hockney visited China with Stephen Spender, he met a nine-year-old prodigy: 'and then he drew pictures for us, cats, done in the Chinese manner with brushes, which were stunning. Watching him do them was something:

the way they were placed on the paper... [my italics]' How you place the image is crucial in art – the image can be cropped, or allowed to luxuriate in space, but it has to be deliberate and unhesitant. It is fatal to miscalculate. Hockney (again referring to the 'non-problem' of joins): 'if you haven't got a big piece of paper, you use two smaller pieces of paper. Any artist would do that, just stick another piece there.' It sounds attractively pragmatic, but we've all looked at drawings that have run out of road and continued, with an impression of ineptitude, on an extra added piece.

I said there were exceptions. *Winter Timber, 2009* is one. The colours are so boisterous, so vehement, the joins aren't an issue. In the foreground are loud tractor tracks in purple chevrons. There is a dead tree trunk straight out of panto – in pink with navy wrinkles. The standing trees are bright turquoise. The form of the picture is a splayed M. At its centre are three loads of logs next to a pink-and-grey-striped road, heading to vanishing point, while the logs river towards you – a spate of gold, intended, I think, to remind the viewer of molten steel, great girders of shuddering metal, at once arranged and chaotic, from nature's fiery furnace. I was unpersuaded. They came across as confectionery-coloured, like marshmallow lengths, those cylindrical sweets called flumps.

In the big paintings, the rhetoric-count is high, but the masterpieces on show here are mostly smaller scale, in an area where Hockney has always excelled – drawings. *Timber Gone, 2008* is a perfect charcoal drawing of absence, the redolent minimal detritus left by the logs in a clearing, an asymmetrical circus ring of sawdust. His charcoal drawings can be miraculous and certainly superior to the paintings. For example, there is a quartet of paintings of three *Thixendale Trees*, through the seasons, *Spring, 2008, Winter, 2007, Autumn, 2008, Summer, 2007.* Each has eight panels. They are competent, old-fashioned paintings of the kind you could see routinely in railway compartments in the fifties. Only the scale is gigantified.

And scale is part of the problem. Look at the brilliant charcoal preparatory drawings on deliciously thick Aquarelle Arches paper, *Autumn Thixendale, October 21st, 2008* and *October 18th.* Charcoal is a difficult medium, but Hockney avoids the coarseness always on offer, achieving instead concentrate, burnish and delicacy. In the foreground the plough-land is thin free-hand lines. In front there are a few spindly plants, set down swiftly, economically, suggestively. And notice the line for the road and the other single line for the horizon – both simply set down so that the trio of trees are perfectly *placed.*

Hockney tells Gayford: 'If you were told to make a drawing of a tulip using five lines, or one using a hundred, you'd have to be more inventive with the five. After all, drawing in itself is always a limitation.' Compare this effortless charcoal spontaneity with the laboured quartet of *Thixendale Trees* and their formulaic summer-leaf canopies. There is another crucial thing to notice in a further charcoal drawing, *October 28th* – with its working instructions, 'chalk in soil', colour notes and marked-in grid – the appearance of a hill into the right of the composition, presumably to expand the scale. In all four of the *Thixendale* paintings that hill is dead space, the pictorial equivalent of a brown-fill site, irredeemably dull.

Yet his iPad prints are ravishing, if a little over-dependent on the road as a compositional device. They exploit the back-lighting of the iPad, a sort of dimmer switch, an under-glow that works like the wet white ground in pre-Raphaelite paintings. Room 9 is dominated by a large oil, *The Arrival of Spring in Woldgate, East Yorkshire*, which, again, is an old-fashioned picture except for its scale. It aims to capture the explosion of spring and, in a measure, does so. Its main device is free-floating leaves the shape of bicycle saddles, some on big bendy twigs. There is a framing candelabra of branches to the right and left of the painting. (Hockney isn't shy enough of the theatrical Claude Lorrain curtains. In *A Closer Grand Canyon, 1998*, a queer picture in sixty sections that captures the unnaturalness of the Canyon, Hockney uses two curtains of nougat-like rock as compositional parentheses.)

The iPad drawings are more charming because less insistent. You feel the marks more than you do in the big oil. *1 January* has puddles on a pink-and-mauve road like Calder taking a wire for a whirl. (By comparison Hockney's watercolours are workmanlike. True, his clouds are good, but watercolour was made for clouds. Not even a Sunday painter could fluff clouds. In *Trees and Puddles, East Yorkshire 30.11.04* the wooden puddles are straight out of art block.) *3 January* captures what Debussy, the composer of 'Brouillards', called the poetry of fog. Apart from the odd failure (the irrelevant scribbles across *8 January*), the iPad prints represent Hockney on a roll, one smash hit after another. In the next room are two large iPad masterpieces, both of Yosemite, in which the single vertical joins are virtually invisible. *Yosemite II, October 5th 2011* is like something from a Chinese scroll – an ocean of mist in blue mountains, rendered with breathtaking boldness. I thought of Wordsworth's description of mist on Mount Snowdon at the end of *The Prelude*: 'the sea, the real Sea, that seem'd / To dwindle, and give up its majesty, / Usurp'd upon as far as sight could reach.' A great peroration in paint – except it isn't paint as such.

Yosemite III, October 5th 2011 reuses the road curving out of sight, reuses the tree curtains from Claude, but transmits the sublime sensation of the endless redwood mounting the length of the picture and continuing out of sight.

Hockney's eleven nine-camera films (on eighteen screens) are marvellous, too. They splice the seasons, they bring movement to nature – especially the bold callisthenics of a hedgerow cavorting in a stiff wind – and use the join to advantage by exploiting repetition, overlap, disappearance and discontinuity.

A qualified success, then, but with splendid highpoints. Miss the reworking of Claude's *Sermon on the Mount* – disastrously scaled up – with its wooden worshippers listening deafly to Jesus like play-people. Don't miss the brilliant earlier photo-collages, especially *The Grand Canyon, Looking North, September 1982* and *Pearblossom Highway 11th–18th April 1986*. Allow four hours at least. There's a lot to look at, a lot to think about.

Damien Hirst Retrospective
(2012)

In March 1986, I was in Australia at the Adelaide Writers' Week. One night at dinner, I was telling the outraged and incredulous Cuban novelist-in-exile, Guillermo Cabrera Infante, that Baudelaire had plagiarised his famous essay on Edgar Allan Poe from two essays in the *Southern Literary Messenger* by John R. Thompson and John M. Daniel. And that Daniel, in turn, had plagiarised his piece from Griswold's obituary of Poe. Alain Robbe-Grillet, whose luggage had been lost several days before by Quantas, was preternaturally composed and charismatic in a rumpled linen safari suit. His only piece of clothing a paradox – soiled yet chic. He was also at a remove, chauvinistically silent, refusing to descend to English. *'Nous causons au sujet de plagiarisme,'* explained Cabrera Infante. Robbe-Grillet was suddenly alert: *'J'approve,'* he said crisply, *'je suis voleur.'* It was a strikingly original counter-intuitive statement.

There are two – but only two – remarkable works in this Damien Hirst retrospective. One is *A Thousand Years* (1990). The title refers to Hitler's claim (to a British journalist in March 1934) that the National Socialist Third Reich would last a thousand years. But the idea is stolen from William Golding's *Lord of the Flies*.

It is in two glass sections. In the air is a storm of flies, a blizzard of black holes. The left-hand compartment contains a hollow white cube with a circular hole in each visible plane. The pane dividing the sections has four holes, so that the gross, wrinkled meat flies bred there can fly into the further section – where there is a partially flayed cow's skull on the floor, poised in a brown pool of blood the colour of gravy, so viscous it looks as if it might be synthetic, like a magician's spill of ink, something you could peel off. The angry crimson skull has stiff white eyelashes and sodden fur still on its muzzle. Its tongue, the colour of Irn-Bru, protrudes, as if the thing were thinking hard. There is, above this head, a blue Insect-O-Cutor and an angled tray filled with two stirring wedges of dying flies. The flies are dying like flies. Looking at this piece is like looking at eczema. It is the weight of numbers. Your brain itches.

Neither the title's characteristically glib, melodramatic allusion to the Third Reich, nor the debt to Golding, can affect the power of this piece – or its evident originality. I first saw this piece in *Sensation!*, the Saatchi show at the Royal Academy in 1997. I was unimpressed – because I understood only the concept, the

Damien Hirst, Tate Modern, 4 April–9 September 2012.

realised idea, but resisted the actuality. Importantly, then there were far fewer flies. *A Thousand Years* is now all actuality, the very texture, the unflinching feel and the flinch of disgust. It is gruesome and brilliant.

Whereas the famous shark, shackled to its coffee-bar-existentialist title – *The Physical Impossibility of Death in the Mind of Someone Living* – seems ever more delapidated, more fairground side-show, with every dowdy showing. What clichéd menace it once may have theoretically possessed has evaporated. Not just yawning, but drowning – saved from going belly-up only by its tough nylon threads – its front fins like stabilisers. I gave it a good long look and noticed that it seems *dusty*. Next time, some cleaning lady should hoover it. There is another, smaller, replacement shark, in better nick (*The Kingdom*, 2008) – but it is a tiddler and the loss of scale is fatal.

The other show-stopper is *Pharmacy* (1992), which owes debts to Warhol's use of Brillo packaging, something to Joseph Cornell, and something to those laborious, pedantic reconstructions by Ed Keinholz. This is a larger-than-life pharmacy, down to its apothecary bottles on the counter filled with different coloured liquids – blue, red, lime and emerald. There is even a green-neon Hermes sign. All this literalism is beside the point, however. Hirst, rather in the manner of Claes Oldenburg, has simply noticed how something ordinary and familiar has beauty and charisma. With Oldenburg, it might be a baseball bat. For Hirst, it is the great frieze of pharmaceuticals in their packaging. He understands pattern very well in this piece. For example, there are five opaque white plastic jars of Theo-Dur – but there is also a jar in a smaller size. And the five larger jars show their blue labels at different angles. Theme and variations: a simple thing, you might think, but the scale of this piece is crucial. As it always is. The Zovirax packets provide another theme and variations. And so on. All these patterns exist, disappear, reappear, overlap. The walls become orchestral, a great polyphony of colours, a symphony of signs – creating something calm and beautiful that everyone has experienced in a French or Italian chemist's, if not in their local Boots. I was reminded of Elizabeth Bishop's charming poem, 'Filling Station', where the oil-cans are arranged to say 'ESSO-SO-SO-SO / to high-strung automobiles'.

Though all the smaller pharmaceutical cabinet pieces are given 'intriguing' titles, pilfered from the Sex Pistols – *EMI, God, Seventeen, Pretty Vacant, Bodies, No Feelings, Submission* (featuring Anusol), *New York, Holidays, Anarchy* – the diminished scale gives them the feel of a preparatory sketch. They are negligible. You wouldn't miss them, but Hirst has so few ideas he tends to milk them. The spot paintings are a case in point. Null and repetitive, with the artist apparently unable to decide which pieces work best. One of the earliest works here is *8 Pans* (1987), done when Hirst was at Goldsmiths. The circular undersides of the pans are coloured differently, with household gloss paint. They are the first spot painting, however different they might seem at first. And the later butterfly paintings – real butterflies arranged on more gloss paint – are sometimes also spot paintings, naturally camouflaged with dark polka dots. Others are the starting point for Hirst's spin paintings, with throws and smears of brilliance. The spin paintings also arrive via Jackson Pollock, of course. Just as the spot paintings emulate Gerhard Richter's Pantone colour charts. Art historians see this as artists in dialogue with each other, but sometimes it is just derivative.

Lullaby, The Seasons (2002) is four arrangements of ampoules and pills. In 2007, the *Spring* arrangement was sold for a record price of £9.6 million. I prefer Cy Twombly's *Quattro Stagioni*, recently shown at the Dulwich Gallery, but the Hirsts are simply and beautifully decorative. Each is like a bead curtain hanging sideways, in the horizontal. The pills and ampoules rest on glass shelving, with mirror backing. Think of sifted, sorted tiny pebbles, or beading on a dress, or sequins. They are the *height* of fashion: the season of each is a matter of colour tone and it is quite subtle. Winter, for example, is a grey-blue; autumn a hint of overall russet. The set of four is, despite the glittering setting, rather restrained and tasteful. Which is a relief from the overstatement of, say, *The Black Sun* (2004), which is a circular targe composed of flies in resin. Or the dove suspended in formaldehyde which ends the show. It is titled *The Incomplete Truth* and draws a glib contrast between the religious connotations of the dove and the physical reality of the bird. If you look closely, you will see that tiny bubbles are clinging to its beak – the Steradent effect. I think he should give formaldehyde a good long rest.

He should also stop relying on those inflated, aereated ideas that go down so well in the megaphonic art-world. A giant fibreglass ash-tray is filled with fag ends, filthy fag packets, the odd KP salted peanuts packet, an empty ketchup tube, etc., and given the title *Crematorium* (1996) – a *memento mori*, you see. Hirst could have been an advertising copywriter. There are also two separated friezes of fag ends in different rooms. One is rather beautiful, actually, because the 'cork' tips are intuitively well spaced and mostly laid on their sides, their yellow colour a kind of thick darning, coming and going, appearing and disappearing. In the second arrangement, the fag ends are standing and crowded – so they look like fag ends and nothing else. Another idea over-exploited. It may be all right, on occasion, to be a thief, but it isn't a good idea to steal from yourself – though it may be commercially lucrative.

The catalogue includes an interview with Nicholas Serota. Hirst emerges as an engaging, obliging motor-mouth. But his answers return, nervously, obsessively, to the subject of painting. 'The void of a painting is always a difficult thing.' 'When I was painting, it used to be a big catalogue of disasters.' 'Whereas in a painting, I'd get lost.' 'I'd spend so much time on shit paintings.' This is a representative sampling. It isn't by any means exhaustive. There's more. Yet, interestingly, revealingly, apart from the spot non-paintings, there are no paintings in the Tate Retrospective. Not even the Bacon-derivative 'Blue' paintings that bombed at the Wallace Collection in 2009.

In August 2006, I saw several Hirst paintings at the Palazzo Grassi in Venice, alongside *Infinity* (2001), a glass cabinet full of pills, row on row. My notebook records: 'Good joke about tachisme, pointillisme – his own spot paintings.' My next note: 'his *terrible* oil paintings'. I record three titles, including *Skull in Slaughtered Cow* (2005) – a flagrant Picasso derivative, repeated in the Tate Modern Retrospective in the two sheep skulls, *Stimulants (and the Way They Affect the Mind and Body)*, (1991). However, what I remember is Hirst's sequence of paintings, done from Polaroids, of a birth. I managed to find one on-line, *Untitled*. It shows the moment when the child is being lifted from the birth canal on to the mother's stomach. The umbilical cord, coiling back to the vagina, is plausibly pearlescent, like an oyster-shell in a Dutch still life. It is competently painted, which is surprising, because the rest of the picture is an unmitigated disaster. The mother appears to have given birth to a papier-mâché baby, the colour intending to represent protective vernix on the skin, waterproofing for the womb's amniotic fluid. The expression on the newborn face, instead of being simply crumpled, looks as if Hirst has cribbed it from Munch's *Der Schrei*. There is no technique.

In an interview for *Turps Banana* (Issue 1, November 2004) Hirst speaks of his figurative painting as something accomplished by hired 'technicians'. He puts in the black lines. His role is to organise – like a film director. By 'technicians', despite the demotion implied, he means artist-hirelings with technique he doesn't possess. Years ago, a very skilled artist, Mark Alexander, was told by one of his tutors at the Ruskin that art wasn't about skill. John Updike, reviewing a show of Van Gogh drawings in New York at the Metropolitan Museum in 2005, commented: 'his skills are uncertain but his spirit is determined.' And Updike's final verdict? 'In his paintings, the sunflowers, the workers' worn shoes, the famous chair … seem indeed to have arrived from another world, as freshly and startlingly *there* as the annunciatory angel, full of their news.'

I have to say that when I saw the 2010 Royal Academy exhibition, *The Real Van Gogh: The Artist and His Letters*, I was struck by Van Gogh's unevenness, his uncertainty, his clumsiness, and the occasional descent into the ludicrous. These pictures arrive with a patina of fame and expectation. But take a painting like *Wheatfield behind St Paul's Hospital*, with its irresistible signature turbulence – and then consider the central figure of the man with the scythe. It is botched and inept. GCSE, actually.

And Hirst? True, great art *isn't* about skill. It isn't about clumsiness either. You have to have skill before you can dismiss it. Picasso was a virtuoso. In *Bailey's Democracy*, David Bailey photographed a raft of people in the nude, including Damien Hirst, pulling his prepuce and mugging at the camera. A telling image of Hirst's skills – not that much, stretched not very far.

Acknowledgements

These essays have appeared in *Areté*, the *Times Literary Supplement*, the *Kipling Journal*, the *Financial Times*, Peter Lang, Penguin Books, the *New Statesman*, the *Daily Telegraph*, the *Guardian*, *Another Magazine*, the *London Review of Books*, *Modern Painters* and *Memory: An Anthology* (edited by Harriet Harvey Wood and A. S. Byatt).

More Dynamite was copyedited by Donna Poppy, whose meticulous genius and preternatural alertness are legendary.

When I was a young lecturer in Oxford, undergraduates had to spend two terms on Milton for prelims. One student, I remember, compared everything to *Bleak House* or *Othello*. 'Il Penseroso' was less amusing than *Bleak House*. *Comus* was a dramatic work similar to *Othello*, another dramatic work, by Shakespeare. After a month of this, I asked the undergraduate why *Bleak House* and *Othello* were such invariable points of reference. They were his A-level set-texts.

In this collection of essays, there are, I know, some touchstones to which I return. For example, *To the Lighthouse* and Mrs Ramsay's thoughts about the *bœuf en daube*. Or Tom Stoppard's account, in *Talk* magazine, of discovering his Jewishness. There are others. Over a decade of occasional literary journalism, there are bound to be recurrent argumentative tropes and preoccupations. It isn't that Donna Poppy didn't notice. Many repetitions have been weeded out. In some cases, the argument would limp if the connective cartilage were removed, so it has been allowed to remain. I ask the reader's understanding.

A Note on the Author

Craig Raine was born in 1944 and educated at Exeter College, Oxford. He became editor of *Quarto* in 1979 and was subsequently Poetry Editor at Faber from 1981 to 1991. He is now an emeritus Fellow at New College, Oxford, and has been the editor of *Areté* since 1999. He is the author of three collections of literary essays, six works of poetry and two novels, *Heartbreak* and *The Divine Comedy*, published by Atlantic Books. His *Collected Poems 1978–1999* were published in 2000 and his verse drama, '*1953*' was directed by Patrick Marber at the Almeida Theatre in 1996. His critical study *T. S. Eliot* was published in 2007.

Index